PLUTARCH'S
ETHICAL WRITINGS AND
EARLY CHRISTIAN LITERATURE

STUDIA AD
CORPUS HELLENISTICUM
NOVI TESTAMENTI

EDIDERUNT

H. D. BETZ • G. DELLING

W. C. VAN UNNIK

VOLUMEN QUARTUM

HANS DIETER BETZ

PLUTARCH'S
ETHICAL WRITINGS AND
EARLY CHRISTIAN LITERATURE

LEIDEN
E. J. BRILL
1978

PLUTARCH'S ETHICAL WRITINGS AND EARLY CHRISTIAN LITERATURE

EDITED BY

HANS DIETER BETZ

LEIDEN
E. J. BRILL
1978

ISBN 90 04 05659 9

PRINTED IN THE NETHERLANDS

TABLE OF CONTENTS

PREFACE

The present volume on Plutarch's ethical writings is the result of a research project begun after the completion of a previous volume in this monograph series, *Plutarch's Theological Writings and Early Christian Literature*, SCHNT 3 (Leiden, 1975). Due to unforeseen complications (the total amount of extant material in Plutarch's ethical writings, the diversity of topics, problems of authenticity, unresolved questions of sources, etc.), the original plan to investigate all of Plutarch's ethical writings was soon in need of modification. The lack of adequate *Vorarbeiten* for most of the essays meant that a thorough investigation of the essays to be included was first needed in order to make possible a meaningful comparison with early Christian ethical material. In addition the team has tried to respond positively to criticisms expressed toward the first volume. Thus, the study of the historical background of Plutarch's ethics and the formal structure and composition of the essays has been given more attention than in the first volume. As a result of all this, the present volume contains rather lengthy studies on some of Plutarch's ethical works. The selection is incidental and represents personal interests of the authors or assignments made by the project. It is our hope that the studies show that much can be learned from the careful investigation of Plutarch's ethical writings and that more such investigations are needed.

This volume would not have come into being without the gracious support of many institutions and persons, to whom we express our most sincere gratitude. The *National Endowment for the Humanities* supported the project by substantial grants during the years 1973-1977. The *Institute for Antiquity and Christianity*, especially its Assistant Director, Dr. James Brashler, was of great help in solving administrational problems. Much of the editorial work lay in the hands of Dr. William C. Grese, Research Associate at the Institute. The Indexes were compiled with the help of Howard M. Jackson, Marjorie Menaul, and Professor Edward N. O'Neil who also gave permission to make use of the unpublished *Index Verborum Plutarcheus*.

Claremont, California, USA — H. D. Betz
January 1978

ABBREVIATIONS

Abbreviations of early Christian and other ancient literature are given in the indexes.

AC	*L'Antiquité classique*
AJPh	*American Journal of Philology*
Almqvist	H. Almqvist, *Plutarch und das Neue Testament* (Uppsala, 1946)
AnBib	Analecta Biblica
Bauer	W. Bauer, *A Greek-English Lexicon of the New Testament and Other Early Christian Literature,* trans. W. F. Arndt and F. W. Gingrich (Chicago, 1957)
BDF	F. Blass and A. Debrunner, *A Greek Grammar of the New Testament and Other Early Christian Literature,* trans. and ed. R. W. Funk (Chicago, 1961)
Betz, *Lukian*	H. D. Betz, *Lukian von Samosata und das Neue Testament* (Berlin, 1961)
Betz, *Paulus*	H. D. Betz, *Der Apostel Paulus und die sokratische Tradition* (Tübingen, 1972)
Bill.	H. L. Strack and P. Billerbeck, *Kommentar zum Neuen Testament aus Talmud und Midrasch* (Munich, 1961-63)
BR	*Biblical Research*
BT	Bibliotheca Teubneriana
Bultmann, *Der Stil*	R. Bultmann, *Der Stil der paulinischen Predigt und die kynisch-stoische Diatribe* (Göttingen, 1910)
Bultmann, *HST*	R. Bultmann, *The History of the Synoptic Tradition,* rev. ed. (New York and Evanston, 1968)
Bultmann, *TNT*	R. Bultmann, *Theology of the New Testament,* 2 vols. (New York, 1951-55)
CAH	*Cambridge Ancient History*
CBQ	*Catholic Biblical Quarterly*
ClQ	*Classical Quarterly*
CPh	*Classical Philology*
Diels-Kranz	H. Diels and W. Kranz, *Die Fragmente der Vorsokratiker,* 9th ed. (Berlin-Charlottenburg, 1959-60)
ECL	Early Christian Literature
Edmonds	J. M. Edmonds, *The Fragments of Attic Comedy* (Leiden, 1957-61)
EvT	*Evangelische Theologie*
ExpT	*Expository Times*
Goodwin-Gulick	W. W. Goodwin and C. B. Gulick, *Greek Grammar* (Boston *et alibi,* 1930)
Griffiths	J. G. Griffiths, *Plutarch's De Iside et Osiride* (Cambridge, 1970)
GRBS	*Greek, Roman and Byzantine Studies*
G&R	*Greece & Rome*

Helmbold and O'Neil	W. C. Helmbold and E. N. O'Neil, *Plutarch's Quotations* (The American Philological Association, 1959)
HNT	Handbuch zum Neuen Testament
HR	*History of Religions*
HSCP	*Harvard Studies in Classical Philology*
HTR	*Harvard Theological Review*
HUCA	*Hebrew Union College Annual*
IDB	*Interpreter's Dictionary of the Bible*
IDBSup	Supplementary volume to *IDB*
Int	*Interpretation*
JAAR	*Journal of the American Academy of Religion*
JBL	*Journal of Biblical Literature*
JHPh	*Journal of the History of Philosophy*
JQR	*Jewish Quarterly Review*
JRS	*Journal of Roman Studies*
JSJ	*Journal for the Study of Judaism in the Persian, Hellenistic and Roman Period*
Lampe	G. W. H. Lampe, *A Patristic Greek Lexicon* (Oxford, 1961)
LCL	Loeb Classical Library
LSJ	H. G. Liddell, R. Scott, H. J. Jones, et al., *A Greek-English Lexicon* (Oxford, 1968)
LXX	Septuagint
NH	Nag Hammadi
Nilsson, *GGR*	M. P. Nilsson, *Geschichte der griechischen Religion*, vol. 1: 3d ed.; vol. 2: 2d ed.; 2 vols. (Munich, 1961-67)
North, *Sophrosyne*	H. North, *Sophrosyne: Self-Knowledge and Self-Restraint in Greek Literature* (Ithaca, New York, 1966)
NovT	*Novum Testamentum*
NT	New Testament
NTD	Das Neue Testament Deutsch
NTS	*New Testament Studies*
OCD	*Oxford Classical Dictionary*, 2d ed. (1970)
OT	Old Testament
PECL 1	*Plutarch's Theological Writings and Early Christian Literature*, ed. H. D. Betz (Leiden, 1975)
PG	*Patrologia Graeca*, ed. J.-P. Migne
PGM	*Papyri Graecae Magicae*, ed. K. Preisendanz, 2d ed., A. Henrichs (Stuttgart, 1973-74)
PhR	*Philosophical Review*
PhW	*Philologische Wochenschrift*
PW	*Pauly's Real-Encyclopädie der classischen Altertumswissenschaft*
RAC	*Reallexikon für Antike und Christentum*
RecSR	*Recherches de science religieuse*
RGG	*Die Religion in Geschichte und Gegenwart*
RhM	*Rheinisches Museum für Philologie*
RHPhR	*Revue d'histoire et de philosophie religieuses*
Rist, *Stoic Phil.*	J. M. Rist, *Stoic Philosophy* (Cambridge, 1969)
SCHNT	Studia ad Corpus Hellenisticum Novi Testamenti

SIG	*Sylloge Inscriptionum Graecarum*, ed. W. Dittenberger (Leipzig, 1898-1901)
SJT	*Scottish Journal of Theology*
Smyth-Messing	H. W. Smyth and G. M. Messing, *Greek Grammar* (Cambridge, Mass., 1956)
SVF	*Stoicorum Veterum Fragmenta*, ed. H. von Arnim (Stuttgart, 1964)
TAPhA	*Transactions and Proceedings of the American Philological Association*
TAPhS	*Transactions of the American Philosophical Society*
TDNT	*Theological Dictionary of the New Testament*
TGF	*Tragicorum Graecorum Fragmenta*, ed. A. Nauck, supplemented by B. Snell (Hildesheim, 1964)
TLZ	*Theologische Literaturzeitung*
TU	Texte und Untersuchungen
ZAW	*Zeitschrift für die alttestamentliche Wissenschaft*
Ziegler	K. Ziegler, *Plutarchos von Chaironeia*, 2d ed. (Stuttgart, 1964) [1st ed. in PW, 21.1 (1951): 636-962]
ZNW	*Zeitschrift für die neutestamentliche Wissenschaft und die Kunde der älteren Kirche*
ZTK	*Zeitschrift für Theologie und Kirche*
ZWT	*Zeitschrift für wissenschaftliche Theologie*

INTRODUCTION

BY

HANS DIETER BETZ

Claremont Graduate School and School of Theology
Claremont, California

The study of ethics in the period of Graeco-Roman and early Christian antiquity is at present in a state of transition. Inevitably, this transition is accompanied by confusion and a host of problems.

To begin with, there is the question of terminology and definition.[1] Contrary to scholars of former times who spoke of Christian ethics with a certain naivété, theologians have recently begun to question whether ethics is the proper term to be applied to early Christian moral demands and whether Christianity can or even ought to have an ethic at all.[2] Ethics as a term tends to be defined either on the model of modern ethical theory as a general and scientific theory of moral obligations, or on the model of classical philosophical ethics as a rational system of moral virtues necessary to bring raw human nature up to the level of εὐδαιμονία. If these are the only admissible definitions of ethics, primitive Christianity did not and could not have had such ethics. But the question then is whether these definitions are satisfactory. Leaving the philosophical and theological side of the proper definitions to those who are competent to deal with them, we should say that historically they do not fit the phenomena of the period of history that is of concern to us.

Phenomenologically, the ethical world of the Graeco-Roman period was very complex, and it is important to distinguish among

[1] See on this problem Eduard Schwartz, *Ethik der Griechen*, ed. W. Richter (Stuttgart, 1951) 14ff. The confusion is well demonstrated by H. D. Wendland, *Ethik des Neuen Testaments*, NTD Ergänzungsreihe 4 (Göttingen, 1970) 2-4. Cf. also W. Schrage, "Ethics in the NT," *IDBSup* (1976) 281-89, 281: "It is not proper to speak of *the* NT ethic because, in spite of all the lines of convergence and the constant elements, it is necessary to treat the various writings and authors separately and to inquire into their ethical motifs and criteria and the way these are applied..."

[2] See on this point the discussion by V. P. Furnish, *Theology and Ethics in Paul* (Nashville, 1968) 208ff.: "Is there a 'Pauline ethic'?" Cf. J. T. Sanders, *Ethics in the New Testament* (Philadelphia, 1975).

several levels of ethical material found in the writings extant from the period. Greek and Roman philosophers continued to present in their works theoretical systems of ethics, based on metaphysical assumptions for which the groundwork had been laid by earlier philosophers. These theories represent high-level philosophical reflection, although their goal, more than at any other time, was to ensure the best possible life to the individual and the community. In the Hellenistic and Roman periods especially, philosophers were engaged in the practice of what we would call today "psychological counseling" or "psychotherapy," that is, using ethical theory in a simplified and practical form in order to educate themselves and others to accept and carry through a reasonable way of life.[3] This practice was, of course, primarily oral, although we also find it in the form of written works, including some of Plutarch's, but not in ECL.

Another level is known as "popular morality," a name which scholarship usually applies to apparently unsystematic collections of moral principles which are shared by particular communities.[4] The principles are semi-philosophical and are often derived from philosophy, or from folk-wisdom, or from both. Their *Sitz im Leben* is primarily oral instruction within the community in which the material functions, but it is also found in writings, as in Plutarch and in ECL.

Still different is the type of material which comes from social customs and religious rituals. Often this material assumes the status of ethical principles. For example, the social customs of friendship have been elevated from the level of family relationships to that of ethical-philosophical principles governing the relationships between philosophers in Plutarch, and Christians in ECL. Similarly, vegetarianism, originally based on a ritual taboo, becomes for Plutarch a philosophical problem.

Finally, societal units of every kind possess what is called an "ethos," a distinguishable but implicit life-style based upon cultural values and represented mostly by attitudes and symbols. This

---

[3] See especially I. Hadot, *Seneca und die griechisch-römische Tradition der Seelenleitung* (Berlin, 1969); and the reviews by G. Maurach, *Gnomon* 43 (1971) 87-89; H. D. Betz, *JHPh* 9 (1971) 86f.; also H. G. Ingenkamp, *Plutarchs Schriften über die Heilung der Seele* (Göttingen, 1971); and the review by D. Babut, *AC* 91 (1972) 671-73.

[4] Cf. K. J. Dover, *Greek Popular Morality in the Time of Plato and Aristotle* (Berkeley & Los Angeles, 1974).

"ethos" functions to identify cultural groups and to set them off from each other.[5] Plutarch's "ethos," which expresses itself in everything he says and does, is that of a member of the Greek aristocratic and cultural elite. By comparison, the early Christian "ethos" originated in Judaism, a cultural minority. By the time of the New Testament, the early Christian "ethos" was still in the process of formation and is therefore quite diversified in comparison with Plutarch's.

It should be clear that all of these levels are part of the total behavior pattern of people and that the various levels do not exclude one another. At every level the other levels are to some degree represented. Philosophical ethics, e.g., often begins by questioning what is assumed to be the custom or the consensus of popular morality. Philosophical value judgments which are often made at this point should not, however, be accepted uncritically. After all, customs and popular morality have often prevailed over philosophical ethics, and this not always for the wrong reasons. In the same way, simple folk-wisdom can be elevated to the highest philosophical level. Conversely, highly original creations of philosophical thought can be popularized and even become part of the accepted, everyday morality.

Because of this character of ethics as a "mixture," [6] caution should be exercised with regard to nomenclature. Graeco-Roman and early Christian ethics should not be approached with narrow definitions, but rather with the broad picture of the phenomena in mind. It is a dubious method when scholars attribute theory only to the philosophers who make it explicit.[7] Theory is also found

[5] See J. H. Schütz, "Ethos in Early Christianity," *IDBSup* (1976) 289-93.

[6] This term is used by A. Dihle, *RAC*, s.v. Ethik. Dihle gives an excellent survey about the ethical situation and developments in the Greek, Roman, and Patristic periods. On his concept of "Misch-Ethik" see 666ff.

[7] Cf. Dihle, *RAC* 6:706, who distinguishes sharply between the " 'ungesetzliche', personale Charakter der sittlichen Forderungen aus der Predigt Jesu," which on account of the imminent eschatology was in no need of ethical objectivation, and the "zwangsläufige Entwicklung zu einer objektiven Sittenlehre" and the "immer kompliziertere System einer christlichen Ethik." What Dihle calls "christliche Sonder-Ethik" begins, according to him, only in the early Church, not with Jesus, and continues without developed reflection or categorical clarity well into the second century. "Bis dahin gab es im wesentlichen nur eine mehr oder weniger naive Anknüpfung an synagogale und popularphilosophische Paränese, eine praktische Umsetzung des Inhaltes der Verkündigung Jesu in sittliche Einzelvorschriften und sich in ebenfalls in praktischen Einzelvorschriften dokumentierende Lösungsversuche der Fragen der Lebensgestaltung..." (707).

where it is not spelled out.[8] On the other hand, ethical actions should not be denied to philosophers just because they are philosophizing. Nor should Graeco-Roman ethics be identified with the sum-total of its philosophical theory. Recent studies, particularly the one by K. J. Dover, have rightly emphasized the importance of the so-called "popular morality" over against the ethical systems of the philosophers.[9]

Furthermore, research on Plutarch's ethics is presently in a state of transition. Since the work by O. Gréard[10] no comprehensive treatment of the subject has been published. This situation is understandable because of the negative judgment pronounced on Plutarch by historians of philosophy in the last 100 years. Authoritative works have again and again pointed out that Plutarch's philosophy is eclectic and lacks the intellectual acumen of the classical period of Plato and Aristotle. Readers have no doubt concluded that Plutarch was an epigone who deserves no further study.[11] Hence, Plutarch's ethics is characterized as that of an idealistic and philanthropic psychologist and physician of the soul.[12] Ziegler stands for many when he prefers Plutarch's warm, kind, and human personality to his writings, for which he uses, somewhat disrespectfully, the name of "sermons."[13] Ziegler's

[8] See, e.g., R. Bultmann's essay "Das Problem der Ethik bei Paulus," *ZNW* 23 (1924) 123-40, reprinted in his *Exegetica* (Tübingen, 1967) 36-54, in which he treats Paul's ethic as a "theory" (*Exegetica*, 37). An English translation by K. R. Crim can be found in R. Bultmann, *The Old and New Man in the Letters of Paul* (Richmond, Va., 1967) 7-32.

[9] Dover (*Greek Popular Morality*, 1ff.) rightly objects against the confusion of the philosophical systems of ethics with "Greek morality." His study provides an important new approach to reconstruct the popular morality from the non-philosophical literature (rhetoric, tragedy, comedy, etc.).

[10] O. Gréard, *De la morale de Plutarque* (Paris, [2]1874).

[11] This negative value judgment was summed up by K. Ziegler in his article in PW which first appeared in 1949: "Plutarch ist kein originaler Denker gewesen. Das lag nur zum kleineren Teil an der Zeit, in die er hineingeboren wurde, zum grösseren Teil an der Beschaffenheit des Geistes und des Charakters, mit dem er geboren worden ist. Es fehlte ihm die Schärfe und Energie des Denkens, die geistige Schöpferkraft, die den überragenden und originellen Denker ausmacht, es fehlte ihm auch der unbedingte Wille zur Klarheit" (301).

[12] Ibid., 305f.

[13] "Auf diesem Gebiet wie überhaupt in seiner Ethik und mit seiner φιλανθρωπία, die sich von der christlichen Nächstenliebe wenig oder garnicht unterscheidet, mit seiner ganzen priesterlich-milden Gesinnungsweise *wirkt P. christlich*, und es ist nicht verwunderlich, wenn schon die Frage aufgeworfen worden ist, ob P. etwas vom Christentum gewusst und vielleicht Einflüsse von daher erfahren habe." (Ibid., 306; the emphasis is Ziegler's.)

opinion, representative as it is, is a mistaken judgment nevertheless. It lacks the willingness to consider with seriousness anything not conforming to the classical period and to the clichés of 19th century intellectualism. Yet, judgments like Ziegler's and Zeller's [14] have prevented scholars from paying much attention to Plutarch. For the same reason, histories of ethics, because of their emphasis upon the great classical systems of ethics, often neglected any development after the emergence of the Stoa.[15] In addition philologists were discouraged from studying Plutarch by the poor results yielded by *Quellenforschung*, another obsession of the time.

Only in recent years has a new understanding of the post-classical Hellenistic and Roman period of philosophy been gradually emerging. Historians of philosophy have again become interested in the developments between Plato and Neoplatonism.[16] In this development Plutarch is a key figure.[17] His numerous writings provide a good view of first-century Middle Platonism in Greece. These writings are also storehouses of philosophical traditions not otherwise extant. This material is especially important for the field of ethics.

Stimulation has also come from the adjacent fields of literary criticism and the history of psychology and pedagogy.[18] Rather

---

[14] The description of Plutarch's ethics in E. Zeller, *Die Philosophie der Griechen in ihrer geschichtlichen Entwicklung* (Leipzig, [5]1923) 3.2:200-04 is entirely negative. Zeller never asks why Plutarch says what he says. Instead he judges Plutarch's ethics to be personally charming but historically irrelevant: "Die Reinheit seiner Grundsätze, die edle und feinsinnige Auffassung sittlicher Verhältnisse, wie das Familienleben und die Freundschaft, die schöne und menschenfreundliche Gesinnung, welche sich in ihnen ausspricht, hat diesen Abhandlungen von jeher viel Freunde erworben; aber neue und eigentümliche Gedanken sind darin kaum zu finden" (203).

[15] See, e.g., F. Jodl, *Geschichte der Ethik als philosophischer Wissenschaft* (Stuttgart & Berlin, [4]1930) who concludes the ethics of antiquity with Cicero and devotes to Plutarch about half a page. Schwartz, *Ethik der Griechen*, also concludes with the Stoa but does not mention Plutarch at all. The older work by L. Schmidt, *Die Ethik der alten Griechen* (Berlin, 1882), has a few pages on him (1:40-42).

[16] See Ph. Merlan, "Greek Philosophy from Plato to Plotinus," *The Cambridge History of Later Greek and Early Medieval Philosophy*, ed. A. H. Armstrong (Cambridge, 1967) 10-132.

[17] Ibid., 58-63. See also H. J. Krämer, *Der Ursprung der Geistmetaphysik* (Amsterdam, 1964); id., *Platonismus und hellenistische Philosophie* (Berlin, 1971); D. Lemke, *Die Theologie Epikurs* (Munich, 1973); H. Dörrie, *Platonica Minora* (Munich, 1976); Ph. Merlan, *Kleine philosophische Schriften* (Hildesheim, 1976); J. Dillon, *The Middle Platonists* (London, 1977).

[18] See P. Rabbow, *Seelenführung* (Munich, 1954); and Hadot, *Seneca* (see n. 3, above).

than trying to isolate sources, scholarship has been increasingly attentive to the questions of the literary forms, genres, and composition of Plutarch's ethical writings. In this area of research, interest in Plutarch has no doubt profited from analogous studies on Seneca.[19] The study of rhetorical forms and composition is, of course, closely related to the question of their function. H. G. Ingenkamp in particular has demonstrated that Plutarch's ethical writings serve the purpose of "Seelenheilung." [20] This purpose grew out of older philosophical concerns, but took on new importance because of the situation and circumstances of the time. Instead of judging this emphasis to be due to a lack of interest in philosophy itself and the result of epigonic fatigue, one ought to see its necessity and purpose. Greece had come a long way since Plato and Aristotle. Plutarch testifies to the far-reaching cultural changes and to the economic depression which had beset his country. To neither condition could he remain oblivious. Several hundred years of ethical reflection had refined and conflated the great ethical systems of the past. The society and political role of Greece presupposed by these systems were no longer a reality. Plutarch well understood the changes and their implications and tried to make the best of the new situation. Most important was the task of interpreting the Greek philosophical and ethical traditions to the educated society of his own time and especially to the powers that be, the Romans.

In his ethics Plutarch stands in the tradition of the Platonic Academy. Although precious little is known of the state of the Academy at his time, it is safe to say that Plutarch made use of the developments which had taken place in the Academy since Plato. Elements drawn mainly from the Platonic, Peripatetic and Stoic schools had become amalgamated to form a conglomerate of ideas which Plutarch shared.[21] The transition from the aristocratic society of Athens to the cosmopolitan panorama of the Roman Empire was still in progress. Most importantly, however, Plutarch was fully devoted to bridging the gulf between philosophical-ethical theory and practice. Even Socrates had been aware of this

---

[19] See W. Brinckmann, *Der Begriff der Freundschaft in Senecas Briefen* (Philosophische Dissertation, Cologne, 1963); H. Cancik, *Untersuchungen zu Senecas Epistulae morales* (Hildesheim, 1967), with the review by G. Maurach, *Gnomon* 41 (1969) 472-76; id., *Der Bau von Senecas Epistulae morales* (Heidelberg, 1970); id., review of Hadot, *Seneca*, in *Gnomon* 43 (1971) 87-89.

[20] See n. 3, above.

[21] See D. Babut, *Plutarque et le Stoïcisme* (Paris, 1969).

dichotomy, but it was the Stoics who first attacked the problem and provided some solutions. Philon of Larissa may have been the one who introduced the teaching of philosophy as an analogy to the work of the physician into the Academy,[22] but Plutarch's ethical writings show that he wholeheartedly embraced this concept. Medical language and metaphors are found throughout his ethical writings. In addition, the analogy of the physician affects the entire range of language, genre, and composition. His works provide more than intellectual instruction; they offer ethical guidance through healing the soul of its illnesses.

For these reasons, the literary investigation of Plutarch's metaphors and images gains new and significant purpose.[23] The same must be said with regard to the rhetorical and compositional analysis of his individual writings, a process which has barely begun.[24]

On the whole, Plutarch's ethic is negative. He acknowledges that mankind and society are "sick" internally in their souls as well as externally in their behavior. In his view, health can only be restored by the expulsion of both internal and external evils. This goal is accomplished by training that is mental and intellectual, as well as behavioral. In contemporary terms, one would call Plutarch's methods types of "psychotherapy." The reading of his works is subservient to this purpose. It was perhaps for this reason that Plutarch kept his arguments closely connected with widely shared popular morality and wisdom. He consciously stayed in touch with the people of his social milieu, the intellectual and political leadership of his hometown and of other Greek cities, his many friends all over the world, and especially with influential Roman officials.[25] Plutarch places great emphasis on religion. This emphasis is peculiar because Plutarch seems to have had no illusions

---

[22] See the excerpt from Areius Didymus in Stobaeus, *Eclogae* II. 7. 2 (ed. Wachsmuth & Hense, vol. 2, pp. 39-41). See K. von Fritz, "Philon von Larissa," PW 19 (1938) 2535-44; G. Maurach, *Gnomon* 43 (1971) 88.

[23] See F. Fuhrmann, *Les Images de Plutarque* (Paris, 1964).

[24] See especially the commentaries on individual treatises of Plutarch, by D. Babut, *Plutarque, De la vertu éthique* (Paris, 1969), with the review by H. G. Ingenkamp, *Gnomon* 44 (1972) 250-55; H. Görgemanns, *Untersuchungen zu Plutarchs Dialog De facie in orbe lunae* (Heidelberg, 1970); J. Hani, *Plutarque, Consolation à Apollonius* (Paris, 1972); L. J. R. Heirman, *Plutarchus "De audiendis poetis"* (Proefschrift, Leiden, 1972); B. Bucher-Isler, *Norm und Individualität in den Biographien Plutarchs* (Bern & Stuttgart, 1972).

[25] See C. P. Jones, *Plutarch and Rome* (Oxford, 1971).

about the decline of traditional Greek religion in his time. Observing the superficial religious activities of the masses, he stresses the need for deep religious convictions. Repeatedly the last sections of his writings have a religious theme.

These new approaches to Plutarch research provide promising opportunities to the student of the history of ethics. The corpus of Plutarch's ethical writings—that is, those which are extant—allows a nearly full vision of the ethical landscape of the Greek culture at the time of primitive Christianity. What is true for the situation in religion is certainly also true for the situation in ethics. Plutarch's ethical writings are storehouses for ethical material of all levels, from archaic customs and rituals to popular morality to philosophical arguments. Besides the information he provides, Plutarch also reflects the ethical concerns of the educated people of his time and the methods by which he, as one of the most respected philosophers, hoped to assist the individuals and society of his time to grow ethically. The historians of Christianity have always been struck by the close similarities between Christian ethics and Plutarch's ethics. In the past these similarities have often led scholars to believe that Plutarch was influenced by Christianity. There is, however, not the slightest evidence to confirm such influence. The closeness between Plutarch and early Christianity can be explained by their dependence upon common traditions and by their sharing in common ethical concerns. Only after this dependence is understood can the original and peculiar features of both sides become clear.

This assessment of the general situation takes for granted that the study of early Christian ethics is also at present going through a revolution. To describe in detail all the changes and developments in this field is impossible here. But some of the general concerns of present research ought to be mentioned. It is now generally recognized that the early Christian writers made extensive use of Graeco-Roman popular ethics. This ethical material is, however, of quite diverse origin and character. To a large extent, the material had its origin in philosophical ethics. Mostly through the Cynic-Stoic schools it became "popularized" and part of the morality of the urban population. In this form philosophical ethics influenced early Christianity. This influence was in part mediated by Hellenistic Judaism, which had appropriated Greek philosophical material several centuries before Christianity. Therefore we find ethical material of this kind both in early and in late New Testament sources. In addition, there were influences of general popular morality, customs and rituals, which early Christianity shared with the Judaism from which it came. One should keep in mind, however, that in many instances this popular morality was shared by antiquity as a whole, including Judaism, Hellenistic culture, and early Christianity. Further complication is caused by the fact that scholarship has only now begun to turn its attention to the interrelationships between Judaism and Hellenism.[26] Whatever results these studies yield will affect the understanding of early Christian ethics.

It should be obvious from these remarks that the term "early Christian ethics" covers a great variety of material. There is no single system that can take up all of these various concepts and harmonize them. In analogy to christology and to other *loci* of early Christian theology, ethics also represents a variety of concepts describing what the Christian ethical life is all about.

Somewhat in analogy to the Platonic philosophy of Plutarch, early Christian ethics is based upon a theological foundation, the Christian message and faith. Both Plutarch's philosophical tradition and primitive Christian theology are the result of reflection, and both integrate various types of ethical material by interpreting and even changing them. New ethical insights occur when confrontations between inherited morality and philosophy or theology demand new ethical reflection and action. As a result, the difference between Plutarch's ethics and early Christian ethics is the greatest whenever the tensions and conflicts between the ethical traditions and the doctrinal requirements are the strongest.

Therefore, Plutarch and ECL differ not only in their hermeneutical frameworks, but as a result they also subject their ethical traditions to a different process of selection, evaluation and inter-

---

[26] See M. Hengel, *Judaism and Hellenism*, 2 vols. (Philadelphia, 1974); Th. Middendorp, *Die Stellung Jesu ben Siras zwischen Judentum und Hellenismus* (Leiden, 1973); R. Braun, *Kohelet und die frühhellenistische Popularphilosophie* (Berlin, 1973); B. L. Mack, *Logos und Sophia: Untersuchungen zur Weisheitstheologie im hellenistischen Judentum* (Göttingen, 1973); H. A. Fischel, *Rabbinic Literature and Greco-Roman Philosophy: A Study of Epicurea and Rhetorica in Early Midrashic Writings* (Leiden, 1973); B. Z. Wacholder, *Eupolemus: A Study of Judaeo-Greek Literature* (Cincinnati, 1974). For further literature, see G. Delling, "Perspektiven der Erforschung des hellenistischen Judentums," *HUCA* 45 (1974) 133-76; and the continuing annotated bibliographies in *JSJ* and *Studia Philonica*.

pretation. In ECL this process differs from author to author and results in the great diversity within Christian ethics. The same diversity, therefore, should be expected in a comparison between Plutarch and early Christian ethics.

In many ways the fourteen contributions assembled in this volume reflect the state of transition characteristic of present research on ancient ethics. The authors come from different fields of historical study. Some have had more contact with neighboring fields than others. Ancient History is represented by Mr. Smith and Mrs. Wicker; Classics by Messrs. Dillon, Hershbell, Martin, O'Neil, and Miss Phillips; and New Testament studies by Messrs. Aune, Beardslee, Betz, Grese, and Lührmann. Due to the different backgrounds of the authors, the papers show considerable variety in methods, presuppositions, questions and interests. They provide neither a consensus nor the last word on any of the subjects discussed. The authors' goal is, however, not simply to represent their established fields of study but to learn from one another. As a result of group discussions and the exchange and mutual critique of preliminary drafts, the papers are evidence of changed views and new insights. This situation is both realistic in terms of the present state of research and hopefully stimulating in terms of future developments.

DE PROFECTIBUS IN VIRTUTE (MORALIA 75A - 86A)[1]

BY

WILLIAM C. GRESE

Institute for Antiquity and Christianity
Claremont, California

I. INTRODUCTION

The ostensible purpose of this essay is to defend the perceptibility of progress towards ἀρετή and to describe how such progress can be recognized.[2] Such a defense Plutarch considered a necessary response to the ancient Stoic position which he interpreted as making progress impossible. According to the Stoics, man was either φαῦλος[3] or σοφός/τέλειος. There was no intermediate state between the two, and all sins were considered equal, just as all moral acts were also equal. Since there were no degrees of vice or of virtue, the Stoics further argued that the change from φαῦλος to σοφός was a sudden change that could happen without the person who had been changed even being aware of it.[4]

This position is unsatisfactory, as Plutarch explains, because it does not conform to reality. People are not totally bad or totally good, but there are different degrees of both κακία and προκοπή.[5] In fact, one can and does perceptibly progress from a worse state to

---

[1] The text used here is the one by F. C. Babbitt, *Plutarch's Moralia*, LCL, vol. 1 (1927). The text by W. R. Paton and I. Wegehaupt and revised by H. Gärtner (BT, vol. 1 [1974]) was also consulted.

[2] See the introductory question, 75A-B. The so-called Lamprias Catalog (no. 87 [LCL 15:16]) entitles this treatise: Πῶς ἄν τις αἴσθοιτο ἑαυτοῦ προκόπτοντος πρὸς ἀρετήν;

[3] For the use of φαῦλος (75E, 82D, 85F, also 75D) in ECL, see Bauer, s.v., 1.

[4] 75C-D: καὶ γὰρ ἀκαρεὶ χρόνου καὶ ὥρας ἐκ τῆς ὡς ἔνι μάλιστα φαυλότητος εἰς οὐκ ἔχουσαν ὑπερβολὴν ἀρετῆς διάθεσιν μεταβαλὼν ὁ σοφός. Here Plutarch gives the ancient Stoic position together with its technical terminology. The technical name for one who has become wise unknowingly is ὁ διαλεληθώς. For an explanation of the Stoic position, see Rist, *Stoic Phil.*, 81-96. Cf. also *SVF*, III, 524-43 (pp. 140-45). The Stoicism that Plutarch here describes is the ancient Stoic position and does not take into account the revisions of the middle and late Stoics. According to D. Babut (*Plutarque et le Stoïcisme* [Paris, 1969] 15-18), it was customary at Plutarch's time to define Stoicism in this narrow way.

[5] 75F-76B.

a better one.[6] An even more basic problem with the Stoic position is that it offers no criteria by which one can recognize if he is progressing, and thus it gives no guidance to those who want to know how to improve.

In this essay Plutarch does not feel obligated to spend much time in arguments against the Stoics. Apparently these arguments were well-known to his readers.[7] Instead Plutarch concentrates on providing practical advice for those who want to be able to evaluate their own conduct [8] and in giving useful guidance to the readers who want to improve their lives.[9] He accomplishes both objectives by listing the ways by which such progress can be recognized. These ways include: continual, regular advancement (76C-E); the increasing desire to spend more of one's time on philosophy (76F-77D); a growing ease in one's studies coupled with a reduction in the number and duration of periods of dejection and uncertainty (77D-78A); the recognition of the superiority of philosophy over what οἱ πολλοί admire (78A-E); the change from ostentatious language to language dealing with character and feeling (78E-79B);[10] going beyond the form of what the philosophers have said to get at the substance (79B-D); learning from what is seen as well as from what is heard (79D-F); putting what is learned into effect in one's life (79F-80A); making speeches for the improvement of the speaker and of the listeners, not for display purposes (80B-E);

---

[6] 76B; the proof for this assertion makes up the rest of the essay, 76C-86A.

[7] On the basis of this observation, Babut (*Plutarque et le Stoïcisme*, 47-52) suggests that *prof. virt.* is later than those works (*Stoic. repug.*, *Stoic. absurd.*, *adv. Stoic.*) in which Plutarch presents his arguments against the Stoics in greater detail. C. P. Jones ("Towards a Chronology of Plutarch's Works," *JRS* 56 [1966] 61-74) does not suggest dates for Plutarch's other works against the Stoics, but he does place *prof. virt.* at the end of Plutarch's career.

[8] Plutarch describes a variety of signs by which a person can tell if he is progressing in virtue. Cf. ἐπιλογισμός in 76C (on which see H. G. Ingenkamp, *Plutarch's Schriften über die Heilung der Seele* [Göttingen, 1971] 99-105); τεκμήριον in 76C; σημεῖον in 76F, 77B, 78B, 82A, E, 84A, 85B, E; δήλωμα in 77D, 78E, 84B; ἴδιον in 84B, E; ἐπισκοπέω in 80B, E; κρίνω in 83E; ὁράω in 79B.

[9] 76C-86A. Cf. Ziegler, sec. III.4.c (col. 136).

[10] 79B: ὁ ἁπτόμενος ἤθους καὶ πάθους λόγος. This is the kind of discourse that philosophers should use. It is of value because it affects the inner character of the individual (cf. 79C: ἐπανόρθωσις ἤθους, πάθους κουφισμός). As such it contrasts with the language of those who are only interested in how their language sounds or on the kind of momentary impression that their speech makes (cf. 78E-F, 80A, B).

not needing to publicize one's virtues because one is content with knowing that one has done what is right (80E-81F); the readiness to accept correction (81F-82F); reason's control of the soul's emotive element even during sleep (82F-83E); moderation of τὰ πάθη (83E-84B); the desire to imitate the deeds of the virtuous (84B-85B); the desire to let oneself and what one has done be seen by one's family and those one admires (85B-D); the recognition that all sins, even small ones, are important (85E-86A).

II. Plutarch and Early Christian Literature

In opposing the ancient Stoic teaching of a sudden conversion, Plutarch actually finds himself in agreement with his contemporary Stoics and using their technical term for describing someone in this intermediate state, προκόπτων. Both Plutarch and his contemporary Stoics would agree that the earlier theories of a sudden conversion to perfection were too simple and did not conform to reality.[11] Similarly Paul rejects the claims of the Corinthian enthusiasts that they had been transformed, probably through baptism, to a state of complete perfection.[12] Against such a position Paul argues that perfection is to be had only eschatologically (1 Cor 13:12; 15:42-46; Phil 1:6; 3:12-14; Rom 6:4, 8), and until then the Christian must be on guard against temptations (1 Cor 10:1-13) and needs ethical guidance (1 Cor 5-8; 10-14; Rom 6:12-19; 12-15; Gal 5:13-6:10).[13] In short, the view of the enthusiasts, like that of the Stoics, was too simple.

There are, however, two other elements in ECL which, at least in theory, come closer to the Stoicism that Plutarch rejects than to Plutarch's argument for a gradual change. First, when the law of

[11] Cf. A. Bonhöffer, *Die Ethik des Stoikers Epictet* (Stuttgart, 1894) 144-53. We cannot here go into the relationship between Plutarch and Stoicism. On this topic, see Babut, *Plutarque et le Stoïcisme*.

[12] Cf. the use of τέλειος (75C, 76A, 84D) in 1 Cor 2:6; 14:20; Phil 3:15; also σοφός (75D, E) in 1 Cor 1:20, 26f.; 3:18. For a brief discussion of the Corinthian theology and its relation to Paul, cf. J. M. Robinson, "Kerygma and History in the New Testament," *Trajectories through Early Christianity* (Philadelphia, 1971) 30-39. Such a sudden transformation also has parallels in the miracle stories and conversion stories. See below on 75D.

[13] For the relationship between the Pauline "indicative" and "imperative," together with a comparison of Paul with the Stoics, see R. Bultmann, "The Problem of Ethics in the Writings of Paul," *The Old and New Man in the Letters of Paul* (Richmond, Va., 1967) 16-30.

God is seen as a complete whole, it cannot be kept only partially (Jas 2:10; Rom 13:8-10; Gal 5:14; Matt 5:19; 22:34-40//Mark 12:28-31//Luke 10:25-28).[14] Second, where the new life of the Christian is seen as a product of the divine spirit, one either lives by the spirit or one does not (Gal 5:18-25; Rom 8:12-14).[15] In neither case is there room for the concept of a gradual improvement.

Plutarch, as we have seen, argues against his interpretation of the Stoic position with a list of ways by which one can recognize his own progress. Although Paul also recognizes the need for self-evaluation (cf. 1 Cor 11:28, Gal 6:4 [16]), he bases his evaluation not on what he has achieved (1 Cor 3:18; 4:7; Phil 3:13), but on what God has given him (1 Cor 4:7; Rom 6:11; 2 Cor 3:5; 13:5). In fact, the only true evaluation will be the final eschatological evaluation by Christ (1 Cor 3:13-15; 4:3-5).[17]

In this treatise Plutarch's basic purpose is to provide his readers with guidance on how to improve their lives. The guidance that he gives compares, as we shall see in section III, with ethical advice given in ECL. In addition, *prof. virt.* with its instruction on how to achieve perfection needs to be compared with the Sermon on the Mount, which gives the conditions for entrance into the Kingdom of Heaven; [18] the instruction concerning the two ways in Did 1-6, which promises life instead of death; and the Mandates of Hermas, which claim that those who follow the Mandates will receive all the promises of God (Vis 5:7).

Nevertheless, there is a basic difference between Plutarch and ECL. Plutarch's objective is the achievement of ἀρετή, the development of perfect character (cf. 75C: ἄκρατον τὸ ἀγαθὸν καὶ τέλειον). Such self-centeredness is generally absent from ECL where Plutarch's stress on the achievement of one's own individual προκοπή is replaced with an emphasis on ἀγάπη and concern for the neighbor.[19] Yet, in some of ECL the motivation for such love can be the

[14] Yet, cf. Did 6:2-3: ὃ δύνῃ, τοῦτο ποίει.

[15] Cf. also in this connection the light-darkness contrast in John 8:12; 11:9f. One is either in the light or in the darkness.

[16] On Gal 6:4 see H. D. Betz, *Galatians*, Hermeneia (Philadelphia, forthcoming) ad loc.

[17] In this connection cf. also the unexpected judgments in Matt 7:21-23/ Luke 13:25-27; Matt 25:31-46; Herm Sim 9:6:3-5.

[18] See H. Windisch, *The Meaning of the Sermon on the Mount* (Philadelphia, 1951) 27-29.

[19] Cf. A. Dihle, *RAC*, s.v. Ethik, B.I.a.2, b.5; also V. P. Furnish, *The Love Command in the New Testament* (Nashville, 1972).

individual's own desire for salvation (1 Tim 6:17-19; Herm Man 2:4-6; Sim 1; 5:3:7f.; cf. also Matt 6:4, 19f.).

Plutarch's encouragement to his readers to improve towards ἀρετή by letting the divine λόγος increasingly rule their lives compares to an extent with Paul's teaching that the Christian life is produced by the divine spirit (Gal 5:22f., 25; Rom 8:14). Yet for Plutarch such improvement is the result of the individual coming to realize his own potential. For Paul, on the other hand, man by himself cannot obey God (Rom 7:14-24; Phil 3:7-9). Only the added gift of the spirit makes obedience possible.[20] Claims of self-improvement Paul would consider πεποίθησις ἐν σαρκί [21] or καύχησις.[22] It is therefore not surprising that προκοπή and προκόπτω are relatively infrequent in ECL.[23]

III. Other Parallels

Ch. 1

(75A)

ὦ Σόσσιε Σενεκίων. With this address or dedication of the essay, cf. Luke 1:3; Acts 1:1. For information about Sosius Senecio, see R. H. Barrow, *Plutarch and His Times* (Bloomington, Indiana, 1969) 41; C. P. Jones, *Plutarch and Rome* (Oxford, 1971) 54-57.

[20] Cf. John 15:4f.: χωρὶς ἐμοῦ οὐ δύνασθε ποιεῖν οὐδέν, Herm Man 12:4:4f., where having the Lord in the heart makes it possible to keep the commandments. Contrast, however, the views of Luke-Acts (Luke 7:1-10; Acts 10:1-2) and Ps-Clem Hom (1:1:1 and 13:5:1-2) that non-Christians can come close to Christianity and lead a virtuous life. On the contrast between ECL and Plutarch's understanding of ἀρετή, see H. Jonas, *The Gnostic Religion* (Boston, 1963) 266-81; the article by Hershbell in this volume, pp. 136, 144f., 150.

[21] Phil 3:4.

[22] Cf. R. Bultmann, *TDNT*, s.v. καυχάομαι κτλ., C.

[23] See προκοπή (*prof. virt.* 75B, C bis, 76A, B, D, E, 77D, 78A, B, 79B, 81D, 82A, B, E, 83D, E bis, 84A, B, E) in 1 Tim 4:14f., where it describes progress as a minister; προκόπτω (*prof. virt.* 75C bis, 77C, 78E, 79B, D, 80C, 81A, 82D, E, F, 84A, C, D, F, 85B, 86A) in Luke 2:52 (Καὶ Ἰησοῦς προέκοπτεν ἐν τῇ σοφίᾳ καὶ ἡλικίᾳ καὶ χάριτι παρὰ θεῷ καὶ ἀνθρώποις); Gal 1:14 (προέκοπτον ἐν τῷ Ἰουδαϊσμῷ); 2 Clem 17:3 (προκόπτειν ἐν ταῖς ἐντολαῖς τοῦ κυρίου); Just Dial 2:6, which ironically describes progress in Platonism; see also G. Stählin, *TDNT*, s.v. προκοπή, προκόπτω. On βελτιόω (*prof. virt.* 75B, 85C) cf. Diogn 6:9, where it describes the improvement of the soul through asceticism, and Diogn 1, where the intended result of reading Diogn is βελτίω γενέσθαι. In ECL οἰκοδομέω usually refers to the upbuilding of the community (cf. O. Michel, *TDNT*, s.v. οἰκοδομέω, B.2), but it is used for individual improvement in Barn 16:7-10; Pol Phil 3:2. Cf. also W. A. Beardslee, *Human Achievement and Divine Vocation in the Message of Paul* (London, 1961) 66-78.

(75D)

ἀκαρὲς χρόνου καὶ ὥρας. The suddenness of the conversion was a *topos* in conversion stories (see *PECL* 1:219) and in other miracle stories (see Betz, *Lukian*, 157). Cf. τάχος in 75D.

τὰ μὲν ἀφαιροῦντι τὰ δὲ προστιθέντι. Such talk of "putting off" and "putting on" in an ethical context is reminiscent of Col 3:9-14.

(75E)

ἐκ τῆς ψυχῆς μεθεικότα τὰς χθιζὰς ἀβελτερίας καὶ ἀπάτας. According to Plutarch, the Stoic position was that one becomes perfect through the sudden removal of evil. A similar understanding appears in gnosticism (e.g., Corpus Hermeticum XIII, 8-9) and in exorcism stories (e.g., Mark 1:23-28//Luke 4:33-37). Like Plutarch, the Pauline school realized that sin was not something that could be removed so quickly and completely. Cf. Rom 6:3-19; Col 3:1-9; also above part II.

ἐκλάμπω. Here the attainment of understanding is called "illumination" (cf. 76B, 77D, 81D-E). On such use of light terminology, see H. Conzelmann, *TDNT*, s.v. φῶς κτλ.

γενόμενος κατ' εὐχὴν ἀνὴρ ἐκ γυναικός. This example is based on the opinion that it is better to be a man than to be a woman. Cf. Copt Gos Thom log. 114. For an analysis of this widespread view and an examination of the Christian response, see Wayne A. Meeks, "The Image of the Androgyne: Some Uses of a Symbol in Earliest Christianity," *HR* 13 (1973-74) 165-208.

(75F)

μεταβαλὼν εἰς θεῖον ἐκ θηριώδους βίον. The change from ὁ φαῦλος to ὁ σοφός is described as a change from bestial to divine existence. For a comparison of vice with animal behavior, cf. Rev 22:15; Sent Sext 270; also Phil 3:2. For a comparison of virtue with divine behavior, cf. 1 John 4:7. On μεταβολή cf. *PECL* 1:149.

Ch. 2

(76A)

εἰς μίαν ὁμοῦ κακίαν πάντας ἀνθρώπους πλὴν ἑνὸς τοῦ τελείου τιθεμένης. This Stoic view Plutarch considers foolish because it places almost all men into the same category. Paul is closer to the Stoics than to Plutarch in that he sees sin as something that dominates all men (Rom 1-3, esp. 3:19-20) except for those in

Christ, who have been freed from sin (Rom 6:1-11). However, Paul's position is more comparable to Hellenistic mystery religions and to Hellenistic mysticism. Cf. R. Bultmann, "The Problem of Ethics in the Writings of Paul," *The Old and New Man*, 16-30. Cf. also 1 John 3:4-10.

(76A-B)

ἐν μὲν ταῖς σχολαῖς ... ἐν δὲ τῷ βίῳ καὶ τοῖς πράγμασιν. Plutarch criticizes the Stoics for the inconsistency between what they do and what they preach. Cf. Betz, *Lukian*, 114f.; also Sent Sext 177; Matt 7:15-20; 1 Clem 38:2; Did 11:8; Bauer, s.v. ἔργον, 1.a. Such a criticism of Paul may lie behind his defense in 2 Cor 1:15-20; 4:7; 10-13 (cf. the interpretation by Betz, *Paulus*).

Ch. 3

(76C)

οὕτως ἄν τις ἐν φιλοσοφίᾳ τὸ ἐνδελεχὲς καὶ τὸ συνεχὲς τῆς πορείας ... λείως καὶ ὁμαλῶς τοῦ πρόσθεν ἐπιλαμβανόμενον ... τεκμήριον ἑαυτῷ ποιήσαιτο προκοπῆς (cf. 77D). For examples of the use of "way" and "walk" as names for ethical activity or philosophical life, see Bauer, s.v. ὁδός, 2 (cf. also 76D, 77D, 83A), ὀρθοποδέω, περιπατέω, 2, πορεία, 2 (cf. also 75D, 83B), πορεύω, 2.c, στοιχέω.

ὁμαλῶς. Here "smoothness" in the walk is a sign of progress. Herm Man 6:1:4 uses ὁμαλῶς to describe travel along the path of the Christian life; cf. also the use of ὁμαλός in Herm (Bauer, s.v., 2). However, the same image is used to describe the way of sin in Ps-Clem Hom 7:7:2; cf. also Matt 7:13f.

ἀπταίστως. Cf. the similar figurative usage in Jude 24.

(76D)

ἔθος (συνηθεία in 79D; ἐθισμός in 83B). Good habits help one to progress in virtue by making one accustomed to a virtuous life (cf. H. G. Ingenkamp, *Plutarchs Schriften über die Heilung der Seele*, 105-15). Such ideas are rare in ECL because of ECL's stress on man's need for divine help (see above part II). However, see Sent Sext 412, 414, 445, 129; Ps-Clem Hom 5:25:1.

τῆς κακίας ἐπιτιθεμένης κτλ. A halt in the progress towards virtue brings the danger of an attack by κακία. Such talk of attacks is reminiscent of Eph 6:10-17.

(76E)

χρησμός. See *PECL* 1, index, s.v.

συνειδῆς σεαυτὸν ἡμέρας τε καὶ νύκτωρ ἀεὶ τῇ κακίᾳ διαμεμαχημένον. On the "spiritual" warfare of Christians, cf. Eph 6:12; G. Stählin, *TDNT*, s.v. ἡδονή, E.3.a; Bauer, s.v. πανοπλία, 2. On the necessity for constant vigilance, cf. 1 Pet 5:8.

Ch. 4

(76F)

πόνος καὶ ἄσκησις (cf. 83B-C). Use of athletic imagery to describe the struggle to lead a virtuous life is a common *topos* in diatribes. In line with ECL's general view that salvation depends on God and not on man, Paul et al. do not use the athletic imagery in the same way as Plutarch does here. On this whole question see V. C. Pfitzner, *Paul and the Agon Motif: Traditional Athletic Imagery in the Pauline Literature* (Leiden, 1967). However, cf. ἄσκησις in Mart Pol 18:3; Athenag Res 15:7; ἀσκέω in Acts 24:16; 2 Clem 20:2-4; Herm Man 8:10; Sent Sext 51, 64, 69, 98 = 334, 120.

τῆς προθυμίας οἷον ἀπομαραινομένης. On the threat that weariness offers to the ethical life, cf. Gal 6:9; 2 Thes 3:13. The danger of weariness is also a concern in apocalyptic contexts: Matt 10:22; 24:13//Mark 13:13; Rev 1:9; 2:2f., 19.

(77A-B)

οὕτως ὅσοι τὸ πρῶτον . . . τελευτῶντες ἐξέκαμον καὶ ἀπηγόρευσαν. The eagerness of beginners in philosophy is contrasted with their later weariness. Cf. Gal 3:3 (ἐναρξάμενοι . . . ἐπιτελεῖσθε); Matt 13:20-22 //Mark 4:16-19//Luke 8:13f. Cf. also 76F above.

(77B)

πράγματα ἄλλα. These lead astray from philosophy. Cf. τὰ βιωτικὰ πράγματα in Herm Vis 3:11:3; Man 5:2:2. Cf. also Matt 13:22// Mark 4:19//Luke 8:14; Matt 8:18-22//Luke 9:57-62; Matt 19:21f.//Mark 10:21f.//Luke 18:22f.; Ps-Clem Hom 1:8:1-3; 1:14:6-15:1.

(77C)

πόθος ὁ πρὸς φιλοσοφίαν. On this desire for philosophy see *PECL* 1:87.

πεῖνα καὶ δίψα. With this use of hunger and thirst to describe the desire for philosophy, cf. Matt 5:6; also John 6:35. Cf. also Bauer, s.v. διψάω, 2.

γάμος, πλοῦτος, φιλία, στρατεία. Cf. Luke 14:18-20. "Die wichtigsten Verrichtungen, die den Menschen in Anspruch nehmen, werden exemplifiziert. Gemeinsam für Plut. und das N.T. ist nur ὁ γάμος. Auf den übrigen Punkten macht sich der kulturelle Unterschied bemerkbar; πλοῦτος, φιλία und στρατεία spielen keine entscheidende Rolle in der Umwelt Jesu" (Almqvist, 67).

Ch. 5

(77D)

πλάνη. For conversion as a turn from πλάνη, cf. Tit 3:3; 1 Pet 2:25; Tat 29:1-2. Cf. also H. Braun, *TDNT*, s.v. πλανάω κτλ.

(77E)

περιφέρω. Cf. the similar figurative usage in Eph 4:14; Heb 13:9 v.l.

ἀφεικότα τὰς ἐν τῇ πόλει τιμὰς καὶ ἀρχὰς διὰ φιλοσοφίαν. With this conversion to philosophy (on which see O. Gigon, "Antike Erzählungen über die Berufung zur Philosophie," *Museum Helveticum* 3 [1946] 1-21; A. D. Nock, *Conversion* [Oxford, 1933] 164-86), cf. Jesus' call to his disciples to leave their possessions and to follow him in Matt 4:18-22//Mark 1:16-20; Matt 8:18-22//Luke 9:57-62; Matt 19:21f.//Mark 10:21f.//Luke 18:22f.; Matt 19:27-29//Mark 10:28-30//Luke 18:28-30; Luke 5:27f. Cf. also Sent Sext 81, 264a.

διὰ φιλοσοφίαν. For Plutarch, all is to be sacrificed for the sake of philosophy. With this cf. esp. Matt 19:29 (ἕνεκεν τοῦ ἐμοῦ ὀνόματος) //Mark 10:29 (ἕνεκεν ἐμοῦ καὶ ἕνεκεν τοῦ εὐαγγελίου)//Luke 18:29 (εἵνεκεν τῆς βασιλείας τοῦ θεοῦ). Cf. also Matt 5:10; Matt 5:11//Luke 6:22; Matt 10:18//Mark 13:9//Luke 21:12; Matt 10:22, 39; 16:25//Mark 8:35//Luke 9:24; Matt 19:12; 24:9// Mark 13:13//Luke 21:17; Acts 9:16; 1 Cor 4:10; 9:23; 2 Cor 4:5, 11; 1 Pet 3:14.

(77F)

ἀπ' οὐδεμιᾶς ἀνάγκης. Contrast Diogenes' view that he had chosen philosophy for himself with Paul's statement in 1 Cor 9:16.

τῶν ἀγαθῶν ἁπάντων ἐστερημένος. Lack of wealth was conventional for some philosophical schools; cf. Betz, *Paulus*, 100-17. Cf. also Matt 10:9f.//Mark 6:8f.//Luke 9:3; Did 11:6, 12; Sent Sext 18; Ps-Clem Hom 12:6:4; 77E above.

(77F-78A)

When Diogenes was dissatisfied with his poverty, the sight of a mouse feasting in his left-overs taught him to be satisfied. An incident in the story of the prodigal son (Luke 15:14-19) is just the opposite. There the feeding pigs convince the prodigal to give up his present life-style and to return to the wealthy father he had left.

With this use of nature to teach contentment, cf. Matt 6:25-34// Luke 12:22-32.

Ch. 6

(78B)

διαφόρων ἀντιλήψεις ἐν γέλωτι καὶ παιδιᾷ. The philosopher has to endure scoffers. Cf. Matt 9:24//Mark 5:39f.//Luke 8:52f.; Matt 27:38-43//Mark 15:27-32//Luke 23:35-37; Acts 17:32.

τὸ μὴ ταραττόμενον κτλ. One sign of progress in philosophy is not being disturbed by the worldly success of non-philosophers. Cf. 2 Clem 20:1.

(78E)

ὀρθῶς γιγνώσκει περὶ θεῶν. This, according to Aristotle, is what is most important. Cf. *PECL* 1:37f.

Ch. 7

(78F)

τῷ νομίσματι τοὺς Ἕλληνας πρὸς οὐδὲν ἕτερον ἢ τὸ ἀριθμεῖν χρωμένους. This famous description of the Greeks by Anacharsis is comparable with the rich fool in Luke 12:16-21 in that both describe a foolish misuse of wealth.

(79A)

συμβαίνω. Cf. the use of συμβαίνω to introduce a proverb in 2 Pet 2:22.

Antiphanes' story of Plato's acquaintances who only much later understood the meaning of Plato's words is comparable to Jesus' disciples who did not understand Jesus' sayings until after his resurrection. Cf. Luke 24:6-9; John 2:22; 12:16; also Acts 11:16.

Ch. 8

(79B-C)

ὅρα . . . τὸ χρήσιμον καὶ σάρκινον καὶ ὠφέλιμον (cf. 79E: τὸ οἰκεῖον καὶ χρήσιμον). For Plutarch what is important about a writing is that it should offer something χρήσιμον . . . καὶ ὠφέλιμον. Cf. 2 Tim 3:16; 2:14. Cf. also ἐπανόρθωσις in 2 Tim 3:16; ὄφελος and χρηστός in Just Dial 1:2. σάρκινος is used here positively, but in ECL it is primarily negative. Cf. Bauer, s.v., 2.

(79D-E)

οὐκ ἀπὸ λόγων μόνον κτλ. From his daily experiences a philosopher is able to gain insights into what makes a life virtuous (77F-78A; 82F). Cf. the illustrations from nature in Matt 6:25-34//Luke 12:22-32.

(79F-80A)

ἂν τοὺς λόγους ταῖς πράξεσι μιγνύωσι κτλ. Those who apply their concepts of virtue to their daily lives are more apt to gain an understanding of virtue from their daily experiences. Behind this lies the common idea that one cannot be virtuous simply in the abstract, but that virtue must also show up in one's daily life (also 76A-B, 84B). Cf. John 15:14; Rom 2:13; Jas 1:22-25; 2:22-26; 1 John 1:6; 1 Clem 38:2; Sent Sext 225; cf. also 1 Cor 9:27.

(79F)

ἀλλὰ καὶ πρὸς ἡδονὰς καὶ πρὸς ἔριδας καὶ περὶ κρίσεις καὶ συνηγορίας καὶ ἀρχάς. The list describes various areas of life in which one should manifest his virtue. Cf. Eph 5:15ff.; Col 3:18ff.; 1 Pet 2:11ff. The differences between the NT lists and that of Plutarch reflect the different sociological backgrounds of the two. Cf. 77C above. More in line with Plutarch, Sextus seems to direct some of his maxims towards the upper class; cf. H. Chadwick, *The Sentences of Sextus*, 102f.

(80A)

ὃ λαβόντες ἐκ φιλοσοφίας εὐθὺς εἰς ἀγορὰν κτλ. Plutarch questions the progress of those who want to sell philosophy or use it for display. On the question of whether philosophers should accept payment and its parallels in ECL, see Betz, *Paulus*, 100-17; *Lukian*, 112-14. Cf. also the criticisms of religion being used for show in Matt 6:1-18; Luke 18:9-14; also Sent Sext 341-42.

Ch. 9

(80B)

μὴ δόξης εἰκαίας ἕνεκα μηδ' ἐκ φιλοτιμίας. One who is motivated by a desire for glory is not a true philosopher; cf. 1 Thes 2:6. John contrasts the δόξα of men with the δόξα given by God: John 5:44; 7:18; 8:54; 12:43. Cf. also 78E; 80B and ch. 10.

τὸ φιλόνεικον καὶ δύσερι περὶ τὰς ζητήσεις ὑφεῖται (cf. 78F; 84E). See the similar rejection of such conduct in 1 Tim 6:4f. Cf. also Chadwick, *The Sentences of Sextus*, p. 104.

(80C)

μήτε . . . ὑπὸ δειλίας ἀναδυόμεθα. This, for Plutarch, shows progress in virtue. Cf. the portrait of the apostles in Acts 2:14ff.; 4:13; 14:3; 17:22ff.; and the view of Paul's opponents (1 Cor 2:3f.; Betz, *Paulus*, 44-57). Cf. also Sent Sext 170 and the use of παρρησία, H. Schlier *TDNT*, s.v. παρρησία, παρρησιάζομαι, C.2-3.

Ch. 10

(80E)

Οὐ μόνον δὲ δεῖ τοὺς λόγους ἀλλὰ καὶ τὰς πράξεις ἕκαστον ἐπισκοπεῖν εἰ τὸ χρειῶδες τοῦ πανηγυρικοῦ κτλ. The last few chs. spoke about the importance of τὸ χρειῶδες in one's language. This ch. says that one's actions should also have τὸ χρειῶδες. On the importance of πρᾶξις corresponding to λόγος, cf. 76A-B.

ζητεῖ μάρτυρας. Cf. the similar expressions in Mark 14:55//Matt 26:59.

ἔτι μᾶλλον. Conclusion *a minore ad maius*. See *PECL* 1, index, s.v. Conclusion.

(80F)

ὥσπερ οὖν ὁ καλῶν ἐκεῖνος κτλ. With this example of illusory pride, cf. Luke 18:9-14; Matt 19:20-22//Mark 10:20-22//Luke 18:21-23; Luke 15:25-32; 1 Cor 8:2; Gal 6:3; 1 Clem 38:2. On self-praise, cf. the article by Betz in this volume, pp. 367ff.

(81A)

δόντα τῷ φίλῳ κτλ. That a friend helps a friend was a well-known friendship *topos*, cf. Cicero *Off.* 1. 17. 56; 3. 10. 43; *Amic.* 8. 26; 13. 44; 16. 56-59. For Plutarch, helping one's friends is a virtuous act, but it is considered insignificant in Matt 5:43-48//

Luke 6:27f., 32-36; 14:12-14, because it is only what everyone does (contrast Gal 6:10).

πρὸς ἔντευξιν αἰσχρὰν πλουσίου κτλ. Preferential treatment for the rich is opposed here and Jas 2:2-5.

ἐν ἑαυτῷ κατασχεῖν καὶ σιγῆσαι. Cf. 80F above. Progress can be recognized when one is satisfied with keeping his achievements to himself. Other witnesses are not needed because one sees oneself as a good enough witness. Contrast Matt 6:3f., where one does not even want oneself as a witness because God should be the only witness. See Almqvist, 34; also 80A above and *cup. divit.* 528A.

οὗτος γὰρ αὐτὸς εὐδοκιμῶν παρ' ἑαυτῷ. Cf. the recommendation for self-evaluation in Gal 6:4.

(81B)

τὸν λόγον ἐντὸς ἤδη τρεφόμενον καὶ ῥιζούμενον ἐν ἑαυτῷ. Cf. ὁ ἔμφυτος λόγος, Jas 1:21 (on which see M. Dibelius and H. Greeven, *James* [Philadelphia, 1976] ad loc.). Cf. also the terminology similar to Plutarch's in Eph 3:17; Col 3:15f.

οἱ μὲν οὖν γεωργοὶ κτλ. This comparison with the attitude of farmers towards grain vividly portrays the "emptiness" of the ἀλαζών. On the ἀλαζών see *The Characters of Theophrastus*, ed. R. G. Ussher (London, 1960) 193; and cf. Jas 4:13-16; 1 Clem 21:5; 38:2. On κενός, cf. Jas 2:17-20; Herm Man 11:3-4; 12:4:5; Sim 9:19:2. For a comparison of humans with plants (also 77A), see Matt 13:24-30, 36-43; 13:1-9, 18-23//Mark 4:1-9, 13-20// Luke 8:4-8, 11-15; John 15:1-8, etc.

(81B-D)

τῶν φιλοσοφεῖν βουλομένων νέων κτλ. The contrast between real philosophers and those who only look like philosophers was a common *topos*. On the use of the *topos* in 2 Cor 10-13, cf. Betz, *Paulus*, 44-57. On the arrogant behavior of the young, cf. 1 Clem 3:3; 1 Tim 3:6; 1 Pet 5:5; also 79B, 81D-F.

συλλέγειν καρπὸν ἀπὸ τῶν λόγων. καρπός is frequently used in a similar figurative way in ECL, cf. Bauer, s.v. 2. a-b; Almqvist, 52.

(81C)

καθάπερ ἀγγείων κενῶν κτλ. For the body described as an ἀγγεῖον, cf. Herm Man 5:2:5. For man as an empty vessel to be filled, cf. Herm Man 5:2:7; 12:4:5.

πώγων καὶ τρίβων. A caricature of the philosopher's appearance not found in the NT. Cf. Just Dial 1:2.

(81C-D)

τὸ δὲ φιλοσοφίας ὄνομα κτλ. The refusal of honorific titles is a sign of virtue. Cf. Mark 10:18//Luke 18:19; John 1:20; also Matt 23:8-10. Cf. the use here of ἁρπάζω with Phil 2:6ff., on which see Almqvist, 117f.

"οὔ τίς τοι θεός εἰμι· τί μ' ἀθανάτοισιν ἐίσκεις;" (Homer *Od.* 16. 187). For refusal to be considered divine, cf. Acts 3:12; 10:25f.; 14:11-15; Rev 22:8f. Contrast Acts 12:21-23.

(81D-E)

ὥσπερ γὰρ οἱ τελούμενοι κατ' ἀρχὰς κτλ. The interpretation of philosophical "progress" by comparison with and in terms of mystery cult language (cf. A. D. Nock, *Conversion*, 181f.; G. Bornkamm, *TDNT*, s.v. μυστήριον, A.2) has parallels in ECL where Christian "faith" is interpreted in that way. Cf. Rom 6:1-14; Col 2:11-15; 3:1-17; Eph 4:22-24. Cf. also H. D. Betz, "The Mithras Inscriptions of Santa Prisca and the New Testament," *NovT* 10 (1968) 71f.; *PECL* 1:55f.

οἱ τελούμενοι. On this technical term see *PECL* 1:39.

ἐν θορύβῳ καὶ βοῇ. Cf. the clamor and confusion of the unbelieving crowds in Matt 9:23//Mark 5:38; Matt 27:24; Acts 17:13; 20:1; 21:30, 34; Mart Pol 8:3; 9:1.

δρωμένων δὲ καὶ δεικνυμένων τῶν ἱερῶν. This technical terminology does not occur in ECL (cf. G. Schrenk, *TDNT*, s.v. ἱερός, E-F). On δείκνυμι see *PECL* 1:293.

μετὰ φόβου καὶ σιωπῆς. Fear is also a common response to the supernatural in the gospels; see H. Balz, *TDNT*, s.v. φοβέω κτλ., D.2. On silence see *PECL* 1:185.

ἡ δόξα. In discussing 2 Cor 3:18 (μεταμορφούμεθα ἀπὸ δόξης εἰς δόξαν), R. Reitzenstein (*Die hellenistischen Mysterienreligionen* [Stuttgart, 1927] 357-61) suggested that mystery religions might be the basis for the use of δόξα in the 2 Cor passage (cf. also Rom 8:29f.; Phil 3:21). The predominant view in NT studies, however, has been that the NT concept of the divine δόξα comes from the OT כבוד יהוה (see G. Kittel, *TDNT*, s.v. δόξα, F-G). Does this passage in Plutarch, which uses δόξα in a mystery religions context, support Reitzenstein? Or is δόξα used here, as elsewhere in the essay (78E, 80B, F, 81C), simply in the sense of "fame" or "repute" as Babbitt (ad loc.) has translated?

μέγα φῶς. Cf. 75E, s.v. ἐκλάμπω.

ἀνακτόρων ἀνοιγομένων. Cf. the open temple in Rev 11:19; 15:5; Barn 16:9. ἀνάκτορον is the technical name for the Eleusinian shrine. It does not occur in ECL.

σιωπὴ καὶ θάμβος. The response to the supernatural; cf. above s.v. μετὰ φόβου καὶ σιωπῆς. Cf. also Mark 1:27//Luke 4:36; Mark 9:15; 10:24; 16:5f.; Luke 5:9; Acts 3:10, 11; 9:6 t.r.; Apoc Pet 8, 11.

ὥσπερ θεῷ τῷ λόγῳ. Philosophy is here compared to a mystery religion in which ὁ λόγος functions as the deity. Elsewhere Plutarch can identify Osiris and Hermes as ὁ λόγος, cf. *PECL* 1:68, 71.

(81E-F)

Menedemus ridicules the typical student of philosophy by characterizing improvement in a student as a change from a σοφός to a φιλόσοφος to a ῥήτωρ until finally one becomes an ἰδιώτης. In this connection cf. Paul's criticism of the σοφία of the Corinthians with ἡ μωρία τοῦ κηρύγματος (1 Cor 1:18-31; cf. 3:18-20), his denial of being a ῥήτωρ (1 Cor 2:1-5, 13; 2 Cor 10:10), his admission to being an ἰδιώτης (2 Cor 11:6; cf. also Acts 4:13), and his teaching that the Christian is "only human" (cf. Betz, *Paulus*, 138-48).

ἅπτονται τοῦ λόγου . . . τὸν τῦφον κατατιθεμένους. Cf. 1 Tim 6:3f. where τυφοῦσθαι is contrasted with προσέρχεσθαι ὑγιαίνουσιν λόγοις τοῖς τοῦ κυρίου ἡμῶν Ἰησοῦ Χριστοῦ. Cf. also τυφοῦσθαι as a temptation for beginners in 1 Tim 3:6.

Ch. 11

(81F-82A)

On this comparison of ἁμαρτάνοντες with the sick, cf. 1 Tim 6:4; Herm Sim 6:5:5; A. Oepke, *TDNT*, s.v. νόσος κτλ., A.

δέονται βοηθεῖν. Cf. the requests for help in NT miracle stories: Matt 8:2//Mark 1:40//Luke 5:12; Matt 9:18//Mark 5:23//Luke 8:41f.; Matt 9:27//Matt 20:30f.//Mark 10:47f.//Luke 18:38f.; Matt 15:22, 25//Mark 7:26; Mark 8:22; 9:22; Luke 17:12f.; John 11:3; cf. also 2 Cor 12:8.

(82A)

ἀνήκεστοι μέν εἰσιν οἱ πρὸς τοὺς ἐλέγχοντας κτλ. Those who object to being corrected are worse off than those who are willing to accept correction. This is conventional ethical advice; see Prov 12:1; 13:1, etc.; 2 Clem 19:2; Sent Sext 245. Cf. 2 Cor 7:8-11; F. Büchsel, *TDNT*, s.v. ἐλέγχω, 2; J. Behm, *TDNT*, s.v. νουθετέω, νουθεσία. Thus the response of the Pharisees (Matt 12:14// Mark 3:6; Matt 21:45f.; Luke 7:30; 16:14f.), the Jews (John 5:18; 8:59) and the Epicureans (Acts 17:32) shows them to be incurable (cf. John 3:20).

τὸ δ' ἑαυτὸν ἁμαρτάνοντα παρέχειν κτλ. Confession of faults (ὁμολογέω) is a sign of progress. Cf. Matt 3:6//Mark 1:5; Luke 15:21 (contrast vs. 29); 18:9-14; Acts 19:18; 1 John 1:9; Barn 19:12; 1 Clem 51:3; 52:1-4; 2 Clem 8:1-3; Did 4:14; Herm Vis 1:1:3; 3:1:5; Sim 9:33:3.

που. For the similar use of που with quotations, cf. Bauer, s.v., 1.

(82B)

We have here a caricature of the hypocrite who displays his outer defects while covering up his inner faults. Cf. Matt 23:1-36 (esp. the ἐντός/ἐκτός contrast in vss. 25f.//Luke 11:39-41). On the list of vices, see *PECL* 1, index, s.v. Lists of vices, virtues.

(82C)

ἀλλ' ὁ τούτοις ὁμόσε χωρῶν κτλ. With this description of contrition, cf. the publican in Luke 18:13, and with ὁ δὲ τὴν οὐσίαν κτλ., cf. Luke 18:14.

(82F)

The story about Pyrrho describes the ideal response to danger, an ideal to which Paul conforms in Acts 27:21-38.

Ch. 12

ὅρα. Used to call attention to what follows as in Herm Man 6:2:4.

(83A)

τῆς φύσει τυραννικῆς ψυχῆς τὸ φανταστικὸν καὶ ἄλογον οἷα κατὰ τοὺς ὕπνους δρᾷ. Elsewhere in Plutarch sleep is a time for the soul to escape the evil of the body (cf. *PECL* 1:268), but here with Plutarch's interpretation of Plato (*R.* 571C; also in *virt. et vit.*

101A) it provides an opportunity for the irrational part of the soul to escape the restrictions imposed upon it by daily life. *ECL* does not seem to share this view about dreams.

"μητρί τε γὰρ ἐπιχειρεῖ μίγνυσθαι" καὶ περὶ βρώσεις ὁρμᾷ παντοδαπάς. These specific evils arising in dreams are part of a longer list mentioned by Plato (*R.* 571D). The Corinthian libertines claimed the freedom to do these very things; see 1 Cor 5:1f.; 8:1ff.

ἃς μεθ' ἡμέραν ὁ νόμος αἰσχύνῃ καὶ φόβῳ καθείγνυσιν. Plutarch sees νόμος as preventing the irrational part of the soul from accomplishing what it desires (see also in *virt. et vit.* 101A). For Paul in Rom 7:7f. νόμος gives ἁμαρτία the opportunity to awaken desire.

(83A-C)

ὥσπερ οὖν τὰ πεπαιδευμένα καλῶς τῶν ὑποζυγίων κτλ. The virtuous person is compared to a well-trained animal which does not leave the ὁδός even when αἱ ἡνίαι have been released. On the comparison of human conduct with reining an animal, cf. Jas 3:2f. and *PECL* 1:190, 191. Cf. 76C above on πορεία, ὁδός, 76D on ἔθος, 76F on ἄσκησις.

(83C)

πῶς οὐ μᾶλλον κτλ. Conclusion *a minore ad maius*. See *PECL* 1, index, s.v. Conclusion.

κατὰ τοὺς ὕπνους. For NT examples of God giving messages to people in their sleep, see A. Oepke, *TDNT*, s.v. καθεύδω, C.1.b.

ὀργιζόμενον . . . τὸν Ποσειδῶνα. On the anger of God, see *PECL* 1:218.

(83C-D)

Stilpo criticizes Poseidon's demands for offerings because the demands do not conform to Delphic theology. Stilpo's small offerings should be acceptable because they are μέτριος. In Mark 12:41-44//Luke 21:1-4 the small offerings of the widow are acceptable because, in conformity to the teachings of Jesus, she has given all that she had.

μεμψιμοιρέω. Cf. the complaints of God in Rom 9:19; Heb 8:8; Herm Sim 9:10:4.

(83D)

πλαττομένης ἔτι δόξαις καὶ νόμοις. Cf. on 83A above.

(83E)

ἕξεως ἤδη βεβαιότητα καὶ κράτος ἐχούσης ἐπὶ τοῖς λόγοις ἀσάλευτον. Plutarch here uses the Aristotelian term ἕξις (*EN* 2. 5. 1105[b] 19ff.; also *prof. virt.* 82E) for the disposition of the wise man which leads him to live in accordance with virtue. The Stoic term διάθεσις (*virt. mor.* 441B-C; also *prof. virt.* 75D, 84E) is almost equivalent. Cf. Rist, *Stoic Phil.*, 2f. Of these two terms only ἕξις occurs in ECL, Heb 5:14 (cf. Bauer, s.v.). For the NT, according to R. Bultmann (*TDNT*, s.v. αἰδώς, C), "The essence of the believer . . . is not a relationship to himself, a ἕξις or ἀρετή, but a being before God and towards his neighbour." Cf. the figurative use of βέβαιος (Bauer, s.v.) and ἀσάλευτος (Bauer, s.v., 2; σαλεύω, 2), cf. also κράτος in Eph 6:10; 1:19.

Ch. 13

(83E-84A)

ἡ παντελὴς ἀπάθεια μέγα καὶ θεῖον κτλ. To reach the Stoic goal of complete ἀπάθεια (see 82F) one would have to become divine. Plutarch therefore concerns himself with the more practical Aristotelian goal of trying to moderate τὰ πάθη and to avoid excesses (ὑπερβολαί) and thus εἰς τὸ μέσον καθίστασθαι. ECL's different view of τὰ πάθη did not allow for such moderation (see the article by Hershbell in this volume, pp. 143f., 151). The term μέτριος is, however, used in 1 Clem 1:3. Because God is ἀπαθής, Ignatius has difficulty explaining the sufferings of Jesus; cf. Ign Eph 7:2; Pol 3:2; *PECL* 1:151.

(83F)

εἰ Δωρίοις κτλ. Musical comparisons (cf. 84A) were a diatribe *topos*; cf. 1 Cor 14:7f.

θαυμασταὶ παρ' ὃ δεῖ λόγων καὶ ἀνθρώπων ἢ καταφρονηταί. Excessive θαυμάζειν is preferable to καταφρονεῖν. This should be compared with προσωπολημψία, which God is denied as having in Rom 2:11; Eph 6:9; Col 3:25 (also Acts 10:34) and which is rejected for Christians in Jas 2:1-9.

Ch. 14

(84B)

A sign of progress is when one's κρίσεις result in ἔργα (cf. also the λόγος/πρᾶξις comparison here and in 79F-80A, 80E, 84D). A similar indication is the μιμεῖσθαι of the virtuous (84C, cf. 85B) or ὁ πρὸς τὰ ἐπαινούμενα ζῆλος καὶ τὸ ποιεῖν εἶναι προθύμους ἃ θαυμάζομεν. Cf. Tit 2:14 (ζηλωτής); Herm Man 12:5:1 (πρόθυμος); Herm Sim 5:3:4 (προθυμία).

(84C-E)

μίμησις. The ἀνὴρ ἀγαθὸς καὶ τέλειος (cf. 75C) is one who has achieved ἀρετή, and to admire him means to imitate him and to become like him: τῷ ἀγαθῷ μονονουχὶ συμφῦναι γλιχόμενος (cf. σύμφυτος in Rom 6:5), also συναρμόττειν καὶ συγκολλᾶν ἑαυτοὺς ὦμεν πρόθυμοι. For the history of religions background to the μίμησις terminology and an analysis of its use by Paul, see H. D. Betz, *Nachfolge und Nachahmung Jesu Christi im Neuen Testament* (Tübingen, 1967) 48ff. Cf. also 2 Thes 3:7-9; 1 Tim 4:12; Heb 13:7; 1 Clem 17:1; Ign Eph 10:3; etc. In addition, cf. 85A-B, παράδειγμα in 82D, *PECL* 1, index, s.v. Example.

ἀργός. Cf. the similar use of ἀργός in Jas 2:20; 2 Pet 1:8.

νύττω. Cf. κατανύσσομαι in Acts 2:37.

ζῆλον ἐπὶ τοῖς καλοῖς. Cf. Gal 4:18; 1 Pet 3:13 and 84B above.

(84D)

τὴν καρδίαν στρέφεσθαι. With this statement of Alcibiades (Plato *Smp.* 215E) cf. Acts 2:37; 7:54; cf. also J. Behm, *TDNT*, s.v. καρδία, B-D.

ἔργοις καὶ πράξεσιν ἀνδρὸς ἀγαθοῦ καὶ τελείου παραβάλλων ἑαυτόν. In order to learn how to progress one should compare himself with his superiors. Paul points out the foolishness of those in Corinth who compare themselves to themselves; cf. 2 Cor 10:12 and Betz, *Paulus*, 118-32.

Ch. 15

(84E)

κατὰ Πλάτωνα μακάριον μὲν αὑτὸν ἡγεῖσθαι τὸν σώφρονα, "μακάριον δὲ τὸν ξυνήκοον τῶν ἐκ τοῦ σωφρονοῦντος στόματος ἰόντων λόγων." With this macarism of Plato (*Lg.* 711E), cf. Matt 13:16//Luke 10:23; John 20:29. With Plutarch's expansion, cf. John 13:17; Jas 1:25. Cf. also F. Hauck and G. Bertram, *TDNT*, s.v. μακάριος κτλ.

θαυμάζω. The typical reaction to a divine man. Cf. *PECL* 1, index, s.v.

(84F)

ἂν μὴ μόνον εὐημεροῦντας κτλ. ἀρετή is to be admired, welcomed and "imitated," even when it is accompanied by afflictions. Cf. Paul's theology of the cross, on which see E. Güttgemanns, *Der leidende Apostel und sein Herr* (Göttingen, 1966); Betz, *Nachfolge und Nachahmung*, 143ff.

(85A)

"φεῦ, τοῖσι γενναίοισιν ὡς ἅπαν καλόν." With this quotation from Euripides (fr. no. 961, *TGF*), cf. 1 Cor 9:19-23; 3:21-23; Tit 1:15.

πρὸ ὀφθαλμῶν. Cf. κατ' ὀφθαλμούς in Gal 3:1.

τί δ' ἂν ἔπραξεν ἐν τούτῳ Πλάτων; Plato and others who function as examples are not always applicable to current situations. Therefore, one has to ask what they would have done in the new situation. Similar questions were one reason why the early Church expanded and interpreted the sayings of Jesus and felt the need for the deutero-Pauline literature. Cf. 84C-E above.

(85B)

πρὸς ἔσοπτρα κοσμοῦντας ἑαυτούς. Jas 1:23-25 uses ἔσοπτρον in a similar metaphorical way, but there the mirror is not heroes from the past, but the law of God. On κοσμέω, cf. Bauer, s.v., 2.b.α.

Ch. 16

(85C)

ἀνδρὸς ἐνδόξου καὶ σώφρονος ἐξαπίνης ἐπιφανέντος. For response to a great man as an evaluation of one's virtue, cf. Jas 2:2-4.

(85D)

ἔρως ἐμφύεται. Cf. the implanted λόγος (Jas 1:21), τῆς δωρεᾶς πνευματικῆς χάρις (Barn 1:2), δωρεὰ τῆς διδαχῆς (Barn 9:9).

παρασχεῖν οἰκίαν αὑτοῦ καταφανῆ κτλ. One's virtue is evident in his homelife. Cf. 1 Tim 3:1-13 and the household codes (Eph 5:21-6:9; Col 3:18-4:1; 1 Tim 2:8-15; Tit 2:1-10; 1 Pet 2:18-3:7).

λόγους λεγομένους ἢ γραφομένους. Cf. the criticism of Paul by his opponents in 2 Cor 10:10 (on which see Betz, *Paulus*, 44-69).

Ch. 17

(85E)

τὸ μηδὲν ἔτι μικρὸν ἡγεῖσθαι. Considering all sins to be important is a sign of progress because it is the only way one will be able to avoid all sins. Generally speaking, for ECL all sins are important because they separate man from God (cf. Hershbell, *virt. mor.*, p. 147). Yet, cf. the distinctions between sins in Matt 12:31f.//Mark 3:28f.; 1 John 5:16f.

On the importance of μικρόν for μεγά, cf. Matt 25:21//Luke 19:17; Luke 16:10; 1 Cor 5:6; Gal 5:9; Jas 3:2-5.

τί γὰρ τὸ παρὰ τοῦτο; With this expression cf. Jas 2:16 (τί τὸ ὄφελος;); 1 Cor 15:32 (τί μοι τὸ ὄφελος;).

(85F-86A)

καὶ γὰρ αἱμασιάν κτλ. This essay concludes with an illustration from the construction trade to show the care that one should take in building his life. Cf. the similar illustration that is used to end the Sermon on the Mount in Matt 7:24-27//Sermon on the Plain in Luke 6:47-49.

DE TUENDA SANITATE PRAECEPTA
(MORALIA 122B - 137E)

BY

MORTON SMITH
Columbia University
New York, New York

I

This tractate, entitled Ὑγιεινὰ παραγγέλματα (henceforth *sanit. praec.*), was no. 94 in Lamprias' catalogue. Extracts from it were included in an early fourth century collection by Sopatros of Apamea which was read by Photius (codex 161, on Sopatros' book eight). Photius says Sopatros got them from a yet older collection of extracts by an unspecified author. Nine passages from Plutarch's tractate were cited by Stobaeus in the early fifth century.[1] A Latin translation by Erasmus, *Plutarchi Chaeronensis de tuenda bona valitudine precepta*, was printed in London in 1513 and an English translation of this by R. Wyer appeared about 1530.[2]

The text used here is that edited by I. Wegehaupt and W. Sieveking in *Plutarchi Moralia* 1 (ed. W. Paton and I. Wegehaupt, revised by H. Gärtner, BT [1974] 253-283). I have also consulted the translations by Babbitt and by Xylander as revised by Wyttenbach, and Wyttenbach's commentary.[3] The dissertation of G. Böhm, *Plutarchs Dialog* Ὑγιεινὰ παραγγέλματα *analysiert und auf seine Quellen untersucht* (Giessen, 1935) is chiefly concerned with tracing Plutarch's medical ideas to their sources (mainly Plato

---

[1] 122E in 4. 38. 8 (vol. 5, p. 900); 125E in 3. 16. 23 (vol. 3, pp. 485f.; both this and the preceeding are cited as Πλουτάρχου ἐκ τῶν Ὑγιεινῶν Παραγγελμάτων) and seven selections from 125F to 130A, cited simply as Πλουτάρχου, in 4. 37. 6-12 (vol. 5, pp. 880-82), which is Stobaeus' section "On health, and the foresight to preserve it."

[2] *The gouvernaunce of good helthe, by the moste excellent phylosopher Plutarche* (London, n.d.). I owe the date to the Columbia University Library catalogue.

[3] F. Babbitt, *Plutarch's Moralia*, LCL, vol. 2 (1928) 214-293; D. Wyttenbach, *Plutarchi Chaeronensis Moralia* (Oxford, 1795-1830) 8 vols. in 15. Translation, 1.2.481-540; commentary, 6.2.803-869.

and Asclepiades of Bithynia),[4] but is also valuable for its explanations of technical medical terms.

The literary form of *sanit. praec.* is that of a Platonic dialogue of the type in which, after a brief initial conversation, one of the speakers reports at length and without substantial interruption the teaching of someone absent.[5] The dialogue form in general is unknown to ECL, which, however, contains numerous stories of conversations and reports of speeches. The dialogue was mainly a philosophical or literary form and almost invariably upper-class; Lucian's *Dialogues of Sailors* and *Dialogues of Prostitutes* are upper-class parodies. In the present example, Plutarch seems to have departed from convention by making the speaker, Zeuxippos, report his own teachings, but this is not perfectly clear and the influence of the Platonic examples has led commentators to suppose that the teacher referred to is Plutarch.[6] In any event,

---

[4] Asclepiades of Bithynia = A. of Prusa = *Asklepiades* 39 in PW 2.2 (1896) 1632f. An early first century B.C. advocate of "natural" and agreeable regimen for the sick, Asclepiades was widely influential.

[5] On Plutarch's dialogues in general, C. Kahle, *De Plutarchi Ratione Dialogorum Componendorum*, Göttingen, 1912 (diss.); the form of *sanit. praec.* is discussed on pp. 26-29. On the speakers and characteristics of *sanit. praec.*, Böhm 1ff. and Ziegler, sec. 3.4.O.

[6] Zeuxippus tells his interlocutor (Moschion) that one Glaucus has attacked "us," i.e., Z. himself, βοῶν . . . ἡμῖν σύγχυσιν ὅρων τετολμῆσθαι διαλεχθεῖσι περὶ διαίτης ὑγιεινῆς (122C). Moschion asks to hear these things Glaucus attacked (122F). Z. replies, Ἔφη τοινυν ὁ ἑταῖρος ἡμῶν ἀκοῦσαί τινος λέγοντος ὡς (ibid.) and hereon follow the teachings attacked (122F, end, to 124C). After stating them, Z. concludes (124C-D): Ταῦθ' ἡμῖν ὁ Γλαῦκος ἐν γέλωτι προύφερεν ὡς παιδαγωγικά· τῶν δ' ἄλλων οὐ πάνυ πρόθυμος ἦν ἀκούειν, οὐδ' ἡμεῖς ἐκείνῳ διηγεῖσθαι. σὺ δ' ἐπισκόπει τῶν λεχθέντων ἕκαστον. From here on his exposition continues as if he were giving an account of his own opinions. There are numerous expressions in the first person (e.g., 125D, 126D, 127B, 130A and F, 132D and E, 133D, etc.); the tractate concludes with a reference to ἄνδρες φιλόλογοι καὶ πολιτικοί, πρὸς οὓς ἐνέστηκεν ἡμῖν ὁ λόγος (137C). If this were all the evidence, we should suppose that ὁ ἑταῖρος in 122F was Glaucus. But in 135B and D there are two sentences interrupted by ἔφη as if the speaker (Zeuxippus) were reporting somebody else's statements. Wyttenbach (ad loc.) took the latter of these to indicate that Zeuxippus was summarizing a lecture of Plutarch's; he therefore supposed that in 122F ὁ ἑταῖρος ἡμῶν was Plutarch. In this supposition he was followed uncritically by Babbitt, 215 and 220 n.a, Böhm, 3 (who negligently referred to ὁ ἑταῖρος as mentioned in ch. 24, 135B-136A, where it does not occur), and Ziegler, sec. 3.4.O, col. 152. But this is almost certainly false because (1) what ὁ ἑταῖρος says is concluded by ταῦθ' ἡμῖν ὁ Γλαῦκος . . . προύφερεν (124C); (2) ὁ ἑταῖρος is *not* the speaker whose medical opinions are reported, on the contrary ἔφη . . . ὁ ἑταῖρος . . . ἀκοῦσαί τινος λέγοντος. So ὁ ἑταῖρος is almost certainly Glaucus, the word being used either sarcastically or as meaning

since Plutarch is the author, the teachings are those he has chosen to present. He has drawn them from a variety of sources (this Böhm has shown), and he may have augmented them by some thoughts of his own.

The formal difference of *sanit. praec.* from the works of ECL is matched by its difference in content. *Sanit. praec.* is a treatise on how to preserve health by rational regimen. No treatise of ECL deals with this subject nor even discusses it at any length. Indeed, throughout the whole of ECL there are only two occasions in which writers clearly, albeit in passing, recommend certain practices as healthy: 1 Tim 5:23 "No longer drink only water, but use a little wine because of your stomach and your frequent illness;" Herm Vis 3:9:2ff., urging readers to share their food with the poor, "For some people, because they eat so much, bring sickness on their bodies and damage them, while the bodies of those who do not have food are damaged by their lack of sufficient nourishment." As dubious cases one may add John 11:12, where the disciples say of Lazarus, who is ill, "If he has slept he will get well" and Acts 27:33f., where Paul urges his fellow travellers to eat something before landing because they have been fourteen days without food, (!) "for this is good for you" (τοῦτο γὰρ πρὸς τῆς ὑμετέρας σωτηρίας ὑπάρχει). Hermas was warned by an angel (Vis 3:10:7f.) that too many or great revelations might be bad for his health. Prayer alone (in Mark 9:29 B ℵ* it[k] georg[1] Clement) or prayer and fasting (*rell*) are said to be necessary for certain types of exorcism, but this takes us out of the realm of rational hygiene and into that of miracle and magic.

To this latter realm belong the reports of Jesus' proceedings in exorcisms and cures, e.g., Mark 7:33f. "He put his fingers into his ears, and spat and touched his tongue and looked up to heaven,

---

merely "interlocutor," as in Matt 20:13; 22:12. (Hippocrates, *Letter to Damagetos*, ed. Littré, 9.354, shows this usage is not limited to strangers whose names are unknown, cf. Bauer, s.v.) If Plutarch must be dragged in to fit the Platonic paradigm, it would be more plausible to find a reference to him in τινός. But since Glaucus was attacking what Zeuxippus had said, τινός probably refers to Z. This leaves the two instances of ἔφη, in 135B and D, to be explained. The first may refer to Homer, as Wyttenbach, followed by Babbit, seems to have supposed (ad loc.), or to Zeuxippus, as Böhm thought (27, n. 1). The second probably refers to Zeuxippus and may have been added by a copyist who understood the first as Böhm did and imitated it to soften an awkward transition. If so, the dialogue contains no reference to Plutarch.

sighed, and said to him 'Εφφαθα," cf. Mark 8:23; John 9:6; Acts 9:17ff. Here, too, belongs the prescription of anointing and prayer for cure of the sick, in James 5:14ff.: anointing is no less familiar as a magical than as a medical technique; [7] its conjunction here with prayer shows the type of efficacy expected; and the context specifies that the prayer, not the natural consequences of the anointing, will effect the cure (5:51: ἡ εὐχὴ τῆς πίστεως σώσει τὸν κάμνοντα). Jesus is said to have ordered that Jairus' daughter, after her resurrection, be given something to eat (Mark 5:43) and that Lazarus, after his, be loosed from the graveclothes and allowed to walk (John 11:44); these reports may also reflect magical beliefs (eating in this, the upper world binds the returned spirit to stay here; loosing from the graveclothes and walking separate the body from death), or may be merely naturalistic narrative inventions. Even in the very early churches resurrection from the dead can hardly have been so common as to result in the development of a rational regimen for the resurrected (*contra* Irenaeus 2:48:2 ed. Harvey, *saepissime*!). The relapses of persons exorcised are of course explained, like the exorcisms, entirely in demonological terms (Matt 12:43ff.//Luke 11:24ff.). Jesus' command to the disciples, "Heal the sick," is coupled with "Raise the dead; cleanse lepers; cast out demons" (Matt 10:8; abbreviated by Luke 10:9 //Copt Gos Thom log. 14).

Not only are the healings consistently miraculous—θεραπεύω in this literature normally means "cure by a miracle" [8] and "cures" are among the gifts of the spirit (1 Cor 12:9, 28, 30)—but also the causes of sickness are commonly conceived to be supernatural. The insane are "demoniacs"; "fever" and "leprosy" are demons (Luke 4:39//Mark 1:31//Matt 8:15; Mark 1:42//Luke 5:13); birth defects are caused either by divine punishment or divine providence (John 9:2ff.); mutism, blindness, and infestation by parasites result from encounters with supernatural beings (Luke 1:20ff.; Acts 9:8; 12:23); Paul's own physical affliction was an angel of Satan sent by God to keep him humble (so he was proud of it, 2 Cor 12:6-9); and he attributed the sickness and the deaths that had occurred among the Corinthian Christians to their unworthy communions (1 Cor 11:29ff.). Moreover, he and his imita-

---

[7] *PGM* I. 224, 256; II. 19, 160; IV. 746, 802, 1091, 1338, etc.
[8] So H. Beyer, *TDNT*, s.v., 4.

tors claimed to be able to cause sickness by handing their opponents over to Satan (1 Cor 5:3ff.; 1 Tim 1:20; cf. Rev 2:22). The converse also holds true; those in a state of grace are exempt from illness. If one is born of God "the Evil One does not touch him" (1 John 5:18); the saints of old were healed of their illnesses by faith (Heb 11:34); the martyrs in paradise will not suffer hunger, thirst, sunstroke, or sunburn (Rev 7:16); Paul was immune to snakebite (Acts 28:3-6) and Justus Barsabba to poison (Pap 2:9 = Eusebius *h.e.* 3:39), as the risen Lord said all believers would be (Mark 16:18; this makes possible a clear and simple demonstration of faith, which fundamentalists might well require of their candidates for ordination).

All this does not result from the fact that the authors of ECL were wholly ignorant of rational medicine. It is true that the attempts to find in "Luke's" work typically "medical language" and evidence of special medical training, knowledge, or interest (and so to identify the author as "Luke the doctor" of Col 4:14) were unjustified.[9] But there are a fair number of ECL passages that do show knowledge of the common medical (or, first-aid) practices and opinions of the times. For example, the good Samaritan "bound up the wounds (of the thieves' victim) pouring on oil and wine" (Luke 10:34); the jailer at Philippi, after his conversion, washed the wounds left on the apostles by their beating (Acts 16:33); Paul recognizes that if one member of the body suffers the whole body is affected (1 Cor 12:26), and that the appropriate diet for infants is milk, for adults, solid food (1 Cor 3:2; again Heb 5:12f.; 1 Pet 2:2; Barn 6:17); Hermas knows the syndrome and symptoms of old age, and also, how these can be briefly interrupted by good news—as of a large inheritance (Vis 3:11:3f.; 3:12:2).

[9] See the classic discussion by H. Cadbury, *The Style and Literary Method of Luke* (Cambridge, Mass., 1920) 39-72, with a note on the history of the question by G. Moore, pp. 51-54. Of the eighteen "medical words" which Cadbury says were alleged by Harnack, Zahn, and Moffatt as evidence of Luke's medical knowledge, only three are cited from *sanit. praec.* in Wyttenbach's *Index Graecitatis* to Plutarch. These are κραιπάλη, ῥῆγμα, and τραῦμα. On the common usage of κραιπάλη see Moore's note, p. 54. Ῥῆγμα and τραῦμα are equally common, as are many of the other items in the list, some of which surely occur in *sanit. praec.* though Wyttenbach did not think it worth while to cite them, nor I to search for them. This is not to deny that in the Greek of Plutarch's time there were some technical medical terms (see below, on 129D), but merely to say that their occasional occurrence in Plutarch or in ECL does not generally deserve attention.

Besides such, and even commoner,[10] commonplaces, there are also traces of the equally common medical disillusionment: the woman with an issue had "suffered many things from many doctors and wasted everything she had and got no better, but rather went down hill" (Mark 5:26//Luke 8:43); POxy 1 (= Copt Gos Thom log. 31) parallels "No prophet is accepted in his own country" with "And no doctor can cure those who know him." But such disillusionment does not suffice to explain the almost total absence of rational medical advice from a body of material so rich as ECL in precepts for everyday life; nor, as shown above, can the absence be explained as resultant from total ignorance of medical practice.

Looking for other explanations, we of course think first of the gospels' miracle stories, since many of them are stories of cures and exorcisms and therefore testify to a lively interest in physical and mental health and to the importance of health as a theme in Christian propaganda.[11] The testimony is undeniable and is confirmed by the continuance in Acts and many apocryphal acts and gospels of stories about miraculous cures. Yet further evidence of the same interest appears in many details; for instance, the promise in Rev 22:2 that the leaves of the tree of life will be for the healing of the nations, the prayer in 1 Clem 61:1 that God give health to "our rulers and leaders," the descriptions of the saviour and God as ἰατρός in Diogn 9:6 and Ign Eph 7:2, and the many promises of "life" [12] which carries with it, by implication, "health" —at least sufficient for survival. The saints in paradise will presumably be healthy.

But no writer of ECL thought it worth while to make this presumption explicit. The nearest approach to this is Rev 7:16, cited

[10] E.g., for knowledge that people say, "The healthy don't need a doctor" (Mark 2:17//Matt 9:12//Luke 5:31); that there are different sorts of eunuchs (Matt 19:12); that congenital blindness was thought incurable (John 9:32); that the symptoms of glossolalia are like those of insanity (1 Cor 14:23); that salve is used for the eyes (Rev 3:18); that there is a medical instrument for examining structures buried in folds of fat (Pap., fr. 3, edd. Gebhardt, Harnack, Zahn).

[11] On this see Harnack, *Die Mission und Ausbreitung des Christentums*, 4 ed. (Leipzig, 1924) 1: 129-150, "Das Evangelium von Heiland und von der Heilung."

[12] Mark 9:43,45 //Matt 18:8f.; Mark 10:30//Matt 19:29//Luke 18:30; Matt 7:14; 19:17; 25:46; John 3:15, 16, 36; 4:14, 36; and passim; Acts 2:28; 3:15; 11:18; 13:46, 48; Rom 2:7; 5:17, 21 and often in Paul's letters; frequent also in the Pastorals, Catholic Epistles, and Rev and throughout the Apostolic Fathers.

above. ὑγ(ί)εια is almost never mentioned—never in the NT, only twice in the Apostolic Fathers (1 Clem 20:10 the marvels of creation include springs created for men's pleasure and health; 61:1 the blessing of health is asked for rulers), never in the early apologists. The adjective ὑγιής is fairly frequent in the gospels and Acts, in reports of cures; [13] Hermas uses it half a dozen times metaphorically to mean "in good shape" of trees, shoots, and building blocks; [14] in Titus it once describes "sound" teaching (2:8). Ὑγιαίνω is used in the NT four times of actual health,[15] eight times of teaching or belief [16] (it never occurs in the Apostolic Fathers or early apologists). This last, metaphorical sense is also implied by many of the uses of related terms, noticed above. When God is recommended as a doctor in Ign Eph 7:1f. it is because of his success in curing heretic bite; when the same attribute is applied to the saviour in Diog 9:6 it is one of a long string (τροφέα, πατέρα, διδάσκαλον, σύμβουλον, ἰατρόν, νοῦν, φῶς, etc.) and the other members suggest that its meaning is metaphorical. Particularly significant is the rarity of ὑγίαινε and the like as a wish at the beginning of Christian letters, or a valediction at the end. In the NT the wish appears only in 3 John 2 (εὔχομαί σε . . . ὑγιαίνειν). Similarly ἔρρωσο/ἔρρωσθε stands at the end of only two letters, of which one is a pagan's (Acts 15:29; 23:30 t.r.). In the Apostolic Fathers ὑγιαίνω never appears. Ignatius regularly used ἔρρωσθε at the ends of his letters, but always with some addition (ἐν χάριτι θεοῦ, ἐν Χριστῷ Ἰησοῦ, etc.) to give it a metaphorical meaning.[17] Otherwise it never appears in the Apostolic Fathers. In the Zenon Papyri, by

[13] Mark 5:34; Matt 12:13; 15:31 (see B. Metzger, *A Textual Commentary on the Greek New Testament* [New York, 1971] ad loc.); John 5:(4), 6, 9, 11, 14f.; Acts 4:10.

[14] These are mostly symbols of believers, so the meaning is really the same as that in Titus, viz., "sound *in faith*;" Herm Sim 8:1:3f. *ter*; 3:1; 6:3; 9:8:3, 5, 7.

[15] Luke 5:31 (the healthy don't need a doctor); 7:10 (cure); 15:27 (the prodigal's father rejoiced to get him back safe and sound); 3 John 2 (epistolary greeting). Cf. also Matt 8:13 v.l.

[16] 1 Tim 1:10; 6:3; 2 Tim 1:13; 4:3; Tit 1:9, 13; 2:1f.

[17] Ign Eph 20:2; Magn 15:1; Trall 13:2; Rom 10:3; Phil 11:2; Smyrn 13:1f.; Pol 8:3 *bis*. Ignatius was imitated by Polycarp, Phil 14, *incolumes estote in domino Iesu Christo*. The greeting ἐρρῶσθαι ὑμᾶς εὐχόμεθα in Mart Pol 22:1 is bracketed by Zahn as a later addition, see his note in *Patrum Apostolicorum Opera*, edd. O. de Gebhardt, A. Harnack, T. Zahn, ed. 3, fasc. 2 (Leipzig, 1876) XLIX. Zahn is followed in this by T. Camelot, *Ignace d'Antioche*, 4 ed. (Paris, 1969) 208 (who thinks it fourth century), and W. Schoedel, *The Apostolic Fathers*, 5 (Camden, N.J., 1967) 80.

contrast, almost every fully preserved letter ends with ἔρρωσο/ἔρρωσθε, and additional wishes for the recipients health are common.[18] In the many letters of ECL (except for 3 John 2, the ambiguous σώζεσθε in Barn 21:9, and the metaphorical expressions of Irenaeus and Polycarp) there is none which either begins or ends by wishing the recipient physical health.

The same silence about health prevails throughout the contents. Ἴασις in the NT refers only to miraculous cures (Luke 13:32; Acts 4:22, 30); and ἰατρός appears only in the sayings "The healthy don't need a doctor" (Mark 2:17//Matt 9:12//Luke 5:31); "Doctor, heal yourself" (Luke 4:23); the story of the sick woman who had wasted her money on doctors (Mark 5:26//Luke 8:43 v.l.); and the reference to "Luke the doctor" in Col 4:14. In the Apostolic Fathers ἴασις is normally "healing of sins;" [19] ἰάομαι normally refers to such cures; [20] and we have already seen the figurative uses of ἰατρός.[21] Much the same is true of σῴζω and σωτηρία. In ECL they refer either to miraculous cure or deliverance from death (the sense that prevails in the synoptics) or to Christian salvation (in the rest of the NT and the Apostolic Fathers); the common Greek reference to "being healthy" is never found in the NT and is very rare in the rest of ECL.[22] Health is almost never among the things prayed for,[23] or the things for which authors give thanks, or urge others to give thanks. Sickness is not among the works of the flesh, nor is health among those of the spirit (Gal 5:19-23; 1 Clem 35:1ff.).

---

[18] On the frequency of ὑγίαινε (*et sim*) as an epistolary greeting see Bauer, s.v., F. Preisigke, *Wörterbuch* (Berlin) 1927, s.v.

[19] Herm Man 4:1:11; 12:6:2; Sim 5:7:3f. (*bis*?); 7:4; 8:11:3. The solitary exception is Barn 12:7 referring to Moses' cure of snake bite. Ἰάματα, v.l. in Barn 3:4, refers to cure of sins.

[20] 1 Clem 16:5; 56:7(?); 59:4 (Gebhardt's emendation of ἀσεβεῖς to ἀσθενεῖς is needless; Harnack's argument that the prayers are *pro sanctis* is not valid, since by this time some of the *sancti* had become ἀσεβεῖς, as the following petition shows, "bring back the errant"; A. Hilgenfeld, *Clementis Romani Epistulae*, 2 ed. [Leipzig, 1876] reads ἀσεβεῖς); 2 Clem 9:7; Barn 5:2; 14:9; Herm Vis 1:1:9; Sim 9:23:5; 28:5. The only references to physical healing are Barn 8:6 and Herm Vis 1:3:1, both somewhat dubious.

[21] Above, p. 38. There is one literal use, the statement in Pap, fr. 3, that even a doctor with an instrument could not get through the fat around Judas' eyes.

[22] See W. Foerster's articles on σῴζω and cognates in *TDNT*.

[23] Exceptional occurrences: 1 Clem 59:4 ἐξανάστησον τοὺς ἀσθενοῦντας (for ἴασαι see above, n. 20); 61:1.

Yet in spite of all this, and in spite of the appearance of χαρίσματα ἰαμάτων in Paul's lists of the gifts of the spirit (1 Cor 12:9, 28, 30), and in spite of dominical commands to heal the sick (Matt 10:8; Luke 10:9; Copt Gos Thom log. 14) and of Acts stories of the apostles' miracles, and Paul's own insistence that he had done plenty (2 Cor 12:12)—nevertheless, Paul and his imitators and early Christian writers in general often refer to Christians being ill,[24] and care of the sick is among the Christian duties frequently specified,[25] though never with any indication of what one is to do for them except visitation and, in Jas 5:14f., unction and prayer.

In sum, the early Christian attitude towards health and illness has produced a paradoxical body of evidence:

(1) many stories of miraculous cures by Christ and the apostles;

(2) evidence from Paul himself that he and other apostles claimed to perform miracles, cause sickness, and (presumably) cure it;

(3) evidence, also from Paul, that he himself was a sick man, and, from Paul and others, that sickness was not rare in the Christian communities and that care of the sick was an important community problem;

(4) common neglect of this problem in the prayers and/or thanksgivings preserved; and

(5) almost total neglect of rational means for preventing and dealing with illness; this in spite of

(6) evidence that some such rational means were known in the community.

To explain this tangle of contradictions we may posit several contradictory causes:

(1) a strong tradition that the body is contemptible and to be neglected (Matt 6:25 and such like material—this prevented expression of concern for health in the literature);

(2) the common human concern for health, and strong community feeling (this produced the communal care for the sick and injunctions about it);

(3) the origin of the movement in the enthusiasm aroused by Jesus' "miraculous" power as a healer (this made such miracle

---

[24] 1 Cor 2:3; 11:30; 2 Cor 4:10ff.; 11:30; 12:5, 7-10; Gal 4:13f.; Phil 2:26f.; 3:10; Col 1:24; 1 Tim 5:23; 2 Tim 4:20.

[25] Matt 25:43f.; Acts 20:35; 1 Thes 5:14; Heb 13:3; 1 Tim 5:10; Jas 5:14f.; Pol Phil 6:1.

stories part of the core of the tradition; popular hopes and love of the miraculous preserved and developed them):

(4) the fact that Paul and his competitors had nothing like Jesus' success as miracle workers, but were not wholly unsuccessful (this made more acute the essential problem of miraculous healing—Why doesn't it work on everybody?). Hence Paul's claim to do miracles and his unwillingness to talk about them. We may well believe *both* that he had done a few, *and* that he had good reason to fear he might not be able to do one again—particularly not when one was most needed for public relations.

If this analysis of the early Christian attitude towards health and illness is correct, we can understand why *sanit. praec.* and ECL have basically so little in common. The rational hygiene with which *sanit. praec.* is concerned was not wholly unknown to the Christian communities, but was kept out of the literature of those communities on the one hand by the teaching that it was unworthy of Christian concern, on the other by the tradition of miraculous cures that claimed to make it unnecessary (Jas 5:14f.). Moreover, ECL generally avoided the subject of health because Christians' private prayers for it (of which there must have been many) commonly and conspicuously went unanswered, and this raised embarrassing questions as to their merits and their saviour's power and concern. This was a particularly difficult form of the problem of evil. Consequently it was consistently neglected. Consequently we can look for no more than occasional contacts between *sanit. praec.* and ECL.

II

The outline of *sanit. praec.* is as follows:

Ch. 1 *Introduction* (122B-E)
Dialogue between Moschion, a doctor, (*qu. conv.* 658A) and Zeuxippus, a philosopher, in which Z explains to M his refusal to discuss with one Glaucus, another doctor, who had been ridiculing some of Z's teachings.[26] M asks to hear the statements ridiculed and Z's other opinions on medical subjects.

[26] On the question, whether the teachings were Zeuxippus' or Plutarch's, see above, pp. 33f., n. 6.

Chs. 2-27 *Body* (122F-137E)
A speech by Zeuxippus, in two parts:

Chs. 2-5 1. (122F-124D) Report of the two propositions attacked by Glaucus, viz.: that one should be careful to keep the hands warm, and that, while healthy, one should both get used to the regimen imposed on the sick and, generally, practice moderation, especially in eating and drinking.

Chs. 6-27 2. (124D-137E) The rest of Z's medical opinions, arranged as follows:

Chs. 6-7 (a) More on moderation. Natural, unstimulated appetite should be the limit of indulgence (124D-126B).

Chs. 8-9 (b) Overindulgence deprives us of many pleasures (126B-127B).

Ch. 10 (c) Overindulgence aggravates illness produced by other causes (127B-C).

Chs. 11-15 (d) Watch for premonitory symptoms and abstain in advance (127C-130A).

Ch. 16 (e) Exercises suitable for scholars, especially declaiming and reading (130A-131B)

Ch. 17 (f) Baths, better warm (131B-D).

Ch. 18 (g) Food, better light. Eat little meat (131D-132A).

Ch. 19 (h) Milk is a food, not a beverage. Wine is to be used in moderation, with lots of water (132A-F)

Chs. 20-21 (i) Literary conversation, during and after meals, moderates appetite and aids digestion (132F-134A).

Ch. 22 (j) Avoid emetics and cathartics; if necessary, use natural ones (134A-F).

Chs. 23-25 (k) Avoid the sort of strict regimen that cuts off its adherent from public affairs. Health is to be sought for the sake of humane activities. For this end the body's needs, including pleasure, should be satisfied (134F-136D).

Chs. 26-27 (l) Observe your body carefully, learn its needs, tastes, capacities, and limitations, and care for it accordingly (136D-137E).

This outline presents nothing unusual save the pseudodialogue of the introduction, which reminds one of the false front—the gothic or palladian façade—on a warehouse. Behind it, the treatise is simply an expository barn where the topics are stacked one after another in no observable order. A similar composition (façade and warehouse) is found in ECL, notably in Jas and Barn, though in them the façades are epistolary and not nearly so developed as Plutarch's. Heb reverses the arrangement, having a systematic treatise in front and an epistolary lean-to at the rear. Such literary false façades, especially the epistolary, continued popular in Europe through the eighteenth century and were often used even in the nineteenth, for example, in the many "letters" on learned subjects to prominent patrons, which fill the memoirs of European learned societies, notably those of France, Italy, and the Netherlands.

III

Comments on individual passages of *sanit. praec.*:

(122 B-C)

Zeuxippus' reported refusal to discuss with Glaucus is in accord with the pseudapostolic precepts to avoid contentious men, whose unreasonable vanity is shown by their obstinate adherence to their own opinions when they ought to accept yours (1 Tim 6:3f.; Tit 3:10f.; cf. Acts 19:9).

(122D)

The metaphorical interpretation of the "house" in *Od* 4. 392 as the body occurs twice in Plutarch (fr. 179. 9 [LCL 15:334] = Eusebius *p.e.* 1.8.9). It is found also in Philo *De Somniis* 1. 10. 57 and perhaps in Dio Chrys. *Or.* 40. 5, von Arnim. (The other passages cited as parallels by Wyttenbach take the verse literally.) The great example of the same metaphor in the NT is 2 Cor 5:1 for which—though particularly for the term σκῆνος—many classical and a few Biblical parallels are cited by Wettstein, ad loc., and referred to by E. Allo, *Saint Paul. Seconde Épitre aux Corinthiens* (Paris, 1956) 138; to which add Luke 11:33f. In the NT, however, the body is more often thought the house of a demon or spirit, Mark 3:27//Matt 12:29; Matt 12:44// Luke 11:24; Rom 8:9; 1 Cor 3:16; 6:19; 2 Cor 6:16.

(122D)

σωτηρία in the sense of "physical well being" (Wyttenbach, *incolumitatem corporis*) not in the NT and rare in the Apostolic Fathers, see above, p. 39.

(122F)

ἑταῖρος, of a mere interlocutor, so Matt 20:13; rare; see above, p. 33, n. 6.

(123B-C)

That fasting should be done privately and not made a public demonstration is a teaching attributed to Jesus by Matt 6:16-18. Jesus recommends modesty because it will be rewarded; Plutarch, for its own sake.

(123D)

That one should not be scrupulous about washing before meals is Jesus' teaching according to Mark 7:1-23//Matt 15:1-20. But both the types of washing and the motives of the speakers differ. Plutarch, against Greek refinement, points out that it is sometimes healthy to forego a bath. Jesus, against Jewish legal requirements, declares washing the hands before meals uncessary.

(123E)

ἑστίασιν [βασιλικὴν καὶ (vΠΘ)]ἡγεμονικὴν (*rell*): Plutarch's attitude towards a dignitary's dinner (or, more likely, a dinner for a dignitary) is the realistic one of a man who has gone to such parties; he anticipates indigestion. Contrast Matt 22:1-14. Since Christians never had to face the real thing, ECL could use the royal dinner as a picture of perfect bliss. This contrast epitomizes not only the writers' difference in social station, but also the difference between the temporary asceticism (for the sake of future indulgence) advocated by ECL, and the permanent asceticism (as a means of adjustment to the limits of human nature, but also as a matter of good taste, 126B) advocated by *sanit. praec.* The insertion of βασιλικὴν καὶ before ἡγεμονικὴν probably shows the influence of the NT on the transmission of Plutarch's text.

(123E)

συνουσίαις καὶ φιλοφροσύναις: *Hendiadyoin*, NT parallels and literature noted by Almqvist, 79.

(123E)

ἐπαχθῆ φανέντα: The importance of politeness in the success of Christianity versus more observant forms of Judaism deserves notice. It is illustrated, for instance, by 1 Cor 10:27 = Luke 10:8, "Eat what is put before you." Any diet raises the same difficulty and Plutarch inclines to the same solution, though he admits exceptions (124B-C).

(123F-124A)

The story of Philip is in effect a parable although it happens to be true (or, Plutarch thought it so). It is complete with application, introduced by οὕτω, as often in the gospels (which, however, use οὕτως, e.g., Matt 13:40, 49; 18:35; 20:16). Plutarch's example proves that the application, though formally distinct, may be part of the original structure. Bultmann, *HST*, 178, n. 1, predictably discovered a philosophical distinction between parables and stories told as examples; but this "example" could be transformed into a "parable" simply by the substitution of "a king" for "Philip."

(124C)

τῇ κύλικι καὶ τῇ τραπέζῃ: Almqvist, 98, compares 1 Cor 10:21: ποτήριον κυρίου . . . καὶ ποτήριον δαιμονίων . . . τραπέζης κυρίου . . . καὶ τραπέζης δαιμονίων, and notes other examples of the same conjunction in Plutarch *sept. sap. conv.* 159E (τράπεζαι καὶ κρατῆρες) and *qu. conv.* 612E (τραπέζης καὶ κύλικος).

(124Dff.)

With this long discussion of diet contrast Matt 6:25-32//Luke 12:22-30: "Do not worry about yourselves, as to what you may eat . . . So do not worry, saying, 'What can we eat?' or 'What can we drink?' or 'What can we wear?' For all these things are concerns of the gentiles."

(124D-E)

In contrast to Plutarch's approval of pleasure (within its proper limits, cf. 126B-127B; 132B; 137B), ἡδονή occurs in ECL only 17 times and is always pejorative, except in Herm Man 10:3:3 and 12:5:3 where it means "good taste" (of wine, in comparisons), 2 Clem 15:5 and Herm Sim 6:5:7 which speak of the pleasure of doing good, and 2 Pet 2:13 which implicitly contrasts the true pleasure to come with τὴν ἐν ἡμέρᾳ τρυφήν. ἥδομαι occurs only once in the whole literature, Ign Rom 7:3 οὐχ ἥδομαι τροφῇ φθορᾶς, οὐδὲ ἡδοναῖς τοῦ βίου τούτου. ἡδύς as an adjective appears only once, Herm Sim 8:9:1, pejorative. (Adverbial forms meaning "willingly," ἥδιον, ἥδιστον, ἡδέως, are found in Mark 6:20; 12:37; 2 Cor 11:19; 12:9, 15; 1 Clem 2:1; 62:3). Ἡδυπαθεία is twice mentioned, 2 Clem 16:2; 17:7, both pejorative. ἡδέως is used seven times, of which three are favorable (1 Clem 31:3; Herm Sim 8:10:3; 9:27:2), four pejorative (Ign Trall 6:2; Herm Man 2:2; Sim 6:5:5 [!]; Acts 13:8 v.l.). There are no other uses of the root in NT and Apostolic Fathers.

(124E)

ἀπέχοντα, "having received": Wyttenbach, ad loc, following Wettstein, notes as parallel Matt 6:2 ἀπέχουσιν τὸν μισθὸν αὐτῶν, and also parallels Epictetus *Diss.* 3. 24. 17 τὸ γὰρ εὐδαιμονοῦν ἀπέχειν δεῖ πάντα ἃ θέλει with Phil 4:18 ἀπέχω δὲ πάντα καὶ περισσεύω. He cites many other classical parallels.

(125B)

The battle between the body and its inhabitant appears in 1 Cor 9:27 ὑπωπιάζω μου τὸ σῶμα καὶ δουλαγωγῶ. But for Plutarch, in this tractate (cf. 135E-137E) the body is the source both of healthy pleasures and healthy moderation, the inhabitant is the source of excesses and unhealthy practices, and the happy outcome of the battle is an ultimate victory by the body and its built-in natural law. Contrast Paul, for whom the body is the seat, if not the source, of sin and therefore of death (Rom 6:12; 7:24) and the desired outcome is its subjugation to the inhabitant. This latter notion, a commonplace of ancient asceticism, of course occurs in Plutarch too, for instance, immediately below in 125D-E.

(126E-F)

The theme, that for brief pleasure one may lose eternal happiness, is frequent in ECL, e.g., Luke 6:24ff.; 16:25; 1 Tim 6:9; Jas 5:1ff.; 2 Pet 2:13. Equally common in ECL is the converse theme, that brief troubles will produce eternal joy, e.g., 2 Cor 4:17; 1 Tim 4:8; Jas 1:2; 1 Pet 1:6f.; 5:10.

(127F)

ὡς οἴνῳ δὴ τὸν οἶνον, κραιπάλῃ δὲ τὴν κραιπάλην ἐξελῶντας: Almqvist, 50, compares Mark 3:22f. (//Matt 12:24//Matt 9:34//Luke 11:15) ἐν τῷ ἄρχοντι τῶν δαιμονίων ἐκβάλλει τὰ δαιμόνια . . . πῶς δύναται σατανᾶς σατανᾶν ἐκβάλλειν; A. thinks all these are parodies of the principle *similia similibus curentur* (many examples), and he sees in the juxtaposition of two different cases of the same word, in Mark 3:23, a fashionable rhetorical device not found in the example from Plutarch.

(129A)

Both Plutarch and the gospels (Matt 16:2f. in the western text and koine//Luke 12:54ff.) ridicule the careful observance of signs of coming weather, by contrast with neglect of signs of something more important—Plutarch, ill health, in the gospels, the end of the world. In all three passages signs of coming rain or storm are among those ridiculed; both Luke and Plutarch use forms of ὄμβρος. Evidently this sort of argument was no less fashionable than feeble.

(129C-D)

τὸ τοὺς φίλους ἐπισκεπτόμενον ἀσθενοῦντας. This was a pagan politeness and a Jewish duty; ECL repeatedly enjoins it: Matt 25:36, 43; Acts 20:35; 1 Thes 5:14; 1 Tim 5:10; Jas 5:14ff.; Pol Phil 6:1. The frequency indicates the importance of community care for the poor Christians. Plutarch comes from and writes for the rich; he never thinks of community care; his visit is purely polite. His advice that while visiting one should not show off one's knowledge of medical jargon is evidence that there was such a jargon, and that it was not readily comprehensible to the average hearer. The same fact appears, e.g., from Galen's praise of Hippocrates φαίνεται συνηθεστάτοις τε καὶ διὰ τοῦτο σαφέσι τοῖς ὀνόμασι κεχρημένος.[27] (Had everybody done this, and had there been nothing else that one could do, this would have been no reason for special praise—and in fact Galen goes on to give some examples of the sort of jargon he disliked.) Such passages refute Moore's claim that since Greek medical terms were formed from Greek roots "with that creative freedom in which Greek surpasses all other tongues" their "meaning . . . if not their technical definition, was at once evident to every Greek." [28] Actually the creative freedom of Greek had given many roots so

---

[27] Galen, *Comm. in Hipp. de epidemiis*, 3.32, ed. Kühn 17.1.678.

[28] G. Moore, "*Editorial Note,*" in H. Cadbury, *The Style and Literary Method of Luke*, 54.

many meanings, and formed words from them in so many different ways for so many different purposes, that new formations must often have been seriously ambiguous, as Galen complains they were. Moore's argument was written in a good cause—to refute the silly claims of Hobart and his imitators that Luke's style shows a physician's peculiar vocabulary—but the cause could have been served better by a better statement of the facts, to wit, that in the second century A.D. there were lots of peculiarly medical terms, and they do not commonly appear in Luke's vocabulary.

(130Aff.)

περὶ γυμνασίων: In ECL γυμνασία appears only once (1 Tim 4:8) and γυμνάζω only five times (1 Tim 4:7; Heb 5:14; 12:11; 2 Pet 2:14; 2 Clem 20:2). None of the uses of the verb refer to actual gymnastics or even physical exercise (Heb and 2 Pet use the participle to mean, generally, "practiced in," and 1 Tim and 2 Clem speak metaphorically of "practicing" or "training oneself" in virtue). Thus the only early Christian reference to physical exercise is that of 1 Tim 4:8, "Physical exercise is useful <only> for a little while" (by contrast with exercise in virtue which gives hope of eternal rewards).

(130B)

Again the notion of the body as the house of an indwelling spirit, see above on 122D and 125B.

(131E)

Plutarch's advice τοῖς δὲ λεπτοῖς ἐμφύεσθαι . . . οἷα τὰ πολλὰ τῶν λαχάνων has only accidental similarity to Paul's permission ὁ δὲ ἀσθενῶν λάχανα ἐσθίει (Rom 14:2). Paul's ἀσθενῶν is a man weak in faith, who avoids meat for fear of violating purity laws; Plutarch fears overnourishment, and his advice is intended for everyone.

(132A)

Like Plutarch, the writers of ECL think of milk rather as a food than as a beverage. This is true even of 1 Cor 3:2, though it has ἐπότισα (contrast 9:7, ἐσθίει), and of Heb 5:12f. where milk is τροφή as it is in 1 Pet 2:2 and Barn 6:17 (which shows how the author understood the citations in 6:8, 10, 13). These instances in

ECL suffice to suggest a reason for this common attitude, viz., that milk was mainly baby food. It was messy to handle, hard to keep sweet (there was practically no refrigeration) and therefore mostly made into cheese. Relatively little reached the cities.

(132B)

Plutarch's recommendation of wine is paralleled by that of Pseudo-Paul, 1 Tim 5:23, the only clear instance of medical advice in the NT (see above, introduction). Significantly, Christian commentators, as reported by Cornelius a Lapide, ad loc.,[29] commonly neglected the medical significance of the verse. Jerome, *Ad Eustochium*, and Chrysostom used it to show that hitherto Timothy had abstained from wine; he was therefore an example of asceticism. Ambrosiaster looked at the matter as an episcopal administrator: Paul prescribed wine for Timothy because God needs healthy servants, therefore we should take care of ourselves. Luther returned to the question of asceticism and argued on the contrary side: Paul told Timothy to take *a little* wine because his stomach was feeble and not able to take more; those of us who are healthy need not be so limited. This was too much for Cornelius a Lapide,[30] who replied *Paulus vinum permittit non ad voluptatem, sed ad necessitatem*; *ideoque dicit "utere", non "fruere"*—an argument from bad evidence, but it reminds us that the pleasant qualities of wine, which partly persuaded Plutarch to recommend it, are not noticed by the NT text. Bengel said nothing about the subject. By the time of E. Scott (*The Pastoral Epistles* [London, 1936] ad loc.) Protestantism had come full circle: "It has to be noted that the verse is meant, not to advocate the use of wine, (!) but to protest against a type of doctrine which would rule out the whole physical side of man's life as evil." Actually Pseudo-Paul's opinion that a little wine was good for the stomach was shared by Plutarch (*qu. conv.* 652B) and by many ancient writers cited by Wettstein, ad loc.

(134D)

The implicit contrast between Greeks and inferior races (Arabs,

---

[29] *Commentaria in Scripturam Sacram*, ed. A. Crampon (Paris, 1858) 19.249f.

[30] "Bacchica ergo bacchantis Lutheri, quam sua inter pocula effudit, est interpretatio" (ibid.).

Scythians) was one which Paul, not being a Greek, vigorously rejected: In Christ "there is neither Jew nor Greek, slave nor free, male nor female" (Gal 3:28); cf. Col 3:11: In Christ "there is neither Greek nor Jew, circumcision nor uncircumcision, barbarian, Scythian, slave, freeman." (Is the change of order significant?)

(135E-F)

The opinion attributed to Jason, "that one must act unjustly in little things in order to act justly in great ones," is compared by F. Babbitt (LCL, ad loc.) to the opinions Paul rejects in Rom 3:8, "Let us do evil that good may come," and 6:1 "Let us remain in sin, that grace may abound." (Paul says the former of these was attributed to him, and quotes the latter as if it was, too.) Since the contexts and therefore the meanings of all three statements are uncertain, comparisons are hazardous, but it seems likely that the Christian ones were based on eschatological expectations alien to the pagan.

SEPTEM SAPIENTIUM CONVIVIUM (MORALIA 146B - 164D)

BY

DAVID E. AUNE

St. Xavier College
Chicago, Illinois

I. INTRODUCTION

While recent scholarship has been virtually unanimous in ascribing this treatise to Plutarch (listed as No. 110 in the so-called Lamprias Catalogue), the authenticity of Συμπόσιον τῶν ἑπτὰ σοφῶν was a matter of lively debate during the Nineteenth Century.[1] The work is in fact pseudonymous; while Plutarch is undoubtedly the actual author, the ostensible author is one Diokles, a μάντις in the court of the sixth century Corinthian tyrant Periander (146C, 149D).[2] The composition is addressed to an equally fictitious Nikarchos, a supposed contemporary of Diokles. Since the name "Nikarchos" is one found in Plutarch's recent ancestry (his great grandfather, according to *Ant.* 68. 7), it may well be his intention to guarantee the validity of this version of the Banquet of the Seven Sages by implying that the composition had been in the possession of his family since the Sixth Century.[3]

The purpose of the composition is given in the προοίμιον (146B-C):

---

[1] The arguments for and against authenticity are rehearsed, together with the citation of relevant literature, in R. Hirzel, *Der Dialog* (Leipzig, 1895) 2:132, n. 4; J. Defradas, *Plutarque: Le Banquet des Sept Sages* (Paris, 1954) 7-12 (a particularly excellent summary); Ziegler, sec. III. 12.a (cols. 246ff.). R. Volkmann's arguments against authenticity (*Leben und Schriften des Plutarch von Chaeronea* [Berlin, 1869] 1:188-209), particularly with regard to stylistics, were ably refuted by G. Hermann, *Quaestiones Criticae de Plutarchi Moralibus* (Halle, 1875). Defradas argues that Platonic inspiration is the best proof of authenticity (p. 15).

[2] On the general subject of literary pseudonymity in antiquity see the superb study by W. Speyer, *Die literarische Fälschung im heidnischen und christlichen Altertum* (Munich, 1971). In Speyer's discussion of "Die einzelnen Fälschungen und ihre Motive" (pp. 131-49), the only motive applicable to *sept. sap. conv.* (a work which, along with *gen. Soc.*, is not mentioned by Speyer) is "Wirkungswille", pp. 132f.: "Berühmte Namen der Vorzeit wurden in solchen Fällen bevorzugt, da man besonders seit hellenistischer Zeit dem Altüberlieferten grosse Verehrung entgegenbrachte."

[3] Hirzel, 2:144.

Diokles, who was both present and a participant at the Banquet of the Seven Sages, desires to provide Nikarchos with a true account of what transpired on that famous occasion. Diokles thinks this an important task in view of the many false accounts of the Banquet which are in circulation, and he wishes to tell his version of what occurred before old age impairs his memory. In view of the fact that at least three literary techniques characteristic of pseudonymous works pretending authenticity are found in this προοίμιον (pseudonymity; first person, eyewitness report; warnings against other literary falsifications),[4] Plutarch's real purpose must be inferred. Many scholars have supposed that Plutarch's purpose was generally to praise and delineate the Greek ideal of practical and intellectual wisdom through the presentation of a collection of sayings and stories which tradition had generally associated with the legend of the Seven Sages.[5] While this general assessment of Plutarch's purpose cannot be denied, it would appear that *sept. sap. conv.* was composed with more specific intentions in mind. Plutarch seems to have two primary, yet interrelated, purposes in view:

(1) He wishes to create an exemplary symposion to serve as a model for those held in his own day with regard to: (a) the intellectual and experiential level and breadth of the guests, (b) the active participation of all who are present, (c) the focus on important moral, philosophical and religious issues without prejudice to the more banal subjects, (d) the emphasis on conviviality and fellowship rather than on intoxication, (e) the elements of wit and spontaneity, (f) the necessity for variety in both guests and subjects discussed, and (g) the emphasis on orderliness and decorum.[6]

(2) While the conversation appears desultory, a careful examination of the content and structure of *sept. sap. conv.* (see below under II. Content and Structure) indicates that the recurring central theme of the composition is the οἰκονομία or proper management of states (kingdoms, tyrannies and democracies), households and the cosmos.[7] The relationship between the first two was

---

[4] Speyer, 44-84 ("Die Mittel der Echtheitsbeglaubigung").

[5] Hirzel, 2:140ff.; Defradas, 12-15.

[6] Plutarch's views on these matters are expressed in the first book of *qu. conv.* (612C-629A).

[7] E. David, Πλουτάρχου τῶν ἑπτὰ σοφῶν συμπόσιον: κείμενον, μετάφρασις καὶ ἑρμενεία (Athens, 1936) 10f., considers the discussions on the management of states and households to be central in *sept. sap. conv.*, yet he omits

a topos of frequent discussion in the Graeco-Roman period, while the latter was in itself a subject of central importance during the same period.

The literary genre of *sept. sap. conv.* is the symposion, a rather loosely defined literary form which used the social custom of the dinner party as the framework for anything from a relatively unified philosophical discussion (for which the earliest and most influential example is the *Smp.* of Plato) to discrete collections of miscellaneous lore and learning (Xenophon *Smp.*; Athenaeus *Deip.*; Plutarch *qu. conv.*). While Plutarch frequently used the literary convention of the dialogue, *sept. sap. conv.* is the only authentic instance in which the dialogue is set within the context of a symposion. In choosing this genre, Plutarch's scope of creativity was delimited by the literary tradition of the symposion [8] as well as by the parameters of the symposion as a living social custom.[9] The intellectual character of the colloquies in the symposia of Plato and Xenophon is certainly idealized, and in Plutarch's own day it seems clear that high levels of intellectual and philosophical discussion were deemed out of place at a symposion (Plutarch *qu. conv.* 1. 1 [612E-615C]). In several respects, Plutarch follows the literary exemplar provided by Plato's *Smp.*: (1) he uses the device of reported conversation, (2) he uses the device of interruptive events to add interest and the appearance of verisimilitude, and (3) he accomodates the style and diction of the conversations to the profession and character of the various participants. In other respects, however, *sept. sap. conv.* differs markedly from Plato and approximates what is known of the dialogue-style of Heracleides of Pontus,[10] i.e., in the use of imaginative dramatizations in ancient settings with ancient worthies as ostensible participants. Further, the composition of *sept. sap. conv.* has an episodic construction which is a probable consequence

---

the cosmic dimension. He concludes, on p. 11, with the following: «Ἡ κεντρικὴ λοιπὸν ἰδέα τοῦ Συμποσίου τῶν 7 Σοφῶν εἶναι ἡ κοινωνικὴ ζωὴ ὑπὸ τὴν γενικωτέραν καὶ τὴν μερικωτέραν της ἔννοιαν.»

[8] J. Martin, *RAC*, s.v. Deipnonliteratur; F. Ullrich, *Entstehung und Entwicklung der Literaturgattung des Symposion* (Würzburg, 1908-9); Hermogenes *Meth.* 36 (Rabe, pp. 455ff.).

[9] W. A. Becker, *Charicles: Illustrations of the Private Life of the Ancient Greeks*, 8th ed. (London, 1889) 333-47; Mau, "Convivium," PW, 4:1201-1208; R. Arbesmann, *RAC*, s.v. Gefrässigkeit.

[10] W. von Christ, *Geschichte der griechischen Literatur*, rev. O. Stählin and W. Schmid (Munich, 1920) 2.1:72, 492.

of the incorporation of large segments of traditional sayings and stories. Finally, extended speeches in *sept. sap. conv.* are rare, not only in consequence of the discrete traditional materials which Plutarch has used, but also because he places a positive value on sayings and anecdotes, with their characteristic brevity and spontaneity, as reliable indicators of a man's true character (ἦθος).[11]

In choosing the symposion genre as the framework for an imaginative dramatization incorporating various legendary sayings and anecdotes associated with the Seven Sages, it is unclear whether Plutarch had any literary exemplars which might have served as models for his composition.[12] While Diogenes Laertius (I. 40) refers to an account of Archetimos of Syracus, who supposedly wrote as an eyewitness of a meeting of the Seven Sages at the court of Kypselos, no mention is made of the genre used by Archetimos. In fact, Hirzel (2:138) doubts whether the priority of Archetimos' account can be presumed. However, in view of Plutarch's reference to the λόγοι ψευδεῖς (146B) in opposition to which Diokles is setting forth his own account, it would seem that he is aware of antecedent literature which is similar in genre and content to *sept. sap. conv.*[13]

The legend of the Seven Sages, both as individuals and as a collectivity, became the focus for various romantic legends and folktales which produced biographies, collections of sayings or apophthegmata and letters attributed to various members of the canonical group of Seven. While unambiguous evidence is lacking, it is probable that biographies of the Seven Sages were already being produced in the fifth century B.C.[14] In an analysis of *Pap. Soc. It.* IX, 1093, Bruno Snell expressed the opinion that a poetic version of the Banquet of the Seven Sages originated in the fifth century.[15] Further, it seems likely that the six drinking songs

---

[11] A. Wardman, *Plutarch's Lives* (Berkeley and Los Angeles, 1974) 227 (cf. pp. 105-52, which deal with "The Analysis and Description of Character").

[12] Hirzel, 2:138.

[13] In light of the extant evidence, Bohren's thesis that Archetimos' account served as an exemplar for Plutarch seems probable in spite of Hirzel's demurrer (F. E. Bohren, *De septem sapientibus* [Bonn, 1867] 20f., 61ff.).

[14] A. Momigliano, *The Development of Greek Biography* (Cambridge, Mass., 1971) 28: "The existence of fifth-century biography of poets and Wise Men is conjectural, but, I should say, altogether likely."

[15] B. Snell, "Zur Geschichte vom Gastmahl der Sieben Weisen," *Gesammelte Schriften* (Göttingen, 1966) 118.

attributed to six of the Seven Sages, preserved by Diogenes Laertius, also go back to the fifth century.[16] While these poems were apparently excerpted from Lobon of Argos' composition "On Poets" (third century B.C.), the opinion that Lobon fabricated much of his material has long been suspected.[17] Many such songs, as well as many individual sayings and apophthegmata, must have been in oral circulation prior to incorporation into various collections.[18] Most attributions of such sayings or apophthegmata to particular ancient worthies are tendentious, based rather on what an ideal wise man should have said than on what he in fact actually said. Diogenes Laertius summarizes the confusion which existed in his own day with regard to the attribution of particular sayings to particular sages: διαφωνοῦνται δὲ καὶ αἱ ἀποφάσεις αὐτῶν καὶ ἄλλου ἄλλο φασίν (1. 41).

Finally, a few remarks should be devoted to the subject of the Greek legend of the Seven Sages which forms the basis for *sept. sap. conv.* Both individually and collectively they exemplified the archaic Greek ideal of σοφία, i.e., a judicious combination of practical and intellectual wisdom. While legends regarding the Seven probably reach back into archaic times, the ideal of the sage was renewed in popularity when the image of the sage was transformed in Cynic and Stoic thought. The earliest reference to the Seven is Plato *Prt.* 343Aff., where they are named (Thales of Miletus, Pittakos of Mytilene, Bias of Priene, Solon of Athens, Kleobulos of Lindos, Myson of Chen and Chilon of Sparta), where reference is made to their short memorable sayings (indicative of a love for Spartan culture), and where mention is made of their assembly at Delphi where they inscribed such maxims as "Know Thyself" and "Nothing Overmuch" on the Temple of Apollo. While the number

---

[16] Diogenes Laertius 1. 35, 61, 71, 78, 85, 91; n.b. the stock formula which introduces each song: τῶν δὲ ᾀδομένων αὐτοῦ εὐδοκίμησει ἐστι τάδε. Cf. B. Snell, *Leben und Meinungen der Sieben Weisen* (Munich, [4]1971) 62ff.; *idem*, "Zur Geschichte vom Gastmahl der Sieben Weisen," 118; Momigliano, 27.

[17] Speyer, 129; W. Kroll, "Lobon," PW, 13:931-33.

[18] Stobaeus has preserved such a collection of sayings in a composition attributed to Demetrios of Phaleron entitled τῶν ἑπτὰ σοφῶν ἀποφθέγματα, in which strings of unconnected sayings are introduced with the name of the sage, the name of his father, his birthplace and the verb ἔφη (1. 172 [Hense]). A similar collection attributed to Sosiados is entitled τῶν ἑπτὰ σοφῶν ὑποθῆκαι and contains 144 short, unattributed maxims (Stobaeus 1. 173 [Hense]). Several other such collections are referred to by David, p. *25.

seven remains constant,[19] the list of specific sages which make up the group varies considerably.[20] In *sept. sap. conv.*, the list of sages is almost identical to that of Plato except that Anacharis replaces Myson. A frequent motif in the legends involves various meetings of the Seven Sages. Ephoros mentioned a meeting of the Sages at the court of Croesus in Sardis (Diogenes Laertius 1. 40), an event which seems to be implied in Herodotus 1. 29. Other authors, according to Diogenes Laertius, have the Sages meet at Delphi (1. 40; cf. Plato *Prt.* 343A; Plutarch *Sol.* 4. 1), at the pan-Ionian festival at Mykale or at Corinth (Diogenes Laertius 1. 40; Plutarch *Sol.* 4. 1). In all the variants of the legend handed down the Seven Sages functioned as paradigmatic images of the Greek ideal of wisdom and virtue with complete consistency between word and deed.

II. Outline and Structure

The following outline of the content of *sept. sap. conv.* will serve as an introduction to the structure of the composition.

I. Historical προοίμιον (Ch. 1; 146B-C)
II. Introductory Narrative Setting (Ch. 2; 146D-148B)
  A. Dialogue with subsidiary narrative
    1. Setting for banquet: hall near the Lechaeum outside of Corinth
    2. Occasion: festival of Aphrodite, whom Periander was honoring after a period of neglect
    3. *Peripatos* participated in by Thales, Diokles and Neiloxenos
      a. Though transportation had been arranged by Periander, the group chose to walk

[19] The fact that the number seven was sacred to Apollo, in combination with the close association of the Seven Sages with Delphi, may account for the constancy of the number (see Barkowski, PW, 2. Reihe, 4:2247). Other suggestive associations of the wisdom concept with the number seven include Pindar's reference to the seven wise sons of Helios (*O.* 7. 71) and the NT reference to the seven "deacons," chosen because they were πλήρεις πνεύματος καὶ σοφίας (Acts 6:3). The idealized portrait of the seven deacons in Acts is only part of Luke's presentation of the ideal experiences enjoyed by the primitive community in its earliest days.

[20] Diogenes Laertius (1. 41) reports that Hermippos enumerated no less than seventeen sages from whom the Seven were invariably drawn.

b. Neiloxenos has brought a letter to Bias from Amasis of Egypt; this serves to remind Thales of the former question which Bias successfully answered for Amasis.
c. Conversation proceeds on the topic of the mutual attitudes of sages and tyrants toward one another
d. Conversation continues on the more appropriate subject of the proper preparation of dinner guests

B. Arrival at the Banquet Site (Ch. 3; 148B-149F)
1. Preliminary baths and sightseeing
2. Episode 1: Eumetis, who is learning from Anacharsis, provides an exemplary attitude of a disciple to a sage
3. Episode 2: the group meets Alexidemos of Miletos, who objects to the seating arrangements and is reproached by Thales, who provides an exemplary attitude toward such superficial honors
4. Episode 3: Periander has Thales and Diokles inspect a prodigy; as a mantic, Diocles takes it seriously, while Thales humorously discounts its significance, thereby exemplifying the rationalism of the sage in contrast to the religious superstition of the mantic

C. The Banquet (Chs. 4-5; 149F-150F)
1. The seating of the guests
2. Thales, attempting to prod Bias into answering Amasis while sober, is told by Bias that his wisdom will be improved through the wine of Dionysos
3. Emphasis is placed on the simplicity and restraint of the banquet in contrast to normal banquets given by Periander
4. The banquet ends with the removal of the tables, the pouring of libations to the accompaniment of a flute and the distribution of garlands

III. The symposion: the main conversation over wine (Chs. 6-21; 150F-164D)

A. The Governance of States
1. Bias answers a riddle for Amasis and then the Seven Sages give Amasis some unsolicited advice on how a king or tyrant might best be held in repute (Chs. 6-7)
2. The remainder of Amasis' letter is read, containing the Ethiopian king's responses to nine riddles; Thales

disagrees with the answers and provides his own (Chs. 8-9)
3. Cleodoros objects to the trivial nature of such questions and riddles, but is put down by Periander and Aesop (Ch. 10)
4. Mnesiphilos suggests, and each sage responds to, the question of how a democracy might best succeed (Ch. 11)

B. The Governance of Households
1. Diokles suggests, and each sage responds to, the question of how a household might best be managed (Ch. 12)
2. The question of why Solon does not drink is discussed; the natural wisdom and conviviality of the guests makes the usual function of wine superfluous (Ch. 13)
3. The subject of household management is resumed, and the proper proportion of property and food necessary for men is discussed (Chs. 14-16)

C. The Governance of the Cosmos
1. The story of the miraculous rescue of Arion by dolphins as an example of divine justice (Chs. 17-18)
2. Solon's story of Hesiod's murder and the miraculous rescue of the corpse by dolphins (Ch. 19)
3. Pittacus relates the story of Enalos and the daughter of Smintheos who were miraculously rescued by dolphins (Ch. 20)
4. Anacharsis briefly summarizes the ways in which the will of the gods is achieved in the world, arguing that both men and animals are as much divine instruments as the inorganic elements (Ch. 21)

D. Concluding discussion on the Delphic maxims and the final libation to the Muses, Poseidon and Amphitrite (Ch. 21; 164A-D)

The structure of *sept. sap. conv.* is broadly determined by the literary context provided by the history of Greek and Roman symposion literature and by the living social custom of the symposion. If, as we have suggested above, one of the primary purposes of Plutarch was to present a model symposion, then we would expect the author to be as sensitive to the structures of the current social custom as to the literary tradition which began with Plato's *Smp.* Since the coherent conversation at a symposion (if such high intellectual levels were attained) occurred during the πότος which immediately followed the δεῖπνον, we find that the focal themes of *sept. sap. conv.* are located in precisely that position (Chs. 6-21; 150F-164D). Plutarch shows himself to be extremely genre-conscious when, in Ch. 2 (147D) he makes Thales comment on the inappropriateness of discussing the relationship between sages, kings and tyrants on the way to dinner. Within the symposion section proper of *sept. sap. conv.* there is a constant tension between what we have described as the central theme of the composition (i.e., the three levels of management or governance of the cosmos) and the episodic structure of the section which presumably reflects the desultory nature of conversation at actual symposia. In consequence, the central theme of the composition recurs or is resumed several times during the apparently variegated discussions of Chs. 6-21. The apparent digressions from the central theme are intercalated into the focal subject, however, at carefully determined intervals. According to the content outline which we have formulated above, the central theme is treated in III. A. 1, 4; B. 1, 3; C. 1, 4. Thus, in III., section A. on "The Governance of States," both begins and ends with that subject, with the apparent digressions centrally located in A. 2, 3. The same elementary form of "ring composition" is found in section B. on "The Governance of Households," and in section C. on "The Governance of the Cosmos." The consistency of Plutarch's structural mechanisms in each of these sections, if the above analysis is accepted as valid, makes the thematic unity of *sept. sap. conv.* a virtual certainty on the basis of formal as well as material criteria.

Plutarch has several formal ways for indicating whether a particular episode is beginning or has concluded. At the beginning of Ch. 12 (154F), he uses the phrase τέλος δὲ καὶ τούτου τοῦ λόγου λαβόντος as a formal indication that the subject of the governance of states, the focal theme in Chs. 6-11, has come to an end. A similar phrase is used at the beginning of Ch. 13 (155E) to indicate that the first phase of the discussion on household management has come to an end. After the digression on Solon's abstinence in Ch. 13, the subject of household management is formally resumed again by Chersias at the beginning of Ch. 14 (157A). The entire section on household governance (Chs. 12-16) is formally concluded at the end of Ch. 16 (160C) with the following sentence: τὰ μὲν οὖν ῥηθέντα περὶ τροφῆς, ὦ Νίκαρχε, ταῦτ' ἦν. Devices which Plutarch uses to introduce new subjects or to resume subjects which had already been partially discussed include: (1) the formulation of a question or topic for discussion by one of the participants, (2) the use of a letter (in this case from Amasis, king of Egypt) to suggest appropriate topics for discussion, and (3) the use of interruptive events which require explanation and elaboration.

III. Relationship to Early Christian Literature

Aside from the more particular features of *sept. sap. conv.* which have interesting parallels or contrasts with ECL (these are dealt with *seriatim* in section IV below), there are two separate and significant subjects which require extended consideration. The first is Plutarch's technique of composition, a topic which would appear to have numerous parallels to the various stages in the process of composition which eventuated in the canonical Gospels (particularly in light of the disciplines of Form Criticism and Redaction Criticism). The second is the Graeco-Roman literary genre and social institution of the symposion, which has parallels in ECL both as a literary device and as a social structure which influenced the patterning of early Christian gatherings for sacral meals and worship.

A. *Tradition and Composition in 'sept. sap. conv.' and the Canonical Gospels*

In many respects, the literary task which Plutarch had set for himself in composing this work was a complex one. It involved the organization and presentation of a diverse body of traditional sayings and stories traditionally associated with the Seven Sages within the formal boundaries set by the symposion genre and within the material boundaries set by his selection of a central theme and his delineation of an ideal symposion. However, even within the framework of these limitations, it will become evident that Plutarch exercised a great degree of editorial and literary freedom in shaping both the composition as a whole as well as its various constituent components in a manner commensurate with his own literary, philosophical and religious inclinations.[21]

[21] Not all classical scholars have regarded *sept. sap. conv.* as a literary "achievement." Cf. Becker, 333: "It was an unhappy thought of Plutarch's—if indeed the work be his—to range beside these masterpieces [i.e., Plato's

In order to facilitate a comparison between the process of composition presupposed by *sept. sap. conv.* and the canonical Gospels, it is necessary that we provide a brief summary of the contemporary *communis opinio* on the nature of the interplay between traditional materials and literary composition in the Gospels: (1) The evangelists were forced to confine their narratives to the traditional temporal and geographical frame of the life of Jesus; this limitation, which was both self-imposed and externally imposed by literary convention, is characteristic of the literary genre "gospel." (2) The evangelists were the recipients (perhaps even active collectors) of a considerable body of traditional sayings and stories which had been associated with Jesus of Nazareth. Many of these traditions were discrete, others had already been assembled in oral and/or written collections; almost all of them were what A. Jolles would describe as "simple forms." [22] (3) The greater part of this early Christian folklore (the term is appropriate, since authentic folklore must meet the test of existing in varying versions in oral circulation) had already undergone "communal re-creation," [23] i.e., the gradual transformation through reiteration of orally circulating material into stereotyped forms, styles and structures. (4) Due to the difficulties of incorporating generally non-narrative simple forms into narrative contexts, the evangelists necessarily exercised considerable editorial freedom in adapting the traditional materials which they introduced into new contexts. (5) In addition, the evangelists introduced various modifications in the constituent sayings and stories which they utilized in order to bring them into harmony with the overall thematic emphases of their compositions. (6) The biographical technique of the evangelists, if it can be called such, while broadly chronologically-oriented, was almost totally unconcerned with character development; Jesus is presented essentially as a static personality. (7) The evangelists structured their narratives in an essentially episodic manner. Individual episodes were frequently created by collecting originally diverse Christian folklore into topically unified narrative segments. The

Smp.; Xenophon's *Smp.*] the tedious disputation of his seven sages, whose wire-drawn subtleties are only exceeded by the tasteless absurdities of the Deipnosophists in Athenaeus."

[22] A. Jolles, *Einfache Formen* (1930); cf. R. Scholes, *Structuralism in Literature* (New Haven, 1974) 42-50.

[23] This term has become widely accepted among American folklorists; cf. J. H. Brunvand, *Folklore: A Study and Research Guide* (New York, 1976) 13f.

fact that the oral forms out of which the synoptic Gospels were fashioned are so easily isolatable by the form critic is indicative of a tension in those Gospels between the individual, constitutive oral unit and the literary narrative considered as a whole.

The literary history of Plutarch's *sept. sap. conv.* is as illuminating for the study of the canonical Gospels as that of the Gospels is for the study of Plutarch. The following statements are an attempt to summarize the literary task and process which eventuated in *sept. sap. conv.*: (1) In consequence of Plutarch's decision to produce an imaginative dramatization involving the Seven Sages, he was of necessity limited to selecting one of the legendary traditions of their joint meeting; one suspects that he selected the environs of Corinth for several reasons: (a) legends included Corinth as the site where one of the gatherings of the Seven Sages occurred, (b) Plutarch may have wished to correct the account written by Archetimos of Syracuse, (c) Plutarch may have wished to show that Periander, sometimes named as one of the Seven, was in fact not a member of the group, (d) the story of Arion's miraculous rescue had always been associated with Corinth, and (e) Dolphin stories (*sept. sap. conv.* contains three) were closely associated with Corinth. (2) Plutarch's selection of the symposion genre as the literary framework for his composition would appear to be an almost unavoidable choice in view of his desire to depict a gathering of the Seven Sages. (3) Plutarch was an active collector of both oral and written sayings and stories which he lavishly used to illustrate the character of great personages and to make various philosophical, scientific, religious and ethical points.[24] In addition to having a prodigious memory (the importance and value of memorizing and techniques for memorizing were emphasized in the Graeco-Roman rhetorical schools), Plutarch also made use of collections of notes (ὑπομνήματα) which he and his assistants had carefully collected on various subjects.[25] While a great many of

[24] The breadth of Plutarch's erudition is evident in Helmbold and O'Neil, *Plutarch's Quotations*. In checking the number of quotations which Helmbold and O'Neil list for *sept. sap. conv.*, I found no less than fifty-three citations listed; nevertheless, most of the sayings and stories used by Plutarch in this short composition are not listed since the attributions, when given, are for the most part legendary. Parenthetically it might be noted that the modern study of folklore has had a minimal influence on classical scholarship.

[25] Plutarch *tranq. an.* 464F; *cohib. ira* 457Df.; *coniug. praec.* 145E; *Lyc.* 19f.; *Luc.* 41; *Them.* 11. 18; *Cat. Ma.* 7. 2; 9. 7. The kind of material which Plutarch and others had assiduously collected is exemplified in two collections of sayings traditionally ascribed to Plutarch: *reg. et imp.* and *Lacon.*

these sayings and stories (Plutarch favored "simple forms") had been excerpted from literary contexts, a great many others seem to have enjoyed varying and largely indeterminate periods of primarily oral circulation.[26] (4) A great many of the sayings and stories which Plutarch drew upon had already assumed a stereotyped form, style and structure through the process which we have labeled as "communal re-creation" (a morphological analysis of some of this material will be attempted below). (5) In Plutarch's utilization of sayings and stories relating to the Seven Sages, many (if not most) of which existed in non-narrative contexts (e.g., collections of apophthegmata mentioned above), the requirements of adaptation to a narrative context necessitated the introduction of modifications into individual sayings and stories. (6) Further modifications were demanded if such material was used to develop the central themes of *sept. sap. conv.* (7) The biographical technique of Plutarch, one of the great biographers of late antiquity, generally subordinates chronological considerations and character development to the static exposition of an individual's ἦθος by means of illustrations of his words and deeds. (8) In consequence of the important function of "simple forms" in Plutarch's *sept. sap. conv.* (as well as in the *Vitae*) the composition has an episodic structure which has impeded critics from seeing the thematic unity of the composition.

A careful consideration of the implications of these areas of similarity in the process of composition lying behind both Plutarch's *sept. sap. conv.* and the canonical Gospels easily leads to the conclusion that the various processes and forces which eventuated in the composition of each of these documents have more points of agreement than of disagreement. If this assessment is correct, it means that the commonly accepted notion that the canonical Gospels were an entirely new and unique literary form developed by early Christianity in late antiquity stands in need of reassessment.[27] Perhaps one factor which has contributed to the impregnability of this *communis opinio* is the fact that the form critical method has been rigorously applied only to Biblical litera-

[26] The relationship between oral and written transmission of traditional sayings and stories is of course much more complex in the periods of classical and Hellenistic antiquity than for early Christianity.

[27] W. G. Kümmel, *Introduction to the New Testament*, rev. ed. (New York and Nashville, 1975) 35-37.

ture.[28] In the remainder of this section we shall attempt to provide a morphological analysis of some of the "simple forms" out of which Plutarch has fashioned *sept. sap. conv.*

In analyzing the form and structure of the traditional sayings and stories which Plutarch has incorporated into *sept. sap. conv.*, one is aided by the fact that not infrequently such material is used elsewhere in the corpus of Plutarch's writings. As in the case of the first three canonical Gospels, therefore, a synoptic comparison is made possible. Since *stories* (i.e., relatively brief narratives which do not culminate in a saying or pronouncement) are polymorphic and generally resistant to morphological analysis,[29] our investigation will focus on those traditional *sayings* which Plutarch has used in *sept. sap. conv.* Further, in our classification of various types of sayings, the ancient Greek terminology for such sayings (e.g., χρεῖαι, ἀποφθέγματα, γνῶμαι, ἀπομνημονεύματα, etc.) has been studiously avoided. The incorporation of such terminology into a modern system of classifying ancient Greek sayings is inherently problematical, since the terms are more or less synonymous.[30] When distinctions between these terms are made, as for example in the progymnasmata of the later rhetoricians (e.g., Theon *Prog.* 5 [Spengel, pp. 96-106]; Hermogenes *Prog.* 3-4 [Rabe, pp. 6-10]; Aphthonius *Prog.* 3-4 [Spengel, pp. 23-27]), such distinctions are generally academic and fail to reflect the vagaries of popular

---

[28] While a great deal of effort has gone into the analysis of the oral/literary units out of which the Gospels were fashioned, and recent progress has been made in the form critical analysis of rabbinic literature (J. Neusner), little effort has been expended on a similar analysis of Greek literature. In the words of J. M. Robinson, "... a more thorough investigation of Greek literature with regard to this gattung [i.e., "logoi sophon"] is still a further need" ("LOGOI SOPHON: On the Gattung of Q," *Trajectories through Early Christianity*, ed. J. M. Robinson and H. Koester [Philadelphia, 1971] 74).

[29] In NT research, the form critical classification "Stories about Jesus" is generally recognized as possessing no definite structural form (V. Taylor, *The Formation of the Gospel Tradition* [London, 1953] 31f., 142). In folklore studies, the great exception to the general lack of success in analyzing the structure of stories is V. Propp's formulation of the thirty-one functions found sequentially in Russian Märchen (*Morphology of the Folktale* [Austin, 1970]).

[30] D. A. Russell, *Plutarch* (London, 1973) 100-117. R. M. Grant has excellent discussions of these various terms in *The Earliest Lives of Jesus* (New York, 1961) 14ff., 119ff. (see index). The Greek terminology is also discussed by W. Gemoll, *Das Apophthegma: Literarhistorische Studien* (Vienna and Leipzig, 1924) 1-6, 6-17.

usage.[31] For present purposes it would appear useful to designate those sayings which are frequently called χρεῖαι (which characteristically lack any narrative framework), as *wisdom sayings*, and other forms of ἀπομνημονεύματα or ἀποφθέγματα (which possess narrative frameworks and additional structural elements of varying complexity), as *wisdom stories*.[32]

The wisdom saying consists in a single structural element, generally an observation concerning man or the world, the profundity and astuteness of which is self-evident. Such sayings are a universally popular "simple form" of folklore; their circulation is primarily oral and they resist confinement to literary contexts. The wisdom story consists in two structural elements: (1) the problem, question or problematic situation, and (2) the solution proposed by the sage. Unlike the wisdom saying, the pronouncement with which the wisdom story culminates cannot stand alone; it would be incomprehensible without its brief (but extremely functional) narrative context. Such wisdom stores are frequently found in the stereotyped two-part structure ἐρωτηθείς ... εἶπε. In the collection of wisdom stories attributed to the Seven Sages in Diogenes Laertius, that style is used in stories attributed to Thales (1. 26), Solon (1. 59), Chilon (1. 69), Bias (1. 86, 87), Periander (1. 97), and Anacharsis (1. 103, 104, 105). In *sept. sap. conv.* 147B, Neiloxenos relates a wisdom story concerned with Thales which is structured in an identical manner: ἐρωτηθείς ... ἀποκρίναιο. Elsewhere (e.g., 153C-D; see commentary below), Plutarch has apparently elaborated the single structural element in the wisdom saying into the two-part structure characteristic of wisdom stories.

Since both wisdom sayings and wisdom stories circulated in non-narrative collections, the requirements for adapting such material to narrative contexts appears to have produced stereotyped patterns of expansion and adaptation appropriate for such contexts. The demands of narrative made the presence of an audience

---

[31] For examples of Plutarch's own imprecision, see *Them.* 18. 1, with which compare 18. 5.

[32] Gemoll (p. 6) defines the apophthegm as "eine kurze, ernste oder witzige, auf jeden Fall treffende Streitrede. Eine entsprechende Tat kann sie begleiten oder zum Ausdruck bringen." This definition is a bit too restrictive for what we have termed the wisdom story. Elsewhere, Gemoll (p. 2) describes the fundamental structure of the apophthegm: "Zum Apophthegma gehören also gewöhnlich zwei Personen, eine, die fragt, und eine, die antwortet, eine, die reizt, und eine, die gereizt erwidert."

necessary, even if it consisted only in the interlocutor of the sage. In narrative contexts the impersonal interlocutor (cf. the use of the passive verb ἐρωτηθείς) tends to be identified. The presence of an audience in narrative contexts partially accounts for the addition of a third structural element which is used to embellish the two-part wisdom story, the *acclamation*. The acclamation is an expression of delight and approval, perhaps even amazement at the sagacious response of the sage (see 146F, 147A, 152E-153E, 153E-154C). An inductive study of the use of wisdom sayings and wisdom stories in *sept. sap. conv.* demonstrates that there is a direct correlation between the presence of the acclamation and the purpose of the wisdom story. Wisdom stories appear to be used for two primary purposes in Plutarch's *sept. sap. conv.*: (1) to emphasize the particular content or conventional wisdom expressed in the saying with which the story culminates, or (2) to emphasize the astonishing wisdom of the sage. The acclamation is found appended only to those wisdom stories whose purpose it is to emphasize the wisdom of the sage. Finally a fourth structural element is occasionally found only in those wisdom stories which conclude with an acclamation, and that is the *false solution*. The false solution, when used, is always inserted immediately following the statement of the problem and functions in such a way that the wisdom of the sage, who provides the correct solution, is both highlighted and enhanced (see 149C-F; 152E-153E).

While this morphological analysis applies to all wisdom stories found in *sept. sap. conv.*, when such stories are analyzed from the perspective of their function, three distinct types of wisdom story may be differentiated: (1) The *gnomic wisdom story* consists of the basic two-part wisdom story structure (with the possible addition of the two secondary structures discussed above) within which the opinion of a sage is solicited and instantaneously obtained by a friendly and admiring interlocutor (see 147B, 149C-F, 151Eff., 154F-155E [omitting 155A-C which has been intercalated by Plutarch], 155A-B, 156A). (2) The *agonistic wisdom story* consists of the basic two-part wisdom story structure (with the possible addition of the two secondary structures) within which the sage is (unsuccessfully) challenged by a difficult question, problem or situation for the specific purpose of testing his reported sagacity (see 146F, 147A, 150Fff., 152E-153E, 153E-154C). (3) The *paradigmatic wisdom story* consists of the basic two-part wisdom story structure (with the possible inclusion of the two secondary structures) within which the sage exemplifies his theoretical wisdom through practical action or conduct (see 148E-149B).

The present state of research makes any detailed comparison between the constituent simple forms of *sept. sap. conv.* with those of the synoptic Gospels inherently problematical, not to say foolhardy. While NT scholars have intensively analyzed the rather limited literary corpus of the canonical Gospels using the method of form criticism for the past fifty years, little or no comparable work has been done on the vast corpus of Graeco-Roman literature. Those limited comparisons which we have chosen to make have been limited to the two literary forms which we have analyzed above, the wisdom saying and the wisdom story.

The wisdom sayings in *sept. sap. conv.* have many formal parallels with what form critics have generally designated as "sayings of Jesus" (i.e., sayings wholly lacking a narrative framework). In view of the universality of proverbs and aphorisms as vehicles for expressing conventional wisdom, this fact is hardly surprising. In R. Bultmann's discussion of "dominical sayings," he distinguishes five types of such sayings, one of which he descriptively calls "Logia (Jesus as the Teacher of Wisdom)." [33] It is these sayings which bear the closest resemblance, both formally and materially, to Graeco-Roman wisdom sayings.

Surprisingly, the wisdom stories of *sept. sap. conv.* have few close parallels, either in form or substance, with analogous forms in the synoptic Gospels. The closest parallel to the wisdom story in the synoptic Gospels is what scholars have generally called the "pronouncement story," i.e., a saying of Jesus set in a brief narrative framework (n.b. that a problem or question is not necessarily a universal feature of this form). Originally called apophthegmata by R. Bultmann, he went on to distinguish three types of apophthegmata, (1) controversy dialogues, (2) scholastic dialogues, and (3) biographical apophthegms. With regard to both form and function, the controversy dialogues correspond rather closely to agonistic wisdom stories, just as scholastic dialogues closely correspond to gnomic wisdom stories. However, with regard to subject matter, the proverbial or aphoristic character of the wisdom story is only rarely paralleled in synoptic pronouncement stories.

---

[33] Bultmann, *HST*, 69-108.

In fact, I have found only three pronouncement stories in the synoptic Gospels which might (*mutatis mutandis*) be regarded as parallels to the Graeco-Roman wisdom story with regard to form, function and content. Each of these pronouncement stories has been classified by Bultman as a controversy dialogue, and would therefore correspond to what we have called the agonistic wisdom story: (1) the question about the greatest commandment (Mark 12:28-34//Matt 22:34-40//Luke 10:25-28), (2) the question concerning tribute money (Mark 12:13-17//Matt 22:15-22//Luke 20:20-26), and (3) the question concerning the resurrection (Mark 12:18-27//Matt 22:23-33// Luke 20:27-40). To suppose that these three pronouncement stories, with their close parallels to the Graeco-Roman wisdom stories, were fortuitously placed together in the twelfth chapter of Mark strains credulity. Further, each of these pronouncement stories contains a final acclamation, a feature which corresponds to the third (optional) structural element in the wisdom story structure;[34] none has anything resembling the fourth (optional) structural element in the wisdom story, i.e., the false solution.

Paradoxically, the oral form in the synoptic Gospels which is most closely related to the wisdom story, with regard to both form and function, is the "miracle story." The three structural elements characteristic of the miracle story (occasionally the third element is absent) include: (1) the circumstances or problem, (2) the healing or solution, and (3) the impression of onlookers, or confirmation of healing or acclamation.[35] Eight of the twenty-eight miracle stories in the four canonical Gospels contain the final element of acclamation, expressed either in terms of the amazement of the onlookers or their spontaneous glorification of God.[36] Further,

---

[34] The literary nature of the final element of acclamation is evident in the fact that, while the acclamation is found at the conclusion of Mark 12:28-34, it is absent from the parallel sections of Matt 22:34-40 and Luke 10:25-28. Matt postpones using the acclamation until the conclusion of the next pericope, the question about David's son (Matt 22:41-46).

[35] V. Taylor, *The Formation of the Gospel Tradition* (London, 1953) 121; P. Achtemeier, "Miracles and the Historical Jesus: A Study of Mark 9:14-29," *CBQ* 37 (1975) 472.

[36] Miracle stories which conclude with an acclamation, i.e., an expression of amazement from onlookers or the spontaneous glorification of God, include (1) the demoniac in the synagogue (Mark 1:23-27/Luke 4:33-36), (2) the paralytic (Mark 2:1-12//Luke 5:17-26//Matt 9:1-8), (3) the Gerasene demoniac (Mark 5:1-20//Luke 8:26-39), (4) the deaf mute (Mark 7:31-37//

two miracle stories, the woman with the issue of blood (Mark 5:25-34//Luke 8:43-48) and the epileptic lad (Mark 9:14-29// Matt 17:14-20//Luke 9:37-43) contain the fourth (optional) element of the wisdom story, the false solution. In the former story the physicians were unable to cure the woman, and in the latter story the disciples were unable to cure the epileptic lad. Both the acclamation and the false solution function in such a way that the divine power of the healer is further emphasized. The formal and functional similarity of the Graeco-Roman wisdom story and the miracle story of the synoptic Gospels may perhaps be partially accounted for if it is realized that both function (in their respective cultures and/or social levels) in a revelatory manner. The wisdom of the Graeco-Roman sage is indicative of his status as a divine man, just as the miraculous powers of Jesus were thought to be indicative of his possession of divine power and authority.[37]

B. *The Deipnon-Symposion in Early Christianity*

1. *The Literary Genre*

ECL contains no examples of the symposion as a literary genre, a fact which underlines the independence of early Christianity from Graeco-Roman *Hochliteratur*. The dialogue, a literary genre which, like the symposion, originated (for all practical purposes) with Plato, had always been a characteristic feature of symposion literature. Early Christianity adopted the dialogue form fairly rapidly, but was slower to adopt the symposion as a literary genre. Discounting the spurious *Cena Cypriani*, Jerome reports that Lactantius had composed a symposion (*vir. ill.* 100), while the earliest extant example of Christian symposion literature was written by Methodius. In the NT, however, there are several instances in which a δεῖπνον is used as a literary vehicle for organizing and framing a number of the sayings of Jesus. While the Synoptic tradition does contain reminiscenses of Jesus' meals with disciples and acquaintances (Mark 2:13-17//Matt 9:9-13//Luke

Matt 15:29-31), (5) blind Bartimaeus (Luke 18:35-43), (6) the dumb demoniac (Luke 11:14-15//Matt 12:22-23), (7) the young man at Nain (Luke 7:11-17), and (8) the stilling of the storm (Mark 4:35-41//Luke 8:22-25//Matt 8:23-27).

[37] Cf. D. L. Tiede's thesis that wisdom and miracle constitute two distinct traditions constitutive of the Graeco-Roman figure of the divine man (*The Charismatic Figure as Miracle Worker* [Missoula, 1972]).

5:27-32; Mark 14:18-26//Matt 26:21-30//Luke 22:15-23; Mark 14:3-9//Matt 26:6-13//Luke 7:36-50), the phenomenon which we are presently discussing is strictly a literary technique used by the evangelists Luke and John. The most extensive single example of the δεῖπνον as a literary device is found in John 13-16, the so-called Farewell Discourses of the Johannine Jesus, which is framed by a meal setting with table-talk occasionally inserted into the narrative. While the basic framework is based on the tradition of the Last Supper (Mark 14:12-26//Matt 26:17-30// Luke 22:7-38), the meal framework is nevertheless consciously used by the Fourth Evangelist to unify an important section of his gospel. The other examples of the use of a dinner as a literary device are limited to Luke: (1) In Luke 14:1-24, the dinner setting is used as a framing device for four literary units, (a) the healing of the man with dropsy (14:1-6), (b) the parable of the wedding feast (14:7-11), (c) Jesus' teaching on humility (14:12-14), and (d) the parable of the great supper (14:15-24). This device was apparently suggested to Luke by the nature of the material which he wished to place together; the second and third unit deal with banquet etiquette, while the fourth uses a banquet as the setting for a parable. (2) Luke 11:37-54 is similarly framed by a dinner setting which is clearly the result of Lukan editorial activity (Luke 11:3f., 53f. were obviously added by the evangelist), since the parallels in Matt contain no such emphasis. (3) Luke 7:36-50 also uses a dinner as the context for a pronouncement story; n.b. the presence of an *umbra* or σκιά (an uninvited guest; cf. Plutarch *qu. conv.* 707A). A consideration of the synoptic parallels (Mark 14:3-9//Matt 26:6-13) reveals the way in which Luke had enlarged the material included in the meal setting found in his Markan exemplar. (4) In Luke 24:13-32 we find the combination of a peripatos with a dialogue, which closes with a meal in vss. 28-32; however, the meal does not serve as a framework for the dialogue. (5) Similarly, the Lukan resurrection appearance of Jesus to the assembled disciples, accompanied by his explanation to them of the meaning of the OT (Luke 24:36-49) is apparently set in the context of a meal (cf. vss. 41ff., and Acts 1:4).

2. *The Social Custom*

The symposion was an immensely popular and ubiquitous social custom in classical antiquity, particularly in the Graeco-Roman period.[38] The basic structure of the symposion seems to have remained relatively unchanged from Homer to the end of antiquity. While symposia could be held on both private and public occasions, our discussion will focus on the structure and character of private symposia. Symposia were generally set in the context of the largest meal of the day, the Greek δεῖπνον (or the Roman *cena*), which began about the ninth or tenth hour of the day and could last three or more hours (well into the night). The Roman *convivium* was relatively small in scale, normally consisting of 6, 9 or 12 guests, while the Greek symposion frequently consisted of 36 or more guests. Normally,[39] wine was not served with the meal, but was reserved for the πότος which followed the δεῖπνον proper. In both tradition and practise, the symposion was regarded as a social expression of Greek religion (Athenaeus *Deipn.* 5. 192), and so was begun with offerings of food-portions to appropriate divinities (Athenaeus *Deipn.* 5. 179) and concluded with libations and the singing of hymns to appropriate divinities (Athenaeus *Deipn.* 5. 149). Frequently meat from sacrificial animals appears to have been preferred for the δεῖπνον proper (Athenaeus *Deipn* 4. 140, 173; 11. 459; 12. 534).[40] After the guests had finished the meal, the tables were removed and the πότος or symposion itself was begun with three libations to (1) the Olympian divinities generally, (2) the heroes, and (3) Zeus Soter; after the first libation a hymn in praise of Dionysos (the god of wine and intoxication) was sung.[41] Crowns were distributed during these rites (Athenaeus *Deipn.* 3.

---

[38] The following literature discusses the symposion as a social custom: Hug, "Symposion," PW, 2. Reihe, 4:1266-70; Mau, "Convivium," PW, 4:1201-1208 (an excellent article); Becker, *Charicles*, 333-47 (an excellent description of the symposion in the fifth and fourth centuries B.C. with copious references to primary sources).

[39] For an exception, see Lucian *Symp.* 14f.

[40] Pliny *Ep.* 10. 96. 10 refers to the sale everywhere of sacrificial meat. On the preference of sacrificial meat for meals of a religious nature, see *Vita Aesopi* (Vita G), 51, 54 (Perry, pp. 52f.), and *Vita Aesopi* (Vita W), 51 (Perry, p. 90). According to M. Isenberg ("The Sale of Sacrificial Meat," *CPh* 70 [1975] 273: "As the case stands . . . the problem of the sale of sacrificial meats still awaits its proper solution.")

[41] H. Blümner, *The Home Life of the Ancient Greeks* (New York, 1966) 212-13 (referring to classical Greek customs). While the basic structure of the symposion remained the same through the time of Plutarch, the specific deities invoked and honored exhibits wide variety in the sources. Dionysos, however, was customarily honored at symposia because of intimate association with wine, intoxication and ecstasy (W. F. Otto, *Dionysus: Myth and Cult* [Bloomington and London, 1965] 143ff.).

101; 9. 409; Plutarch *qu. conv.* 615B; *sept. sap. conv.* 150D), and the presence of a flute girl (generally a prostitute) was considered indispensable for the proceedings (Lucian *Symp.* 46; Athenaeus *Deipn.* 4. 129, 131, 150; 8. 349; Plutarch *sept. sap. conv.* 150D).[42]

Private symposia could be family affairs held on such occasions as wedding or memorials (Lucian *Symp.* 8), or they could be invitational affairs hosted by a man in his home (or another appropriate location), or they could be regularly scheduled events participated in by members of a particular club or association (commonly designated ἔρανοι or θίασοι).[43] Women were customarily excluded from all symposia other than those which were exclusively family affairs (Plutarch *qu. conv.* 612F).[44] Women who held religious offices in religious societies would of course also be present at cult symposia (Poseidippos as summarized in Athenaeus *Deipn.* 9. 377).[45]

Basically, a symposion was a drinking party and frequently tended to end in intoxication (Lucian *Symp.* 17; Athenaeus *Deipn.*

[42] Plato claimed that flute girls, dancing girls, and harp girls were unnecessary at a symposion (*Smp.* 176E; *Prt.* 347C), while Plutarch assumes that, in fact, a harp girl might not necessarily be present (*qu. conv.* 616A). More often than not flute girls and harp girls were prostitutes (Lucian *DMeretr.* 1, 3, 6, 12, 15) who were indispensable for the libations and hymns. They remained in attendance throughout the entire symposion (Becker, *Charicles*, 241-50, 344; Blümner, op. cit., pp. 171, 216). Greek vase paintings, particularly on drinking cups and wine bowls, attest to the ubiquity of flute girls at symposia as well as to their talents as prostitutes.

[43] Private symposia were of two major types, those for which the cost was divided among the participants, and those to which the guests were freely invited (PW, 4:1201f.). Family symposia and invitational symposia belong to the latter group, while the religious meals of various clubs or associations belong to the former group. Cf. Athenaeus *Deipn.* 8. 362: ἔρανοι δέ εἰσιν αἱ ἀπὸ τῶν συμβαλλομένων συναγωγαί, ἀπὸ τοῦ συνερᾶν καὶ συμφέρειν ἕκαστον. The fact that an ἔρανος and a θίασος cannot be differentiated from each other in this regard is clear from the sentence immediately following the above quotation from Athenaeus: καλεῖται δ' ὁ αὐτὸς καὶ ἔρανος καὶ θίασος καὶ οἱ συνιόντες ἐρανισταὶ καὶ θιασῶται.

[44] PW, 4:1203. Ordinarily, the presence of women at a symposion would be indicative of the fact that they were prostitutes. An exception to this is found in *sept. sap. conv.* where Melissa and Eumetis stay for part of the symposion, but leave well before its conclusion (155E). In spite of the fact that they were present from 150D to 155E, they maintained strict silence (154B).

[45] P. Foucart, *Des associations religieuses chez les Grecs* (Paris, 1873) 148-52 (while Foucart is correct in maintaining that women were not excluded from the state cults and consequently their inclusion in religious societies was hardly innovative; nevertheless, the inclusion of women in some cultic activities [notably religious symposia] constituted a considerable innovation).

2. 36). For this reason they were forbidden in Sparta and Crete,[46] and elsewhere the office of symposiarch was intended to mitigate this almost inevitable result (Plutarch *qu. conv.* 620A-622B). Gluttony was another form of self-indulgence characteristic of many symposia (Lucian *Par.* 5; Athenaeus *Deipn.* 5. 178; 12. 527).[47] While the nature of the sources makes confident conclusions difficult, it would appear that the social class, profession and education of the guests had a direct bearing on the intellectual level and degree of decorum characteristic of individual symposia.[48] Cultivated and serious conversation appears to have been rare at most symposia; many thought that philosophers made exceptionally poor guests (Lucian *Par.* 51; Plutarch *qu. conv.* 612E-615C). They tended to bore other guests, who would start singing, telling stories or just leave (Plutarch *qu. conv.* 614F-615A); the result was (according to Plutarch) that good fellowship was thereby destroyed and "Dionysos is displeased" (*qu. conv.* 615A). To such cultivated persons as Plutarch, the danger of disorder (ἀταξία) was a constant threat to symposia (*qu. conv.* 615E, 618C; Athenaeus *Deipn.* 10. 420). Frequently, at larger symposia, people would come and go depending on what was being served (Athenaeus *Deipn.* 10. 419), or on the nature of the conversation or entertainment (Pliny *Ep.* 9. 17. 3). Custom indicated that guests should be seated in positions commensurate with their honor or reputation (Lucian *Symp.* 9); lack of definite seating arrangements could contribute to disorder (Plutarch *qu. conv.* 615C-D). Plutarch frequently emphasizes the point that there should be equality among the guests (ἡ ἰσότης τοῖς ἀνδράσι, *qu. conv.* 613F). Many thought that the guests at a symposion should vary in age and outlook (Athenaeus *Deipn.* 5. 177), a factor which might add both interest and variety to the proceedings. Occasionally both slaves and masters found themselves at the same symposion (Athenaeus *Deipn.* 4. 149). For Plutarch the question of order and propriety at symposia was sufficiently important for him to toy with the idea

---

[46] Becker, *Charicles*, 334.

[47] R. Arbesmann, *RAC*, s.v. Gefrässigkeit.

[48] According to Plutarch (*qu. conv.* 716D-E [Loeb translation]), ". . . if ignorance and lack of culture keep company with wine, not even that famous golden lamp of Athena could make the party refined and orderly . . . The outcome of undisciplined chatter and frivolity, when it reaches the extreme of intemperance, is violence and drunken behavior—an outcome wholly inconsistent with culture and refinement."

of reinstating the office of symposiarch (*qu. conv.* 620A-622B). The activities at a symposion, in addition to drinking and serious and witty conversation, could include dancing (Lucian *DMeretr.* 15; Athenaeus *Deipn.* 4. 134), singing (Plutarch *vit. pud.* 531B; *qu. conv.* 622C; Lucian *Par.* 51), games (Athenaeus *Deipn.* 11. 479), recitations of various kinds and the extemporaneous composition of verse (through the inspiration provided by Dionysos; Athenaeus *Deipn.* 2. 39). On a lower level, various forms of sexual promiscuity appear to have been common (Lucian *Symp.* 46; Athenaeus *Deipn.* 4; every conceivable form of sexual liaison is depicted at such gatherings on vase paintings), a factor facilitated by the quenching of the lights (Plutarch *qu. conv.* 761D). Brawls and violence were not unknown to ancient symposia (Lucian *Symp.*; Plutarch *qu. conv.* 716F).

In summary, Greek symposia of the Graeco-Roman era, while retaining a basically similar formal structure, were characterized by immense variety with regard to the constituent elements. Such occasions functioned as physical and emotional outlets and were couched in formal religious customs and practises. The average individual might participate in a symposion one or two times per month, while others made a profession of them (Lucian *Par.* 15).

While Greek clubs or associations could have political, economic or religious overtones and purposes, the symposia which they sponsored tended to assume a structure and content similar to the general symposia which we have discussed above.[49] The symposia of religious θίασοι or ἔρανοι (Athenaeus *Deipn.* 5. 185f.) appear to be most fruitful for the purpose of comparison with early Christian cultic associations which characteristically held sacral meals as an integral part of Christian worship.[50] Referring to early Christian groups in the Graeco-Roman world, Ziebarth has, I think, correctly observed that "es ist daher eine naheliegende Vermutung, dass sie sich bei Bildung ihrer Verfassung an das Muster der heidnischen Kultvereine angelehnt haben." [51] Ziebarth's "Vermutung," which

[49] On the subject of Greek religious societies, see Foucart, *Des associations religieuses chez les Grecs*; E. Ziebarth, *Das griechische Vereinswesen* (Leipzig, 1896); F. Poland, *Geschichte des griechischen Vereinswesens* (Leipzig, 1967 [1909]); E. A. Judge, *The Social Pattern of Christian Groups in the First Century* (London, 1960) esp. pp. 40-48 on "Unofficial Associations: Koinonia"; M. N. Todd, *OCD*, s.v. Clubs, Greek.

[50] Ziebarth, op. cit., 192.

[51] Ziebarth, op. cit., 130.

is unsupported in his study, is nevertheless particularly appropriate for understanding the structure of the association(s) [52] of Corinthian Christians, who seem to have been largely Gentile. To pagan observers Christian groups were conceptualized as θίασοι (Lucian *Peregr.* 11) and individual members as θιασῶται (Origen *Cels.* 3. 23). Our scanty knowledge of early Gentile Christianity will make it necessary to limit our discussion to evidence drawn from Paul's Corinthian correspondence.

The information which can be gleaned from Paul's discussion of the particular situation of the Corinthian Christians in 1 Cor indicates that the observance of the Lord's Supper, together with the attendant activities and phenomena of Christian worship, conforms (*mutatis mutandis*) to the socio-religious pattern of sacral meals or symposia customarily held by Graeco-Roman religious societies.[53] In addition to the existence of αἱρέσεις and σχίσματα among the Christians at Corinth (1 Cor 1:10; 11:18),[54] many of Paul's difficulties with the Corinthian community seem to have arisen from the fact that they had not been adequately resocialized into the traditions and customs of their newly adopted religion. Some still participated in religious meals at temples (1 Cor 8:10; 10:20-21), and many were invited to dinners and symposia where sacrificial meat was served (1 Cor 10:27-32). It would be surprising indeed if Greek social customs, particularly with regard to Greek symposia within the context of religious societies, did not exercise a considerable degree of influence on the structure, customs and decorum of sacral meals eaten at Christian gatherings. Several points may be made in support of this contention.

1. Paul explicitly compares the Christian sacral meal with pagan sacral meals with regard to their mutual implications for the participant (1 Cor 10:14-22). The force of this analogy is dependent on the actual similarities between the Lord's Supper and other religious meals. It seems clear that the Corinthian Christians

[52] R. Reitzenstein, *Die hellenistischen Mysterienreligionen* (Stuttgart, [3]1927) 333; G. Heinrici, "Die Christengemeinde Korinths und die religiösen Genossenschaften der Griechen," *ZWT* 19 (1876) 465-562.

[53] While the patterns of Jewish religious associations are frequently presumed to have had the greatest influence on nascent Christian socio-religious structures, a caveat must be registered against the tendency to find single socio-cultural explanations for the polymorphous organization of Christian groups throughout the Mediterranean world.

[54] G. Theissen, "Soziale Integration und sakramentales Handeln: Eine Analyse von I Cor. XI 17-34," *NovT* 16 (1974) 182-86.

understood the Lord's Supper in terms of the same conceptual framework that they brought to bear on other sacral meals within their experience.

2. One of the central reasons for which the Corinthian Christians assembled was to have dinner together (1 Cor 11: 33: ὥστε ... συνερχόμενοι εἰς τὸ φαγεῖν). Even though Paul is of the opinion that members ought to satisfy their appetites at home (1 Cor 11:22, 34), that does not mean that the sacral meals at Corinth were not real meals.[55] Further, the common distinction between two kinds of Christian meals, the eucharist and the agape (love) feast appears to be artificial in the case of the Corinthian community. The centrality of the sacral meal is emphasized in 1 Cor 11:20-21, where Paul stresses the point that when the Corinthians assemble, it is not the *Lord's* dinner that they eat, it is their *own* dinner.[56] Paul is clearly offended by the structure and decorum which marked the sacral meals of the Corinthian community; one suspects that the root of the conflict lies in Paul's perception of the antithesis of Greek versus Judaeo-Christian socio-religious traditions and customs. What offends Paul most is the inequality and disorder of the proceedings.

3. One of Paul's primary emphases in 1 Cor 10-14 is the necessity of order and decorum in the Christian assemblies. Paul, like Plutarch, is concerned that the proceedings exhibit such qualities as moderation, fellowship, order and decorum. This general concern may be broken down into several constituent elements: (a) disorderly procedures in partaking of the "common" meal (1 Cor. 11:18-22, 27-34),[57] (b) the behavior of women in the assembly (1 Cor 11:2-16; 14:33b-36), (c) preferences and competition regarding various spiritual gifts together with their relative value and desirability (1 Cor 12:4-31), (d) orderliness and decorum in the exercise of various spiritual gifts which are expressed during

[55] Paul's recommendation that members of the community satisfy their rapacious appetites at home seems to be related to the issue of decorum and order at the symposia of the Corinthian congregation. A similar situation is found in Antigonus of Carystus' *Life of Menedemus* (non-extant), who reports that the symposia held by the philosopher Menedemus were so Spartan in their fare that guests had to dine at home before coming (Athenaeus *Deipn.* 10. 419).

[56] See the excellent discussion in Theissen, op. cit., 182-86.

[57] The analysis provided by Theissen (op. cit.) centers on the problems connected with 1 Cor 11:17-34.

the service (1 Cor 14:6-50, esp. vs. 40: πάντα δὲ εὐσχημόνως καὶ κατὰ τάξιν γενέσθω).[58]

With regard to the disorderliness of the common meal, we have adequately demonstrated in our discussion of the Greek symposion above that such occasions were primarily outlets for physical and emotional needs rather than for intellectual ones. The same problem, i.e., disorderliness at meals, is treated by Plutarch in *qu. conv.* 642F-644D. The advantages and disadvantages of allotting each guest a specific quantity of food is discussed (a Homeric practise, one which is met occasionally in Plutarch's day and a characteristic practise at public sacrificial feasts) versus the practise of allowing each guest to share in the common fare to whatever extent he wishes. The upshot is that people can end up satiated and hungry in both situations. The similarity of this situation to Paul's assessment of that at Corinth becomes clear in these words attributed to Lamprias (644C): ἀλλ' ὅπου τὸ ἴδιον ἔστιν ἀπόλλυται τὸ κοινόν ("But where each has his own portion, fellowship is destroyed"). The presence of women in the assembly was undoubtedly necessitated by the voluntary and open nature of the Christian sect, together with the fact that many independent women of status seem to have been attracted to nascent Christianity (Acts 13:50; 16:14; 17:12; Rom 16; 1 Cor 1:11); Paul is faced with the dilemma that, while women are ordinarily not participants in the sacral meals of religious societies, they are at the Christian assemblies in Corinth. In the matter of the preferences for certain spiritual gifts together with the dominance in the community of certain powerful individuals, Paul's advice in 1 Cor 12:4-31 in many respects echoes Plutarch's desire that complete equality prevail at symposia (supra, p. 73), and that all who are present should actively participate in the proceedings. Finally, with regard to decorum and orderliness in the exercise of various spiritual gifts during the service, we note that while Plutarch is of the opinion that philosophers should avoid dominating symposia with incomprehensible discussions, Paul recommends that glossolalia, unless it be accompanied by rational interpretation, be restrained in Christian assemblies. From our discussion of the nature of the activities at

[58] Cf. Plutarch's advice that philosophers should join in on the spirit of the symposion as long as the bounds of propriety are not exceeded (*qu. conv.* 613F: ἐφ' ὅσον μὴ ἐκβαίνει τὸ εὔσχημον).

typical symposia, the "disorder" at Corinth seems fairly representative of the real nature of such occasions.

4. From what we have thus far observed of typical Greek symposia of the Graeco-Roman period, the phrase ὃς δὲ μεθύει (1 Cor 11:21b) appears to be a note of realism, not merely rhetorical exaggeration. Wine was a cheap commodity available to all in first century Greece, and it seems to have flowed freely during Christian assemblies. The conviction of Paul, which he shared with the Corinthian Christians, that ὄντως ὁ θεὸς ἐν ὑμῖν ἐστιν (1 Cor 14:25) would be closely associated by Greeks with the phenomenon of vinous intoxication (see commentary under 150B-C). The two elements appear to be brought together in 1 Cor 12:13: πάντες ἓν πνεῦμα ἐποτίσθημεν. The same combination occurs in Eph 5:18 (pseudo-Pauline, yet certainly reflecting ecclesiastical practises in areas formerly under Pauline influence): μὴ μεθύσκεσθε οἴνῳ, ἐν ᾧ ἐστιν ἀσωτία, ἀλλὰ πληροῦσθε ἐν πνεύματι; since the context (cf. Eph 5:19f.) is that of Christian worship, it would appear that the presence of Dionysos has not entirely been barred from Christian gatherings. The presuppositions characteristic of pagan religious symposia again appear to have been imported into Christian sacral assemblies.

5. Finally, it seems that the very structure of the assemblies of the Corinthian Christians has been influenced by symposia patterns. The δεῖπνον is clearly set at the beginning, and begins with what might easily be construed to be a "sacrifice" of a portion of the food to be eaten and concludes (μετὰ τὸ δεῖπνον, 1 Cor 11:25) with a ceremony involving wine (1 Cor 11:20-26). Irregardless of the Jewish order of these proceedings, they were obviously adaptable to the structure of the Greek symposion. While there is no evidence to support the contention that wine continued to be drunk during the worship service which followed (but, cf. Eph 5:18), the spiritual ecstasy which characterized the proceedings would appear to have an *oinogenesis*. The various phenomena characteristic of Christian worship which are enumerated by Paul in 1 Cor 14 have many parallels with the kinds of activities which were engaged in at Greek symposia (*mutatis mutandis*).

IV. Commentary

Ch. 1

(146B-C)

Historical prologue; the Banquet of the Seven Sages is cast in the form of a symposion which is being reported in written form by Diokles to Nikarchos, both of whom are fictitious personnages. While most literary works of this type start with a προοίμιον, this particular προοίμιον, in both form and content, most closely resembles the historical προοίμια which had become a stereotyped literary convention with Greek historical writers; cf. Lucian *Hist.Conscr.* 23; K. Lorenz, *Untersuchungen zum Geschichtswerk des Polybios* (Stuttgart, 1931) (this dissertation centers on a detailed analysis of the προοίμια of Books 1 and 3 of Polybios; references to other historical prologues are made on p. 73, n. 1). While the obvious parallel in ECL is the historical preface of Luke-Acts (Luke 1:1-4; Acts 1:1-2 [both parts should be taken together]), the peculiar nature of the προοίμιον in *sept. sap. conv.* requires some explication. This is particularly true since H. J. Cadbury's singularly important article on the Lukan prologue ("Commentary on the Preface of Luke," *The Beginnings of Christianity* [London, 1922] 2:489-510) appears not to have been regarded seriously by many commentators on Luke. Cadbury argues that, since the use of a historical prologue had become a stereotyped literary convention, the implications of Luke 1:1-4 cannot be pressed literally. Two such recent attempts are D. J. Sneed, "An Exegesis of Luke 1:1-4 with Special Regard to Luke's Purpose as a Historian," *ExpT* 83 (1971-72) 40-43, and R. Morgenthaler, *Die lukanische Geschichtschreibung als Zeugnis: Gestalt und Gehalt der Kunst des Lukas* (Zürich, 1948) 2:105: "Criticism of Luke has not taken the prooimion of Luke's work seriously," The προοίμιον of *sept. sap. conv.* is an example of a historical prologue which cannot be taken seriously: (1) It serves as a prologue to a pseudonymous literary production. (2) Diokles, the fictive author, is made out to be an eyewitness and participant in the events and conversations which are narrated. (3) The fictitious recipient of the account, Nikarchos (a name found in Plutarch's lineage), is an apologetic device to further guarantee the verisimilitude of the narrative. (4) Both the events and the conversations which form the substance of the symposion constitute an imaginative dramatization of a selection of legendary sayings and stories which clustered about the figures of the Seven Sages. Consequently, the προοίμιον is but one of a number of devices which Plutarch uses (certainly with tongue in cheek) in an apologetic manner to lend credence and verisimilitude to an imaginative literary *tour de force*. Aside from the obvious parallel in Luke 1:1-4 and Acts 1:1-2, a parallel of equal significance, but one which seems to have escaped the notice of most commentators, is the fragmentary evidence of Papias' προοίμιον to his lost composition Λογίων κυριακῶν ἐξηγήσεως (preserved in Eusebius *h.e.* 3. 39. 2-4; cf. the section on "Papiasfragmente" in Funk-Bihlmeyer, *Die Apostolischen Väter*, 2d ed. [Tübingen, 1956] 133-40). While the προοίμιον of Papias' lost treatise has many parallels with the προοίμιον of Luke-Acts and *sept. sap. conv.* (see the table of parallels which follows), this similarity (to my knowledge) has not hitherto been observed. W. R. Schoedel has called attention to the stock rhetorical devices of Papias' προοίμιον (*Polycarp, Martyrdom of Polycarp, Fragments of Papias*, Vol. 5 of *The Apostolic Fathers: A New Translation and Commentary*, ed. R. M. Grant [London, 1967] 100f.), and J. Munck has called attention to the conventionality of Papias' expressions ("Presbyters and Disciples of the Lord in Papias," *HTR* 52 [1959] 230). Several general observations might be made regarding the implications of the specific comparisons made in Table I: (1) Papias' utilization of the stereotyped form of the historical προοίμιον would indicate that, as in the case of Luke 1:1-4, the constituent statements of the προοίμιον should not be pressed into reconstructions of the historical situation within which Papias wrote (a point which J. Munck makes in the article cited above). (2) That fragment of Papias quoted by Eusebius in *h.e.* 3. 39. 15 belongs, on the basis of both form and style, to the προοίμιον of Papias' lost work. (3) Since the closest parallel in ECL to Papias' προοίμιον is found in Luke-Acts, and since the extant fragments of Papias show no knowledge of Luke-Acts (R. Heard, "Papias' Quotations from the New Testament," *NTS* 1 [1954-55] 130-34), it could be inferred that Papias wrote in conscious opposition to the kind of continuous historical narrative represented by Luke. (4) Papias' preference for short "authentic" sayings stemming from Jesus with the addition of short interpretive

TABLE I. Synoptic Comparison of the Historical *Prooimia* of

Plutarch *sept. sap. conv.* 146B-C	Luke 1:1-4/ Acts 1:1	Papias [Eusebius *h.e.* 3. 39. 2-4]	Papias [Eusebius *h.e.* 3. 39. 15]
1 ὦ Νίκαρχε	σοι κράτιστε Θεόφιλε ὦ Θεόφιλε [Acts 1:1]	σοι	
2 πράγμασι	πραγμάτων ποιεῖν τε καὶ διδάσκειν [Acts 1:1]	ὅσα [ἐμνημόνευσα]	ὅσα [Μάρκος] ἐμνημόνευσεν τὰ ὑπὸ τοῦ κυρίου ἠλεχθέντα ἢ πραχθέντα
3 λόγοι ψευδεῖς συντεθέντες	πολλοὶ ἐπεχείρησαν ἀνατάξασθαι διήγησιν	οὐ γὰρ τοῖς τὰ πολλὰ λέγουσιν ἔχαιρον ὥσπερ οἱ πολλοί οὐ γὰρ τὰ ἐκ τῶν βιβλίων	
4 ἐν οἷς καὶ αὐτὸς ἤμην	αὐτόπται ὑπηρέται	τὰ παρὰ ζώσης φωνῆς καὶ μενούσης [cf. αὐτόπτην (3. 39. 2)] τί [7 disciples] εἶπεν ἅ τε [2 disciples] λέγουσιν	
5 οὔτε τοὺς λόγους ὀρθῶς ἀπεμνημόνευσεν		τὰς ἀλλοτρίας ἐντολὰς μνημονεύουσιν	ὡς ἀπεμνημόνευσεν
6	παρέδοσαν ἡμῖν [διήγησιν περὶ τῶν πεπληροφορημένων]	τὰς παρὰ τοῦ κυρίου . . . δεδομένας	τῶν κυριακῶν λογίων
7	παρηκολουθηκότι ἀκριβῶς	παρηκολουθηκώς	παρηκολούθησεν ἀκριβῶς
8 ἀπ' ἀρχῆς	ἀπ' ἀρχῆς ἄνωθεν ὧν ἤρξατο	παρὰ τοῦ κυρίου	τὰ ὑπὸ τοῦ κυρίου
9 ὑμῖν ἅπαντα διηγήσομαι	περὶ πάντων λόγον ἐποιησάμην [Acts 1:1]		
10 ὁ διηγούμενος	ἔδοξε κἀμοί . . . σοι γράψαι		
11	ἵνα ἐπιγνῷς . . . τὴν ἀσφάλειαν ἀκριβῶς	ἀλήθειαν τἀληθῆ ἀληθείας	
12	καθεξῆς		οὐ μέντοι τάξει

comments would seem to indicate that the literary form which Papias preferred resembled a collection of χρεῖαι or apophthegmata. Referring to Peter, Papias states ὃς πρὸς τὰς χρείας ἐποιεῖτο τὰς διδασκαλίας (Eusebius *h.e.* 3. 39. 15), a phrase which Schoedel accurately translates as "who presented his teachings in *chria*-form" op. cit., p. 107); cf. J. Kürzinger, "Irenäus und sein Zeugnis zur Sprache des Matthäusevangeliums," NTS 10 (1963-64) 109, n. 2.

Ch. 2

(146D)

Because of certain dreams of Melissa, Periander set about to honor and worship the goddess Aphrodite. Dreams are regarded as a vehicle for divine revelation, and it is here implied that Periander's neglect of Aphrodite might be the cause for divine reprisals, hence the tyrant's zeal to "honor and worship" the goddess. Plutarch disapproves of this attitude toward the gods which he would describe as δεισιδαιμονία (cf. *PECL* 1:1-35; H. Braun, "Plutarch's Critique of Superstition in the Light of the New Testament," *Occasional Papers of the Institute for Antiquity and Christianity*, No. 5 (n.d.). On dreams, see *PECL* 1:15, 207, 254, 268, 293. On dream revelations in ECL, cf. A. Oepke, *TDNT*, s.v. ὄναρ, B (Oepke's article is chiefly valuable for citations from ancient literature; his theological evaluation of the religious significance of dreams in ECL is seriously deficient). No adequate study exists on the subject of dreams as a facet of the larger subject of divination in ECL (but, see A. Wikenhauser, "Die Traumgesichte des NT in religionsgeschichtlicher Beleuchtung," *Pisciculi*, Antike und Christentum, Suppl. Vol. 1 (Münster, 1939), 320-33. The closest parallel in NT to the ominous dream of Mellissa appears to be Luke 12:20, where the phrase εἶπεν δὲ αὐτῷ ὁ θεός seems to presuppose a dream as the medium of divine communication. The rich man in the parable had a life-style which angered the deity, and a dream prepared the way for divine punishment.

Thales, seeing the fancy transportation which Periander had prepared for his guests, refuses it and walks to the banquet site with Neiloxenos and Diokles. On the *peripatos* as a narrative device, see *PECL* 1:88, 104f., 131, 141, 291. This avoidance of luxury set the tone for the symposion, i.e., sages exemplify their teachings in their life-styles. In the NT, Jesus is depicted not only as demanding that people surrender their wealth and worldly possessions, but also as an example of that mode of life. In the Q sayings (Matt 8:20//Luke 9:58), Jesus is made to say that foxes and birds have dwellings, but not the Son of Man. See M. Hengel, *Property and Riches in the Early Church* (Philadelphia, 1974), where both the Jewish and Greek philosophical attitudes toward property and riches are discussed in terms of their joint influence on early Christianity (an excellent bibliography is found on pp. 89-92).

(146E)

Neiloxenos, who has brought a letter from Amasis, king of Egypt, has been instructed by that monarch to give Bias the first chance to solve the problem posed; should he fail, it should be passed *seriatim* to the other six sages. Plutarch has apparently modelled this challenge on analogy with the legendary Beaker of Bathycles (mentioned in *sept. sap. conv.* 155E; cf. Diogenes Laertius 1. 28), or the legendary tripod which is to be given to the wisest of the Greeks. Each of the Seven, beginning with Thales, passes the prize on to the next until it again reached Thales, who dedicated the object to Apollo. Some of the variants of this folktale are recorded in Diogenes Laertius 1. 28f.

(146F)

The problem posed by Amasis to Bias. Using the literary device of secondary narration, Plutarch has Thales repeat an *agonistic wisdom story* concerning Bias. In terms of our analysis above (pp. 66ff.), this story consists of three structural elements: (1) the problem: Amasis sent Bias a sacrificial animal requesting that he return the worst and the best portion, (2) the solution: Bias returned the tongue, (3) the acclamation: Bias was, in consequence, held in high esteem by the monarch. In another use of the same anecdote (*aud.* 38C), Plutarch does not use the acclamation and explains Bias' selection of the tongue by stating that human speech contains the greatest benefits as well as injuries. There the form of the anecdote (or agonistic wisdom story) is determined by the fact that he is stressing the content of the anecdote (the importance of human speech), whereas in the present context he uses the anecdote merely to emphasize the sagacity of Bias. In *garrul.* 506C, Plutarch uses the same wisdom story in a manner identical to its use in *aud.* 38C, except that he attributes the story to Pittacus, thereby demonstrating the unimportance of the specific ascription of such a wisdom story in comparison with the importance of the kind of person to whom such a story was attributed. It is natural to compare this kind of agonistic wisdom story with analogous forms found in the Synoptic gospels (cf. supra, pp. 67ff.).

(147A)

The story of Thales' measurement of an Egyptian pyramid. Again Plutarch uses the device of secondary narration. This particular agonistic wisdom story concerning Thales is of interest in that it is found here in a unique form. Another version of the story is found in Diogenes Laertius 1. 27 (quoting Hieronymos of Rhodes) and in Pliny *HN* 36. 82, in which it is said that Thales waited until the time of day when it is known that the length of a shadow is equal to the height of the object which casts it; at that moment, Thales measured the shadow. Here, Thales is said to set his walking stick at the edge of the shadow cast by the pyramid, thus applying the theorem (also attributed to Thales) that a triangle is determined if its base and the angles relative to the base are given. Plutarch (or his source) has reformulated this wisdom story about Thales in conformity with one of the latter's well-known geometric theorems. Thus it is the feat itself which is stressed, not the particular method by which it was achieved. Plutarch has cast this wisdom story into the form of an agonistic wisdom story: (1) the problem: the difficulty of ascertaining the height of a pyramid is implicit (by implication there is a gathered crowd of onlookers), (2) the solution: Thales measures the pyramid's height by means of geometrical principles, (3) the acclamation: the wisdom story is introduced with this feature: "the king finds much to admire in you, and in particular he was immensely pleased with ...." Again Plutarch has used the wisdom story, not for its content, but rather as a means of heightening the sagacity of yet another of the Seven Sages.

(147B)

Again using the technique of secondary narration, Plutarch has Neiloxenos relate a gnomic wisdom story concerning Thales centering on a question of Molpagoras: τί παραδοξότατον εἴης ἑωρακώς; This wisdom story appears in the classic form ἐρωτηθείς . . . ἀποκρίναιο (to which we have called attention above supra, pp. 65ff.). In *gen. Soc.* 578D the basic form of the wisdom story is retained (ἐρωτώντων . . . ἔφη) yet the setting is different and the question (ὅ τι καινότατον ἱστορήκοι) is posed by "friends" of Thales after he had returned from a long journey. This wisdom story consists only of a problem and a solution; the acclamation is absent (according to our theory expressed above, p. 66) because the reason for Plutarch's use of this story is to emphasize its content: the bad reputation which Thales had with tyrants and kings. Note that Thales is made to deny the attribution of this wisdom story to himself in 147B, while Plutarch definitely attributes the saying to Thales in *gen. Soc.* 578D (See B. Einarson, Review of *Plutarque: Le Banquet des Sept Sages*, by J. Defradas, *CPh* 51 [1956] 276-79).

Neiloxenos is made to attribute to Thales a wisdom saying to the effect that of wild animals the worst was the tyrant, and of tame animals the worst was the flatterer. Elsewhere (*adul. et am.* 61C), Plutarch attributes an identical wisdom saying to Bias, again illustrating the relative unimportance of exact attribution so long as the character of the speaker is appropriate. Further, the saying in *adul. et am.* 61C includes both a question and an answer, i.e., it has the basic two-part structure of the wisdom story. Here Plutarch has truncated the form for literary reasons. The absence of some form of acclamation may again be attributed to the fact that the content of the saying is the primary reason for its use by Plutarch: Thales' bad reputation with tyrants.

(147C)

χαλεπὸν ἐσθλὸν ἔμμεναι; Plutarch's Thales attributes this wisdom saying to Pittacus. Though brief, the saying needs no further embellishment to be fully comprehensible. Plutarch may attribute this saying to one of the Seven Sages because he recalls Plato's opinion that this saying is an example of Laconic brevity "privately handed about with high approbation among the sages" (Plato *Prt.* 343B). Elsewhere Plutarch uses an unattributed variant of this saying, which he describes as a παροιμία: χαλεπὰ τὰ καλά (*lib. ed.* 6c).

(147D)

Thales is made to interrupt the foregoing conversation for the ostensible reason that it is unsuitable for those on their way to dinner; this device indicates the genre-consciousness of Plutarch.

(147E)

The discussion in this *peripatos* dialogue now turns to the subject of the proper preparation for attending dinners (147E-148B). As Defradas observes (*Le Banquet,* 93, n. 28) one of the primary themes of *sept. sap. conv.* (here he exaggerates slightly) finds expression in this conversation: the primacy of the spirit over the body (a basic feature of Plutarch's Platonic idealism).

(147E-F)

Thales cites the Sybarites as an example of improper preparation for dinners: they present invitations to women a year in advance of the occasion so that sufficient time will be available for securing appropriate apparel and jewelry. He emphasizes the difficulty of the far more important task of finding appropriate adornment for the ἦθος rather than the σῶμα. The sensible person (ὁ νοῦν ἔχων) comes prepared to participate in whatever topic might arise in the course of the conversation; symposia can be wrecked by boors (cf. supra, p. 73). 1 Pet 3:3-4 contains an essentially parallel thought: adornment should not be physical (elaborate coiffures, wearing of fine jewelry and exquisite apparel—of these three, Plutarch neglects to mention only the coiffures), but rather seek to adorn ὁ κρυπτὸς τῆς καρδίας ἄνθρωπος ἐν τῷ ἀφθάρτῳ τοῦ πραέος καὶ ἡσυχίου πνεύματος (cf. Tertullian *Apol.* 6). A similar conception is expressed in 1 Tim 2:9f.: women should adorn themselves modestly, not with braided hair or gold or pearls or costly attire, but by good deeds (δι' ἔργων ἀγαθῶν).

(148A-B)

Thales mentions the Egyptian custom of displaying a σκελετός at symposia in order to remind guests of what their end will be; this encourages φιλία and ἀγάπησις. Life, which is short with regard to time, should not be made long by evil conduct. The σκελετός which is mentioned (cf. a more accurate description of the Egyptian custom in Herodotus 2. 78, certainly Plutarch's primary source) was in all probability a mummy-like statuette (described in *Is. et Os.* 357F as an εἴδωλον ἀνθρώπου τεθνηκότος). On this see S. Morenz, *Egyptian Religion* (Ithaca, 1973) 195f., 329, nn. 58ff.). Herodotus 2. 78 states that after showing the statuette to guests, the following saying is repeated: ἐς τοῦτον ὁρέων πῖνέ τε καὶ τέρπευ· ἔσεαι γὰρ ἀποθανὼν τοιοῦτος. Cf. Lucian *Luct.* 21; Petronius *Satyr.* 34. In 1 Cor 15:32, Paul, quoting Isa 22:13 (cf. Isa 56:13), says "Let us eat and drink, for tomorrow we die." A similar sentiment is expressed in Luke 12:19ff. in the parable of the rich fool (Luke 12:13-21). Paul sees sensual and self-indulgent enjoyment of life as a consequence of believing that death is the end and that there will be no final resurrection. But the Egyptian, in the words of Morenz, "could not free himself from the consciousness of death even when he was calling on his fellow-men to enjoy life" (Morenz, op. cit., 196). Plutarch gives this Egyptian custom a moralistic interpretation which is close to the meaning of the parable of the rich fool, i.e., one who accumulates wealth and property should be aware that they are ultimately meaningless.

A sensible man doesn't go to a dinner just to gorge himself, but rather to participate intelligently in the discussion. In 1 Cor 11:20-22, 33-34, Paul criticizes the Corinthian community for their boorish behavior at common meals; some are drunk while others are still hungry. He finally advises them to hold to decorum at their meals, and if any are ravenously hungry they ought to eat at home. Paul wants edification to be the hallmark of Christian symposia, nothing else. Similarly, Jude 12 speaks of "heretics" who by nature act like irrational animals (ὡς τὰ ἄλογα ζῷα, Jude 10); n.b. the description of a person who acts properly as a sensible man in *sept, sap. conv.* 147F (ὁ νοῦς ἔχων), 148A (νοῦν ἔχοντος ἀνδρός). Jude 12 further describes these "heretics" as "those who are stains in your love feasts, feasting together shamelessly, concerned for themselves alone" (οὗτοι εἰσιν οἱ ἐν ταῖς ἀγάπαις σπιλάδες συνευωχούμενοι ἀφόβως ἑαυτοὺς ποιμαίνοντες). 2 Pet 2:12f. (based on Jude 12) contains the same sentiments. The position of Plutarch's Thales and Paul appears essentially the same; both argue for moderation and decorum at symposia, the primary purpose of which is not to eat, drink and carouse, but to have fellowship within the context of enlightening discussion and mutual sharing.

Ch. 3

(148D)

The Eumetis episode. Eumetis is given the highest praise by Thales for three outstanding qualities: wonderful sense (φρόνημα θαυμαστόν), political astuteness (νοῦς πολιτικός) and a philanthropic character (φιλάνθρωπον ἦθος). φιλανθρωπία is a very significant ethical concept in Plutarch (cf. "Philanthropie," Ch. 4 of R. Hirzel, *Plutarch* [Leipzig, 1912] 23-32) and was an outstanding virtue in Middle Platonism and later Stoicism. Philanthropia is particularly important as a characteristic of rulers which in Tit 3:4 is applied to God, as it is in Diogn 8:7; 9:2. See H. Martin, "The Concept of *Philanthropia* in Plutarch's *Lives*," *AJPh* 82 (1961) 164-75.

(148E)

The Alexidemos episode. The character of Alexidemos is juxtaposed to that of Eumetis and is set forth by Plutarch as an example of those qualities of character which one should studiously avoid. A bastard son of the tyrant Thrasybulos, Alexidemos storms out of the banquet hall angry at the inappropriate seat which he has been given. In form, this is a paradigmatic wisdom story since the episode culminates in the exemplary behavior of Thales. The story contains five major elements: (1) the problematic situation: Alexidemos' pompous exit from the dinner because of an imagined slight to his honor in the matter of seating arrangements. (2) To this Thales gives a two-fold response: (a) your place at the table will not make you better or worse than you were before, and (b) one should try to find some positive benefit to be derived from those with whom we sit, since our objections will make us hateful to both our fellow guests and our host. (3) Alexidemos rebuts Thales advice by claiming that wise men make it their chief occupation to be honored. (4) To explain Alexidemos' bizarre behavior, Thales claims that he is "senseless and uncouth by nature" (ἔμπληκτος καὶ ἀλλόκοτος φύσει [149B]), (5) Later (149F), Thales intentionally takes the seat abandoned by Alexidemos with the observation that he would have paid to sit next to Ardalos. The entire episode turns on the question of τιμή, a concept which is important in earliest Christianity in view of the central significance of honor in near eastern customs and cultures. Cf. E. R. Dodds on "shame-culture" vs. "guilt-culture" in *The Greeks and the Irrational* (Berkeley, 1951) 28-63; this subject is related to earliest Christianity in J. D. M. Derrett's discussion of "relationship and prestige" in *Jesus's Audience: The Social and Psychological Environment in Which He Worked* (New York, 1973) 38-45. There are a few NT passages which explicitly deal with the relationship between seating arrangements and the question of honor. Jas 2:1-7 deals with the problem of giving undue attention and honor to the rich, while the poor are ignored and given inferior seating (cf. M. Dibelius and H. Greeven, *James* [Philadelphia, 1976] 128ff., who emphasize the rhetorical nature of this example; it does not, they claim, represent the real situation in the Christian community in which Jas arose, but is an exaggerated and flagrant instance of partiality). In the parable of the choice of places at table (Luke 14:7-14), it is argued that places of honor at table should be bestowed, not presumptuously taken. The advice in Luke 14:10: "go, sit in the lowest place," conforms to the paradigmatic action of Thales.

(149A)

Thales compares Alexidemos with a Spartan, who, being given the last place in a chorus, responded, "Good! You have found out how this may be made a place of honor." In form, this is a gnomic wisdom story consisting of (1) a problematic situation, and (2) a solution. Again, one suspects that the acclamation is not used because it is the content of the gnomic wisdom story which is being stressed. Elsewhere, pseudo-Plutarch in *Lacon.* 208D names Agesilaos as the particular Spartan who made this retort, and later in *Lacon.* 219E the same saying in precisely the same setting is assigned to Damonidas. The saying is also attributed to Aristippos in a setting wherein he has been assigned the last place at dinner (Diogenes Laertius 2. 73). The saying has been carefully preserved in tradition, while the setting and the attribution of the saying show great variety and fluidity.

(149B-C)

Thales explains Alexidemos' boorish behavior by claiming that he is "senseless and uncouth by nature," and gives an example of how in his youth Alexidemos' senseless behavior earned his father "enmity in place of friendship" (ἔχθραν ἀντὶ φιλίας). Plutarch carefully distinguishes between a person's φύσις and ἦθος (cf.

Alc. 2. 1); in contrast to the earlier Stoa, he, in the Platonic tradition, sees in man both the elements of intelligence and irrationality, reason and emotion. In *num. vind.* 551Cff., Plutarch affirms that each soul has an innate measure of virtue which is capable of both repression and near obliteration or of training and encouragement in the path of moral goodness (cf. *PECL* 1:199ff.). Later, in 562B, he argues that while animals have an ἦθος which constantly reveals itself for what it is, human nature (ἡ ἀνθρώπου φύσις) "can enter into customs and doctrines and laws of conduct and thereby frequently conceal its failings and imitate a virtuous course, with the result that it either wipes out an inherited stain of vice, or else eludes detection for a long time" (cf. *PECL* 1:217). A basic hindrance to virtuous conduct can lie in the φύσις and/or in one's youth (cf. B. Bucher-Isler, *Norm und Individualität in den Biographien Plutarchs* [Bern und Stuttgart, 1972] 46). Ethical virtue, for Plutarch then, consists in the regulation of the passions by reason and education (R. M. Jones, *The Platonism of Plutarch* [Menasha, Wisconsin, 1916] 13). The contrast between the anthropology of ECL and Plutarch could hardly be greater. Unlike Plutarch, ECL does not assume that non-Christian man has an innate divine element which needs only to be trained and directed. Generally, ECL assumes that unaided man has a natural tendency to sin and that even human virtues are as vices (here one sees an agreement with Stoicism). In several instances in ECL, evil behavior is seen as conclusive proof that particular individuals were never truly Christians. Cf. 2 Pet 2:12-22//Jude 8-13; 1 John 2:19 ("They went out from us but they were not of us"); 3:4-10. However, though the Christian assumption that man by nature has no divine element pervades early Christianity, once Christianization has occurred and the Spirit of God or of Jesus is thought to dwell in Christians, many parallels between Plutarch's φύσις-ἦθος dichotomy begin to appear, particularly in the underlying assumptions behind the paraenetical traditions in ECL (cf. *PECL* 1:314).

(149C-E)

Diokles and Thales are invited to examine a prodigy (an infant centaur) to determine whether its birth is a sign and portent or is without significance. In this third episode, Plutarch's purpose appears to be to contrast the rationalism of Thales with the δεισιδαιμονία of Diokles; Periander is neutral in that, while he fears that the prodigy may have negative significance, he is persuaded that this is not the case by Thales. The entire episode appears to be a free literary creation of Plutarch in the form of a gnomic wisdom story. It consists of four elements: (1) the problematic situation (the birth of an infant centaur), (2) the false solution, which is jestingly suggested to Diokles by Thales, i.e., the prodigy is a sign of divine wrath indicating the necessity for various rites of ritual propitiation, (3) the real solution, proposed by Thales, is that wives ought to be provided for stableboys, (4) the acclamation consists of Periander's approval of Thales' witty solution.

ἤ τι σημεῖόν ἐστι καὶ τέρας; these two terms are frequently found together in ECL: Matt 24:24//Mark 13:22; John 4:48; Acts 2:19, 22, 43; 4:30; 5:12; 6:8; 7:36; 14:3; 15:12; 2 Thes 2:9 [with δύναμις]; Heb 2:4; Rom 15:19; 2 Cor 12:12 [with δυνάμις]; Did 16:4; Barn 4:14; 5:8; 1 Clem 51:5. In ECL τέρας is always found in the plural, and always with σημεῖον in the plural; this is undoubtedly due to the rather strange fact that the phrase is *always used generically*, never with respect to a particular event (as it is here in Plutarch). Plutarch's use of this stock expression in the singular is certainly due to the fact that a specific prodigy is in view. Defradas (*Le Banquet*, 96) claims that "the first [term] designates prophetic signs given by the gods; the second designates that which deviates from the normal." Against this, the fact that the terms are used together in a stereotyped manner seems to indicate that they are essentially synonymous. Further, in ECL these terms seem to refer to events which are clearly and obviously revelatory and miraculous; here whether the prodigy is auspicious is precisely the question.

(149D)

Diokles has interpreted the sign as an indication of strife and discord and also as a result of the fact that the entire group has not yet had a chance to atone or propitiate Aphrodite's wrath for a previous offense: πρὶν ἢ τὸ πρῶτον ἐξιλάσασθαι μήνιμα. The view of Diokles is one that Plutarch would regard as superstitious; cf. *PECL* 1:1ff. Plato held that the gods cause no evil (Plato *R.* 377ff.), and Plutarch as a good Platonist held that god was absolutely good and therefore could not be responsible for causing evil (Jones, *The Platonism of Plutarch*, 81).

ἐξιλάσκομαι ("propitiate, atone") is not found in the NT and only twice in the Apostolic Fathers (1 Clem 7:7; Herm Vis 1:2:1). ἱλάσκομαι without the prepositional intensifier is found twice in NT (Luke 18:13; Heb 2:17); cf. the verb ἱλατεύομαι (Herm Vis 1:2:1), the nouns ἱλασμός (1 John 2:2; 4:10), ἱλαστήριον (Rom 3:25; Heb 9:5). καθαρμός is purification from cultic and moral defects, while ἱλασμός (in this case) is the propitiation of the gods whose wrath has been provoked. On some of the procedures for καθαρμοί, cf. *PECL* 1:15f., 26f. One major difference between the early Christian and Hellenistic conceptions of propitiation is that, as evidenced in such passages as 1 John 4:10, it is apparently God, not man, that has taken the initiative in making propiation (cf. F. Büchsel, *TDNT*, s.v. ἱλασμός [3:317]). However, since the viewpoint which sees Jesus' coming and death as an act of propitiation is essentially the metaphorical use of the cultic language of propitiation, the differences are more apparent than real.

(150A)

Aesop was also present, having been sent by Croesus to Periander and then to Delphi (Herodotus 2. 134). This feature adds interest to the narrative, since legend held that Aesop was killed at Delphi (cf. A. Wiechers, *Aesop in Delphi* (Meisenheim am Glan, 1961); on Aesop and his role in *sept. sap. conv.* see Defradas, *Le Banquet*, 23ff.

(150B-C)

Thales suggests that Bias deal with Amasis' problem while sober. Bias responds that Dionysos is called Lysios ("solver") because of his wisdom, so that if he is filled with the god he will not compete less adequately. Dionysos was traditionally regarded as functionally identical with wine and its intoxicating effects (*qu. conv.* 705B, 715E). Not infrequently, intoxication was regarded as a mantic state. In early Christianity the parallel between wine and Dionysos on the one hand and eucharistic wine and Jesus on the other immediately suggests itself (cf. M. Smith, "On the Wine God in Palestine," *Salo Wittmayer Baron Jubilee Volume* [Jerusalem, 1975] 815-29). John 6:53, 55 refer to drinking the blood of the Son of Man, in an obvious reference to the eucharist (whether the references are interpolations by a later hand makes little difference for the early Christian history of religious thought); yet there is no explicit reference in ECL to the drinking of eucharistic wine which will result in being filled with God (or Jesus) to my knowledge. However, cf. Eph 5:18; 1 Cor 12:13; 11:21b (supra, p. 78).

θεοῦ μεστός; while this phrase refers explicitly to the intoxicating presence of Dionysos, there are nevertheless many formal parallels to this expression in ECL, none of which, however, (as we have observed above) make this condition dependent upon consumption of eucharistic wine. The closest parallel appears to be Ign Magn 14:1: θεοῦ γέμετε; cf. Ign Eph 15:3 (αὐτὸς ἐν ἡμῖν θεὸς ἡμῶν); Ign Rom 6:3 (εἴ τις αὐτὸν [i.e., θεὸν] ἐν ἑαυτῷ ἔχει); Ign Magn 12:1 (Ἰησοῦν γὰρ Χριστὸν ἔχετε ἐν ἑαυτοῖς). On this question see D. E. Aune, "The Presence of God in the Community: the Eucharist in Its Early Christian Cultic Context," *SJT* 29[1976] 451-59. In spite of the formal similarities in expression, the differences seem significant: (1) the inner presence of Dionysos through wine is an individual experience with no moral or cultic prerequisites, and (2) the divine presence for Ignatius, as for Paul, is primarily a corporate experience which has elaborate cultic and moral requirements (cf. D. E. Aune, *The Cultic Setting of Realized Eschatology in Early Christianity* [Leiden, 1972] 142-52). A further parallel with the expression θεοῦ μεστός is found in Acts 2:13: γλεύκους μεμεστωμένοι, which is the judgment of observers that the disciples ἐπλήσθησαν πάντες πνεύματος ἁγίου (Acts 2:4), i.e., the filling of the Holy Spirit resembled intoxication (cf. Acts 2:15: "we are not intoxicated, as you presume"). These parallels become more significant in the light of 1 Cor 11:21b, where we find some boorish participants in the sacral meals of the Corinthian congregation (ὃς δὲ μεθύει; cf. W. Schmithals, *Gnosticism in Corinth* [New York and Nashville, 1971] 253). While Schmithals does not take this statement at face value (with H. Conzelmann, *1 Corinthians* [Philadelphia, 1975] 195), in view of the nature of Greek religious symposia, we have every indication of the literalness of the expression (cf. A. Robertson and A. Plummer, *A Critical and Exegetical Commentary on the First Epistle of St Paul to the Corinthians*, 2nd ed. [Edinburgh, 1914]). Schmithals falsely distinguishes between a profane feast and a cultic meal;

the situation in Corinth would seem to presuppose a syncretism which combined pagan with Christian traditions; thus wine as a vehicle for divine possession in Corinth is not simply a wild inference.

Ch. 5

(150D)

The tables are removed, the garlands distributed, and libations were poured to the accompaniment of the music provided by a flute-girl (cf. supra, p. 72, n. 42). These cultic actions bring the first part of the banquet to a close and initiate the second part, the symposion proper.

Ch. 6

(151Aff.)

Periander bids Neiloxenos to read the letter from Amasis king of Egypt to Bias. In his letter Amasis states that the Ethiopian king is engaged in a contest of wisdom (σοφίας ἅμιλλαν) with him; if he can find a solution to the king's demand that he drink up the ocean, many villages and cities will be his reward. After some preliminary bantering, Bias answers that the Ethiopian king must stop the rivers emptying into the ocean so that the ocean which *is* may be drunk, not the one which will be. "As soon as Bias had said this, Neiloxenos for joy hastened to embrace and kiss him. The rest of the company also commended the answer and expressed their satisfaction with it" (151D). The present unit under consideration may be called an agonistic wisdom story, consisting of three structural elements: (1) the problem (in this case a riddle proposed by the Ethiopian king), (2) the solution offered by Bias, and (3) the acclamation of Neiloxenos and the rest of the gathered company. Both the trifling nature of the riddle and its solution, together with the added element of the acclamation, combine to indicate that this agonistic wisdom story functions in such a way as to underline the wisdom of the sage Bias.

(151D-E)

Chs. 6-7 constitute a unit, the focus of which is on the responses of each of the Seven Sages to the apodosis "a king or a tyrant could best gain esteem if ..." The transition to that focal section, which is found in Ch. 7, is put into the mouth of Chilon. He suggests that Neiloxenos should take word back to Amasis, not on the subject of how to drink brine, but rather on the subject of how to make his kingship more potable to his subjects. The trivial concerns of king Amasis are contrasted with the kind of serious concerns which the Seven Sages think ought to characterize such a monarch. In effect, the Sages set themselves to answering the kind of question which Amasis should have asked. That which follows is a literary compilation of Plutarch which has the basic structural form of a gnomic wisdom story: (1) the problem: a single statement forming an apodosis, "a king or a tyrant will be held in esteem if . . ." (2) the solution: a series of seven protases, each introduced with the conditional particle εἰ (with the exception of the last statement by Chilon). The expression of consternation expressed by Periander (representing tyrants) and Aesop (representing kings) cannot be regarded as a third structural element, that of acclamation. The primary purpose of the inclusion of this complex and extended gnomic wisdom story, therefore, is not to demonstrate the wisdom of the Seven Sages, but rather to focus on the content of their advice to rulers. If this supposition is correct, the importance and centrality of this subject as a major theme in *sept. sap. conv.* is confirmed.

(151F)

πολλά γ' . . . ἑτοίμως; in a brief tangential section, Neiloxenos is made to comment to Diokles privately that many things have been fabricated about the Seven Wise men, and most people delight in producing such fabrications and accepting them from others. Here Plutarch is strengthening the claims made in the προοίμιον (supra, 146B-C). In Papias' προοίμιον similar statements are made regarding those who concoct oracles of the Lord (Eusebius *h.e.* 3. 39. 3); cf. 2 Pet 1:16; 1 Tim 1:4; 4:7; 2 Tim 4:4; Tit 1:14.

(152D)

συμποσίου δ' ἀρετὴν νομίζεις τὸ πάντας διαλέγεσθαι καὶ περὶ πάντων. The thought is that within the framework of a symposion equality ought to prevail, and full participation on the part of all is regarded as appropriate (cf. supra, p. 77). The Corinthian congregation was drawn from various strata of Corinthian society (1 Cor 1:26-29; cf. W. H. Wuellner, "The Sociological Implications of I Corinthians 1:26-28 Reconsidered," *Studia Evangelica*, vol. 6,

TU, 112 [Berlin, 1973] 666-72), a factor which contributed to community rivalries and conflicts against which Paul argues (1 Cor 11: 17-22, 27-32; cf. G. Theissen, *Nov T* 16 [1974] 182-86). In Paul's advice in 1 Cor 12:4-31, culminating in 1 Cor 13, he essentially argues for equality despite various apparent forms of diversity. τῷ λαλεῖν ἐν οἴνῳ βρεχόμενον; cf. supra, 150B-C.

Chs. 8-9

(152E-153D)

Periander suggests that the second part of Amasis' letter be considered by the group. Amasis, reports Neiloxenos, as part of the wisdom contest previously mentioned, had asked the Ethiopian king nine "superlative" questions, i.e., what is the oldest thing, the most beautiful, etc. Neiloxenos then proceeds to read the question posed by Amasis, together with the responses given by the Ethiopian king to the assembly of sages. Thales observes that no single answer can stand uncontested, and after a brief explanation of what he means, Thales himself undertakes to answer each of the nine questions. This section, while it appears to be a free composition of Plutarch, nevertheless incorporates a great deal of traditional material in the form of a collection of χρεῖαι. The entire episode is constructed in the form of a complex agonistic wisdom story: (1) the problem(s): the nine "superlative" questions posed by Amasis, (2) the false solution(s): the unsatisfactory answers given by the Ethiopian king, (3) the true solution(s): provided *seriatim* by Thales, and (4) the acclamation: given by the assembly of Sages and friends (ἀποδεξαμένων δὲ πάντων τὸν Θαλῆν, 153E). Both elements (2) and (4) fit the present narrative setting and formally indicate that the focus of this collection of sayings is the sagacity of Thales rather than the content of the sayings themselves. Further, many of these sayings (here attributed to Thales by Plutarch) were similarly attributed to that sage in collections which had been in circulation for some time. In Diogenes Laertius 1. 35, six of the wisdom stories used by Plutarch are attributed to Thales, but in a different form. For example, the question about the oldest thing is found in this form: πρεσβύτατον τῶν ὄντων θεός· ἀγένητον γάρ [n.b. the inferential particle γάρ which ends a sentence here as it does in Mark 16:8], while Plutarch's version is found in this form: τί πρεσβύτατον; θεός, ἔφη Θαλῆς· ἀγέννητον γάρ ἐστι (153C). Apparently Plutarch has taken the simple single structure of the wisdom saying and transformed it into the basic two-part structure of the wisdom story so necessary for narrative contexts.

In Mark 12:28-34//Matt 22:34-40//Luke 10:25-28 we find a general parallel to the kind of "superlative" questions found here in Plutarch: ποία ἐστὶν ἐντολὴ πρώτη πάντων;//ποία ἐντολὴ μεγάλη ἐν τῷ νόμῳ; (Mark 12:28b//Matt 22:36). However, this question probably represents a reiterative attempt, in a religion which had a plethora of religious laws, to reduce them to a manageable whole by discovering the foci of the entire body of legal material. In Plutarch the "superlative" questions are strictly based on Greek intellectual curiosity, though it must be admitted that the philosophic quest relating to the one and the many lurks behind many of these questions. Nevertheless there is a similarity between these NT questions and those found here in Plutarch in that in both cases the questions are regarded as appropriate for sages.

(153C)

θεός ... ἀγέννητον γάρ ἐστι. The adjective ἀγέννητος ("unborn, unbegotten") is applied to Jesus in Ign Eph 7:2 where he is described paradoxically as γεννητὸς καὶ ἀγέννητος; this at least indicates that by the time of Ignatius Christians were beginning to make use of the language of popular Greek philosophical theology (cf. R. M. Grant, *The Early Christian Doctrine of God* [Charlottesville, 1966] 14f.). For the use of this adjective in ECL, see J. Lebreton, "ἀγέννητος dans la tradition et dans la littérature chrétienne du IIme siècle, *RecSR* 16 (1926) 431-43; G. L. Prestige, *God in Patristic Thought* (London, [2]1952) 37-54. Ordinarily the term is reserved for God alone in ECL, and it is so used in Justin (cf. E. F. Osborn, *Justin Martyr* [Tübingen, 1973] 21f.).

Ch. 10

(153E-154C)

Cleodoros objects to the trivial nature of some of the questions and riddles which have just been discussed. Plutarch appears to be setting up a straw man in that he himself exhibits constant curiosity in his writings with trivial as well as weighty issues.

Both elements are appropriate at a symposion in Plutarch's view. Periander responds (for Plutarch) that the "wisdom contest" is a traditional Greek preoccupation. To demonstrate this fact he cites the famous story of the *Certamen Homeri et Hesiodi*. The formal structure is that of an agonistic wisdom story composed of the following structural elements: (1) the problem: a riddle propounded by Homer, (2) the solution: a response immediately offered by Hesiod, and (3) the acclamation: Hesiod gained great admiration from all and won the prize of a tripod.

(154B)

Eumetis, who is still present at the symposion (cf. supra, p. 72, nn. 44, 45), appears desirous of responding to Cleodoros, so Aesop, as it were, answers for her. Plutarch, who violates custom by having a woman (non-prostitute) present at a symposion, is nevertheless careful to have her remain silent in spite of his views on the equality of those present at symposia and his notion that all present should participate. The parallel in the NT is 1 Cor 11:5, 13; 14:33ff., where Paul deals with the silence of woman in Christian assemblies. On this subject, see W. O. Walker, Jr., "1 Corinthians 11:2-16 and Paul's Views Regarding Women," *JBL* 91 (1975) 94-110. Many scholars are of the opinion that 1 Cor 14:33-36 is a post-Pauline gloss (Walker, p. 95, n. 6 summarizes the views on this matter). In 1 Cor. 11:5, 13 women are apparently allowed to prophecy in the Corinthian assembly (Walker, pp. 101-110, argues that 1 Cor 11:2-16 is a post-Pauline interpolation). Whether or not modern feminists will allow Paul to escape characterization as a male chauvinist through such hypotheses of post-Pauline interpolations, it seems clear by the manuscript testimony that such views, even if non-Pauline, were sufficiently widespread and popular so that no doubt of their authenticity was occasioned until comparatively recently. Clear post-Pauline injunctions for women's silence in the assembly are voiced in 1 Tim 2:12; Eph 5:22. To conclude this brief discussion, however, we should mention the assessment of F. Poland, *Geschichte des griechischen Vereinswesens* (Leipzig, 1909) 27: "Schon das ist bezeichnend für einen religiösen Verein, dass die Frauen gelegentlich als völlig gleichberechtigt neben den Männern mit besonderem Namen genannt werden ....."; Poland emphasizes the slight place of women in Greek associations on pp. 289-98.

Ch. 11

(154C-F)

Mnesiphilos now suggests a new topic; just as they formerly dealt with kings and tyrants, now the subject should concern itself with republican forms of government. Each of the Seven Sages is asked to contribute a predicate to the subject "the best democracy is ..." (κρατίστην εἶναι δημοκρατίαν ...). Beginning with Solon, each of the Sages makes the requested contribution. In form, this section is a literary adaptation of the gnomic wisdom story containing the basic two structural elements (1) the problem: expressed in the subject, and (2) the solution: the predicate contributed by each Sage. Here again the absence of the third element of acclamation is indicative of the fact that the content of this complex gnomic wisdom story is the reason why Plutarch has inserted it into the narrative.

(154E)

φοβοῦνται τὸν νόμον; in context this phrase means that one should respect the law as one does a tyrant. While fearing the law is never found in the NT, God is frequently the object of verbs meaning "to fear," a religious conception which springs from the OT and Judaism (Acts 10:2, 22; 13:16, 26; 1 Pet 2:17; Rev 14:7; 19:5; cf. Col 3:22; Rev 15:4). In Ign Magn 2:1 the recipients of the letter are advised to "submit yourselves to the presbytery as to the law of Jesus Christ," a notion which is precisely the opposite to that found here in Plutarch. In ECL the expression "to fear the law" is found only once in Diogn 11:6: φόβος νόμου ᾄδεται. In Rom 13:3 it is said that rulers are a fear (terror) to evil deeds, not good deeds; one should not therefore fear political authority (ἐξουσία).

Ch. 12

(154F)

τέλος δὲ καὶ τούτου τοῦ λόγου λαβόντες; Plutarch uses this expression to formally indicate the end of the preceding section and the start of a new topic of conversation. Similar devices are used at the beginning of Ch. 13 (155E) and the end of Ch. 16 (160C), cf.

supra, pp. 59f. Matt uses a similar formula to formally conclude each of the five main discourses of his gospel (7:28; 11:1; 13:53; 16:1; 19:1; cf. K. Stendahl, *The School of St. Matthew* [Philadelphia,[2] 1968] 24ff.).

(154F-155F)

Diokles now introduces a new subject, that of household management, which he relates to the management of kingdoms and states; the subject is appropriate, he claims, for while all do not manage kingdoms or states, all have a hearth and home. The subject of household management is raised a number of ways in ECL, particularly in the so-called *Haustafeln* (rules for the household): Col 3:18-4:1; Eph 5:22-6:9; 1 Tim 2:8-15; 6:1-2; Tit 2:1-10; 1 Pet 2:13-3:7; Did 4:9-11; Barn 19:5-7; 1 Clem 21:6-9; Pol Phil 4:2-6:3 (for a full discussion with an excellent bibliography see E. Lohse, *Colossians and Philemon* (Philadelphia, 1971) 154ff).

(154F-155A)

Aesop observes that Anacharsis the Cynic maintains a homeless state. In a logion from Q (Matt 8:20//Luke 9:58), Jesus is made to claim that he has no permanent home. Aesop further says of Anacharsis that he moves about from place to place in a wagon. Jesus is depicted in the gospels as an itinerant preacher (Luke 4:43//Mark 1:38; Matt 9:35; cf. Mark 6:6, 56), and the same is affirmed of the disciples (Matt 10:11; 9:6; Luke 8:1; 9:56; 10:38; 17:12). The Cynic attitude toward one's home is reflected in Diogn 5:5: πατρίδας οἰκοῦσιν ἰδίας, ἀλλ' ὡς πάροικοι; cf. Diogn 6:3: καὶ Χριστιανοὶ ἐν κόσμῳ οἰκοῦσιν, οὐκ εἰσὶ δὲ ἐκ τοῦ κόσμου. Peregrinus Proteus led an itinerant Cynic mode of life prior to becoming a Christian and after his Christianization and subsequent release from prison continued to lead an itinerant life (Lucian *Peregr.* 10, 15f.). The same mode of life characterized Paul and his companions. Itinerant apostles and prophets are discussed in Did 11-13.

(155C)

The anecdote of Solon's visit to Croesus is found in the form of an expanded gnomic wisdom story in Herodotus 1. 30, and is further expanded and embellished in Plutarch *Sol.* 27. Here the gist of the story is repeated, while its form is severely truncated, and its meaning is altered. In the first two references, the point is that a man should not be judged happy until his entire life has been completed; here the contrast is between the inner virtue of a man in contrast to his external luxury (cf. Defradas, *Le Banquet*, 104, n. 118).

(155D)

The best home, maintains Bias, is that in which the head of the house maintains the same character which he maintains outside of it. This emphasis on consistency in domestic and non-domestic roles is paralleled in 1 Tim 3:4-5. In Pol Phil 11:2 a man who wishes to be a presbyter must control himself before he can enjoin the same things on others.

The best home is that in which the head of the household has more who love (φιλοῦντας) than fear (φοβουμένων) him, says Kleobulos. Eph 5:25//Col 3:19, within the context of *Haustafeln*, exhorts husbands to love (ἀγαπᾶτε) their wives; this exhortation is repeated in Eph 5:33, while wives are in turn exhorted to respect (φοβῆται) their husbands. Similarly, slaves are told to submit to their masters μετὰ φόβου καὶ τρόμου (Eph 6:5). In the lists of household rules in ECL, wives are rarely told to "love" their husbands (the single exception is Tit 2:4: ἵνα σωφρονίζωσιν τὰς νέας φιλάνδρους εἶναι), children and/or servants are never told to "love" their father or master (cf. Phlm 16 where Paul exhorts Philemon to receive the slave Onesimus back, not as a slave, but as an ἀδελφὸν ἀγαπητόν). Fear, discipline and punishment appear to have been much more a feature of Israelite-Jewish pedagogy than of Greek pedagogy. The notion "fear" is ubiquitous in the *Haustafeln*; cf. Col 3:22; Eph 5:33; 6:5; 1 Pet 2:17, 18; 3:2, 6; Did 4:9, 10, 11; Barn 19:5, 7; 1 Clem 21:6, 7, 8; Pol Phil 4:2; 6:3 (most of these references relate to the fear of God).

(155E)

ἐπεὶ δὲ καὶ οὗτος ἔσχεν ὁ λόγος τέλος; see 154F.

(156A)

Aesop's fable about a wolf seeing some shepherds eating a sheep can be classified as a gnomic wisdom story: (1) the problematic situation is the shepherd's eating of a sheep, (2) the solution, offered by the wolf, is "What an uproar you would make if I were doing that!"

(156B)

In Mnesiphilos' defense of Solon's abstinence from wine, he observes that the end, not the means, is the objective of every art and faculty. In Rom 6:1f. Paul argues against the position that one should continue in sin in order that the resultant grace might be more plentiful.

Ch. 14

(157Aff.)

Chersias swings the discussion back to the subject of household management and suggests a topic which he claims was omitted from the previous conversation, namely the acquisition of that measure of property which should be regarded as sufficient and adequate. This subject, which occupies the whole of Chs. 14 through 16 (157A-160C) finally focuses on the question of food in Ch. 17.

Ch. 15

(158B-C)

Solon expresses the opinion that the next best thing to the greatest and highest of all good is to require the minimum amount of food; he claims that it is general opinion that the greatest good is to require no food at all. On early Christian asceticism see *PECL* 1:306ff.

(158C)

τραπέζης ἣν ἀναιροῦσιν αἱρομένης τροφῆς φιλίων θεῶν βωμὸν οὖσαν καὶ ξενίων; Cleodoros argues against Solon's contention that the greatest good is to require no food at all. If the table (synecdoche for the οἶκος) is done away with, other things must also go: (1) the altar fire on the hearth, (2) the hearth itself, (3) the wine-bowls, (4) all entertainment and hospitality. Here it is clear that the τράπεζα in Greek homes serves at least a formal religious function, particularly at meals where guests were present such as symposia. Generally, in discussions of 1 Cor 10, emphasis is given to Greek festivals or to temple restaurants as the places where the Corinthian Christians were tempted to share in sacrificial meats and other offerings. In 1 Cor 10:14-30 we find Paul drawing an analogy between the Israelite altar (θυσιαστηρίον), the table of the Lord (τραπέζης κυρίου) and the table of demons (τραπέζης δαιμονίων), cf. 1 Cor 10:18, 21. From his statement in 1 Cor 10:20b, it seems clear that to him, eating food sacrificed to pagan divinities is a meal shared with those divinities (cf. D. Gill, "*Trapezomata*: A Neglected Aspect of Greek Sacrifice," *HTR* 67 [1974] 117-37).

(158F-159A)

ἀλλ' οἴχεται τὸ πρεσβύτατον ἡμῖν μαντεῖον. On the dream as a major form of divination, see 146D.

Ch. 16

(159E-160C)

Diokles attempts to refute the physician Kleodoros' contention that food is necessary so that there might be tables, wine-bowls and sacrifices to Demeter and Kore. Actually, food is taken as a necessary antidote to hunger, yet is conducive to death as well as life. If we could be freed from bodily needs, the soul could then concentrate on using its freedom to focus on the truth without distraction. This opinion is probably that of Plutarch himself, since it comes at the end of the discussion on food, is not contradicted, and resembles opinions which Plutarch expresses elsewhere. In Plutarch's view, the σῶμα is an obstacle and an impediment to the concerns of the ψυχή. This dichotomous anthropology has few clear parallels in ECL (cf. the article by Hershbell, in this volume, pp. 145-47), at least in terms of the bipartite division of man into σῶμα—ψυχή. Diogn 6:1-9 (probably a late third century document) elaborates on the ψυχή—σῶμα dichotomy of Hellenistic anthropological dualism; cf. R. Brändle, *Die Ethik der 'Schrift an Diognet'* (Zürich, 1975) 148-55. While adherents of the older history of religions school interpreted Paul in terms of Hellenistic anthropological dualism (cf. R. Reitzenstein, *Die hellenistischen Mysterienreligionen* [Stuttgart, 1927] 333ff.), the last generation of NT scholars has tended to interpret Paul's anthropology in terms of a monism derived from his Hebraic heritage. The best treatment of the subject, which carefully examines the Hellenistic presuppositions of Paul's anthropological thought is W. C. Stacey, *The Pauline View of Man In Relation to Its Judaic and Hellenistic Background* (London, 1956). In a carefully balanced article, S. Laeuchli takes the plurality and polarity in many of Paul's statements seriously, though he admits that Paul's terminology does not presuppose a staging within man of various ontological values ("Monism and Dualism in the Pauline Anthropology," *BR* 3 [1958] 15-43). More recently the view that Paul holds an essentially monistic anthropology as been attacked in detail by R. H. Gundry, *Sōma in Biblical Theology: With Emphasis on Pauline Anthropology* (Cambridge, 1976).

(160C)

τὰ μὲν οὖν ῥηθέντα περὶ τροφῆς; see 154F.

Ch. 18

(160Eff.)

The story of Arion's miraculous rescue by dolphins. Arion was coming by boat to Corinth and learned that the crew had planned to kill him. When they finally made their attempt, he cast himself into the sea and was borne up by a school of dolphins who eventually deposited him safely on shore. He realized that his rescue was divinely caused. This story, as told by Plutarch, is an example of his belief in the overruling activity of deity in the lives of individuals and communities. On this see B. S. MacKay, "Plutarch and the Miraculous," *Miracles*, ed. C. F. D. Moule (London, 1965) 95-111. The NT miracle closest to this is found in Acts 27:1-44, in which the survival of Paul and the entire crew occurs because God has determined that Paul must go to Rome (Acts 27:24f.). While the rescue of all on board is clearly viewed by the author of Luke-Acts as a divine intervention, there is nothing in the event itself which is incredible in natural terms. Perhaps one could surmise that Plutarch would have been sympathetic to this "miracle."

Ch. 20

(163A)

Pittacus narrates the story of the daughter of Smintheos who was chosen by lot to be sacrificed as a living virgin to Amphitrite and the Nymphs of the sea. Enalos, her lover, clasped her and both fell into the sea. Later Enalos appeared at Lesbos unharmed and related how dolphins had rescued the couple and put them on shore unharmed. He concludes that one must recognize the difference between the impossible (ἀδύνατος) and the unfamiliar (ἀσυνήθης), between the unexpected (παράλογος) and the incredible (παράδοξος) and neither believe nor remain skeptical haphazardly. This is apparently Plutarch's way of classifying the previous dolphin stories as perhaps unfamiliar and unexpected, but not inherently impossible. ECL exhibits no similarly sophisticated and skeptical view of the miraculous.

Ch. 21

(163D)

Finally, Anacharsis supplies a philosophical framework for seeing the natural world as a place for perceiving the active will of deity. This activity is naturally good, reliable and just in accordance with Plutarch's Platonic framework. The ψυχή, claims Anacharsis, exists in the most dominant and important parts of the cosmos; little wonder then that the most excellent things occur through the will of God (θεοῦ γνώμῃ).

ἐν πᾶσιν εἶναι τοῖς κυριωτάτοις μέρεσι τοῦ κόσμου καὶ μεγίστοις ψυχήν; this statement is attributed to Thales by Anacharsis, and seems to be inferred from Aristotle *de An.* 411a7ff.: καὶ ἐν τῷ ὅλῳ δέ τινες αὐτὴν [τὴν ψυχὴν] μεμῖχθαί φασιν ὅθεν ἴσως καὶ Θαλῆς ᾠήθη πάντα πλήρη θεῶν εἶναι. The saying is unattributed in Plato *Lg.* 899B: θεῶν εἶναι πλήρη πάντα.

(164D)

The closing libations are not for Aphrodite as one might expect, but rather to the Muses (cf. 158D); they are the ones instrumental in inspiring discussion among sages, not Dionysos. The fact that the libations are also in honor of Poseidon and Amphitrite probably springs from the fact that the last three stories in *sept. sap. conv.* relate to dolphins and miraculous rescues at sea.

MULIERUM VIRTUTES (MORALIA 242E - 263C)

BY

KATHLEEN O'BRIEN WICKER

Scripps College
Claremont, California

I. INTRODUCTION

The *Mulierum virtutes*,[1] no. 126 in the Lamprias catalog, is generally considered an authentic work of Plutarch.[2] Ziegler does not date this work, but a date between 115-125 A.D. has been suggested by some scholars.[3] Plutarch dedicated the *Mulierum virtutes* to Clea, a priestess at Delphi, to whom he had also dedicated the *De Iside et Osiride*.[4] Plutarch's stated purpose is to provide a fitting commemoration for Leontis, ἡ ἀρίστη who had recently died.[5] The treatise is also undoubtedly meant to honor Clea to whom it was dedicated. After Leontis' death, Plutarch and Clea had discussed the unity of virtue, and Plutarch wrote the work, at Clea's request, in an attempt to complete his own ideas on the topic.

---

[1] Bibliography: M. Dinse, *De libello Plutarchi gunaikôn aretai inscripto* (Berlin, 1863); North, *Sophrosyne*; P. A. Stadter, *Plutarch's Historical Methods: An Analysis of the Mulierum Virtutes* (Cambridge, 1965); Ziegler, sec. III.10.a.

The edition used here is that of F. C. Babbitt, *Plutarch's Moralia*, LCL vol. 3.

[2] Stadter, 1-2 and n. 2-3.

[3] Ibid., 213 and n. 4-9.

[4] Ziegler, col. 41, and Stadter, 2-3.

[5] Ziegler (col. 41) suggests that she may have been the mother or a relative of Clea, but cf. also Stadter, 9 and n. 42. In choosing to follow the Roman custom of giving women a fitting commemoration at the end of their lives (242F), Plutarch rejects the view of Thucydides that the best woman is the one who is unknown outside her home (242E). For a discussion of the Roman practice, cf. S. Pomeroy, *Goddesses, Whores, Wives, and Slaves* (New York, 1975). Plutarch is somewhat more sympathetic to the view of Gorgias who suggests that it is better for a woman's fame to be known than her form (242F). The view of Thucydides agrees with the conservative view of women's place in Ps 128:3; Prov 31:27; Sir 26:16. ECL does not take this extreme view, though the Household Codes which will be discussed below do tend to view woman's proper place as in the home. Gorgias' view is similar to that expressed in 1 Pet 3:3-4; 1 Tim 2:9f. that a woman should be more concerned with her virtue than her appearance. For an interesting reference in ECL to the spread of a woman's fame, cf. Mark 14:9//Matt 26:13.

The opening words of the treatise state its theme: Περὶ ἀρετῆς . . . γυναικῶν.[6] Plutarch formulates his thesis more specifically in 242F: "the virtue of men and women is the same" (εἰς τὸ μίαν εἶναι καὶ τὴν αὐτὴν ἀνδρὸς καὶ γυναικὸς ἀρετήν). He says in 243B-D that the best way to prove that the ἀρετή of men and women is the same is to compare the similarity and difference (ὁμοιότης καὶ διαφορά) in their lives and actions. He does not develop this method of demonstrating his thesis, however. Instead, after considering and affirming the idea that ἀρετή, though it has an essential unity, is expressed in different ways in the lives of specific individuals (243D), he assembles a diverse collection of historical and semi-historical accounts of the deeds of Greek and non-Greek women to support his thesis. These accounts do not directly demonstrate that there is no difference in ἀρετή between the sexes, but only that women can perform deeds traditionally considered masculine. The reverse case, that men also demonstrate traditionally feminine characteristics, is not made.

The composition of the treatise is simple. The introduction of the topic (242E-243E) is followed by fifteen separate accounts of the deeds of groups of women acting together (243E-253E). After a brief transition paragraph (253E-F), twelve accounts about the deeds of individual women are presented (253F-263C).

II. Plutarch's Treatise and Early Christian Literature

Plutarch draws his examples for the *Mulierum virtutes* from a wide range of written sources. A study of these examples and their sources shows that he did not rely uncritically on only a single version of an event but frequently selected and combined the various accounts available to him. ECL also draws heavily on earlier oral and written traditions, but the gospel writers, unlike Plutarch in this treatise, set their collection of Jesus traditions in a geograph-

[6] There is a discrepancy between the theme of the treatise expressed in the opening sentence and the titles in the Lamprias catalog, Γυναικῶν ἀρεταί and Περὶ τοῦ πῶς δεῖ ζῆν γυναῖκα πρὸς ἄνδρα. The second of these titles is clearly not descriptive of the treatise. The use of ἀρεταί in the other title and the occurrence of ἀρετή in the opening line of the treatise raise the question of what Plutarch intends as the theme of the treatise, ἀρετή or ἀρεταί. A study of the treatise indicates that the theme is ἀρετή. The possession of ἀρετή by an individual is reflected in the practice of specific virtues (αἱ ἀρεταί) which ultimately result in the perfection or achievement (ἡ ἀρετή) of the individual. Cf. also *aud. poet.* 24C-D and *Alex. fort.* 332C-D.

ical and chronological framework. Evidence of the redactional activity of both Plutarch and the ECL writers is discernible in the texts.[7] Examples of this activity are the moral lessons which Plutarch draws at the end of some stories to relate them more effectively to his thesis (cf. 247A, 249C-D) and the interpretations of the parables which the gospel writers provide (cf. Mark 4:13-20// Matt 13:18-23//Luke 8:11-15; Matt 13:36-43). Both Plutarch and ECL attempt to appear factual in their accounts, but since they are often working with materials of more or less questionable reliability, their value as historical sources cannot be uncritically accepted.

In ECL the closest parallels to Plutarch's method of using a collection of diverse historical examples to demonstrate a thesis are found in Hebrews and 1 Clement. The author of Hebrews recalls the faith of many outstanding OT figures (ch. 11), the suffering and glory of Jesus (12:1-3; 13:12) and the faith of Christian preachers (13:7) to exhort his audience to remain strong in their faith. 1 Clement also refers to a variety of exemplary figures from the OT, NT, early church history and the pagan literature in an attempt to resolve the problems of the Christian community in Corinth. Included are references to the faith and obedience of the patriarchs, particularly Abraham (chs. 10; 31:2), the piety of Lot (ch. 11), the faith and hospitality of Rahab (ch. 12), the humility of David (ch. 18) and of Christ (ch. 16), the suffering of Peter, Paul and the Christian martyrs (chs. 5:1-6:1), and the loving self-sacrifice of heathen kings and rulers, and of the Jewish heroines Judith and Esther (ch. 55).

Rhetoricians, as well as ethical and religious teachers in the ancient world, commonly wrote historical, semi-historical or even pseudo-historical accounts about distinguished individuals for the purpose of extolling their virtues.[8] While these aretalogies differ according to the characteristics of their subjects, they also have

---

[7] Stadter's study analyzes the sources Plutarch probably used for the stories in this treatise and his redactional activity upon them. The major redaction-critical studies of the synoptics are W. Marxsen, *Mark the Evangelist* (New York, 1969); G. Bornkamm, G. Barth and H. J. Held, *Tradition and Interpretation in Matthew* (Philadelphia, 1963); H. Conzelmann, *The Theology of St. Luke*, 2nd ed. (New York, 1961).

[8] Cf. M. Hadas and M. Smith, *Heroes and Gods* (New York, 1965) for a discussion of the literary aretalogy in the ancient world. Cf. also M. Smith, "Prolegomena to a Discussion of Aretalogies, Divine Men, the Gospels, and Jesus," *JBL* 90 (1971) 174-88.

some common features. Generally they praise the teachings and deeds of divinely gifted persons who are concerned with the spiritual welfare of humanity, who live moral lives, and who often die as martyrs. Their purpose is propagandistic, leading to the cultic worship of their subjects or the authentication of their teachings.

These literary aretalogies of philosophers and religious figures appear to have influenced the manner in which historians like Plutarch present the lives of outstanding political figures.[9] The accounts in the *Mulierum virtutes* seem to reflect this influence as well. They are recounted specifically to emphasize the moral qualities and virtuous actions of their subjects. Taken as a whole, the stories constitute a composite picture[10] of the ideal woman: virtuous in private moral behavior; concerned with the good of the community; able to contribute intelligently, justly and piously to its welfare; courageous and resourceful in defending it against enemies; and willing to die and to see her husband and children killed rather than to endure tyranny. While it is not uncommon to find aretalogies of women as exemplars of household virtue in the ancient world, aretalogies of women as models of political and social virtue are unusual. Only a few collections of accounts about the public deeds of famous women are known from the ancient world before Plutarch.[11]

The actions of the women in the *Mulierum virtutes*, unlike the aretalogies of religious figures, are not attributed to a divine agent. The two exceptions may be the report about the women of Phocis, who were divinely inspired (ὁρμὴ καὶ τόλμα δαιμόνιος) to defend the city under the leadership of Telesilla (254D), and the strange rash of suicides among the women of Miletus (249B-D). On the other hand, the women who act or die nobly for the freedom of their

[9] Cf. Hadas and Smith, 73-81, 87-88.

[10] A parody of the method of praising the ideal woman by combining the characteristics of a number of different individuals is provided by Lucian in his *Imagines*. Cf. the study of Lucian's literary method by J. Bompaire, *Lucien écrivain: Imitation et création* (Paris, 1958).

[11] Stadter (7-8) cites references in the ancient literature to the *Accounts of Deeds Done Courageously by Women* by Artemon of Magnesia; *Women Who Were Philosophers or Otherwise Accomplished Something Noteworthy, or through Whom Houses Were Joined in Good Will* by Apollonius the Stoic; the anonymous collections *Women Lifted up to Great Fame and Brilliant Reputation* and *Women Intelligent and Courageous in Warfare*, and a four volume work of biographies of women by Charon of Carthage. Stadter has also demonstrated that Polyaenus' *Strategemata*, often considered to be Plutarch's source for the *Mul. virt.*, is actually dependent upon Plutarch.

people often receive praise and acclaim which must have approximated divine honors if they were not actually such: τιμὴ καὶ χάρις (247A); δόξα καὶ τιμή (254B); μετὰ χαρᾶς καὶ στεφάνων ὑποδεχόμενοι καὶ θαυμάζοντες (254E); ἡρωικαὶ τιμαὶ ... ὡς θεῷ θύειν (255E); μετὰ χαρᾶς καὶ δακρύων, ὥσπερ ἀγάλματι θεοῦ προσπίπτοντες (257D). Xenocrite, who did not accept the honors and gifts offered her, was made a priestess of Demeter by the people (262C-D). Other virtuous women had statues erected in their honor (245E, 250F) and were remembered at annual religious celebrations commemorating the events in which they were involved (244D-E, 245E-F).

Within ECL the life of Jesus is, of course, the subject of the most developed aretalogy,[12] though the lives of Paul and the other apostles are also treated in an aretalogical fashion.[13] Aretalogies of women in ECL are rarer and more limited in scope. The piety of Elizabeth and Anna is praised.[14] Outstanding women from the OT and Hellenistic Judaism are also praised in ECL: Rahab for her faith and hospitality and good works; Sarah as the virtuous wife and woman of faith; Judith, Esther and Susanna for their courage in facing physical danger; the mother in Maccabees for her steadfastness and fidelity.[15] The acts of the early Christian martyrs, however, contain the most striking aretalogies of women in ECL.[16] They

---

[12] See Hadas and Smith, 161-63; H. Koester, "One Jesus and Four Primitive Gospels," in J. M. Robinson and H. Koester, *Trajectories Through Early Christianity* (Philadelphia, 1968) 187-91; Smith, *JBL* 90 (1971) 195-98.

[13] Cf. Koester, 191-93.

[14] Cf. Luke 1:6; 2:36-37.

[15] Cf. Jas 2:25; Heb 11:11, 31; 1 Pet 3:5-6; 1 Clem 12:1-8; 55:4-6. Christian mothers are also praised for enduring the deaths of their children like the mother in Maccabees, see Mart Mar et Jam 13 [p. 212], Mart Mont et Luc 16:4 [p. 230]. Another woman praised in the Jewish tradition but who is not referred to in ECL is Asenath in Joseph and Asenath. She does not begin as a heroine but becomes one through her conversion.

[16] All references to the martyr literature in this paper are to H. Musurillo, ed. and tr., *The Acts of the Christian Martyrs*, Oxford Early Christian Texts (Oxford, 1972). The following abbreviations will be used for the texts in this volume which are cited in this paper:

Mart Pol = The Martyrdom of Polycarp (1)
Mart Carp et Soc = The Acts of Carpus, Papylus, and Agathonicê (2)
Mart Just et Soc = The Acts of Justin and Companions (4)
Mart Lougd = The Letter of the Churches of Lyons and Vienne (5)
Acta Scill Mart = The Acts of the Scillitan Martyrs (6)
Mart Apoll = The Martyrdom of Apollonius (7)
Mart Perp et Fel = The Martyrdom of Perpetua and Felicitas (8)
Mart Pot et Basil = The Martyrdom of Potamiaena and Basilides (9)
Mart Pion = The Martyrdom of Pionius (10)

present the women martyrs as virtuous, strong in their faith, courageous in giving testimony, able to endure tremendous physical suffering, and willing to die and leave behind their children and families rather than renounce their faith. These accounts were influenced by the narratives of Jesus' passion (see especially Mart Pol 1:2 [p. 2], 17:3 [p. 16]), the examples of the martyrs of Hellenistic Judaism [17] (2 Mac 6:18-31// 4 Mac 5-7; 2 Mac 7//4 Mac 8-18) and the deaths of the pagan martyrs, particularly Socrates.[18]

With the exception of Jesus, Christian heroes and heroines were not divinized after death (see, e.g., Mart Pol 17:1-3 [pp. 14-16]). Nevertheless the martyrs had an important place in the Christian tradition and their burial sites and death anniversaries were held in special honor.[19]

The aretalogies of outstanding individuals not only served the propagandistic purposes of establishing the divinely inspired character of their subjects, of authenticating their teachings or of providing a record of their notable accomplishments. They were

Mart Cypr = The Acts of Cyprian (11)
Mart Mar et Jam = The Martyrdom of Marian and James (14)
Mart Mont et Luc = The Martyrdom of Montanus and Lucius (15)
Mart Fel = The Martyrdom of Felix the Bishop (20)
Mart Das = The Martyrdom of Dasius (21)
Mart Agap et Soc = The Martyrdom of Agapê, Irenê, Chionê, and Companions (22)
Mart Iren = The Martyrdom of Irenaeus Bishop of Sirmium (23)
Mart Crisp = The Martyrdom of Saint Crispina (24)
Acta Phil = The Acts of Phileas (27)

Different recensions of a text are indicated by the use of A, B, C, following Musurillo's text.

[17] Hadas and Smith (pp. 87-97) have demonstrated that 4 Mac was modeled upon the Socratic tradition and that the Mart Pol as well as other Christian martyr literature was subsequently influenced by 4 Mac.

[18] Three passages from the acts of the Christian martyrs are of particular interest in this regard. "Christians are not the only ones who are concerned for their souls; pagans are too. Take Socrates, for example. When he was being led to his death, even with his wife and children present, he did not turn back, but eagerly embraced death." (Acta Phil [B] 4:2) [p. 349]. "Were Socrates and Aristides and Anaxarchus and all the rest fools in your view because they practiced philosophy and justice and courage?" (Mart Pion 17:3) [p. 159]. "The Athenian informers convinced the people and then unjustly condemned Socrates, so too our Saviour and teacher was condemned by a few malefactors after they had him bound." (Mart Apoll 41) [p. 101].

[19] Cf. Mart Pol 18:1-3 [p. 16]; 21 [p. 18]; Mart Carp et Soc 47 [p. 28]; Mart Just et Soc (B) 6:2 [p. 52]; Mart Apoll 47 [p. 102]; Mart Pion 23 [pp. 164ff.]; Mart Cypr 5:6 [p. 174]; Mart Fel 31 [p. 270]; Mart Das 12:1 [p. 278]; Mart Agap et Soc 7:2 [p. 292]; Mart Iren 6 [p. 300]. See also *PECL* 1: index, s.v. Tombs, cults of and Burial, rites of.

also used as models of behavior to be emulated or avoided.[20] The general belief of antiquity, which Plutarch also shares, is that παραδείγματα (243A, 253E), examples of virtuous behavior, are more effective than logic or physical force in encouraging persons to perform the kinds of actions through which habits of virtue are acquired. In several of the *Lives* as well as in some of the essays of the *Moralia* Plutarch states the idea that an understanding of virtuous behavior can best be arrived at through a study of the lives and deeds of notable persons.[21] He also frequently provides in his writings examples of persons whose lives effectively embody the characteristics of virtue or vice which he wishes to praise or condemn. The use in the *Mulierum virtutes* of multiple examples to demonstrate the nature of ἀρετή provides an illustration of the value of παραδείγματα for theoretical as well as practical ethical considerations.

ECL also follows the practice of antiquity in using παραδείγματα to teach practical ethical behavior. Jesus, as he is depicted in the gospels, is the primary model for imitation (see, e.g., John 13:15; Phil 2:5-11; 1 Pet 2:21; Heb 12:1-4; 13:12-13; 1 Clem 16; Mart Pol 1 [p. 2]; 17:3 [p. 16]; Mart Apoll 36-41 [p. 100]). Outstanding figures of the OT and early Christianity including the martyrs are also recommended as worthy of imitation (see, e.g., 1 Pet 3:5-6; Heb 6:11-12; 13:7; 1 Clem 9:2; 17:1; 46:1; Mart Pion 1 [p. 136]; Mart Mont et Luc 14:9 [p. 228]). 1 Pet 3:1-2 suggests that the exemplary behavior of Christian wives may bring about the conversion of their pagan husbands to a life of virtue.

While παραδείγματα usually serve the function of providing models of specific virtuous behavior, Plutarch, as has been noted above, uses them in this treatise primarily to demonstrate his understanding of the nature of ἀρετή. The term ἀρετή has various shades of meaning in the ancient literature.[22] Generally human ἀρετή referred "to excellence of achievement, to mastery in a specific field, on the one side, or to endowment with higher power on the other, or often to both together." [23] In the Homeric period ἀρετή was often associated with manliness or courage in battle and

---

[20] Cf. A. Lumpe, *RAC*, s.v. Exemplum, and H. Schlier, *TDNT*, s.v. ὑπόδειγμα.

[21] Cf. *Alex.* 1; *Pomp.* 8; *Nic.* 1; *Cim.* 2; *Per.* 1-2; *garrul.* 505A-511E; *frat. am.* 488D-489F; *amat.* 768B-D; 770D-771C; *prof. virt.* 84B-85B.

[22] O. Bauernfeind, *TDNT*, s.v. ἀρετή.

[23] Ibid., 1:458.

came also to mean the δόξα which accompanied distinguished deeds. Frequently the courage and excellence of the hero were considered divine endowments. The Greek philosophers used the term ἀρετή to denote intellectual and moral excellence or virtue. Only slight reference, if any, was made to its divine character.

The concept of ἀρετή which Plutarch uses in the *Mulierum virtutes* embraces both the Homeric concept of courageous achievement and the notion of intellectual and moral excellence found in the philosophical tradition.[24] Like the latter, Plutarch understood ἀρετή as human excellence, not divine achievement.

Apparently because ἀρετή was such an important concept in the heroic and ethical thought of the ancient world, ECL tends to avoid using the term. When it does occur, its meaning is strongly influenced by the Jewish use of ἀρετή as an equivalent for δικαιοσύνη. In 1 Pet 2:9 it appears to be synonymous with δόξα. The ECL use of ἀρετή, with its emphasis on the divine character of justification, thus appears to be closer to the Homeric than to the philosophic meaning of the term.

The fundamental issue underlying Plutarch's assertion about the unity of ἀρετή is whether or not women have the same nature as men and, by implication, the same kind of perfection. Until Socrates, due to the subordinate social position of women in Classical Greece, it was almost universally assumed that there was one ἀρετή proper to women and another to men because of an essential difference in their natures. Socrates, however, seems to have taught that some women might be as capable as men of achieving human excellence.[25] One of his pupils, Antisthenes, is credited with saying that "virtue is the same for women as for

[24] It has been common to interpret ἀρετή in this treatise as bravery. Cf. Babbitt's translation cited above. At times bravery is a component of the outstanding accomplishment, but, given the diversity of deeds Plutarch praises in this treatise, to view its theme as the bravery of women is too limiting. In ten of the passages in which ἀρετή occurs in the *Mul. virt.* it clearly has the meaning of moral virtue or excellence in general (cf. 242E, 243A-C, 249C, 250A, 252B, 257F, 259E). In the other seven instances it can best be interpreted as accomplishment or achievement resulting from the extraordinary exercise of moral or intellectual virtue (cf. 244B, 245B, 250D, 253F, 254C, 255E, 260D, 262C). 262C is particularly helpful in understanding Plutarch's idea of ἀρετή in this treatise. Here both the woman who inspired the overthrow of the tyrant by her words and the one who carried out the activity which led to his death are praised for their ἀρετή.

[25] Plato, *R.* 457B-466D; *Men.* 73A-B; Aristotle, *Pol.* 1260a21; Xenophon, *Smp.* 2.9.

men" (ἀνδρὸς καὶ γυναικὸς ἡ αὐτὴ ἀρετή).[26] Aristotle rejects this view, claiming that men have a superior nature and therefore a superior virtue, while, women, because of their weaker nature, can attain only an inferior virtue.[27]

With the breakdown of the polis at the end of the fourth century B.C., the traditional role of women underwent important modifications.[28] New models for the public involvement of women were available in the behavior of the Hellenistic queens and the activities of the women whose new economic power made them a significant factor in their communities. These changes in the roles of women in Hellenistic society are also reflected in the teachings of the philosophical schools.[29] Epicureans, Cynics, Stoics, Neo-Pythagoreans and Academicians all tended toward the recognition of the equality of women of philosophical ability in their schools. None of these schools, however, seem to have suggested that all women were by nature the equals of men.

Plutarch's views of the ἀρετή of women, a topic common in the philosophical discussions of his day, are developed in detail in the *Coniugalia praecepta*,[30] the *Amatorius*[31] and the *Mulierum virtutes*. Only in the last text, however, does he laud the public as well as the private ἀρετή of women. He praises his heroines for their practical wisdom (λογισμός, 243F; τὸ φρονεῖν, 255E; πολιτικῆς δεινότητος οὐκ ἄμοιρος, 255E; σοφή, 262D), good sense (φρόνημα, 258F) and courage and daring which they undertake in defense of freedom (θαρρεῖν, 245B; θυμός, 245B; τόλμα, 245D, 250D, F; θάρσος, 247A; ἀνδρεία, 261D). The heroines show strength to endure danger and to suffer in silence (247A, 251B), even under torture (ἀήττητος, 256D). They can present a vigorous and eloquent defense of themselves when the occasion demands it (252B-C,

---

[26] Diogenes Laertius 6. 1. 12.

[27] *Pol.* 1259b1; 1260a21-24.

[28] Cf. Pomeroy, 120-48.

[29] Cf. Diogenes Laertius 6. 7. 96-98; 7. 1. 33; 7. 5. 175; *SVF*, I, pp. 58-59, fr. 247; III, p. 59, fr. 253-54; C. E. Manning, "Seneca and the Stoics on the Equality of the Sexes," *Mnemosyne* 26 (1973) 170-77; Pomeroy, 131-36; A.-J. Festugière, *Epicurus and His Gods* (Cambridge, 1969) 29-30; C. E. Lutz, *Musonius Rufus: The Roman Socrates*, Yale Classical Studies, 10 (New Haven, 1947) 37-49.

[30] Cf. K. O. Wicker, "First Century Marriage Ethics: A Comparative Study of the Household Codes and Plutarch's Conjugal Precepts," in *No Famine in the Land*, ed. J. W. Flanagan and A. W. Robinson (Missoula, 1975) 141-53.

[31] Cf. the study of this treatise by Hubert Martin, Jr. in this volume, pp. 442-537.

260C-D) and persuade others of the wisdom of their views and actions (243F-244A, 253C). They demonstrate the ability to govern humanely (262D-263C) and to distribute fair and impartial justice (246B-C). They are also recognized as poetesses (243B, 245D), prophetesses (243B) and priestesses (251E, 257F, 262D).

Plutarch also praises his heroines for characteristically feminine qualities. His description of Camma the Galatian best typifies the traditional notion of feminine ἀρετή. She is described as conspicuous for her form and beauty (περίβλεπτον μὲν ἰδέᾳ σώματος καὶ ὥρᾳ), modesty (σώφρων), love of her husband (φίλανδρος), quick wits (συνετή), highmindedness (μεγαλόφρων), and kindness (εὐμενεία) and benevolence (χρηστότης) to her inferiors (257E-F).

Many of these same characteristics of feminine ἀρετή, and others in addition, are attributed to other heroines of the *Mulierum virtutes*: beauty (καλή, 251A, 255E, 256E, 259C), nobility (γενναία, 251B, 260C; εὐγένεια, 253E) natural goodness (εὐφυΐα, 249C), fear of moral disgrace (ἡ τῆς ἀδοξίας εὐλάβεια, 249C), orderly behavior (εὐταξία, 249D), highmindedness (μεγαλόφρων, 251B), high worth (ἀξίωμα, 253C), modesty (σώφρων, 260F), humaneness (φιλάνθρωπος, 260F), self-control (σωφροσύνη, 261D), goodness (χρηστή, 262D), and kindness (φιλοφροσύνη, 244A). They are also praised for their fidelity to their husbands in life and in death (πίστις, 258F; cf. also 250A, 252B-C, 255F, 257F-258C, 258E-F, 260F-261B), their affection for their children (258D), and their willingness to be of service to family (249D) and to the gods (249F).

Plutarch contrasts the courageous, noble and virtuous behavior of his heroines with the behavior of their men, which at times lacks courage and insight (243E-244A; 244F-245B; 246A-B; 246B-C; 253B-D; 262D-263C), and with the ruthless, lawless and exploitative behavior of tyrants (245B-C; 245D-E; 251C-252E; 255F-257E; 257F-258C; 261F-262C) and mercenary soldiers (247B-C; 249E-F; 251A-C; 258E-F; 259E-260D). Only twice does he use negative portrayals of other women as foils for the virtues of his heroines (254B-C; 256B-D).

ECL also contains important passages which reflect upon the question of the nature and perfection of women in relation to men and the appropriate roles and virtues of both sexes in the Christian community.[32] First, there is the example of Jesus who stands in

[32] Cf. C. F. Parvey, "The Theology and Leadership of Women in the New Testament," in *Religion and Sexism*, ed. R. R. Ruether, (New York, 1974) 117-49.

strong contrast to the rabbis of the period in that he has devoted women followers, named and unnamed in the tradition, among his followers.[33] Not only does he address his preaching and promise of the kingdom to women as well as to men, but in Luke 10:38-42 he praises Mary more for her attentiveness to his teaching than Martha for her concern over household chores. He works miracles for women[34] and uses them and their concerns as the subjects of his parables and examples.[35] Women also figure importantly in the birth stories,[36] and in the passion and resurrection narratives[37] in the gospels.

Women like Priscilla, Lydia, Dorcas and others continue to play an important role in the post-Easter Christian community. They are referred to in Acts[38] and in the Pauline and Deutero-Pauline letters, particularly the greetings.[39] These women engage in charitable practices,[40] teach,[41] prophesy[42] and make their homes available for house churches.[43]

Turning from the evidence for the involvement of women within the Christian community to a study of the theoretical considerations about women which are found in ECL, Paul's letters are of particular interest. In Gal 3:26-28 he uses what was probably a pre-Pauline baptismal formula which states that in Christ the distinctions between Jew and Greek, slave and free, male and female are abolished. This statement does not speak just to the social equality of all persons in Christ but even suggests that in Christ such fundamental distinctions among persons as biological sex are eliminated. This is a radical statement, apparently appearing

---

[33] Cf. Luke 7:37-38; 8:1-3; John 4:39; 11:1-44.

[34] Cf. Mark 1:29-31//Matt 8:14-15//Luke 4:38-39; Mark 5:21-43//Matt 9:18-26//Luke 8:40-56; Mark 7:24-30//Matt 15:21-28; Luke 7:11-17; 13:10-17.

[35] Cf. Luke 15:8-9; Mark 12:41-44//Luke 21:1-4; Matt 25:1-13; Luke 7:36-50.

[36] Cf. Matt 1-2; Luke 1-2.

[37] Cf. Mark 14:3-9//Matt 26:6-13//John 12:1-8; Luke 23:26-31; Mark 15:40-41//Matt 27:55-56//Luke 23:49; Mark 15:47//Matt 27:61//Luke 23:55-56; Mark 16:1-8//Matt 28:1-10//Luke 24:1-12//John 20:1-2, 11-18.

[38] Cf. Acts 1:14; 16:13ff.; 17:4, 12, 34; 18:18.

[39] Cf. Rom 16:1-16; Phil 4:2; Col 4:15; 2 Tim 4:19.

[40] Cf. Acts 9:36; 16:15; 1 Tim 3:11.

[41] Cf. Acts 18:26; Tit 2:3-5.

[42] Cf. Acts 21:9; 1 Cor 11:5.

[43] Cf. Acts 12:12; Rom 16:3-5; 1 Cor 16:19; Col 4:15.

here for the first time in ancient literature.[44] It goes far beyond the position Plutarch takes on the univocal nature of ἀρετή in men and women in the *Mulierum virtutes*.[45]

It should be noted, however, that the views Paul expresses in 1 Corinthians on the relationship between the sexes differ in some important respects from those just discussed in the Galatians passage.[46] Paul advocates in 1 Cor 7 a reciprocity of rights and duties in the marriage relationship which presumes the equality of husbands and wives, but in 1 Cor 11:3 he suggests that the wife is subject to the husband who is subject to Christ who in turn is subject to God. This view of the subordination of the wife to her husband is modified by 1 Cor 11:11-12, however, where the mutual dependence of men and women is stressed. In 1 Cor 11:5 Paul criticizes women for praying or prophesying with their heads uncovered. This injunction appears to be directed towards heretical tendencies within the congregation, however, and not to the role of women *per se*. In 1 Cor 14:34-5 Paul insists that women should keep silence in the churches. This passage appears inconsistent with 1 Cor 11 where participation is allowed to women properly attired. Various attempts have been made to deal with the discrepancies between Galatians and 1 Corinthians and within 1 Corinthians itself. Some have tried to reconcile them; others view them as a lamentable inconsistency between Paul's theory and practice. Still others have questioned the authenticity of the problematic passages in 1 Corinthians.[47]

Other views on the relationship between men and women are also

---

[44] See H. D. Betz, *Galatians*, Hermeneia (Philadelphia, forthcoming) ad loc. 3:26-28.

[45] The Pauline idea of the transcendence of sexual distinctions does not become the normative view in ECL but is preserved only in gnostic and heretical Christian Communities. See, e.g., Copt Gos Thom 22, 114. See also Wayne A. Meeks, "The Image of the Androgyne: Some Uses of a Symbol in Earliest Christianity," *HR* 13 (1974) 167-180.

[46] Cf. H. Conzelmann, *1 Corinthians*, Hermeneia (Philadelphia, 1975) ad loc. 7:1-7; 11:2-16; 14.

[47] Cf. R. Scroggs, "Paul and the Eschatological Woman," *JAAR* 40 (1972) 283-303 and "Paul and the Eschatological Woman: Revisited," *JAAR* 42 (1974) 532-37; W. O. Walker, Jr., "1 Cor 11:2-16 and Paul's Views Regarding Women," *JBL* 94 (1975) 94, n. 1; A. Feuillet, "La Dignité et le rôle de la femme d'après quelques textes pauliniens," *NTS* 21 (1974-75) 157-91; E. Pagels, "Paul and Women: A Response to Recent Discussion," *JAAR* 42 (1974) 538-49; D. C. Smith, "Paul and the Non-Eschatological Woman," *Ohio Journal of Religious Studies* 4 (1976) 11-18; Parvey, 123-36.

expressed in ECL. One is that women are by God's design the natural inferiors of men. 1 Tim 2:13 argues that this is proved by Eve's secondary place in the order of creation and her sinful fall. 1 Pet 3:5-6 affirms the Jewish practice of subordinating women to men by presenting the submissiveness of Sarah to Abraham as the appropriate model for the relationship of a wife to her husband. Col 3:18 describes the subjection of a wife to her husband as "fitting in the Lord." 1 Clem 20-21 explains female subordination as part of the order which God imposed on his creation to secure peace and harmony in the universe. Another approach to understanding the relationship between the sexes, found in Eph 5:21-33, is that men and women are different, incomplete in themselves, but complementary to one another. However, in Christ they become an essential unity. Thus, their virtues too, though different, are complementary and have their common origin in ἀγάπη (Eph 4:2, 15-16; 5:2).

Whichever rationale is used to explain the relationship between the sexes, there is a general consensus in ECL that in terms of their practical behavior wives should be subordinate to their husbands and should cultivate the traditional female household virtues. The Household Codes[48] in particular detail the appropriate behavior for husbands and wives. Husbands are expected to be the thoughtful, loving, sensible and considerate leaders, teachers and exemplars of virtue for their wives. Wives in turn are enjoined to be loving (φίλανδρος, Tit 2:4; στέργω, 1 Clem 1:3; Pol Phil 4:2), submissive (ὑποτάσσομαι, Col 3:18; Eph 5:21f.; 1 Pet 3:1; Tit 2:5), obedient (ἔν τε τῷ κανόνι τῆς ὑποταγῆς ὑπαρχούσα, 1 Clem 1:3), and reverent (φόβος, φοβέω, Eph 5:33; 1 Pet 3:2) to their husbands. They are expected to be chaste and pure (ἁγνεία, ἁγνή, Tit 2:5; 1 Pet 3:2; 1 Clem 1:3; 21:7; Pol Phil 4:2), sensible (σώφρων, Tit 2:5), domestic (οἰκουργός, Tit 2:5), capable (ἀγαθή, Tit 2:5), circumspect (σωφρονέω, 1 Clem 1:3), meek (πραΰτης, 1 Clem 21:7) and silent (σιγή, 1 Clem 21:7). They are to love their children (φιλότεκνος, Tit 2:4) and to educate them in the fear of God (Pol

[48] The Household Codes appear in ECL late in the first century. Their original purpose is unknown but it has been suggested that they were initially intended to counteract the radical social practices affecting the household and the community which developed in early Christianity. Cf. J. E. Crouch, *The Origin and Intention of the Colossian Haustafel* (Göttingen, 1972); E. Lohse, *Colossians and Philemon* (Philadelphia, 1971) 154-58; M. Dibelius and H. Conzelmann, *The Pastoral Epistles* (Philadelphia, 1972) 5-8, 139-43.

Phil 4:2). They are promised salvation through bearing children, if they continue in faith, love, and holiness with modesty (σωθήσεται δὲ διὰ τῆς τεκνογονίας, ἐὰν μείνωσιν ἐν πίστει καὶ ἀγάπῃ καὶ ἁγιασμῷ μετὰ σωφροσύνης, 1 Tim 2:15).

The Household Codes, by relegating women exclusively to the roles of wife and mother, deprive them of any significant leadership role within the orthodox Christian community.[49] Subsequently, women emerge only rarely from this subordinate status. In periods of persecution, however, women are recognized as the equals of men in their courage and strength in suffering and dying for their faith (1 Clem 6:2). The women martyrs are described as outstanding for their beauty (Mart Pot et Basil 1 [p. 132], Mart Carp et Soc [B]6:5 [p. 34]; Mart Crisp 3:1 [p. 306]), purity and modesty (ἁγνεία, Mart Pot et Basil 1 [p. 132]; καθαρά, Mart Just et Soc [C] 3:3 [p. 56]), courage in giving testimony or enduring suffering and remaining faithful under torture (Mart Just et Soc [C] 3 [p. 56]; Acta Scill Mart 9 [p. 88]; Mart Lougd 17-19 [p. 66]; 25-26 [pp. 68ff.]; Mart Pot et Basil 1-5 [p. 132], Mart Crisp 1-4 [p. 302]), courage in going to death (Mart Lougd 41-42 [p. 74]; 53-6 [pp. 78ff.]; Mart Perp et Fel 18 [pp. 124-126]) and ability to face suffering and death cheerfully and happily (ἀγαλλιάω, Mart Carp et Soc [A] 44 [p. 28], Mart Lougd 55 [p. 78]; γελάω, Mart Pion 7:5 [p. 146]).

The practice of contrasting the behavior of virtuous women with examples of the opposite behavior, which was noted above in the discussion of the *Mulierum virtutes*, also occurs in ECL. In the gospels, Jesus contrasts the generosity of the widow who gives her mite with that of the rich who give more but not all of their wealth (Mark 12:41-44//Luke 21:1-4); the wisdom of the five maidens who have oil in their lamps with the foolishness of those who have none (Matt 25:1-13); the faith and love of the sinful woman who anoints Jesus' feet with the inattentiveness of Simon the host who neglects to wash Jesus' feet (Luke 7:36-50). The Household Codes, as was noted above, present complementary rather than contrasting behavior patterns. In the martyr literature, however, the integrity and fidelity of the martyrs is contrasted with the cruelty of their oppressors (Mart Just et Soc [C] 1 [p. 54]; Mart

[49] Women do continue to be important in gnostic and Montanist sects, however. Cf. Rev 2:20 and Copt Gos Thom 21, 61, 114. For other examples, see W. Schmithals, *Gnosticism in Corinth* (Nashville, 1971) 245.

Lougd 8-10 [pp. 62ff.], 27 [p. 70], 53 [p. 78]; Mart Mont et Luc 2 [p. 214]) or the lack of courage of other Christians (Mart Pol 4 [p. 4]) or the protestations of their families (Mart Perp et Fel 3,5 [pp. 108-12]).

In the above comparison of ECL with Plutarch's *Mulierum virtutes*, a number of similarities have been noted between the texts in their use of sources, historical orientation, methods of composition, aretalogical influence and use of examples for ethical teaching. But by far their most significant common feature is their concern about the nature, role and ethical behavior of women, a fact which speaks to the common cultural background of the texts.

Plutarch takes a theoretical approach in the *Mulierum virtutes* to the question of women's ἀρετή, stating and defending the thesis that women are capable of the same virtuous activity as men. ECL, on the other hand, has a more practical interest in the problem and generally regards women as having a different virtuousness than men and supports this position with a variety of arguments.

Plutarch does not differ from ECL in valuing the traditional roles of women as wives and mothers. He praises his heroines generously for many of the same virtues which the Household Codes advise women to practice. The major difference between the two, however, is that in ECL the roles of wife and mother are the only appropriate ones for women, while for Plutarch women have the inherent capacity to assume other social roles as well. Yet Plutarch is not necessarily trying to liberate women from their traditional roles in demonstrating their ability to act for the public good,[50] though he clearly is supportive of a more active involvement of women in the public sphere than ECL. But it should be noted that most of his examples in the *Mulierum virtutes* focus on the behavior of women in extraordinary situations, most often when the freedom of the community is being threatened by tyranny. These occasions are most closely paralleleled in early Christianity by the periods of

[50] This position is corroborated by a study of the *Coniug. praec.* where Plutarch expresses great regard for the household virtues of women. Cf. Wicker, 142-49. Cf. also the example of Aretaphila of Cyrene which Plutarch cites in the *Mul. virt.* After she had succeeded in eliminating two tyrants, she was invited to "share with the best citizens in the control and management of the government. But she, as one who had played through a drama of varying sort and of many roles up to the winning of the prize, when she saw the city free, withdrew at once to her own quarters among the women, and, rejecting any sort of meddling in affairs, spent the rest of her life quietly at the loom in company of her friends and family." (257D-E)

persecution when Christians have to decide between resisting tyranny at the cost of their lives or renouncing their faith. In these situations Christian women demonstrate that they are the equals of men in their ability to testify, suffer and die for their faith. ECL shows no hesitation in praising them for their outstanding witness to the faith and in regarding them as models for believers.[51] Plutarch and ECL differ even here, though, in that ECL regards God and not the individual as the ultimate source of all virtuous action, while Plutarch views perfection as a human accomplishment. This may explain why Plutarch is free to arrive at a position on the nature and perfection of women from the observation of their behavior while ECL continues to maintain its position on the subordinate status of women in spite of the contradictory evidence of the outstanding witness of the women martyrs.

III. Other Parallels

(242E)

Περὶ ἀρετῆς. For Paul's use of περί to introduce a topic, cf. 1 Cor 7:1; 8:1; 16:1.

ὦ Κλέα. The literary device of dedicating a treatise to an individual is also found in Luke 1:3; Acts 1:1.

(242F)

ἔπαινος. Cf. Mark 15:39. For a discussion of this practice in Rome, cf. Pomeroy, 182-83.

παραμυθία. For παραμυθία of consolation at the time of death, cf. John 11:31; cf. also 1 Thes 4:13-18.

(243A)

τὸ ἱστορικὸν ἀποδεικτικόν. For ἀπόδειξις as a rhetorical concept in ECL, cf. 1 Cor 2:4.

ἐκ τοῦ φιλοκάλου μάλιστα τῆς ψυχῆς ἀναδούμενος τὴν πίστιν. This philosophical idea from the Platonic tradition does not occur in ECL. πίστις is mainly a religious t. t. in ECL, cf. R. Bultmann, *TDNT*, s.v. πιστεύω κτλ., D. For φιλόκαλος, cf. also 256D.

---

[51] Musurillo (p. liii) suggests that the courage of both sexes, as well as those of slave and free status, in facing martyrdom is a fulfillment of Paul's teaching in Gal 3:28.

(243B)

τὰ Σιβύλλης λόγια. For reference to the Σίβυλλα in ECL, cf. Herm Vis 2:4:1.

(243C)

σύνεσις. An important aspect of ἀρετή in this treatise is intelligence which leads to practical actions. σύνεσις is one of the terms Plutarch uses for this quality. Cf. σύνεσις and its cognates also at 257F, 258F, 261E. Other terms used in this treatise to describe this quality include ἐπίνοια (262C), λογισμός (243F, 256E), νοῦς (249C, 258A), πρόνοια (261E), σοφός (262D), φρόνησις κτλ. (243D, 252B, 255E). The opposite qualities are ἀνόητος (257A, 259E, 263B) and ἀμαθής (258E). Generally ECL connects practical wisdom with divine wisdom acquired through a right relationship with God. It is not a natural capacity as in Plutarch. Cf. the following for more complete discussions of the usages of these terms in ECL: H. W. Heidland, *TDNT*, s.v. λογίζομαι, λογισμός, B; J. Behm, *TDNT*, s.v. νοῦς; U. Wilckens, *TDNT*, s.v. σοφία κτλ., E, F; H. Conzelmann, *TDNT*, s.v. συνίημι κτλ., D, E; G. Bertram, *TDNT*, s.v. φρήν κτλ., D, E.

φρόνημα. The quality of high-spiritedness which leads to the performance of outstanding deeds is another important aspect of ἀρετή in this treatise. For φρόνημα cf. also 258F. Other terms in this treatise which stress a disposition to great deeds as well as the physical capacity to carry them out include: ἀνδρεία κτλ. (243C, 243D, 261D); θάρσος κτλ. (245B, 247A, 250D, 253A, 257C, 262E); θυμός κτλ. (245A, 245B); μεγαλοπραγμοσύνη (243C); ῥώμη κτλ. (250F, 259A); τόλμα (245A, D, 250D, F, 256A, 259C, 260C, 261E); ψυχή (259A); ὁρμή (245D, 262C). θυμός occurs with a negative meaning in 251C as does τόλμα in 253C. Cowardice is regarded as a vice in this treatise, cf. the use of κακίζω κτλ. in 245A, 246A, 247A, 257C. ECL values many of these same qualities, particularly in situations where the faith of Christians is threatened, but God or the Spirit and not the individual is regarded as the source of spirit and courage. In some instances these qualities are considered vices, as in Plutarch. For a fuller discussion of these terms in ECL, cf. Bauer, s.v. ἀνδρεῖος, ἀνδρείως, ἀνδρίζομαι; W. Grundmann, *TDNT*, s.v. θαρρέω; F. Büchsel, *TDNT*, s.v. θυμός; G. Fitzer, *TDNT*, s.v. τολμάω κτλ., D; G. Bertram, *TDNT*, s.v. φρήν κτλ., D, 3; G. Bertram, *TDNT*, s.v. ὁρμή κτλ., C, D.

ἐπειδὴ διαφορὰς . . . διαίταις. For a similar expression of the single source of the various manifestations of virtue in ECL, cf. 1 Cor 12:4-11.

(243D)

δίκαιος. δίκαιος and its cognates refer to the upright moral nature of an individual whose behavior is in accord with his or her character. Cf. also 243D, 250B, 255C. Lack of this quality is considered a vice, cf. 248A. δίκαιος and its cognates in ECL tend to have the Jewish sense of righteousness as a divine gift rather than the Greek notion of human perfection. Cf. G. Schrenk, *TDNT*, s.v. δίκαιος, C; δικαιοσύνη, D, E.

φίλανδρος. Love and fidelity to her husband are important aspects of the ἀρετή of women in this treatise. Cf. also 257F. πίστις is used of marital fidelity in 258F. ECL also affirms these qualities of feminine virtuousness. Cf. Tit 2:4; 1 Clem 1:3; Pol Phil 4:2.

παρίημι Luke 1:1-4 also mentions other works on the same subject at the beginning of his gospel. He does not pass over them, like Plutarch, however, but seems to suggest that they have inaccuracies and require his more accurate work. John 20:30 indicates that there are Jesus traditions which are not included in his gospel.

ἀκοῆς ἄξια. The deed of the woman who anoints Jesus is considered by him to be worthy of remembrance, cf. Mark 14:9//Matt 26:13.

Example 1

(243E)

ὑποτρέχω. This nautical t.t. also occurs in Acts 27:16. Cf. Acts 27 for another discussion of ship travel and shipwreck.

(244A)

φιλανθρώπως. For references to this quality of humaneness, cf. also 249B, 250E, 260F. In ECL φιλανθρωπία is usually a divine quality, cf. Tit 3:4 and Diogn 9:2, but in Acts 27:3 and 28:2 it is used of humans as here. φιλανθρωπία is one of a number of terms which Plutarch uses in this treatise to describe the basic positive disposition of the virtuous person to other persons equal or inferior to themselves. Other similar terms include μεγαλόφρων (251B, 257F); εὐμένεια κτλ. (244A, 250E, 257F); εὔνοια (256C, D); εὐφυΐα (249C); φιλοφροσύνη (244A, 255B, 256D, 261A); φιλόφρων κτλ. (258B, F); χάρις (252A); χρηστός (250B, 255B, 257F, 262D). A number of these terms do not occur in ECL. Of those that do occur, the qualities are frequently considered divine attributes or are connected with the salvation event. Cf. K. Weiss, *TDNT*, s.v. χρηστός, C; H. Conzelmann, *TDNT*, s.v. χάρις κτλ., D, E. In ECL ἀγάπη is the significant virtue which regulates and informs human conduct.

Example 2

(244B)

μαρτυρούμενον ἱεροῖς τε μεγάλοις. This is one of several places where Plutarch refers to religious rituals. Cf. also the use of ἑορτή (244D, 253F, 254A, C, D); πομπή (257F); τελέω (244D, 245E); θυσία (253F, 255C, 257E). The most important ritual celebration in ECL is that of the eucharistic meal, which is a celebration of the Lord's death, according to 1 Cor 11:23-26. Also cf. Mark 14:22-25//Matt 26:26-29//Luke 22:14-20. For the use in ECL of the religious t.t.s listed above, cf. G. Schrenk, *TDNT*, s.v. ἱερός, E; Bauer, s.v. ἑορτάζω, ἑορτή; G. Delling, *TDNT*, s.v. τελέω, C; J. Behm, *TDNT*, s.v. θύω κτλ., B.

δόγματα παλαιά. ECL uses the term δόγμα to refer to the Mosaic law, cf. Eph 2:15; Col 2:14.

(244C)

ἐξανίστημι. This term describing the posture of the orator is often found in historical narrative, cf. Acts 15:5.

(244E)

ἡ Ἄρτεμις. For other references to this goddess, cf. 247E, 253F, 257F. Cf. also references to her in Acts 19:24, 27f., 34f.

Example 3

οἱ δοκοῦντες γνώριμοι. Cf. οἱ δοκοῦντες εἶναί τι in Gal 2:6; cf. also 2:9.

οἱ . . . φίλοι τοῦ γαμοῦντος. Cf. the similar expression in John 3:29.

(244E-F)

μηνιμάτων δὲ τοῖς Χίοις προφαινομένων καὶ τοῦ θεοῦ κελεύσαντος. For the pollution of a city in ECL, cf. Matt 10:14f.//Luke 9:5; Matt 11:21-24//Luke 10:12-15; Matt 23:37-39//Luke 13:34f.

(244F)

ἀνελόντας ἀνελεῖν. A case of *Jus talionis*, cf. Matt 26:52. But for a rejection of this practice in ECL, cf. Matt 5:38-41//Luke 6:27f.; Rom 12:17; 1 Cor 6:7; 1 Pet 3:9. Cf. also the discussion in E. Käsemann, "Sentences of Holy Law in the New Testament," in *New Testament Questions of Today* (Philadelphia, 1969) 66-81.

ἅπαντες ἔφασεν. For similar mass acceptance of guilt, cf. Matt 27:25.

(245B)

σῴζω. This term occurs in ECL for rescuing persons from natural disasters, cf. Bauer, s.v., 1, though more frequently it is used of the salvation event.

ἐκήρυξε κήρυγμα. Cf. also 251D. These terms become t.t.s related to the proclamation of the gospel in ECL, cf. G. Friedrich, *TDNT* s.v. κηρύσσω, D, κήρυγμα, B.

τοὺς οἰκέτας . . . ἐπ' ἐλευθερίᾳ. Here the slaves do not accept the offer of freedom from Philip but remain loyal to their masters. ECL recommends that slaves retain their status as such, serving their masters as they would the Lord. Cf. 1 Cor 7:21f.; Eph 6:5-8; Col 3:22-24; 1 Pet 2:18. Cf. also Phlm.

Example 4

(245C-D)

εἰς θεοῦ πέμψαι περὶ ὑγιείας. For a prayer for physical health in ECL, cf. Mark 1:40//Matt 8:2//Luke 5:12; Mark 5:23//Matt 9:18; 2 Cor 12:8; 1 Clem 61:1. Cf. also H. D. Betz, "Eine Christus-Aretalogie bei Paulus (2 Kor 12, 7-10)," *ZTK* 66 (1969) 288-305.

(245D)

ἀπαλλάσσω. A t.t. in miracle stories, cf. Bauer, s.v.

ταχύ. A miracle *topos*, cf. Bauer, s.v. εὐθύς, παραχρῆμα.

θαυμάζεσθαι. θαυμάζω frequently occurs in ECL in the context of miracle stories, cf. G. Bertram, *TDNT*, s.v. θαῦμα κτλ., C.

μυθολογέω. Cf. also 247F, 248B. Cf. *PECL* 1:135, 113.

δαιμόνιος. Cf. W. Foerster, *TDNT*, s.v. δαίμων, δαιμόνιον for a discussion of the use of these terms in ECL.

παρίστημι A t.t. in demonology, cf. Bauer, s.v., 2.b.α.

(245E)

μέχρι νῦν. Cf. Bauer, s.v. μέχρι, 1.b

Example 5

(246A)

τοὺς πέπλους ἐκ τῶν κάτω μερῶν ἐπάρασι. Cf. also 248B. This practice of self-exposure is totally foreign to ECL. Cf. Stadter, 73 and n. 140-44. Cf. also Teles, 59 H.

Example 6

(246C)

διακρίνω. In ECL women do not appear as arbitrators, as here. διακρίνω occurs as a legal t.t. in ECL, in 1 Cor 6:5. Cf. 1 Cor 6:1-8 for the manner of settling differences among Christians.

ἀμφίβολος. Cf. ἀμφιβολία Did 14:2.

δικαστής. Cf. also the use of δικαστή and κριτής in 250B. Jesus declines the title of judge, cf. Luke 12:14.

Example 7

(246D)

τοῦ δὲ θεοῦ πλεῖν κελεύσαντος αὐτούς. Cf. also 247D. In ECL Paul receives divine guidance for his missionary activities. Cf. Acts 16:6-10; 19:21-22. Cf. also *PECL* 1:140: τὴν Πυθίαν.

(246E)

πολλὴν ἐν ὀλίγῳ χρόνῳ λαμβάνοντας αὔξησιν ὁρῶντες. For the rapid growth of Christianity, cf. Acts 6:7; 12:24; 19:20.

ἐπιβουλεύω. A plot to do away with someone is a common story topic, cf. Acts 9:23ff.; 20:3; 23:30.

(247A)

ἄξιον οὖν ἄγασθαι . . . γενέσθαι. Here the women are praised for not revealing the plot. The related themes of silence in the face of suffering and danger occur in 249F, 250E, 251B, F, 252B, 256D. Cf. the silence of Jesus during his passion, Mark 14:61//Matt 27:12-14.

Example 8

(247D)

θόρυβοι πανικοὶ προσέπεσον. For panic and confusion in a group, cf. Acts 21:34.

(247E)

ξόανον. The term ξόανον is used in a criticism of idolatry in Apoc Pet 18:33 in line with the rejection of images in Jewish-Christian theology. Cf. also Acts 19:23ff.; 17:22ff. See *PECL* 1, index, s.v. idolatry.

περαίνεσθαι τὰ πυθόχρηστα φήσας ἐσήμαινεν. Matthew's gospel frequently interprets events as fulfillments of prophecies, cf. Matt 1:22-23; 3:3//Luke 3:4-6; Matt 4:14-16. Cf. also Luke 24:44-49.

Example 9

(247F)

μαρτυρέω. Cf. H. Strathmann, *TDNT*, s.v. μάρτυς κτλ., E, F for the use of these terms in ECL.

(248A)

εὔξατο . . . ἀνόνητον. Cf. also 248D, 254B. For the power of prayer in ECL, cf. Mark 11:22-24//Matt 21:18-22. The prayers for the forgiveness of offenses in Luke 23:34 and Acts 7:60 are in contrast with the behavior of Bellerophon. Cf. also the rejected prayer in Luke 9:54f. In addition note the woes in Matt 11:20ff.// Luke 10:13-15; Matt 23:13-38//Luke 11:42-52; 13:34f.; Acts 5:1-12. Cf. also the curse as punishment for non-acceptance of the gospel in Gal 1:8f.

κῦμα δὲ διαρθὲν ἐπέκλυζε τὴν γῆν. Jesus performs the opposite miracle of quieting the stormy sea, cf. Mark 4:36-41//Matt 8:23-27//Luke 8:22-24.

(248B)

ὑπ' αἰσχύνης. αἰσχύνη is one of several words used in this treatise of a sense of shame or modesty. Cf. also 249D, 262C. Other terms with a similar sense include αἰδώς κτλ. (248C, D, 251F, 259F, 262B); αἰσχρός (249D, 251B, 253E). These terms often have implicit or explicit sexual connotations. For a fuller discussion of these terms in ECL, cf. R. Bultmann, *TDNT*, s.v. αἰδώς, αἰσχύνη κτλ.

(248D)

πᾶν τὸ πεδίον ἐξήνθησεν ἁλμυρίδα καὶ διέφθαρτο παντάπασι. Cf. Mark 11:12-14, 20//Matt 21:18-19.

ἡ ὀργή. The term is used here of divine anger. ὀργή is also used of

Bellerophon's response to ingratitude (248C) as well as of human passion and rage in a negative sense; cf. 243F, 251B, F, 252D, 263B. For a fuller discussion of ὀργή of both divine and human wrath in ECL, cf. G. Stählin, *TDNT*, s.v. ὀργή κτλ., E. Cf. also *PECL* 1:197.

Example 10

(249A-B)

οἱ δὲ τῶν ὀρῶν ἐπιλαβόμενοι παραχρῆμα μὲν διέφυγον. For the mountains as a place of refuge in times of disaster in ECL, cf. Mark 13:14//Matt 24:16//Luke 21:21.

Example 11

(249B)

δεινὸν πάθος καὶ ἀλλόκοτον κατέσχεν. The behavior of the women is similar to that of people possessed by demons in ECL. Cf. Mark 9:14-29//Matt 17:14-21//Luke 9:37-42 where the demon tries to make the epileptic boy kill himself. Cf. also Mark 5:5. Plutarch also considers this behavior a result of demonic activity, cf. 249C. For κατέχω of possession by a disease in ECL, cf. Luke 4:38 v.l.; John 5:4 v.l.

ἐξαίφνης. For ἐξαίφνης in miracle stories in ECL, cf. Luke 9:39; Acts 9:3; 22:6.

ἐπιθυμία θανάτου. Cf. Paul's desire for death in Phil 1:21-24.

(249C)

κρεῖττον ἀνθρωπίνης βοηθείας. For the miracle story *topos* of the inability of human help, cf. Mark 5:26//Luke 8:43; Mark 9:18//Matt 17:16//Luke 9:40. Cf. also Bultmann, *HST*, 221.

γυμνὰς ἐκκομίζεσθαι διὰ τῆς ἀγορᾶς. Physical modesty was important for women even in death. Cf. also 253E. For the naked exposure of the Christian women martyrs, cf. Mart Agap et Soc 5:8 [p. 290]; Mart Carp et Soc 6:5 [p. 34]; Mart Perp et Fel 20:3-5 [p. 128].

μέγα δὴ τεκμήριον εὐφυΐας καὶ ἀρετῆς ἡ τῆς ἀδοξίας εὐλάβεια. ECL agrees with Plutarch in valuing the modesty of women, cf. 1 Tim 2:9.

Example 12

(249D)

εἰς ἱερά. In ECL, cf. Luke 2:37 for Anna in the temple. ECL uses ἱερόν for pagan temples, cf. Acts 19:27, as well as for the temple in Jerusalem. Cf. G. Schrenk, *TDNT*, s.v. τὸ ἱερόν, E.

διηκονοῦντο τοῖς ἀλλήλων . . . τοὺς πόδας ἀπονίζειν. For an example of service and washing the feet of others cf. John 13:3-17. Cf. also Joseph and Asenath 20.

κόσμιον ἔρωτα καὶ νόμιμον. ECL also approves of orderly love in young men, cf. Tit 2:6.

ἡ εὐταξία τῶν γυναικῶν. Orderly sexual relations were also enjoined upon women in ECL, cf. Tit 2:4-5; Plutarch also uses σώφρων κτλ. of feminine chastity (257F, 260F, 261D) as does ECL. Cf. U. Luck, *TDNT*, s.v. σώφρων κτλ., C.D.

(249E)

μήτε μοιχείαν μήτε φθοράν. Cf. also 254C, 261F. For these two words occuring in combination in ECL, cf. 2 Clem 6:4. Both Plutarch and ECL disapprove of these kinds of sexual excess.

Example 13

μηδέπω τοῦ φρονεῖν παρόντος. For a distinction between inspiration and rationality in ECL, cf. 1 Cor 14:18-19.

(249F)

θεραπεύω. Cf. also 250D and 257C where encouragement is also a way of helping others. ECL also values ministry to the needy. Cf. H. W. Beyer, *TDNT*, s.v. θεραπεία κτλ.; O Schmitz, *TDNT*, s.v. παρακαλέω, παράκλησις, F.

πείσασαι τοὺς ἄνδρας. The persuasive abilities of women are referred to here and in 253C. For a similar theme in ECL, cf. Acts 16:15.

Example 14

(250A)

ὕβρις. This is a negative ethical term in Greek thought. Cf. also 251A, 252C, 253D, 259A, E, 260A, D for the use of ὕβρις and its cognates in this treatise. For its uses in ECL, cf. G. Bertram, *TDNT*, s.v. ὕβρις κτλ., D, E.

Example 15

(250F-251A)

ἐχρῆτο δὲ τῇ δυνάμει πρὸς οὐδὲν ἐπιεικὲς οὐδὲν μέτριον. Plutarch follows the Aristotelian concept of the mean in praising moderation and condemning excess. For ἐπιεικής cf. also 259E; for μέτριος, 262D. Cf. also the use of the term περιττῶς, 262D. This concept from Hellenistic ethics is found in ECL, cf. Heb 5:2; Ign Trall 4:1; 1 Clem 1:3. Cf. H. Preisker, *TDNT*, s.v. ἐπιείκεια, ἐπιεικής; K. Deissner, *TDNT*, s.v. μέτρον κτλ. Plutarch uses a variety of terms in addition to those mentioned above which describe behavior not in accordance with the mean. These include rashness (ἐμπλήκτως, 257A); despotism (δεσποτικῶς, 259A); relentlessness (ἄτεγκτος, 256A, D); jealousy (ἐπίφθονος, 255B, 256C); unlawful behavior (παράνομος κτλ.,* 251B, C, 255F); bellicoseness (πολεμιστής, 247F), cruelty (ὠμός, 247F, 252C); insatiability (ἄπληστος, 262D); irreverence (ἀσεβής,* 255C; ἀνόσιος,* 258C); lack of self-control (ἀκρατής,* 258E); violence (ἀσελγαίνω, 253C); brutishness (θηριώδης, 247F, 256A) and viciousness (πονηρός,* 260E). These negative qualities are all basically contradictory to the Christian ideal of ἀγάπη as well. Those terms which occur in ECL, indicated above with an asterisk, also have negative ethical meanings. Cf. Bauer. Excessive love of wealth is also condemned by Plutarch in this treatise, cf. 258E, 259C, 262D. For a discussion of this topic, see the study of *cup. divit.* by O'Neil in this volume, pp. 289ff. For a condemnation of lust and drunkenness, cf. 251B.

(251A)

ἡ θυγάτηρ καλή. The beauty of the heroines is regularly commented upon in this treatise, the assumption generally being that moral and physical beauty are often found together. Cf. also 251A, 255E, 256E, 257F, 259C. Such comments are rare in ECL, but cf. Mart Pot et Basil 1 [p. 132]; Mart Carp et Soc (B) 6:5 [p. 34]; Mart Crisp 3:1 [p. 306]. Cf. also Joseph and Asenath 23.

(251B)

ἡ δὲ παῖς οὖσα γενναία. The well-born *topos* occurs commonly in the context of feminine praise, cf. also 253E, 260C. For this theme in ECL, cf. *PECL* 1:248.

σπαργῶν καὶ μεθύων. Lust and drunkenness are also frequent vices exhibited by the villains in this treatise. Cf. 251C, 254D, 256E, 258E, 259E-F. ECL also disapproves of these vices. Cf. G. Stählin, *TDNT*, s.v. ἡδονή, φιλήδονος, E; H. Preisker, *TDNT*, s.v. μέθη κτλ. B.

(251E)

οὔτε τοῖς νηπίοις βοηθεῖν ἀπολλυμένοις. Cf. Matt 2:13-18 where the slaughter of infants shows the cruelty of Herod.

ἱκετηρίας καὶ στέμματα τῶν ἀπὸ τοῦ θεοῦ. Cf. also 254C. For these religious t.t.s in ECL, cf. Acts 14:13; Heb 5:7.

(252B)

ὡς κυρίους ἡμῶν. For the husband as κύριος in ECL, cf. 1 Pet 3:6.

(252C)

τὴν τῆς πατρίδος ἐλευθερίαν. The theme of political freedom occurs frequently in this treatise. Most of the situations in which the heroines perform their outstanding deeds are ones where the freedom of the community is being threatened. Cf. also 253B; 256E; 257D, E; 260C; 262A, C. In ECL ἐλευθερία becomes a spiritualized concept of freedom from sin and death. Cf. H. Schlier, *TDNT*, s.v. ἐλευθερία, C. See also *PECL* 1:284.

ἐκέλευσε τὸ παιδίον αὐτῆς ὡς ἀποκτενῶν ἐν ὄψει κομισθῆναι. Children are also used in ECL to attempt to dissuade the Christian women from remaining steadfast in their faith. Cf. Mart Perp et Fel 3:6 [p. 108]; 5:3 [p. 112]; 6:2 [p. 112]. The inspiration of the mother in Maccabees who watched her sons die is referred to in Mart Lougd 55 [p. 78]; Mart Mar et Jam 13:1 [p. 212]; Mart Mont et Luc 16:4 [p. 230].

(252D)

γυναικῶδες. The pejorative use of γυναικώδης in this treatise deserves special note. It may be an indication that Plutarch has taken over another source without modification here.

(252E)

γίγνεται δὲ σημεῖον αὐτῷ μέγα. Cf. *PECL* 1, index, s.v. Omens, portents.

μεσημβρία μὲν γὰρ ἦν. For special revelations at midday in ECL, cf. Acts 10:9-11; 22:6; Luke 23:44.

(252F)

μετεπέμψατο μάντιν. Cf. Matt 2:1-8; Herm Man 11:2.

ὁ δ' ἐκεῖνον μὲν παρεκάλει . . . βοηθοῦντος. For βοηθέω of divine help, cf. 2 Cor 6:2. Cf. also *PECL* 1:119.

τὴν δίκην αἰωρουμένην . . . τῷ τυράννῳ. Jesus interpreted his anointing as a preparation for his death. Cf. Mark 14:3-9//Matt 26:6-13. Cf. also Acts 21:11.

τῆς δὲ νυκτὸς . . . παραστάντα. Cf. Acts 16:9; Mart Pol 22:3 [p. 18]. Cf. also *PECL* 1, index, s.v. Visions, Dreams.

Example 16

(254A)

μετέχω. For the use of μετέχω of participation in religious festivals, cf. 1 Cor 10:21.

Example 17

(254B)

ἐρασθείσῃ δε τῇ Νεαίρᾳ συνῆλθε. For συνέρχομαι in a sexual sense in ECL, cf. Matt 1:18; 1 Cor 7:5 v.l.

(254C)

ἑορτῆς δὲ . . . καθηκούσης . . . καὶ πρὸς πόσιν ἁπάντων. For the association of a religious festival and drinking in ECL, cf. 1 Cor 11:17-34. Cf. also the association of sacrifice and banquet in 255C-D.

(254E)

μετὰ χαρᾶς καὶ στεφάνων ὑποδεχομένους. Cf. *PECL* 1:298.

βασκάνῳ τινὶ τύχῃ. Cf. Mart Pol 17:1 for reference to an envious evil being associated with the death of an outstanding individual.

(254F)

ὅρκον ᾔτησεν. For a discussion of oaths in ECL, cf. J. Schneider, *TDNT*, s.v. ὅρκος, B.

Example 19

(255F)

τὸν ἱερέα τοῦ 'Απόλλωνος αὐτόχειρ ἀνελών. Cf. Matt 23:35 for a reference to the murder of Zechariah the priest.

(256A)

ἡ 'Αρεταφίλα ὑποθεῖσα μόνην τοῖς κοινοῖς ἐλπίδα. For a similar notion in ECL, cf. John 18:14; 1 Clem 55:1. Cf. also R. Bultmann, *The Gospel of John* (Philadelphia, 1971) 641-48.

(257C)

προσήγαγε τῷ βαρβάρῳ καὶ παρέδωκεν. Cf. also 259B. In ECL it is not the guilty but the innocent who are betrayed and handed over to death. Jesus is the supreme example of a person betrayed by a supposed friend. Cf. Mark 14:10-11//Matt 26:14-16//Luke 22:3-6. Cf. also W. Popkes, *Christus Traditus* (Zürich, 1967).

(257D)

τὸν δὲ Λέανδρον ἐνράψαντες εἰς βύρσαν κατεπόντισαν. Cf. Mark 9:42//Matt 18:6//Luke 17:2; 1 Clem 46:8 for references to this kind of punishment.

(257E)

ἡ δ' ὡς ποικίλον τι δρᾶμα καὶ πολυμερὲς ἀγωνισαμένη μέχρι στεφάνου διαδόσεως. ECL does not use the drama competition but rather the race as the context for the winning of the prize. Cf. *PECL* 1:298.

τοῦ πολυπαγμονεῖν ... διετέλεσεν. This statement, as was indicated in the introduction, may reflect Plutarch's sentiments about the appropriate role of women in ordinary circumstances. For a similar ideal of behavior for all Christians, cf. 1 Thes 4:11-12; 2 Thes 3:11f.

Example 20

(257F)

σέβω. A religious t.t., cf. W. Foerster, *TDNT*, s.v. σέβομαι, C.

(258B)

παρὰ τῇ θεῷ. For a similar expression in ECL, cf. Bauer, s.v. παρά, II.2.b.

τὴν θεὸν προσκυνήσασα. Cf. *PECL* 1, index, s.v. προσκυνέω, προσκύνησις.

μαρτύρομαί σε ... ὦ πολυτίμητε δαῖμον. For an invocation of God as witness in ECL, cf. Rom 1:9; 2 Cor 1:23; Phil 1:8; 1 Thes 2:5; Ign Phld 7:2.

(258C)

τὴν ἐλπίδα τῆς δίκης. Contrast the sentiment here of taking justice into one's own hands with that in Rom 12:14-21.

καταβαίνω πρὸς τὸν ἐμὸν ἄνδρα. ECL also thinks of a descent to the realm of the dead in an underworld. Cf. Rom 10:7; 1 Clem 51:4.

Example 21

(258D)

μὴ τίκτουσα ... ὑποβαλλόμενον. A similar story is told of Sarah in the OT, cf. Gen 16:1-6, but it is not reported in ECL.

Example 22

(258E)

ἀπολυτρόω. Ransoming becomes associated with the salvation event in ECL, cf. F. Büchsel, *TDNT*, s.v. ἀπολύτρωσις.

(258F)

ἐκείνου δὲ πεισθέντος ... ἀπήλαυνεν. For a woman arranging for the beheading of a man as a personal vendetta in ECL, cf. Mark 6:24-28//Matt 14:8-11.

Example 23

(259C)

ἣν ὁ δήμιος ἀναίμακτον αὐτῷ καὶ καθαρὰν διαφυλάξαι βουλόμενος. Undoubtedly this was a common practice among executioners, cf. John 19:23-24.

Example 24

(260A)

δαίμονος διδόντος. Here a notion of divine providence, but in 260B the idea is expressed that Fate uses persons as instruments of destruction. Cf. *PECL* 1:223, s.v. μοίρᾳ τινι θεῶν; index, Punishment, divine.

Example 25

(260D)

Βάττου τοῦ ἐπικληθέντος Εὐδαίμονος υἱός. For the use of symbolic names or nicknames, cf. also 261E. In ECL, cf. John 1:42; Matt 16:17f. Cf. also Bauer, s.v. Θωμᾶς; Σίμων, 1; Πέτρος.

DE VIRTUTE MORALI (MORALIA 440D - 452D)

BY

JACKSON P. HERSHBELL
University of Minnesota
Minneapolis, Minnesota

I. INTRODUCTION

According to K. Ziegler, *De virtute morali* belongs to Plutarch's "popularphilosophisch-ethischen Schriften," and its Greek title, Περὶ τῆς ἠθικῆς ἀρετῆς, appears as number 72 in the so-called Lamprias *Catalogue*.[1] With the exception of J. Hartman, who considered the treatise a clumsy and foolish imitation, no one has questioned its authenticity during the present century.[2] Since Plutarch gives no references in the work to events of his life or times, its date cannot be certainly established. Its anti-Stoic polemic, however, has led D. Babut to conclude that it does not belong to Plutarch's youth, but to the period of *prof. virt.*, that is, after 85 and probably not before 95.[3] C. P. Jones does not date *virt. mor.*, but he places *prof. virt.* after 100 and before 116.[4] If Jones is correct, Babut's chronology needs to be somewhat revised.

---

[1] See Ziegler, sec. III.4.a and col. 62. On the catalogue, see M. Treu, *Der sogenannte Lampriaskatalog der Plutarchschriften* (Waldenberg in Schlesien, 1873). The text used in this study is that of D. Babut, *Plutarque, De la vertu éthique* (Paris, 1969). See my review in *AJPh* 93 (1972) 640-41; also the review by H. G. Ingenkamp, *Gnomon* 44 (1972) 250-55. Other texts are: W. C. Helmbold, *Plutarch's Moralia* 6, LCL (1939) 18-87 and M. Pohlenz, *Plutarchi Moralia* 3, BT (1929) 127-56. Studies important for understanding the treatise are: D. Babut, *Plutarque et le Stoïcisme* (Paris, 1969); see my review, *AJPh* 93 (1972) 485-89; S. G. Etheridge, *Plutarch's 'De virtute morali.' A study in extra-Peripatetic Aristotelianism* (Cambridge, Mass., 1961). Resumé in *HSCP* 66 (1962) 252-4; M. Pinnoy, *Aristotelisme en Antistoicisme in Plutarchus' 'De virtute morali'* (Louvain, 1956); M. Pinnoy, *De peripatetische thema's in Plutarchus' 'De virtute morali'* (Diss. Leuven, 1966); M. Pinnoy, "Het begrip 'Midden' in de ethica van Plutarchus," *Zetesis, Album amicorum . . . aangeboden aan . . . E. de Strycker* (Antwerp/Utrecht, 1973) 224-233.

[2] J. J. Hartman, *De Plutarcho Scriptore et Philosopho* (Leyden, 1916) 203ff. See also Ziegler, 133-34.

[3] Babut, *Vertu*, 80ff.

[4] See his "Towards a Chronology of Plutarch's Works," *JRS* 56 (1966) 73, and his *Plutarch and Rome* (Oxford, 1971) 137.

That the purpose of the treatise is to refute Stoic doctrine on the relation of πάθη to λογισμός and to defend Platonic-Aristotelian teachings on the soul, virtue, and emotions, is obvious. The treatise's structure, however, is less clear: sometimes the argumentation appears loose, incoherent, and tedious. Since Babut has devoted much study to the composition of *virt. mor.*, his outline will be used in summarizing its contents. Following this, the work will be compared with early Christian literature and thought, and specific passages and significant terms will be discussed. One reason for this procedure is that in order to make any meaningful comparison of Plutarch's treatise with early Christian literature, it is necessary to understand it fully, and this involves viewing it in the context of a long philosophical tradition, a tradition which was seemingly ignored by or unknown to early Christian authors. The only occurrence of φιλοσοφία in the NT is in Col 2:8 where Paul links it with "empty deceit." Presumably, of course, it is used with reference to heretical opponents who called their doctrines "philosophy" to give them weighty authority.[5] Paul's use of the term is thus not necessarily disparaging. Nonetheless, there are remarks in other early Christian works, e.g., those on the "empty and silly discourses" of philosophers in Diogn 8:2f., or those which contrast God's wisdom with the "babblings of foolish philosophers," Theophilus of Antioch *Autol.* 2. 15. 43-48. If O. Michel's observations on φιλοσοφία are correct, the central convictions of early Christianity are "neither related to philosophy nor dependent on it." [6] Moreover, whereas Plutarch envisioned a perfecting of the self into a harmonious whole, a work of which one might be justly proud, the early Christians thought that perfection could only be attained by increasing reliance on God, and seeing His perfection as a paradigm (cf. Matt 5:48). The Sermon on the Mount (Matt 5-7), however, in which the closest parallel to perfection occurs, has a Jewish and not a Greek background.[7]

According to Babut, *virt. mor.* has two main parts: Pt. I on ethical virtue includes chs. 1-6 to 445B; Pt. II from ch. 7, 446E through ch. 11 contains the refutation of the Stoic theory of the emotions. These parts are separated by an interlude or transitional

[5] See O. Michel, *TDNT*, s.v. φιλοσοφία D.2 (9:185f.).

[6] Ibid.

[7] Cf. Matt 5:48 with Lev 19:2 or see G. D. Kilpatrick, *The Origins of the Gospel According to St. Matthew* (Oxford, 1946).

section (ch. 6, 445B to ch. 7, 446E) on the distinction between temperance and self-control and between incontinence and intemperance. Ch. 12 concludes the work with the view that the emotions are part of human nature, and indispensable to moral development.

Chapter Summaries

In ch. 1, the treatise's introduction, Plutarch announces his purpose to consider ethical virtue (ἠθικὴ ἀρετή), which, in contrast to theoretical virtue (θεωρητικὴ ἀρετή), has the emotions as its matter (ὕλη) and λόγος or the rule fixed by reason as its form (εἶδος). In order to clarify his own teachings, he sketches the opinions of other philosophers at the outset, and this doxography extends through chs. 2 and 3.

Menedemus of Eretria is mentioned first in ch. 2. He and Ariston of Chios believed in the unity of virtue. According to Menedemus, σωφροσύνη, ἀνδρεία, and δικαιοσύνη are identical. Ariston also made virtue one in being and called it "health"; but it received different names when exercised in different circumstances, e.g., "self-control" when desires or pleasures are involved. Zeno of Citium had a similar view and made prudence (φρόνησις) the basis of all virtues, but Chrysippus multiplied the names of virtue to absurdity.

In ch. 3 Plutarch claims that all these thinkers agree that virtue is a certain disposition (ἕξις) of the soul's hegemonic part, and a faculty (δύναμις) engendered by reason, or rather is itself reason that is harmonious, firm and unshaken. The irrational or passionate part of the soul is not distinct from the rational, but the same part of the soul, the διάνοια or ἡγεμονικόν, is changeable and becomes either virtue or vice; it has nothing irrational within itself, and it can be considered so only if it acts contrary to reason as a result of an overpowering impulse. Even passion (πάθος) is a perverted and disordered reason, the result of defective and erroneous judgment which has acquired vehement force. According to Plutarch, this conception is false. It overlooks the fact that as man is a composite of body and soul, so the soul, human as well as cosmic, consists of two parts, the intelligent and rational (νοερὸν καὶ λογιστικόν) and the passionate and irrational (παθητικὸν καὶ ἄλογον). The latter is again split up into the ἐπιθυμητικόν and θυμοειδές. This is the teaching of Plato which Aristotle initially followed, later modified, but maintained in essence.

Ch. 4 begins with a digression until 443C... ἀναπιμπλάμενον ὑπὸ συνηθείας, on the many examples which show that reason rules the irrational part of the soul not by force, but by sympathetic guidance and persuasion. At 443C Plutarch takes up his discussion of ethical virtue which lasts until ch. 6, 445A. Moral character (ἦθος) is well named because it is a quality of the irrational part (ποιότης τοῦ ἀλόγου) formed by reason by means of habit (ἔθει). Reason does not destroy πάθος completely, but orders and limits it, thus implanting the ethical virtues which are not negations, but due proportions of the passions, and just means (οὐκ ἀπαθείας ... ἀλλὰ συμμετρίας παθῶν καί μεσότητας). Of the soul's three states, capacity or potentiality (δύναμις), passion (πάθος), and a settled disposition (ἕξις), it is from the last that ethical virtue results, it being "a force and state of the capacity proper to the irrational part, which is bred by habit, and which is vice, if passion has been educated badly, but virtue if it has been educated well by reason."

Having affirmed, contrary to Stoic apathy, that ethical virtue is a mean between the passions, Plutarch defines the notion more precisely in ch. 5 by distinguishing it from theoretical virtue (σοφία). The latter is concerned with things that exist absolutely (ἁπλῶς ἔχοντα), e.g., earth, heavens, stars. There are also things that exist in relation to us (πῶς ἔχοντα πρὸς ἡμᾶς), e.g., pleasures and pains. Prudence or practical reason (φρόνησις) has to deal with these, and more specifically, to do away with defects and excesses of the passions, and to find the proper mean, μεσότης, between the ἔλλειψις and ὑπερβολή which, according to Aristotelian teaching, is the characteristic of ethical virtue.

Ch. 6 deals with the notion of ethical virtue as a mean until 445A. "Mean" (τὸ μέσον) is used in different senses, but none of its three usual meanings apply to virtue: it is neither a mixture of vices, nor an arithmetic mean, nor a middle term without relation to the extremes. Virtue is a mean (μεσότης) much like that of musical sounds and harmonies. Its role is to prevent the releases and tensions, the excesses and defects of impulse (ὁρμή), and to reduce each passion to moderation and faultlessness (εἰς τὸ μέτριον καὶ ἀναμάρτητον). Courage, for example, is a mean between cowardice and rashness; temperance is a mean between lack of feeling (ἀναισθησία) and intemperance.

This last example, in which the difference between the rational and irrational, the reason and passion, is especially clear, leads

Plutarch to distinctions between temperance (σωφροσύνη) and self-control (ἐγκράτεια), incontinence (ἀκρασία) and intemperance (ἀκολασία), and his discussion from ch. 6, 445B to ch. 7, 446E forms a transition between the two parts of the treatise. Now, if the same part of the soul desired and formed judgments, self-control would not differ from temperance, nor incontinence from intemperance. But they do differ: in a temperate person the irrational power of the soul obeys and cooperates willingly with the reason; in the self-controlled, the irrational resists and is mastered only by the force of reason. In a parallel way, incontinence is viewed as an inability of reason to impose its authority on the passions, whereas intemperance is a perversion of reason which destroys even the awareness of wrongdoing. The poets provide numerous examples of these affections of the soul.

From 446E to 447A of ch. 7, Plutarch expounds the Stoic doctrine that passion is not different from reason, and from 447B to the chapter's end, he presents his first argument against it. According to the Stoics, there is no conflict between two forces, reason and passion, in the soul, but only the pull of reason in opposite directions; in fact, the passions such as desire and fear are only perverted opinions and judgments of the reason. Because of their diversity and swiftness, however, the passions are not perceived as activities (ἐνεργείας) of the reason. But, according to Plutarch, this doctrine is contrary to experience. For the beginning or cessation of a passion never reveals a change from desiring to judging or vice-versa, but always the co-existence of two forces (even if the one is momentarily dominated by the other). To confuse these is as absurd as to identify a hunter with his quarry since in both cases there is not a changing of one thing, but two things struggling and fighting with one another. Against this observation the Stoics object that one and the same deliberative faculty is often torn between contrary opinions about the expedient. But their objection is specious because the soul's thinking part (τὸ φρονοῦν) cannot conflict with itself. Proof of this is that purely intellectual debates are never painful, and never accompanied by feelings of constraint. If they are, this is because of secretly attached emotions, and not the reasonings themselves. In general, when one reasoning (λογισμός) seems opposed to another, there is no perception of two different entities, but of a single one manifest in different sense impressions. Only the struggle, necessarily painful, of the irrational with reason, splits the soul into two and gives evidence of its dual nature.

Ch. 8 contains Plutarch's second argument against the Stoics: the different natures of the rational and irrational can be seen not only in their conflict, but also in the subordination of emotion to reason. For example, just as there is irrational anger in which passion and reason struggle, so there is justified anger in which the two agree. Or, since there is a good and a bad modesty (αἰδώς), it can be seen that emotion sometimes submits to reason, and sometimes acts against it.

Arguments from the notion of right sensibility to feelings (εὐπάθειαι) and from Stoic definitions of moral terms form the whole of ch. 9. The Stoics concur partially with the observations of chs. 7 and 8 and call shame "modesty," pleasure "joy," and fears "precautions." These euphemisms would not be objectionable if they were referred to the same emotions, distinguished only by their relations to reason. But, in fact, Stoic terminology is confusing and only obscures the basic inconsistency of their conceptions, e.g., sometimes they call "joys" and "precautions" (εὐλαβείας) "right sensibilities to emotion" (εὐπάθειας) instead of ἀπαθείας, using the terms correctly. For they thus affirm that in the souls of the temperate (τοῖς σωφρονοῦσιν), the passions are not suppressed, but only disciplined by reason's action.

Ch. 10 is basically an argument taken from variations in the intensity of passions and is directed against the famous Stoic doctrine that all errors or faults (τὰ ἁμαρτήματα . . . τὰς ἁμαρτίας) are equal. In the case of the emotions, this view is contrary to the evidence. For, according to the Stoics, every emotion is an error. Yet there are great differences in emotions according to their intensity, e.g., Plato's grief at Socrates' death and that of Alexander at Cleitus' death. To minimize this kind of evidence, the Stoics deny that variations of intensity in emotions affect the judgment (κρίσις) in which lies the ability to error (τὸ ἁμαρτητικόν). According to them, only the psychic disturbances which accompany judgment are subject to variations of intensity. There are, nevertheless, differences of degree even between erroneous judgments, e.g., some consider poverty not to be an evil, others regard it a great evil, and still others think it to be the greatest evil. Judgments of value also vary considerably about death and health. Thus it appears that even in judgments there is greater and lesser error. But, finally, the Stoics themselves concede that the irrational is essentially different from judgment. It is in accord with the irrational, they say, that emotion becomes more or less strong. Chrysippus, for example, in claiming that reason is often rejected when we are under the impulsion of another more violent force, recognizes, if not the principle, at least the consequences of the separation between reason and passion.

The division between chs. 10 and 11 is barely discernible, and Plutarch's discussion of Chrysippus reminds him that Plato thought expressions such as "to be better than oneself" or "to be master of oneself" were paradoxical unless there is duality in human nature, a better and a worse part. It is thus clear that he who holds the worse in subjection to the better is "self-controlled," and he who allows the better to be subject to the irrational part of his soul is incontinent and in a state contrary to nature (παρὰ φύσιν). For nature requires that reason, which is divine, have authority over the irrational which arises directly from the body and shares in its passions. That the irrational is merged with the body is shown by impulses which become strong or weak in accord with the body's changes. Thus there are differences of temperament among young and old, the former being more susceptible to the force of desire because of their abundant, hot blood, the latter becoming more rational as the passionate element accompanies the body in its decline. Moreover, the different passions of animals don't depend on the rightness or wrongness of opinions, but on purely physical factors. In human nature also, blushing, paleness, and trembling show that the body takes part in the movements of emotion. But when intellect (τὸ διανοητικόν) acts alone, not accompanied by emotion, the body remains in repose. This fact also makes it clear that there are two parts in the soul which differ from each other in their functions.

The point of departure for ch. 12, the treatise's conclusion, is furnished by the Stoic classification of things according to their principles of organization: a cohesive force (ἕξις), a principle of growth (φύσις), an irrational soul (ἄλογος ψυχή), and a rational soul (ψυχὴ λόγον ἔχουσα). Man participates in all these organizing principles: he is held together by a cohesive force, nurtured by a principle of growth, and as a rational creature he has a portion of the irrational which ought not to be completely eliminated, but only cultivated and educated in a manner that preserves what is good and useful, but suppresses what is harmful and excessive.

The emotions ought to be for reason like subdued and docile horses whose power ought to be used wisely, and not destroyed. Thus cultivated, the emotions become valuable auxilliaries of the virtues, e.g., anger (ὁ θυμός) contributes to courage, hatred of evil (μισοπονηρία) to justice, and righteous indignation (νέμεσις) opposes insolence. In dealing with the emotions, it is necessary, as in all things, to avoid excess: moral virtue arises when equity and moderation (ἐπιείκεια καὶ μετριότης) are produced by reason in the emotional faculties and activities. Desire, fear, pleasure, pain are not blameable in themselves, but only in their excessive manifestations. In fact, if passions were done away with, reason would be too inactive and dull in many persons. This possibility has been recognized by many legislators, Plato and Homer were aware of it, and even Plutarch's opponents, the Stoics, take account of it in their ethics and pedagogy. Also philosophy ought not to neglect the emotions, but to cultivate them, and hence to lead the young on to delight in the honorable and to hate the dishonorable. The education which is fit for the free-born has no greater or fairer end.

II. Plutarch's Treatise and Early Christian Ethics

Plutarch's *virt. mor.* is very much in the Platonic-Aristotelian ethical tradition, a tradition which will have great influence on later Christian thinkers, notably Clement of Alexandria,[8] but which presents a different anthropology and basis for ethical conceptions than is found in the New Testament and the Apostolic Fathers. Plutarch's notion of the bipartite soul, for example, enables him to make subtle distinctions between ἀκρασία-ἀκολασία and σωφροσύνη-ἐγκράτεια, distinctions which seem to have been nonexistent for the early Christians. Yet the emphasis Plutarch places on σωφροσύνη-ἐγκράτεια is one which finds its way into Christian ethics.[9] More specifically, although the term ἐγκράτεια is used only rarely in the New Testament, great importance seems given to it when in Acts 24:25 the moving theme of Paul's address to Felix and Drusilla is "righteousness and self-control" (δικαιοσύνη καὶ ἐγκράτεια). Also in 2 Clem 15:1 the author claims to have given his readers weighty advice concerning "self-control," and this is in

---

[8] See E. F. Osborn, *The Philosophy of Clement of Alexandria* (Cambridge, England, 1957) 96ff.

[9] On σωφροσύνη, see H. North's detailed study, *Sophrosyne*.

keeping with his admonition to "keep the flesh pure." In Herm (Man 1:2 and 6:1) the first commandment after that of "faith" and "reverence of God" is "self-control," and in the dance of the Virtues, "Self-Control: is the daughter of "Faith" and generatrix of all ensuing virutes (Vis 3:8:4f.).[10]

It is, of course, in connection with ethical terms, many of which are taken from popular philosophy, probably the Cynic-Stoic diatribes,[11] and especially with catalogues of vices and virtues, that parallels between Plutarch's treatise and early Christian literature can be found. Catalogues of vices were made by Paul, of the desires and sins that one must avoid, and frequently as in Gal 5:19-23 they are paralleled with a contrasting catalogue of virtues (e.g., Col 3:5-14; Eph 4:31f.; 1 Tim 6:4-11; Jas 3:15-18; cf. also 1 Clem 35:15; 2 Clem 4:3; Herm Sim 9). Compare these with, for example, 447A . . . καὶ γὰρ ἐπιθυμίαν καὶ ὀργὴν καὶ φόβον καὶ τὰ τοιαῦτα πάντα δόξας εἶναι καὶ κρίσεις πονηράς. . . , which is, according to Almqvist, a "zusammenfassender Abschluss eines Tugend- oder Lasterkataloges." [12] Despite the doubtful assumption of Almqvist, as though Plutarch could not think of terms such as these without copying them from some catalogue, the passage in *virt. mor.* is a parallel to catalogues in early Christian literature. These catalogues are often pareneses, and some pareneses are developed with homiletical breadth according to ethical catch-words, e.g., the warning against vices and the exhortation to exercise virtues in 1 Clem is organized about terms such as ζῆλος (chs. 3-6) or ὁμονοία (chs. 20-22). Apropos the Cynic-Stoic diatribe, it is interesting to note that its influence on 1 Clem seems to be great.[13] In these pareneses, however, there is no doctrine of the mean,[14] and whereas Plutarch conceives of moral virtue as a mean between the excesses and defects of the passions, e.g., courage is a mean between cowardice and foolhardiness (see chs. 5 and 6 of this study), for the early Christians, virtues always seem opposed to vices without any

[10] Cf. the use of ἐγκράτεια in the Acts Paul Thec 5 and in *The Sentences of Sextus* (index, s.v.).

[11] See Bultmann, *Der Stil*, and W. Capelle and H. Marrou, *RAC*, s.v. Diatribe, esp. 999ff.

[12] *Plutarch und das Neue Testament*, 116.

[13] See Marrou, *RAC*, s.v. Diatribe, 999-1000, where he cites "Exempla," 1 Clem 55:1; "Aufzählung," 1 Clem 35:5, and "Verbannung," 1 Clem 5:6.

[14] The mean may also have been absent from the diatribe; it is, for example, not attested in Teles; see O. Hense's edition of the fragments, 1909.

thought of excess or defect; instead of the mean, early Christian ethics often uses the "Two Ways" concept which by definition rules out the mean.[15] In the Mandata, for example, Hermas often contrasts virtues against vices: "simplicity" and "evil speaking" (Man 2), "purity" and "adultery" (Man 4), "long-suffering" and "quickness to anger" (Man 5), or "grief" and "joyfulness" (Man 10); cf. Plutarch's lists of means with corresponding excesses and defects at 445. In general, the catalogues of virtues in early Christian literature are not derived from ethical ideals, e.g., that of the mean, nor are they determined by any systematic order. The lists are often associative and loose, generated primarily by the need to advise or warn the Christian community. Plutarch's primary purpose, however, in *virt. mor.* is to refute Stoic ethical theory while maintaining Platonic-Aristotelian doctrines, and whatever parenetic elements there may be are subsidiary to his polemic.

Plutarch has, of course, a pedagogical interest in moral virtue. At the conclusion of the treatise, for example, he declares that there is no nobler end than to have the young "delight in honorable and to be annoyed with dishonorable things" (452). A similar concern with character education is evident even earlier in the treatise, notably 443D where Plutarch accepts the Aristotelian notion of ethical virtue as a settled condition (ἕξις) of the soul's irrational capacity which has been educated well by reason (ὑπὸ τοῦ λόγου παιδαγωγηθῇ, 443D); cf. the very different sentiment of Barn 21:6, "and be taught of God (γίνεσθε δὲ θεοδίδακτον), seeking out what the Lord requires of you." Aristotle's discussion of goodness of character in *EN* 1103a14-b25 immediately comes to mind: as we learn to be builders by building or harp players by playing the harp, we become just or temperate by just or temperate acts. Morality is a matter of skill, ἐπιστήμη or "know how" as Socrates had taught, and it is hard, if not impossible, to find a similar conception in early Christian thought where ἐπιστήμη is a "gift of God," not something acquired by man on his own initiative, e.g., at Barn 21:5.[16] Moreover, although "good works" are demanded, it is often in conjunction with abstention from "passions of the flesh," e.g., 1 Pet 2:11f., not the proper education of these passions (see the comments on ch. 12 of this study). Ultimately, of course, all ethical demands are related to the commandment of

[15] See W. Michaelis, *TDNT*, s.v. ὁδός, esp. C.2.a and D (5:70 and 93ff.).
[16] See Bauer, s.v. ἐπιστήμη.

love: "beloved, let us love one another . . . herein is love, not that we loved God, but that he loved us, and sent his son. . . ," 1 John 4:7f. In other words, virtue seems understood both under the demand for sanctification and as a requirement for love.[17] Thus the virtues are not singled out as traits of character, but as modes of conduct in fellowship with others. On the whole, there seems to be no thought of character education in early Christian thought, and it is probably significant that ἦθος appears seldom in early Christian literature, and that one of its few occurrences is in Paul's quotation from a play of Menander: φθείρουσιν ἤθη χρῆσθ' ὁμιλίαι κακαί (1 Cor 15:33).

For the early Christians, virtues are basically not derived from an ideal concept of humanity, though account should be taken of Christ as "the Second Man" (1 Cor 15:45ff.; cf. the notion that Adam is a τύπος of "him that was to come," Rom 5:14), but are ultimately rooted in the salvation drama initiated by God, and herein is a significant difference between Plutarch's view of ethical virtue and early Christian views on virtue.[18] Granted Plutarch would also claim that his ethical doctrine is ultimately rooted in God, there is nonetheless a difference of emphasis. Certainly in this treatise Plutarch's ethical conceptions are based primarily on an ideal concept of humanity, and this is perhaps best shown by his acceptance of the Platonic-Aristotelian doctrine of the bipartite soul, a soul in which reason controls, but does not destroy the emotions, and in which an inner harmony is achieved by habit and as a result of the subservience of the emotions to reason (see, for example, 445Bf.) Plutarch's thought in this treatise is, without doubt, dualistic. Not only is the soul two-fold, but man's nature is two-fold, a blend of body and soul (see 441D-E). There is, of course, in Plutarch's thought, especially in ch. 11, a close connection between the irrational part of the soul and the body, the irrational deriving its origin from the body (450E), but in general, Plutarch's dualism of body-soul and irrational-rational is clear and emphasized in the treatise. It is, however, difficult to compare this dualism with early Christian concepts of body and soul largely because the usage of these terms is fairly complex, and σῶμα, in particular, has

[17] See Bultmann's discussion in *TNT*, 2:218ff.

[18] See esp. R. Bultmann's remarks in *Jesus and the Word* (New York, 1958) 108ff., 133-37, and 198ff. Cf. H. Conzelmann, *An Outline of the Theology of the New Testament* (New York, 1969) 90ff.

a number of religious meanings, e.g., the immortal body or the church as the body of Christ, which would perhaps be incomprehensible to Plutarch. There are, of course, sayings such as Matt 10:28 that persecutors can kill the body but not the soul, or Heb 13:3 according to which man is in the body: . . .αὐτοὶ ὄντες ἐν σώματι; cf. 13:17, "they watch for your souls." The thought of these verses is close to the Platonic distinction of body and soul, yet the terminology seems to embrace the whole man as seen from different perspectives.[19] By the time of the Christian apologists, the division into σῶμα and ψυχή is common, and there is even reference to the irrational passions of the soul which the body follows.[20] But it is difficult to find any clear emphasis on the σῶμα-ψυχή division in the NT and Apostolic Fathers with the exception of Diognetus' famous simile (ch. 7) to wit, that what the soul is in the body, Christians are in the world. The soul is not of the body, it is invisible, immortal, and though the soul loves the body, it is hated by the latter. Apart from Diognetus' letter, there is no clearly formulated division of man into body and soul in early Christian thought. Even Paul who uses σῶμα as the most comprehensive term to characterize man's existence, did not dualistically put body and soul in opposition to each other. In sum, the "body-soul" contrast is rarely found in early Christian literature; instead, there is the σάρξ-πνεῦμα dualism.[21]

Not only is man not conceived of dualistically in early Christian thought, but the ψυχή, which for Paul at least is the knowing, willing self, is not viewed as bipartite or tripartite in nature. If Bultmann's analysis of Paul's anthropology is correct, man can be viewed as either ψυχή, σῶμα, or πνεῦμα, but he is basically a living unity. Νοῦς, for example, occurs in Paul, but it does not mean "mind" or "intellect" as a special faculty or part of the soul.[22] Potentially, of course, it designates man's higher nature as opposed to flesh or σάρξ, but it too is capable of being corrupted (Rom 1:28). In general, according to Bultmann's elaborate analysis, the "mind" in Pauline thought means the whole of self conceived as subject of its thinking, feeling, and judging, whereas

---

[19] See E. Schweizer's discussion in *TDNT*, s.v. σῶμα, D.1, 3-4 (7:1058f.).

[20] Athenag Leg 1:4 and 36:1f.; see also E. Schweizer, *TDNT*, s.v. σῶμα, E.2.a (7:1084).

[21] See Bultmann, *TNT*, 1:192f. and 232ff. and 330ff.

[22] Ibid., 209-211.

the "body" is the same self regarded as the object of these activities.

In some respects, early Christian conceptions of the body-soul are closer to the Stoic position which Plutarch attacks in the treatise. First, the Stoics, at least of the old Stoa and those mentioned specifically by Plutarch, Zeno and Chrysippus, were not dualists, and mind or soul was, according to them, ultimately reducible to the corporeal, or more precisely, reason is a body because it acts and the thing that is subjected to its action or acted upon is also a body and called "matter." [23] Moreover, the soul consists of pure reason, and one does not explain passion by attributing it to an irrational faculty. Passion is a reason or judgment, but it is an "irrational reason." [24] In other words, just as there is no real distinction between soul and body, so there is no distinction between reason and passion. These are simply "modes" of one and the same substance viewed from different standpoints. It is, of course, the Stoic failure to distinguish reason from passion which most concerns Plutarch in this treatise, and insofar as the Stoic view is similar to early Christian thought, it is legitimate to assume that Plutarch would have polemicized against Christian authors on this matter as well.

There is another similarity between Stoic views and early Christian doctrines, and that concerns the notion of wrong-doing or "sin" (ἁμαρτία). In ch. 10 of the treatise, Plutarch mentions the Stoic belief that all sins are equal, and although he does not attack the view in detail in this treatise, it is clear that Plutarch is against it (see 449D and *prof. virt.*, esp. 76A-B). In early Christianity the problem of sin after baptism was especially of great concern, e.g., in Hermas, and if sin is an offense or rebellion against God, there can be no basis for a more or less (that all sins were equal seems to have been believed by most Christians, and some rabbis; see the commentary on ch. 10). Sin is, of course, universal (Rom 3:23), and is often bound up with the flesh (σάρξ). If Bultmann's exegesis of Phil 3:3-7 is correct, the attitude which orients itself by "flesh" is the self-reliant attitude of the one who trusts in his own strength and in what he considers controllable by himself.[25] And human self-reliance and self-seeking are bound up with "passions" and "desires" which, according to Gal 5:24,

[23] See Diogenes Laertius 7. 134-139.
[24] See *SVF*, III, nos. 377-420.
[25] Bultmann, *TNT*, 1:240.

the man of faith has crucified. This human attitude so bound up with sin is specifically described by Paul in the verb "desire": the divine law is "you shall not desire" (οὐκ ἐπιθυμήσεις). But according to Paul (Rom 7:7f.), this law only arouses sinful desires. That these Christian views of sin have some similarity to Stoic doctrines, seems clear. In particular, the negative judgment on passions and desires is not unlike the Stoic ideal of apathy. The universality of sin is like the Stoic belief that all men are fools or at best progressing to virtue; if one ever attains virtue, "it is late and at the very sunset of his days." [26] Lastly, the Stoic view that all sins are equal is like the basically uncompromising attitude to degrees of sin found in early Christianity.

One value of this treatise for students of early Christian thought lies in its transitional nature, that is, it employs a terminology and concepts, especially of a Platonic-Aristotelian provenance, which will be incorporated into later Christian thought, e.g., Clement of Alexandria, but which are often not found in the New Testament and Apostolic Fathers. It is primarily insofar as the latter drew on popular philosophical terminology that significant points of contact can be established between them and Plutarch. It may well be that the main vehicle for the philosophical ethical concepts of early Christianity was the diatribe, and there is thus a common terminology to the extent that the Platonic-Aristotelian and the Cynic-Stoic traditions overlap. Certain doctrines, however, such as the dualism of the body and soul or the bipartite nature of the latter, are not clearly present in most early Christian literature. M. Pohlenz has observed that Stoicism probably takes its impetus from a Semitic culture, especially its monotheism,[27] and it is thus not surprising that there are perhaps significant similarities between the Stoic position attacked by Plutarch in this treatise and early Christian views. There are, of course, also similarities between notions of Plutarch and those of early Christianity, e.g., the emphasis on ἐγκράτεια, but these are probably due to whatever common culture existed between the Hellenic world and the Christian community. To be sure, it seems to be the case that the more Platonic and Aristotelian Plutarch is, the farther he is from

[26] *SVF*, I, 529.

[27] *Die Stoa* (Göttingen, 1948) 1:1f. A. A. Long, however, sees nothing in Stoicism which requires the hypothesis of Semitic influences. See his *Hellenistic Philosophy* (London, 1974) 113.

early Christian thought, while the more Cynic-Stoic he is, the closer he comes to early Christianity. In this treatise and others, he opposes Stoicism. He attacks its intellectualism, because it fails to take the emotions seriously. In the diatribes of the early itinerant preachers, the same case was made against the Stoics, and early Christianity was also opposed to Stoic intellectualism. Certainly a major similarity between Plutarch and the early Christian thinkers was a serious regard for human emotions. The more practical and the less theoretical Plutarch is, the closer he comes to early Christian ethical thought.

The following commentary attempts, chapter by chapter, to illustrate in more detail the differences and similarities between this treatise and early Christian literature. The commentary is based on the chapter summaries given at the beginning of this study where the treatise is analyzed in its own terms. In the attempt to establish parallels, linguistic and conceptual, it is easy to lose sight of the fact that despite his appeal for later Christian authors, Plutarch, as a priest of Delphi, was probably not an *anima naturaliter christiana*.

Ch. 1

Although Plutarch is obviously thinking of the Aristotelian distinction between ethical and intellectual virtue at the outset of his treatise, the terminology coincides only partially with Aristotle's: for Aristotle θεωρητικός applies only to a kind of life,[28] and the virtue opposed to ethical virtue is always called διανοητική. Plutarch's substitution of θεωρητικός for διανοητικός probably reflects the influence of the Stoic Panaitios who seems first to have used the expression θεωρητικὴ ἀρετή.[29] Moreover, Plutarch's formula for ethical virtue which has passion for its matter (ὕλη) and the rule fixed by reason (λόγος) for its form (εἶδος), is not found in Aristotle. Nevertheless, the first chapter seems to show Peripatetic influence, especially the doxographical examination announced at the chapter's end.[30]

Plutarch's traditional notion of ethical virtue (cf. λεγομένης καὶ

[28] See *EN* 1.5.1095 where the life of contemplation is listed with those of pleasure and politics.

[29] See Diogenes Laertius 7. 92.

[30] Doxographies are also found in other works of Plutarch, notably *Is. et Os.* 360Eff., *def. or.* 415Aff., *Is. et Os.* 369Dff., *an proc.* 1026Bf., and ibid. chs. 2-8.

δοκούσης) and many of the concepts employed in ch. 1, as well as in the rest of the treatise, bear little, if any, clear correspondence to early Christian notions. The key term, ἀρετή, in the sense of moral excellence or virtue, appears infrequently in early Christian literature, and no distinction is made between ethical and intellectual or theoretical virtue (ἠθική and θεωρητική do not occur in Bauer). Only twice in the NT ἀρετή refers to human virtue (its occurrences in 1 Pet 2:9 and 2 Pet 1:3 refer probably to manifestations of divine power). Thus in Phil 4:8 . . . εἴ τις ἀρετὴ καὶ εἴ τις ἔπαινος ταῦτα λογίζεσθε, where Lohmeyer tried unsuccessfully to divorce ἀρετή and the preceding words, ἀληθῆ, σεμνά, δίκαια, ἁγνά, κτλ., from non-Jewish religious and philosophical thought and to keep them wholly within the OT milieu, on the basis that every term occurs in the LXX.[31] But the LXX is not identical with the OT milieu, and Phil 4:8 may show the influence of diatribe language.[32] O. Bauernfeind thought the reference to ἀρετή in Phil 4:8 more religious than secular and also saw an echo of the LXX usage in which ἀρετή describes, notably in Mac, the "fidelity of heroes of faith in life and death." [33] But his contrast of "religious" and "secular" is of little use.[34] In the other NT occurrence where ἀρετή means moral virtue, 2 Pet 1:5: ἐπιχορηγήσατε ἐν τῇ πίστει ὑμῶν τὴν ἀρετήν, ἐν δὲ τῇ ἀρετῇ τὴν γνῶσιν, the term is closely connected with the holiness of God. In Christian literature after the NT, ἀρετή is found in Herm Man 1:2, Sim 6:1:4 and Sim 8:10:3, but with a sense approximating δικαιοσύνη, and contrary to the classical doctrine of the cardinal virtues which makes δικαιοσύνη logically subordinate to ἀρετή.[35] In brief, what the early Christians emphasized in connection with "virtue" is not human achievement or merit, but the acts and being of God, and although Plutarch, in accord with his Platonic-Aristotelian heritage, affirmed the divinity of reason (see 450D), virtue remains basically a human accomplishment. In other words, a basic difference between Plutarch and the early Christians concerns not so much what ἀρετή is, but how to obtain it.

---

[31] E. Lohmeyer, *Der Brief an die Philipper*, 9th ed. (Göttingen, 1953).

[32] See A. Oltramare, *Les Origines de la diatribe romaine* (Geneva, 1926) 13f., on the use of exhortation, and *PECL* 1:310-11.

[33] See *TDNT*, s.v. ἀρετή, B.

[34] See M. Smith's incisive critical remark on Bauernfeind's discussion, *PECL* 1:30.

[35] In 2 Clem 10:1 ἀρετή is connected with belief in God and doing his will.

No distinction is made between ethical and theoretical virtue in early Christian literature, and thus it is not surprising that Plutarch's corresponding distinction between matter and form is without parallel. Ὕλη occurs, but primarily in the sense of earthly, perishable stuff, sometimes with the connotation of what is hostile to God, e.g., Ign Rom 6:2, and never as the philosophical complement of εἶδος which is used only of outward appearance or shape, sight or vision, and once of kind, ἀπὸ παντὸς εἴδους πονηροῦ, 1 Thes 5:22.

Plutarch considers the emotions or passions (πάθη) the matter of ethical virtue, and λόγος, the rule fixed by reason (not reason itself) to be its form.[36] Now, the term πάθος occurs in the NT only in the Pauline literature, and primarily with a sexual reference: in Rom 1:26 the πάθη ἀτιμίας are the vices of homosexuality, and in Col 3:5, it probably denotes erotic passions.[37] In neither case is the term specifically oriented to the Stoic concept, [38] and the ἐν πάθει ἐπιθυμίας of 1 Thes 4:5 doesn't mean ἐπιθυμία as πάθος, but πάθος, as sexual passion arising from ἐπιθυμία. In brief, ἐπιθυμία is a subjective, not an appositional genitive. In the Apostolic Fathers, πάθος often refers, for example, fifteen times in Ignatius, to "suffering" or "death," with special reference to Jesus' death. It can also refer to the evil of adultery or bad temper, e.g., Herm Man 4:1:6 and Sim 6:5:5, but the Aristotelian concept of the emotions or passions of anger, fear, confidence, joy, etc., which forms the basis for understanding Plutarch's use of the term,[39] is wholly lacking in early Christian literature.

Finally, although the early Christian use of λόγος covers a number of somewhat different meanings connected with the basic idea of "word" or "speech," there seem to be only two occurrences which have a sense similar to Plutarch's use, i.e., the rule fixed by reason. Both occur in Acts and seem to refer to "rational consideration" or "the result of deliberation": τίνι λόγῳ, "for what reason," in 10:29 and κατὰ λόγον "with reason," in 18:14.

Plutarch's πάθη/λόγος = ὕλη/εἶδος is thus without parallel in early Christian thought, and although he affirmed, in accord with

[36] See Babut, *Vertu*, 130.

[37] On the Cynic condemnation of sexual passion, see Diogenes Laertius 6. 67.

[38] See W. Michaelis, *TDNT*, s.v. πάσχω-πάθος, 4-5 (5:928) and M. Pohlenz, "Paulus und die Stoa," *ZNW* 42 (1949) 82.

[39] See, for example, *EN* 2.4.1105b 19f.

his Platonic-Aristotelian heritage, the divinity of reason (see 450E), virtue is for him basically a human accomplishment and very much bound up with his concept of the human ψυχή which will be examined later.

Ch. 2

There is nothing in early Christian literature comparable to the doxography of this chapter.[40] According to B. Wyss, the earliest Christian author who shows familiarity with doxographical literature is Athenagoras (177 A.D.), and part of the interest in doxography was sparked by the Gnostic heresy.[41] The inventory of moral terms used by various Stoic thinkers, especially Chrysippus, has perhaps a superficial resemblance to the ethical lists of the NT which may go back to Stoic teachings.[42] But the classical doctrine of the four cardinal virtues, which forms the background for Plutarch's survey of previous thought on the nature of virtue, has little or no parallel in early Christian writers (however, in Wis 8:7 there does seem to be a reference to them: σωφροσύνη, δικαιοσύνη, ἀνδρεία, and φρόνησις or σοφία). For of these virtues mentioned by Plutarch, ἀνδρεία is found not at all in ECL. Paul does, of course, admonish Christians to ἀνδρίζεσθε (perhaps echoing the LXX) in the face of the powers of darkness, 1 Cor 16:13, and the neuter plural, ἀνδρεῖα, appears, perhaps paradoxically, in 1 Clem 55:3 in connection with women's heroic deeds, e.g., Judith and Esther. But at least as a word, ἀνδρεία is not found in ECL. The other cardinal virtues are found in ECL, and a discussion of their meanings is in order.

Σωφροσύνη occurs in early Christian literature often with other virtues, e.g., with ἁγνεία in Ign Eph 10:3, with ἁγνεία, ἐγκράτεια, and other virtues in 1 Clem 64. The latter passage is one of the early Christian ethical lists, and the linking of ἐγκράτεια with σωφροσύνη is especially interesting since it seems reminiscent of Plato's view of self-control (σωφροσύνη) as the mastery (ἐγκράτεια) of pleasures and desires (*R.* 430E). The notion that σωφροσύνη is a special virtue of women (see Plut. *coniug. praec.* 139C and 140C and *amat.* 767E and 769B) and that it tends to be understood especially

[40] That it is doxographical is shown by Babut, *Vertu*, 3.
[41] See B. Wyss, *RAC*, s.v. Doxographie, esp. 204ff.
[42] For bibliography on ethical lists, see *PECL* 1, index, s.v. Lists of vices, virtues, and *IDB*, s.v. Lists, 5.

as the restraint and control of sexual desires, thus taking on the sense of "chastity," seems to be widespread in the early church. But the meaning of "moderation" or "self-control," as in 1 Clem 62:2,[43] seems closest to Plutarch's in this treatise.

The concept of δικαιοσύνη has a long history prior to Plutarch and, beginning with Plato until the early Christian authors, has a complexity of meanings. In the NT there are contexts where the term becomes almost equivalent to Christianity, e.g., Matt 5:10, 1 Pet 2:24. In the Pauline writings, it does not seem connected with Hellenistic doctrines of virtue, δικαιοσύνη never occurring in statements about ἀρετή though 1 Tim 6:11 and 2 Tim 2:22 are similar to Greek ethical lists, and in both cases δικαιοσύνη signifies right conduct and is listed with other Christian characteristics like faith, charity, and peace.[44] In passages such as Herm Man 1:2; Sim 6:1:4, however, δικαιοσύνη is mentioned in connection with ἀρετή, and the believer in God shall put on "every virtue of righteousness" (ἐνδύσῃ πᾶσαν ἀρετὴν δικαιοσύνης), and there is in this phrase perhaps a hint of the unity of virtue like that reported by Plutarch concerning Menedemus. Something not unlike the unity of virtue is also found in Paul, who in Gal 5:22ff. calls "virtues" like joy, goodness, faith, meekness, temperance, the "fruit of the spirit" (ὁ καρπὸς τοῦ πνεύματος; cf. 3:20ff., one God . . . one Christ), and in the Sermon on the Mount (pre-Matthean tradition), which sums up Christian ethics in the so-called Golden Rule (Matt 7:12).[45]

The other virtues of Stoic thinkers reported by Plutarch, Ariston's "health" (ὑγίεια) and Zeno's "prudence" (φρόνησις), have no parallels in Christian thought. The primary sense of ὑγίεια seems to be physical health, and with the exception of the Pastorals, ὑγιαίνειν and ὑγιής occur nowhere else in the NT. There they seem to mean "to be sound" and "sound," and characterize the content of Christian preaching (cf. *aud. poet.* 20F, "for these are the sound (ὑγιαίνουσαι) and true opinions about the gods." [46] Φρόνησις occurs

---

[43] For further discussion, see U. Luck, *TDNT*, s.v. σώφρων, C-D (7:1102f.).

[44] See G. Schrenk, *TDNT*, s.v. δικαιοσύνη, E.2.1 (2:210).

[45] Cf. Judaism where rabbis discuss the question as to what is the "unity" in all the prescriptions of the Torah; see Mark 10:17ff.; 12:28ff.; and Gal 5:14.

[46] For further discussion, see M. Dibelius-H. Conzelmann, *The Pastoral Epistles* (Philadelphia, 1972) 24f.

only twice in the NT, and in liturgically shaped texts: Luke 1:17 and in Eph 1:8 where God's grace endows the believer with pure wisdom and understanding. In post-apostolic literature, it occurs in Just Dial 1:6; 23:2; 48:1, etc., esp. in debate with Judaism, and it seems to mean primarily a way of thinking or frame of mind (see Herm Sim 9:18) though it is interesting to note that defenders of Zeno claimed that he used φρόνησις in the sense of knowledge, ἐπιστήμη, and the latter appears as one of the seven women or Christian virtues in Herm Vis 3:8:5.[47]

Of the many virtues in which Chrysippus believed, only two, πραότης and εὐτραπελία, are mentioned in ECL, though the latter term is always used in a bad sense, "coarse jesting" or "buffoonery," Eph 5:4. Πραότης could, of course, be considered a characteristic of the Christian, esp. of the bishop Ign Trall 3:2. A variant form of μεγαλότης, μεγαλειότης, occurs in the sense of grandeur in ECL, but only of a divinity, e.g., Luke 9:43, Diogn 10:5. Chrysippus' other virtues, χαριεντότης, ἐσθλότης, καλότης, ἐπιδεξιότης, and εὐαπαντησία, mentioned by Plutarch, do not appear in ECL.

Much of the vocabulary used by Plutarch in surveying the thought of Stoic thinkers is technical and philosophical, e.g., οὐσία which occurs in ECL only in the sense of "property," "wealth" (Luke 15:21), or ποιότης which does not occur at all. Two words used by Plutarch, λευκοθέα and μελανοθέα, are probably hapax, and he is perhaps the originator of the comparison of virtue with a knife or fire when illustrating Aristotle's doctrine.[48]

Ch. 3

A basic assumption of this chapter, and indeed of Plutarch's concept of ethical virtue, is the two-fold nature of man: man is a blend (μῖξις) of body and soul, 441D, and the soul itself is two-fold, consisting of the rational and passionate elements, the latter subdivided into the appetitive and spirited parts. Neither belief seems to be present in or at least clearly formulated in early Christian thought.

First, although there are passages in the NT suggesting a dualism of ψυχή and σῶμα, e.g., Matt 10:28 and Heb 13:3 according to which man is in the body,[49] these are not simply the Platonic

[47] See G. Bertram, *TDNT*, s.v. φρήν, D.4-E.

[48] See Babut, *Vertu*, 132.

[49] For other references, see Bauer, s.v. ψυχή.

distinction of body and soul since both terms seem to embrace the whole man as seen from different viewpoints,[50] and there is no clear negative evaluation of the σῶμα in early Christian thought. It is not until Diogn 6:1-8 that Stoic and Platonic ideas are used and that there is some parallel to Plutarch's dualism.[51] The soul permeates the whole body (vs. 2) and is an invisible being caught in the visible body (vss. 4 and 7). The author's concern is to envision Christians as the soul of the cosmos: they are in the cosmos, but not of it. There is an obvious influence here of the parallelism between the human body and cosmos, a good example of which is Plutarch's discussion of *Ti.* 35Af. at 441E.

Second, there is no clear indication of the tripartite (or bipartite) soul in ECL. Ψυχή can function, of course, as the seat and center of man's inner life in its various aspects as, for example, the center of feeling and emotion, but Plutarch's vocabulary in describing tripartition, especially the terms τὸ λογιστικόν, τὸ παθητικόν, θυμοειδές or τὸ ἄλογον, is not found in ECL. Moreover, there is also no clear notion of the basic dual nature of the soul, that is, the contrast between the rational and the irrational. The conflict between them briefly mentioned by Plutarch at 442A-B, however, is not unlike that noted by Paul in his discussion of sin, especially Rom 7.[52] According to W. D. Davies, the Rabbinic doctrine of the two impulses, or *yetzer ha-ra* and *yetzer ha-tob*, probably underlies Paul's discussion.[53] This is, however, questionable since Paul does not speak of two impulses, but of the conflict between the flesh (σάρξ) by which he serves the "law of sin" and the mind (νοῦς) by which he serves the "law of God" (7:25) where νοῦς takes up the "inward man" (ἔσω ἄνθρωπος) of vs. 22. Paul's use of νοῦς —it occurs almost exclusively in his writings and in the Pastorals— as the thinking, reasoning, or purposing aspect of man's consciousness, seems to be an equivalent of "mind" or "reason" in the Greek philosophical sense.[54] C. H. Dodd, for example, draws a parallel between Rom 7:15, "I do not act as I want to act; on the contrary, I do what I detest," and Aristotle's view of ἀκρασία in which a person knows what is right, but fails to do it, and further notes

[50] See E. Schweizer, *TDNT*, s.v. σῶμα, D.I.3.
[51] Ibid., E.1.a.
[52] See also Rom 1, 2, and 5:12ff.
[53] W. D. Davies, *Paul and Rabbinic Judaism* (London, 1958) 23ff.
[54] See Bultmann, *TNT*, 1:211ff.

that νοῦς can be characterized as " 'reason' for the Greek word is the one current in this sense in the philosophers." [55] Unlike the "flesh," νοῦς is related to the higher, spiritual order of creation, and vss. 22, 23, and 25 describe the state of one who has reached despair in the moral conflict; he affirms the moral ideal (the law) intellectually with the reason, but has not succeeded in having harmonious desires for the ideal. His impulses remain attached to unworthy sentiments (πᾶσαν ἐπιθυμίαν, vs. 8). Now although Plutarch usually speaks in this treatise of τὸ νοερόν or τὸ λογιστικόν,[56] he, like his master Plato, was aware of the conflict in man's ψυχή between its higher and lower elements. In sum, Plutarch's (and Plato's) view of the human ψυχή or person as divided into two (or three) parts of which the λόγος, τὸ νοερόν, or λογισμός is the highest, finds a parallel in ECL, expecially in Rom 7.

Much of the other ethical and psychological vocabulary used by Plutarch in this chapter is not found in ECL, or if it occurs, it seems to be without technical meaning. For example, in 441C-D, διάθεσις is not found at all in ECL; δύναμις is used in a non-technical sense, "ability," e.g., 2 Cor 8:3, but not as potentiality for rational or irrational capacities;[57] ἡγεμονικόν is used to qualify the Spirit in 1 Clem 18:32; ἕξις is used only once, in Heb 5:45, and there means "exercise" or "practice," not the skill or settled disposition acquired by practice; λόγος and its opposite ἄλογος occur, but not with Plutarch's meanings, the latter term used only in connection with animals, "like unreasoning animals" in 2 Pet 2:12 and Jude 10 (once in the trivial sense of "absurd," "this is absurd to me" in Acts 25:27). Παθητικός doesn't occur and ὀρεξίς exists only in the sense of sexual desire (see Rom 1:27). Διάνοια and ὁρμή occur, but with no special meanings.[58]

There are, however, some similarities of vocabulary, and possibly of thought, which should be noted, and they are as follows:

441C: according to Plutarch, the Stoics agree that virtue is reason which is "firm and unshaken" (βέβαιος καὶ ἀμετάπτωτος); cf. Paul's admonition to his brethren to be firm and unshakeable (ἑδραῖοι. . . ἀμετακίνητοι) in 1 Cor 15:58;

[55] C. H. Dodd, *The Epistle of Paul to the Romans* (New York, 1932) 113f.

[56] Cf. Diogn 2:9, "man has the power to feel (sense) and think" . . . αἴσθησιν ἔχει καὶ λογισμόν; other uses of λογισμός in ECL generally mean no more than "calculations" or "thought"; see Bauer, s.v. λογισμός.

[57] See *EN* 2.1103a 26ff.

[58] See Bauer, s.v. διάνοια and ὁρμή.

442A: Plutarch's ὁμοιοπαθής used in connection with man's soul and the world's soul is found in Acts 14:15 and Jas 5:17, but in regard to human feelings;

Plutarch's use of ἄτακτος to describe the passionate part of the soul is used to describe the undisciplined φορά or impulse in Diogn 9:1;

442B: the nutritive and vegetative parts of man's soul, i.e., its irrational parts, are mere "offshoots of the flesh" (τῆς σαρκὸς ἐκβεβλάστηκε), a notion of σάρξ not unlike that of Paul; [59]

442C: Plutarch uses the verb κατασχηματίζεσθαι to describe the conformity of the soul's passionate part to the rational; cf. Rom 12:2 where Paul admonishes the brethren not to be conformed (συσχηματίζεσθε) to the world, and 1 Pet 1:14.

Ch. 4

In this chapter Plutarch begins to quote from the poets of antiquity in support of and to illustrate his own opinions. He does this not only in the remainder of the treatise, but in many, if not all, of his other works. His knowledge of previous literature was immense,[60] but little of the Greek poetic tradition can be found in early Christian literature.

The examples used to show the conformity of the irrational to reason are taken from sexual experience, dining, music, and animal breeding. Most are, however, without parallel in early Christian literature with the exception of two similarities: a) the mention of unclean and unlawful food in 442F reminds one of Jewish dietary laws (cf. Plutarch's καθαρῶν τι. . .νομίμων with Acts 10:15 and Mark 7:19),[61] though the adjective νόμιμος is not applied to food in ECL; b) Plutarch's mention of lyres, pipes and flutes as void of life (ἄψυχα) is very similar to 1 Cor 14:7 where Paul speaks of flute and "harp" (κιθάρα) without life (ἄψυχα) giving sound. The πηκτίς and λύρα are not mentioned in ECL, but Paul knows the "flute" (αὐλός), and the κιθάρα was an instrument not unlike the "lyre." [62] Plutarch later uses an example from music (444E) to illustrate a point (see also 451F and 452B), and there is a general

---

[59] See Bultmann, *TNT*, 1:239ff.

[60] See, for example, H. Schläpfer, *Plutarch und die klassischen Dichter* (Zürich, 1950) and Helmbold and O'Neil.

[61] On dietary laws, see also *PECL* 1:301ff.

[62] See also *PECL* 1:193.

similarity between his appparent interest in music and Paul's use of instruments for metaphorical or rhetorical purposes.[63]

There are some minor but interesting similarities in language between this chapter and ECL:

442D: cf, Plutarch's use of τυπικαῖς in regard to indirect actions and τυπικῶς ("by way of example") in 1 Cor 10:11;

443E: according to Plutarch, neither reason nor law allows us to "touch" (θιγεῖν) beautiful girls and boys; cf. Col 2:21 with its reference to the human regulations, "grasp not, taste not, touch not" (μηδὲ θίγῃς);

443B: Plutarch's reference to training animals by "breeding and teaching" (τροφῇ καὶ διδασκαλίᾳ) bears a slight similarity to Paul's claim to have been "reared" (ἀνατεθραμμένος) in Tarsus and "taught" (πεπαιδευμένος) in the law of his fathers, Acts 22:3;

443C: cf. Plutarch's use of συνήθεια with 1 Cor 11:16 (see Bauer, s.v.).

But much of the language of this chapter, especially that of the last paragraph (443C-D), cannot be found in ECL, e.g., ὀργιλότης, αἰσχυντηλία, and θαρραλεότης. Indeed the entire conception of ethical virtue as a quality of the irrational (ποιότης τοῦ ἀλόγου), and that ethical virtues are not the absence of emotion (οὐκ ἀπαθείας), but due proportions and means of the emotions (συμμετρίας παθῶν καὶ μεσότητας) is without parallel in ECL. The importance of Plutarch's position is that, unlike the Stoics, he takes human emotions seriously and tries to integrate them into ethics. Christianity has the concept of ἀγάπη to integrate ethics and emotions, and it is interesting that Paul and other early Christian thinkers never espouse the Stoic doctrine of ἀπάθεια.[64]

Ch. 5

Much of this chapter is based on the distinction between σοφία and φρόνησις, or theoretical and practical reason.[65] Both terms occur in ECL, especially σοφία. That they correspond, however, to Plutarch's usage is very doubtful. First, φρόνησις is used in a nontechnical manner and seems to mean primarily a "way of thinking"

---

[63] See 1 Cor 13 and 14:8 with its reference to the σάλπιγξ; also *PECL* 1:193.

[64] See M. Pohlenz, "Paulus und die Stoa," *ZNW* 42 (1949) 69-104.

[65] Cf. *EN* 6.5-8. 1140a 24-1142a 30.

or "attitude" or "insight, intelligence." [66] But for Plutarch a task of φρόνησις (444C) is to eliminate the defects and excesses of the emotions and to deliberate concerning things that can be otherwise or are doubtful, to come down among things that are full of error and confusion (πράγματα πλάνης μεστὰ καὶ ταραχῆς) and to mingle with chance things (τυχηροῖς). These latter terms apply not only to the realm of human action, but probably to the whole sublunary world. Now, human deception, error (πλάνη) was certainly known to the early Christians,[67] but the notion of τυχηρά, the accidental or the realm of chance, and τύχη as a whole, seems foreign to ECL (τύχη occurs only in Mart Pol, "to swear by the fortune of Caesar," 9:2, 10:1, and τυχηρός not at all). Second, although the concept of σοφία is a very complex one in ECL, there is no usage that quite corresponds to Plutarch's notion of it as concerned with things that remain ever the same and are unchanging, although perhaps its use in Barn 6:10, "wisdom and understanding of the Lord's own secrets," . . .σοφίαν καὶ νοῦν. . .τῶν κρυφίων, and the notion of it as the wisdom which God imparts to men,[68] comes close to Plutarch's view of it (444D) as a power by which the most divine (θειότατον) and blessed part of knowledge (ἐπιστήμη) becomes possible for us (the notion of σοφία as originating in the νοῦς is not unlike that in Barn 6:10 where νοῦς occurs with it; also Barn 2:3 and 21:5 where σοφία is linked with ἐπιστήμη). There are also contexts in ECL where σοφία is used in connection with the demands made by life and seems to mean something like good judgment or "practical wisdom" (Acts 6:3 and the other passages cited in Bauer), in which case it is almost the equivalent of Plutarch's φρόνησις and contrary to his understanding of σοφία. In brief, Plutarch's distinction between theoretical and practical wisdom, as well as its corresponding objects, i.e., things absolute and things relative to us, is not found in ECL.

One reason, of course, that there is no clear distinction between φρόνησις and σοφία in ECL is that for the early Christians, many of them with a Jewish background, wisdom is always "practical" (see, for example, Exod 35:30ff. or Eccl 7:23). A similar view is in the Socratic-Cynic tradition,[69] and Paul uses the same term, σοφία,

[66] See Herm Sim 9:17:2a, b, 4; 9:18:4 where the "mind" of the nations is manifold (ποικιλή).

[67] See Bauer, s.v. πλάνη.

[68] See Bauer, s.v. σοφία.

[69] See Diogenes Laertius 6.11ff. and 73.

when distinguishing the "wisdom of this world" from the "wisdom of God" at 1 Cor 1:20.

Other terms used in connection with σοφία and φρόνησις in this chapter also do not occur in ECL: ἐπιστημονικὸν καὶ θεωρητικόν, βουλευτικὸν καὶ πρακτικόν, παθητικόν, αὐτοτελής, and surely the distinction between τὰ μὲν ἁπλῶς ἔχοντα and τὰ δὲ πῶς ἔχοντα is without parallel in ECL. It is also interesting to note that in discussing the nature of theoretical wisdom, Plutarch uses a simile taken from geometry, but no familiarity with geometry is found in ECL.[70]

This chapter introduces the familiar Aristotelian notion of ethical virtue as involving a mean (μεσότης) between excess (ὑπερβολή) and defect (ἔλλειψις). Μεσότης does not occur in ECL, ἔλλειψις is used once in a non-technical sense, "without failing" δίχα ἐλλείψεως 1 Clem 20:10, and although ὑπερβολή occurs, there is only one instance which approximates Plutarch's sense, "beyond measure" "exceeding," εἰς ὑπερβολήν 2 Cor 4:17, but again it is not a *technicus terminus*. But aside from the language in which the doctrine of the mean is expressed, Aristotelian and Platonic,[71] it is difficult to find a comparable notion in ECL (the notion of "self-control" which is expressed in the NT should not be confused with it; see the discussion in connection with ch. 6). The most successful endeavor has been that of H. D. Betz who in his study of Plutarch's *laud. ips.* notes the parallels, and observes that 2 Cor 10:13ff. with its opposition against boasting of things "without measure" (εἰς τὰ ἄμετρα), has something of the notion of μεσότης.[72]

There are some minor linguistic parallels between expressions in this chapter and those in ECL:

443E: πᾶσαν ἀρετήν; cf. πᾶσαν ἀρετήν in Herm Man 1:2; Sim 6:1:4; 8:10:3;

444C: κατὰ φύσιν; cf. κατὰ φύσιν Ign Trall 1:1; Rom 11:24a;

444C: τὸ ἐξαιρεῖν τὰς ἀμετρίας τῶν παθῶν καὶ πλημμελείας cf. θυσίαι περὶ ἁμαρτίας κ. πλημμελείας 1 Clem 41:2 (cf. *superst.* 168D ἁμαρτίαι κ. πλημμέλειαι) and the use of ἐξαιρεῖν in Matt 5:29, "to pluck out," i.e., "eliminate" the offending eye.

---

[70] The example of the geometer is found in a different context in *EN* 6.1142a; Plutarch's use is probably taken from *EN* 3.1112a 21-2; cf. 444E.

[71] The terms μέτριος, ὑπερβάλλειν, ἐγκαταλείπειν, καιρός in 444B reflect Platonic theory; see Babut, *Vertu*, 151 and 75.

[72] In this volume, pp. 367ff.

444C: wisdom (σοφία) is without any needs; cf. ἀπροσδεής, said of the Master in 1 Clem 52:1.

Ch. 6

This chapter is rich in ethical terminology, and the first section which gives several examples of virtues as means is worth study. In the previous chapter (5) it was noted that μεσότης, and τὸ ἐλλεῖπον and τὸ ὑπερβάλλον do not occur in ECL (ἔλλειψις and ὑπερβολή occur but without technical meaning). Similarly τὸ μέσον, and τὸ μᾶλλον and τὸ ἧττον do not occur in ECL, and Plutarch's examples of means are without parallel:

τὸ ἀδιάφορον (the word isn't found in ECL) as the mean between τὸ ἀγαθόν and τὸ κακόν (the extremes are not mentioned as such in ECL);

ἀνδρεία (the noun is not found in ECL; see the discussion of ch. 1), δειλία and θρασύτης occur, but not frequently (see Bauer);

ἐλευθεριότης (not in ECL), μικρολογία only once and in the sense of a "small matter, trifle," Herm Man 5:2:2, and ἀσωτία as "debauchery";

πραότης (πραΰτης is the predominant form in the NT) occurs often, but Plutarch's extremes of ἀναλγησία and ὠμότης are not found;

σωφροσύνη (the term is in ECL), but the extremes, ἀναισθησία and ἀκολασία are never used in ECL;

δικαιοσύνη as the mean in contracts (συμβόλαια) between the more and less of what is due (πλέον . . . τοῦ προσήκοντος . . . ἔλαττον) is conceptually and linguistically wholly foreign to ECL; none of the words except δικαιοσύνη occurs.

Plutarch's central purpose in this chapter is, of course, to show that if the soul did not have rational and irrational parts, there would be no difference between self-control (ἐγκράτεια) and temperance (σωφροσύνη), and incontinence (ἀκρασία) and intemperance (ἀκολασία). Much of his discussion of the conflict in the soul is based on Plato's simile of the horses in *Phaedrus* 253Cff. Now, it has already been seen that Plutarch's Platonic-Aristotelian psychology is foreign to early Christian thought. Moreover, his distinction between ἀκρασία and ἀκολασία, based as it is on this psychology, is not found in early Christian thought, the term ἀκολασία not occurring at all. Σωφροσύνη, ἐγκράτεια, and ἀκρασία are, of course, found in ECL, but it would be a mistake to conclude that these terms mean precisely what they mean in *virt. mor*. For Plutarch σωφροσύνη-ἐγκράτεια and ἀκρασία-ἀκολασία refer to distinct psychic conditions. More specifically, σωφροσύνη denotes the state of the soul when the irrational part is obedient to and cooperates with reason; in ἐγκράτεια reason prevails, but not without conflict between it and the irrational. Ἀκολασία involves not only wicked emotions, but also a depraved reason; in ἀκρασία, however, the reason is sound and preserves (σῴζει) its power of judgment (κρίσις), but is overcome by the emotions.

In NT ethics, σωφροσύνη and ἐγκράτεια are comparatively unimportant. Cognates of σωφρονέω occur only fourteen times and bear such meanings as "soundness of mind" (in Acts 26:25 where Paul defends himself against charges of μανία) and "moderation" or "good sense," e.g., in 1 Tim 2:9 where αἰδώς and σωφροσύνη are expected of women. Generally σωφροσύνη is used of "chastity" and a disciplined or ordered life, e.g., Tit 2:5,[73] and in 2 Tim 1:7 σωφρονισμός is merely one of a list of three virtues given by God: δυνάμις, ἀγάπη, and σωφρονισμός. Its exact meaning is, of course, difficult to determine in this context. Ἐγκράτεια occurs in Gal 5:23 where it is a "fruit of the Spirit" along with ἀγάπη, χαρά, εἰρήνη, μακροθυμία, χρηστότης, ἀγαθωσύνη, πίστις, and πραότης, all of which are opposed to the works of the flesh, πορνεία, ἀκαθαρσία, ἀσέλγεια, . . . μέθαι, κῶμοι. Ἐγκράτεια is especially emphasized in Hermas where Hermas himself is described as ὁ ἐγκρατὴς ὁ ἀπερχόμενος πάσης ἐπιθυμίας πονηρᾶς, Vis 1:2:4, a notion of ἐγκράτεια not unlike that of Plutarch.[74] In 1 Clem 7:9 it refers to sexual restraint and is contrasted (vs. 5) with ἀκρασία which denotes the sexual impulse and its satisfaction. Significantly in 1 Clem 38:2 ἐγκράτεια is a gift bestowed by God, and since biblical thinkers regarded man's life as directed and determined by God, there really was no place for self-mastery in an autonomous ethic.

Ἀκολασία, it was noted above, does not appear in ECL. Ἀκρασία does, but infrequently (only twice in the NT, 1 Cor 7:5 and Matt 23:25). It is thus surprising to find it personified as a maiden clothed in black, and being one of the four more powerful vices in Herm Sim 9:15:3; the others are Ἀπιστία, Ἀπείθεια, and Ἀπάτη. From the context, however, the precise meaning of ἀκρασία cannot

[73] See U. Luck, *TDNT*, s.v. σώφρων, 2.C-D.

[74] See W. Grundmann, *TDNT*, s.v. ἐγκράτεια, 4 (2:341f.) for further discussion of the term in Hermas.

be readily determined. Plutarch's discussion of ἀκρασία and ἀκολασία does contain some interesting possible parallels to ECL. First, according to him, two characteristics of the ἀκόλαστος are to share joyfully in wrongs committed (ἡδομένῳ κοινωνεῖν ὑπάρχει τῶν ἁμαρτανομένων) and to be swept along willingly (ἑκών) to the shameful. Compare this with Paul's description of ἀγάπη in 1 Cor 13:6 which does not rejoice in wrongdoing (ἀδικία) and the implication of Rom 8:20 that man sins willingly.[75] Second, the ἀκρατής, unlike the ἀκόλαστος, betrays the honorable unwillingly (ἄκων). Compare with 1 Clem 2:3 where God's mercy for any unwilling sin (ἄκοντες ἡμάρτετε) is to be implored.

Other interesting points of comparison with ECL are in connection with Plutarch's quotations:

446A: ἔα μ' ἀπολέσθαι τοῦτο γάρ μοι συμφέρει from a comic poet; cf. Phil 1:21 with its sentiment that to die, i.e., to be with Christ, is a good thing;

The quotation from Euripides, fr. 841, ὅταν τις εἰδῇ τἀγαθὸν χρῆται δὲ μή, invited Helmbold's comparison with Rom 7:19 "in the King James Version"; [76]

Lastly, Plutarch's quotation of a simile from a Greek drama, perhaps by Euripides, ὡς ἄγκιστρον ἀγκύρας, is interpreted by him as a reference to that which is not under reason's control; for a similar metaphorical use of ἄγκιστρον, see Ign Magn 11, "to be caught on the fishhooks of error" (κενοδοξίας);

445B: cf. Plutarch's use of τὸ εὔσχημον and 1 Cor 12:24 where it refers to the "proper" or "seemly" parts of the body (there is an emphasis on εὐσχημοσύνη in Paul's discussion).

Ch. 7

In this chapter Plutarch begins his polemic against the Stoics which continues until Ch. 12, the treatise's conclusion. The Stoic position is that there is no conflict between reason and passion, but only a double orientation (τροπή; in ECL the term occurs only in Jas 1:17, probably with an astronomical meaning; see Bauer) of one and the same reason. This Stoic view of the human reason (λόγος) is not unlike the Pauline conception of the νοῦς. For if Bultmann is correct,[77] νοῦς in Paul refers not only to the mind or

[75] See F. Hauck, *TDNT*, s.v. ἑκών.
[76] In his Loeb edition, 49, n. c.
[77] *TNT*, 1:211ff.

intellect as a special faculty, but also to conscious or unconscious volition, understanding, attention. In Rom, esp. chs. 1 and 7, there are uses of νοῦς which suggest that although it is the self which is the subject of "willing" (7:15f. and 19-21) and aims at the good, its "doing" is frustrated by sin dwelling "in the members." Its innate inclination may be to the good, but as "depraved inclination" (ἀδόκιμος νοῦς) in Rom 1:28, the νοῦς may be striving toward the bad and thus having in itself the possibility of heeding or rejecting God's demands. It is especially interesting to note that Paul uses "heart" (καρδία) to a large extent synonymously with νοῦς. Like νοῦς, it is man's personal self, the subject that desires (Rom 10:1), lusts (Rom 1:24), grieves (Rom 9:2), or suffers (2 Cor 2:4), and also like νοῦς, it is not a higher principle in man, but only the purposing, planning self which can turn either to the good or to the bad. The primary difference between νοῦς and καρδία seems to lie in the dominance of striving and being moved by feelings in the latter.[78] Nonetheless, Paul's concepts of νοῦς and καρδία seem much closer to the Stoic view that passions and reason are not essentially different than they do to Plutarch's emphatic differentiation between reason and the emotions.

Plutarch's notion of the conflict (στάσις or μάχη) between reason and the emotions (e.g., 447F, 448C) reminds one, of course, of Paul's "war with the law of his mind" (Rom 7:24; cf. also Gal 5:17) where the flesh desires against the spirit (ἡ γὰρ σὰρξ ἐπιθυμεῖ κατὰ τοῦ πνεύματος) and vice versa.[79] It is interesting to note, however, that μάχη in ECL always refers to battles fought with actual weapons (Paul's term in Rom is ἀντιστρατευόμενον); στάσις which occurs often in 1 Clem means both actual uprisings and revolts, but also dissensions or disputes. Πόλεμος is, of course, used figuratively in ECL as in Jas 4:1, but Plutarch does not use the term in describing reason's battle with the passions.

Two interesting linguistic parallels are Plutarch's use of τί οὖν at 447C; cf. Bauer, s.v. τίς, τί, 3 (it is a dialogical device); and the use of μετατίθεσθαι at 447F, "to change one's view or opinion," should be compared with Gal 1:6, "desert him who called you (and turn) to another gospel" (μετατίθεσθε ἀπὸ τοῦ καλέσαντος. . .).

---

[78] Ibid., 220ff.

[79] See also E. Brandenburger, *Fleisch und Geist* (Neukirchen, 1968).

Ch. 8

Plutarch's contention that the different natures of the rational and irrational can be seen not only in their conflict, but in the subordination of emotion to reason, leads him into a brief consideration of justified anger in which reason and emotion agree. One becomes angry justly, for example, in behalf of parents and children against enemies and despots. There is also, of course, irrational anger. In the NT anger seems to fall under a similar ambivalent judgment. Jesus' prophetic anger or indignation, e.g., Mark 3:5 and John 2:13-21 (cf. Luke 19:45-46), certainly suggests a redemptive use of this human emotion, and it becomes a sign for, and the incarnation of God's anger. Moreover, indignation over wrong can become an instrument of sanctification (2 Cor 7:11). But despite these positive views of anger, there are passages such as Jas 1:19-20, "the anger of man does not work God's righteousness," or Eph 4:26, "do not let the sun go down on your anger," which indicate a negative judgment on human anger.

Plutarch's example of two kinds of "modesty" (αἰδώς) as revealing the distinction between reason and the emotions, is especially interesting since αἰδώς occurs only in 1 Tim 2:9, and not at all in the Apostolic Fathers. In the apologists, the term occurs only in Athenag Leg 30:2, and there is thus little doubt that αἰδώς does not play a significant part in early Christianity. Bultmann observes, "the reason for this is not merely that it had become a highbrow term, but especially that in Greek it had come to be used primarily of a ἕξις. The essence of the believer, however, is not a relationship to himself, a ἕξις or ἀρετή, but a being before God and towards his neighbor." [80]

Ch. 9

In this chapter Plutarch attacks Stoic ethical terms, and it is interesting that two important terms used by the Stoics are not found in ECL: εὐπάθεια and ἀπάθεια. The adjective ἀπαθής is used twice of Christ ("without having suffered") in Ign Eph 7:2 and Ign Pol 3:2. Similarly other terms used by the Stoics do not occur or occur with different meanings, e.g., δῆγμος, συνθροήσις, or Chrysippus' καρτερία (449C) do not occur at all; βούλησις is used

[80] *TDNT*, s.v. αἰδώς C (1:171).

only of God's will,[81] and εὐλάβεια occurs in the sense perhaps of "reverence" or "fear."[82]

Χαρά, which is emphasized to the highest degree in the Johannine literature and the NT generally,[83] is called a "εὐπάθεια" by the Stoics, and in this chapter and elsewhere is regarded simply as an emotion by Plutarch.

Ch. 10

The Stoic doctrine that all "sins" are equal, mentioned by Plutarch at the beginning of this chapter, is clearly not accepted by him (cf. also *prof. virt.* 76A-B). In early Christianity there also seems to have been a distinction between graver and lighter forms of sin, e.g., 1 John 5:16-17 or Matt 12:31-32 (cf. Mark 3:28-29). Yet from a theological point of view, there is a similarity between Stoic and Christian doctrines on the matter of sin or wrongdoing, for if, according to the Christians, sin is an offense or rebellion against God, there can be no basis for more or less. In Christian writings there is a preference for ἁμαρτία in the sing., and that all sins are equal seems to be a majority view. In every instance, however trivial, the offense is incalculable.[84] Despite this similarity between the Stoic and Christian positions on sin, it would be contrary to the early Christians to consider every emotion an error, as did the Stoics.

In observing that there are differences in judgments (κρίσις) as well as emotions, Plutarch attacks the famous Stoic theory that passion is a perverted reason or judgment (the repetition of κρίσις in the treatise is not accidental; cf. 442E, 442F, and 443A).[85] Κρίσις occurs in the NT, but mostly in the sense of penal judgment, human and divine, and, of course, of Christ's world judgment, e.g., John 5:28f. Poverty, death, and health are given by Plutarch as examples of things variously judged. When Plutarch observes that some do not judge poverty to be an evil, he is probably thinking of the Stoics, and perhaps even the Cynics.[86] But poverty was also not an evil for early Christianity. Jesus became poor for the sake of

[81] See Bauer, s.v. βούλησις.

[82] See R. Bultmann, *TDNT*, s.v. εὐλαβής, B (2:753).

[83] See Bultmann, *TNT*, 2:83f.

[84] See Jas 2:10 and the problem of sin after baptism raised in Hermas.

[85] Babut, *Vertu*, 9.

[86] On Plutarch and poverty, see O'Neil's study of *cup. divit.* in this volume, pp. 289ff.

mankind (2 Cor 8:9 and Phil 2:5-6), and the rich young ruler is advised to sell everything (Matt 19:21f.). Health was obviously valued in early Christianity, not however as the greatest good in the world, but as a sign of God's forgiveness and power, e.g., Jas 5:15 and Acts 2:16-21.

Some language in this chapter invites comparison with ECL:

450A: on κολασμοῖς κτλ., see *PECL* 1, index s.v. κόλασις, punishment;

450C: cf. Plutarch's quotations from Chrysippus' book *On the Failure to Lead a Consistent Life* with some of the sentiments expressed by Paul in Rom 7, esp. Chrysippus' "for the passions when once raised, drive out the reasoning processes" with Paul's "for sin, taking the occasion . . . deceived me. . . ."

Cf. Plutarch's quotation from Menander and Rom 7:24, esp. Menander's οἴμοι τάλας ἔγωγε with Paul's ταλαίπωρος ἐγὼ ἄνθρωπος.

Ch. 11

In this chapter the close relationship between the irrational part of the soul and the body is emphasized, and the concept of "nature" (φύσις) is fairly prominent. Plutarch is concerned not only with the nature of the human organism, but with that of animals as well; cf. his τὰς τῶν θηρίων . . . φύσεις with Jas 3:7a, πᾶσα γὰρ φύσις θηρίων. It is interesting to note further that in ch. 3 the author of Jas speaks of the need for bridling the whole body, and especially the tongue that is considered the cosmos of iniquity (vs. 6). For Plutarch the seat of desire is the liver (ἧπαρ, 450F), a term which does not appear in ECL, which tends to identify desire with the heart. In any case, both authors see a connection between an organ of the body and human behaviour.

The concept of "nature" is, of course, operative in Paul, and he uses the phrases "according to" or "contrary to" nature (Rom 1:26, 11:24). Also the Christians of Tralles are said to have a blameless nature οὐ κατὰ χρῆσιν ἀλλὰ κατὰ φύσιν (Ign Trall 1:1), and whereas the concept of nature is not especially prominent in early Christian thought, it probably refers to the providential ordering of the natural world as it did for the Stoics, and even for Plutarch despite his anti-Stoic attitude in this treatise.[87]

---

[87] See Bultmann's brief discussion of φύσις in *TNT*, 1:71.

In connection with 1 Cor 10: 16ff., Almqvist notes a parallel to 451B "zum Wechsel κοινωνεῖν-μετέχειν," but it is quite minor.[88]

Ch. 12

A main idea of this concluding chapter is the need for proper cultivation of the emotions, not their repression. The emotions can be valuable auxilliaries of the virtues if excess is avoided, and moral virtue arises when equity and moderation (ἐπιείκεια καὶ μετριότης) are produced.

The notion that the emotions are sometimes justified is not foreign to early Christian thought, e.g., the righteous anger of Jesus at Mark 3:5, though the emotions are not thought of in connection with specific virtues. For example, Plutarch speaks of θυμός as contributing to the development of courage. Θυμός, however, in the NT connotes the unreflecting passion of anger, e.g., Luke 4:28, whereas ὀργή is the relatively more considered moral indignation, e.g., Jas 1:19. In fact, ὀργή is perhaps closest in meaning to Plutarch's μισοπονηρία (451E), a term not found in ECL. Indeed, in this chapter Plutarch often uses a different moral vocabulary than that of early Christian authors, and in doing so, emphasizes character education. For example, in advocating ἐπιείκεια and μετριότης, Plutarch's use of these terms, and hence conception, is quite different from Christian ἐπιείκεια in which the emphasis is on meekness, and especially the meekness of the Christ, 2 Cor 10:1, ἐπιεικείας τοῦ Χριστοῦ.[89] 'Επιείκεια is also enjoined on the Christian community in the face of hostile slanderers, 2 Cor 10:6. In any case, the notion of what is equitable, right, or fitting is not readily discernible in the term. Μετριότης does not occur in ECL, and the Delphic maxim related to it, μηδὲν ἄγαν (cf. Plutarch's ἄγαν φόβον at 452A), is not expressly stated in ECL; but cf. Rom 12:3, 2 Cor 10:12, Eph 4:7, 13, 16.[90] If, moreover, ἐπιείκεια is to be manifested to all men (see Phil 4:5), Christians are to show φιλοστοργία to one another, Diogn 1. But φιλοστοργία in Plutarch seems to be more general, not confined to the Christian community, and is coupled with φιλανθρωπία at 451E. Again, φιλοτιμία, which in this

---

[88] Almqvist, 98.

[89] See H. Preisker, *TDNT*, s.v. ἐπιείκεια (2:589f.).

[90] See also the passages studied in Betz's *laud. ips.* in this volume, pp. 367ff, and *PECL* 1:90.

chapter (452D) and in ch. 7 at 447D seems to have a bad connotation for Plutarch, "ambition," in its one occurrence in ECL at Diogn 3:5 seems oddly to mean "respect"—"to show the same respect to dumb images." But most important, Nemesis, the great moral force since Homeric times which Plutarch opposes at 451E to foolishness and insolence (ἀνοίᾳ καὶ ὕβρει), is not mentioned at all in ECL, and ἄνοια is used only in the sense of the folly of heretical teachers and human ignorance (the meaning at 2 Clem 13:1, where it is coupled with πονηρία, comes close to Plutarch's meaning), and ὕβρις seems to mean "shame" or "mistreatment." [91]

In sum, many of the great values of the pagan world, especially the emphasis Plutarch places on character education, are not found in or given very little stress by early Christian authors. One reason for this is that character education would be regarded as a form of the "works of the law." [92]

There are some interesting linguistic and conceptual comparisons in this chapter with ECL:

451C: Plutarch claims that the function of reason is not to "cut down" (συνεκκόπτειν) and destroy the emotions; cf. Bauer, s.v. ἐκκόπτω, esp. 1 Clem 63:2, "to root out the lawless anger," and 2 Cor 11:12, "to remove the occasion (ἀφορμὴν); κολοῦσαι; cf. *PECL* 1, index, s.v. κολούω;

451D: on the subduing of the emotions (τοῖς πάθεσι δεδασμένοις), cf. Jas 3:8: "the tongue no man can tame" (δαμάσαι), in contrast to things of the animate world, e.g., birds, beasts, and serpents;

452A: ἄγαν φόβον; see discussion above;

452D: "Than this saying (that of a Spartan tutor), there can be shown (ἀποφῆναι) no greater nor fairer end of such education as befits a freeborn child"; cf. 1 Cor 12:31, "and yet I show you (δείκνυμι) a more excellent way."

---

[91] See Bauer, s.v. ὕβρις.

[92] See Acts 22:3 for a conventional view; cf. Philo, and esp. E. Bréhier, *Les Idées philosophiques et religieuses de Philon d'Alexandrie* (Paris, 1925) 272ff. on "La Nature et l'éducation."

DE COHIBENDA IRA (MORALIA 452E - 464D)

BY

HANS DIETER BETZ
Claremont Graduate School and School of Theology
Claremont, California

AND

JOHN M. DILLON
University of California
Berkeley, California

I. INTRODUCTION

The title of this work [1] in the MSS is περὶ ἀοργησίας (*De cohibenda ira*). It does not seem to figure in the Catalogue of Lamprias, since the entry περὶ ὀργῆς (No. 93), which does occur, almost certainly refers to a different work from which Stobaeus has preserved a fragment.[2] The fragment in question is of very much the same tone as the work before us, but the essay περὶ ὀργῆς may have dealt with the symptoms rather than the cure.

ἀοργησία is a term which, in the sense in which Plutarch is using it here, probably goes back to the early Stoic writers, although it is not attested earlier than Nicolaus of Damascus, a Peripatetic of the Augustan Age.[3] In this "good" sense, it means complete freedom from the passion of anger, such as would be the ideal of the Stoic philosopher. Characteristically, Aristotle, the first attested user of the term, employs it in a bad sense, as denoting an "unnatural," excessive failure to be roused to anger. In *EN* 2. 7. 1108a4ff., he makes ἀοργησία one of the extremes (that of "defect") on either side of the Mean, the other, that of excess, being ὀργιλότης, iras-

[1] The texts used in this study are by W. C. Helmbold in *Plutarch's Moralia* 6, LCL (1931); W. R. Paton, M. Pohlenz and W. Sieveking, *Plutarchi Moralia* 3, BT (1929, repr. 1972). See M. Pohlenz, "Über Plutarchs Schrift περὶ ἀοργησίας," *Hermes* 31 (1896) 321-38; A. Schlemm, "Über die Quellen der Plutarchischen Schrift περὶ ἀοργησίας," *Hermes* 38 (1903) 587-607; H. G. Ingenkamp, *Plutarchs Schriften über die Heilung der Seele* (Göttingen, 1971); P. Rabbow, *Antike Schriften über Seelenheilung und Seelenleitung, I: Die Therapie des Zorns* (Leipzig & Berlin, 1914).

[2] Fr. 148, ed. F. H. Sandbach, *LCL* 15:274-77.

[3] See LSJ, s.v.

cibility. The Mean itself, Aristotle's ideal, is gentleness, πραότης. It is significant, and entirely to be expected, that the word used for one extreme by Aristotle should become the term for the desired ideal in Stoicism.[4] We will note the interplay of these three terms in Plutarch's essay, πραότης [5] being assimilated to ἀοργησία [6] and ὀργιλότης [7] made the extreme opposite to them both. ECL does not employ the word ἀοργησία,[8] but πραότης (or πραΰτης) [9] and ὀργίλος (though not ὀργιλότης) [10] occur. πραΰτης is a frequently mentioned virtue in Paul, often linked with ἐπιείκεια.[11] In Col 3:12 the readers are encouraged to put on πραΰτης, after having been previously urged (3:8) to put off, among other vices, ὀργή and θυμός, the two key words of Plutarch's essay. One feels that Pauline ethics was in fact in agreement with Aristotle, rather than with the Stoics, in leaving a proper place in ethics for righteous indignation (see below 453D on μισοπονηρία), but Paul links πραΰτης in his list of virtues with μακροθυμία, ἐγκράτεια, and ταπεινοφροσύνη, indicating a determination to restrain himself as long as possible.[12]

The doctrine of *cohib. ira* is straightforward and uncompromising. Anger is one of the πάθη (see esp. 453E, 455E, 456F-457A) and, as such, a disease of the soul which must be eradicated. One must seek out the causes and observe the symptoms, and then set about the

---

[4] For a discussion of the Stoic influences in Plutarch's treatise, see D. Babut, *Plutarque et le Stoïcisme* (Paris, 1969) 94-97.

[5] In *cohib. ira,* πρᾶος occurs 453B, C, D; 455B; 456A; 462A; 464D; πραότης 457D; 458C; 459C; 462C; πράως 454B; 458E. The opposites, ὀργή and θυμός, are frequent in this as well as in other treatises of Plutarch; see esp. 454A-B; 456D-E; 457C; 459A-B, D; 464C, and for further references *Index Verborum Plutarcheus,* s.v.

[6] ἀοργησία is rare in Plutarch; apart from the title it occurs only in a variant reading (Θ) in 463A 17-18; ἀοργητός is found in 464C and *lib. ed.* 10C, where it is named as a quality of the wise man and illustrated by an anecdote about Socrates (cf. the parallel anecdote in 461A).

[7] Apart from *cohib. ira* 454B, ὀργιλότης is found only in *virt. mor.* 443D; the adjective ὀργίλος occurs in *cohib. ira* 457B (twice); 463B; *adul. et am.* 56C; *qu. conv.* 618E (opposite of σιωπηλός); 682C.

[8] ἀοργησία is first found in a list of virtues in Athanasius, *Vita Antonii* 17 (*PG* 26: 869B). See Lampe, s.v. But ἀοργητός is attested 1 Clem 19:3; Ign Phld 1:2; Diogn 8:8; Just 1 Apol 16:1, in the "Stoic" sense.

[9] ECL has πραϋπάθεια, πραΰς, πραΰτης (πραότης) frequently. For references, see F. Hauck and S. Schulz, *TDNT,* s.v.; Bauer, s.v. Opposite to "anger" it occurs esp. Jas 1:20f.; Ign Eph 10:2.

[10] Tit 1:7; Did 3:2 have ὀργίλος; Herm Man 12:4:1: ὀργίλως; ὀργιλότης is not attested in Lampe, s.v.

[11] E.g., 2 Cor 10:1; Gal 5:23; Eph 4:2; Col 3:12.

[12] See Gal 5:22f.; Eph 4:2; Col 3:12.

cure. Various techniques for controlling the symptoms are suggested (see the analysis below). Don't answer the call to rant and rave (ch. 5); observe the passion in others (ch. 6); keep the tongue soft and smooth (ch. 7). But one must chiefly analyze its causes. These are identified as (1) a conviction that one is being despised or belittled (ch. 12); (2) luxury, which produces a spoiled self-love and a demand for rare and special things (ch. 13); (3) a tendency to expect too much of people (ch. 16)—this last especially having the air of self-analysis by Plutarch. Once one has unmasked these causes, they can be reasoned away, and occasions of provocation avoided.

Plutarch's essay is the result of a long tradition. We can compare it with another example of the genre in Seneca's essay *De ira* and note various common elements which point back to much earlier sources. Of these, Plutarch mentions only the Peripatetic philosopher Hieronymus of Rhodes, once to disagree with him (454F), once to borrow an image from him (460C).

Although Plutarch makes use of Hieronymus, he is unlikely to be heavily dependent on a Peripatetic source, his tone being so uncompromisingly Stoic. There were, after all, already in Cicero's day,[13] a host of essays on the subject of Anger. In fact, in the case of a man of Plutarch's learning and skill, it is improper to think of a single source, but rather of a great store of maxims, quotations and *exempla,* which he has at his finger-tips and can produce at will. The extent to which Plutarch, or any great Sophist of the second century A.D., is an "oral poet" is not sufficiently appreciated. He can draw on the tradition in general, in this case the diatribe tradition, and not one or another particular source, though he will have read them all.

The *cohib. ira* is formally a dialogue, a form Plutarch may have chosen in order to start a "conversation" with the reader. The beginning of the treatise is a dialogue between Plutarch's Roman friends Sextius Sulla and C. Minicius Fundanus.[14] Fundanus has spent a year abroad, and Sulla now, after visiting with him for five months, raises a question that has been intriguing him. What has become of the temper for which Fundanus was notorious before he went away? Sulla requests that he tell how the "cure"

---

[13] Cf. *Epistula ad Quintum Fratrem* 1. 1. 37.

[14] On the friends, see Helmbold's notes, *LCL* 6:92, 93; also C. P. Jones, *Plutarch and Rome* (Oxford, 1971) 57f., 60.

was achieved. Fundanus responds with a "testimony" of what he has experienced, which is at the same time an essay about the cure for anger.

This rather complex literary form has some surprising similarities with miracle stories, where at times we find a request by those who observe the healing to tell how it was accomplished. The miracle story told may be the answer to such a request. At first sight, Fundanus' testimony seems the very opposite of a religious miracle. Dealing with the cure of an emotion, this cure is not the result of divine intervention but of psychagogic techniques. And yet, there is a curious connection with religious miracles because of the role of the Logos. In the final analysis, the divine Logos, dwelling in the soul, brings about the cure (see 453D-E), so that we have in fact a form of miracle, wrought, to be sure, by the Logos rather than by a miracle-worker. This difference may have also determined the literary form. Rather than a "miracle story" of the type found in ECL, Fundanus' testimony is a set essay, clearly composed and moving from topic to topic in an orderly way. It is embellished with all the art of rhetoric, specifically similes and metaphors, quotations and *exempla*. Medical metaphors, probably Cynic-Stoic in origin, are predominant, describing anger as a disease which must be cured by the right diagnosis and therapy. At the end, the language of religious asceticism takes priority.

The following analysis shows the structure of the work:

452F-453D I. Introductory dialogue between Sulla and Fundanus Ch. 1

452F-453C A. Sulla's address to Fundanus
452F 1. *exordium*
a. the method of ἐπισκοπεῖν used by painters
453A b. the difficulties of human self-observation
c. the service of a friend: observing moral progress
2. *captatio benevolentiae*: a praise of Fundanus' moral progress
453B a. his violent and fiery temper in the past
b. his "miraculous" moral improvement ("healing")
c. his continuing activity and strength
453C 3. reference to the testimony of Eros

4. a request to tell how the "healing" has come about

453C-D B. Fundanus' reply: a display of modesty

453D C. Sulla's refusal to accept that modesty and his renewal of the request

453D-464D II. Fundanus' testimony

453D-455E A. Presuppositions for the therapy Chs. 2-5

453D 1. reference to a philosophical authority: a quotation of a saying of Musonius Ch. 2

453D-455E 2 the concepts of a philosophical therapy

453D-E a. the λόγος

1) its place in the soul

2) its function: watching over the κρίσεις

3) its power

4) its origin "outside" of the soul

453F b. the θυμός

1) its place among the πάθη

2) its effect upon the soul

454A-B c. the situation of the soul

1) comparison with a ship in a sea-storm

2) comparison with a city under siege

454B-C d. the possibilities for the cure

1) the concept of irascibility (ὀργιλότης) Ch. 3

a) definition of the term

b) the symptoms of irascibility

c) the curability of flare-ups

d) Fundanus' testimony of his own experience

454D-F 2) anger is curable because of its small beginnings Ch. 4

454F-455B 3) anger is curable because it is recognizable from the beginning

455B-E e. the general method of the cure Ch. 5

1) the type of cure in general: καθάπερ τυράννου κατάλυσις τοῦ θυμοῦ

2) general non-cooperation: μὴ πείθεσθαι μηδ' ὑπακούειν προστάττοντος αὐτοῦ

3) the general ethical denominator: ἡσυχάζειν, ἡσυχή

455E-464D B. Therapy (ἰατρεία) Chs. 6-16

455E-459B 1. *Epilogismoi* [15] Chs. 6-10

455F-457C a. the "unpleasant examples" (457C: τὰ φαῦλα παραδείγματα) Chs. 6-8

455E 1) the method: observation of the "symptoms" of anger Ch. 6

455F-456E 2) the "symptoms" Chs. 6-7

455F-456C a) the face

456C-E b) the voice

3) observations as to the nature of θυμός Ch. 8

a) rejection of the common opinion

(1) θυμός not εὐγενής, ἀνδρώδης, φρόνημα, μέγεθος

(2) false equations: τὸ ταρακτικόν = τὸ πρακτικόν, etc.

456F-457C b) the "symptoms" are those of μικρότης καὶ ἀσθένεια

457A (1) rage is directed against subalterns (children, women, dogs, horses, mules)

(2) the rage of despots especially shows that its nature is τὸ μικρόψυχον

457B-C (3) anger is a symptom of the ἀσθένεια of the soul: the weaker the soul, the greater the temper

457C-459B b. the "pleasant" examples Chs. 9-10

1) the method: hearing and seeing of famous *exempla* Ch. 9 (457C: κάλλιστα μὲν ἀκούσματα κάλλιστα δὲ θεάματα)

457C 2) the presuppositions

a) rejection of the common opinion

(1) manliness = τὰ παροξυντικά

(2) transferral of "values" from the women's to the men's quarters

---

[15] The term ἐπιλογισμός is technical and refers to an ethical consideration of a theoretical nature. For a discussion, see Ingenkamp, 99ff., 112f., 119ff.

457D	b) introduction of πραότης as the true virtue	
	(1) its relationships with ἀνδρεία and δικαιοσύνη	
	(2) its origin in a "struggle"	
	(3) its character as a victory over anger	
	(4) its evidence of "great and victorious strength"	
	c) the types and function of the *exempla*	
457E	3) the *exempla*	
457E-458C	a) *exempla* demonstrating the beneficial, "divine" character of πραότης	
458C-459B	b) *exempla* demonstrating the destructive, "demonic" character of θυμός	Ch. 10
459B-463B	2. *Ethismoi* [16]	Chs. 11-15
459B	a. The method of ἄσκησις	Ch. 11
459B-462E	b. Exemplaric situations for training	
459B-460C	1) the treatment of the slaves	
459B	a) the social relationship of masters and slaves	
459C-D	b) the critical situation: the punishing of slaves	
	(1) the origin of the situation: accusations of wife and friends against the slaves	
	(2) the common opinion once shared by Fundanus: "Slaves are ruined if they go unpunished."	
	(3) the correct views now held by Fundanus	
	(a) it is better to ruin slaves by forbearance than to ruin oneself by bothering to correct them	

[16] The term ἐθισμός is technical and refers to the practical exercise in ethical therapy. For a discussion, see Ingenkamp, 105ff.

(b) not punishing a slave may create in him a sense of shame which is the beginning of ethical improvement
(c) if punishing is done it must be done εὐκαίρως, μετρίως, ὠφελίμως, πρεπόντως

459E-460C c) Fundanus' attempts (459D πειρῶμαι) to eliminate anger from such situations

460D-E 2) the feeling of being despised and neglected Ch. 12
a) description of the nature of the experience
b) description of the cure
(1) in principle
(2) in practice

461A-462E 3) outbursts of anger Ch. 13
461A-C a) description of the cause
b) general description of the cure
(1) in principle
(2) the symptoms of the "disease"
461C-462E c) the cure in practice
461C-D (1) the use of food
461E-462A (2) the use of utensils
462A-B (3) daily business affairs
462B-E (4) verbal exchanges Ch. 14

462E-463B c. Concluding ethical consideration
462E-F 1) the wrong approach to the "disease"
a) the absurd and inhuman character of anger
b) the human tendency of renaming the evil instead of changing the attitudes

462F-463B 2) definition of the nature of θυμός Ch. 15
463A a) definition of θυμός as τῶν παθῶν πανσπερμία
463A-B b) interpretation of this definition

(1) a catalog of vices
(2) the activity of anger: ἀγωνίζειν
(3) the goal of anger: cause trouble for others
(4) its destructive effects on people
463B 3) the right approach to a cure Ch. 16
463C-464D 3. Fundanus' testimony (first person singular)
463C a. the reasons for his fits of anger
1) his natural disposition
2) his over-extension of love and trust
463C-464D b. the three steps toward the cure
463C-F 1) first step: understanding one's humanity
a) reference to philosophical sayings
b) the implication of human "sinfulness"
463F-464B 2) second step: the avoidance of inquisitiveness
a) identification of inquisitiveness as a source of anger
b) reference to a saying of Euripides
c) application by Fundanus
(1) he leaves nothing to Fate
(2) he applies the rule *Divide et impera*: delegating the small matters which cause anger to others, while keeping control over the important matters
464B-C 3) the third step: "fasting from evil"
464B a) reference to Empedocles' phrase
b) interpretation in terms of asceticism in religion
464C c) ethical application by
(1) gradually increasing the time periods of abstention from anger
(2) constantly maintaining self-observation and self-control
(3) trusting in God's help
464D c. Conclusion: confirmation by experience

II. Early Christian Literature and the Topic of Anger

In ECL one does not find a long analysis of the passion of "anger" or detailed methods for its "cure." One must realise, however, that primitive Christianity also stands within a long tradition which took up various contributions from Jewish religion as well as Hellenistic philosophy.[17] The great difference between Plutarch's essay and the primitive Christian view of anger is that for the Christians God's wrath was a well-known concept,[18] while for the Stoic concept such emotions had to be kept away from the deity. Because of the idea of the imitation of God, there is room for a certain type of anger in Christian ethics,[19] as there is no room for it in Plutarch's essay. There is, however, no doctrinal consistency in early Christianity. Where ethical material from the diatribe literature is taken over, "anger" is usually condemned together with other "vices." [20]

It is surprising to find a rather careful regulation of "anger," in terms comparable to those of Plutarch, in the so-called Sermon on the Mount, which is certainly one of the oldest passages of the NT. In Matt 5:21-26, Jesus interprets the command of the Decalogue οὐ φονεύσεις as excluding not only killing but also ὀργίζεσθαι τῷ ἀδελφῷ. This is then illustrated by exemplary "cases." Anger against the brother is considered incompatible with God's will and with the required δικαιοσύνη (cf. 5:20; see the commentary below on 457D). It is contrary to God's attitude (see 5:43-48//Luke 6:27f., 32-36), and therefore the beatitudes include one for οἱ πραεῖς (Matt 5:5; Did 3:7; cf. 15:3; Barn 19:4).

[17] See F. Büchsel, *TDNT*, s.v. θυμός κτλ.; H. Kleinknecht et al., *TDNT*, s.v. ὀργή κτλ.; Almqvist, 130f.; Betz, *Lukian*, 201; G. Petzke, *Die Traditionen über Apollonius von Tyana und das Neue Testament* (Leiden, 1970) 226; G. Mussies, *Dio Chrysostom and the New Testament* (Leiden, 1972) 187.

[18] The subject is extensively discussed in Plutarch's essay *num. vind.* (see *PECL* 1:181-235). On the whole topic, see G. Stählin, *TDNT*, s.v. ὀργή κτλ., E.II; Bultmann, *TNT*, index, s.v. Wrath; G. H. C. MacGregor, "The Concept of the Wrath of God in the New Testament," *NTS* 7 (1960-61) 101-09; H. Conzelmann, *RGG*, 3d ed., s.v. Zorn Gottes, III; Idem, *An Outline of the Theology of the New Testament* (London & Evanston, 1969) 239-41.

[19] Jesus is reported to have been angry (Mark 3:5; cf. the problematic ἐμβριμάομαι in John 11:33, 38; cf. also Matt 23:13ff.). So is Paul in Acts 17:16. See also Rom 10:19 (Deut 32:21); 12:19; 2 Cor 7:11 (ἀγανάκτησις); Eph 4:26 (Ps 4:5): ὀργίζεσθε καὶ μὴ ἁμαρτάνετε· ὁ ἥλιος μὴ ἐπιδυέτω ἐπὶ παροργισμῷ ὑμῶν, μηδὲ δίδοτε τόπον τῷ διαβόλῳ.

[20] See 2 Cor 12:20; Gal 5:20; Eph 4:31; 6:4; Col 3:8; 1 Tim 2:8; Tit 1:7; Did 3:2; 15:3; 1 Clem 13:1; 39:7; 45:7; 46:5; 63:2; Ign Eph 10:2; Phld 8:1; Pol Phil 6:1; Herm Man 5.

Jas 1:19-21 is close to Plutarch, as well as to the Sermon on the Mount. After the exhortation βραδὺς εἰς ὀργήν the reader is told that human ὀργή and divine δικαιοσύνη are irreconcilable. All evil must be eliminated ἐν πραΰτητι. Puzzling is the phrase that ὁ ἔμφυτος λόγος should be "received" because it is capable of saving souls.[21] The expression ὁ ἔμφυτος λόγος can refer to the missionary preaching implanted in the believers, to an originally Stoic concept, or to both.[22] The language suggests that it refers to both, and that a "Stoic" concept has been taken up by James,[23] possibly through the medium of Hellenistic Judaism.[24]

Even more detailed is Herm Man 5, which is devoted entirely to "anger" and its avoidance. Anger (ὀξυχολία)[25] is identical with τὸ πονηρὸν πνεῦμα, which is related to the devil (5:1:3; 6:2:4f.) and opposed to τὸ πνεῦμα τὸ ἅγιον. It is incompatible with δικαιοσύνη (5:1:1-3). Hermas provides a lengthy explanation of how "anger" works; as in Plutarch we are given the symptoms and causes. Among the servants of God who are filled with faith and the power of the Holy Spirit, "anger" has no real chance. But in the ἀπόκενοι καὶ δίψυχοι, it works its way into their hearts (5:2:1f.), overwhelms them, chokes the Holy Spirit and drives it out (5:1:3; 5:2:4-7). How can one escape "anger"? The answer is: through being μακρόθυμος, because μακροθυμία is the opposite of ὀξυχολία, and where one occupies the place the other has no chance (5:1:1f.; 5:2:3). There is a careful balance between assistance by the Shepherd (5:1:7), the indwelling Holy Spirit (5:1:2; 5:2:1; 5:2:5-7), ἡ δύναμις τοῦ κυρίου (5:2:1), protection by the angel (5:1:7), and obedience to the Lord's commandments (5:2:8).

There is no doubt that Hermas comes closest to Plutarch, but there are also obvious differences in concept. It appears that Plutarch and ECL are in contact not directly, but indirectly

---

[21] See below on 453B; 453E, where Plutarch's "Stoic" concept is discussed.

[22] For a discussion of the problem, see M. Dibelius, *James* (Philadelphia, 1976) 108-14; F. Mussner, *Der Jakobusbrief* (Freiburg, [2]1967) 99-103; Bauer, s.v. ἔμφυτος.

[23] Cf. the use of ἔμφυτος Barn 1:2; 9:9; Ps-Clem Hom 3:15:1; 3:26:1; 20:6:4; Just 2 Apol 8:1; 13:5 (with reference to the Stoics).

[24] Cf. Wis 12:10; Ps.-Phocylides 128; Philo, *deus imm.* 101; *fug.* 122; *spec. leg.* 3:138; *virt.* 23; *praem. poen.* 5. In all these passages, however, ἔμφυτος is connected with something representing an "innate" evil.

[25] The terminology occurs exclusively in Hermas and not in Plutarch: ὀξυχολέω Herm Man 10:2:3; ὀξυχολία Man 5:1:3, 6f.; 5:2:1, 4, 8; 6:2:5; 10:1:1f.; 10:2:3f.; Sim 9:15:3; ὀξύχολος Man 5:2:7; 6:2:4; Sim 6:5:5.

through the philosophical terminology which had entered into Hellenistic Judaism prior to Christianity. In ECL there is as strong a concern about anger as in the rest of the ancient world. Beginning with the Sermon on the Mount we find traces of ethical theory and practice which show increasing similarity with Plutarch. Notably, these traces are found in those parts of ECL which are attributed to Jewish Christianity and not in typically Hellenistic passages.

The basic differences between Plutarch and these early Christian traditions are indicated by Plutarch's systematic and complete treatment in the Platonic-Stoic tradition of the Logos, while in ECL we find eclectic and ad hoc references connected mostly with the indwelling of the Holy Spirit. Yet, the Christian side shows that there was extensive reflection, as well as practice, on how to deal with "anger".

III. Commentary

Ch. 1

(452F)

ἐπισκοπέω. The introductory section is built around the notion of ἐπισκοπεῖν. Plutarch begins by discussing the method of painters: prior to finishing their work they step back from it periodically, in order to inspect it critically from a distance. This method, however, cannot be applied to human self-inspection because we cannot step outside of ourselves, in order to look at ourselves from a distance. Plutarch's somewhat skeptical view of the possibilities of human self-judgment are noteworthy in view of the general importance of self-knowledge; on this see *PECL* 1:85, 90, 128.

(453A)

ἕκαστον αὑτοῦ φαυλότερον κριτὴν ἢ ἑτέρων. That one is a better judge of others than of oneself was a common view in antiquity and is reflected also in Matt 7:3-5//Luke 6:41-42; Luke 18:9-14.

τὸ τοὺς φίλους ἐφορᾶν διὰ χρόνου καὶ παρέχειν ὁμοίως ἐκείνοις ἑαυτόν. This well-known friendship-*topos* does not seem to occur in ECL, but cf. 1 Pet 3:2; Phil 3:17; 1 Thes 4:1; etc. See I. Hadot, *Seneca und die griechisch-römische Tradition der Seelenleitung* (Berlin, 1969) 164ff.

τὸν τρόπον καὶ τὸ ἦθος ἐπισκοπεῖν. This language is technical. In ECL, τρόπος occurs Heb 13:5; ἦθος 1 Cor 15:33 (quotation from

Menander); ἐπισκοπέω Heb 12:15; 1 Pet 5:2 v. l.; Ign Rom 9:1; Ign Pol inscr.; Herm Vis 3:5:1; etc. See H. W. Beyer, *TDNT*, s.v. ἐπισκέπτομαι κτλ.

τῶν φαύλων ἀφῄρηκεν. For ἀφαιρέω in connection with the removal of vices, see Rom 11:27 (LXX Isa 27:9); Heb 10:4; 1 Clem 8:4 (Isa 1:16).

εὐφυΐα. The concept ("natural aptitude to virtue") is not found in ECL. It was common in Platonic ethics, cf. Aristotle *EN* 3. 5. 1114b5ff.; Albinus *Didascalicos* ch. 30; it is also frequent in Philo *leg. all.* 1. 55; 3. 249, etc.

(453B)

διάπυρος πρὸς ὀργήν. For similar usage of the metaphor of fire, cf. Ign Rom 7:2; Jas 3:6; Acts 18:25; Rom 12:11; Eph 6:16.

ἡ μαλακότης οὐκ ἀργίαν οὐδ' ἔκλυσιν. The term μαλακότης, which is not found in ECL, denotes a positive "softness," while in ECL related terms, like μαλακία, μαλακός, are negative. ἀργία and ἔκλυσις are not in ECL, but ἀργός and ἐκλύω are found. See Bauer, s.v.

τὸ θυμοειδές. This Platonic term is not found in ECL.

οὐδ' αὐτομάτως ἀπομαραινόμενον. The language looks "medical" and has a parallel in the miracle story Mark 5:29: εὐθὺς ἐξηράνθη ἡ πηγὴ τοῦ αἵματος αὐτῆς. μαραίνω is used of the spirit in Herm Vis 3:11:2. For αὐτόματος in miracles, see Acts 12:10; cf. Mark 4:28.

ὑπὸ λόγων τινῶν χρηστῶν θεραπευόμενον. Plutarch refers of course to philosophical precepts, but the parallels with miracles should not be overlooked. "Healings" by Jesus' words are esp. emphasized in Matthew; see Matt 8:8, 16. Matthew also likes θεραπεύω (4:23f.; 8:7, 16; 10:1; etc. See G. Strecker, *Der Weg der Gerechtigkeit* [Göttingen, [3]1971] 175-77).

ἀπαγγέλλων ὕποπτος ἦν. Eros serves as the "witness" of Fundanus' change. Cf. the role of witnesses in miracle stories. For a collection of passages, see Bultmann, *HST*, 225f.

(453C)

ἐπιμαρτυρέω. See the similar context in 1 Pet 5:12, where the term occurs as a hapax legomenon in ECL.

διελθ' ἡμῖν ὥσπερ ἰατρείαν τινὰ σεαυτοῦ ... The request made by Sulla that Fundanus tell the story of his healing has parallels in

NT miracle-stories: Mark 5:16, 20//Luke 8:36, 39; John 9:10, 15, 26. Cf. Plutarch *num. vind.* 563ff. (*PECL* 1:219-21).

(453D)

μισοπονηρία ("righteous indignation"), which is also used by Plutarch in 456F; 462E; 463B, E, is not found in ECL, despite the suitability of the concept. Cf. Barn 4:10: μισεῖν τὰ ἔργα τῆς πονηρᾶς ὁδοῦ, etc.; for other similar expressions, see Bauer, s.v. μισέω, 2.

Ch. 2

"τὸ δεῖν ἀεὶ θεραπευομένους βιοῦν τοὺς σῴζεσθαι μέλλοντας." The saying of Musonius recommends "constant medical treatment" for the mind as the way of "survival" in life. The saying also expresses Plutarch's view, which he unfolds in the following essay. For the form of the saying, cf. sayings of Jesus in Mark 13:13//Matt 10:22; 24:13; Mark 8:35//Matt 16:25//Luke 9:24//John 12:25; also Acts 16:30f.; Rom 10:9. For the content and the medical images, cf. 2 Clem 9:7: ὡς ἔχομεν καιρὸν τοῦ ἰαθῆναι, ἐπιδῶμεν ἑαυτοὺς τῷ θεραπεύοντι θεῷ. . . .

(453E)

τὸν λόγον . . . ἐμμένοντα τῇ ψυχῇ συνέχειν τὰς κρίσεις καὶ φυλάσσειν. The λόγος is located in the soul as an inner watch-dog. The analogy of the νοῦς in Rom 7:23 is apparent, but in Paul's view the νοῦς is helpless; cf. also Paul's concept of conscience Rom 2:15.

φαρμακοῖς . . . οὐκ ἔοικεν ἀλλὰ σιτίοις ὑγιεινοῖς ἡ δύναμις αὐτοῦ. The comparison of the λόγος with medicine is rejected in favor of a comparison with a healthy diet, which, when maintained constantly, engenders a constant excellent state. Cf. the concept of the Eucharist as φάρμακον ἀθανασίας in Ign Eph 20:2; λόγος ὑγιής and synonyms in the Pastoral Epistles (cf. 1 Tim 1:10; 6:3; 2 Tim 1:13; 4:3; Tit 1:9, 13; 2:1, 2, 8).

μετ' εὐτονίας ἕξιν ἐμποιοῦσα. The Stoic term εὐτονία is not attested in ECL, but ἕξις is found in Heb 5:14 with a similar meaning.

τὰ πάθη is the concept under which "anger" is subsumed. So also Herm Sim 6:5:5 v.l.; cf. Rom 1:26; Col 3:5; 1 Thes 4:5; and *PECL* 1, index, s.v. πάθος.

παραινέσεις καὶ νουθεσίαι. ECL is also full of "ethical exhortation"; for νουθεσία see 1 Cor 10:11; Eph 6:4; Tit 3:10; Ign Eph 3:1; παραίνεσις does not occur in ECL, but παραινέω does.

νόσημα. Plutarch treats "anger" as a "disease" throughout the essay. On the metaphor of the "disease of the soul" see *PECL* 1: 200.

βοηθοῦντα λόγον ἔξωθεν εἰς τὴν ψυχήν. The λόγος enters into the soul from the outside. In ECL the equivalents are the Redeemer Christ (Gal 2:20; Col 1:27) and the Spirit (Gal 4:6; Rom 5:5; and often) entering into the human heart "from outside." A strange parallel is Jas 1:21: δέξασθε τὸν ἔμφυτον λόγον τὸν δυνάμενον σῶσαι τὰς ψυχὰς ὑμῶν.

ὁ . . . θυμὸς . . . ἐξοικίσας τελείως καὶ ἀποκλείσας. "Anger" completely expels and locks out reason, and this absence is what makes anger so difficult to cure. Cf. the "choking" of the Spirit in Herm Man 5:1:3 and the incapacity of the νοῦς in Rom 7:23.

(453F)

ὥσπερ οἱ συνεμπιπράντες ἑαυτοὺς ταῖς οἰκίαις. The situation of those possessed by anger is compared to those who burn themselves in their own houses. Cf. the human body as οἰκία 2 Cor 5:1f.; also "burning with passion" 1 Cor 7:9.

διὸ μᾶλλον ἐν χειμῶνι καὶ πελάγει ναῦς . . . The comparison with the ship is found in diatribe literature. Cf. the metaphorical language in Matt 8:23ff.; Jas 3:4; Jude 13. Christ is called κυβερνήτης of the body Mart Pol 19:2.

(454A)

ἐν θυμῷ καὶ ὀργῇ σαλεύων. For the figurative use of σαλεύω cf. Acts 2:25 (LXX Ps 15:8); 2 Thes 2:2. See Bauer, s.v., 2.

ὥσπερ οἱ πολιορκίαν προσδεχόμενοι. . . . For a comparison with a city under siege, see 1 Clem 57:4. Very similar also is The Teachings of Silvanus (NH VII, 4) 84, 15ff., where the city is identical with the soul (p. 85, line 2). For military imagery, cf. also 2 Cor 10:4-6; Eph 6:10ff. The term παρεισάγω also belongs to military language and is used in 2 Pet 2:1; cf. παρεισάκτος Gal 2:4.

καθάπερ κελευστὴν ἔνδοθεν ἔχῃ τὸν αὐτῆς λόγον. The λόγος is compared to a boatswain. See above on κυβερνήτης.

(454B)

ὑπερήφανος καὶ αὐθάδης . . . ὁ θυμός. Anger is compared to a strong tyranny, which can be overthrown only by a revolt from within (sc. the λόγος). Cf. for the imagery Mark 3:24//Matt 12:25// Luke 11:17; cf. Copt Gos Thom 21; 35. The moral adjectives have a parallel esp. in 1 Clem 57:2: ὑπερήφανος, αὐθάδεια. Cf. Bauer, s.v. ὑπερήφανος, αὐθάδης, for further references.

Ch. 3

ἡ . . . συνέχεια τῆς ὀργῆς. Plutarch explains that the persistence of anger creates an evil "condition" (ἕξις) in the soul, which is termed ὀργιλότης and which culminates in ἀκραχολία, πικρία and δυσκολία. The θυμός then becomes very sensitive. This psychology is not found in ECL, but some of the concepts do occur: ὀργίλος Tit 1:7; Did 3:2; ὀργίλως Herm Man 12:4:1; πικρία is found in a list of vices in Eph 4:31, together with θυμός and ὀργή (cf. Bauer, s.v. πικρία, πικρός, for more passages); ὀξυχολία κτλ. is prominent in Herm Man 5:1:3-6; 6:2:4f.; 10:1:1-2; 10:2:3f.; for further references, see Bauer, s.v.

(454D)

οὐδὲ . . . ἀρχὰς ἔχει μεγάλας ἀεὶ καὶ ἰσχυράς. Anger is considered curable because at the beginning of an attack it is weak and powerless. Examples to prove the point are provided in 454D-455B. Cf. Jas 3:5, where the smallness of the tongue is contrasted with its enormous power which nobody can tame.

Ch. 4

(454E)

καθάπερ . . . τὴν φλόγα θριξὶ λαγῴαις ἀναπτομένην. Anger is compared to a flame that is beginning in a hare's fur, etc. (Cf. *conjug. praec.* 138F for the same comparison.) See above 453B.

(455A)

θυμούμενον . . . βραδέως. For "slowness of anger" see Jas 1:19: βραδὺς εἰς ὀργήν.

Ch. 5

(455B)

τυράννου κατάλυσις τοῦ θυμοῦ. The rule of anger over a person is compared with that of a despot, whose dethronement is identical with the ethical task. This view comes close to Pauline tradition, where "evil" is considered a demonic despot ruling man by the many vices. See esp. Eph 2:1-3; 6:12; Rom 3:9; 6:7-14; 7:13; Gal 3:22; 5:13-24; etc. Cf. Ign Trall 4:2: καταλύεται ὁ ἄρχων τοῦ αἰῶνος τούτου.

μὴ πείθεσθαι μηδ' ὑπακούειν. The general method for fighting the despot "anger" is to disobey its orders. Similar language is used by Paul; see Rom 6:12-18; also 2:8; Gal 5:7.

μέγα βοᾶν καὶ δεινὸν βλέπειν καὶ κόπτειν ἑαυτόν. Cf. the description of a demon-possessed person in Mark 5:3-5; 9:17f.//Luke 9:39//Matt 17:15.

(455C)

ἀτρεμεῖν οὖν κράτιστον ἢ φεύγειν καὶ ἀποκρύπτειν καὶ καθορμίζειν ἑαυτοὺς εἰς ἡσυχίαν. The verbs describe ways to escape from anger. Only φεύγειν is used by ECL in this connection. Cf. 1 Cor 6:18; 10:14; 1 Tim 6:11; 2 Tim 2:22; etc. See Bauer, s.v., 3.

(455D)

ὀργιζόμεθα καὶ πολεμίοις καὶ φίλοις καὶ τέκνοις καὶ γονεῦσι καὶ θεοῖς νὴ Δία καὶ θηρίοις καὶ ἀψύχοις σκεύεσιν. Contrary to love, anger is indiscriminately directed against everybody and everything. Cf. Col 3:19, where anger against wives is prohibited; cf. also Col 3:21. See also below 455F; 457A.

(455E)

διὸ καὶ μισεῖται καὶ καταφρονεῖται μάλιστα τῶν παθῶν. Anger is considered the worst of the passions. The prominence of anger among the vices is reflected also in ECL; cf. esp. Matt 5:22; Eph 4:31; Col 3:8; Jas 1:19f.; Did 3:2; Ign Phld 8:1; etc.

Ch. 6

εἰ μὲν ὀρθῶς οὐκ οἶδα. For this rhetorical parenthesis, cf. 2 Cor 12:2f.: εἴτε . . . οὐκ οἶδα . . .

κατεμάνθανον τὴν ὀργὴν ἐν ἑτέροις. This activity Plutarch considers to be an important part of the therapy. Cf. the warnings Matt 7:3-5//Luke 6:41-42.

(455F)

τὸ πρόσωπον. Plutarch describes vividly the distorted face of a person overcome by anger. There is no parallel in ECL, but cf. the anger of Herod Matt 2:16 (also 22:7; Luke 14:21), and of the older brother Luke 15:28.

φωνή. Another symptom of anger is the change of the voice. Plutarch cites the example of the orator Gaius Gracchus who had a musician help him modulate his voice properly. For the rhetorical *topos*, see Gal 4:20: ἀλλάξαι τὴν φωνήν.

(456B)

παρὰ φύσιν. See *PECL* 1:289, 311, 314, 321.

(456C)

πικρὰ καὶ σπερμολόγα ῥήματα. Cf. Rom 3:14 (LXX Ps 9:28): τὸ στόμα ... πικρίας γέμει. For σπερμολόγος cf. Acts 17:18.

Ch. 7

(456D)

ἡ γλῶττα. Plutarch compares the healing of anger and fever with the treatment of the tongue. The example of the tongue was popular in diatribe literature and is found also in Jas 1:26; 3:5-12; etc. For further references, see Bauer, s.v. γλῶσσα.

(456E)

οὐδὲν γὰρ ὁ ἄκρατος ἀκόλαστον ... ὁ θυμὸς ἀναδίδωσι. The association of unmixed wine with anger is found in Rev 14:10; also 14:8; 16:19; 18:3; 19:15. Cf. Tit 1:7: μὴ ὀργίλον, μὴ πάροινον.

Ch. 8

τὸ προσέχειν ἀεὶ τοῖς ἁλισκομένοις ὑπ' ὀργῆς. Cf. on 456D.

(456F)

τὴν ἄλλην τοῦ θυμοῦ κατανοεῖν φύσιν. Plutarch presents his view on the nature of anger, a view that is contrary to the judgment of the masses who take anger to be a sign of nobility, manliness, pride and greatness, and who use euphemistic epithets like πρακτικόν for ταρακτικόν, etc. (cf. also 462F). One should remember that for the Peripatetics anger had potentially noble connotations. It is not clear, however, that Plutarch turns against the Peripatetics at this point. ECL has no discussion of this kind, but Eph 4:26f. does not completely eliminate anger.

τὰ ... ἔργα. The term here refers to the activities of angry persons. Cf. Paul's concept of τὰ ἔργα τῆς σαρκός Gal 5:19-21; etc. See Bauer, s.v. ἔργον, l.c.β.

(457B)

διὸ καὶ γυναῖκες ἀνδρῶν ὀργιλωτέραι. Plutarch interprets anger as a sign of physical and emotional "weakness" and, as a consequence, considers women to be naturally more prone to anger than men.

The view that women are morally "weaker" than men is reflected also in 1 Pet 3:7 (ὡς ἀσθενεστέρῳ σκεύει τῷ γυναικείῳ); 1 Cor 11:2-16; 1 Tim 2:9-15.

Ch. 9

(457D)

ἡ ... ἀνδρεία ... τῇ δικαιοσύνῃ συμφερομένη περὶ μόνης μοι δοκεῖ διαμάχεσθαι τῆς πραότητος. Plutarch goes against the common opinion that "courage" and "justice" go together, but that "gentleness" is unrelated to them. Interestingly, the Sermon on the Mount also relates polemically οἱ πραεῖς (Matt 5:5) and δικαιοσύνη (cf. 5:6, 10, 20; 6:1, 33); similarly Jas 1:20f.; 3:13, 18; Herm Man 5:1:1f.

τὸ ... ἐν τῇ ψυχῇ στῆσαι κατὰ θυμοῦ τρόπαιον. A typical military image to describe a moral victory over anger. ECL does not have this language, but beginning with Just 1 Apol 55:3 the cross of Christ is called a τρόπαιον. See Lampe, s.v.

διὸ καὶ συνάγειν ἀεὶ πειρῶμαι καὶ ἀναγινώσκειν ... τὰ τῶν φιλοσόφων ... Plutarch's words state the reason for collecting and reading the *exempla* of the philosophers. They are evidence of their moral strength and victory. Cf. the purpose of the words of Jesus and the apostles; see *PECL* 1:88, and index, s.v. Word(s).

(458B)

μειλίχιος. Plutarch refers to this attribute of Zeus as evidence that "mercy" and "gentleness," the opposite of anger, are θεῖος and ὀλύμπιος. ECL also relates God and "mercy," although by different terms (cf., e.g., Matt 5:7; Luke 1:50, 54, 58, 72, 78; Eph 2:4; Col 3:12; 1 Tim 1:2; 2 Tim 1:2; Tit 3:5; Jas 2:13; 3:17; 1 Pet 1:3; 2 John 3).

(458C)

τὸ ... κολαστικὸν ἐρινυῶδες καὶ δαιμονικόν. Punishment, however, is related to "anger," and therefore to the Furies and Demons. On this topic, see *PECL* 1:224, and index, s.v. Punishment.

Ch. 10

ἀνατρέφει ... καὶ διαφθεῖραι καὶ καταβαλεῖν. The work of "anger" is purely destructive. Early Christians would certainly agree; cf. Matt 5:21-26; 1 Clem 63:2; etc.

ἀναστῆσαι . . . καὶ σῶσαι καὶ φείσασθαι καὶ καρτερῆσαι. The work of πραότης with συγγνώμη and μετριοπάθεια is constructive and beneficial. Early Christians would again agree. See esp. Did 15:1; Ign Eph 10:2; Trall 3:2; 4:2 (even the devil is impressed!); Gal 6:1. On συγγνώμη see Ign Rom 5:3; μετριοπαθέω occurs Heb 5:2.

σκοπῶν τὸν δι' ὀργῆς τρόπον ἄπρακτον εὑρίσκω. Plutarch finds that anger is ineffectual as a method of defense and gives a vivid description of the ridiculous behavior of such an angry person. Among the things mentioned is "gnashing the teeth," which is found also in Acts 7:54. On the whole, the descriptions of the Pharisees and other Jewish leaders in the Gospels and Acts again and again demonstrate Plutarch's point of view.

Ch. 11

(459B)

οἷον δαμάζοντος καὶ καταθλοῦντος ἀσκήσει τὸ ἄλογον καὶ δυσπειθές. The phrase describes the method of ἄσκησις, a fundamental concept in Hellenistic ethics. For a discussion of the concept, see Ingenkamp, *Plutarch's Schriften über die Heilung der Seele*, 99ff., 121. While early Christian authors mostly presuppose, rather than explain, the theory of ἄσκησις, at least Jas 3:7f. has the term δαμάζειν. The term ἄσκησις is first attested in Mart Pol 18:2; ἀσκέω occurs in Acts 24:16; 2 Clem 20:4; Herm Man 8:10; Pol Phil 9:1 v.l.; Diogn 5:2; 12:5. See H. Windisch, *TDNT*, s.v.; Bauer, s.v.; V. Pfitzner, *Paul and the Agon Motif* (Leiden, 1967) 23-35 and passim.

ἐγγυμνάσασθαι τοῖς οἰκέταις. Plutarch pays special attention to the treatment of slaves, because there is no better way to learn to control one's anger. The section 459B-E (see also 463B) is of great interest because of the ethical and social information contained in it. The treatment of slaves was also seen as a great challenge to the Christian faith by early Christian authors. See esp. Gal 3:28; 1 Cor 7:21ff.; 12:13; Eph 6:5-9; Col 3:11, 22-4:1; 1 Tim 6:1f.; Tit 2:9f.; Phlm passim; 1 Pet 2:18f.; 2 Pet 2:19 (?); Ign Pol 4:3. For literature, see H. Conzelmann, *First Corinthians* (Philadelphia, 1975) 127f.; E. Lohse, *Colossians and Philemon* (Philadelphia, 1971) 154-63; S. Bartchy, ΜΑΛΛΟΝ ΧΡΗΣΑΙ: *First Century Slavery and the Interpretation of 1 Corinthians 7:21* (Missoula, Montana, 1973); D. Lührmann,

"Wo man nicht mehr Sklave oder Freier ist," *Wort und Dienst* 13 (1975) 53-83.

οὔτε . . . φθόνος οὔτε φόβος οὔτε φιλοτιμία. Plutarch's view is that these attitudes do not affect the relationship of the master to his slave. Eph 6:5; 1 Pet 2:18 recommend φόβος for the slaves towards their masters; cf. Eph 5:21: ὑποτασσόμενοι ἀλλήλους ἐν φόβῳ Χριστοῦ. φθόνος is generally regarded as a "vice" in ECL.

διὰ τὴν ἐξουσίαν. The greatest ethical danger threatening the slave master is his absolute power over the slave. In the Christian literature dealing with the slaves, the masters are put under the ἐξουσία of Christ and God; see esp. Gal 3:26-28; 1 Cor 7:21-24; Eph 6:9; Col 4:1.

(459C)

ἐπὶ τοὺς οἰκέτας ὡς τῷ μὴ κολάζεσθαι διαφθειρομένους. Plutarch states and rejects the common view that not punishing slaves will spoil them. Cf. Eph 6:9, where the slave masters are told: ἀνιέντες τὴν ἀπειλήν. Similarly Col 4:1: τὸ δίκαιον καὶ τὴν ἰσότητα . . . παρέχεσθε. Paul's letter to Philemon has only one purpose, to prevent the punishment of Onesimus (esp. 17f.).

διαστρέφειν ἑαυτὸν εἰς ἑτέρων ἐπανόρθωσιν. Plutarch's first reason for rejecting punishment of slaves is that it is better to ruin slaves than to ruin oneself through bitterness and anger, as a result of the correction of others. Cf. the anecdotes about Plato and the slave *lib. ed.* 10D; *num. vind.* 551B (cf. *PECL* 1:198); *adv. Col.* 1108A.; also Cato's saying, *reg. et imp.* 199A. Remarkably, Paul makes a similar point in Gal 6:1 (σκοπῶν σεαυτόν, μὴ καὶ σὺ πειρασθῇς). The technical term ἐπανόρθωσις is found also in 2 Tim 3:16. See also Did 15:3: ἐλέγχετε δὲ ἀλλήλους μὴ ἐν ὀργῇ, ἀλλ' ἐν εἰρήνῃ. . . .

(459D)

ἐπειθόμην ἡγεμονικώτερον εἶναι τοῦ θυμοῦ τὸν λογισμόν. Plutarch's second reason for rejecting punishment of slaves is that their education can be better accomplished by "reason." He has observed that slaves, precisely because they were pardoned and not punished, often developed "shame," which is the beginning of moral improvement and better performance as slaves. For the background of these ideas and their implications for Matt 5:38-48//Luke 6:27-36, see L. Schottroff, "Gewaltverzicht und Feindesliebe in der urchristlichen Jesustradition," in *Jesus*

Christus in Historie und Theologie, ed. G. Strecker (Tübingen, 1975) 197-221, esp. 208-13.

οὐ μετάνοιαν ἐμποιεῖ τοῦ κακουργεῖν ἀλλὰ τοῦ λανθάνειν πρόνοιαν. Harsh treatment of slaves does not result in repentance, but in planned deceit. Cf. the implication of the Christian faith for slaves: they are supposed to become better slaves (Eph 6:5ff.; Col 3:22ff.; 1 Tim 6:1; Tit 2:9f.; 1 Pet 2:18; Ign Pol 4:3; Did 4:10-11).

εὐκαίρως τοῦτο ποιεῖν καὶ μετρίως καὶ ὠφελίμως καὶ πρεπόντως. Thirdly, if slaves are to be punished, it should be done with these guidelines in mind. The reason is that the guidelines are designed to remove anger from the one who is doing the punishing. This can be done by giving the slave a chance to defend himself and by listening to his plea. Delaying and limiting the punishment are also ways of eliminating anger and of preventing the embarrassing situation that the slave appears to be more just than the master. Plutarch's long deliberations (to 460C) have no parallel in ECL, but there is good reason to assume that early Christians would have approved of them.

Ch. 12

(460D)

δόξα τοῦ καταφρονεῖσθαι καὶ ἀμελεῖσθαι. One of the sources of "anger" is a person's belief that he is being despised or neglected. As a "cure" Plutarch recommends that others help to remove the source of such a belief, that is, the elimination of arrogance which creates the impression of contempt and neglect. A lengthy discussion of the point follows. ECL does not have this kind of discussion, but Paul's exhortation against σκανδαλίζειν of fellow Christians (Rom 14-15) is very similar; cf. also 1 Cor 13:5: οὐ ζητεῖ τὰ ἑαυτῆς, . . . οὐ παροξύνεται.

Ch. 13

(461A)

φιλαυτία καὶ δυσκολία μετὰ τρυφῆς καὶ μαλακίας are "vices" which describe another source of "anger." A vivid portrait of such behavior is given in 461B. The "cure" is indicated by the opposite qualities of εὐκολία —and ἀφέλεια in connection with the principle of συμφέρεσθαι τοῖς παροῦσι καὶ μὴ δεομένῳ πολλῶν καὶ περιττῶν. This principle refers to the goal of αὐτάρκεια and introduces asceticism into the discussion. For the adoption of the "principle" ἀρκεῖσθαι τοῖς παροῦσι, see Heb 13:5; also Phil 4:11f. The conventional vices, except δυσκολία, occur in ECL: 2 Tim 3:2 (φίλαυτος); τρυφή κτλ. occurs 2 Pet 2:13; cf. Jas 5:5 and often in Hermas, where μαλακία is also found (for passages and parallels see Bauer, s.v.). For the peculiar usage of μετά, cf. Eph 4:2; 6:23; Col 1:11; 1 Tim 2:15.

(461C)

ἐθιστέον οὖν τὸ σῶμα δι' εὐτελείας πρὸς εὐκολίαν αὔταρκες ἑαυτῷ γινόμενον· οἱ γὰρ ὀλίγων δεόμενοι πολλῶν οὐκ ἀποτυγχάνουσιν. The statement sums up Plutarch's ethical recommendations. Cf. 1 Clem 2:1; also 2 Cor 12:9; 1 Tim 6:8. The principle of αὐτάρκεια is adopted in 2 Cor 9:8; Phil 4:11f.; 1 Tim 6:6; Herm Man 6:2:3; Sim 1:6. See Dibelius and Conzelmann, *The Pastoral Epistles*, 84f.

(461C-D)

ἀρξαμένους ἀπὸ τῆς τροφῆς. The exercises are to begin with getting one's eating habits under control. The ideal is σιωπῇ χρήσασθαι τοῖς παρατυγχάνουσι. In ECL cf. Luke 10:8: ἐσθίετε τὰ παρατιθέμενα ὑμῖν. See also Matt 6:25-34//Luke 12:22-32; Rom 14:2ff.; 1 Cor 8:8; 10:25; Phil 3:19 (ὁ θεὸς ἡ κοιλία); Rom 16:18; etc.

(461E-F)

ἐθιστέον δὲ καὶ σκεύεσιν εὐκόλως ὁμιλεῖν ἅπασι . . . The use of utensils is another good area for exercises. Examples show what Plutarch is castigating as a cause of "anger." The "cure" is to stay away from using a multitude of precious objects and to be content with a few, ordinary ones. In ECL polemics of this kind are found only infrequently. See Jas 2:2ff.; 5:2f. and Betz, *Lukian*, 194-99.

(462B)

ὁ . . . τοῦ θεοῦ νάρθηξ ἱκανὸς κολαστὴς τοῦ μεθύοντος. Plutarch appears to discuss the possible connection between "anger" and wine drinking. He explains apologetically that the Dionysiac μανία alone is harmless, but that when "anger" is added to the potion, it produces τραγῳδίαι καὶ μῦθοι. Cf. Tit 1:7 which requires that a bishop be μὴ ὀργίλος, μὴ πάροινος; Eph 5:18; also cf. John the Baptist, Luke 1:15; 7:33//Matt 11:18. See also below 464B.

Ch. 14

δεῖ δὲ μήτε παίζοντας αὐτῇ διδόναι τόπον . . . If "anger" is mixed into the jesting which we use in discussions and conversations, it results in ἔχθρα instead of φιλοφροσύνη. In learned discussions it turns φιλολογία into φιλονεικία, etc. Cf. the rejection of εὐτραπελία in Eph 5:4. See Almqvist, 90f.

Ch. 15

(463A)

τῶν παθῶν πανσπερμία τις ὁ θυμὸς εἶναι. Applying Zeno's view that semen is a mixture drawn from all δυνάμεις of the soul, Plutarch calls anger a πανσπερμία out of λύπη, ἡδονή, ὕβρις. It is even worse than φθόνος because its ἀγωνίζειν is not to avoid suffering, but to destroy the other person, and its ὄρεξις is λυπεῖν. Early Christian theology would agree with many of the concepts although a precise parallel is not found in ECL. Paul's discussion of the ἔργα τῆς σαρκός in Gal 5:19-21 is at least similar.

Ch. 16

(463C)

τὸ δ' ἐμὸν ἦθος, οἶσθα . . . Fundanus concludes his report with a "testimony" explaining first how his former fits of anger had come about and how he is now attempting to combat them. For "testimony" in ECL, cf. Gal 1:13ff.; Phil 3:4ff.; etc. On the whole subject, see P. Tachau, *"Einst" und "Jetzt" im Neuen Testament* (Göttingen, 1972).

ὥσπερ . . . οἱ κατὰ κενοῦ βαίνοντες. Cf. Gal 2:2: εἰς κενὸν τρέχω.

ὅσῳ μᾶλλον ἐπερείδω τῷ φιλεῖν ἐμαυτόν, ἁμαρτάνω μᾶλλον . . . Fundanus' first step of recovery was the recognition that his "anger" had its main source in his excessive love of other people. Not being sure whether he was able to curtail his φιλεῖν, he attempted at least to cut down on his "excessive trust" (πιστεύειν). Cf., by contrast, 1 Cor 13, esp. 13:7: πάντα πιστεύει.

(463D-E)

ἄνθρωποι καὶ σπέρματα ἀνθρώπων ὄντες ἐκφήνωσί που τῆς φύσεως τὴν ἀσθένειαν. Plutarch's concept of human "weakness" is derived from Plato, to whom he refers. This "weakness," however, does not lead him to go as far as Sophocles does in viewing man as wholly evil. Rather, Fundanus says, it is sudden and unexpected events which jolt people into fits of anger. Instead of being driven into anger by his disappointment in someone else, Fundanus realizes the person's mortal, and therefore faulty, nature. When one puts himself, using Plato's words, into the same position: ἦ που ἄρ' ἐγὼ τοιοῦτος; (cf. Luke 18:9-14), this comparison ("syncrisis motif") makes us humble and cautious. The more we recognize how much συγγνώμη we need ourselves, the less we will be engulfed by μισοπονηρία towards others. The principle involved here (leniency towards others brought about by the recognition of one's own "weakness") has no parallel in ECL, but it is rejected in Herm Sim 5:7:2: βλέπε, μήποτέ σου ἐπὶ τὴν καρδίαν ἀναβῇ τὴν σάρκα σου ταύτην φθαρτὴν εἶναι .... There is, however, a similar connection between the recognition of one's own sinfulness and the readiness to forgive others. See esp. Matt 6:12// Luke 11:4; Matt 7:1-5//Luke 6:37-42; Matt 18:23-35; Rom 2:1ff.; 14:4; Jas 4:11f.; 5:9; etc.

(463F)

πειρῶμαι καὶ τοῦ πολυπράγμονος ἀφαιρεῖν ... The second step of his "cure" was Fundanus' constant attempt to stay away from moral inquisitiveness, that is, τὸ ... ἐξακριβοῦν ἅπαντα καὶ φωρᾶν.... Abstention from πολυπραγμοσύνη is attributed to Christians by Diogn 4:6; cf. 5:3. See also Plutarch's essay entitled περὶ πολυπραγμοσύνης (515B-523B).

(464A)

πιστεύειν δὲ καὶ χρῆσθαι τὰ μὲν γυναικὶ τὰ δ' οἰκέταις τὰ δὲ φίλοις οἷον ἄρχοντ' ἐπιτρόποις τισὶ καὶ λογισταῖς καὶ διοικηταῖς, αὐτὸν ἐπὶ τῶν κυριωτάτων ὄντα τῷ λογισμῷ καὶ μεγίστων. Plutarch's words briefly describe his "method" for ruling the household: instead of getting bogged down by every trivial concern, the master of the house should entrust and delegate the minor affairs to the members of the family, while retaining control over the important decisions. Plutarch's policy is, of course, an application of the Roman political rule of *Divide et impera*. Cf. the image of the feudal lord in Matt 25:14-30//Luke 19:12-27. It seems that the author of the Pastoral Epistles implicitly applies the rule to the church by entrusting the gospel to the addressees of the letters (see esp. 1 Tim 1:11, 18; 6:20; 2 Tim 1:12, 14; 2:2; Tit 1:3).

(464B)

"νηστεῦσαι κακότητος." The final step towards the ethical goal leads into the area of religion. As various of his treatises show, this step is characteristic of Plutarch's ethics. Here he takes up the "great and divine" phrase of Empedocles about "fasting from evil" (Diels-Kranz, I, 369, fr. B 144; see Helmbold and O'Neil, 26). The "spiritualized," ethical interpretation of the ritual of fasting has very close parallels in Philo's treatment of the festivals (*spec. leg.* 2. 193-203) and in ECL in Barn 3:1-3; Herm Sim 5 (see esp. 5:1:4f.; 5:3:6); for further passages in the Fathers, see Lampe, s.v. νηστεία, A.4; in Gnosticism, see *Epistula ad Floram* 3. 13 (W. Foerster, *Gnosis* [Oxford, 1972] 1:159); cf. also Epiphanius *Panarion* 26. 5. 8 (Foerster, *Gnosis* 1:320).

ἐν εὐχαῖς ὁμολογίαι. Plutarch interprets "fasting from evil" in analogy to "vows made in prayers." This original general meaning of ὁμολογέω/ὁμολογία is found in ECL only in Matt 14:7, where Herod μεθ' ὅρκου ὡμολόγησεν αὐτῇ (sc., to the daughter of Herodias). But in ECL the term has taken on the specific meaning of "confession" of Christ (2 Cor 9:13).

ἀφροδισίων ἐνιαυτὸν ἁγνεῦσαι καὶ οἴνου. For temporary sexual abstinence see 1 Cor 7:5 and Conzelmann, *First Corinthians*, 117. Ritual abstinence is, of course, attested frequently in ECL. See J. Behm, *TDNT*, s.v. νῆστις κτλ. On the abstinence from wine, see above on 462B.

τιμῶντας ἐγκρατείᾳ τὸν θεόν. On ἐγκράτεια see *PECL* 1:264, 315.

ψευδολογίας . . . ἀπέχεσθαι. Cf. 1 Tim 4:2.

(464C)

οὐχ ἧττον θεοφιλῆ καὶ ἱεράν. Plutarch emphasizes that this "ethical" fasting is not inferior to the ritual fasting. Cf. the polemic against ritual fasting in Herm Sim 5:1:1-5 (see on 464B above).

ἡμέρας πρῶτον ὀλίγας ἀοργήτους οἷον ἀμεθύστους καὶ ἀοίνους διαγαγεῖν . . . Fundanus' moral progress is, of course, gradual. The term ἀόργητος, found only here in the treatise itself, occurs also in 1 Clem 19:3; Ign Phld 1:2, where it refers to God.

ὥσπερ νηφάλια καὶ μελίσπονδα θύοντα. Fundanus declares his ethical asceticism as a "spiritual" sacrifice. Cf. Rom 12:1. See *PECL* 1, index, s.v. Spiritualization. The term νηφάλιος occurs in a similar context in 1 Tim 3:2; Tit 2:2.

πειρώμενος ἐμαυτοῦ. "Making trial of myself" is the method of measuring moral progress. See 2 Cor 13:5: ἑαυτοὺς πειράζετε . . . ., ἑαυτοὺς δοκιμάζετε, also 1 Cor 11:28; Gal 6:4.

κατὰ μικρὸν οὕτω τῷ χρόνῳ προὔβαινον εἰς τὸ πρόσθεν τῆς ἀνεξικακίας. The words describe the idea of moral progress. It is not found in ECL. On ἀνεξικακία, cf. ἀνεξίκακος in 2 Tim 2:24.

ἐγκρατῶς προσέχων καὶ διαφυλάττων μετ' εὐφημίας ἵλεω καὶ ἀμήνιτον ἐμαυτόν. Moral progress is virtually identical with self-preservation. Cf. the exhortation προσέχετε ἑαυτοῖς in Luke 17:3; 21:34; cf. Acts 20:28; Barn 2:1; 4:6. See also 1 Tim 5:22 (σεαυτὸν ἁγνὸν τήρει); 1 John 5:21; Jude 21. For the opposite, see John 12:25: ὁ φιλῶν τὴν ψυχὴν αὐτοῦ ἀπολλύει αὐτήν . . .//Matt 10:39// Luke 9:24; 17:33.

ἁγνεύοντα καὶ λόγων πονηρῶν καὶ πράξεων ἀτόπων καὶ πάθους. Plutarch also describes the process of getting "anger" under control in terms of "spiritualized" religious language (for ἁγνεῦσαι, see also 464B above). Similarly Barn 19:8; cf. ἁγνεία in 1 Tim 4:12: ἐν ἀγάπῃ ἐν πίστει ἐν ἁγνείᾳ. See furthermore Jas 4:8; 1 Pet 1:22; 1 John 3:3; Barn 5:1; 8:3; etc. (for further references see also Bauer, s.v. ἁγνεία).

(464D)

καὶ θεοῦ τι συλλαμβάνοντος. Divine assistance in the process is considered of some importance, but nowhere in the treatise does Plutarch spell out in what sense that divine assistance becomes effective. Thus, the reference here comes in almost as an afterthought to an ethics which is fundamentally man's own achievement. In ECL the concept of divine "help" is not as prominent as one might expect. Cf. esp. Heb 2:18; Gal 5:22f.; 1 Clem 36:1; 59:3, 4.

ἐσαφήνιζεν ἡ πεῖρα τὴν κρίσιν. The method of testing oneself serves to confirm the theoretical κρίσις by experience. Reflections of the method may be behind 1 Clem 1:2.

τὸ ἵλεων τοῦτο καὶ πρᾶον καὶ φιλάνθρωπον. Plutarch interprets "divine assistance" by the principle of ὅμοιος τῷ ὁμοίῳ: those who possess the divine endowment of τὸ πρᾶον and τὸ φιλάνθρωπον have the greatest chance of reaching the moral goal by the method Plutarch is suggesting. In Plutarch the concept of divine endowment is, of course, traditionally Platonic; in ECL this concept is not prominent (see 2 Pet 1:4), but its place is filled by the concept of the divine Spirit (see, e.g., 1 Cor 2:12-16; Gal 5:22f.; 6:1). The difference from Plutarch is also sharply expressed by Tit 3:4f.: ἡ χρηστότης καὶ ἡ φιλανθρωπία ἐπεφάνη τοῦ σωτῆρος ἡμῶν θεοῦ, but then human works of righteousness are rejected in favor of the saving ritual of baptismal regeneration.

DE TRANQUILLITATE ANIMI (MORALIA 464E - 477F)

BY

HANS DIETER BETZ
Claremont Graduate School and School of Theology
Claremont, California

I. INTRODUCTION

Plutarch's essay "On Tranquillity of Mind" (περὶ εὐθυμίας, no. 95 in the Lamprias catalog, LCL 15:16) [1] discusses a subject that was popular among philosophers of his time. This can be inferred from the request of his Roman friend Paccius that he write the work [2] and from Seneca's *De tranquillitate animi*, which has much in common with Plutarch's work. The beginning of the tradition is said to rest with Democritus, who introduced the Greek philosophical concept of εὐθυμία [3] into ethics and wrote a work on it, some fragments of which are extant.[4] Whether his student Epicurus used the notion is not altogether clear,[5] but Epicurus' notion of

[1] Bibliography. The text used here is by W. C. Helmbold, *Plutarch's Moralia* 6, LCL (1962). Translations of *tranq. an.* quoted here are taken from Helmbold's translation. The edition by M. Pohlenz & W. Sieveking (*Plutarchi Moralia* 3, BT [1929]) was also consulted. M. Pohlenz also wrote two important articles: "Plutarchs Schrift περὶ εὐθυμίας," *Hermes* 40 (1905) 275-300; "Philosophische Nachklänge in altchristlichen Predigten," *ZWT* 48 (1905) 72-95. There are two valuable commentaries: G. Siefert, *Plutarchs Schrift* περὶ εὐθυμίας, Programmschrift Pforta 1908 (Naumburg, 1908), and H. Broecker, *Animadversiones ad Plutarchi Libellum* περὶ εὐθυμίας (Bonn, 1954). Broecker's dissertation also has a bibliography, to which the following works should be added: Ziegler, sec. III.4.n; I. Hadot, *Seneca und die griechisch-römische Tradition der Seelenleitung* (Berlin, 1969); H. G. Ingenkamp, *Plutarchs Schriften über die Heilung der Seele* (Göttingen, 1971); H. Adam, *Plutarchs Schrift Non posse suaviter vivi secundum Epicurum* (Amsterdam, 1974).

[2] 464E.

[3] For passages see Diels-Kranz, 68. B. 3-4. On the Democritean concept see G. Vlastos, "Ethics and Physics in Democritus (Part One)" *PhR* 54 (1945) 582-85; Horst Steckel, "Demokritos," PW, Suppl. 12 (1970) 208-12.

[4] See R. Hirzel, "Democrits Schrift περὶ εὐθυμίας," *Hermes* 14 (1879) 354-407.

[5] See C. W. Chilton, *Diogenes of Oenoanda: The Fragments* (Oxford, 1971) 29f.; H. J. Krämer, *Platonismus und hellenistische Philosophie* (Berlin & New York, 1971) 201, 203.

ἀταραξία is very similar and might have taken the place of the Democritan term.[6] Beginning with the Stoic Panaetius' essay περὶ εὐθυμίας,[7] the notion played an important role in Stoicism.[8] Yet another work on the subject is said to have been written by the Pythagorean Hipparchus.[9]

The problem discussed by Plutarch is on people's minds today more than ever before. Only the names and methods have changed. The old name "tranquillity of mind" seems to have acquired a bad taste, the connotations of petty complacency and television commercials. For better or worse, the whole matter is presently in the hands of psychology and the pharmaceutical industry, not to mention the drug culture.

Plutarch's work is a letter-essay (λόγος, 464F)[10] on the topic of (περί)[11] εὐθυμία. It is addressed to his Roman friend Paccius,[12] at whose request it was written.[13] In this connection the author makes an interesting remark about how he went about creating his piece. Since their mutual friend Eros[14] was about to leave for Rome at the urgent request of Fundanus, Plutarch did not want to let him go "with empty hands"[15] but took the opportunity to send the requested work. He then excuses himself, saying that he did not have sufficient time but: ἀνελεξάμην περὶ εὐθυμίας ἐκ τῶν ὑπομνημάτων ὧν ἐμαυτῷ πεποιημένος ἐτύγχανον. He believes, however, that Paccius had asked him to write: οὐκ ἀκροάσεως ἕνεκα θηρωμένης καλλιγραφίαν ἀλλὰ χρείας βοηθητικῆς (464F-465A).[16]

[6] See A. R. Neumann, "Epikuros," PW, Suppl. 11 (1968) 624f., with further literature; also Ph. Merlan, *Studies in Epicurus and Aristotle* (Wiesbaden, 1960), ch. 1.

[7] See M. van Straaten, *Panaetii Rhodii Fragmenta* (Leiden, 1952) fr. 45. Cf. also his earlier book, *Panétius* (Amsterdam, 1946) 296ff.

[8] See A. Bonhoeffer, *Epictet und die Stoa* (Stuttgart, 1890) 293-98, who treats εὐθυμία as part of χαρά; but in his *Die Ethik des Stoikers Epictet* (Stuttgart, 1894) 46-49, he treats it as among the notions belonging to ἀπάθεια. Cf. Andronicus' definitions, Περὶ παθῶν 6 (*SVF*, III. 432); Diogenes Laertius 7. 116 (*SVF*, III. 431).

[9] See H. Dörrie, *Der Kleine Pauly* (1967), s.v. Hipparchos, 5.

[10] Cf. the prooemium of Acts (1:1) and Bauer, s.v. λόγος, 1.a.ζ.

[11] Cf. Luke 1:1-4, and Bauer, s.v. περί, 1.

[12] On Paccius, see Ziegler, sec. I.8.

[13] It is probable that in some cases Paul wrote at the request of his churches. Cf. 1 Cor 5:9-11; 7:1, 25; 8:1; 12:1; 16:1, 12; 1 Thes 5:1-2.

[14] On Eros, see Ziegler, col. 38 (I.8). Cf. Acts 15:22f.; 1 Cor 16:3.

[15] 464F: μηθ' ὑπομένων κεναῖς παντάπασιν τὸν ἄνδρα χερσίν. For this expression see Mark 12:3//Luke 20:10; Luke 1:53; also Bauer, s.v. κενός, 1.

[16] Cf. 1 Cor 2:4f.; 2 Cor 10:10; 11:6. See Betz, *Paulus*, 57ff.

Whether this remark reflects the true situation or is simply a stylistic device does not need to concern us here.[17] More important is the method it reveals, a method which we must assume Plutarch also used on other occasions. He collected "material" called ὑπομνήματα, from which he then composed his works whenever he saw fit.[18] This method is obvious from *tranq. an.* itself, where we can distinguish between "source-material" of diverse origin and tendencies, and the author's own "redactional" contributions of arrangement, composition and interpretation.

It should be noted that in spite of Plutarch's excuse this work is of no less quality than his other works.[19] This means that his redactional contribution is considerable. It is not possible to isolate any one special source, as the failure of the old "Quellenforschung," which sought such a source, has demonstrated.[20] On the contrary, Plutarch's excerpts must have come from a wide variety of sources, including specific works on the subject. In addition he shows an intimate knowledge of the subject matter itself, and therefore his own work is much more than what he took out of his reference files. His own synthesis is clear, and so is the purpose of the work. His aim, he assures us, is not for elegance of style,[21] but to provide help in the form of "therapy by word" [22] in face of the problems of daily life.

Plutarch's advice does not provide "new wisdom," but it reminds the reader of what we all know and experience: πολλάκις ἀκηκοὼς μνημονεύεις (465A). Because of our peculiarly stubborn stupidity as human beings, we need to go through an extensive learning process, a preventive mental therapy,[23] before we can hope to bring our

---

[17] See Ziegler, col. 149 (III.4.n).

[18] For a similar method see 2 Tim 4:13; also *Acta Pilati* A, *prooemium* (ed. C. Tischendorf, *Evangelia Apocrypha* [Leipzig, 1876] 210): ταῦτα εὗρον τὰ ὑπομνήματα ἐν ἑβραϊκοῖς γράμμασιν. On ὑπομνήματα see H. Martin, "Plutarch's Citation of Empedocles at Amatorius 756D," *GRBS* 10 (1969) 57-70; G. Avenarius, *Lukians Schrift zur Geschichtsschreibung* (Meisenheim, 1956) 85ff.; J. Hani, Plutarque, *Consolation à Apollonios* (Paris, 1972) 41-42; H. Cherniss, LCL 13:398f., who refers to *cohib. ira* 457D-E.

[19] So Ziegler, col. 149 (III.4.n).

[20] On the whole question, see the commentaries by Siefert and Broecker; Ziegler, col. 151 (III.4.n); Helmbold, LCL 6:163f.

[21] 464F.

[22] See on this subject P. Laín Entralgo, *The Therapy of the Word in Classical Antiquity* (New Haven & London, 1970).

[23] 465B; 476E-F.

emotions under control. This is what Plutarch's παρακαλεῖν[24] amounts to: through meditation (ἐπιλογισμοί)[25] and exercise Paccius will arrive at the λόγος εἰθισμένος καὶ μεμελετηκώς[26] and develop the attitude Plutarch sums up in the *peroratio*: . . .τοῖς παροῦσιν ἀμέμπτως συνοίσονται καὶ τῶν γεγονότων εὐχαρίστως μνημονεύσουσι καὶ πρὸς τὸ λοιπὸν ἵλεω τὴν ἐλπίδα καὶ φαιδρὰν ἔχοντες ἀδεῶς καὶ ἀνυπόπτως προσάξουσιν (477F).

The composition of the essay is fairly clear.[27] It follows the traditional structure of rhetoric.[28] Within a section, Plutarch usually states a philosophical principle or problem first, then illustrates it by a series of quotations, apophthegms, anecdotes, examples, and comparisons,[29] in order to conclude by another philosophical statement expressing his position.

I. Exordium	Ch. 1
A. Address (464E)	
B. Excusatio (464F)	
C. Captatio benevolentiae (465A)[30]	
II. Quaestiones (465A-B)	
III. Statement of utilitas (465B-C)	
IV. Probatio	Chs. 2-5
A. Refutation of false ethical theories	Chs. 2-4
B. Presentation of Plutarch's own ethical theory	Ch. 5
V. Exhortatio (467C: ἀσκεῖν καὶ μελετᾶν)[31]	Chs. 6-19
VI. Peroratio[32]	Ch. 20

[24] 477F.

[25] See 471C; 476B; and Ingenkamp, *Plutarchs Schriften*, 99ff.

[26] 465B; cf. ἀσκεῖν καὶ μελετᾶν 467C; and Ingenkamp, *Plutarchs Schriften*, 105ff., 113f.

[27] The composition was discussed esp. by Siefert (cf. 3f.) and Pohlenz, *Hermes* 40 (1905) 275-84. Cf. also Broecker, 23-25.

[28] It belongs to the γένος συμβουλευτικόν.

[29] Their function is to stimulate their imitation, in order to guide the student toward ἕξις (*facultas*), that is, the acquisition of ἀρετή. See on this, H. Lausberg, *Handbuch der literarischen Rhetorik* (Munich, 1960) secs. 1-8.

[30] Cf. 1 Thes 5:1-2; Acts 17:22; Luke 23:12; Phil 4:22.

[31] See on this Lausberg, *Handbuch*, sec. 6; Ingenkamp, *Plutarchs Schriften*, 99ff.

[32] Cf. Gal 6:12-17; and H. D. Betz, "The Literary Composition and Function of Paul's Letter to the Galatians," *NTS* 21 (1974-75) 356f.; also Jas 5:19f.

II. "Tranquillity of Mind in Plutarch and Early Christianity

The subject matter discussed under the term εὐθυμία is difficult to understand. This difficulty is reflected by the fact that even the translation of the term εὐθυμία has its problems.[33] The English title goes back to Latin renderings. Cicero *Fin.* 5. 87, proposes: "εὐθυμίαν ... id est animum terrore liberum," or, ibid., 23: "Democriti autem securitas, quae est animi tranquillitas." Most revealing is Seneca *De tranquillitate animi* 2. 3:

> Hanc stabilem animi sedem Graeci euthymian vocant, de qua Democriti volumen egregium est; ego tranquillitatem voco: nec enim imitari et transferre verba ad illorum formam necesse et; res ipsa, de qua agitur, aliquo signanda nomine est, quod appellationis Graecae vim debet habere, non faciem.

One must realize, however, that these considerations belong to the philosophical-ethical interpretation of the term. Originally the term denoted "cheerfulness, contentment" in the secular sense, especially in association with banquets.[34] Depending upon the context, therefore, the term could express a variety of "cheerful" feelings: from the joyfulness coming from a good dinner to the philosophical notion to "spiritual" cheerfulness at religious festivals.[35]

By the time of Plutarch, the concept had become part of the program of psychagogy, and it is in this context that Plutarch's work must be interpreted.[36] Since a variety of philosophical schools used the concept, one cannot expect that the older meanings were any longer distinguishable within specialized systems of ethics. Instead, a kind of common understanding emerged, which was shared by authors belonging to quite different schools. It is, therefore, understandable that Plutarch's concept was not simply derived from one of the older schools, but was "eclectic."

[33] On this question see Broecker, 20-22.

[34] Cf. Xenophon *Cyr.* 1. 3. 12; 4. 5. 7; Pape, *Griechisch-Deutsches Handwörterbuch*, s.v. The secular meaning is confirmed by Hesychius, *Lexicon* (ed. K. Latte) 2:226, who gives: εὐθημοσύνη, ἀμεριμνία, χαρά.

[35] Pindar, fr. 155, has Euthymia as a goddess together with Zeus and the Muses. On an amphora from Ceglie, which is decorated by the wedding of Heracles and Hebe, Euthymia appears as the name of a Maenad (cf. Waser, "Euthymia," PW 6.1 [1907] 1511-12).

[36] See Hadot, *Seneca*, 135-41.

Although Plutarch's philosophical concept of εὐθυμία is based upon the philosophical tradition which he had at his disposal and which he used, his own contributions are even more important. His treatment shows how serious the question had become at his time. Plutarch fully recognized that the historical situation of his day did not allow the simple repetition of the old answers. Radical skepticism loomed large in his mind. He seems to have been aware of what one may call the "gnostic" option.[37] There is pessimism when he speculates about the impact which traditional religion and philosophy, including his own, can make upon the masses.[38] On the other hand, Plutarch rejects as illusions the claims of the Stoics (462A) that they already possess εὐθυμία. Trying to steer between these Stoic claims and the radical dualism of the "gnostic" variety, Plutarch tries to find his own way and thereby reaffirm the older Platonic interpretation.[39]

His discussion shows deep insights into the nature of man. The steady climax of his argument is fed primarily by his psychological observations. Beginning with the relatively easy problems of ethical behavior, he finds his way through those that are increasingly intricate, until he reaches the heavy subjects of fear of death, conscience, and purification of the soul. Characteristic of Plutarch is his strong emphasis upon religion, not the religion of the masses but that of the wise man.[40]

Plutarch is extremely cautious in making any claims or promises for possessing "tranquillity of mind." If there is a possibility for man to experience it, it is at the end of serious intellectual and mental training. Then the philosopher—only for him does such a possibility exist at all—can be grasped by an enthusiastic inspiration which leads to a purification of his soul and a life of virtue.[41] For such a person Diogenes' dictum "πᾶσα ἡμέρα ἑορτή" will come true, and he will enjoy tranquillity of mind.[42]

The relationship between Plutarch's concept of εὐθυμία and primitive Christian thought is difficult to determine. There are puzzling problems not only in ECL, but also in the Jewish environment, where Jewish literature presents a somewhat complicated

[37] See below p. 225.
[38] See below on 477E-F.
[39] See ch. 5, 467A-C.
[40] See 465B-C and ch. 20, 477C-E.
[41] 477A-B.
[42] 477C-D.

picture. In the LXX the term εὐθυμία is not attested,[43] but Symmachus' translation uses it in some places to render the Hebrew שִׂמְחַת גִּילִי as εὐφροσύνη τῆς εὐθυμίας.[44] The question may be raised whether the LXX knew of the philosophical doctrine transmitted under the term and for that reason avoided it. The LXX could have used the term to translate a number of Hebrew terms, but it preferred other concepts which have no philosophical connotations. Apart from this, the OT has many parallels to the subject matter discussed by Plutarch,[45] but to work these out would require a special study.

The situation in the LXX is all the more puzzling in comparison with Philo, where we have a number of highly interesting passages containing the term εὐθυμία.[46] In some instances they are even parallels to Plutarch.[47] Philo constantly uses the term when he describes the joy at festivals, both secular and religious.[48] These passages are also helpful because of the synonyms Philo most graciously supplies.[49] Apart from the secular usage we find εὐθυμία in Philo used in the context of psychology and psychagogy [50] and even in connection with the mysteries of Dionysus.[51] The spectrum of meanings is very similar to Plutarch's, while Plutarch's treatise is more systematic and, of course, has a different religious frame of reference.[52]

In ECL, the term εὐθυμία is not attested. It does, however, occur in Sent Sext 262: μετ' εὐθυμίας εἰ θέλεις ζῆν, μὴ πολλὰ πρᾶττε· πολυπραγμονῶν γὰρ κακοπραγμονῶν ἔσῃ. The verb εὐθυμέω is found only in Jas 5:13; Acts 27:22, 25; εὔθυμος in Acts 27:36; Ign Pol 7:1; Herm Man 8:10. In all of these passages the terminology is on

---

[43] According to Hatch-Redpath, *A Concordance to the Septuagint*, s.v.

[44] See Origin's *Hexapla*, ed. F. Field, ad loc. Ps 42 (43):4; cf. similarly 50 (51):10; εὐθυμεῖν: Ps 31 (32):11; Prov 15:15; also εὔθυμος 2 Mac 11:26.

[45] Prov 15:15 is even a parallel to Plutarch (see below on 477C).

[46] According to G. Mayer, *Index Philoneus* (Berlin, 1974) s.v.

[47] The parallels are noted below.

[48] See *congr.* 161; *som.* 2. 144, 167; *vit. Mos.* 2. 211; *decal.* 161; *spec. leg.* 1. 69; 2. 42f., 156; *Flacc.* 118.

[49] Cf. in a "list of virtues" *sacr. A.C.* 27; also *leg. all.* 3. 215; *plant.* 92; 166; *congr.* 161; *som.* 2. 167; *vit. Mos.* 1. 333; *spec. leg.* 2. 98; etc.

[50] Cf. esp. *plant.* 90-92; 116; *migr. Abr.* 165; *mut. nom.* 131; *som.* 2. 249; *Jos.* 113; 245; *spec. leg.* 1. 69; 2. 42f., 98; *virt.* 67; *praem. poen.* 31f.; 71.

[51] *Som.* 2. 249; *leg. Gai.* 82.

[52] Note, e.g., how Philo relates the term to Abraham (*deus imm.* 4), Jacob (*plant.* 90-92), Aunan (*migr. Abr.* 165), Isaac (*mut. nom.* 131; *praem. poen.* 31f.), and Moses (*virt.* 67).

the level of popular morality but not necessarily without the influence of philosophy.[53] At this level there are some distant parallels to Plutarch.[54] On the whole, however, primitive Christianity, like Judaism except Philo, has carefully avoided the term εὐθυμία as well as the psychagogic doctrine associated with it.[55] One can, of course, only speculate why this is so. Primitive Christianity did not share one of the decisive presuppositions of the philosophical doctrine, the concept of the immortal soul. There may also be a sociological reason. Plutarch and Seneca express concerns which belong to the highly privileged upper classes of the Roman empire. This social world was refined and wealthy enough to afford the idea of mental tranquillity. On the other hand, this society was increasingly unsure of its own values and goals, so that disengagement from the turbulent affairs of business and politics became more and more desirable for the more sensitive minds.

In order to understand the relationship between Plutarch's work and primitive Christianity, we must go beyond the term εὐθυμία κτλ. There can be no doubt that the issues which are behind the request of Paccius were also well-known to the early Christians, and we would assume that they also developed means of dealing with them.

It is obvious that primitive Christianity experienced these issues at a different level and in different ways than did Plutarch and his social class. They experienced far more severely than did Plutarch that "this world" does not provide any hope for something Plutarch calls εὐθυμία. When Paul implies that "this world" is characterized by ἀκαταστασία and contrasts it with "the God of peace," he

[53] In Jas 5:13 εὐθυμεῖ is contrasted with κακοπαθεῖ, a term prominent in popular philosophy; for passages see Bauer, s.v. The sea-voyage story in Acts 27 depicts Paul as a "divine man" who acts prudently in this dangerous situation and does what Herm Man 8:10 in a "list of virtues" calls εὐθύμους ποιεῖν. In Ign Pol 7:1 the phrase εὐθυμότερος ἐγενόμην ἐν ἀμεριμνίᾳ θεοῦ has a parallel in 477E.

[54] See below, part III.

[55] The philosophical traditions rejected in early Christianity enter into church and theology together with the emergence of mysticism and quietism. See Pohlenz' article, mentioned above note 1, which deals mainly with Basil and Chrysostom; cf. also briefly his article in *Hermes* 40 (1905) 299f.; G. Bardy, *Dictionnaire de Spiritualité* (1932) s.v. Apatheia; P. Pourrat, *Dictionnaire de Théologie Catholique* (1936) s.v. Quiétisme; E. Beyreuther, *RGG*, 3d ed., s.v. Quietismus; F. Heiler, ibid., s.v. Gelassenheit; the article on "Heiterkeit" in *RAC* is not yet published.

expresses what most Christians at the time believed.[56] Although Plutarch is aware of the dismal life most people must put up with (see 477E), he rejects such pessimism (see 475D). The ordinary Christian's negative experience of life was more than that of neutral "distractions." It was the experience of demonic tumult and confusion both within and without. Only the fool says to himself: ἀναπαύου, φάγε, πίε (Luke 12:19). Real life was nothing but θλῖψις.[57] Primitive Christians longed for "tranquillity of mind," just as any human being does. However, their understanding of the way to gain such tranquillity was quite different from that of Plutarch and of the philosophical tradition in which he stands. In order to delineate this understanding, we must take other terminology into account.

The earlier, non-philosophical understanding of εὐθυμία does have a parallel in the notions of εὐφραίνω, εὐφροσύνη and χαίρειν, χαρά. These terms are frequently found in ECL, where they are also connected with the joys of meals and festivals, both secular and religious.[58]

Turning to theological reflection, the terminology of "peace" (εἰρήνη κτλ.) plays a significant role. Only God has "peace," [59] and giving it to man is part of salvation.[60] Strictly speaking, God's peace is a possibility for man only eschatologically. The realm of "heaven" is identical with "peace." Here the terms of ἀνάπαυσις κτλ.[61] and κατάπαυσις [62] are also important. The work of Christ was interpreted in terms of establishing "peace" both in heaven and on earth.[63] In anticipation of the eschatological peace of the saints in heaven,[64] the gift of the Spirit carries the "peace of God" into the human heart and into the life of the Christian community.[65] Therefore, the Christian is enabled to experience peace already now.

---

[56] 1 Cor 14:33: οὐ γάρ ἐστιν ἀκαταστασίας ὁ θεὸς ἀλλὰ εἰρήνης.

[57] See esp. John 16:33; Rom 5:3; 12:12; 2 Cor 1:4; 2:4; 7:4; etc.

[58] See R. Bultmann, *TDNT*, s.v. εὐφραίνω κτλ.; H. Conzelmann, *TDNT*, s.v. χαίρω κτλ.

[59] Cf. esp. Rom 15:33; 1 Cor 14:33; 2 Cor 13:11; Phil 4:7; 1 Thes 5:23; 2 Thes 3:16; etc. On the whole, see W. Foerster, *TDNT*, s.v.

[60] See esp. Rom 5:1.

[61] See Vielhauer mentioned below, note 70.

[62] See O. Hofius, *Katapausis* (Tübingen, 1970).

[63] See esp. Col 1:20; Eph 2:14-17; Heb 3-4; Barn 15. Christ's promise in Matt 11:28 includes this life and the hereafter: ἐγὼ ἀναπαύσω ὑμᾶς.

[64] See esp. the macarism, Rev 14:13; also 6:11; 2 Clem 5:5; 6:7. For the condemned there is no rest: Herm Sim 6:2:7.

[65] See esp. Gal 5:22; Rom 5:1-5; 8:6; 14:17; 15:13; Col 3:15: ἡ εἰρήνη τοῦ Χριστοῦ βραβευέτω ἐν ταῖς καρδίαις ὑμῶν.

This enabling gift is then made the basis for ethical responsibility: the Christian is charged with the task to "make peace" and to live in peace with his fellow men.[66] Plutarch's view is somewhat similar at this point because he, although coming from a different direction, recognizes the need for ἐνθουσιασμός (see 477B).

It is noteworthy that Paul himself dispenses peace through his epistolary blessings,[67] just as he receives relief from his anxieties by the encouragement of other Christians. The "setting at rest of the spirit" and the "refreshing of the heart" is mentioned several times in Paul and Ignatius.[68] In this sense, it is possible to experience peace of mind even under the severe conditions of θλῖψις.[69] But the typically eschatological character of the early Christian view is summed up best much later by Augustin, at the beginning of his Confessions: inquietum est cor nostrum, donec requiescat in te. There were, however, gnostics who did promise the full realization of ἀνάπαυσις now as part of their concept of salvation.[70]

Another strand of tradition related to the theme of ἀνάπαυσις is connected with the terms ἡσυχία, ἡσυχάζω, ἡσύχιος, ἡσυχῶς. This terminology is employed by ECL, mostly in its later phases, and points to popular morality. The general tenor is that life should be conducted in a quiet way,[71] especially by the women.[72] The rejection of rebellion is a particular concern of 1 Clement.[73] The "spirit" of an authentic prophet should be ἡσύχιος,[74] and church officials are approved by 1 Clement when they conduct their business ἡσυχῶς καὶ ἀβαναύσως.[75] Beyond this, the word-family is

---

[66] For passages see W. Foerster, *TDNT*, s.v. εἰρήνη κτλ.; esp. F.4, and s.v. εἰρηνεύω.

[67] Rom 1:7; 1 Cor 1:3; 2 Cor 1:2; 13:11; etc.

[68] See 1 Cor 16:18: ἀνέπαυσαν γὰρ τὸ ἐμὸν πνεῦμα καὶ τὸ ὑμων, also 2 Cor 7:13; Phlm 7; 2 Tim 1:16; Ign Eph 2:1; Magn 15:1; Trall 12:1 (κατὰ πάντα με ἀνέπαυσαν σαρκί τε καὶ πνεύματι); Rom 10:2; Smyrn 9:2; 10:1; 12:1; Ign Pol 7:1.

[69] See Rom 15:13: ὁ δὲ θεὸς τῆς ἐλπίδος πληρῶσαι ὑμᾶς πάσης χαρᾶς καὶ εἰρήνης..., 2 Cor 2:13; 7:5; 8:13; 2 Thes 1:7; 1 Clem 59:3; Barn 10:11; etc.

[70] For gnostic passages, see Ph. Vielhauer, "ΑΝΑΠΑΥΣΙΣ: Zum gnostischen Hintergrund des Thomasevangeliums," in *Aufsätze zum Neuen Testament* (Munich, 1965) 215-34; W. Foerster, *Gnosis* (Oxford, 1974) 2, index, s.v. rest, repose. Strange is Barn 4:2.

[71] 1 Tim 2:2: ἤρεμον καὶ ἡσύχιον βίον διάγωμεν ἐν πάσῃ εὐσεβείᾳ καὶ σεμνότητι. 2 Thes 3:12: μετὰ ἡσυχίας ἐργαζόμενοι τὸν ἑαυτῶν ἄρτον ἐσθίωσιν.

[72] 1 Tim 2:11f.; 1 Pet 3:4.

[73] See esp. 1 Clem 61:1.

[74] Herm Man 11:8.

[75] 1 Clem 44:3.

found in "lists of virtues." [76] Ignatius can also speak mystically of the ἡσυχία θεοῦ and about ἡσυχία as part of the Christian life.[77] Luke is very close to Plutarch when he makes ἡσυχάζειν the result of giving in to the will of God.[78]

Of special interest is the "slogan" εἰρήνη καὶ ἀσφάλεια, to which Paul refers in 1 Thes 5:3, rejecting the attitude described by it. Paul does not indicate from which source he has gotten this "slogan" or who, in his view, fits the description. Previous studies have related it to the Epicureans,[79] the gnostics,[80] and the prophetic tradition.[81] The "slogan" of 1 Thes 5:3 could be related in some way to εὐθυμία. Its words and its form correspond to the Latin "tranquillitas atque securitas," [82] which, according to Cicero (*Fin.* 5. 23),[83] were used to render the meaning of εὐθυμία in the Latin philosophical tradition. Thus Seneca (*Epist.* 92. 3) defines: "Quid est vita beata? Securitas et perpetua tranquillitas." It may be that Paul has these claims in mind when he refers to the "slogan." The interesting fact is, however, that we find an equivalent "slogan" in the O.T., using different terms but expressing the same meaning: שָׁלוֹם וֶאֱמֶת.[84] The LXX does not translate these as εἰρήνη καὶ ἀσφάλεια, but uses different terms in almost every case.[85] Again, we find parallels in the Hebrew OT referring to "peace" and "security" in contexts comparable to Plutarch's concept of εὐθυμία.[86] This picture increases the possibility that the notion of εὐθυμία was intentionally avoided by the LXX translators and, perhaps, also by ECL.

---

[76] See 1 Thes 4:11; Herm Man 5:2:3, 6; 6:2:3; 8:10; Did 3:8; Barn 19:4.

[77] Ign Eph 19:1; 15:2.

[78] Acts 21:14.

[79] N. W. DeWitt, *Epicurus and His Philosophy* (Minneapolis, 1954) 336ff.; Id., *St. Paul and Epicurus* (Minneapolis, 1954) 7, 41f.

[80] W. Schmithals, *Paul and the Gnostics* (Nashville & New York, 1972) 166f.

[81] W. Harnisch, *Eschatologische Existenz* (Göttingen, 1973) 78ff.

[82] For a treatment of the concepts, see Hadot, *Seneca*, 126-35, 135-41.

[83] See the quotation above, p. 202.

[84] 2 Kgs 20:19; Isa 39:8; Jer 33:6; Esth 9:30.

[85] See LXX 4 Kgs 20:19; Isa 39:8; Jer 40:6; Esth 8:12h; also 1 Chr 4:40; 22:9; 1 Mac 10:66; Ezek 38:11; etc.

[86] Cf. esp. Job 12:6; Pss 4:8; 16:9-11; 122:6-9; 123:4; Prov 1:33; 3:23f.; 10:9f.; 11:15; Jer 6:14; 7:10; 30:10; 46:27; Ezek 28:25f.; 38:11; Amos 6:1; Zeph 2:15; cf. Wis 4:17; 7:23 (βέβαιον, ἀσφαλές, ἀμέριμνον). I am indebted for advice here to Rolf Knierim.

III. Plutarch's Essay

Ch. 1

The position which Plutarch himself takes in regard to the question of tranquillity of mind is based on the way in which he states the problem. It is not without reason that at the outset he presents the fundamental assumptions in form of two questions (465 A-B). "For what power is there in money or fame or influence (465A)
at court to help us to gain ease of soul or an untroubled life, if it is not true that the use of them is pleasant to us when we have them and that we never miss them when we have them not?" The answer to the question is obvious:[87] There is no power in money, fame, or influence at court, and no one in his right mind expects help from these cliché achievements of the culture [88] when it comes to the question of ἀλυπία ψυχῆς,[89] and βίος ἀκύμων.[90]
The answer to the second question is equally obvious: "And how (465B)
else can this be achieved except through reason, which has been carefully trained quickly to hold back the passionate and irrational part of the soul when it breaks bounds...?" Of course, there is no other means than the λόγος.[91] This was *communis opinio* among all philosophers of the time, although the terminology appears to be close to Stoicism.[92]

If the matter is that clear, why is there a problem? Perhaps at this point we can grasp the dilemma underlying the philosophy of

---

[87] See *PECL* 1:208, and index s.v. wealth. Broecker (37f.) has a collection of parallels of this *locus communis diatribae*, among them *virt. et vit.* 100D; 101D; *cons. ux.* 611C. Cf. Matt 16:26//Mark 8:36//Luke 9:25.

[88] See also 471B; 474C; 477A. There is no exact parallel in ECL where the three concepts are joined.

[89] This concept is discussed by Broecker, 189f. In Christian literature it is found in Just Dial 45:4. Cf. also 2 Clem 19:4; Matt 11:29: ἀνάπαυσις ταῖς ψυχαῖς; Herm Sim 9:5:4; 1 Cor 16:18; 2 Cor 7:13; Phlm 20.

[90] βίος ἀκύμων is a common philosophical ideal, as parallels in Broecker (38f.) illustrate. There seems to be no parallel in ECL, but Clement of Alexandria, *paed.* 2. 7 (p. 193, 30 [Stählin]) says: ὁ Χριστιανὸς . . . γαλήνης καὶ εἰρήνης οἰκεῖός ἐστιν. Cf. the figurative use of κύματα in Jude 13; Matt 8:23-27.

[91] τί δὲ τοῦτ' ἐστὶν ἄλλο ἢ λόγος . . . See also 475C; 475A, and the discussion in Broecker, 40-42. The primitive Christian Logos christology is, on the whole, different, but the point of connection with the philosophical tradition is made in Ker Pet 1: Christ as νόμος καὶ λόγος. Cf. Acts 4:12: οὐδὲ γὰρ ὄνομά ἐστιν ἕτερον . . .

[92] λόγος εἰθισμένος καὶ μεμελετηκώς. Not attested in ECL, but cf. Chadwick, *The Sentences of Sextus*, index, s.v. ἐθίζω.

Plutarch's time. The answers to the problems were well-known, if one cared to search for them, but at the same time the problems appeared to get worse. Plutarch illustrates the problem by a reference to Xenophon,[93] who gave the advice that "in prosperity we should be particularly mindful of the gods and should honour them, so that, when some need comes upon us, we may invoke them with the confidence that they are already well-disposed and friendly." [94] In other words, we all know the answer, but we tend to forget it. As a result, when we fall into a situation of need we are caught unprepared. Plutarch then concludes that we must do the same as
(465C) with the worship of the gods: [95] the human λόγος must be kept in continuous training until a habitual attitude is developed,[96] so that in times of an emotional crisis the λόγος will be able to keep the πάθη in check.[97] The preventative training must utilize philosophical-ethical λόγοι,[98] and this is what Plutarch had in mind when he sent his work to his friend in Rome.

Ch. 2

In the first part of the argumentative section Plutarch refutes false opinions about how to achieve tranquillity of mind (see above, p. 201). First, he takes issue with Democritus. Quoting from Democritus' work on the subject,[99] Plutarch goes beyond Democri-

---

[93] *Cyr.* 1. 6. 3.

[94] Xenophon summarizes a belief shared by most people in antiquity, including Christianity: One should worship the deity at all times properly, so that when need comes one can turn to them with confidence. Only the fool forgets to honor the deity in a time of good fortune. On God's goodness cf. Matt 6:7-8, 25-33//Luke 12:22-31; Matt 7:11//Luke 11:13; Matt 19:17// Mark 10:18//Luke 18:19; Acts 14:17; 17:23; Rom 1:19-23. For expressions of continuous gratitude, cf. 2 Cor 9:15; Eph 1:6; 5:20; 1 Tim 2:1. See esp. Luke 6:35 (Matt 5:45): God is χρηστὸς ἐπὶ τοὺς ἀχαρίστους καὶ πονηρούς. Also Phil 4:6; Col 2:7; 1 Tim 2:1f.

[95] It is interesting that Plutarch starts here with an observation from religion, because he will also end with a chapter on religion.

[96] This is done by οἱ νοῦν ἔχοντες (on this concept cf. *PECL* 1 index, s.v. νοῦς). By contrast, οἱ χαλεποί, those driven by the πάθη, are comparable with savage dogs (465C). This comparison is found also in Ign Eph 7:1; Did 9:5; Phil 3:2; Rev 22:15; Matt 7:6; Gal 5:15. See Grese, on *prof. virt.* in this volume, p. 16.

[97] τὰ πάθη τὰ τῆς ψυχῆς διαγριαινόμενα. This concept is not found in ECL, but cf. ἀγρία . . . ἐστιν ἡ ἐπιθυμία, Herm Man 12:1:2; cf. 12:4:5; Sim 9:26:4. For a collection of parallels, see Broecker, 43-45.

[98] See also *cohib. ira* 453D; 454B, and Broecker, 45.

[99] See Helmbold's note, LCL 6:170, ad loc.; Siefert, 9f.; Broecker, 45-52, for discussion of the problem.

tus himself by taking his warning against πολλὰ πρήσσειν[100] as a recommendation for complete ἀπραξία. It has been suggested that this radical interpretation of Democritus may be Epicurean. Plutarch regards ἀπραξία not only as too expensive but also as unrealistic.[101] Just as ἀναισθησία σώματος is no therapy for madness, (465D) so also the ψυχῆς ἰατρός[102] cannot hope to cure τὸ ταραχῶδες ... καὶ λυπηρόν of the soul by prescribing such "remedies"[103] as ῥᾳθυμία καὶ μαλακία καὶ προδοσία φίλων καὶ οἰκείων καὶ πατρίδος. Life itself shows that inactivity does not guarantee tranquillity: For example, women do not become more tranquil than men by staying home most of the time,[104] but on the contrary their quarters are full of λῦπαι δὲ καὶ ταραχαὶ καὶ κακοθυμίαι διὰ ζηλοτυπίας καὶ δεισιδαιμονίας καὶ φιλοτιμίας καὶ κενῶν δόξων, ὅσας οὐκ ἂν εἴποι τις.[105] Laertes is another example: he lived in solitude[106] for 20 (465E) years, but λύπη was his steady companion. In fact, for some natures it is precisely inactivity which causes ἀθυμία.[107] This was acknowl- (465F) edged even by Epicurus, who did not recommend ἡσυχάζειν for (466A) everybody. Finally, it is not the quantity of accomplishments

[100] Democritus' warning is against πολυπραγμοσύνη, a common *topos* in Hellenistic ethics. See Plutarch's work on the subject, *curios.* In ECL, a similar warning is found in Herm Sim 4:5. Cf. also Diogn 4:6; 5:3.

[101] On ἀπραξία (cf. also *non posse* chs. 15-19 [1097A-1100D]; *adv. Col.* 1122A; *lat. viv.* 1129A; 1130E; etc.) and ἀπραγμοσύνη (466A; 472B; etc.), see Broecker, 51f. In ECL, the terminology does not appear until Gregory Nazianzen and Chrysostom, where it is applied to the monastic life (so according to Lampe, s.v. ἀπραγμοσύνη). However, it is interesting that 2 Thes 3:10-12 has a warning against "idleness" (cf. also 1 Tim 5:13), perhaps referring to gnostics; cf. Schmithals, *Paul and the Gnostics*, 197ff.

[102] On this concept see *PECL* 1:193 (on 550A) and a collection of passages in Broecker, 55.

[103] Actually it is a "catalog of vices." Some of the terms have parallels in ECL: ῥᾳθυμέω is cited once by Bauer in Herm Vis 1:3:2; cf. Sent Sext 126; μαλακία a few times (cf. Bauer, s.v.); Judas Iscariot is the prime example of προσδοσία φίλων (Luke 6:16; see Bauer, s.v. προσδότης).

[104] γυναῖκας ... οἰκουρίᾳ τὰ πολλὰ συνούσας. On οἰκουρία and ἀπραξία see Broecker, 56. Cf. the Haustafel in Tit 2:5.

[105] A "catalog of vices" characteristic of women; cf. also ζηλοτυπέω applied to men in 473B, and further parallels in Broecker, 57f. The judgment on women is very harsh in most of the work. On δεισιδαιμονία of women see Broecker, 57f.

[106] μετ' ἀπραξίας καὶ κατηφείας. Broecker (59) refers to the parallel in *lat. viv.* 1129D-E. κατήφεια occurs also in Jas 4:9.

[107] Cf. *Index Verborum Plutarcheus*, s.v. In ECL ἀθυμία occurs in 1 Clem 46:9; ἀθυμέω in Col 3:21.

but the quality that leads to τὸ εὔθυμον or to τὸ δύσθυμον.[108] The failure to perform a good act is as bad as the performance of an evil act: τῶν γὰρ καλῶν ἡ παράλειψις οὐχ ἧττον ἢ τῶν φαύλων ἡ πρᾶξις ἀνιαρόν ἐστι καὶ ταραχῶδες, ὡς εἴρηται.[109]

Ch. 3

Next, Plutarch [110] refutes those who believe that one particular form of life makes all the difference: τοὺς ... ἀφορισμένως ἕνα
(466B) βίον ἄλυπον νομίζοντας.[111] The proof for this refutation is given in the form of two quotations from Menander, in which the poet ridicules the instability of the wealthy—a diatribe *topos*.[112] Also, a comparison is brought in pointing out the foolishness of people at sea who want to escape sea-sickness by transferring from one size of boat to another.[113] Plutarch's view is that a mere change of external
(466C) life-style does not relieve the soul of its anxieties: αἱ τῶν βίων ἀντιμεταλήψεις οὐκ ἐξαιροῦσι τῆς ψυχῆς τὰ λυποῦντα καὶ ταράττοντα.[114] Whatever external difficulties may exist, the cause of unhappiness is internal:[115] ἀπειρία πραγμάτων, ἀλογιστία, τὸ μὴ δύνασθαι μηδ' ἐπίστασθαι χρῆσθαι τοῖς παροῦσιν ὀρθῶς.[116] Depending upon the inner disposition, external circumstances appear as agreeable or disagreeable.[117]

---

[108] This term is not found in ECL.

[109] Broecker's parallels (60f.) show that the sentence has connections with Democritus as well as with proverbial material. The sentence could be illustrated by Matt 12:9-14//Mark 3:1-6//Luke 6:6-11.

[110] Broecker (50f.) points to the parallels.

[111] Plutarch mentions farmers, bachelors, kings. The Jewish concept of "despised trades" is comparable; cf. Luke 18:11; 3:12ff. On "despised trades" see J. Jeremias, *Jerusalem in the Time of Jesus* (London, 1969) 303ff. The term μονάζω (Barn 4:10; Herm Sim 9:26:3) goes even further.

[112] See *virt. et vit.* 101C and H. Herter, "Zur ersten Satire des Horaz," *RhM* 94 (1951) 11f., with many references.

[113] For parallels see Broecker, 62-64. Cf. the behavior of the sailors in Acts 27:30, which, in effect, exemplifies what Plutarch ridicules.

[114] Cf. the skepticism against external appearance in the polemics against the Pharisees (Matt 6:1f., 5, 16; 23:25-28//Luke 11:39-40, etc.) and against Christian "heretics" (2 Cor 11:13-15; Matt 7:15). See also J. Reiling, *Hermas and Christian Prophecy* (Leiden, 1973) 58ff. and passim.

[115] Early Christians would agree. Cf. the great emphasis in ECL upon man's "inner" renewal (see esp. Rom 12:2).

[116] Cf. Heb 13:5: ἀρκούμενοι τοῖς παροῦσιν. See Bauer, s.v. ἀρκέω, 2.

[117] Cf. Phil 4:11f.

Ch. 4

Positively speaking, it is Reason (ὁ λογισμός)[118] which creates in us εὐκολία [119] and thereby the ability to adjust to the conditions of life. The point is then illustrated by an apophthegm of Anaxarchus,[120] the examples of Crates [121] and Agamemnon, an anecdote about Diogenes, and two more examples of Socrates and Phaeton. Finally, a comparison shows what Plutarch is driving at: As the shoe is moved about together with the foot and not vice versa,[122] so the inner disposition creates the life-style that corresponds to it. Plutarch refutes those who think that ἡ συνήθεια determines what is best,[123] pointing out his own view that τὸ φρονεῖν ἅμα τὸν αὐτὸν βίον ποιεῖ καὶ ἄριστον καὶ ἥδιστον.[124] From these presuppositions, he then concludes what we must do:[125] διὸ τὴν πηγὴν τῆς εὐθυμίας ἐν αὐτοῖς οὖσαν ἡμῖν ἐκκαθαίρωμεν, ἵνα καὶ τὰ ἐκτός, ὡς οἰκεῖα καὶ φίλια, μὴ χαλεπῶς χρωμένοις συμφέρηται.[126]

(466D) (466E) (466F) (467A)

---

[118] The concept is Platonic (cf. τὸ φρονεῖν in 466F; 467B; οἱ φρόνιμοι in 467C). See Broecker, 67f. In ECL cf. first Diogn 2:9. See Bauer, s.v.; Lampe, s.v.

[119] See also *cons. ux.* 608D. Cf. εὐκόλως in Herm Man 12:3:5 v.l.

[120] For the parallels see Broecker, 68: Alexander, Agamemnon, and Phaeton are examples of δυσθυμία; Crates, Diogenes, and Socrates of εὐθυμία. Alexander's complaint that "we have not yet become lords of one single world" may be compared with Matt 4:8-10//Luke 4:5-8; Mark 10:35-45// Matt 20:20-28; 1 Cor 4:8; Copt Gos Thom 2.

[121] . . . πήραν ἔχων καὶ τρίβωνα παίζων καὶ γελῶν ὥστερ ἐν ἑορτῇ τὸν βίον διετέλεσε. The wallet and the cloak are the standard equipment of the Cynic; for parallels see Broecker, 68 (cf. Matt 10:10//Mark 6:8//Luke 9:3; etc.). See Bauer, s.v. πήρα. On the attitude cf. Matt 6:16-18; Matt 9:14//Mark 2:18//Luke 5:33; 1 Cor 5:8. See further ch. 20 below.

[122] The comparison was popular in diatribe literature, and parallels are given by Broecker, 70. For the symbolic use of ὑπόδημα, cf. Matt 3:9// Mark 1:7//Luke 3:16//John 1:27; Acts 13:25; Eph 6:15.

[123] The polemic could be directed against Pythagoras or a Stoic (cf. Helmbold's note ad loc.; Broecker, 71-74). Reflections on συνήθεια are found in 1 Cor 8:7; 11:16; Herm Man 5:2:6.

[124] Broecker (71-74) shows that the juxtaposition of συνήθεια and φρόνησις is anti-Stoic (cf. *adv. Stoic.* 1073C-D, and the lost treatise Περὶ συνηθείας πρὸς τοὺς Στωϊκούς, Lamprias Catalog no. 78).

[125] This paraenetical conclusion, introduced by διό (cf. often in the NT; e.g., Acts 20:31; Rom 13:5; 15:7; 2 Cor 6:17), is the basis for the following discussion.

[126] On this notion of πηγή, see 477B, *virt. et vit.* 100C, and further parallels in Broecker, 74f. In ECL, cf. Mark 7:15; 1 Cor 6:18-20; πηγή is used figuratively in John 4:14; 2 Pet 2:17, etc. See Bauer, s.v., 2-3. On the figurative use of ἐκκαθαίρω cf. 2 Tim 2:21.

Ch. 5

Alluding to Plato's comparison of human life with a game of
dice (κυβεία),[127] Plutarch formulates man's ethical task as involving two things: βάλλειν δεῖ τὰ πρόσφορα καὶ βαλόντα χρῆσθαι καλῶς
τοῖς πεσοῦσι. What is important in this is the distinction between
τὰ ἐφ' ἡμῖν and τὰ παρὰ τῆς τυχῆς.[128] Our task [129] amounts to τὸ . . .
(467B) προσηκόντως δέχεσθαι τὰ γινόμενα παρὰ τῆς τυχῆς. This is achieved,
if we do the following: τὸ οἰκεῖον ὠφελήσει μάλιστα καὶ τὸ ἀβούλητον
ἥκιστα λυπήσει τοὺς ἐπιτυγχάνοντας.[130]

As he often does in this work, Plutarch contrasts the positive
with the negative. Here, failure in life [131] is illustrated by a comparison with sickness and an anecdote about Theodorus the Athe-
(467C) ist.[132] On the other hand, the way the φρόνιμοι [133] act is aptly
compared with bees who gather honey even from thyme, the
driest and the harshest of all plants. Like the bees, the φρόνιμοι
too achieve benefits, even under adverse circumstance.[134]

Ch. 6

In this chapter, Plutarch brings us closer to the purpose of the
(467D) treatise as he begins what he calls ἀσκεῖν καὶ μελετᾶν.[135] First he
uses several, sometimes funny examples to illustrate the wise-man
reacting to an unwanted situation by exclaiming, "Not so bad
after all!" Such a reaction in effect changes the impact of unwanted
circumstances.[136] The illustrations are then followed by rhetorical

---

[127] *R.* 10. 604C. The comparison was very popular, as the parallels in Broecker (76f.) show. Cf. Eph. 4:14: ἡ κυβεία τῶν ἀνθρώπων.

[128] Both concepts are prominent in Hellenistic philosophy (see Broecker, 77f.), but absent from ECL.

[129] ἔργον. Cf. Gal 6:4, and Bauer, s.v.

[130] τὸ ἀβούλητον occurs also in 467C; 474E; 475A. Cf. Luke 22:42: πλὴν μὴ τὸ θέλημά μου ἀλλὰ τὸ σὸν γενέσθω. See Lampe, s.v. ἀβούλητος, esp. for the interpretation of Christ's passion.

[131] οἱ ἀπαίδευτοι. Cf. 1 Clem 39:1.

[132] The proverbial expression τῇ δεξιᾷ τοὺς λόγους ὀρέγοντος αὐτοῦ τῇ ἀριστερᾷ δέχεσθαι τοὺς ἀκροωμένους (cf. *lib. ed.* 5A) has a parallel in Matt 6:3.

[133] οἱ φρόνιμοι is found often in ECL. See Bauer, s.v.

[134] The comparison of the prudent with bees is a common-place; see Broecker (79), who refers to *aud. poet.* 32E(!); *aud.* 41F-42A. Cf. the related comparison with honey in Herm Man 5:1:5-6.

[135] See above p. 201. The combination of the terms is Cynic-Stoic (see Broecker, 80) and has no parallel in ECL, but individually both terms do occur (see Bauer, s.v.).

[136] ἔξεστι γὰρ μεθιστάναι τὴν τύχην ἐκ τῶν ἀβουλήτων. The doctrine is Cynic-Stoic; for parallels see Broecker, 80f.

questions, supplied with the proper answers, which call for the
imitation of these examples.[137] Such questions are typical of the
diatribe style.[138] Next, examples of famous men are introduced to (467E)
demonstrate [139] that one does not really suffer a disadvantage
from evils like failure to get an office,[140] loss of a tyrant's friendship,[141] childlessness, [142] poverty,[143] or the seduction of one's
wife.[144] The chapter ends with a longer apophthegm, a debate (467F)
between Stilpo and Metrocles [145] in which Stilpo argues that one (468A)
person's ἁμάρτημα cannot become another's ἀτύχημα.[146]

Ch. 7

Next, Plutarch considers the principle: Do not make it your (468B)
business to straighten out the faults of others! (468C: τὸ μὲν οὖν ἀπευθύνειν ταῦτα μὴ νόμιζε σὸν ἔργον εἶναι),[147] which is the opposite of what people ordinarily do: τοὺς δὲ πολλοὺς οὐ μόνον τὰ τῶν φίλων καὶ οἰκείων ἀλλὰ καὶ τὰ τῶν ἐχθρῶν ἀνιᾷ καὶ παροξύνει κακά (468B).[148] In as much as we are surrounded by a host of

---

[137] Τί οὖν κωλύει μιμεῖσθαι τούτους; On the phrase τί κωλύει; see *PECL* 1, index, s.v. κωλύω; on "imitation" see *PECL* 1, index, s.v.

[138] For parallels, see Broecker, 82. See also Almqvist, 41.

[139] 467E states the function of examples: διὸ καὶ τοῦτο πρὸς εὐθυμίαν μέγα, τὸ τοὺς ἐνδόξους ἀποθεωρεῖν. Cf. Heb 12:1 and the story of Abraham in Rom 4.

[140] 467D. The alternative is the ideal of the simple life: ἐν ἀγρῷ διάξεις ἐπιμελόμενος τῶν ἰδίων. Cf. *praec. reip.* 798D-E. See Broecker, 81f. Cf. 1 Thes 4:11: πράσσειν τὰ ἴδια καὶ ἐργάζεσθαι ταῖς χερσίν.

[141] 467D. The hazards connected with the friendship of the powerful are a commonplace, esp. in the diatribe literature. See E. Bammel, "φίλος τοῦ Καίσαρος," *TLZ* 77 (1952) 205-10; H. Donner, "Der Freund des Königs," *ZAW* 73 (1961) 269-77. Broecker (82) refers to *exil.* 602E; cf. John 19:12.

[142] 467E: ἀπαιδία. Cf. the example of Sarah's sterility (Gal 4:21-31; Rom 4:19; 9:9; Heb 11:11; Barn 13:2; 2 Clem 2:1); also Luke 1:7, 36. However, the macarism in Luke 23:29 is in line with Plutarch (cf. also Matt 24:19//Mark 13:17//Luke 21:23 and the whole concept of "virginity" in primitive Christianity).

[143] πενία. Cf. Luke 6:20; 4:18; Jas 2:1ff.; etc. See O'Neil, in this volume, pp. 289ff.; Broecker, 84.

[144] This remarkable view has no parallel in ECL; 1 Tim 2:14 (in context) and Matt 5:27-29 show that the matter was not taken lightly in primitive Christianity.

[145] For a discussion and parallels, see Broecker, 85f.

[146] Cf. Gal 6:5: ἕκαστος γὰρ τὸ ἴδιον φορτίον βαστάσει. Also cf. John 9:2-3.

[147] On the whole chapter and its parallels with Seneca, see Broecker, 87-92. Comparable in ECL is the doctrine in Matt 5:39: μὴ ἀντιστῆναι τῷ πονηρῷ (see also Rom 12:19-21; 1 Cor 6:1-11; 1 Thes 5:15; 1 Pet 2:23; 3:9; Did 1:4; 1 Clem 2:1; Just 1 Apol 16:1-2). On ἔργον see above n. 129.

[148] Cf. 1 Cor 13:5 where it is said of ἀγάπη that it οὐ παροξύνεται, and by contrast Acts 15:39; 17:16. See also Matt 7:3-5//Luke 6:41-42.

evils,[149] only οἱ ἀνόητοι will be bothered and become angry because
of that. The wise-man knows that, given the state of affairs in the
world, such evils and evildoers are all one should expect. To react
in anger and bitterness is irrational. Rather, Plutarch recommends
(468C) that one react to evil like a physician [150] does to a disease: Instead
of getting angry he applies the necessary remedies gently and with
self-control.[151] One should look at the wicked as a bunch of barking
(468D) dogs, who only fulfill their nature.[152] Getting emotionally involved,
however, means becoming infected by the same disease which up-
sets us.[153] According to Plutarch, there are philosophers (i.e.,
the Stoics) who for this reason even forbid feeling pity for people
in misfortune.[154] They advise providing concrete help, but without
becoming emotionally involved in the misfortunes.[155] As we are
(468E) advised to cure our own shortcomings ἄνευ λύπης,[156] so it is only to
be expected that we will not encounter only those who are ἐπιεικεῖς
καὶ χαρίεντες.[157]

Plutarch also observes that people who become excessively upset at the evil they see arouse the suspicion that they do so ὑπὸ φιλαυτίας . . . οὐ μισοπονηρίας.[158] Their excessive concern about "circumstances" can easily engender enmity against those one

---

[149] This is expressed by a "list of vices": βλασφημίαι γὰρ καὶ ὀργαὶ καὶ φθόνοι καὶ κακοήθειαι καὶ ζηλοτυπίαι μετὰ δυσμενείας. Some of the concepts appear in ECL lists (βλασφημία, ὀργή, φθόνος, κακοήθεια); ζηλοτυπία is found in Did 5:1. For the connection with μετά in lists, see Col 1:11; 1 Tim 2:15. See Almqvist, 124.

[150] On the comparison with the physician see above, p. 7.

[151] ἤπιος φαίνῃ καὶ μέτριος . . . εὐφρανῇ τῇ σῇ διαθέσει. Cf. 1 Thes 2:7 and A. Malherbe, "Gentle as a Nurse," *NovT* 12 (1970) 203-17; Gal 6:1; 2 Tim 2:24f.

[152] Cf. Matt 7:6; Phil 3:2; Rev 22:15; Gal 5:15.

[153] ἀλλοτρίων ἀναπιμπλάμενος κακῶν. This doctrine is also behind 1 Cor 15:33; Gal 6:1; Rom 12:2; also 1 Pet 1:14, etc.

[154] See on this R. Bultmann, *TDNT*, s.v. ἔλεος κτλ. (2:4), who cites the passage in n. 16; ECL takes a different position (ibid., sec. C).

[155] οὐ τοῦ συναλγεῖν καὶ συνενδιδόναι τοῖς πλησίον. Contrast Rom 12:15; 1 Cor 12:26; 2 Cor 11:29; Luke 10:33 (ἐσπλαγχνίσθη); 1 Pet 3:8 (συμπαθής); Col 3:12; etc.

[156] Cf. 2 Clem 19:4: μὴ . . . λυπείσθω ὁ εὐσεβής, also Herm Man 10:1-3; 3:4; Sim 9:15:3; Vis 4:3:4; Rom 14:15. On this whole concept see R. Bultmann, *TDNT*, s.v. λύπη κτλ.

[157] Cf. the Christian warning in Rom 12:17: μηδενὶ κακὸν ἀντὶ κακοῦ ἀποδιδόντες (see Rom 12:14-21; 13:10; and the passages above n. 146); Matt 5:44//Luke 6:28; Luke 23:34; Acts 7:60; 1 Cor 4:12f.

[158] Cf. 2 Tim 3:2: φίλαυτος; μισοπονηρία is not listed in Bauer; cf. Heb 1:9 (Ps 44:8 LXX).

suspects of having deprived him of something he wanted. In the last sentence Plutarch states his own ideal of political involvement. The language is rather conventional, but what he really means is "non-involvement":[159] ὁ δὲ τοῖς πράγμασιν ἐθισθεὶς ἐλαφρῶς συμ-
περιφέρεσθαι καὶ μετρίως εὐκολώτατος ἀνθρώποις ὁμιλεῖν γίνεται (468F)
καὶ πραότατος.[160]

Ch. 8

Returning to the matter περὶ τῶν πραγμάτων,[161] Plutarch discusses the attitude of complaining and recommends: τοῖς πράγμασι (469A)
παυσόμεθα μεμφόμενοι καὶ δυσχεραίνοντες.[162] The reason is that
what we perceive as ἀβούλητα συμπτώματα are, in fact, a mixture of
good and bad.[163] The way to εὐθυμία is to not overlook the good:
ὅσα προσφιλῆ καὶ ἀστεῖα πάρεστιν ἡμῖν.[164] Instead of excessive con- (469B)
centration upon one's own problems,[165] Plutarch suggests: ἀγαθοῖς
δὲ παροῦσιν οὐ προσάγεις τὴν διάνοιαν;[166] There is no reason to (469C-D)
complain and despair about everything because we are troubled
by Tyche in only one thing. As usual Plutarch exemplifies this
doctrine by comparisons and anecdotes.[167]

---

[159] The concepts are Stoic; see the parallels in Broecker, 92. But Plutarch comes close to the Pauline doctrine of ὡς μή, 1 Cor 7:29-31.

[160] Cf. the requirements for church officials in Did 15:1; Ign Trall 3:2; Gal 6:1; furthermore Ign Eph 10:2.

[161] Cf. 466F-467C. On the flow of thought see Broecker, 92ff.

[162] Cf. Jude 16.

[163] Cf. Matt 5:45; 22:10; 25:31-46. Cf. Matthew's concept of the church as *corpus mixtum*; see G. Strecker, *Der Weg der Gerechtigkeit*, 3d ed. (Göttingen, 1971) 217-19; cf. "mixtures" of good and bad implicit in Rom 7:18-21; 12:21; 13:3f.; Heb 5:14; 1 Pet 3:11; 3 John 11. Hermas also has a doctrine of "mixture" (Man 5:1:6; 10:3:3).

[164] Cf. Luke 6:35 (quoted above, n. 94); Rom 2:4; furthermore, 1 Thes 5:21; Phil 4:8.

[165] Plutarch quotes first from Attic Comedy (for passages see Helmbold, LCL 6:193, n. a): τί τἀλλότριον, ἄνθρωπε βασκανώτατε, κακὸν ὀξυδορκεῖς, τὸ δ' ἴδιον παραβλέπεις; The verse is also quoted by Horace *sat.* 1. 3. 25, and has a parallel in Matt 7:3-5//Luke 6:41f. Plutarch then turns against blaming oneself excessively.

[166] Instead of: ἀγαθῶν . . . παρόντων, κακὸν ζητοῦντα. Cf. Matt 6:25-34// Luke 12:22-32.

[167] 496C tells about the man from Chios who sold old and good wine to others while he was looking for sour wine for his own luncheon (cf. John 2:10); 469D compares human foolishness with the behavior of children, a diatribe *topos* (cf. Matt 11:16f.//Luke 7:31f.). Contrast Matt 18:10-14// Luke 15:3-7; Luke 15:8-10. Cf. Almqvist, 92f., on ἀπολλυμένοι . . . σῳζομένοι.

Ch. 9

Plutarch takes up another familiar question: καὶ τί . . . ἔχομεν;
τί δ' οὐκ ἔχομεν;[168] The most respected possessions are: fame, a
(469E) house, a wife, a good friend. But it is important not to overlook the
ordinary things we have, for which we should also be grateful:[169]
ζῶμεν, ὑγιαίνομεν, τὸν ἥλιον ὁρῶμεν.[170] Consider the absence of evils
like war or riots, or the availability of simple things we can do or not
(469F) do.[171] Usually these small things are taken for granted and become
(470A) desirable only when we no longer have them. Rather than over-
looking or despising them, we should take account of them and use
them for our benefit. Most people,[172] to be sure, do just the opposite: Instead of looking carefully at the things they have, the
tendency is to look at others and their possessions.[173]

Ch. 10

(470B) Another major source of tranquillity of mind is self-examination:
τὸ μάλιστα . . . αὑτὸν ἐπισκοπεῖν καὶ τὰ καθ' αὑτόν.[174] However, self-
examination leads to tranquillity only if one compares oneself
with those whose fortunes are worse,[175] and not, as most people
foolishly do, with those whose situation is better.[176] This well-
known doctrine of comparison with others Plutarch discusses
(470C) especially in his work *laud. ips.* Applied in the wrong way, self-

---

[168] Cf. 1 Cor 4:8; Matt 13:12//Mark 4:25//Luke 8:18, where the same question is presupposed.

[169] χάριν ἔχειν also occurs in 470B, C. The doctrine of gratefulness is part of the philosophical tradition; Broecker (101) mentions Epicurus *Ep.* 3 (p. 59, 9 Usener) and Cicero *Fin.* 1. 62. In ECL it occurs frequently: 1 Tim 1:12; Heb 12:28, etc. (see Bauer, s.v. χάρις, 5); also Eph 5:20; 1 Thes 5:18; 1 Tim 4:4, etc.

[170] Cf. the *conditio Jacobaea* (Jas 4:15); for ὑγίεια see 3 John 2; 1 Clem 61:1; for the "sun" cf. Matt 5:45.

[171] Among them: ἡ γῆ παρέχει γεωργεῖν—a *topos* also in Jas 5:7; Matt 6:25-32//Luke 12:22-30.

[172] This is attributed to Arcesilaus.

[173] Esp. to external things: ἔξω βλέποντες. Cf. Matt 23:25//Luke 11:39f.; Jas 2:1ff.

[174] Cf. 472C, which also deals with the Delphic maxim. On *laud. ips.* see below, pp. 367ff.

[175] τοὺς ὑποδεεστέρους ἀποθεωρεῖν. This is parodied in Luke 18:11. See also Diogn 10:5; Rom 14:10; Jas 2:6, etc.

[176] πρὸς τοὺς ὑπερέχοντας ἀντιπαρεξάγειν. Cf. Phil 2:3; Paul's refusal to make such a comparison in 2 Cor 10:12 and Betz, *Paulus*, 118ff. The *topos* is turned into irony in 1 Cor 4:10.

examination easily turns into collecting προφάσεις ἀχαριστίας ἐπὶ τὴν τύχην and engaging in self-punishment.[177] In this connection, Plutarch mentions the Chians, Galatians[178] and Bithynians as people who are known to be dissatisfied with whatever political lot has fallen upon them. Peace, however, enters the mind when one (470D) learns to appreciate the relatively good life which one enjoys as compared with myriads of others far worse off. Such a man is moved to the point where he ὑμνῶν τὸν ἑαυτοῦ δαίμονα καὶ τὸν βίον ὁδῷ πρόεισιν.[179] Plutarch's examples are taken from the Olympic (470E-F) Games, from Herodotus, and from the pool of anecdotes about Socrates.[180] He concludes with a praise of the life that comes from a tranquil mind: ἔξεστιν εἰπεῖν, "λαμπρὰ τὰ καθ' ἡμᾶς πράγματα καὶ ζηλωτὸς ἡμῶν ὁ βίος· οὐ προσαιτοῦμεν οὐκ ἀχθοφοροῦμεν οὐ κολα- (471A) κεύομεν." [181]

Ch. 11

Plutarch continues the discussion of μεμψιμοιρία begun in the previous chapter.[182] He criticizes that instead of doing what he had recommended there, we are accustomed to doing the opposite. This happens because τὸ δύσζηλον ἡ φύσις ἔχουσα καὶ τὸ βάσκανον.[183] Instead of being satisfied with our own blessings, we are jealous of what we see others have.[184] Yet, such jealousy admires only the pretty outside appearance.[185] If we would only look behind the

---

[177] See also on 469E. Cf. Luke 6:35; 2 Tim 3:2; Ker Pet 2 (p. 14, 21).

[178] It was often thought that this proverbial character of the Galatians is reflected in Paul's letter to the Galatian churches. See, esp. Lightfoot, *Galatians* (London, 1881) 13-16.

[179] The reference complies with the rules for "self-praise": the wise man does not praise himself, but his δαίμων.

[180] The stories about Socrates and about expenses in Athens were common, esp. in the diatribe literature. See Broecker, 110f.

[181] As Broecker (111) points out, begging, carrying burdens, and flattering the rich and powerful mean an existence *between* that of a freeman and that of a slave. See also *exil.* 604B. Nevertheless, the "praise" is paradoxical. Cf. 2 Cor 11:29; 12:10; 2 Cor 13:3-4, 9, and the whole concept of καυχᾶσθαι ἐν ταῖς ἀσθενείαις, for which see Betz, *Paulus*, 73ff. Luke 18:11 is a parody of such self-praise. Cf. also the "antitheses" in 1 Cor 4:9-13; 2 Cor 4:7-10; 6:4-10; and the "catalog of περιστάσεις," 11:23-27.

[182] Cf. above, p. 218.

[183] δύσζηλος is a hapax legomenon. Broecker (112) refers to parallels. For βάσκανος cf. Mart Pol 17:1; Ign Rom 3:1; 7:2.

[184] For this ethical *topos*, see Gal 6:4.

[185] The juxtaposition of splendid outside and disgusting inside is a diatribe *topos*; see Broecker (112) for passages. Cf. Matt 23:25-28//Luke 11:39f. esp., but also Mark 7:14-23; Rom 2:28f.; 2 Cor 4:16; 5:12; 7:5; 2 Tim 3:5; 1 Pet 3:3f.; etc.

beautiful curtain, we would see many disgusting things. Plutarch says, αἱ . . . τῶν παθῶν φωναὶ πρὸς τὴν κενὴν δόξαν ἔνδοθεν ἀντιμαρ-
(471B-C) τυροῦσι.[186] After some illustrations [187] and quotations he concludes this discussion by saying that it might help to reduce the major obstacle to tranquillity of mind: τὸ θαυμάζειν τὰ τῶν πλησίον ἐκταπεινοῦντος τὰ οἰκεῖα καὶ καταβάλλοντος.

Ch. 12

(471D) One of the ways to destroy tranquillity of mind is letting our impulses run wild, instead of coordinating them with our abilities: τὸ μὴ συμμέτροις χρῆσθαι πρὸς τὴν ὑποκειμένην δύναμιν ὁρμαῖς.[188] This kind of foolishness can take various forms. Overblown hopes, when they cannot be realized, turn into complaints against δαίμων καὶ τύχη, but not, as they should, into complaints against one's own stupidity.[189] To attempt the impossible is folly and stupidity. Again, the real force behind it is: ἡ φιλαυτία μάλιστα, φιλοπρώτους ποιοῦσα καὶ φιλονίκους ἐν πᾶσι καὶ πάντων ἐπιδραττομένους ἀπλήστως.[190]
(471E) The foolish goal of being first in everything [191] can only result in ἀθυμεῖν.[192] The same is true of the claim to be everything at the same time.[193] Plutarch's illustrations include a comparison with a sailor artfully managing his sails,[194] a list of proverbial ἀδύνατα,[195] a caricature of the megalomaniac behavior of the rich and the

[186] On κενὴ δόξα cf. Gal 5:26; also 465D; on αἱ τῶν παθῶν φωναί cf. Rom 7:23f.; 8:26.

[187] The apophthegm of Pittacus is interesting because it is also transmitted in connection with other names (see Broecker, 112f.). The saying ἑκάστῳ τι ἡμῶν κακόν ἐστιν· ᾧ δὲ τοὐμόν, ἄριστα πράττει has a partial parallel in Gal 6:5.

[188] This doctrine, for which parallels are found in Broecker (116-119), is nothing but an application of the Delphic maxim μηδὲν ἄγαν (see below, p. 375). Cf. 2 Cor 10:13-15 and the Pauline doctrine of μέτρον in Rom 12:3; Eph 4:7, 13.

[189] See Herm Man 9:8: σεαυτὸν αἰτιῶ καὶ μὴ διδόντα σοι, also Sim 6:3:5. For parallels to this commonplace, see Broecker, 119f.

[190] On φιλαυτία, see on 468E. φιλοπρωτεύειν is also rejected in 3 John 9; Matt 23:6//Mark 12:39//Luke 20:46; Luke 22:27; 14:7-11; also Matt 20:27//Mark 10:44; Mark 9:35. See Bauer, s.v. πρωτο-, φιλοπρωτεύω. On φιλόνικος cf. 1 Cor 11:16.

[191] Cf. the christology in Col 1:18: ἐν πᾶσιν αὐτὸς πρωτεύων.

[192] ἀθυμεῖν and ἀνιᾶσθαι are the opposites of εὐθυμεῖν. For parallels see Broecker, 121. In ECL ἀθυμέω occurs in Col 3:21; also Just Dial 107:3.

[193] Cf. Paul's claim in 1 Cor 9:19-23. See H. Conzelmann, *First Corinthians* (Philadelphia, 1975) ad loc.

[194] ὥσπερ ἱστίοις. See on 466B, where foolish behavior at sea is mentioned.

[195] Cf. Matt 7:16//Luke 6:44; Matt 19:24//Mark 10:25//Luke 18:25; Luke 9:62; Matt 6:27//Luke 12:25; Jas 3:11f.

mighty, and a number of historial examples of such megalomania,[196] (471F-
including well-known anecdotes about Dionysius of Syracuse, 472A)
Alexander the Great, Achilles and Megabyzus the Persian.[197] Finally, Plutarch turns against the Stoics and their claim: τὸν σοφὸν παρ' αὐτοῖς μὴ μόνον φρόνιμον καὶ δίκαιον καὶ ἀνδρεῖον ἀλλὰ καὶ ῥήτορα καὶ ποιητὴν καὶ στρατηγὸν καὶ πλούσιον καὶ βασιλέα προσαγορευόμενον.[198] The one who is prudent, however, recognizes that abilities are divided among people, as they are even among the
gods: ἄλλος ἄλλην ἔχων δύναμιν.[199] Thereby, he maintains his tran- (472B)
quillity of mind.

Ch. 13

Elaborating on the doctrine introduced at the end of ch. 12, (472B)
Plutarch points out that certain occupations are by nature opposite
to others because they require a different way of life.[200] Not every- (472C)
thing is good for everyone.[201] Instead one must obey the Pythian inscription [202] and αὐτὸν καταμαθεῖν, εἶτα χρῆσθαι πρὸς ἓν ὃ πέφυκε, instead of ἄλλον ἄλλοτε βίου ζῆλον ἕλκειν καὶ παραβιάζεσθαι τὴν
φύσιν.[203] This advice is then illustrated by quotations, historical (472C-E)
examples, an apophthegm of Strato and Menedemus,[204] and a
quotation from Aristotle's letters to Antipater.[205] Nature teaches (472F-
us [206] that as certain fruits belong to certain plants [207] and different 473A)

[196] Broecker's parallels (121-24) show that the names attached to the anecdotes may vary.

[197] The anecdote illustrates Paul's gnome, Gal 6:3; cf. 1 Cor 3:18; 8:2.

[198] Such excessive claims are offensive; cf. δεδικαιωμένος in Barn 4:10; see on *laud. ips.* below, pp. 367ff. Broecker (125) has parallels. Cf. above n. 193.

[199] Paul uses a similar argument, adapted into Christian conceptuality, in his discussion of the χαρίσματα in 1 Cor 12:4ff.

[200] For the same principle, cf. Matt 6:24//Luke 16:13.

[201] Cf. 1 Cor 6:12; 7:35, 38; 10:23.

[202] For a collection of passages, see *PECL* 1, index, s.v. Delphi; also below, p. 375.

[203] Cf., again, Paul's doctrine of the χαρίσματα in Rom 12:3ff.; 1 Cor 7:7; 12:4ff.; 1 Pet 4:10, etc.

[204] See *laud. ips.* 545A-F and the parallels in Broecker, 173.

[205] See on this *prof. virt.* 78D; *laud. ips.* 545A, where it is addressed to Alexander instead of to Antipater. See also Broecker, 133. The point is that Alexander had no more right to be proud because he ruled over many people, than does someone who has the true notions about the Gods. Cf. Matt 4:8-10//Luke 4:5-8.

[206] 473A: τὴν φύσιν ὁρῶμεν ὑπομιμνήσκουσαν ἡμᾶς. On "nature" see also 472C πέφυκε; 476B φύσις ψυχῆς. Cf. 1 Cor 11:14: ἡ φύσις . . . διδάσκει.

[207] νῦν δὲ τὴν μὲν ἄμπελον σῦκα φέρειν οὐκ ἀξιοῦμεν οὐδὲ τὴν ἐλαίαν βότρυς. The form βότρυς is strange. Helmbold (LCL 6:213, n. c) has noted the parallel in Matt 7:16//Luke 6:44; Jas 3:12. See Almqvist, 36.

foods are good for different animals,[208] so also different occupations
(473B) fit different people.[209] Failure to follow the pattern of Nature ends
inevitably in ζηλοτυπεῖν and unhappiness.[210]

Ch. 14

(473B) Plutarch now turns from external matters to the internal matters of the soul, declaring: ἕκαστος ἐν ἑαυτῷ τὰ τῆς εὐθυμίας καὶ δυσθυμίας ἔχει ταμιεῖα.[211] His anthropology is quite dualistic, although he is opposed to another, even more radical dualism. The ταμιεῖα contain good and evil and correspond to the variety of
(473C-D) πάθη. The use of the vessels determines whether one is ἀνόητος or φρόνιμος, for the "fools" ignore present goods because of their excessive concern for the future, while the "wise men" can utilize even the goods of the past. Plutarch then explains this more fully in a section on "memory" and "time." [212] The "wiseman" has a "historical" relationship to time because he remembers things of the past and thus makes them present reality. He looks at life as one historical sequence in which past, present, and future hang together and yet are distinct.[213] The "fool," on the other hand, does not remember anything.[214] He exists merely in the present and therefore experiences life as a succession of disconnected moments The chapter concludes with a polemic against an anthropology

---

[208] The subject is discussed at length by Athenag Res 5:1-6:6. Comparison with the animals was popular; cf. Matt 6:26//Luke 12:24; Matt 8:20// Luke 9:58; Jas 3:7; 2 Pet 2:12; Jude 10. See Bultmann, *Der Stil*, 91.

[209] With this entire argument cf. Paul's doctrine of vocations, Rom 12:6-8; 1 Cor 12:28-30; Eph 4:11f.

[210] This verb is not found in ECL (on the noun, see above, p. 216). The opposite is true of the wisemen: τοὺς γὰρ οὕτω τὰ οἰκεῖα σεμνύνοντας οὐκ ἐνοχλήσει τὰ τῶν πλησίον (472E). Cf. Exod 20:17; Deut 5:21 (LXX); Rom 7:7, 13:9. Almqvist (37) refers to ἐν αὐλαῖς βασιλέων (473B) as a parallel to Matt 11:8.

[211] On the origin of the doctrine, see Broecker, 136-39. Plutarch's dualism, although using Platonic-Stoic concepts, comes close to the primitive Christian dualism of σάρξ and πνεῦμα. Cf. esp. Gal 5:17; Rom 7:15, 23; Jas 4:1, 5; 1 Pet 2:11 (αἱ σαρκικαὶ ἐπιθυμίαι) . . . στρατεύονται κατὰ τῆς ψυχῆς.

[212] The doctrine of μνήμη τῶν ἀγαθῶν is Epicurean and Stoic. See Broecker, 138. Cf. Philo, *virt.* 67; Luke 16:25 is a peculiar Jewish (Christian) parallel.

[213] τὸν βίον ἕνα γενέσθαι, συμπλεκομένων τοῖς παροῦσι τῶν παρῳχημένων . . . See Broecker, 140f. Cf. Heb 13:8 and Bauer, s.v. εἷς, 2.a.

[214] 473C: ἀναίσθητος καὶ ἀχάριστος . . . λήθη. See Broecker, 141. Cf. 2 Pet 1:9.

which teaches radical discontinuity between man's existence (473E)
yesterday, today, and tomorrow.[215]

Ch. 15

If the absence of a μνήμη τῶν ἀγαθῶν is detrimental to "tranquillity of mind," so is excessive preoccupation whith only ἡ τῶν κακῶν μνήμη.[216] In Plutarch's view we certainly cannot ignore (473F)
that we also have ἡ τῶν κακῶν μνήμη. At this point, Plutarch (474A)
introduces his doctrine of "mixture": since there is nothing pure and unmixed in the universe, we should not expect total purity in our lives either.[217] There are contrasting forces at work in our affairs,[218] but it is also possible to achieve harmony between them. Getting the right "mixture" by encompassing the bad with the (474B)
good is the formula for εὐθυμία.

Ch. 16

"Mixture" also means that at birth we received τούτων ἑκάστου (474C)
σπέρματα τῶν παθῶν ἀνακεκραμένα and with that πολλὴν ἀνωμαλίαν.[219] The wiseman, therefore, will expect from the future good and bad, and taking heed to the μηδὲν ἄγαν, he will deal with them both.[220] This disposition serves to avoid "fear," which is the greatest impediment to "tranquillity of mind." At this point, Plutarch takes up the discussion of fear,[221] using Epicurus, whom he also quotes,[222]

---

[215] It is interesting that the anthropology rejected here is virtually the same as the one affirmed in *de E* 392D (see *PECL* 1:98); also my paper, "Observations on Some Gnosticising Passages in Plutarch," *Proceedings of the International Colloquium on Gnosticism, Stockholm, August 20-25, 1973* (Stockholm, 1977) 169-78.

[216] Two illustrations come from animal behavior: the flies slipping away when walking on a mirror and the beetles at Olynthus. Cf. Broecker, 148.

[217] τῶν ἀνθρωπίνων καθαρὸν οὐδὲν οὐδ' ἀμιγές. See *Is. et Os.* 369B-D (*PECL* 1:64) and Broecker, 149-51. Examples are taken from music (cf. 1 Cor 14:7-9) and painting. For the opposite to Plutarch's idea of mixture, see Rom 14:20: πάντα . . . καθαρά, also Tit 1:15.

[218] ἀντιστοιχίαι. It is interesting that the ἀντιστοιχίαι are identified in 474B, following Empedocles, as the two μοῖραι καὶ δαίμονες. See Broecker, 153; *PECL* 1:101f. (on 394A). Cf. 2 Cor 6:14-16.

[219] See Broecker, 154ff., for a discussion of the sources and a collection of parallels.

[220] For this Delphic maxim, see below, p. 375.

[221] The object of chs. 16-18 is ἡ πρὸς τὴν τύχην ἀφοβίαν (Broecker, 154).

[222] "ὁ τῆς αὔριον ἥκιστα δεόμενος, ἥδιστα πρόσεισι πρὸς τὴν αὔριον" (Fr. 490, Usener). See Broecker, 158. Cf. Matt 6:34; 1 Cor 15:32; Jas 4:13, 14, all of which include proverbial material.

in order to show that those who are least afraid of the bad things[223] in life are most able to enjoy the good things.[224] Absence of fear
(474D- is, therefore, one of the absolute prerequisites of εὐθυμία.[225] This
475A) is further exemplified by an apophthegm (Anaxagoras),[226] philosophical sayings,[227] and examples (Carneades, Perseus and Aemilius,[228] Odysseus).

Ch. 17

(475B) Generally speaking, the way man faces the ἀβούλητα depends as much upon φύσις as upon δόξα.[229] To be sure, there are painful experiences which cause φύσει τὸ λυποῦν καὶ βαρῦνον, but most of the time our distress comes from false opinions (δόξαι) through which we learn and become accustomed.[230] The latter, however, touch neither σάρξ nor ψυχή[231] and primarily involve matters of social prestige and prejudice, such as: δυσγένεια πατρὸς ἢ μοιχεία γυναικὸς ἢ στεφάνου τινὸς ἢ προεδρίας ἀφαίρεσις.[232] None of these prevent a man

[223] τοὺς ἥκιστα τἀναντία ταρβοῦντας. The terminology is Epicurean, for which see Broecker, 160. See above on 465A.

[224] Listed are: πλοῦτος . . . καὶ δόξα καὶ δύναμις καὶ ἀρχή. See 465A. Cf. Rev 5:12.

[225] 474D: It is a gift of Reason: ᾧ δὲ δίδωσι πρὸς τὴν τύχην ἀδεῶς καὶ ἀτρόμως εἰπεῖν ὁ λογισμός. See Broecker, 160f. Cf. Rom 8:15; 2 Tim 1:7; 1 John 4:18.

[226] The point is the realization of mortality. Cf. Acts 14:15; Heb 9:27, etc.

[227] Plutarch imitates Anaxagoras' saying by adding other sayings all beginning with οἶδα. The same form is used by Paul in Phil 4:12. Plutarch's sayings deal with the insecurity of wealth (cf. Jas 5:2 and often in ECL), political power (cf. John 19:11; Rom 13:1; 1 Pet 2:13-17, etc.), marriage, and friendship (τὸν φίλον ἄνθρωπον ὄντα, cf. 1 Cor 3:4; also Broecker, 163, who refers to Teles 59, 10).

[228] Here Plutarch uses the method of *syncrisis* which is so predominant in the "Lives." For the phrase δυστυχέστατος ἀνθρώπων γεγονέναι καὶ βαρυποτμότατος, cf. 1 Cor 15:19.

[229] On this subject, see Broecker, 167-69. On τὰ ἀβούλητα see on 474E.

[230] The doctrine is Stoic; see Broecker's commentary, 168f. Early Christianity does not share it, but does teach that the same experiences Plutarch talks about must be "mastered" by the Christian "through faith." This explains why there are parallels with ECL in spite of the differences.

[231] Interestingly, an earlier (Epicurean?) anthropology of σάρξ (σῶμα)-ψυχή is reflected here (see Broecker, 170).

[232] They are commonplace in the diatribe literature. On δυσγένεια πατρός, cf. 1 Cor 1:26 (also *PECL* 1:248); on the taking away of a crown, cf. Rev 3:11; on προεδρία, cf. Luke 14:7-14; Matt 23:6//Mark 12:39//Luke 20:46; 11:43; Herm Man 11:12. Interestingly, distress over the adultery of one's wife is treated here merely as a prejudice. ECL is much more rigorous, but John 7:53-8:11 is comparable, and the Corinthian "gnostics" may have treated the matter as an adiaphoron (cf. 1 Cor 5:1ff.).

from having his body and soul in good condition. However, even when we must face those things that are inherently (φύσει) painful, such as νόσοι καὶ πόνοι καὶ θάνατοι φίλων καὶ τέκνων,[233] our reaction (475C) is to a great extent a matter of our conceptuality. If we let the λόγος remind us that such experiences are part of the κοινὴ καὶ φυσικὴ ἀνάγκη [234] and that they result from our body being a "mixture," then we can bear the suffering by leaving the physical body to Tyche, but "standing secure" [235] as far as our most important part, the mind, is concerned.[236]

After interrupting the discussion by an apophthegm about (475D) Stilpo,[237] Plutarch continues the discussion of the anthropological problem. He appears to be familiar with the "gnostic" possibility of a radical dualism, in which φύσις is considered completely evil, having: μηδὲν ἰσχυρὸν μηδὲ μόνιμον μηδ' ὑπὲρ τὴν τύχην.[238] He tries to avoid such a conclusion by asserting that the "rotten and mortal" part, which is subject to Tyche, is "small" in comparison with our better part, the soul, in which are located τὰ μέγιστα τῶν ἀγαθῶν ἱδρυθέντα, δόξαι τε χρησταὶ καὶ μαθήματα καὶ λόγοι τελευτῶντες εἰς ἀρετήν.[239] Because these blessings possess ἀναφαίρετον ... τὴν οὐσίαν καὶ ἀδιάφορον, we have ample reason to face up to Tyche with confidence,[240] Plutarch then exemplifies his doctrine by an apophthegm [241] involving Socrates and by an interpretation of the (475E) well-known comparison of the philosopher with a ship's pilot in

---

[233] Cf. Rev 21:4; 2 Cor 11:26f.; 6:4f.

[234] For parallels to this *topos*, see Broecker, 171.

[235] ἀσφαλὴς ἕστηκεν. Cf. Rom 11:20; 1 Cor 7:37; 10:12; Heb 6:19; 2 Clem 6:6. These passages show that while Plutarch points to the soul, primitive Christianity is able to be unconcerned about the present because of their hope in the future.

[236] The wiseman's struggle against Tyche is a *topos*. For parallels, see Broecker, 171f.

[237] The apophthegm is often recorded and states the principle "Omnia bona mea mecum sunt" (Seneca *Ep.* 9. 18). See Broecker, 172. Cf. Matt 10:28//Luke 12:4f.; 2 Clem 5:4; Just 1 Apol 19:7; also Matt 16:26//Mark 8:36//Luke 9:25.

[238] Again, this doctrine corresponds to *de E* 392E-393A (see *PECL* 1:98f.).

[239] See also 476B.

[240] See 475F: θαρραλέως καὶ ἀτρόμως. Cf. Rom 5:1-5; 8:38; 1 Cor 3:22; 1 Thes 4:15; 5:23; 2 Thes 3:3ff.; Jas 5:7ff., etc.

[241] The apophthegm is developed from Plato *Ap.* 30C; for parallels, see Broecker, 173f.; Helmbold, LCL 6:229, n. 6. The saying: ἀποκτεῖναι μὲν Ἄνυτος καὶ Μέλητος δύνανται, βλάψαι δ' οὐ δύνανται. Cf. the references in n. 236 above, also 1 Pet 3:13ff.; Rev 2:10.

(475F) stormy weather.[242] As a last resort, Plutarch points to the pos-
(476A) sibility of suicide:[243] If the pilot (i.e., the "wiseman") is overwhelmed by irrational and unmanageable disasters, he can simply swim away from the body, as from a leaky ship, because: ἐγγὺς ὁ λιμήν.[244]

Ch. 18

The final chapters of the work focus upon the greatest obstacle
(476B) to peace of mind, the fear of death (ὁ τοῦ θανάτου φόβος).[245] Plutarch is convinced that "tranquillity of mind" is virtually identical with overcoming the fear of death (ἡ πρὸς τὸν θάνατον ἀφοβία).[246] Chs. 18-20 explain how, in his view, this can be achieved.

It is not the longing for life (ὁ τοῦ ζῆν πόθος), but the fear of death that makes the "fool" hang on to his body. The beginning of "fearlessness" comes when we contemplate the nature of the soul: τὴν τῆς ψυχῆς φύσιν ἁμωσγέπως ἐπινοῶν. We begin to realize that death means the transformation of the soul for the better and not for the worse: εἰς τὸ βέλτιον αὐτῆς . . . μεταβολή.[247] This realization provides the means [248] by which we can achieve πρὸς τὸν θάνατον ἀφοβία and, thereby, πρὸς τὸν βίον εὐθυμία. The extreme form of such an attitude is, as Plutarch again points out, suicide.[249] But for those who think in this way there is nothing left which is
(476C-D) χαλεπὸν ἢ δύσκολον ἢ ταραχῶδες.[250]

The problem, however, is that the attainment of the attitude recommended by Plutarch is prevented by the superficial attitude

---

[242] For parallels to this *topos* see Broecker, 174f. In ECL, see Matt 8:23-27//Mark 4:35-41//Luke 8:22-25; Acts 27. See also *PECL* 1:221f. (on 563E); Bauer, s.v. κυβερνήτης, 2. Note also the catalogs of vices and virtues in 475E.

[243] So correctly Helmbold, LCL 6:231, n. c; Broecker, 177f. Cf. Matt 27:3-10.

[244] Cf. *non posse* 1103E. For further parallels see Broecker, 177-79. Cf. Herm Sim 8:9:4 (ὁ θάνατος ἐγγύς); and Bauer, s.v. ἐγγύς, 2-3. On the figurative use of λιμήν cf. Ign Pol 2:3; Ign Smyrn 11:3.

[245] See Broecker, 179f.; *PECL* 1:98, 321-24. Cf. Phil 1:23.

[246] Cf. chs. 16-17 on ἡ πρὸς τὴν τύχην ἀφοβία. See above, p. 225. In ECL, see 1 Clem 57:7; Luke 1:74; Phil 1:14; 1 Cor 16:10; and the passages mentioned above, p. 225. Cf. also Philo *plant.* 90-92; *virt.* 67.

[247] On this doctrine see *PECL* 1:321, 322 and index, s.v. μεταβολή.

[248] Note the term ἐφόδιον, also 472C. For parallels, see Broecker, 127f. Cf. 1 Clem 2:1 and Bauer, s.v.

[249] See above, on 476A.

[250] The matter is stated as a rhetorical question. Cf. Rom 8:31-39; 1 Cor 15:54f.

called γλυκυθυμία τῆς ψυχῆς,[251] which in effect supplants τὰ ἀβούλητα by sweet niceties while maintaining a posture of agnosticism and disbelief.[252] Instead of disbelief we need to be "grasped" and moved by θαυμάζειν καὶ ζηλοῦν καὶ συνενθουσιᾶν.[253] Only a hard and heavy learning process can achieve this goal in which our notions and preconceptions are changed by the λόγος.[254]

Ch. 19

While in ch. 18 Plutarch had come close to the Stoic claims he (476D)
had previously ridiculed (472A), he avoids such a misunderstanding by quoting Menander's warning against over-extension of oneself, "No man alive may say, 'I shall not suffer this.'" [255] Plutarch agrees that such a denial is Hybris, and that making such state- (476E)
ments would lead only to φαντασίας ... ὥσπερ ἐνσκιατροφούμενον πολλαῖς ἐλπίσιν ὑπεικούσαις ἀεὶ καὶ πρὸς μηθὲν ἀντιτεινούσαις.[256] However, it is within our power to make ethical decisions [257] and to say: τοῦτ' οὐ ποιήσω· οὐ ψεύσομαι, οὐ ῥᾳδιουργήσω, οὐκ ἀποστερήσω, οὐκ ἐπιβουλεύσω.[258]

This capability is also the way to tranquillity of mind, as Plutarch explains by referring to the concept of "conscience," which he defines as the ineradicable memory of the evil deeds one has committed.[259] This memory works in the soul as an everlasting instrument of torture, like an ulcer in the flesh.[260] The λόγος must (476F)

[251] The term γλυκυθυμία comes from Plato (*Lg.* I. 635C) and is synonymous with ἀτονία and μαλακία. Plutarch uses γλυκυθυμία also in *soll. an.* 970B; *non posse* 1104C; *Them.* 10. See Broecker, 188.

[252] 475C: ἀπογινώσκειν, ἀπιστεῖν. Cf. Bauer, s.v.

[253] Remarkably, Plutarch refers here to ἐνθουσιασμός. The three notions also occur in *prof. virt.* 85A; for a collection of parallels see also Broecker, 186f. See *PECL* I, index, s.v. Cf. Philo *som.* 2. 249; *leg. Gai.* 82.

[254] μελετῶσα φαντασίαν ὑφίστασθαι καὶ προσβιαζομένη τῷ λογισμῷ. For parallels see Broecker, 188f. On πεῖραν ... λαμβάνειν ἑαυτοῦ cf. 2 Cor 13:5.

[255] See Edmonds no. 355, v. 4 (vol. 3 B, p. 698).

[256] See Broecker (190), who cites *exil.* 606D. On "empty hopes" in ECL, cf. Luke 24:21a; Rom 5:5; I Cor 15:12ff.; Eph 5:6; Col 2:8; I Thes 4:13; I Tim 6:17, etc.

[257] At this point we have Plutarch's basis for ethics: it is man's ethical will and decision in cooperation with the self-purification of his soul through his λόγος, which in the last analysis is divine.

[258] Cf. Luke 19:8; but cf. Matt 8:19f.//Luke 9:57f., where an analogous approach to discipleship is rejected.

[259] He introduces it by way of Euripides *Or.* 396. Cf. *PECL* I:206.

[260] οἷον ἕλκος ἐν σαρκί. Broecker (191) refers to other passages. Cf. 2 Cor 12:7: σκόλοψ τῇ σαρκί.

deal with the conscience in a way different from that with which it handles the other λῦπαι, for the λόγος itself produces "regret" (μετάνοια) [261] in the soul.

(477A) Plutarch continues his discussion of conscience with a praise of the virtuous life, almost poetic in tone and reaching back to the beginning of the treatise. Certainly, it cannot be the external possessions which grant tranquillity to the soul.[262] Also, one must recognize that the "inner" pains, which lead to a "purified soul," are more distressful than external calamities.[263] It is Plutarch's view that in the last analysis, only μετάνοια brings about ψυχὴ καθαρεύουσα πραγμάτων καὶ βουλευμάτων πονηρῶν.[264] Such a soul can then become a source of life for τὸ ἦθος ἀτάραχον ἔχουσα καὶ ἀμίαντον,
(477B) and from such a soul flow αἱ καλαὶ πρᾶξεις . . . καὶ τὴν ἐνέργειαν ἐνθουσιώδη καὶ ἱλαρὰν . . . ἔχουσι.[265] Plutarch concludes by asserting that the good deeds of the wiseman leave behind in his soul a lingering memory, like a censer [266] that keeps its fragrance long after the fire has burnt out. This is what produces and sustains the wiseman's tranquillity of mind: κεχαρισμένην καὶ πρόσφατον . . . τὴν ἐπίνοιαν, ὑφ' ἧς τὸ χαῖρον ἄρδεται καὶ τέθηλε. . . .[267] This also enables the wiseman to look with contempt at those who only complain about life as a land full of evils or a place of exile to which
(477C) the soul has been assigned.[268]

Ch. 20

The final chapter is devoted entirely to religion. Such a conclusion is especially characteristic for Plutarch.[269] He introduces his theme

---

[261] In other writings of Plutarch, this is the point of connection between ethics and the mythology of the afterlife. See *PECL* 1:200; Hans-Gottfried Schönfeld, METANOIA (Diss., Heidelberg 1970 [unpublished]). Cf. also 2 Cor 7:9f.; Rom 2:4; Col 3:23; Almqvist, 107.

[262] See above, p. 209.

[263] On the contrast between ἔξωθεν and ἔνδοθεν see 467A.

[264] The corresponding Christian concept is that of the purification of the heart. Cf. Acts 15:9; Matt 5:8; Luke 5:12; 1 Tim 1:5, etc. See Bauer, s.v. καθαρίζω, 2.b; καθαρός, 3.b.

[265] Cf. John 7:38.

[266] On the term λιβανωτρίς see Broecker, 195. Cf. 2 Cor 2:15.

[267] Cf. 477A: εὐδίαν παρέχει βίῳ καὶ γαλήνην. Cf. the probably metaphorical language in Matt 8:26//Mark 4:39//Luke 8:24.

[268] Again, Plutarch is aware of the "gnostic" option and avoids it. Cf. above 468C; 475D.

[269] Plutarch had the religious climax in mind from the beginning and mentioned the ἐνθουσιασμός before (476C; 477B). On the whole chapter, see Broecker (196-200), who notes the similarity to (usurpation by?) John Chrysostom. See also above, p. 204 on Philo.

by way of an apophthegm illustrating Diogenes' famous dictum: πᾶσα βίος ἑορτή.[270] The rest of the chapter is something like a sermon on this theme. Plutarch distinguishes sharply between the true religion of the σώφρων and the public festivals the crowds (οἱ πολλοί) celebrate, which he subjects to scathing criticism.

The universe is a "holy temple": ἱερὸν μὲν γὰρ ἁγιώτατον ὁ κόσμος ἐστὶ καὶ θεοπρεπέστατον.[271] Through birth man is introduced into this temple as a "spectator" (θεατής)[272] οὐ χειροκμήτων οὐδ' ἀκινήτων ἀγαλμάτων [273] but οἷα νοῦς θεῖος αἰσθητὰ μιμήματα νοητῶν. They
include sun, moon, stars, rivers, earth, flora and fauna.[274] Life (477D)
itself is an initiation into and a celebration of these "mysteries": ὧν τὸν βίον μύησιν ὄντα καὶ τελετὴν τελειότατην.[275] In such a life-long festival tranquillity of mind abounds: εὐθυμίας δεῖ μεστὸν εἶναι καὶ γήθους.

It is for this reason that the deity originally instituted the (477E)
festivals and initiations.[276] The true meaning of the festivals, however, is obscured by the ways in which public religion now celebrates them.[277] The crowds wait for the scheduled festivals of Cronus, Zeus, the Panathenaea. On such days they have fun with the hired mimes and dancers. The celebrants perform the proper behavior during the festivals, and at the performances the crowds are silent when they ought to be silent, happy when they ought to be happy, etc. But they fail to carry these experience over into

---

[270] Plutarch had referred to the same dictum in connection with Crates (466E). Cf. the striking parallel in Prov 15:15: πάντα τὸν χρόνον οἱ ὀφθαλμοὶ τῶν κακῶν προσδέχονται κακά, οἱ δὲ ἀγαθοὶ ἡσυχάζουσιν διὰ παντός. The last part of the sentence in Hebrew is even closer to Plutarch: טוֹב־לֵב בִּשְׁתֶּה תָּמִיד (cf. 477D: πίνειν ἐν Κρονίοις). This was recognized by Symmachus who translates εὐθυμῶν ὡς ἐν πότῳ διαπαντός. Philo *spec. leg.* 2. 42, is also parallel; see also I. Heinemann, *Philons griechische und jüdische Bildung* (Hildesheim, 1962) 106ff. In Christian literature, the idea was not adopted before Clement of Alexandria (see Lampe, s.v. ἑορτή, A.3). Cf. 2 Cor 6:2.

[271] Broecker (198f.) notes the Platonic character of the notion and quotes Philo *vit. Mos.* 2. 74 as a parallel; ECL does not have a parallel.

[272] Cf. Rom 1:20; Acts 14:15, 17; 17:23ff.

[273] This polemic against statues is commonplace in ECL. See *PECL* 1, index, s.v. God(s), statues.

[274] Cf. the passages in n. 272 above.

[275] ECL applies μυστήριον to the Christian message and life. See G. Bornkamm, *TDNT*, s.v. μυστήριον, C; cf. Phil 4:12.

[276] 477E. See *PECL* 1, index, s.v. Mysteries; cf. also Philo's discussion of the meaning of festivals, *plant.* 90-92, 166; *somn.* 2. 249; *virt.* 67.

[277] For this criticism of religion, cf. primitive Christian criticism of the Jewish and heathen worship, esp. Matt 6:1-18; Rom 14:15; Gal 4:9f.; 2 Cor 6:16, etc. Cf. also Philo *Flacc.* 118. See Almqvist, 92.

their daily lives, and therefore a person who has enjoyed a festival still regards his own life as a misery.[278] Thus these religious festivals fail to do what they intend to do. They fail to provide tranquillity.[279]
(477F) However, if the common people do not learn it there,[280] they will not accept the philosopher's παρακαλεῖν either. With this note of seeming resignation and its implicit appeal to Paccius, together with a summary of Plutarch's concept of tranquillity of mind, the work has reached its conclusion.[281]

---

[278] Cf. Matt 6:16-18 (σκυθρωπός!); Matt 9:14//Mark 2:18f.//Luke 5:33.

[279] Nevertheless, Plutarch also puts in a strong admonition against such pessimism. Cf. the Christian concept of "joy in suffering," Matt 5:11f.// Luke 6:22f.; and the enormous importance of χαρά in ECL (for which see H. Conzelmann, *TDNT*, s.v.); Rom 12:15; 1 Cor 13:6; Col 1:24 and often (cf. Conzelmann, *TDNT*, s.v. χαίρω, D.2-3).

[280] Such people still live ἐν ὀδυρμοῖς τὰ πολλὰ καὶ βαρυθυμίαις καὶ μερίμναις ἐπιπόνοις . . . 477E describes the unjustified misery quite vividly. Cf. Matt 6:25-34//Luke 12:22-32; Matt 13:22//Mark 4:19//Luke 8:14; Luke 15:25ff. (the elder son); Luke 24:17 (σκυθρωποί).

[281] See above, p. 201.

DE FRATERNO AMORE (MORALIA 478A - 492D)

BY

HANS DIETER BETZ
Claremont Graduate School and School of Theology
Claremont, California

I. INTRODUCTION

In his essay "On Brotherly Love" (περὶ φιλαδελφίας) [1] Plutarch discusses an important chapter of Hellenistic—and one must include Roman—family ethics. As usual he draws on a wide variety of traditions and source materials, and consequently his work has the nature and purpose of a consensus. He presents to his Roman friends what he believes to be the best of the Hellenic tradition, a tradition which the Roman friends not only welcome but even represent as living examples.[2]

The subject of "brotherly love" was not discussed frequently by Greek philosophers.[3] But we can see quite clearly that the topic must have been discussed widely in the so-called "popular morality." [4] Plutarch presents his doctrine as a combination of family ethics [5] and friendship ethics,[6] a combination which had

[1] The essay is No. 98 in the Lamprias Catalogue. The edition used here is by W. C. Helmbold, *Plutarch's Moralia* 6, LCL (1962) 243-325. The edition by M. Pohlenz and W. Sieveking (*Plutarchi Moralia* 3, BT [1929] 221-254) has also been consulted. There is no commentary or any other satisfactory discussion of the work. A few pages are devoted to the question of the sources in C. Brokate, *De Aliquot Plutarchi Libellis* (Göttingen, 1913) 17-24.

[2] See below 478B.

[3] Cf. esp. Xenophon *Mem.* 2. 3; *Cyr.* 8. 7. 14ff. (see on this H. R. Breitenbach, "Xenophon," PW, 2. Reihe, 9.A.2: 1778, 1798-1800); Hierocles, *De fraterno amore* (Stobaeus [ed. Hense] 4:660-664).

[4] See the basic study by F. Dirlmeier, *Φίλος und Φιλία im vorhellenistischen Griechentum* (Munich, 1931).

[5] There does not seem to exist a special study on the subject of brotherhood as part of family ethics. E.g., K. H. Schelkle (*RAC*, s.v. Bruder) does not even mention it.

[6] For a survey and the older literature, see G. Stählin, *TDNT*, s.v. φιλέω κτλ.; K. Treu, *RAC*, s.v. Freundschaft; F.-A. Steinmetz, *Die Freundschaftslehre des Panaitius: Nach einer Analyse von Ciceros "Laelius de amicitia"* (Wiesbaden, 1967); J.-C. Fraisse, *Philia: La Notion d'amitié dans la philosophie antique* (Paris, 1974).

its roots in the archaic Greek family ethics, where συγγένεια and φιλία are intimately related.[7] Plutarch's elaborations, however, presuppose that extensive reflection had taken place, and there are traces of such reflection here and there in ancient literature.[8] On the whole, however, one can say that Plutarch's treatise is the only *systematic* presentation of what antiquity had to say about the ethics of "brotherly love." [9]

We can assume that the family ethics upon which his essay is based was widely shared in antiquity, including, to as extent, Judaism [10] and primitive Christianity. Plutarch spells out what most other writers simply presuppose as commonly shared morality or life experience. Therefore, his essay is of great value not only for the understanding of Hellenistic ethics, but also all ancient ethics, including the OT, Judaism, and Christianity. In Biblical literature terms and concepts related to "brotherly love" appear again and again. Their meaning is rarely discussed, because its knowledge could simply be presupposed.

Surprisingly, however, Plutarch's work has been almost completely neglected by New Testament scholars. Most treatments simply mention the terms φιλαδελφία and φιλάδελφος, and leave it at that.[11]

The terminology might have entered Christian literature through the mediation of Hellenistic Judaism,[12] but there is no explanation of why this terminology was assumed proper in the Christian context.[13] Apparently it was considered part of ἀγάπη, and thus there was no further need for them to explain it.[14] This fact, how-

[7] See on 478C-D. On the relationship of συγγένεια and φιλία, see Dirlmeier, 7-21, with many references.

[8] See LSJ, s.v.; Bauer, s.v. φιλαδελφία.

[9] According to *Index Verborum Plutarcheus*, s.v., φιλαδελφία is found in the title, 478B, C; 480C, F; 483C; 491A; φιλάδελφος occurs 478B; 489A; *aet. Rom.* 267E; *Solon* 93f.; *Lucullus* 520f.

[10] A satisfactory comparison with the OT and Judaism would require a special study. We have, however, noted especially interesting parallels below.

[11] So, e.g., H. von Soden, *TDNT*, s.v. ἀδελφός κτλ. (1:146).

[12] Cf. terminologically 2 Mac 15:14; 4 Mac 13:21, 23, 26; 14:1; 15:10; Philo *leg. Gai.* 87; 92; Josephus *AJ* 4. 26.

[13] C. H. Ratschow ("Agape, Nächstenliebe und Bruderliebe," *Zeitschrift für systematische Theologie* 21 [1950/52] 160-82) noticed that the concepts have problematic relationships, but he did not pay attention to the original meaning of "Bruderliebe." Similarly K. H. Schelkle, *Die Petrusbriefe. Der Judasbrief*, 3d ed. (Freiburg, 1970) 51-53, 93, 190.

[14] See Rom 12:9-13, esp. vs. 10; 1 Thes 4:9; Heb 13:1; 1 Pet 1:22; 3:8; 2 Pet 1:7; 1 Clem 47:5; 48:1. For later passages, see Lampe, s.v.

ever, implies that the terms have already been transformed and no longer refer to family relationships, but to Christian "brotherhood." Apart from a few instances, ECL is not interested in the family relationship of "brotherhood," but instead "brotherhood" almost throughout ECL means "spiritual brotherhood." [15] Along with this transformation, older *topoi* of family ethics now appear simply as Christian church ethics,[16] the congregation becoming the "household of God." [17] This development explains why the terms of "brotherly love" could be taken over into Christian ethics without further discussion.[18]

This widening of originally limited family ethics in ECL leads into two directions. For one thing, family relationships are made second in importance or are even rejected as incompatible with the Kingdom of God: the Christian "brother" is given preference over against the "natural" brother. This, however, does not violate the older rule, not to give priority to the friend instead of the brother, because fellow-Christians are for the most part, called "brothers" and not "friends." [19] The concept of "spiritual brotherhood" could also easily overcome the old limitation of φιλαδελφία to only the male members of the family. The notion of Christian "brotherhood" in the NT includes the "sisters in Christ," giving them equal status even when only "brothers" are mentioned.[20]

On the other hand, one can see how the concept of Christian "brotherhood" served to confirm the bonds within the family. Brothers in Christian families were related to each other not only "by nature," but as Christians.

The crisis of family relations, of which Plutarch speaks so pessimistically at the end of the first chapter of his essay, is reflected also in ECL. Both Plutarch and primitive Christianity admit that the natural bonds do not hold, given the pressures of the times. Both recognize that a religious bond must undergird the natural status of brotherhood if a lasting and proper relationship between

[15] See H. von Soden, *TDNT*, s.v. ἀδελφός κτλ.

[16] See below, part III.

[17] Cf. Gal 6:10; Eph 2:19. See O. Michel, *TDNT*, s.v. οἶκος κτλ.

[18] Cf. von Soden, *TDNT*, s.v. ἀδελφός κτλ., 2 (1:146): "There are no examples of this more general use of φιλαδελφία and φιλάδελφος outside Christian writings."

[19] μὴ προτίμα τοὺς φίλους τῶν ἀδελφῶν (*Corpus Paroemiographorum Graecorum* [ed. Leutsch and Schneidewin], II, 524. 15; cited by Dirlmeier, 9). See below.

[20] See, esp. Gal 3:26-28.

brothers is to be achieved. Plutarch despairs when he looks at his own people.[21] The Roman brothers, to whom he dedicates his essay, are his hope. The early Christians realized and accepted the crisis in family relations as part of the eschatological crisis and as a consequence of Jesus' message.[22] They overcame the crisis with the help of the new concept of ἀγάπη, which for them was identical with Christian "brotherhood" and could give new meaning even to the natural family relations at a later stage of the development. The Christian *Haustafeln* at least implicitly confirm the family relations, including brotherhood.[23] The reception of the concept of "brotherly love" by ECL shows how Christianity was able to perpetuate the older family ethics in a new way, in spite of the cultural crisis at its beginning.

II. Composition [24]

I. *Exordium* Ch. 1
- A. Captatio benevolentiae [25] (478A-B [p. 221.4-7])
- B. Dedication [26] (478B [p. 221.8-10])
  - 1. Address [27]
  - 2. Title of the essay
- C. Statement of purpose [28] (478B [221.10-222.4])

---

[21] See below on 478C-D. Cf. also The Teachings of Silvanus (NH VII, 4) 98: "Es gibt keinen <Freund>, und es gibt keinen Bruder; nach seinem (eigenen) Vorteil strebt ein jeder." (I follow the translation of H. M. Schenke et al., *TLZ* 100 [1975] 15.)

[22] See below, on ch. 4.

[23] See especially 1 Pet 3:8; 1 Tim 5:8; cf. 5:1.

[24] This analysis has taken into account the attempt made by Brokate, 17-24. Compared with Brokate, our analysis is more detailed and avoids the confusion between composition analysis and source criticism. The page and line numbers are those of the Teubner edition.

[25] The *captatio benevolentiae* consists of a brief epideictic description of representations of the Dioscuri. On this element of an exordium, see H. Lausberg, *Handbuch der literarischen Rhetorik* (Munich, 1960) sec. 271. Acts 17:23, the beginning of Paul's speech at Athens, is a NT example.

[26] For NT examples of such a dedication, see Luke 1:1-4; Acts 1:1. See also Helmbold's note b in LCL 6:246.

[27] The words οὕτω δὴ καὶ αὐτὸς ὑμῖν . . . ἀνατίθημι indicate that Plutarch treats the addressees as imitators of the Dioscuri who represent τὸ φιλάδελφον τῶν θεῶν. Cf. 2 Cor 10:7: . . . καθὼς αὐτὸς Χριστοῦ, οὕτως καὶ ἡμεῖς. Cf. also Eph 4:20; Phil 2:5; etc.

[28] The general purpose is said to be protreptic (προτρέπεσθαι [478B]). But the exhortation is not directed toward the Roman noblemen! They are the recipients of the work, but the exhortation addresses the general public.

II. *Propositio* (478B-D [222.4-16])
  A. The moral decay of the time (478B-C [222.4-12])
  B. Two basic definitions upon which the argument rests (478C-D [222.13-16])
    1. a definition of brotherhood
    2. a definition of friendship
III. *Probatio* — Chs. 2-6
  A. The great paradigm of the human body — Ch. 2
  B. μισαδελφία and φιλαδελφία and their effect upon human relations in the family — Chs. 3-6
    1. Hatred of one's brother makes friendship impossible — Ch. 3
    2. Hatred of one's brother is incompatible with being a philosopher — Ch. 4
    3. Hatred of one's brother leads to hatred of parents — Ch. 5
    4. Love of one's brother leads to greater love of parents and to better parenthood — Ch. 6
IV. *Paraenesis* — Chs. 7-20
  A. General statement of the ethical task — Ch. 7
  B. Discussion of specific ethical problems — Chs. 8-20
    1. "προοίμια" [29] — Ch. 8
    2. "διδασκαλία" [30] — Chs. 9-20
      a. The relationship to the parents — Chs. 9-11
        1) while the parents are alive — Chs. 9-10
        2) when the father has died: the division of the parental property — Ch. 11

Avidius Nigrinus and Avidius Quietus, being already imitators of the Dioscuri, serve as a living testimony: ταῦτα πράττοντες ἤδη μαρτυρεῖσθαι μᾶλλον ἢ παρακαλεῖσθαι δόξετε. They serve, one may say, as a living ethical aretalogy—an interesting concept, which ECL also uses; cf. 1 Thes 4:10 (in the context of φιλαδελφία!); 5:11 (καθὼς καὶ ποιεῖτε); 2 Thes 3:4; Phil 4:9; Phlm 21; etc. The expected result, as far as the brothers are concerned, is this: ποιήσει τῇ κρίσει τὴν ἐπιμονὴν βεβαιοτέραν (cf. Luke 1:4; 1 Cor 1:6, 8; 2 Cor 1:21; Phil 1:6-7; etc.).

[29] It is not entirely clear what Plutarch has in mind by the words προοίμια τοῦ λόγου παντός (482D). Cf. Brokate, 18, n. 1: " 'προοίμια' hic non significare libri praefationem, sed prooemia, qualia legibus praeponi solebant ac de utilitate harum legum agebant (velut Platonis προοίμια νόμων) Pohlenz me monuit."

[30] 482D—Plutarch states that he now begins the διδασκαλία, the *ethical* instruction. This understanding is shared by ECL; cf. esp. Mark 7:7// Matt 15:9; Col 2:22; 1 Tim 4:13; etc.

b. The concepts of "inequality" and "equality" — Chs. 12-15
  1) the nature of inequality — Ch. 12
  2) the ethical task
    a. for the brother in the superior position — Ch. 13
    b. for the brother in the inferior position — Chs. 14-15
c. The existence of "differences" between brothers — Chs. 16-20
  1) the difference in age — Ch. 16
  2) the difference in "πάθη" — Ch. 17
  3) the difference in "πράγματα"
  4) (a digression: a ring-composition of exempla)[31] — Ch. 18
  5) the difference of friends and enemies — Ch. 19
  6) the sharing of friends and enemies — Ch. 20

V. *Peroratio*: a "Haustafel" [32] — Ch. 21

III. Plutarch's Treatise and Early Christian Literature

Ch. 1

(478C) Plutarch's concept of "brotherly love" grew out of his perception of the problem, which he outlines at the end of the first chapter. As the components of the term φιλαδελφία indicate, the concept touches upon two areas of ethics, family ethics and friendship ethics. This fact is demonstrated by the two definitions, with which Plutarch concludes the chapter. The first definition defines the proper relationship of brothers in the family: τὸ χρῆσθαι κοινῶς τοῖς πατρῴοις χρήμασι καὶ φίλοις καὶ δούλοις.[33] In 482Dff Plutarch

[31] On this literary form, see H. Conzelmann, *1 Corinthians* (Philadelphia, 1975) 39.

[32] On this literary form and bibliography, see W. Schrage, "Zur Ethik der neutestamentlichen Haustafeln," *NTS* 21 (1974-75) 1-22.

[33] The definition appears to be a variation of the famous maxim attributed to Pythagoras: κοινὰ τὰ φίλων (Aristotle *E.N.* 9. 8, p. 1168b 6-8; Diogenes Laertius 8. 10; etc.). For a collection of passages, see G. Bohnenblust, *Beiträge zum Topos* ΠΕΡΙ ΦΙΛΙΑΣ (Berlin, 1905) 41f.; Stählin, *TDNT*, s.v. φίλος κτλ., A.II.2. In ECL, the literary *topos* of father and sons is present esp. in the so-called "Parable of the Prodigal Son" (Luke 15:11-32), as

discusses the implications of this definition. The second definition defines true friendship: τὸ χρῆσθαι μίαν ψυχὴν δυεῖν σωμάτων χερσὶ καὶ ποσὶ καὶ ὀφθαλμοῖς.[34] The difference between "brotherhood" and "friendship" is that the former is a matter of physical kinship, while the latter is one of voluntary choice.[35] Both are, however, intimately related "by nature." In Plutarch's view φιλαδελφία is not confined to the given relationship of natural kinship, and it is different from the voluntary relationship of friendship. It is a combination of both. As such, φιλαδελφία is an ethical task and challenge. Whether or not one has a brother is a fact one must accept as given, but whether the relationship to a brother is one of φιλαδελφία or μισαδελφία depends upon the question, whether or not one has mastered the ethical task.

As Plutarch shows in the second part of the essay, this ethical task amounts to reasonable conduct in the face of the many human problems in a family (481Fff.). But the more serious dilemma he mentions in the beginning. The greatest problem comes from the general moral decay of his time: ἐγὼ δ' ὁρῶ καθ' ἡμᾶς τὴν φιλαδελφίαν οὕτω σπάνιον οὖσαν ὡς τὴν μισαδελφίαν ἐπὶ τῶν παλαιῶν.[36] As Plutarch sees it, "modern man" [37] has become utterly estranged from the

L. Schottroff ("Das Gleichnis vom verlorenen Sohn," *ZTK* 68 [1971] 27-52) has rightly emphasized (pp. 44-47); for a critique of Schottroff and further bibliography, see C. E. Carlston, "Reminiscence and Redaction in Luke 15:11-32," *JBL* 94 (1975) 368-90. See also Matt 21:28-31; Gal 4:1-2, 22. The maxim κοινὰ τὰ φίλων influenced primitive Christianity; cf. Acts 2:44; 4:32; Gal 6:6, and the whole ecclesiological concept of κοινωνία (see F. Hauck, *TDNT*, s.v. κοινωνός κτλ.); cf. 1 John 1:3.

[34] The definition was famous. For passages see Bohnenblust, *Beiträge*, 40; Stählin, *TDNT* 9:149f.; Thraede, *Brieftopik*, 122f. See on μία ψυχή Acts 4:32; Phil 1:27 (cf. E. Schweizer, *TDNT*, s.v. ψυχή κτλ., D.II.3.), and esp., the saying of Jesus in 2 Clem 12:2 and its interpretation 12:3: τὰ δύο δὲ ἕν ἐστιν, ὅταν λαλῶμεν ἑαυτοῖς ἀλήθειαν [cf. *frat. am.* 483A-C] καὶ ἐν δυσὶ σώμασιν ἀνυποκρίτως εἴη μία ψυχή. In ECL cf. also the φίλος christology of the Fourth Gospel (esp. John 15:14-17; 1 John 3:14-17; etc.). It is interesting that feet, hands, and eyes appear also in 1 Cor 12:15-21, the chapter on the "Body of Christ." A variation of the definition is used in Gal 4:12a.

[35] See below 479B-C; 481E. Cf. the christological application in Heb 2:14-18.

[36] This theory of moral decay is shared by apocalyptic Judaism and Christianity. See also *PECL* 1:142. Cf. Rom 5:12; Gal 3:22f.; Rom 1:18-3:20; 1 John 2:18; etc.

[37] οἱ δὲ νῦν ἄνθρωποι πάντες. Cf. Jesus' judgment of ἡ γενεὰ αὕτη (Matt 11:16//Luke 7:31; Matt 12:39//Luke 11:29; Matt 16:4; Mark 8:12; etc. (see Bauer, s.v. γενέα, 2). Often in ECL the term νῦν refers to the evil present (cf. Bauer, s.v.).

(478D) moral values and standards of the ancestors,[38] and even from "nature" itself. Today, brothers who are friendly towards each other cause an amazement like that caused by the "siamese twins" of Molione.[39] The phenomenon of "brotherly love" and "true friendship" is taken by most as something ἄπιστον . . . καὶ τερατῶδες.

Ch. 2

The *probatio* (chs. 2-6) demonstrates that "brotherly love" is in accordance with "nature" (ἡ φύσις).[40] Plutarch's argumentation begins with the closest "paradigm" for "brotherly love," the human body: τὸ παράδειγμα τῆς χρήσεως τῶν ἀδελφῶν ἡ φύσις οὐ μακρὰν ἔθηκεν.[41] Characteristically, he ends with the reference to Heracles, the "paradigm" superior to man which, however, man must strive to emulate (492C). The human body[42] is constructed in a way that its most important organs exist as διττὰ καὶ ἀδελφὰ καὶ δίδυμα.[43] Examples given include hands, feet, eyes, ears, nostrils. This fact must be taken as a moral lesson "nature" wants to teach us. The purpose of the division is certainly this: ἐδίδαξεν ὅτι ταῦτα σωτηρίας ἕνεκα καὶ συμπράξεως κοινῆς οὐ διαφορᾶς καὶ μάχης οὕτως
(478E) διέστησεν.[44] Plutarch then illustrates the point by an excursus on the human hand, that most important tool of which man has two.[45]

---

[38] οἱ παλαιοί. The belief that in the old times people were morally superior, compared with those of the present, seems to be universal. In primitive Christianity, this view of the ideal past is not emphasized strongly. Cf., however, Gal 1:14; 2 Thes 2:15, etc. Mostly, the "new" is preferable; cf. Ign Magn 9:1; Mark 1:27; John 13:34; Acts 17:19; Rom 6:1f.; 2 Cor 5:17; etc. See P. Tachau, *"Einst" und "Jetzt" im Neuen Testament* (Göttingen, 1972); also *PECL* 1:305.

[39] See on this *adv. Stoic.* 1083C and Helmbold's note, LCL 6:248.

[40] On φύσις see 478D, E, F; 479D, F; 480B; 482B, F; 489C. Cf. 1 Cor 11:14: ἡ φύσις αὐτὴ διδάσκει ὑμᾶς; cf. furthermore Jas 3:7; 2 Pet 1:4; Almqvist, 99.

[41] Cf. terminologically Ign Trall 1:1: οὐ κατὰ χρῆσιν ἀλλὰ κατὰ φύσιν. On οὐ μακράν cf. Acts 17:27; Eph 2:13, 17.

[42] Paul also uses the human body as a paradigm, but in a different way (cf. 1 Cor 12:14ff.; Rom 12:4). See E. Schweizer, *TDNT*, s.v. σῶμα, A.1-5, D.II.2.a. (c).

[43] Helmbold (LCL 6:248, n. b) refers to Hierocles, fr. *De Fraterno Amore* in Stobaeus (ed. Hense) 4:663. This particular version of the paradigm with the doubling of organs is not found in ECL.

[44] Cf. 1 Cor 12:24-27; Rom 12:5.

[45] See Helmbold's notes, LCL 6:249. Cf. Ps 115:4-7; Wis 15:15; 13:19.

Coming from one seed and one source the two hands are like two brothers,[46] operating οὐ πρὸς διαφορὰν καὶ ἀντίταξιν, ἀλλ' ὅπως χωρὶς ὄντες ἀλλήλοις μᾶλλον συνεργῶσιν.[47]

What this separation and yet cooperation entails Plutarch (478F)
describes in greater detail. The forms of separation between brothers may be many,[48] but their relationship must always remain the
same: εὔνοια,[49] συμφωνία[50] (478F), ὁμόνοια,[51] συμφωνία, κρᾶσις and
ἁρμονία (479A). The adverse relationship amounts to πλεονεξία and (479A)
στάσις (479A);[52] it is παρὰ φύσιν (478F)[53] and self-destructive
(479A).[54] The concord of brothers is the foundation of a healthy
family life: οὕτως ἀδελφῶν ὁμοφροσύνῃ καὶ γένος καὶ οἶκος ὑγιαίνει καὶ
τέθηλε, καὶ φίλοι καὶ συνήθεις ὥσπερ ἐμμελὴς χορὸς οὐθὲν οὔτε πράσ-
σουσιν ἐναντίον οὔτε λέγουσιν ἢ φρονοῦσιν.[55] Such a healthy family
will also be able to protect itself against such typical enemies as
οἰκέτης διάβολος[56] ἢ κόλαξ παρενδὺς θυραῖος[57] ἢ πολίτης βάσκανος,[58] (479B)
people who introduce and spread "diseases" of two sorts: ἡ πρὸς
τὸ συγγενὲς διαβολὴ καὶ ὑφόρασις which leads to ὁμιλίαι φαυλαὶ καὶ
πονηραί flowing in from the outside and filling up the deserted
place.[59]

---

[46] ἀπὸ σπέρματος ἑνὸς καὶ μιᾶς ἀρχῆς . . . cf. Gal 3:16.

[47] Cf. 1 Cor 12:24-27; 1 Thes 4:9: τὸ ἀγαπᾶν ἀλλήλους (cf. 480C: φιλεῖν ἀλλήλους).

[48] The contrasts used are μένειν — ἀποδημεῖν, πολιτεύεσθαι — γεωργεῖν. Cf. ἀποδημεῖν in Luke 15:13; ἐν ἀγρῷ in Luke 15:25; on μένειν cf. Luke 15:29-31.

[49] This term plays an important role in relation to friendship. See Bohnenblust, *Beiträge*, 35, 36. Cf. Eph 6:7; Ign Rom 4:1; Matt 5:25f.; Mart Pol 17:3. See J. Behm, *TDNT*, s.v. εὐνοέω, εὔνοια.

[50] Cf. Matt 18:19; 1 Cor 7:5.

[51] Cf. esp. Ign Eph 4:2 and Bauer, s.v.

[52] The terms are common in ECL, see Bauer, s.v. Cf. 1 Thes 4:6: πλεονεκτεῖν ἐν τῷ πράγματι τὸν ἀδελφόν.

[53] Cf. Rom 1:26 and *PECL* 1:311, 314, 321.

[54] A typical example is the older brother in Luke 15:25-32.

[55] Cf. the conclusion of the Haustafel in 1 Pet 3:8-9; also Luke 15:24, 32, where a principle of family ethics is expressed. See also the use of χορός in Ign Eph 4:2.

[56] In ECL, slander is often connected with the women. Cf. 1 Tim 3:11; 2 Tim 3:3; Tit 2:3; Pol Phil 4:3. On slaves, cf. 1 Pet 2:18.

[57] Cf. the parallel in 2 Tim 3:6, again related to women; also Gal 2:4f.; Tit 1:11; 2 Pet 2:1; Jude 4; Barn 2:10; 4:10. On "flattery" see above.

[58] Cf. esp. Gal 3:1; also Mart Pol 17:1.

[59] Cf. Paul's quotation from Menander in 1 Cor 15:33. In Gal 5:9 he makes the same point using another proverb.

Ch. 3

In chs. 3-6 Plutarch shows how φιλαδελφία or the failure to practice it (μισαδελφία) [60] affect other human relations within the family. He states his thesis at the end of chs. 3-5, and then in ch. 6 he concludes with impressive historical examples.

The main point in ch. 3 is that hatred of one's brother makes friendship impossible.[61] Plutarch begins with this point because "friendship" is phenomenologically as well as terminologically close to "brotherhood." However, the differences between the two
(479B) relationships are also fundamental. The brother is like a natural limb of one's own body,[62] while the ἑταῖρος is a μέλος ἀλλότριον, not a gift of "nature" but acquired ἑκουσίως, not received at home but ἐξ ἀγορᾶς ἢ παλαίστρας.[63] A brother who in quarreling with his brother replaces him with a friend is like the prophet Hegisistratos of Elis who made himself a wooden foot after losing his natural one. Although this sounds rather negative, Plutarch does not intend to devaluate friendship as a relationship in its own right.
(479C) It is *another* human relationship which nonetheless is necessary because no person can live alone: ὡς ἀφίλους καὶ ἀμίκτους καὶ μονοτρόπους ζῆν μὴ δυναμένους μηδὲ πεφυκότας.[64] How then are "brotherhood" and "friendship" related? According to our author, friendship is not an "original" but only a "derivate" relationship. It is
(479D) a "shadow and imitation" [65] of the original natural relationship children have with their parents and with one another. This means

[60] μισαδελφία occurs in Plutarch only in *frat. am.* (478C; 480F; 481B; μισάδελφος 482C). It is not found in ECL; but T Benj 7:5; 8:1 has μισαδελφία. Hatred of one's brother is commended in Luke 14:26, rejected in 1 John 2:9; 3:15; 4:20. Cf. Eph 5:29a; Matt 5:43.

[61] Cf. the older brother in Luke 15:29 who, we must conclude, has never invited his "friends."

[62] Cf. Paul's concept of the Christian "brothers" as "limbs" of the body of Christ (Rom 12:4f.; 1 Cor 6:15; 12:12ff.; Eph 4:16, 25; 5:23, 30). Cf. also the principle in Matt 19:6//Mark 10:9; 1 Cor 12:24.

[63] The comparison with the ἑταῖρος is a *topos*. See Dirlmeier, 22ff.; Bohnenblust, *Beiträge*, 39. Often the comparison is used to attack "flattery" and πολυφιλία. Cf. the accusations against Jesus in Luke 7:34//Matt 11:19. Cf. also the invitation in the Parable of the Supper, Matt 22:8-10//Luke 14:21-23.

[64] On this old idea see Bohnenblust, *Beiträge*, 42f.; A. Bonhöffer, *Die Ethik des Stoikers Epictet* (Stuttgart, 1894) 118, n. 70, with many passages. Cf. Gen 2:18; Tob 8:6; also John 8:29; 16:32.

[65] On the comparison with a shadow, see Bohnenblust, *Beiträge*, 32; cf. Col 2:17, Heb 8:5; 10:1.

ethically that a relationship like friendship cannot possibly be authentic if the foundational relationship of brother toward brother is in disorder.[66] Consequently, cultivating a friendship while hating one's brother is unhealthy, unnatural, and sacrilegious [67]

Ch. 4

Hatred of one's brother is incompatible with claiming to be a philosopher.[68] Plutarch documents this thesis by personal testimony, (479E)
a "Streitgespräch" which he once had in Rome when he tried to reconcile two hostile brothers, one of whom claimed to be a philosopher.[69] Plutarch failed, but his reasoning is interesting. He appealed to the philosopher by suggesting to him that really two relationships were out of order: that between brother and brother and that between philosopher and layman (ἰδιώτης). Plutarch's strategy was to reconcile the former with the help of the latter.[70] Once the philosopher realized his relationship to his brother as a layman, both relationships should have been restored. Interestingly, the attempt failed when the philosopher took refuge in the Cynic-Stoic position that natural relationships like that to a brother are irrelevant.[71] This may be acceptable, but the man failed to face up to Plutarch's challenge that he ought to behave towards his brother in the way in which a philosopher ought to act to a layman, and thus his claim to philosophy became "hypocritical."

Conversely, "all other philosophers" affirm "brotherly love" (479F)
as unconditionally good. The reasoning is this: next to the gods, "nature" and the "law of nature" have assigned the greatest honor

[66] Plutarch uses as an example the address of a friend in a letter as "brother." How can this be honest, if the man cannot "walk the same way with his brother." (For this phrase, see Matt 5:41; Did 1:4.) Cf. the frequent use of ἀδελφός in Christian letters.

[67] It is interesting that much of what Plutarch says about one's relationship to a physical brother, primitive Christianity has transferred to the Christian "brother"; cf. Matt 5:22-24; 7:3-5//Luke 6:41f.; 1 John 2:9; 3:14, 17; 4:20f.

[68] Cf. the similar argument that being a Christian and hating the brother are incompatible, esp. 1 John 2:9, 11; 3:15; 4:20.

[69] Cf. Luke 12:13-15 (// Copt Gos Thom 72), where Jesus rejects such a request; however, the language is very similar to Plutarch.

[70] An analogous reasoning is presupposed in the NT Haustafeln: the Christian faith is the compelling motivation to maintain proper family relations.

[71] Cf. Matt 12:48-50//Mark 3:34f.//Luke 8:21; Gos Eb 4; 2 Clem 9:11; Copt Gos Thom 99. Cf. also Luke 2:49f.

to the parents.[72] There is nothing more acceptable to the gods than the honoring of one's parents,[73] as there is nothing more "godless" than their neglect.[74] This law goes beyond the general ethical demand to abstain from doing harm to other people (τοὺς . . .
(480A) ἄλλους κακῶς ποιεῖν ἀπείρηται).[75] It is considered ἀνόσιον . . . καὶ ἄθεσμον if we fail to continuously provide pleasure (εὐφραίνειν) to our parents, both in deed and word. The greatest pleasure sons can present to their parents is: πρὸς ἀδελφὸν εὐνοίας βεβαίου καὶ φιλίας.[76]

(480A-D) Ch. 5

Hatred of one's brother, however, leads to hatred of one's parents: ὁ γὰρ μισῶν τὸν ἀδελφὸν αὐτοῦ καὶ βαρυνόμενος οὐ δύναται μὴ τὸν γεννήσαντα μέμφεσθαι καὶ τὴν τεκοῦσαν.[77] Parents are grieved by a variety of misbehavior in which sons may engage, but they become most upset when their sons hate each other.[78] The reason is shown by a climax leading to mutual extinction of the sons: . . . υἱοῖς διαφερομένοις καὶ μισοῦσιν ἀλλήλους καὶ κακῶς λέγουσι καὶ πρὸς ἔργα καὶ πράξεις ἀντιταττομένοις ἀεὶ καὶ καταλυομένοις ὑπ' ἀλλήλων.[79]

On the other hand, through "brotherly love" sons provide their parents ἡδεῖαν καὶ μακαρίαν . . . γηροτρόφον. It presents the father who is φιλότεκνος with the greatest encouragement.[80] All other

---

[72] The law to love the parents was inscribed in the temple of Apollo at Delphi. See A. Lumpe and H. Karpp, *RAC*, s.v. Eltern, where the evidence is collected. In the OT it is part of the Decalog (Exod 20:12; Deut 5:16 and often). ECL continues it: Mark 10:19//Matt 19:19//Luke 18:20; Mark 7:10//Matt 15:4; Luke 2:51; Eph 6:1-3 (ἐντολὴ πρώτη); Col 3:20; 1 Tim 5:4; Herm Vis 1:3:1; 2:2:2.

[73] In Judaism, it is regarded as the most difficult of the commandments. See Bill., 1:705-709. Cf. also Pseudo-Phocylides 8: Πρῶτα θεὸν τιμᾶν, μετέπειτα δὲ σεῖο γονῆας.

[74] Cf. Mark 7:10//Matt 15:4 (Lev 20:9); Mark 13:12b//Matt 10:21b; Rom 1:30 (γονεῦσιν ἀπειθεῖς); 2 Tim 3:2; Herm Vis 1:3:1; 2:2:2.

[75] ECL, of course, affirms this: cf. Luke 6:27f.; Rom 12:17; 2 Cor 7:2; Gal 6:10; 1 Thes 5:15; 2 Pet 1:7; etc.

[76] Cf. Luke 15:23, 24, 32.

[77] 1 John 4:20b shows how the principle was applied to the love of God (cf. Mark 12:30f.//Matt 22:37-39//Luke 10:27; etc.).

[78] Cf. Luke 15:29-32.

[79] Cf. 1 John 3:15: πᾶς ὁ μισῶν τὸν ἀδελφὸν αὐτοῦ ἀνθρωποκτόνος ἐστίν . . . The idea is also implicit in Matt 5:21f. The greatest example in the Bible is, of course, Cain's fratricide mentioned in 1 Clem 4:7 (ἀδελφοκτονία).

[80] Plutarch contrasts this with φιλόλογος, φιλότιμος, φιλοχρήματος. Cf. Tit 2:4; Herm Vis 1:3:1: φιλότεκνος.

successes, such as oratory, wealth and power, which sons proudly show their parents, will be set aside by the parents in favor of mutual love between the brothers. Plutarch then illustrates this and the opposite by historical examples, concluding with a quotation of Euripides declaring: χαλεποὶ πόλεμοι γὰρ ἀδελφῶν.[81]

Ch. 6

As hatred of one's brother leads to hatred of one's parents, so (480D)
love among brothers leads to greater love for parents and even to being a better parent. Plutarch begins by referring to the example of Peisistratus, who married a second time when his sons were grown, so that he could have more sons like them. "Brotherly love" not only makes sons χρηστοὶ . . . καὶ δίκαιοι but also enhances (480E)
a variety of family relationships. Brothers love one another more because of their love toward their parents, but they also love their parents more because of one another: τοῖς γονεῦσιν ἀντὶ πολλῶν χάριν ὀφείλοντες μάλιστα διὰ τοὺς ἀδελφοὺς ὀφείλουσιν. . . .[82] In fact, of all the inheritance they receive from their parents the brother is the most precious and the most delightful.[83] Plutarch illustrates this by contrary evidence: by reference to Telemachus, who regarded being brotherless a misfortune, and by arguing against Hesiod's advice to make "an only son" (μουνογενῆ παῖδα) the heir, because the very etymology of the name "Muses" contradicts that advice.[84]

If "brotherly love" is proof of love toward one's parents,[85] (480F)
it also becomes the best educational δίδαγμα καὶ παράδειγμα a father can provide to his own sons.[86] The reverse is of course

[81] *TGF*, no. 975. The προδοσία is an old friendship *topos*; see Dirlmeier, 30. Cf. the apocalyptic *topos* in Mark 13:12: . . . παραδώσει ἀδελφὸς ἀδελφὸν εἰς θάνατον (//Matt 10:21//Luke 21:16).

[82] Cf. 2 Cor 12:14: οὐ γὰρ ὀφείλει τὰ τέκνα τοῖς γονεῦσιν θησαυρίζειν, ἀλλὰ οἱ γονεῖς τοῖς τέκνοις. Cf. also Luke 15:31f.

[83] In a spiritualized form we have this doctrine in ECL in connection with the κληρονομία. E.g., in Gal 3:6-29 that concept is developed in a way that Abraham's inheritance consists of the "brotherhood" of the "sons of God" in the "body of Christ" (3:26-29).

[84] Cf. Gal 3:16 with Gal 3:26-28. On the term μονογενής cf. *PECL* 1:165, 296.

[85] τὸ φιλεῖν ἀδελφὸν εὐθὺς ἀπόδειξιν εἶναι τοῦ καὶ τὴν μητέρα φιλεῖν καὶ τὸν πατέρα. Cf. the early Christian doctrine, that the love of one's fellowman is the test for the love of God; cf. esp. 1 John 2:9; 3:14; 4:8, 20f.; 5:1f.

[86] Cf. the educational function of the Parable of the Two Sons, Luke 15:11-32. Paul can also serve as an example of "parental love," 2 Cor 12:14f., and programmatically in 1 Tim 1:2, 18; 2 Tim 1:2.

(481A) equally true: a father who has grown old practicing μισαδελφία in battling his brother ἐν δίκαις καὶ στάσεσι καὶ ἀγῶσι [87] will fail to convince his children when he admonishes them to ὁμονοεῖν.[88] His word is not to be believed because it is contradicted by his deeds.[89] He becomes a "healer of others, full of sores himself" as the saying
(481A-B) goes.[90] Two historical examples demonstrating Plutarch's point in an almost appalling way conclude the section.

Ch. 7

(481B) Plutarch sums up the first part of his argument and formulates what he sees as the ethical task: Διὸ καὶ γονέων κακὴν γηροτρόφον οὖσαν καὶ κακίονα παιδοτρόφον τέκνων ἐκκαθαίρειν προσήκει τὴν μισαδελφίαν.[91] This statement is peculiar because of the negative way in which Plutarch conceives of the ethical task. Rather than straightforwardly demanding "brotherly love," he introduces purification from "hatred of one's brother" as the way to love of the brother.[92] The reason for stating the matter in this way becomes clear when we remember Plutarch's description of the moral decay of his day and the overwhelming presence of μισαδελφία (ch. 1, 478C). This situation makes a simple demand for "brotherly love" impossible. The cultic language of "purification" is, therefore, not improper.[93]

Plutarch underscores the seriousness of the threat by another elaboration of the destructive effects of hatred among brothers. As one would expect from a Greek, this description is most vivid and psychologically most accurate. There are several ways in which hatred among brothers leads to their self-destruction (cf. 479A, B). First, such hate generates self-destruction from the outside, since hostile brothers trigger slander against themselves in the com-

---

[87] Cf. Matt 5:25//Luke 12:58; 1 Cor 6:1-11.

[88] Cf. 1 Tim 3:2-5, 12; 5:3f., 10.

[89] On this ethical topos, cf. esp. 1 Cor 9:27, and Betz, *Lukian*, 114-16.

[90] See the references in Helmbold's note, LCL 6:262f., among them ἰατρέ, θεράπευσον σεαυτόν (Luke 4:23). Cf. also Mark 15:31: ἄλλους ἔσωσεν, ἑαυτὸν οὐ δύναται σῶσαι (//Matt 27:42//Luke 23:35).

[91] Ethical conclusions introduced by διό are found in Acts 15:19; 20:31; Rom 13:5; 15:7; 1 Cor 12:3; 14:13; 2 Cor 6:17, etc.

[92] This concept is very similar to primitive Christian theology, where the "indicative" precedes the "imperative." See on this Bultmann, *TNT*, secs. 38, 50.

[93] ECL also uses καθαίρω, καθαρίζω κτλ. extensively in the figurative sense. See Bauer, s.v. ἐκκαθαίρω is found in 1 Cor 5:7; 2 Tim 2:21.

munity. When their fellow-citizens see that brothers hate each other, they assume that those brothers have an intimate knowledge of each other's character and misdeeds and that the fierceness of
their enmity stems from their awareness [94] of each other's involve- (481C)
ment with evil. This then leads to slander and accusations against them.

Reconciliation of hostile brothers is extremely difficult,[95] more difficult than gluing together broken pieces and more difficult than reuniting friends after a long time of separation. Once what was united by nature has fallen apart, it can never be fully restored to what it was before.[96] Plutarch again compares this with the human body and its limbs (cf. ch. 2, 478D-479B) which require extraordinary efforts of healing in order to restore them to the body if they get severed from it: . . .ἔργον ἐστὶ κόλλησιν εὑρεῖν καὶ σύμφυσιν.[97] Even when hostile brothers become reconciled, wounds remain: . . .ῥυπαρὰν καὶ ὕποπτον οὐλὴν αἱ διαλύσεις ἐφέλκονται.

The other form of self-destruction comes from the inside. Enmity (481D)
between brothers goes deeper emotionally than other hostility between people: πᾶσα μὲν οὖν ἔχθρα πρὸς ἄνθρωπον ἀνθρώπῳ μετὰ τῶν μάλιστα λυπούντων ἐνδυομένη παθῶν, φιλονεικίας ὀργῆς φθόνου μνησικακίας, ὀδυνηρόν ἐστι καὶ ταραχῶδες.[98] Beyond ordinary enmity, hatred between brothers goes so much deeper because it includes the necessary sharing of sacrifices [99] and other family religious rites, as well as sharing the family house or neighborhood, and eventually sharing the family grave. Such hatred means having the trouble before one's eyes all the time and being reminded of the madness daily. Seeing the most delightful and closely akin face becomes an ordeal,[100] and listening to the most beloved and
long familiar voice a thing to be dreaded. Such hatred includes (481E)
seeing other brothers who are able to use the same house, table,

---

[94] . . . πολλὰ καὶ πονηρὰ συνειδότας ἀλλήλοις. On "brotherly love" with regard to the outside, see 1 Thes 4:12; John 13:34f.

[95] Note that the Parable of the Two Sons (Luke 15:11-32) leaves the matter unresolved.

[96] Cf. the similar argument in connection with marriage in Mark 10:6-9// Matt 19:4-6; cf. also 1 Cor 6:16; 7:10f.; 12:24; Eph 5:30-33.

[97] Cf. 1 Cor 12:25: . . . ἵνα μὴ ᾖ σχίσμα ἐν τῷ σώματι. Cf. also 1 Cor 12:21-23.

[98] The terminology of the "catalog of vices" is conventional, but the connection with ἐνδύεσθαι is interesting. Cf. Bauer, s.v. ἐνδύω, 2.b.

[99] Cf. Matt 5:23f.

[100] πρόσωπον . . . σκυθρωπότατον. Cf. for this expression Matt 6:16; Luke 24:17.

undivided land and slaves, while the hostile brothers divide everything, even friends [101] and guests. Everything dear to one brother the other considers inimical.[102] Such ἄνοια καὶ παραφροσύνη (481D) is carried on, although a brother is a unique gift, impossible to replace, just as it is impossible to replace a hand or an eye once the natural one is gone.[103]

Plutarch concludes by approving the decision of the Persian woman to save her brother rather than her children. She could have other children, but never another brother since her parents were dead.

Ch. 8

(481F) A new section clearly begins in ch. 8. Plutarch changes his style to engage in a debate with a fictitious partner [104] who is made to ask the leading question to be dealt with in the following chapters: τί δῆτα χρὴ ποιεῖν, . . . , ὅτῳ φαῦλος ἀδελφὸς γένοιτο; [105]

Before discussing the various forms of this problem, Plutarch sets forth some principal considerations in ch. 8. He calls this section προοίμια τοῦ λόγου παντός, and the content of the λόγος his διδασκαλία (482D). It is surprising for a remark like this to occur in the middle of the work, and it has given rise to some questions.[106]

The first principal consideration is a "reminder" [107]: πρῶτον ἐκεῖνο μνημονεύειν, ὅτι παντὸς ἅπτεται γένους φιλίας ἡ φαυλότης. All human experience, we are reminded, is a "mixture" of good and bad.[108] This anthropology determines the concept of friendship: No human relationship, whether τὸ συγγενικόν or τὸ ἐρωτικόν, can ever be expected to be "perfect": εἰλικρινὲς καὶ ἀπαθὲς καὶ καθαρὸν . . . κακίας.[109] This qualification means that the relations between

101 Cf. μετὰ τῶν φίλων μου, Luke 15:29.

102 The older brother in Luke 15:25-30 is an example of this.

103 Cf. Luke 15:32.

104 This is a common motif in diatribe literature. See *PECL* 1:304.

105 Cf. Acts 2:38: τί ποιήσωμεν . . . ; 16:30; Matt 19:16: τί ἀγαθὸν ποιήσω . . . ; (//Mark 10:17//Luke 18:18).

106 See above , p. 235.

107 See *PECL* 1, index, s.v. Remembering.

108 Early Christianity does not share this philosophical doctrine, but Matthew comes close to it when he conceives of the church as *corpus mixtum*. See G. Strecker, *Der Weg der Gerechtigkeit*, 3d ed. (Göttingen, 1971) 214ff.

109 Early Christianity would agree that "sinfulness" prevents such perfection. Cf. esp. the Sermon on the Mount (Matt 5:43-48). It is noteworthy that in 482A Plutarch mentions the principle of "choosing the least of the evils."

brothers must be seen in a similar way. Taking into account the
existence of evil, the brotherly relationship means τὰ οἰκειότατα
τῶν κακῶν ὑπομένειν,[110] instead of acquiring a "friend" and, thereby, (482A)
πειρᾶσθαι τῶν ἀλλοτρίων. Tolerating a brother's faults is ἀνέγκλητον
ὡς ἀναγκαῖον, while taking on the unfamiliar faults of a friend
is ψεκτὸν ὡς αὐθαίρετον. Plutarch then determines the meaning of
ὑπομένειν as ἐπιχωρεῖν ἔνια καὶ παρείκειν, that is, cautious exhortation but clear abstention from harsh punishment.[111]

Plutarch goes on to apply the friendship principles of Theo- (482B)
phrastus to brotherhood. Whereas friendship must follow the
principle of "first judgment and then love," brotherhood follows the reverse rule, because here φιλία has priority by nature: ἡ φύσις . . . συγγενέννηκε τὴν ἀρχὴν τῆς φιλίας. Therefore, the rule for ethical conduct must be: δεῖ μὴ πικροὺς εἶναι μηδ' ἀκριβεῖς τῶν ἁμαρτημάτων ἐξεταστάς.[112]

In the following, Plutarch illustrates these principles by examples
of absurdity, which demonstrate the "ignorance" and "irrationality" of the "foolish crowds." It is absurd [113] for people to tolerate
generously the wrongdoings of drinking and sports companions (482C)
while being δύσκολοι καὶ ἀπαραίτητοι toward their own brothers. It is also absurd when those who breed and "love" all kinds of dangerous and vicious animals [114] ἀδελφῶν οὐχ ὑπομένουσιν ὀργὰς ἢ ἀγνοίας ἢ φιλοτιμίας. There are even people who make over whole houses and estates to concubines and prostitutes, while they fight with their brothers over a little lot or a corner of a piece of land. In short, such people justify "hatred of the brother" as one and the same with μισοπονηρία.[115] These people περινοστοῦσιν ἐν τοῖς ἀδελφοῖς τὴν κακίαν προβαλλόμενοι καὶ λοιδοροῦντες, while they are not bothered by the very same evils in others[116] but χρώμενοι πολλῇ καὶ συνόντες.[117]

---

110 In early Christianity, constant readiness to forgive and to bear the weakness of "brothers" has been transferred to the fellow-Christian generally. Cf. Matt 6:12//Luke 11:4; Matt 6:14f.//Mark 11:25f.; Matt 18:21f.// Luke 17:4; John 20:23//Matt 16:19//Matt 18:18; Rom 14:1ff.; 15:1ff.; 1 Cor 9:12; 13:7; Gal 6:2, 10; Eph 4:2, 32-5:2; Col 3:13; etc.

111 Cf. Matt 18:15-17; Gal 6:1; 2 Tim 4:2; Tit 3:10f.; Jas 5:14-16.

112 Cf. Col 3:19; Eph 4:31; Jas 3:11, 14; etc. See Bauer, s.v. πικρία, πικρός. Cf. also 1 Cor 13:4-7; Gal 6:1.

113 Cf. the analogous absurdity in Matt 7:3-5//Luke 6:41f.

114 Cf. Gal 5:15.

115 The term is not found in Bauer; cf. Lampe, s.v. μισοπόνηρος; for similar expressions, cf. Bauer, s.v. μισέω, 2.

116 Again, a contradiction of word and deed (cf. above, p. 244).

117 Cf. the Menander quotation in 1 Cor 15:33; cf. also Matt 16:6//Mark 8:15//Luke 12:1; 1 Cor 5:6; Gal 5:9.

Ch. 9

(482D) The section called ἡ διδασκαλία begins by postponing the discussion of the most important problem affecting the relationship between brothers, the division of the parental property (ἡ νέμησις τῶν πατρῴων).[118] We remember that this is also the basis for the definition of good brotherhood (cf. 478C). Plutarch, however, is interested not in the legal aspects of the problem, but only in the psychagogic aspects. First, he takes up τὴν ἔτι ζώντων ἁμαρτανομένην τῶν γονέων ἅμιλλαν καὶ ζηλοτυπίαν (cf. ch. 11, 483C).[119] This problem is broken down further into the description of improper (482D-E) and proper (482E-483A) conduct. Plutarch begins with what, in analogy to political demagoguery, he calls καταδημαγωγεῖν τοὺς ἀδελφούς. With great psychological awareness he shows how such strategy works. Basically, it is the care for one's parents with the intention to monopolize their goodwill (εὔνοια) and to divert
(482E) it from the brother.[120] The motive is simply πλεονεξία.[121] The objective is to ruin the brother's standing by ἀνελευθέρως καὶ πανούργως ὑποτρέχειν,[122] utilizing the parents' ἀσχολία καὶ ἄγνοια, and presenting himself as perfect: εὐτάκτους καὶ κατηκόους ... καὶ σώφρονας, ἐν οἷς ἐκείνους ἁμαρτάνοντας ἢ δοκοῦντας ὁρῶσι.[123]

On the other hand, Plutarch defines as proper conduct assuming the role as "mediator" (διαλλάσσειν [483A]). If the father is angry with the brother, one should share the burden with his brother: συνεκδέχεσθαι καὶ συνυποδύεσθαι καθάπερ τῷ συνεργεῖν ποιοῦντα κουφοτέραν, ὑπουργίαις δὲ καὶ χάρισι συνεισποιεῖν ἁμωσγέπως τὸν ἀδελφόν.[124] Plutarch discusses even more specifically what to do if the father's anger is justified by the brother's faults (472F-483B) or if the brother is accused but innocent (483B-C).[125]

(482F) If a shortcoming occurs, it is proper to explain and excuse the

[118] Cf. Luke 12:13-15; 15:12. See Bauer, s.v. διαιρέω.

[119] Luke 15:11-32 falls into this category.

[120] This attitude is exemplified by the older brother in Luke 15:25-30.

[121] Cf. Luke 15:29f. In ECL, πλεονεξία is often the opposite of ἀγάπη. See Bauer, s.v.

[122] Cf. Luke 15:25-27: the older brother is "caught by surprise," and "finds out what happened."

[123] Cf. Luke 15:29.

[124] Cf. Gal 6:2 of Christian love.

[125] Cf. Luke 15:11-32, where the father's anger would be justified, but he forgives the Prodigal, whereas the older brother accuses his father and his brother.

brother: καιρὸν ἢ πρᾶξιν ἑτέραν ἢ τὴν φύσιν αἰτιᾶσθαι, ὡς πρὸς ἄλλα
χρησιμωτέραν καὶ συνετωτέραν οὖσαν. Often, a mere substitution of
terms [126] will accomplish the purpose (ἡδέως . . . τῶν ὀνομάτων τὰς (483A)
μεταθέσεις οἱ πατέρες προσδέχονται): a brother's ῥαθυμία becomes his
ἁπλότης, his σκαιότης becomes ὀρθότης, his φιλόνεικον his ἀκαταφρόνη-
τον. In this way, the anger of the father is lessened, and at the same
time the father's goodwill for oneself is increased.[127]

Ch. 10

After the ἀπολογεῖν before the father comes the admonition (483A)
(νουθέτησις [483B]) of the brother, defined as: τὸ ἁμάρτημα καὶ
τὸ ἔλλειμμα μετὰ παρρησίας ἐνεικνύμενον.[128] As Plutarch points out,
such admonition is necessary and dangerous.[129] It is necessary
because otherwise there would be complete "permissiveness"
(ἐφιέναι . . . τοῖς ἀδελφοῖς) resulting in compliance with evil (συνεξ-
αμαρτάνειν).[130] The danger is that the admonition can easily turn (483B)
into "trampling on the sinner" (ἐπεμβαίνειν) and into an enjoyment
of admonishing the brother. Rather, the admonition must be an
expression of one's care for the brother: ὡς κηδομένῳ καὶ συν-
αχθομένῳ χρῆσθαι τῇ νουθετήσει. Anything else leads to self-contra-
diction: the defender of his brother before the parents would turn
into his even more vehement accuser: the συνήγορος would become
the κατήγορος.

If, however, the father's anger against the brother is unjust [131]
because the brother has done nothing wrong, παρρησιάζεσθαι ὑπὲρ
ἀδελφοῦ (483C) is called for—the command to obey the parents
and be subservient to their anger notwithstanding: αἱ δ' ὑπὲρ ἀδελφοῦ
παρ' ἀξίαν κακῶς ἀκούοντος ἢ πάσχοντος ἀντιδικίαι καὶ δικαιολογίαι . . .
ἄμεμπτοι καὶ καλαί. The psychagogic "benefit" is that when the (483C)
parents are proved wrong about their son, the "defeat" is "sweeter"
to them than "victory": καὶ γὰρ αὐτοῖς ἡ τοιαύτη δίκη τοῖς ἐλεγ-
χομένοις ποιεῖ τὴν ἧτταν ἡδίω τῆς νίκης.

[126] The older brother uses this method in the negative sense when he accuses his brother: Luke 15:30a.

[127] This is what the older brother in Luke 15:11-32 should have done. Instead, he complains about his father's lack of anger.

[128] Note that in Luke 15:28 the older son refuses to enter the house and meet his brother. Cf. also Matt 18:15-18//Luke 17:3; Did 15:3.

[129] Cf. esp. Gal 6:1.

[130] Cf. the "accusation" implied in Gal 2:17; Rom 6:1.

[131] Cf. Eph 4:26, where anger itself is not called sin: ὀργίζεσθε καὶ μὴ ἁμαρτάνετε (Ps 4:5).

Ch. 11

(483C) The second (cf. ch. 9, 482D) and even more serious situation arises when the father dies.[132] It is imperative to preserve the state of εὔνοια between the brothers, first of all, in the crisis of the father's death itself. Then good brothers share the tears and the pains: εὐθὺς μὲν ἐν τῷ συνδακρύειν καὶ συνάχθεσθαι κοινούμενον τὸ φιλόστοργον.[133] They reject the insinuations of slaves and the gossip of friends. At this point Plutarch commends the example of brotherly love shown by the Dioscuri.

(483D) The critical moment, however, comes with the division of the father's property (ἡ νέμησις τῶν πατρῴων). It is at this time, that, οἱ πολλοί usually declare war against each other.[134] The ethically responsible person, on the other hand, carefully prepares for this situation, knowing that it can be the beginning of incurable enmity or of φιλία καὶ ὁμόνοια. Plutarch proposes some concrete procedures: the brothers should carry out the division either alone by themselves or in the presence of a mutual friend. The distribution should be done, to use Plato's words, δίκης κλήροις, which means: τὰ φίλα καὶ προσήκοντα λαμβάνοντας καὶ διδόντας. Plutarch also proposes to divide up the administration of the properties, but not their ownership and usage: τὴν ἐπιμέλειαν νέμεσθαι καὶ τὴν οἰκονομίαν,
(483E) χρῆσιν δὲ καὶ κτῆσιν ἐν μέσῳ κεῖσθαι κοινὴν καὶ ἀνέμητον ἁπάντων.

Following this advice, Plutarch sets forth examples of irresponsible behavior which destroys brotherly love. One example is the attempt to cut the brother out by shrewd maneuvers and to separate him from old family slaves. When φιλονεικία overwhelms people, the end is splitting up of silver cups and cutting apart of
(483F) cloaks.[135] Worst, of course, is the brother who boasts of having outfoxed the other by his πανουργία καὶ δριμύτης καὶ παραλογισμός. Instead, the proper way is this: δέον ἀγάλλεσθαι καὶ μέγα φρονεῖν ἐπιεικείᾳ καὶ χάριτι καὶ ὑπείξει. . . .[136] Finally, Plutarch introduces
(484A-B) as an illustration the example of Athenodorus' admirable love for his irresponsible brother Xenon.[137]

---

[132] Cf. the legal comparison in Gal 4:1-2.

[133] The whole theme is applied to the relationship between Christians: cf. 1 Pet 3:8 (. . . συμπαθεῖς, φιλάδελφοι); Rom 12:15.

[134] Cf. again Luke 15:11-32, where all following ethical principles are violated.

[135] Cf. Matt 27:35//Mark 15:24//Luke 23:34//John 19:23.

[136] Cf. Luke 15:32. Contrast 1 Cor 6:7.

[137] Athenodorus behaves as the older brother in Luke 15:11-32 should have behaved.

Ch. 12

Chs. 12-15 contain an extensive discussion of the concept of ἰσότης and its opposite, ἀνισότης, in application to brotherhood.[138] The notions are political in origin, as the references to Solon and Plato show. Applied to brotherhood, equality implies either the removal of the distinction between "mine" (τὸ ἐμόν) and "not mine" (τὸ οὐκ ἐμόν),[139] or at least: τὴν ἴσην ἀγαπᾶν καὶ τῆς ἴσης περιέχεσθαι. (484B)

This amounts, Plutarch explains, to laying a good and lasting foundation for ὁμόνοια καὶ εἰρήνη.[140] After proving this point by an apophthegm about Pittacus, Plutarch turns to the notion of ἀνισότης.[141] Again he refers to Plato's doctrine, which states that (484C)
as an "anomaly", inequality produces "movement" (κίνησις), while ὁμαλότης implies a state of στάσις καὶ μονή. Therefore, in regard to brothers: οὕτω πᾶσα ... ἀνισότης ἐπισφαλής ἐστι πρὸς διαφορὰν ἀδελφῶν.

What then is to be done about existing inequality? [142] First of all, Plutarch assumes that: ἐν πᾶσι δ' ἴσους γενέσθαι καὶ ὁμαλοὺς ἀδύνατον. The reason is that the natural dispositions (αἱ φύσεις) of brothers are unequal, and that further inequalities are acquired later: αἱ τύχαι φθόνους ἐμποιοῦσαι καὶ ζηλοτυπίας, αἴσχιστα νοσήματα καὶ κῆρας οὐκ οἰκίαις μόνον ἀλλὰ καὶ πόλεσιν ὀλεθρίους.

If such inequalities cannot completely be removed, the ethical (484D)
task requires the prevention and therapy of their evil effects upon the brotherly relationships: δεῖ καὶ ταῦτα φυλάττεσθαι καὶ θεραπεύειν, ἂν ἐγγένηται.[143] Consequently, two types of brotherly inequality and the corresponding paraenesis must be considered: the ethical task for a brother in a superior position (ὁ ὑπερέχων [484D-485C]), as well as the task for a brother in an inferior position (ὁ λειπόμενος [485C-486D]).

---

[138] The concept of ἰσότης occurs only infrequently in ECL; cf. 2 Cor 8:13f.; Col 4:1; also Gal 4:12a. See G. Stählin, *TDNT*, s.v. ἴσος κτλ.

[139] Cf. Luke 15:31, where the father says: ... πάντα τὰ ἐμὰ σά ἐστιν. Cf. John 16:15; 17:10.

[140] This phrase is used also in 1 Clem 20:10, 11; 60:4; 63:2; 65:1.

[141] The term is not listed in Bauer; cf. Lampe, s.v. It is interesting that the following section has a close parallel in Cicero's *Amic.* See Steinmetz (above, note 6), 128ff., who thinks the source was Theophrastus' περὶ φιλίας, an author whom Plutarch quotes twice (482B; 490E).

[142] Again, Luke 15:11-32 should be compared as a whole.

[143] On φυλάττομαι, see below on 486E.

The basic advice to the ὑπερέχων[144] applies the concept of "equality" in conjunction, it seems, with the old friendship maxim κοινὰ τὰ φίλων[145] and yields this rule: πρῶτον μὲν ἐν οἷς δοκεῖ διαφέρειν, ταῦτα κοινὰ ποιεῖν τοῖς ἀδελφοῖς. Plutarch then shows what this means *in concreto*: . . . συνεπικοσμοῦντα τῇ δόξῃ καὶ συνεισποιοῦντα ταῖς φιλίαις· κἂν λέγειν δεινότερος ᾖ, χρῆσθαι παρέχοντα τὴν δύναμιν, ὡς ἐκείνων μηθὲν ἧττον οὖσαν· ἔπειτα μήτ' ὄγκον ἐμφαίνειν τινὰ μηθ' ὑπεροψίαν, ἀλλὰ μᾶλλον ἐνδιδόντα καὶ συγκαθιέντα τῷ ἤθει τὴν ὑπεροχὴν ἀνεπίφθονον ποιεῖν καὶ τὴν τῆς τύχης ἀνωμαλίαν ἐπανισοῦν, ὡς ἀνυστόν ἐστι, τῇ μετριότητι τοῦ φρονήματος.[146]

As examples Plutarch names Lucullus, who refused to bypass
(484E) his brother for office, and Polydeuces, who preferred to become
only a demigod (ἡμίθεος) together with his brother Castor, instead
of becoming a god (θεός) by himself. In reality, however, the
ὑπερέχων need not give up any of the blessings he enjoys when he
(484F) shares them with his inferior brothers. This is shown by the example
of Plato who shared his fame with his brothers by introducing
their names into his best writings.

Ch. 13

(484F) Furthermore, the anthropological concept of "mixture" makes it
impossible to assume that one brother is "superior" in *all* respects:
. . . ἐν πᾶσι καὶ πάντως ὑπερέχειν τὸν ἕτερον ἀδύνατόν ἐστι. At this
point Plutarch inserts another polemic against the Stoics: One has
(485A) never seen two brothers[147] stemming from the same parents, one
σοφόν, ὁμοῦ καλὸν εὔχαριν ἐλευθέριον ἔντιμον πλούσιον δεινὸν εἰπεῖν
πολυμαθῆ φιλάνθρωπον,[148] and the other αἰσχρὸν ἄχαριν ἀνελεύθερον
ἄτιμον ἄπορον ἀσθενῆ περὶ λόγον ἀμαθῆ μισάνθρωπον.[149] Rather,

---

[144] In Luke 15:11-32, the older brother considers himself "superior" (vs. 29). Cf. Phil 2:3; also 1 Cor 2:1 (οὐ καθ' ὑπεροχὴν λόγου ἢ σοφίας); 1 Clem 57:2; also 1 Tim 2:2.

[145] For this rule, see Bohnenblust, *Beiträge*, 41; G. Stählin, *TDNT*, s.v. φίλος κτλ., A.II.2. Cf. Acts 4:32; 2:44; Gal 6:6.

[146] This paraenesis is similar in many ways to Paul's exhortations with regard to the "weak brothers" (cf. Rom 14-15; 1 Cor 8; 9:22; etc.).

[147] Cf. the two sons of Abraham in Gal 4:21-31, who represent absolute opposites. The "list of vices and virtues" in Gal 5:19-23 is related to the two types of sons.

[148] Cf. the claim of the older brother in Luke 15:29: οὐδέποτε ἐντολήν σου παρῆλθον. Cf. also Paul's opposition to claims of perfectionism: 1 Cor 3:18; 4:8, 10; 8:2; 10:12; 14:37; Gal 6:3. Cf. also Rom 15:1.

[149] The "lists of virtues and vices" conform to the conventional expectations of the culture. The concepts in the two lists are precise contrasts, a type of contrast not used in ECL.

everyone has at least some μοῖρα . . . χάριτος ἢ δυνάμεως ἢ πρός τι καλὸν εὐφυΐας.[150] It is, therefore, the duty of the "superior" brother always to point out the areas where the "inferior" is better and more useful.[151] Plutarch also shows the political advantages of (485B) making one's lesser brother one's συνεργός[152] and σύμβουλος. In this way one can only increase the brother's status[153]: . . . τῶν (485C) καλῶν πάντων κοινωνὸν ἀποφαίνων καὶ χρώμενος παρόντι καὶ περιμένων ἀπόντα. . . .[154]

Ch. 14

What advice should then be given to the "inferior" brother (485C) (ὁ λειπόμενος)?[155] He should consider the fact ὡς οὐχ εἷς οὐδὲ μόνος αὐτοῦ πλουσιώτερος ἢ λογιώτερος ἢ λαμπρότερος εἰς δόξαν ὁ ἀδελφός ἐστιν.[156] There are, to be sure, a multitude of people superior to him: πολλάκις πολλῶν ἀπολείπεται καὶ μυριάκις μυρίων. Whether he envies all of them or only his brother makes no difference, for in either case it will make him the most wretched of all: ὑπερβολὴν ἑτέρῳ κακοδαιμονίας οὐ λέλοιπεν.[157] The proper attitude corresponds (485D) to the example of Metellus: Everyone should pray that he himself might be more successful than anyone else, and if he is not to have such success, that his brother may: εἰ δὲ μή, τὸν ἀδελφὸν αὐτοῦ τὴν ζηλουμένην ἔχειν ὑπεροχὴν καὶ δύναμιν.

Plutarch then provides proof for this advice *e contrario* in the

[150] Cf. Paul's doctrine of the χαρίσματα, esp. Rom 12:3, 6, 7-8; 1 Cor 12:7-11, 18, 24, 28.

[151] Cf. Rom 12:10b: τῇ τιμῇ ἀλλήλους προηγούμενοι, 16; 1 Cor 12:7: πρὸς τὸ συμφέρον, 22-25.

[152] Paul often calls his "brother"-missionaries συνεργοί. Rom 16:3, 9, 21; Phil 2:25; 4:3; Phlm 1, 24 etc. See Bauer, s.v.

[153] For this strategy cf. Rom 12:20 (Prov 25:22): τοῦτο γὰρ ποιῶν ἄνθρακας πυρὸς σωρεύσεις ἐπὶ τὴν κεφαλὴν αὐτοῦ; 1 Cor 9:22; 10:33; etc. Cf. further ἡ καθ' ὑπερβολὴν ὁδός, 1 Cor 13.

[154] This statement includes an important *topos* of friendship, which has also become an epistolary formula. Cf. Gal 4:18; 1 Cor 5:3; 2 Cor 10:11; Col 2:5; etc.

[155] This term is not typical of ECL, although Jas 1:4 should be compared. The type of brother is, of course, exemplified by the younger brother in Luke 15:11-32. (Cf. esp. vss. 24, 32.) Cf. also concepts like οἱ μικροί in Matthew's theology (10:42; 18:6, 10; 25:40; etc.); οἱ ἀσθενεῖς in Paul's theology (Rom 14:1ff.; 15:1ff.; 1 Cor 8:7ff.). Paul consciously assumes the position of ὁ ἐλάχιστος (1 Cor 15:9; cf. 1 Cor 4:10; 9:22), and thereby he imitates Christ (2 Cor 13:3f.).

[156] Again, the parallel to Paul's doctrine of the διαιρέσεις τῶν χαρισμάτων should be noted (1 Cor 12:4ff., esp. vss. 14-25, 29f.).

[157] With this phrase cf. 1 Cor 15:19: ἐλεεινότεροι πάντων ἀνθρώπων.

form of absurdities and contradictions in which οἱ ἀτυχεῖς πρὸς τὸ καλόν engage. They praise famous friends, foreign commanders and men of wealth,[158] but take their own brothers' brilliance as a
(485E) darkening of their own. They are elated when telling of the good fortunes of their fathers and greatgrandfathers, things from which they had no benefit and in which they did not take part, but ἀδελφῶν . . . κληρονομίαις καὶ ἀρχαῖς καὶ γάμοις ἐνδόξοις ἀθυμεῖν καὶ ταπεινοῦσθαι. Ideally, one should not φθονεῖν anyone,[159] but, if this is not possible, at least one should select an external target for one's hostility: εἰ δὲ μή, τρέπειν ἔξω καὶ πρὸς τοὺς ἑτέρους ἀποχετεύειν τὸ βάσκανον.[160]

Ch. 15

(485E) On the other hand, the "inferior" brother should not simply remain in the lower position, leaving his brother higher, but instead
(485F) he should: συναύξειν ἅμα καὶ συναύξεσθαι τοῖς ἀγαθοῖς.[161] Examples from mathematics and from the functioning of the human hand
(486A) (cf. 478D) illustrate how this happens in nature and also in history (486A).

But what should be done when the "inferior" brother has an
(486B) ambitious character (οἱ φιλοτίμοι . . . τῶν ἠθῶν)[162] and is endowed by nature with φθόνοι καὶ ζηλοτυπίαι πρὸς τοὺς πλέον ἔχοντας ἐν δόξῃ καὶ τιμῇ? Those people, Plutarch advises, should not compete with their "superior" brothers in the same activities, but in others.[163] Proof is found in the behavior of wild animals[164] who are hostile to each other only if they depend on the same food. Among the athletes, only those who compete in the same category of sports are antagonists, whereas boxers are friendly to pancratiasts, etc. Again Polydeuces is brought in: he won in boxing,

---

[158] Cf. Jas 2:2ff., a polemic against favoring the rich instead of the poor "brothers."

[159] Cf. Gal 5:26; 1 Pet 2:1; etc. See *PECL* 1, index, s.v. φθονέω, φθόνος.

[160] Plutarch's ethics are clearly limited to the family, including friends, while "the others" are of far less concern for him. Early Christianity was more universalistic, as Paul's remark in Gal 6:10 shows: ἐργαζώμεθα τὸ ἀγαθὸν πρὸς πάντας, μάλιστα δὲ πρὸς τοὺς οἰκείους τῆς πίστεως.

[161] Cf. the concept of αὔξησις together with Christ in Eph 4:15f.; 2:21; Col 1:6, 10; 2:19; 1 Pet 2:2; 2 Pet 3:18.

[162] Cf. the younger brother in Luke 15:12f.

[163] Cf., again, Paul's doctrine of χαρίσματα in Rom 12:3ff.; 1 Cor 12:4ff.

[164] On the comparison with wild animals cf. above, p. 247.

and Castor in running.[165] Among other examples, government (486C)
illustrates how various officials must excel in different functions,
and all must support each other for the common good.[166] Examples (486D)
from history show how this has worked in the past. Thus an "inferior" brother can neutralize his envy by choosing a career different from his brother so that both brothers can succeed. Plutarch concludes this section with this summary: ὅθεν ἀπωτάτω δεῖ ταῖς ἐπιθυμίαις τρέπεσθαι καὶ ταῖς φιλοτιμίαις τῶν ἀδελφῶν τοὺς ἀφθόνως δόξης καὶ δυνάμεως κοινωνεῖν μὴ πεφυκότας, ὅπως εὐφραίνωσιν εὐημεροῦντες ἀλλήλους ἀλλὰ μὴ λυπῶσι.[167]

Ch. 16

The words παρὰ πάντα δὲ ταῦτα φυλακτέον ἐστί . . . introduce a new (486E)
section of the treatise, reminding us of the division of paraenesis into φυλάττεσθαι καὶ θεραπεύειν (484D). The following chapters are primarily concerned with φυλάττεσθαι,[168] that is, preventive ethics.

A major danger to guard against comes from family members (relatives, members of the household, the wife).[169] It is their stimulation of φιλοδοξία by challenging language, which Plutarch calls λόγοι πονηροί. As an example of such language, Plutarch points to the nagging criticism that unfavorably compares a person with this brother. Then he adds a proper answer to such criticism, and a reference to Socrates as an example.

The greater danger to brotherly love, however, comes from (486F)
διαφοραί existing between the brothers,[170] in particular the difference in age.[171] The older brother is used to domination and preference in all kinds of ways,[172] while the younger tends to rebel

---

[165] On the agon motif cf. 1 Cor 9:24-27, which also mentions running and boxing.

[166] Cf. Paul's concept of the church "offices" in Rom 12:5-8; 1 Cor 12:5, 8-11, 28-30; Eph 4:11.

[167] Cf. Gal 5:26: μὴ γινώμεθα κενόδοξοι, ἀλλήλους προκαλούμενοι, ἀλλήλοις φθονοῦντες, Phil 2:1ff.

[168] See also the use of the concept in 483D; 487E; 488B; 491B. For φυλάσσομαι as "guarding against" ethically, cf. Luke 12:15; 2 Pet 3:17; etc. See Bauer, s.v., 2.a.

[169] Cf. the behavior of Jesus' family, Mark 3:31-35//Matt 12:46-50// Luke 8:19-21.

[170] Cf. the χαρίσματα διάφορα in Rom 12:6; διαιρέσεις χαρισμάτων in 1 Cor 12:4.

[171] This applies to Luke 15:11-32 (cf. vs. 25).

[172] Cf. Luke 15:29f.

(487A) against him.[173] If this is allowed to go unchecked, it will destroy
the good relationship between the brothers.[174] In order to prevent
(487B) such a disruption, Plutarch develops a strategy which is essentially
the application of a rather conventional educational philosophy.
(487C) This is followed by a number of impressive historical examples:
Cato and Caepio, Epicurus and his brothers, more recently Apollonius the Peripatetic and Sotion. Finally—something not often
done by him—Plutarch points to his own brotherly relationship
(487D) with Timon,[175] calling upon the addressees as witnesses.[176]

Ch. 17

(487E) Among brothers of the same age there are differences of con-
stitutional πάθη which must be kept under control. These differences may in themselves be insignificant, but if they are allowed
to go unchecked, they may undermine brotherly relations by
constantly eating away the natural gift of love. The beginnings
may be trivial, different interests in children's games, but later
these differences are carried into the palaestra, into hunting and
horse-racing. Rising to the level of φιλόνεικον ... καὶ φιλότιμον,
(487F) they can easily push the brotherly relationship εἰς ἀνήκεστα μίση
καὶ κακοθυμίας (487E).[177]
Plutarch points to the fact that many powerful Greeks have
(488A) ruined themselves in this fashion. The most tragic example is "the
Cadmean victory," the expedition of the Seven against Thebes, in
which the sons of Oedipus, Eteocles and Polyneices, killed each
other in combat.[178] Such tragedy can be avoided, if matters are
kept under control from the beginning: ὅθεν οὐχ ἥκιστα δεῖ περὶ
τὰ μικρὰ καὶ πρῶτα παραδυομένῃ τῇ πρὸς τοὺς ἀδελφοὺς φιλονεικίᾳ
καὶ ζηλοτυπίᾳ διαμάχεσθαι.[179] These are the ways suggested: μελε-

[173] In Luke 15:11-32 the younger brother is the "rebel" who leaves the family (vs. 13). Cf. 1 Tim 5:1; Tit 2:6; 1 Clem 1:3; 3:3.

[174] Again this applies to Luke 15:11-32.

[175] He acknowledges his brother's εὔνοια towards him as Tyche's greatest gift to him.

[176] For this epistolographic *topos*, cf. 1 Thes 2:10; Gal 4:13; 2 Cor 13:5f.; cf. also 1 Tim 6:12; 2 Tim 2:2.

[177] For φιλονεικία as a threat to Christian "brotherhood," cf. Luke 22:24; 1 Cor 11:16. Cf. also the φιλονεικία of the Jews against Christians in Mart Pol 18:1.

[178] On ἀδελφοκτονία cf. above, p. 242.

[179] Cf. Paul's proverb in Gal 5:9: μικρὰ ζύμη ὅλον τὸ φύραμα ζυμοῖ. See also Jas 3:4f.

τῶντας ἀνθυπείκειν καὶ ἡττᾶσθαι καὶ χαίρειν τῷ χαρίζεσθαι μᾶλλον αὐτοῖς ἢ τῷ νικᾶν.[180]

Another source of trouble comes from "business affairs" (τὰ πράγματα),[181] which can alienate even those brothers who generally behave ἐπιεικῶς . . . καὶ πράως. In Plutarch's view, personal and (488B) emotional involvement in such business affairs is really unnecessary. His advice is to let the affairs fight it out themselves: . . . φυλακτέον, ὅπως τὰ πράγματα μάχηται καθ' αὑτά.[182] This means ethically: to abstain from emotional engagement, to keep one's eyes fixed on Justice, and to quickly turn over a disputable matter to the courts. Beyond this, one ought to imitate the Pythagoreans who are not by nature brothers but share their κοινὸς λόγος.[183] If they get carried away into anger, they find a way of reconciliation before the sun goes down: εἴ ποτε προαχθεῖεν εἰς λοιδορίαν ὑπ' ὀργῆς, πρὶν ἢ τὸν ἥλιον δῦναι τὰς δεξιὰς ἐμβαλόντες ἀλλήλοις καὶ ἀσπασάμενοι διελύοντο.[184] After comparing the situation with a disease,[185] (488C) Plutarch concluses the section with this consideration: If the dissension between brothers is caused simply by διαφορὰ τοῦ πράγματος, it will disappear with the settlement of the issue; if it lingers on after the settlement, however, the πρᾶγμα itself was only a pretext of a deeper source of evil.[186]

---

180 Cf. esp. Paul's concern for the "weak brothers" in Rom 14-15; also Rom 12:14-21, and the early Christian doctrine of mutual forgiveness (cf. above, p. 247).

181 For this term, cf. Matt 18:19; 1 Cor 6:1; 2 Cor 7:11; 1 Thes 4:6; Jas 3:16; 2 Tim 2:4 (αἱ τοῦ βίου πραγματεῖαι). See Bauer, s.v. πρᾶγμα κτλ.

182 The advice given here by Plutarch is characteristically different from 1 Cor 6, where Paul does not recommend going to court. Cf. also Matt 5:21-25, 38-42. For further materials, see Conzelmann, *First Corinthians*, on 1 Cor 6:1-11.

183 Cf. Helmbold, LCL 6:302, n. a: "No doubt the 'Ακροάματα of the Master . . ." They correspond to the early Christian λόγοι of Jesus. See *PECL* 1, index, s.v. Words.

184 Cf. Eph 4:26: ὀργίζεσθε καὶ μὴ ἁμαρτάνετε· ὁ ἥλιος μὴ ἐπιδυέτω ἐπὶ παροργισμῷ ὑμῶν . . . Pol Phil 12:1 quotes from the "Scriptures": *irascimini et nolite peccare, et sol non occidat super iracundiam vestram.* Cf. also CD 9:5-8; 7:2f.; 1QS 5:26. The Qumran passages are mentioned in J. Gnilka, *Der Epheserbrief* (Freiburg, 1971) 235. Commentaries on Ephesians (also Helmbold, LCL 6:302, n. b) normally mention the Plutarch passage; cf. also Almqvist, 114. For the handshake cf. Gal 2:9.

185 Cf. above, p. 239.

186 Cf. 1 Cor 6:1-11 where Paul goes further than Plutarch and assumes that having πράγματα against the Christian brother is itself ἀδικία (cf. esp. 6:7f.).

Ch. 18

(488D-F) Before moving to the next problem (ch. 19), Plutarch inserts
a "ringcomposition"[187] of famous examples from history to
prove the doctrine just set forth. He begins with the ἀρχέτυπον . . .
καθαρὸν καὶ ἀμώμητον εὐμενενείας καὶ μεγαλοφροσύνης (489A),
the story of Ariamenes and Xerxes, the succession of the younger
Xerxes to the throne of their father Darius. That this example
comes from the "barbarians" and shows their superior morality
is no accident (488D-F).[188] Next comes the example of Antiochus
and Seleucus, which has the motif of the brother believed dead and
(489A) then found alive (489B-C).[189] The third example is taken from
(489B) mythology (489B-C). According to Plutarch, the Athenians
"corrected" the myth of the quarrel between Poseidon and Athena,
which for them had become a case of mythological ἀτοπία.[190]
They omitted the second day of Boedromion as ἀποφράς, for on
that day the quarrel had occurred.[191]

(489C) Plutarch then suggests[192] that we should regard all days when
we quarrel with relatives as ἡμέραι ἀποφράδες, thus consigning
them to oblivion. He also inserts a strong appeal for mutual forgiveness,[193] an appeal strangely parallel to the Lord's Prayer.[194]

[187] On this literary form, see Conzelmann, *First Corinthians*, 39.

[188] The ethical superiority of "barbarians" was a commonplace in Hellenistic ethics and must have been one of the forces that helped Christianity gain attention. Cf. the typical scene in Acts 17:18ff. The formula Ἕλληνες καὶ βάρβαροι is another expression of the high esteem of barbarians in the eyes of the Greeks (cf. Rom 1:14; also Col 3:11; etc.). See J. Jüthner, *RAC*, s.v. Barbar.

[189] This motif is also found in Luke 15:24, 32. When Antiochus heard that his brother was alive, he brought a sacrifice (τοῖς . . . θεοῖς ἔθυσε) and ordered a festival (cf. Luke 15:23-25).

[190] These moral "embarrassments" of Greek mythology were used in Jewish and Christian apologetics. Cf. the πόλεμος ἐν τῷ οὐρανῷ in Rev. 12:7. See H. D. Preuss, *Verspottung fremder Religionen im Alten Testament* (Stuttgart, 1971); Betz, *Lukian*, 23ff.

[191] See *PECL* 1, index, s.v. Days, observation of.

[192] He introduces his suggestion with the words: τί οὖν κωλύει . . . ; cf. Acts 8:36, and *PECL* 1, index, s.v. κωλύω.

[193] οὐχ ἧττον δὲ τοῦ διδόναι συγγνώμην ἁμαρτοῦσι τὸ αἰτεῖσθαι καὶ λαμβάνειν αὐτοὺς ἁμαρτόντας εὔνοιαν ἐμφαίνει καὶ φιλοστοργίαν. Plutarch also suggests that one should grant forgiveness before the brother asks for it (cf. Matt 6:8 of God; of the father in Luke 15:20).

[194] Matt 6:12//Luke 11:4; Matt 6:14-15; 18:15-20, 21-22//Luke 17:3-4; Matt 18:23-35; John 20:23; Did 15:3 (further parallels are listed in *Synopsis Quattuor Evangeliorum*, ed. K. Aland, 9th rev. ed. (Stuttgart, 1976), 253f.); 2 Cor 2:10; Eph 4:32; Col 3:13; etc.

The following example deals with the Socratic Eucleides and his (489D)
brother, in which two conditional self-curses[195] show how a case of (489D-
διαφορά is superceded by brotherly love. The example of Eumenes 490A)
and Attalus of Pergamum contains another illustration of the
motif of the brother thought dead but then found alive.[196] Plu- (490A)
tarch closes the chain by an example *e contrario*[197]: When Cambyses, who had killed his brother, died, the throne passed from the family of Cambyses to that of Darius, a man who was worthy in terms of brotherly love and friendship.

Ch. 19

Plutarch now returns to the discussion of φυλάττειν in regard to (490A)
existing differences between brothers. The fact that brothers have both friends and enemies is another potential source of trouble.[198] Plutarch reminds (μνημονεύειν)[199] his readers of the rule: τὸ τοῖς φίλοις αὐτῶν ὁμιλεῖν καὶ πλησιάζειν τότε μάλιστα, φεύγειν δὲ τοὺς
ἐχθροὺς καὶ μὴ προσδέχεσθαι.[200] (490B)

He considers the rule an imitation of the Cretan "syncretism" (συγκρητισμός).[201] The Cretans were known for always fighting among themselves, but when an external enemy turned up, they made peace quickly and turned against him together. As Plutarch points out, a good brotherly relationship can be ruined if the rule is not obeyed. Notably, we are touching here upon another ethical
theme, that of true and false friends.[202] Association with the (490C)
brother's enemies easily opens the door to slander.[203] So one should (490D)
stay away from the brother's enemies, especially when bearing a grudge against the brother, and should instead confine oneself to the household, the friends, and the wives, in order to talk the matter over with them.

---

195 Cf. the conditional self-curses in Gal 1:8-9; Rom 9:3; Mark 14:71// Matt 26:74; Acts 23:12f., 14, 21. See W. Speyer, *RAC*, s.v. Fluch (7:1208f., 1211, 1217).

196 See n. 189, above.

197 Cf. esp. the series of examples in 1 Clem 4.

198 Cf. Luke 15:29, 30.

199 On this, see above, p. 246.

200 Cf. Jas 4:4: οὐκ οἴδατε ὅτι ἡ φιλία τοῦ κόσμου ἔχθρα τοῦ θεοῦ ἐστιν;

201 A hapax legomenon in Greek literature. See LSJ, s.v. For the bad reputation of the Cretans, see also Tit 1:12.

202 See Plutarch: *adul. et am.*; *ex inim. util.*; *am. mult.*

203 Cf. Prov 16:28; Sir 6:9; 37:1ff.

Ch. 20

(490E) Plutarch continues this line of thought by quoting a saying of Theophrastus: εἰ κοινὰ τὰ φίλων ἐστί, μάλιστα δεῖ κοινοὺς τῶν φίλων εἶναι τοὺς φίλους.[204] This saying in itself is interesting, because it is an exegesis of the old friendship maxim κοινὰ τὰ φίλων, which it includes and applies to the friend's possession of friends.[205] Plutarch now applies it to brotherhood. If brothers do not share their friends, but keep separate friendships, they will by necessity drift apart: τῷ γὰρ φιλεῖν ἑτέρους εὐθὺς ἕπεται τὸ χαίρειν ἑτέροις καὶ ζηλοῦν ἑτέρους καὶ ἄγεσθαι ὑφ' ἑτέρων. The reason is based upon another experience of life: ἠθοποιοῦσι γὰρ αἱ φιλίαι.[206]

(490F) Consequently: μεῖζον οὐθέν ἐστιν ἠθῶν διαφορᾶς σημεῖον ἢ φίλων αἱρέσεις διαφερόντων.[207] This is why τὸ συμφιλεῖν καὶ συνεχθραίνειν is the best way to preserve the brotherly ὁμόνοια.[208] If a conflict
(491A) should arise between brothers, the mutual friends will do everything they can to reconcile the brothers and restore εὔνοια. Thus approving of this theory of mutual friends as a σύνδεσμος . . . τῆς
(491B) φιλαδελφίας,[209] Plutarch finds reason to reject the contrary views of Hesiod, but this reminds us that Plutarch's constant reference to life experience could be matched by other life experience.

Even if sharing of one's friends is accepted among brothers, brotherly love is still in danger if the brothers begin to prefer their friends instead of each other.[210] This is especially important at public events, where the rule must be: ἀεὶ τὰ πρωτεῖα τἀδελφῷ φυλάττειν . . . τὸ προσῆκον ἀξίωμα τῇ φύσει καὶ γέρας ἀποδιδόντας.[211]

Violating this principle means that one is neglecting his brother.

---

[204] Fr. 75; cf. also *prof. virt.* 65A. See Helmbold and O'Neil, 70.

[205] See on this above, p. 236. Cf. Sir 6:14-16.

[206] Cf. the different friends of the two brothers in Luke 15:11-32: vss. 15(?), 29, 30.

[207] Cf. the Menander quotation in 1 Cor 15:33.

[208] Cf. Phil 1:27; 2:25; 4:3; Col 4:12; contrast Sir 37:4-5; 6:7-13.

[209] For this expression cf. Col 3:14, where ἀγάπη is called σύνδεσμος τῆς τελειότητος. See further Bauer, s.v. σύνδεσμος, 1.b; M. Dibelius, *An die Kolosser*, HNT 12, 3d ed. (Tübingen, 1953) 43f.; G. Fitzer, *TDNT*, s.v. (esp. n. 9); E. Lohse, *Colossians and Philemon* (Philadelphia, 1971), ad loc.

[210] The preference for one's brother corresponds to the natural order. Cf. above, p. 238.

[211] Cf. Herm Sim 8:7:4 where it is foolish to ἔχειν . . . ζηλόν τινα ἐν ἀλλήλοις περὶ πρωτείων (cf. vs. 6). On concern for the first place in the synoptics, see Matt 23:6; etc. (see above on *tranq. an.* 473D).

Preference of the friend should never imply neglect of the brother.[212]
Plutarch remarks at this point that he has explained his views on (491C)
the subject more fully elsewhere, but it is an open question where that might be.[213] He concludes the section with a quotation from Menander [214] and comparisons from nature (horse and dog and their masters; [215] body and soul), all demonstrating that neglect is detrimental to love.

Ch. 21

The final chapter first sums up the previous deliberations under (491D)
the term ἐπιμέλεια . . . τῶν ἀδελφῶν (cf. 491C). However, an even better way to express and preserve brotherly love is by care and love for the family of the brother. After all, the brotherly relationship is embedded in the larger family, and φιλαδελφία belongs to family ethics. Therefore, Plutarch very appropriately concludes the essay with a "Haustafel," apparently specifically designed for brothers.[216]

Consideration is first given to the brother's in-laws, their families, servants, physicians and faithful friends, all of whom should be treated with εὔνοια. Then Plutarch turns to the brother's wife, who must be treated ὡς ἁπάντων ἱερῶν ἁγιώτατον. . ., καὶ σεβόμενον.[217] In concise sentences Plutarch states what should be done in various situations: . . . τιμῶντα μὲν τὸν ἄνδρα κατευφημεῖν, ἀμελουμένῃ δὲ συναγανακτεῖν, χαλεπαίνουσαν δὲ πραΰνειν· ἂν δ' ἁμάρτῃ τί τῶν μετρίων, συνδιαλλάττειν καὶ συμπαρακαλεῖν τὸν ἄνδρα· κἂν αὐτῷ τις
ἰδίᾳ γένηται διαφορὰ πρὸς τὸν ἀδελφόν, αἰτιᾶσθαι παρ' ἐκείνῃ καὶ (491E)
διαλύεσθαι τὴν μέμψιν.[218] If the brother is unmarried, Plutarch advises to get him married.[219]

---

[212] Cf. Christianity's preference for the spiritual "brother" over against the "natural" brother (for passages see above, p. 233). Cf. also 1 Tim 6:2; Phlm 16.

[213] See Helmbold's note (LCL 6:318) where he suggests Plutarch refers "perhaps" to chapter 5.

[214] Fr. 757: οὐδεὶς ἀγαπῶν αὐτὸς ἀμελεῖθ' ἡδέως (see Helmbold and O'Neil, 51). Cf. 2 Cor 12:15b: εἰ περισσοτέρως ὑμᾶς ἀγαπῶ, ἧσσον ἀγαπῶμαι.

[215] Comparisons with animals were common, esp. in the diatribe literature. See Betz, *Lukian*, 188, n. 2, with further literature. See esp. Jas 3:7; 2 Pet 2:12; Jude 10; etc.

[216] On the *Haustafel* generally, see Schrage, *NTS* 21 (1974-75) 1-22.

[217] Cf. Paul's notion of the human body as a temple, 1 Cor 3:16f.; 6:19f. Cf. also in regard to holiness of women: 1 Cor 7:14, 34; Eph 5:26-28; 1 Pet 3:5; etc.

[218] Cf., esp. in regard to the forms of expression, Rom 12:9-15; 1 Cor 7:29-31.

[219] Cf., by contrast, Paul's advice to the ἄγαμοι in 1 Cor 7:8-40: if at all possible, they should remain unmarried. Cf. also 1 Tim 5:1-16 (4:3); Matt 19:10, etc.

Finally the brother's children should be treated in a way which combines εὔνοια toward the brother and τιμή toward his wife. The children should be treated as one's own, but with additional gentleness: τοῖς δὲ παισὶν εὔνουν μὲν ὥσπερ ἰδίοις, ἤπιον δὲ μᾶλλον εἶναι καὶ μειλίχιον. This, is so that when they commit a misdeed, as youngsters do, they will not run away for fear of the parents and get into bad company, but can take refuge with their uncle who will give them friendly counsel and who will intercede on their behalf with the parents: ... ἀλλ' ἀποστροφὴν καὶ καταφυγὴν ἅμα νουθετοῦσαν εὐνοίᾳ καὶ παραιτουμένην ἔχωσιν.[220]

(491F-492A) As illustrations Plutarch brings in some classic examples of the relationship between uncle and nephew. Plato's relationship with his nephew Speusippus had become for Platonic philosophy the
(492B) prototype of education by example.[221] The Thessalian Aleuas was elected king because his uncle had twice slipped a lot into the lot oracle at Delphi, from which the Pythia chose the king.[222]

(492C) Summing up the uncle's duty in the education of his brother's children, Plutarch mentions especially the possibility for inoffensive praise: It is offensive to praise one's own sons, but not the sons of the brother.[223] The latter is not φίλαυτος[224] but φιλόκαλος καὶ θεῖος ὡς ἀληθῶς, as Plutarch derives from the name "uncle" (θεῖος). The word θεῖος then leads Plutarch to introduce the example
(492D) of Heracles who loved his nephew Iolaüs in spite of his 68 sons.[225] Strangely, the last example is that of a woman, Leucothea, who brought up her sister's child when her sister died, and consecrated it together with herself as a god.[226] Since women are only rarely

---

[220] Cf. Paul's letter to Philemon on behalf of Onesimus, a fine example of family relationships transferred into relationships between Christians.

[221] The words ἐκ πολλῆς ἀνέσεως καὶ ἀκολασίας ἐπέστρεψεν (491F) show that the motif of conversion is also implied. Cf. Jas 5:20 esp. See *PECL* 1, index, s.v. Conversion. For the concept of imitation of Plato, cf. Betz, *Nachfolge und Nachahmung Jesu Christi im Neuen Testament* (Tübingen, 1967) 111, where Plutarch *adul. et am.* 53C; *aud. poet.* 26B are mentioned. See also *PECL* 1:241f.

[222] On the lot-oracle, see *PECL* 1:119, 140.

[223] On the subject of self-praise, see the article by Betz, in this volume, pp. 363-93.

[224] On φιλαυτία, see the article by Betz, p. 371.

[225] Again, the concept is that of imitation, now of a god: δεῖ δὲ καὶ τὰ τῶν κρειττόνων ζηλοῦν. On the imitation of Heracles, see Betz, *Nachfolge und Nachahmung*, 54f.

[226] συνεκθειάζω, a hapax legomenon. Cf. Lampe, s.v. συνεκθεόω. On θείωσις, see *PECL* 1:40.

considered in the essay, the example might have been chosen because it enables Plutarch to conclude with a reference to Roman religion. Leucothea's deed is symbolically repeated in the festival of Matuta, when the Roman women take their sister's children in their arms and honor them.[227]

---

[227] On this festival, see Helmbold's note, LCL 6:325. At this festival, the Roman women imitated Leucothea in this way: οὐ τοὺς ἑαυτῶν παῖδας ἀλλὰ τοὺς τῶν ἀδελφῶν ἐναγκαλίζονται καὶ τιμῶσιν. Cf. Matt 19:13-15//Mark 10:13-16//Luke 18:15-17, a scene which is imitated until today in the Christian baptism ceremony. See also Jesus' presentation in Luke 2:28.

DE GARRULITATE (MORALIA 502B-515A)

BY

WILLIAM A. BEARDSLEE
Emory University
Atlanta, Georgia

I. INTRODUCTION

De garrulitate [1] is no. 36 in the Catalog of Lamprias. In the traditional order of essays it is immediately followed by *De curiositate* with which it has much in common. Both treat a common form of anti-social behavior as an illness to be diagnosed and cured by philosophy. In each essay the first and longer part is made up of a vivid description of the "ailment," while the second part offers the cure available from philosophy. The two essays differ in that *De garrulitate* is much richer in the longer illustrative stories.

The subject matter of garrulity (ἀδολεσχία) seems to go back to ancient popular morality.[2] In the Greek tradition, it is found first in the Old Comedy, where the figure of ὁ ἀδολέσχης seems to have been a stock-character.[3] Already here, however, the ἀδολέσχης has been, probably secondarily, identified with Socrates who is the ἀδολέσχης par excellence.[4] Aristotle [5] deals with the terms in regard to rhetoric and even gives a definition [6] of the concept, but it is interesting that the concept did not become part of the serious philosophical and ethical language. Rather it remained a concept describing a funny and despicable character. Its usage, therefore, was primarily polemic.

This background may explain why we find the ἀδολέσχης among

---

[1] This paper is based upon the edition by W. C. Helmbold, Plutarch's *Moralia*, LCL, vol. 6 (1962).

[2] Cf. K. J. Dover, *Greek Popular Morality in the Time of Plato and Aristotle* (Berkeley and Los Angeles, 1974), 25ff.; "Mistrust of Practised Speakers."

[3] See Aristophanes *Nu.* 1480, 1485; fr. 490 (Edmonds 1:710); Eupolis fr. 352 (Edmonds, 1:430-33); Plato *Phd.* 70C.

[4] See esp. Aristophanes (previous note); Plato *Phd.* 70C; *R.* 6. 488E; *Tht.* 195B-C; *Prm.* 135D; *Sph.* 225D; *Grg.* 486C, 470C, 489B, 490C, 492C; *Hp. Ma.* 304B. On Socrates see H. Reich, *Der Mimus* (Berlin, 1903) 1:354ff.

[5] *Top.* 5. 130a34, 8. 158a28, etc.; *Rh.* 1395b26, etc.

[6] *Top.* 5. 130a34: τὸ πλεονάκις λέγειν τὸ αὐτό.

the characters described by Theophrastus,[7] who developed characterization into brief sketches or pictures, a genre which became quite popular in literature. Theophrastus' characters are primarily descriptive, rather than outrightly prescriptive. But they do serve, at the popular level, a moral purpose. They attempt to be educative by using the medium of literary entertainment. The philosophical foundation remains largely invisible, although it is no doubt there. As in the other characters, Theophrastus presents a brief and vivid picture of the ἀδολέσχης, but he does not develop moral doctrines about the subject of garrulity. Theophrastus' indebtedness to comedy and satire is more obvious than his philosophical and ethical interests.[8] This latter line of tradition is certainly present in Plutarch's essay.

The question remains, however, just how Theophrastus' characters of the ἀδολέσχης and the related λάλος become useful for ethics. In his commentary R. G. Ussher doubts there is any practical utility to these characterizations.[9] But the subject of talk is a major theme in Theophrastus: besides Talkativeness (no. 3), he treats Loquacity (Λαλιᾶς, no. 7), Newsmaking (Λογοποιΐας, no. 8), and Illbreeding (Ἀηδίας, no. 20). He offers subtle distinctions between the ἀδολέσχης, who feels the need of talking and speaks randomly, even to strangers, while the λάλος simply has no control over his desire to talk. The λογοποιός, on the other hand, manufactures news, most of it false, in order to be its bearer.[10] Later, we find the ἀδολέσχης in the popular philosophical literature where the character of the ἀδολέσχης is used to ridicule the Sophists and philosophers, especially Socrates.[11]

Plutarch's essay lifts the notion of ἀδολεσχία from the level of popular ethics to the level of serious philosophical ethics. Originally a social problem,[12] in the urban culture to which Plutarch belonged

---

[7] Character 3. See Theophrast, *Charaktere*, edited with comments by P. Steinmetz (Munich, 1960) 2:53ff.

[8] Cf. the talkative old nurse who gives away the secret of parenthood in Menander *Sam.* 40-55; the saying in *Sententia* 379, ed. S. Jaekel, BT (1964): Ἰατρὸς ἀδόλεσχος ἐπὶ τῇ νόσῳ νόσος. See also Juvenal *Satire* 6. 398-412, 413-33, on the gossiping wife and the link between talkativeness and drinking, two themes which also appear in Plutarch's essay; Martial *Epigramma* 9. 35.

[9] R. G. Ussher, *The Characters of Theophrastus* (London, 1960) 10.

[10] Ibid., 51-52, 82, 89.

[11] See R. Helm, *Lucian und Menipp* (Leipzig and Berlin, 1906) 372ff.

[12] See O. Gréard, *De la morale de Plutarque*, 2d ed. (Paris, 1874) 159ff.: "La petite ville."

talkativeness had become a literary theme. In this essay Plutarch offers philosophy as a means to cure the illness and describes how the cure can be achieved.

An obvious difference between Plutarch's essay and ECL is a result of their different social and cultural milieus. Like the OT [13] and Judaism,[14] early Christianity speaks about talkativeness at the level of popular morality,[15] not at the level of philosophical analysis and therapy.

Another difference between Plutarch and ECL is that early Christianity does not recommend the Christian faith as a means to cure a social illness like garrulity. Rather, it is almost taken for granted that through the new Christian life the Christian will stop all forms of talkativeness. Plutarch and ECL agree that talkativeness is bad and must be avoided. For Plutarch it is a major social problem, for Christianity it is only a minor one (this changes, however, as soon as Christianity moves into the same social circles to which Plutarch belongs).[16] For Plutarch, the cure of talkativeness is a primary philosophical concern. For early Christianity, the cure of talkativeness is more a by-product of the concept of salvation and the Christian life. Yet, both early Christianity and Plutarch would agree in that, for Christianity, ἀδολεσχία is as irreconcilable with being a Christian as it is with being a philosopher for Plutarch.

---

[13] ἀδολεσχέω, ἀδολεσχία are used by the LXX to render שִׂיחַ. For a meaning comparable to Plutarch, see LXX Pss 68:13; 118:85; Sir 7:14; 32:9; 1 Kgs 1:16; 4 Kgs 9:11. The phenomenon of talkativeness is also expressed by other terms, sometimes juxtaposed with the proper behavior of the wiseman. See Prov 7:21; 10:19; 12:18; 14:23; Sir 8:3; 13:11-13; 19:7-12; 20:5; 42:11.

[14] In Rabbinic literature talkativeness is a real concern only with regard to prayer. See Bill. 1:403-6. In Aboth 6:6 the matter is at least mentioned among the forty-eight requirements for learning the Torah: בְּמִעוּט שִׂיחָה. While the concern about talkativeness does not seem to be typical for Rabbinic Judaism, Hellenistic Judaism clearly takes it over from the Greek tradition: Philo *sacr. A.C.* 32 has ἀδολέσχης in a catalog of vices; *det. pot. ins.* 130 uses ἀδόλεσχος in a tirade against empty rhetoric; similarly Aristeas *Epistle* 8.

[15] This is indicated by the fact that ἀδολεσχέω is not attested in ECL, so that Bauer does not list the term. ECL does have the even more common synonym φλυαρέω in 3 John 10; φλύαρος in 1 Tim 5:13. Cf. Bauer, s.v.; Hesychius, *Lexicon*, ed. K. Latte, s.v. ἀδολεσχεῖ, has as synonyms φλυαρεῖ and, in some manuscripts, μακρολογεῖ. For other examples of talkativeness in ECL, cf. esp. Matt 6:7; Eph 5:4; 1 Tim 1:6; 6:20; 2 Tim 2:16; Jas 1:19. See also further discussions below.

[16] See Lampe, s.v., for references.

When Plutarch analyzes ἀδολεσχία[17] philosophically, he can draw upon the traditional discussion about the conflict between philosophy and rhetoric.[18] To Plutarch, ἀδολεσχία results from the separation of the λόγοι from the λόγος.[19] The cure is simply the reversal of this disintegration. But—and this is the problem because of which the essay was written—philosophy, which is considered the proper means of healing the disease, seems paralyzed.[20] In order to cure garrulousness philosophy works through λόγοι which require perceptive listeners. Yet, the talkative person, as common experience shows, does not and cannot listen. The ἀδολέσχης is constantly talking and, therefore, cannot listen to any words. ἀσιγησία, the inability to keep silent, is coterminus with ἀνηκοΐα, the inability to listen.[21] In order for philosophy to be effective, a method must first be devised which will treat the inability to listen and thus open the doors, so to speak, so that philosophy can do her work. Plutarch's essay is an attempt to solve the philosophical-ethical problem by devising a method for dealing with the "deafness of the ears."

In constructing his essay Plutarch has used a number of sources. Although a comprehensive study of the sources has not been undertaken, the rich collection of proverbial, apophtegmatic, narrative material, in addition to quotations[22] from poets and philosophers, is apparent. The form of the essay owes much to the rhetorical tradition, but the original reason for the essay is not known. J. J. Hartman[23] held that the piece was actually delivered as a spoken address and was not intended simply as a written piece. This claim would be difficult to prove, despite the items of oral style which Hartman cites. Certainly the essay bears marks of the rhetorical school, for instance, in the illustration of types of reply

[17] According to the *Index Verborum Plutarcheus*, the family of ἀδολεσχέω κτλ. does not occur too often outside of *garrul*. See ἀδολεσχέω in *qu. conv.* 664D, 707C; ἀδολέσχης in *vit. pud.* 530F, 531B; ἀδολεσχία in *qu. conv.* 697D; *Alex.* 23. 677E; ἀδόλεσχος in *reg. et imp.* 177A; *qu. conv.* 618E.

[18] See on this W. K. C. Guthrie, *The Sophists* (Cambridge, 1971) 176ff.; Betz, *Paulus*, 57ff.

[19] See 502B-D.

[20] This is stated in the very first sentence (502B): Δύσκολον μὲν ἀναλαμβάνει θεράπευμα καὶ χαλεπὸν ἡ φιλοσοφία τὴν ἀδολεσχίαν.

[21] 502C. On this pseudo-medical terminology, see Helmbold's note, p. 396.

[22] See Helmbold and O'Neil, passim.

[23] J. J. Hartman, *De Plutarcho Scriptore et Philosopho* (Leiden, 1916) 260-71. Cf. the cautionary comment by Ziegler, sec. III.4.g, col. 142: "Sehr wohl möglich ist das, aber doch nicht zu erweisen."

to a question which deals with Socrates and in which the extended answer would include the whole of Thucydides' eighth book.[24] The illustration is a parody of exercises which were part of the regular training in the proper use of language.[25] No doubt much of the illustrative material comes from the diatribe tradition, although this essay is not as abundant in typical diatribe rhetoric as are some of Plutarch's other writings.[26]

Plutarch's essay *De garrulitate* has been carefully studied by H. G. Ingenkamp in his *Plutarchs Schriften über die Heilung der Seele.*[27] Ingenkamp has shown that, in addition to our essay, *De curiositate, De cohibenda ira,*[28] *De vitioso pudore* and *De laude ipsius*[29] follow similar patterns of diagnosis and cure. According to Ingenkamp, in all of these essays the person afflicted with the malady is directed to consider the malady's undesirable effects, which Plutarch describes in great detail. Once the person recognizes the distasteful nature of the vice (κρίσις), Plutarch provides him with an exercise program (ἄσκησις), by which he can train himself to avoid situations conducive to such vice and create in himself the habit of avoiding the particular type of misconduct being considered.

Plutarch assumes that people possess rational ability and that the kind of vices he describes are the result of a failure of the reason to exercise its proper control. If the individual can be made to recognize these failures for what they are, and if he is provided with a way to avoid them, it is assumed that he can and will do so.

ECL, on the other hand, views such misconduct not as a failure on the part of man's reason, but as a result of human sinfulness, a concept derived from Judaism. Pointing out the problem and providing an exercise program is not enough. Man needs divine forgiveness as well as ethical exhortation.

The following outline is indebted to Ingenkamp. It does not, however, attempt to show detailed patterns of repetition (a-b-a

---

[24] 513A-B.

[25] See H. Marrou, *A History of Education in Antiquity* (London, 1956) 197-205.

[26] Thus the hearer is addressed in the second person only once (506E-F); the rhetorical questions are few (but cf. the beginning of ch. 10, 506E); the opposing position is not introduced as the view of τίς, etc. On diatribe elements, see Index of Subjects, s.v. Diatribe.

[27] (Göttingen, 1971) 26ff.

[28] See the article by Betz and Dillon in this volume, pp. 170-97.

[29] See the article by Betz in this volume, pp. 367-93.

or a-b-a-b), which Ingenkamp points out as typical of many parts of the essay.[30]

Outline

- I. Introduction: Statement of the problem: The remedy for talkativeness is the word of reason (λόγος), but the talkative never listen (502B-E) — ch. 1
- II. Diagnosis of the harm caused by talkativeness — chs. 2-15
  - A. The talkative miss the benefits of silence (502E) — ch. 2
  - B. Talkativeness produces the opposite of its desired results — chs. 2-6
    - 1. The talkative drive away listeners (502E-503C) — ch. 2
    - 2. The talkative are not believed (503C-D) — ch. 3
    - 3. Talkativeness is worse than drunkeness (503D-504C) — ch. 4
    - 4. Talkativeness makes speech dull through repetition (504C-D) — ch. 5
    - 5. Conclusion: Speech, like wine, requires moderation (504D-E) — ch. 6
  - C. Talkativeness has all the bad qualities of other ailments — chs. 7-14
    - 1. Talkativeness brings ruin to cities and empires — chs. 7-9
      - a. Examples of the destructive effects of loose talk (504E-505D) — ch. 7
      - b. Heroic examples of control in speaking (505D-506E) — chs. 8-9
    - 2. Talkativeness brings danger to the talker (506E-510B) — chs. 10-14
  - D. Conclusion: Talkativeness is a disease (510B-C) — ch. 15
- III. Cure for talkativeness — chs. 16-23
  - A. Transition: Repetition of the above, namely, talkativeness has the opposite of its desired effects (510C-D) — ch. 16
  - B. First step: Recognizing these shameful and painful effects (510C-D) — ch. 16

[30] *Plutarchs Schriften über die Heilung der Seele*, 30, 39.

C. Second step: Remembering the benefits of reticence and examples of controlled speech (510D-511E)	chs. 17-18
D. Habit as a cure	chs. 19-23
1. First exercise: Not rushing to answer questions (511E-512C)	ch. 19
2. Second exercise: Giving careful attention to the content of answers (512C-513C)	chs. 20-21
3. Talkative persons must avoid particular subjects which set them off (513C-514C)	ch. 22
4. Talkative persons may turn to writing instead of talking (514C-D)	ch. 23
5. Talkative persons should associate with their superiors (514D-E)	ch. 23
6. Talkative persons should ask themselves whether a remark is necessary (514E-F)	ch. 23
V. Conclusion: Brief résumé of three points already made	ch. 23
A. Quotation from Simonides reminds that words cannot be unspoken (514F-515A)	
B. Practice is stronger than anything else (515A)	
C. Silence is healing (515A)	

II. De Garrulitate and Early Christian Literature

Ch. 1

Summary. Philosophy has a difficult time curtailing talkativeness, for the remedy, the λόγος, requires listeners, but talkative persons never listen:[31] they blame nature, which gave them one tongue but two ears. Even if such a person listens for a moment, talkativeness at once takes over again. Talkativeness is like the seven voiced portico at Olympia, set off by the least utterance. The talkative are like empty vessels, unable to retain what they hear, yet full of noise.

(502B-C) Commentary. The difficulty of hearing the λόγος is a theme in ECL as here,[32] though the λόγος is very differently conceived.[33]

[31] The difficulty of curing words with words may be compared to the difficulty of casting out Satan by Satan, Matt 12:25f.//Mark 3:23-26// Luke 11:17f.

[32] Matt 10:14//Mark 6:11; Matt 18:15-17; Luke 10:16; John 6:60.

[33] Cf. G. Kittel, *TDNT*, s.v. λέγω κτλ., D.6-13; G. Bornkamm, "God's Word and Man's Word in the New Testament," *Early Christian Experience* (New York, 1969) 1-13; Bultmann, *TNT*, secs. 34.1, 48.

Paul speaks of the importance of the occasion of hearing, and much of his correspondence has to do with right hearing.[34] The Pharisees and other Jewish leaders hear Jesus' message, but do not accept it.[35] Nor do they accept the message of the apostles and of Stephen.[36] The Greeks refuse to hear about the resurrection.[37] Sometimes one's possessions make it hard to accept what is heard.[38] According to John, only those who are "of God" can hear the Christian message.[39] But even those who hear and accept the message are not always able to follow it and to produce the works that are the result of proper hearing.[40]

The term θεράπευμα introduces the medical metaphor for the healing of talkativeness. The same metaphor appears frequently in Cynic-Stoic diatribe material where vices are viewed as a disease that needs to be cured.[41] A related image, that of healing from sin, is common in ECL.[42]

Ch. 2

Summary. Let us remind the talkative of the virtues of silence, especially the merits of hearing and being heard. In contrast to other diseases of the soul, which have a chance of achieving what they want, the talkative can satisfy their desire (ἐπιθυμία) only with great difficulty. They desire listeners but cannot get them. This is demonstrated by two apophthegms of Aristotle. In the first, Aristotle wittily rebukes a boring speaker; in the second, he tells another that he was not bored because he was not listening. The ψυχή does not attend to a talkative person, even when one is compelled to listen.

Commentary. The virtue of silence is introduced with a quotation (502E)
from Sophocles and is valued here only for its pragmatic value. Later (504A) the religious depth of silence will be mentioned, the only way in which the essay suggests a religious grounding for ethics.

---

[34] Cf. Rom 10:13-15; 1 Cor 1-2; 2 Cor 10; Gal 1:6-12.

[35] Matt 15:12; 21:45f.; Mark 11:18; John 10:19-21.

[36] Acts 5:33; 6:9f.; 7:54; 28:23-29; cf. also John 9:27f.

[37] Acts 17:32.

[38] Matt 19:22//Mark 10:22//Luke 18:23; Luke 16:14.

[39] John 8:43-47; 1 John 4:5f.; cf. Heb 4:2 where the hearers do not profit from the word because of their lack of faith.

[40] Matt 7:24-27//Luke 6:47-49; Matt 13:1-9, 18-23//Mark 4:1-9, 13-20// Luke 8:4-8, 11-15; Luke 8:21; 11:28; Jas 1:22.

[41] See the article by O'Neil in this volume, pp. 317f.

[42] Cf. *PECL* 1:87, 200.

(503B) The two apophthegms of Aristotle are typical of the witty Greek apophthegm, a very brief story with two actors which culminates in a pointed saying of the principal actor. Stories of similar pattern, though usually more formally elaborated, are common in the Gospels.[43]

Ch. 3

Summary. Nature has guarded the tongue with the teeth, which check the activity of the tongue by biting it.[44] The talkative, who do not control their tongue, appear to devalue speech and hence are not believed, though gaining belief is the object of speech. Just as wheat loses value as it gains bulk in storage, so the addition of ψεῦδος to a story by the talkative person destroys its credence (πίστις).

(503C) Commentary. The control of the tongue was a familiar ethical theme.[45] It recurs at 505D and 510A. The most extended appearance of this tradition in ECL is in James,[46] which proclaims the difficulty in controlling the tongue [47] at the same time as it exhorts the readers to exercise such control.[48] This same doubleness of presentation is present in Plutarch, where much of the illustrative material shows the uncontrollability of the tongue, while the hortatory sections move toward controlling it.

That this dichotomy was a longstanding one is illustrated by the history of the metaphors for the bit (or bridle or reins) and the rudder. Originally these seem to have been positive images of the control of the whole body by reason. This meaning remains in Plutarch, expressed in quotations from *Iliad* 5. 226 (interpreted to mean the "reins of silence") and Euripides *Bacchae* 386, 388

---

[43] See Bultmann, *HST*, 11-69; R. Spencer, *A Study of the Form and Function of the Biographical Apophthegms in the Synoptic Gospels* (Dissertation, Emory University, 1976).

[44] With this argument from the construction of the body, cf. 1 Cor 12:12-31.

[45] Cf. Ps 34:13; Sir 22:27.

[46] Jas 3:1-12; on this passage see J. H. Ropes, *A Critical and Exegetical Commentary on the Epistle of St. James* (Edinburgh, 1916); H. Windisch, *Die Katholischen Briefe*, 3d ed. rev. by H. Preisker (Tübingen, 1951); M. Dibelius and H. Greeven, *James* (Philadelphia, 1976) ad loc. The storm-driven ship, James' image for the uncontrolled tongue, appears in Plutarch in the context of flying words (507A-B).

[47] Jas 3:8; cf. *garrul.*, esp. chs. 11-14 (507C-510B).

[48] Jas 3:10; cf. *garrul.*, esp. chs. 8 (505D-F), 16-23 (510D-515A).

("disaster is the end of unbridled tongues").[49] But in James this optimistic meaning is overruled by the subsequent context which converts the metaphor into a picture of the destructive control of the tongue.[50] Similarly the rudder image is negative in James (3:4f.), despite its earlier optimistic history. The ship out of control also appears (in a separate passage) in our essay, at 507A-B, also in a negative sense and joined, as in James, to the destructive image of fire, though without specific reference to the rudder.[51]

The question of the believability of speech had long been discussed in Hellenistic culture, ever since rhetoric had been recognized as the art of persuasion.[52] Plutarch's essay embodies a deep ambiguity about the rhetorical arts of persuasion, since his work argues for silence or brevity, but is itself exceedingly lengthy and is deeply indebted to the rhetorical tradition. Perhaps there was some conscious irony here. In ECL the persuasiveness of speech was usually grounded in its representation of divine reality rather than in its rhetorical skill.[53] (503D)

The falsehood (ψεῦδος) which the talkative person adds to a story and thus destroys its believability is intended in a weak sense; intent to deceive is not implied.[54] In contrast, ECL is much concerned with falsehood to which conscious evil intent is attributed.[55] The setting of polite and leisurely speech to which Plutarch addressed himself, in contrast to the setting of an urgent desire to communicate a religious message, lies behind the contrast.

Ch. 4

Summary. The self-respecting person will avoid drunkeness which is akin to madness and which leads to uncontrolled talking; as the proverb has it, what is in a man's heart when he is sober

[49] Passages illustrating the use of these metaphors have been collected by J. J. Wettstein, Η ΚΑΙΝΗ ΔΙΑΘΗΚΗ (Amsterdam, 1752) ad loc.; Betz, *Lukian*, 193 and n. 2; and the commentaries. On the history, see esp. Dibelius-Greeven, ad loc.

[50] So Dibelius-Greeven; others take Jas 3:2-3 in the optimistic sense of exercise of control.

[51] In Plutarch the comparison is concerned with the inability to control words once they have been spoken, rather than with one's inability to control his tongue. The image of fire for the destructiveness of the tongue can also be paralleled elsewhere, e.g., Sir 28:13-26.

[52] See n. 18 above.

[53] Cf. Matt 7:29//Mark 1:22//Luke 4:32//John 7:46; 1 Cor 2:1-5; 14:24f.

[54] So Ingenkamp, 29.

[55] Cf. Bauer, s.v. ψεῦδος, and H. Conzelmann, *TDNT*, s.v. ψεῦδος κτλ.

is on his tongue when he is drunk. There follow two apophthegms, one about Bias, who defended his silence at a party by saying that no fool could hold his tongue when drinking, and a similar, more extended story about Zeno, who could hold his tongue at a drinking party. The profundity and mysteriousness of silence is contrasted with the talkativeness of drunkenness, but while the philosophers define drunkenness as foolish talking, the talkative person is foolish always and not just at times. Two proverbial metaphors (as your physician, he is worse than the disease; as your shipmate, worse than seasickness) are climaxed by the statement: we enjoy being with clever rascals more than with good but talkative persons. We may forgive bad talk of one whose deeds are good, as Nestor speaks to Ajax, but the talkative person destroys all gratitude for his deeds.

Commentary. Plutarch introduces the lack of control in drunkenness[56] as a contrast and comparison to the lack of control in talkativeness. His rhetoric requires him to say that talkativeness, because it is continual, is worse than drunkenness, which is occasional; and this rhetoric culminates in the statement that we enjoy being with a bad but intelligent person more than with a good but talkative person.

(503E) Intoxication is more severely condemned in ECL than by Plutarch, though the consequence of loose talking is not often drawn out.[57] Clement of Alexandria, not surprisingly, introduces the theme of loose speech as a consequence of drunkenness into his *Paedagogus*, illustrating both from classical literature and from Jewish Wisdom literature.[58]

(504A) The βαθύ and μυστηριῶδες of σιγή, as noted above (502E), is one of the few points where distinctively religious language appears in the essay (see also 505F and 510E). Here the religious dimension is only alluded to in passing. Silence is important as a total contrast to talkativeness. ECL also knows the mysterious, religious depth of silence,[59] which, in the silence of Jesus before his accusers,[60]

---

[56] On drunkenness, see the essay by O'Neil in this volume, pp. 333, 338.

[57] 1 Cor 5:11 (where μέθυσος is next to λοίδορος in a vice list), 6:10 (the same combination); 1 Thes 5:7; Eph 5:18.

[58] *Paedagogus* 2. 2.

[59] Cf. the awesome silence which culminates in the opening of the seals, Rev 8:1; Ign Magn 8:2 where Christ is the λόγος proceeding out of silence. See Bauer, s.v. σιγή, and the literature cited there; O. Casel, *De Philosophorum Graecorum Silentio Mystico* (Giessen, 1919). Unfortunately, *TDNT* has no article on σιγή.

[60] Matt 26:62f.//Mark 14:60f.; Matt 27:13f.//Mark 15:4f.; Luke 23:9.

can be related to the strategy of silence advised by Plutarch.

Though rhetorical exaggeration is frequent in ECL, those writings could not say with Plutarch that we take more pleasure in the company of clever rascals than of good but talkative persons. But the rascals can be praised on other grounds.[61]

Ch. 5

Summary. The chapter opens with a story about Lysias whose speech for a litigant was deemed inadequate on repeated reading. Lysias replied: Won't the jurors hear it only once? This story then leads to a comment on Homer's skill in avoiding repetitiousness.

Commentary. The "novelty" (καινότης) of Homer, who is ἀεὶ καινός, illustrates the aesthetic meaning of this group of terms. This meaning is largely bypassed in ECL's extensive usage of them.[62] (504D)

Ch. 6

Summary. Speech like wine is destructive if misused. The talkative produce the opposite of their intended effects: they offend those whom they think they please; they are laughed at for the very things for which they want to be admired; and they are disliked for the things for which they want to be liked. Annoyance and hostility are signs of the misuse of the art of speech.

Commentary. This chapter summarizes and concludes the point made by chapters 2-5. Speech, which is the sweetest and most humanizing intercourse, is made inhuman by those who misuse it, and the result for the talkative is that they actually accomplish the very opposite of what they desired. (504E)

That speech is intended to please is a result of the fundamentally social nature of man. Not unnaturally, Plutarch does not here deal with occasions when speech must offend and displease, a theme frequent in ECL.[63]

Ch. 7

Summary. Of the other passions and illnesses, some are dangerous, some hateful, and some ridiculous, but talkativeness has all these disadvantages at once. The talkative are scoffed at for telling what

---

[61] Cf. the Parable of the Unjust Steward, Luke 16:1-8, esp. vs. 8.

[62] Cf. Bauer, s.v., and J. Behm, *TDNT*, s.v. καινός κτλ.

[63] Cf., e.g., Matt 3:7-10//Luke 3:7-9; Matt 23:1-36; 1 Cor 4:14; 2 Cor 2:1-4; 10:1-6; Rev 2:2-5; 3:15-19.

is common knowledge; they are hated as bearers of bad news; they are in danger for they cannot resist telling secrets. This programatic statement is followed by the story of Anacharsis who when sleeping guarded his genitals with his left hand but his mouth with his right: the tongue needed the stronger restraint. Uncontrolled speech is more destructive than uncontrolled lust. Next, a story about Sulla's destruction of Athens shows how loose talk in a barber shop betrayed the city and how uncontrolled mockery of Sulla during the siege led to Sulla's severe revenge. The chapter concludes with a story of a conspirator against Nero who was betrayed because he hinted his intention to a person being taken as a prisoner before Nero.

(504F) Commentary. The three disadvantages of talkativeness correspond to three quite different traditions about the misuse of speech. The first speaks of common talkativeness which is the main theme of the essay. But to strengthen his point Plutarch here introduces two other forms of uncontrolled or inappropriate speech, the bearing of bad news [64] and the betrayal of secrets. Of these latter two only the second is discussed here. The pragmatic social concern with the keeping of political and military secrets which Plutarch focuses on, however, receives little attention in ECL,[65] which is more concerned with morally reprehensible talk.[66]

Ch. 8

Summary. The chapter begins with a brief episode [67] about Zeno who bit out his tongue to prevent revealing a secret under torture; this is followed by a story about Leaena who guarded the secrets of Harmodius and Aristogeiton. No spoken word has been

[64] The unpopularity of the bearer of bad news was a traditional theme, illustrated by Sophocles *Ant.* (cited at 509C-D) and in the OT (2 Chr 18:14-26; Jer 26:1-9; 38:1-6). It may be part of the meaning of the proverb, "A prophet is not without honor except in his own country" (Matt 13:57//Mark 6:4//Luke 4:24).

[65] 2 Sam 17:15f., 21f. is an example of the revelation of military secrets; for a concern with personal secrets, see Sir 13:12-13; 19:7-12.

[66] Rom 1:30 and 1 Cor 5:11 (lists of vices); 1 Pet 3:10-12 (quoting Ps 34:12-16). With Plutarch's quotation (505C) from Plato (*Lg.* 935A and 717D) about the heavy penalty for the lightest thing, words, is to be compared the saying about rendering account in the judgment for every careless word men utter (Matt 12:36).

[67] Short episodes concluding with a saying are here termed "apophthegms." This one is similar except that it focuses on an action rather than a saying. These will be termed simply "episodes." Longer narratives are called simply "stories."

so useful as many that remained unspoken, for it is possible to speak these later, but once spoken a word cannot be taken back. We have men as teachers of speaking, but gods teach silence, as in initiations to the mysteries. Homer has given Odysseus as a model of reticence in that reason controlled all parts of his body. Most of his companions were similar, as in the episode of the Cyclops. Thus Pittacus did not do badly in returning to the king of Egypt, from a sacrificial animal, the tongue as the best and worst part of the body.

Commentary. The examples which Plutarch gives of the refusal, even under torture, to betray secrets can be paralleled by stories of the Christian martyrs. Despite having to undergo torture, the martyrs still refused to deny Christ.[68] (505D)

The religious dimension of silence is here reinforced with a reference to the silence that is required during initiation into the mysteries.[69] As elsewhere, however, this element is not integrated into the practical dimension of the essay, but only mentioned in passing. (505F)

As an example of the proper self-control, Plutarch points to Odysseus whose λόγος elicited complete obedience from all parts of his body. Here Plutarch gives his first full statement of the psychological theory that serves as the basis for his understanding of the cause of talkativeness and of the cure. The cause is the failure of the λόγος to excercise proper control, and the cure is a program for correcting the problem.[70] (506A)

Ch. 9

Summary. In a line of Euripides, Ino says that the knows how to be silent when necessary and how to speak when speech is safe. Such is the result of an aristocratic education which teaches silence before it teaches speaking. There follows an apophthegm of Anti-

---

[68] Cf. Mart Pol 2:3-4; 11; *The Martyrdom of the Saints Justin, Chariton, Charito, Evelpistus, Hierax, Paeon, and Valerian*, Recension C, 4:3-5:2 (ed. Musurillo, p. 58); *The Martyrs of Lyons* 1:18-19 (ed. Musurillo, p. 66); 25f. (pp. 68-70). Cf. the informer who betrays Polycarp in Mart Pol 6:1; cf. also *The Martyrs of Lyons* 1:14 (p. 66).

[69] On such arcana see *PECL* 1, index, s.v. Such a concern is reflected in the proverbs, "Do not give dogs what is holy, and do not throw your pearls before swine, lest they trample them under foot and turn and attack you" (Matt 7:6). Cf. the silence of the disciples in Matt 17:9//Mark 9:9//Luke 9:36. On initiation cf. *PECL* 1:55f.

[70] On Plutarch's ethical theory, see esp. the article by Hershbell in this volume, pp. 144-45. On ἐγκράτεια, see Hershbell, pp. 138-39.

gonus, who rebuked his son for undue curiosity about the time of breaking camp, and an apophthegm of Metellus, who said he would throw his shirt into the fire if it knew such secrets. Next is a story of Eumenes who did not tell his men that the feared Craterus was approaching but let them believe that it was the ineffectual Neoptolemus. After the victory and the death of Craterus, his friends praised him for this silence. Even if they do blame you, it is better that they do so when saved, rather than accuse you because of your trust in them.

(506D-E) Commentary. Craterus' deception of his followers is hard to parallel in ECL, though there, too, reservation of knowledge is not unknown; cf. Paul's view that not all were ready to know the whole truth.[71] But the language of σωθέντας δι' ἀπιστίαν, with its counter, ἀπολλυμένους διὰ τὸ πιστεῦσαι, would be impossible in ECL.

Ch. 10

Summary. Who has the right to speak out boldly against the one who has not kept silent? If you take refuge in another's faithfulness, you are deservedly ruined if he tells what you told him. If the other is faithful, you are saved beyond expectation. The story increases and multiplies as it is told. Just as the dyad is the beginning of difference, though the monad preserves its integrity, so the story is a true secret if confined to its first possessor, but becomes rumor if told. Homer's "winged" words cannot be taken back. As a ship is hard to control in a storm, words which get out of the harbor shipwreck the man who spoke them.

(506E-F) Commentary. The chapter opens with the essay's only full-fledged address to the hearer in the second person, a typical element of diatribe style.[72] The rhetorical move of "who is free from this fault" also occurs in other discussions of this topic.[73]

(507A) The difference between one and two is used to define a secret. Just as two has given up the indivisibleness of one, so secrets cease being secrets as soon as they are told. Such number symbolism can be found in Revelation, but is not widespread in ECL.[74]

---

[71] 1 Cor 3:1-2.

[72] See above p. 268 and n. 26.

[73] Cf. Sir 19:16. Jas 3:2 also recognizes how widespread sins of the tongue are.

[74] On number symbolism, see Barn 9:7f.; Rev 13:17f.; O. Rühle, *TDNT*, s.v. ἀριθμέω, ἀριθμός. On the images of the ship in a storm and fire, see above on 503C.

Ch. 11

Summary. The chapter opens with a long story about a Roman senator who tricked his wife into revealing her inability to keep a secret. It is followed by another, not quite so extended narrative about Fulvius, the friend of Augustus, whose wife betrayed to Augustus' wife the plan of replacing her son, Tiberius, by Postumius Agrippa as Augustus' successor. The result was that Fulvius had to take his own life, and he was joined in suicide by his wife.

Commentary. The subthesis given in ch. 10 about the dangers (507B-
that talkativeness holds for those who are talkative is exemplified 508B)
in chs. 11-14. Ch. 11 begins the list of examples with two stories portraying the talkativeness of women, a stock theme.[75] The attribution of this trait to women is also reflected in ECL, especially in warnings given in the Pastoral Epistles.[76]

Of the two stories in ch. 11 one is comic and the other heroic. As he does in these stories, so Plutarch generally introduces all varieties of characters into the comic stories, but the heroic stories tend to have exalted personages as their dramatis personae. In this tendency Plutarch is following a tradition of separation of genres from which, as Auerbach has shown, ECL broke sharply.[77]

Ch. 12

Summary. This chapter begins with an apophthegm of Philippides who, when asked by King Lysimachus what he would like to have, replied: Anything but your secrets. The talkative are led into undue curiosity, especially about things which ought not to be made known. These secrets destroy those who use them. There follows a story about Seleucus the Victorious who, for the sake of his own security, was forced to have a farmer who had given him shelter killed. The farmer had indicated that he recognized Seleucus, and he could not be trusted to keep silent. If the farmer had only been able to restrain himself, he would have been richly rewarded.

Commentary. Plutarch discusses curiosity in much greater (508C)
detail in his essay *De curiositate*. Here he simply refers to the close

---

[75] See the article by Wicker in this volume, p. 126.
[76] 1 Tim 5:13; Tit 2:3.
[77] E. Auerbach, *Mimesis* (Princeton, 1953) ch. 2.

connection between curiosity and talkativeness, a connection which is also demonstrated in ECL.[78]

Ch. 13

Summary. Unlike the farmer in ch. 12 who hoped for a reward, most talkative people do not have a reason for destroying themselves. The point is illustrated by three stories about the proverbially talkative barbers. In the first, in reply to a comment about how indestructible the tyranny of Dionysius was, the barber jokingly remarked that he had his razor at Dionysius' throat every few days. When the tyrant heard about it, he had the barber crucified.[79] The second is an apophthegm of King Archelaüs of Macedonia; when asked by a barber how he wanted his hair cut, he replied, "in silence." The third is a longer story about a barber who heard from a slave about the Athenian defeat in Sicily; when he spread the news, he was put to the torture to find out who his informer was (he did not know) and then forgotten on the wheel when the terrible news was confirmed. At evening,[80] finally rediscovered, he could not help asking whether they had heard how Nicias had died. The chapter closes by making the moral explicit: how ἀμαχόν and ἀνουθέτητον talkativeness is.

Ch. 14

Summary. The chapter begins by taking up the point of the unpopularity of the bearer of bad news. There follow two long narratives of self-betrayal. The first tells how a temple robber[81] gave himself away by knowing too much about a clue. The second is the story of the discovery of the murderers of Ibycus. Their laughter at the passing cranes as avengers of Ibycus betrayed them. Plutarch then notes how neighboring parts of the body are attracted to the sick and painful part; so the talkative person's tongue draws to itself that which is better concealed. Therefore the tongue must be fenced in lest we behave less sensibly than geese, who are said to take stones in their mouths in order to be silent while they pass the eagle-abundant area of Mount Taurus.

---

[78] Cf. 1 Tim 5:13; cf. also 2 Thes 3:11; Herm Vis 4:3:1; Sim 9:2:7. The image of children playing with a piece of ice which they cannot hold, yet are unwilling to let go, can be compared with the children who cannot make up their minds whether to play party or funeral, Matt 11:16f.// Luke 7:32.

[79] Cf. Bauer, s.v. ἀνασταυρόω.

[80] The phrase (509C) ὀψὲ δὲ λυθεὶς ἤδη πρὸς ἑσπέραν is to be compared for its repetitive adverbs with Mark 1:32.

[81] Cf. ἱεροσυλέω in Rom 2:22 and ἱερόσυλος in Acts 19:37.

Commentary. The sympathy of the parts of the body for each other was a commonplace, appearing also in ECL.[82] Here this physical phenomenon is used to explain why the talkative reveal their own misdeeds. Their tongue attracts to itself some of the sickness that is within them. Therefore Plutarch suggests that reason must function as a barrier to the tongue. Earlier he applied the same image to the teeth.[83] (510A)

Ch. 15

Summary. It is widely recognized that the traitor (προδότης) is the most wicked man. Famous traitors are listed: Euthycrates, Philocrates, Euphorbus and Philagrus. But the talkative person betrays without even getting paid. Thus the verse applies to him: You are not generous: you are sick, you love to give.

Commentary. Plutarch compares the talkative with the most despised class of people, traitors.[84] In contrast to traitors, who betray for their own profit, the talkative disclose secrets because they love to talk. Their talkativeness is a disease;[85] it is not a result of a generous desire to share. This identification of talkativeness as a disease[86] concludes the analysis of talkativeness (chs. 2-15) and prepares for the subsequent discussion of the cure (chs. 16-23). (510B-C)

Ch. 16

Summary. At this point occurs the main division in the essay; Plutarch turns from κρίσις, diagnosis, to ἄσκησις, treatment. The preceding, pejorative description of talkativeness was required in order to show the need for the difficult work of breaking this strong habit. Then once again, as in 504E, Plutarch shows how talkative-

---

[82] 1 Cor 12:26.

[83] Cf. 503C.

[84] The traitor is a key figure in ECL in the figure of Judas: Matt 26:14-16// Mark 14:10f.//Luke 22:3-6; John 13:27 (cf. John 12:6). These passages, like Plutarch, emphasize the venal aspect of the traitor.

[85] Plutarch here quotes a fragment of Epicharmus (see Helmbold, p. 441, n. h). This verse, which describes the love of giving as a disease rather than as φιλάνθρωπος, was originally applied to someone who squanders his possessions (cf. the article by O'Neil in this volume, pp. 316ff.), as Plutarch correctly notes. Here, however, Plutarch applies it to someone who squanders what he knows but should keep to himself. ECL knows of persons who do good for wrong reasons or by deceit: Matt 6:2-4; Phil 1:15-17; the wasteful giving of Matt 26:6-13//Mark 14:3-9//John 12:1-8 is positively judged.

[86] Cf. above on 502B-C.

ness produces the opposite of what is desired. The talkative are hated when they wish to be liked; they cause annoyance when they wish to please; they are laughed at when they think that they are admired. They spend their money without gain, wrong their friends, and destroy themselves. The recognition of these facts is the first step in healing.

(510D) Commentary. The summary of the diagnosis makes two points, both illustrated at length in the preceding chapters. The first is that talkativeness produces the opposite of its desired effects. The second is that it is extremely anti-social behavior, damaging friends, aiding enemies, and destroying oneself. The preceding examples, though drawn from a different realm than that which will be dealt with in the succeeding chapters, are seen as clearer instances of a process inherent in reckless and uncontrolled talking, even in the more limited social context Plutarch actually has in mind.[87]

Ch. 17

Summary. The second step in healing is to consider the effects of the opposite behavior, noting the praises given to restraint in speech, and the holy, mysterious character of silence, and remembering the virtue of the terse speaker, praised by Plato and encouraged by Lycurgus. Spartan speech was purged of all superfluities and is ἀποφθεγματικός. As examples to the talkative we can refer to some famous Spartan answers and to the brevity of the Delphic oracle.[88] We should also note the praise given those who use signs instead of speech, as did Heracleitus (water and barley meal as signs of being satisfied[89] with what is available) and Scilurus (a bundle of shafts as a sign of the power of unity among his sons.).

(510E) Commentary. The argument relies on two contrasts to talkativenesss: silence, a binary opposite, which is the point, as already noted,[90] that opens the religious dimension, and brief speech, which can be conceived as a mean between silence and prolixity. One reason why silence is repeatedly referred to but never analyzed

[87] Rhetorical use of opposites is typical diatribe style. On diatribe style, see above, p. 268 and n. 26.

[88] To practice brevity in speech is to imitate Apollo. Cf. *PECL* 1, index, s.v. Imitation.

[89] Self-sufficiency is a Cynic *topos*. Cf. ἀρκέω in 1 Tim 6:8; Heb 13:5.

[90] On the mystery of silence, cf. at 504A above. Here Plutarch adds the strong religious term, σεμνός.

in detail is that Plutarch is actually teaching not silence, but brevity.[91]

Plutarch advances the unverbalized sign as even briefer than (511C)
brevity of speech. The acted sign actually has other dimensions; like silence, it is a way of pointing to what cannot be directly expressed. Acted signs are not frequent in ECL, but they do occur.[92]

Ch. 18

Summary. If someone will consider such examples, he may stop taking pleasure in talking nonsense.[93] But I am put to shame by the story of the Roman slave who was trained to reply only to what was asked and therefore did not volunteer the information that the emperor had declined his master's invitation to a feast. Only when the feast was underway did the host find this out by direct questioning.

Commentary. The story of the slave illustrates the powerful (511D-E)
role of training (see next chapter). As a tale about an invited guest who did not come, the story of the Roman slave invites comparison with the Parable of the Marriage Feast.[94]

Ch. 19

Summary. It is not possible to stop a talkative person by pulling up the reins; the illness must be cured by habituation. In the first place, let such a person remain silent when questions are asked until all others have declined to answer. Such conversation is not a race. Don't take the answer away from someone else; this looks like a put down. An error in an answer will be much better received if it is not in a response hastily volunteered.

Commentary. The basic point of Plutarch's section on the cure (511E)
of talkativeness is clearly made here: gaining a disciplined habit

---

[91] Brevity of speech also occurs in ECL; cf. Matt 6:7-13. Cf. also Heb 13:22.

[92] Jesus writes on the ground without speaking, John 8:1-11; the sign of Agabus is accompanied by speech, Acts 21:11.

[93] Here (511D) Plutarch shifts from ἀδολεσχία to the even more negative φλυαρεῖν. This word and its corresponding noun are used at 503F, 505C, 508C, and 510C as well as here. These terms are used in ECL: cf. 1 Tim 5:13; 3 John 10.

[94] Matt 22:1-10//Luke 14:15-24.

of reticence is the only way to overcome talkativeness.[95] The emphasis on a gradual conquest of the irrational part of the soul by habituation was so widespread in Hellenistic popular teaching that Babut can speak of it as "un lieu commun, dont il est vain de chercher à chaque fois l'origine dans l'enseignement de telle ou telle école philosophique." [96] This form of ethical discipline plays little role in ECL, though a kind of progress in character is spoken of from time to time.[97] About Paul, Johannes Weiss makes the following comment: ". . . the idea of training and practical guidance as to what should be done if one would become more and more the master of one's own mind, so strongly evident in the Stoics, is almost wholly wanting in Paul. . . . The deepest reason for this deficiency is clear: even as an ethical teacher Paul is primarily a Spirit-filled man." [98] The Spirit, moreover, is related to the new eschatological situation.[99] Other ECL authors put more emphasis on a legalistic morality, but do not extensively develop the theme of disciplined habituation.

(512A) It is to be noted that the further illustrative material in this chapter deals with reasons for control in answering questions arising from the human situation of interpersonal relations rather than from a philosophical theory of self. The concern here is what kind of impression an answer will make on others.

Ch. 20

Summary. The second matter for practice is in the content of one's answers. They must be appropriate to the question and to the questioner. The timing of the answers should also be considered, so that they are not precipitate. Even if the Pythia gives some oracles without waiting for the question, a hasty human answer

[95] We note the following words in this group: ἔθος, 511E (this instance), 514E; ἐθισμός, 511E, 514E; ἐθίζειν, 511F, 512F; ἐθιστέον, 514C; all of these are in the concluding section of the essay. Cf. also *curios.*, esp. 520D, Μέγιστον μέντοι πρὸς τὴν τοῦ πάθους ἀποτροπὴν ὁ ἐθισμός. ἔθος occurs in ECL, but not in this sense; see Bauer, s.v. On the metaphor of the reins, see above at 503C.

[96] D. Babut, *Plutarque et le Stoïcisme* (Paris, 1969) 321, n. 2.

[97] See esp. Rom 5:3-4. For a discussion of the notion of ethical progress in Paul, see W. A. Beardslee, *Human Achievement and Divine Vocation in the Message of Paul* (London, 1961) ch. 4, and V. Furnish, *Theology and Ethics in Paul* (Nashville, 1968) 239-41.

[98] J. Weiss, *The History of Primitive Christianity* (New York, 1937) 2:576f.

[99] Furnish, op. cit., 214: "The Pauline eschatology is not just one motif among numerous others, but helps to provide the fundamental perspective from which everything else is viewed."

may be ridiculous. One should exercise self-control like that of Socrates who poured out the first bucketful of water so that his irrational part would learn to wait for the time set by reason.[100]

Commentary. With the Pythia's answering before the question is put, compare: "Your Father knows what you need before you ask him." [101] Almqvist notes the parallel between ὁ γὰρ θεός, ᾧ λατρεύει, and Paul's ὁ θεός, ᾧ λατρεύω.[102] (512E)

In this chapter there is an explicit reference to a proverb (παροιμία): "They asked for buckets, but tubs were refused," as at 503F (οἱ παροιμιαζόμενοι): "what is in a man's heart when he is sober is on his tongue when he is drunk." Plutarch usually introduces proverbs, as in both these instances, to introduce an element of irony. The condensed popular wisdom of the proverb articulates elements of complexity which philosophical thought cannot fully contain. In the Synoptic Gospels the characteristic use of the proverb heightens even more the elements of hyperbole or paradox.[103]

Ch. 21

Summary. There are three kinds of answers: the barely necessary, the polite, and the superfluous. Examples of each are given. The prolix answer to the question whether Socrates is at home would run on to recite the whole eighth book of Thucydides. To check the tendency to answer too much one must follow the question step by step. Thus Carneades was given the person with whom he was talking to regulate his loud voice.

Commentary. Plutarch wavers between his admiration for Spartan brevity and his appreciation of the politeness of well-regulated conversation. The concluding summary opts for the polite answer that is in accord with the wishes of the questioner. (513A)

Ch. 22

Summary. Socrates used to warn against food and drink which stimulated the appetite when people were not hungry. So the

[100] Socrates' gesture of pouring out the water recalls the very differently motivated gesture of David in 1 Chr 11:15-19.

[101] Matt 6:8, also in a context urging brevity of speech.

[102] Rom 1:9; Almqvist, 82.

[103] More often proverbs are introduced without explicit reference to their name, as at 513E: "Where one feels pain, there will he keep his hand." On proverbs in the Synoptic Gospels, see W. Beardslee, "Uses of the Proverb in the Synoptic Gospels," *Int* 24 (1970) 61-73.

talkative must avoid particular subjects about which they find it hard to control their talking, whether war stories for the military man or law court stories for those who have had successes there. Just as pain draws the hand to the hurt, so pleasure draws the tongue to dwell on pleasant memories, as, for example, in the talk of lovers. The talkative will talk about anything, yet they should particularly guard against the subjects for which they have the greatest weakness. Cyrus' conduct was admirable; he challenged others to contests in which he was less skilled. But the talkative person thrusts aside subjects of conversation about which he knows nothing and leads the conversation into threadbare subjects. As an example, Plutarch mentions the man in his native town who had read a little of Ephorus and bored everyone with the story of the battle of Leuctra.

Commentary. The chapter deals with excessive self-concern and excessive self-praise, themes which are treated in great detail in *De laude ipsius*.[104] The closing reference to Plutarch's fellow townsman is the only only autobiographical reference in the essay.

Ch. 23

Summary. But conversation in a subject where the speaker is learned is the least of the evils of talkativeness, and the speech of the talkative should be turned into such channels. Those who tend to be talkative should take to writing instead of talking, which is what Antipater the Stoic did. He could not come to grips with Carneades in discussion and so he wrote whole books against Carneades. As a result Antipater was nicknamed "pen-valiant." A talkative person who writes this way will be less of a burden to those he is with. To such exercises in habituation (ἐθισμός) must be added reflection (ἐπιλογισμός), as, for example, the question, Is this remark needed? If it is neither useful nor pleasurable, why make it?

Conclusion. We must keep in mind Simonides' remark that he had often repented of speaking, but never of being silent; and also we must remember that practice is the master of all things. But silence, as Hippocrates says, not only prevents thirst, but also sorrow and suffering.

(514D) Commentary. The mocking nickname of Antipater the Stoic, καλαμοβόας, recalls the mocking of Paul as one who could write powerful letters but was ineffectual when personally present.[105]

---

[104] Cf. the article by Betz in this volume, pp. 367-93. See also H. D. Betz, *Paulus*, 74ff. on the ἀλαζών.

[105] 2 Cor 10:9-11.

Almqvist notes the parallel between Col 4:6, "let your conversation be ἅλατι ἠρτυμένος, and Plutarch's ὥσπερ ἁλασὶ τοῖς λόγοις ἐφηδύνουσι τὴν διατριβήν.[106] (514E-F)

The conclusion masterfully brings together the main emphases of the essay. First the quotation from Simonides summarizes the pragmatic point that one may repent of speaking, but one need not expect to repent remaining silent. This point holds together the vivid, often comic, but also tragic material in the central part of the essay, drawn from the tradition of public life, which is often pessimistic about the possibility of controlling speech, and the hortatory material, focused on the private life of leisure, in the main concluding section. Then the recollection of the power of practice (ἄσκησις) summarizes the main concluding section and voices the philosophical presuppositions of the essay which affirm the possibility of control of the irrational part of the self by the rational part, but do not hold that the irrational part can be totally dominated, only held under control. Finally, the saying of Hippocrates that silence is not only a preventive of thirst, but also does not cause sorrow and suffering, refers back to the conjunction of drunkenness and talkativeness in the first part of the essay, and opposes to that the mysterious depth of silence referred to several times in the course of the essay. (515A)

As a rhetorical achievement, *De garrulitate* must rank high among Plutarch's works.[107] Its skillful combination of the serious and the light-hearted makes it easy reading and makes its practical point crystal clear. It must be said, however, that the philosophical problem of the relation between talkativeness and the λόγος is not thoroughly explicated. Essentially the essay presents a negative or disciplinary morality, which is, however, balanced somewhat by the positive picture of right human intercourse which appears from time to time. The assumption is that if only the talkative person can be stilled sufficiently, he will be able to listen not only to other people, but also to his own rational part. The path to this inner quietness is self-discipline (ἄσκησις, ἐθισμός). The outline of the essay has presupposed that self-discipline may be undertaken once the reason has been persuaded of the point.[108] Typically ECL

---

[106] Almqvist, 122.

[107] Helmbold (p. 395) refers to this essay as "by far the best in the volume."

[108] Cf. K. Westaway, *The Educational Theory of Plutarch* (London, 1922) 76. Cf. also D. Faure, *L'éducation selon Plutarque d'après les oeuvres morales* (Aix-en-Provence, 1960) 2:42ff.

would assert that a more active participation of the divine in the process of transformation would be required if the transformation is to be effective.[109]

Plutarch elsewhere deals extensively with the divine, but he is here restricted from doing so by the fact that his only symbol for the divine is silence, which is not an effective symbol for the λόγος, and which only partly coheres with his practical message—for his final word in the practical sphere is not the counsel of silence, but the counsel of moderation in speech. It may be that the difficulty in achieving a full-fledged expression of the relation between excessive speech, speech which communicates the λόγος, and silence, is related to the fact that Plutarch's chosen subject does not allow him scope to deal with the central area where speech struggles with silence—the area where the tragic event breaks the vision of the wholeness of the world, and silence may better communicate "presence," whether human or divine, than speech can.[110] To bring this dimension of the problem of speech into his discussion, however, would have carried Plutarch far beyond the scope which he set for himself in this essay.

---

[109] For Paul, cf. Furnish, *Theology and Ethics in Paul*, 208-27.

[110] See G. Ebeling, *Introduction to a Theological Theory of Language* (Philadelphia, 1973) 104-28.

DE CUPIDITATE DIVITIARUM (MORALIA 523C - 528B)

BY

EDWARD N. O'NEIL
University of Southern California
Los Angeles, California

I. INTRODUCTION

Both classical and Christian literatures are rich in writings which handle the theme of wealth, greed, miserliness and related ideas.[1] To this tradition belongs Plutarch's *De cupiditate divitiarum* or, more accurately Περὶ φιλοπλουτίας.[2]

Yet, contrary to what some critics have said, Plutarch is not primarily concerned in this treatise with greed *per se*. Rather he concentrates on the irrational desire to possess great wealth, and so his basic theme is not πλεονεξία, φιλοχρηματία, or any other such regular term, so much as it is φιλοπλουτία, the word which appears in the title.

Furthermore, in his treatment of the subject, Plutarch ignores one theme which is a regular feature in ancient discussions of wealth. He does not extol the virtues of poverty in contrast to the evils of

---

[1] In addition to many of the books listed in the general bibliography the following works have been used in the preparation of this study: E. V. Arnold, *Roman Stoicism* (London, 1911; re-issued 1958); E. G. Berry, *Emerson's Plutarch* (Cambridge, 1961); S. Dill, *Roman Society from Nero to Marcus Aurelius* (London 1905; re-issued 1937); L. Edelstein, *The Meaning of Stoicism* (Cambridge, 1966); E. N. Gardiner, *Athletics of the Ancient World* (Oxford, 1955; re-issued 1967); H. A. Harris, *Greek Athletes and Athletics* (London, 1964); J. J. Hartmann, *De Plutarcho Scriptore et Philosopho* (Leiden, 1916); M. Hengel, *Property and Riches in the Early Church* (Philadelphia, 1974); O. Hense, *Teletis Reliquiae* (Tübingen, 1909); E. N. O'Neil, "The Structure of Juvenal's Fourteenth Satire," *CPh* 55 (1960) 251-253; V. C. Pfitzner, *Paul and the Agon Motif* (Leiden, 1967); Rist, *Stoic Phil.*; F. H. Sandbach, *The Stoics* (London, 1975); K. M. Westaway, *The Educational Theory of Plutarch* (London, 1922).

[2] F. H. Sandbach, *Plutarchi Moralia*, BT (1967) 7:9; id. *Plutarch's Moralia*, LCL (1969) 15:26. The texts of the treatise used in this study are the Teubner edition of M. Pohlenz and W. Sieveking (1972) 3:332-346 and the LCL edition of P. De Lacy and B. Einarson (1959) 7:2-38.

money.[3] His contrast is between the possessions of the wealthy and those of modest means: οὐδὲν οὖν πλέον ἔχουσιν οἱ πλούσιοι τῶν μέτρια κεκτημένων (ch. 8, 527B). He concludes this part of the discussion with the thought that those with enough are just as wealthy as those who possess enormous riches. He says nothing in the treatise about the destitute.[4]

This attitude is, of course, an aristocratic one. It is as old as Homer [5] and provides a basis for literary themes and philosophical discussions in many authors, among whom we may single out Pindar,[6] Aristophanes,[7] Plato,[8] and Aristotle.[9] Indeed, so frequently does the subject appear in the writings of the latter two that the Loeb editors (p. 12) have fallen into a trap and say that "The governing ideas of the essay *On Love of Wealth* are Aristotelian, though the source is ultimately Plato."

This statement is misleading and incomplete. It does little more than give a specific example of Alfred North Whitehead's famous remark that "The safest general characterization of the European

---

[3] This omission is probably the strongest argument for a Platonic and Aristotelian basis for the treatise and against any strong Cynic-Stoic influence. Yet, despite the importance of this omission, other features of the treatise point directly to the diatribe. Perhaps Plutarch's chief contribution to the theme is his blending of Platonism, Aristotelianism with the Cynic and Stoic tradition.

[4] This statement is true even with the use of πενία (524E) and πένητες (527B). In the first passage Plutarch says that a man with an insatiable greed suffers from πενία ψυχική, and he contrasts this with πενία χρηματική from which a single friend can bring relief. In the latter passage, the comparison is between the rich and those of modest means, and πένητες is virtually equal to the Latin *pauperes*. Many passages in Latin literature use *pauper* in this sense, and one good example is the first Elegy of Tibullus (cf. vss. 1, 5, 19, 37), where the Augustan poet considers the meaning of the word so obvious that he sees no need to explain his use of it. But unless *pauper* refers to modest means, Tibullus first Elegy is nonsense, and it is not nonsense.

[5] E.g., *Il.* 2. 668-669; 16. 596; 24. 536, 546; *Od.* 14. 206; 24. 485-486.

[6] *Ol.* 2. 53-55; *Py.* 3. 107-111.

[7] The *Plutus* has many points of similarity with later discussions of wealth and may, in fact, have exerted more influence on subsequent literature than even the most avid Aristophanic scholars have realized.

[8] A very few examples must suffice: *R.* 1. 331B; *L.* 3. 679B; 4. 705B; 8. 831B-D. See also the references given by De Lacy and Einarson, 2, n. c; 3, n. b, etc.

[9] Again, a few examples must suffice: *Pol.* 1.3.18-19; 2.3.11; 6.19; *R.* 2.16 and, though it is certainly later than Aristotle, *VV* 6.7-7.12. See also De Lacy and Einarson, 2-4.

philosophical tradition is that it consists of a series of footnotes to Plato." [10]

Plutarch is a Platonist. Every critic has said so, but he is an eclectic Platonist.[11] He is also familiar with the writings of Aristotle, of the Cynics, Stoics, Epicureans, and indeed of many other philosophic sects. He criticizes when he disagrees, he borrows when he approves. One need only look at a list of his citations and quotations, his references and allusions, to the whole gamut of Greek philosophical thought to realize the vast scope of his acquaintance with all the traditions.[12]

In physics and religion Plutarch is more indebted to Plato and Aristotle than to any other system, but in ethics his debt is not so heavy. Ethics had, by Plutarch's day, absorbed many new ideas and had changed direction since Plato and Aristotle. The early Cynics and Stoics had sought to give their own explanations of Socrates' teachings, and in doing so they had frequently disagreed with the Platonic and Aristotelian developments. The later Cynics and Stoics, even the Epicureans, sought to clarify and amplify the teachings of their predecessors, and in the process a kind of syncretism took place.[13]

Many Platonic and Aristotelian concepts, however, met with approval and became a part of the teachings of the later sects. In particular, many of them survived in Stoicism even after Chrysippus, Panaetius and Posidonius. Sometimes the later philosophers retained the original terminology, sometimes they adopted new words. Occasionally, they introduced new variations, new points of emphasis, but much of Platonic and Aristotelian philosophy remained in the teachings of the Cynics and Stoics. All of these philosophers were, to repeat Whitehead's *dictum*, adding footnotes to Plato—and to Aristotle, who had himself provided the first set of footnote.[14]

Plutarch, then, a Platonist who is familiar with Aristotle and with the Cynics, Stoics and Epicureans, has perhaps added a few foot-

[10] *Process and Reality: An Essay in Cosmology* (New York, 1929) 63.

[11] See, for example, R. M. Jones, *The Platonism of Plutarch*, 7ff. and the discussion in n. 1 on p. 7; Dill, *Roman Society from Nero to Marcus Aurelius*, 399-401, 408-409, 414.

[12] See Helmbold and O'Neil, though this collection is far from complete.

[13] Rist, *Stoic Phil.*, 53ff.

[14] For a discussion of one example of this process see North, *Sophrosyne*, 151, 220-221.

notes of his own. Yet the style, the language, the themes, and, just as important, the writings of others with whom he has much in common,[15] point to the clear and unmistakable fact that the *cup. divit.* belongs to the tradition of the Cynic-Stoic diatribe.[16]

Consider first the style.[17] There is the use of an imaginary interlocutor (526A, F; 527A), direct address to the reader (525E), ἀλλά (526A) and ἄγε (525D) or φέρε (527B) to mark transitions, the ironic use of imperatives, hortatory subjunctives, rhetorical questions (523E; 524E, F; 525D; 527F), the use of athletic imagery (523C-D), the imagery of sin and sickness (523E, 524A-D).

The language of the treatise contains some Platonic and Aristotelian terms, but with few exceptions they are also a part of the Cynic and Stoic vocabulary. In particular, πάθος [18] and ἐπιθυμία,[19] which appear frequently in this treatise, are basic to Stoic philosophy and especially to the theories of Chrysippus.[20]

Although several definitions of πάθος appear in the Stoic fragments, at least one which both Zeno and Chrysippus give seems close to Plutarch's understanding of the term: ἡ ἄλογος καὶ παρὰ φύσιν ψυχῆς κίνησις (*SVF*, I, fr. 205, p. 50, 22-23) and ἄλογος ψυχῆς κίνησις καὶ παρὰ φύσιν (*SVF*, III, fr. 391, p. 95, 14-15). With these definitions compare Plutarch's observation (524C) where he describes the man who cannot drink enough and likens him to the man who cannot amass enough possessions. The parallelism in Plutarch's two statements is obvious, and the use of the same participle (ἐνοῦσα) at the end of each merely gives added emphasis. Taken together, the similarity of wording in the passage to Zeno and Chrysippus provides a clear example of the Stoic definition of πάθος.

---

[15] In addition to those discussed later see Teles 2, 4A-B.

[16] E. G. Berry, *Emerson's Plutarch*, 74ff. De Lacy and Einarson partially acknowledge the fact on p. 4. See also Ziegler's appraisal which is quoted below in n. 49. J. J. Hartmann (*De Plutarcho Scriptore et Philosopho*, 295) is so displeased with the attitude expressed in this treatise that he exclaims "Denique Stoicum hic habemus ἀρετάλογον, qui se Plutarchum esse simulat."

[17] For a more detailed discussion of the diatribe, its characteristics and themes, see *PECL* 1:303-305. For the imagery see F. Fuhrmann, *Les Images de Plutarque* (Paris, 1964) and see North, *Sophrosyne*, 380-384.

[18] The noun πάθος occurs in 524B, D, E, F; πάσχω in 524B.

[19] The noun ἐπιθυμία occurs in 523E, F; 524F; 525A, B; 526C, the verb ἐπιθυμέω in 524D. See also ὄρεξις in 523E, F; ὀρέγω in 524C.

[20] On πάθος in Stoicism see Rist, *Stoic Phil.*, 22ff., 37ff.; on ἐπιθυμία see Arnold, *Roman Stoicism*, 331-333, and *SVF*, III, pp. 92ff.; IV, p. 54.

Elsewhere (*SVF*, III, fr. 378, p. 92, 11ff.) Chrysippus connects πάθος and ἐπιθυμία by terming the latter one of the four-basic πάθη. Of course one meaning of ἐπιθυμία is sexual desire, and we find allusions to this idea in the *cup. divit.* (525A, D),[21] but Chrysippus follows Zeno in extending the term to other desires.[22] One such extension which is important to an understanding of Plutarch's treatise appears in *SVF*, III, frs. 394-395. Fr. 394 (p. 96, 3-6) says: ὑπὸ μὲν οὖν τὴν ἐπιθυμίαν ὑπάγεται τὰ τοιαῦτα· ὀργὴ καὶ τὰ εἴδη αὐτῆς . . . , ἔρωτες σφόδροι καὶ πόθοι καὶ ἵμεροι καὶ φιληδονίαι καὶ φιλοπλουτίαι καὶ φιλοδοξίαι καὶ τὰ ὅμοια. And fr. 395 (p. 96, 20f.) defines φιλοπλουτία as ἐπιθυμία πλούτου.

The vocabulary of these definitions is interesting. The word πλοῦτος means "wealth" and occurs many times in Stoic fragments, and Chrysippus himself uses it on numerous occasions. Such words as πλεονεξία, ἀπληστία, αἰσχροκέρδεια, φιλοχρηματία and φιλαργυρία are common in most periods and genres of Greek literature as terms for "greed," "avarice," and the like. Yet for this common idea Chrysippus has chosen to include in his definition φιλοπλουτία, a very rare word.[23]

According to LSJ, φιλοπλουτία appears first in Plutarch, but this is, of course, an error since Chrysippus uses the word in the two fragments quoted above.[24] Yet it seems not to occur anywhere else in Greek literature except Chrysippus and Plutarch. Our author, however, uses the word twenty-eight times, almost equally

[21] See also the erotic vocabulary in 524F, 525B. In ECL the most extended passage in probably Herm Man 12, esp. 12:2:1-3.

[22] See esp. fr. 397 (*SVF*, III, pp. 96-97).

[23] Though, interestingly enough, πλεονεξία does not appear in *SVF*, and πλεονεκτέω appears only once (fr. 548, III, p. 147, 13); ἀπληστία and φιλοκέρδεια are missing, and both φιλοχρηματία (fr. 397, III, p. 97, 15) and αἰσχροκέρδεια (fr. 672, III, p. 168, 14) are limited to a single occurrence each, and the latter is actually in a passage of Plutarch (*Stoic repug.* ch. 25, 1046C). On the other hand, φιλαργυρία appears three times (fr. 104, III, p. 25, 17; fr. 421, III, p. 102, 39; fr. 456, III, p. 110, 39). The other examples which von Arnim lists are in Latin where Cicero has used *avaritia*. We cannot be certain, however, either that Cicero is translating Chrysippus or, if he is, that *avaritia* represents φιλαργυρία. But cf. *SVF*, IV, p. 169.

[24] Nor has the Supplement caught the omission. One may, of course, argue that Stobaeus, who is our source for both fragments and who was familiar with Plutarch's writings, inserted a Plutarchan term when he reported Chrysippus' discussion. The substitution is, however, most unlikely in passages as precisely worded as both fragments appear to be. Besides, LSJ often lists a word of Chrysippus as occurring in another author, and that is the way in which it should have treated φιλοπλουτία.

divided between the *Moralia* [25] and the *Lives*.[26] Its usual meanine in these passages [27] agrees in large measure with its use in the *cup. divit.*, and several passages, notably *Crass.* 543C, help to explain, or at least serve as interesting parallels to, its use here.

The adjective φιλόπλουτος appears first in Euripides (*IT* 411, but apparently not again until Plutarch.[28] He uses it three times (*conjug. praec.*, *Galba* 1053A, and as a neuter substantive in *sen. resp.* 793E). Elsewhere it appears only in Lucian's *De domo* Ch. 5, a passage which contains some common themes of the diatribe.[29] The verb φιλοπλουτέω is even rarer. Again according to LSJ,[30] it occurs only in this treatise (524F) where it is an articular infinitive.

Thus Plutarch's use of these words, as well as πάθος, ἐπιθυμία, etc., is a strong indication that he has used Stoic terminology in the *cup. divit.* This is the second proof of the Cynic-Stoic nature of the work.

The themes provide a third proof. Wealth had of course been a regular theme in Greek literature long before Plutarch. It was still popular in his world and persists today.[31] Furthermore, early

---

[25] In this treatise it appears in 523E; 524C; 525B, E; 526D (and of course in the title as well as in no. 211 of the Lamprias Catalogue). Elsewhere in the *Moralia*: *prof. virt.* 85E; *Lacon.* 239F; *num. vind.* 556B; *gen. Soc.* 584F; 585B, C; *praec. reip.* 806F; 819E.

[26] In the *Lives* it appears in *Lyc.* 58B; *Sol.* 89B; *Tim.* 277A; *Lys.* 434C; *Luc.* 502D, 514E; *Crass.* 543C (three times), 551D; *Cat. Mi.* 784F; *Agis and Cleom.* 801A; *Cic.* 887D; *Demetr.* 904C.

[27] Yet several Loeb translators, including De Lacy and Einarson, frequently treat the word as if it were one of the standard terms for avarice and greed.

[28] In an admittedly hasty search, I have found no commentator on this play who remarks on the apparent rarity of the word.

[29] Several passages in the *Dom.* resemble, or at least on the surface seem to exemplify, Plutarch's discussion of the lavish use of wealth (chs. 8-10, 527A-528B): ch. 3 where Lucian refers to Telemachus and his wonderment of Menelaüs' palace in much the same way as Plutarch does (527E-F). The verbal similarity of the two passages is remarkable and not entirely due to the Homeric origin (*Od.* 4. 71-75).

In ch. 5 Lucian's words ἀλλ' ἦν βαρβαρικὸν τὸ θέαμα, πλοῦτος μόνον καὶ φθόνος τῶν ἰδόντων καὶ εὐδαιμονισμὸς τῶν ἐχόντων are closely akin to the plea of Scopas (527C-D) and to the message of the whole concluding section of Plutarch's treatise. The similarities are almost certainly due to Cynic influence upon both compositions.

[30] So far as Plutarch is concerned, LSJ is correct, for this is the only entry for the word in the *Index Verborum Plutarcheus*.

[31] See F. Hauck and W. Kasch, *TDNT*, s.v. πλοῦτος. For an easily accessible list of works and passages which deal with wealth as a major theme see *Great Books of the Western World* (Chicago, 1952), vol. 3, s.v. Wealth.

writers naturally associated wealth with certain attendant "faults," among which were greed, miserliness, prodigality and ambition.[32] Yet the poets, dramatists and even Plato, Aristotle and their followers were content to treat one fault, or at most two, at a time.[33] It was not until the Stoics turned their attention to the subject that anything like a canon of faults caused by wealth was developed.[34]

The scanty remains of Stoic writings, especially in the period following Chrysippus, and the resulting scholarly disagreements over the meaning of what little is left, makes it virtually impossible to identify the men or even the period responsible for the development of such a canon of faults. Yet the fact remains that the canon does not appear in the Stoic fragments collected by von Arnim, but as early as the first century B.C. it emerges fully developed.

Our evidence for the canon's existence is Horace's *S.* 2.3.[35] In this poem,[36] Horace introduces a bore named Damasippus, who regales the poet with a long sermon which the Stoic Stertinius had recently delivered. The main idea of the sermon, and the point which Horace ridicules, is the Stoic paradox that everyone except the wise man is mad. To demonstrate the paradox Stertinius, in the person of Damasippus, first identifies the faults caused by wealth (vss. 77-80) and then discusses them one by one. First is

[32] A more detailed discussion of the points made in this section appears in the unpublished dissertation of R. C. Barrett, *Tibullus I: Theme and Technique* (Univ. of Southern California, 1974) 101-142.

[33] The following list cites only a very few examples from a limited number of the more important authors. Wealth and Greed: Hesiod, *Op.* 27-41, 311-341; Aristophanes, *Pl.*, esp. 454-626; Plato, *L.* 3. 679B; 4. 705B; 8. 831B-D; 11. 919B; Aristotle, *Pol.* 1. 318; 2.4.11. Wealth and miserliness: Aristotle, *Pol.* 1.3. 18-19; *EN* 2.7.4; 4.1. 37-44; Theophrastus, *Char.* 10 and 30. Wealth and prodigality: Plato, *R.* 8. 560E; *Alc.* 1. 122B-124B; Aristotle, *Pol.* 1.3. 18-19; *EN* 4.1.5; 4.1. 29-36. Wealth and ambition: Plato, *R.* 1. 347B; Aristotle, *Pol.* 2.6. 19; *EN* 4.4. 1-6.

The nearest any of these passages comes to a discussion of a canon of faults is Aristotle, *Pol.* 1.3. 18-19. With this passage cf. *Rh.* 2.16. 1-4.

[34] W. S. Anderson may have been the first to use the word "canon" in connection with the group of faults in his Introduction to *The Satires of Persius*, trans. by W. S. Merwin (Bloomington, 1961) 32. See also Arnold, *Roman Stoicism*, 330, for a canon of "sinful conditions."

[35] The Stoic influence on this poem is obvious, but there is also Cynic influence. In fact, Horace himself refers to his satiric writings as *Bionei sermones* (*Ep.* 1.2.60), and in *S.* 2.3 he ridicules Stoic principles in the spirit of the diatribe.

[36] For an analysis of this poem cf. N. Rudd, *The Satires of Horace: A Study* (London, 1966) 173-178. See also Barrett, *Tibullus* I, 106-111.

avaritia, in the longest section (vss. 82-157);[37] next is *ambitio,* i.e., "ambition" (vss. 165-223); then *luxuria,* i.e., "prodigality", "showiness," etc. (vss. 224-280); and finally *superstitio,* i.e., "superstition." [38] These are the faults, the *scelera,* which result directly from wealth, and they occur when man's reason falls prey to *divitiae* (vss. 94-96). Thus *divitiae* and the improper use of it are the cause of human crime and madness. These faults are also diseases (vs. 80), as they are termed by Plutarch as well.

The theme of *divitiae* appears in another poem which is more similar to Plutarch's *cup. divit.* than Horace's poem. Juvenal's *Sat.* 14, in fact, bears a remarkable resemblance to Plutarch's treatise, and more remarkable than the resemblance is the failure of most critics to see it.

The structure of this poem is like that of several other satires of Juvenal in that it has two major sections which are unequal in length and, at first glance, unrelated.[39] The first section (vss.

[37] The section on *avaritia* is longest for two reasons: it is the deadliest of the faults, and the Latin word represents two faults: greed and miserliness.

[38] Superstition has a curious history and a precarious place in the canon. Neither Plato nor Aristotle associated it with wealth, and even the word δεισιδαιμονία, which later became the standard term for this irrational attitude, did not have a pejorative meaning. For a contrary view, however, see H. A. Moellering, *Plutarch on Superstition* (Boston, 1962) 45-46 where he discusses Aristotle, *Pol.* 5.9.15.

The earliest extant use of δεισιδαιμονία with the meaning "superstition" seems to be in Theophrastus' *Char.* 16. For a discussion of this passage see R. G. Ussher, *The Characters of Theophrastus* (London, 1960) 135-136. After Theophrastus, the Stoics frequently discussed superstition, as even the scanty fragments show, and δεισιδαιμονία was the regular term. In none of the fragments, however, are wealth and superstition associated.

Yet the connection had already been made in the third century, for it appears in the writings of the Cynic Teles. In fr. 4A ("On Poverty and Wealth") he says (p. 39 of Hense's text) that the man who suffers from greed "could never be satisfied, since he is insatiable, thirsting for fame and superstitious." Later (p. 41), "But once you have made yourself pretentious, extravagant, superstitious, athirst for fame, insatiable, you will accomplish nothing even if you spend a lot of money."

In the first passage Teles quotes Bion, and he probably uses the same source in the second. We have already seen that Horace was influenced by Bion, and it is reasonable to assume that the early Cynic is responsible for associating wealth and superstition, at least in Teles and Horace.

There is, however, no such association in Plutarch's *cup. divit.*, or in his *superst.* Yet in the *num. vind.* ch. 11, 556B φιλοπλουτία is the cause of many faults, including δεισιδαιμονία, and this passage concludes with the same general subject as the *cup. divit.*, i.e., ostentation.

[39] For a more detailed analysis of this poem see my article in *CPh* 55 (1960) 251-253.

1-106) deals with the general topic that "Parents teach their children harmful precepts." Among these precepts are gambling, gluttony, cruelty, adultery, wantonness, moral uncleanliness, extravagance and superstition.[40]

At this point Juvenal introduces a lengthy discussion of the most dangerous vice which a parent can teach his son. It is *avaritia*, and consideration of this vice constitutes the second and longer section of the poem (vss. 107-316), which then concludes with a short epilogue (vss. 316-331). The first part of the second section (vss. 107-172) deals with the nature and dangers of *avaritia*, and Juvenal develops the argument in accordance with the double meaning of the word, i.e., greed and miserliness. He shows that the parent by his own actions teaches both vices to his son, and in good Juvenalian fashion embellishes his arguments with interesting and rhetorically powerful examples.

After this argument, he addresses himself to the idea that *avaritia* leads to other vices (vss. 173-255). Among them are excessive ambition, dishonesty, robbery and cheating, and patricide. He concludes the section by pointing out the dangers of acquiring wealth and the difficulties in retaining it. After this discussion comes the epilogue in which he asks "How much money is enough?" and then gives a good Cynic-Stoic answer, "Enough to satisfy nature."

This outline, long as it seems, does not do justice to Juvenal's splendid poem. It does not show the wealth of vivid detail, the clever turns of phrase, the biting wit and keen insight into human emotions. What does appear, however, is the large number of themes which the satirist has taken from the Cynic-Stoic tradition on wealth and its attendant faults.

Moreover, the many points of similarity and even agreement between themes and expressions in Juvenal's poem and Plutarch's *cup. divit.* demonstrate clearly that both authors had access to the same, or at least similar, sources.[41] Furthermore, Juvenal used

[40] In the section on superstition appears Juvenal's famous, or infamous, attack on Jews. To the Roman satirist such religious observances seemed foreign, unnatural and excessive, hence examples of superstition.

[41] For example, 523F = 140ff.; 524C-D = 135ff.; 524D-E = 140ff.; 524F = 284ff.; 526C = 170ff.; 526D = 107ff. and 250ff.; 526E = 303-316; 527B = 316-331. And there are many more points of agreement which a more detailed study of the two works could identify.

these sources in other satires,[42] and Plutarch used them in other treatises.[43] And, to repeat once again, these sources belong to the Cynic-Stoic tradition.

Now we may at last turn to an examination of the *cup. divit.* De Lacy and Einarson (p. 4) seem to fall short of the mark when they introduce their brief and unsatisfactory resumé of the treatise with the words "The plan is simple." The plan is not simple. It is complicated and in some places rather curious.[44] Yet a structural outline [45] shows the unity of the composition: [46]

I. *Exordium* (ch. 1, 523C8-D3)
   A. Some people wrongly judge wealth by its outward show and consider lavish possessions as blessings. They are right only if happiness can be bought (523C8-D13).
   B. Some prefer to be rich and wretched rather than spend their money and be happy (523D14-D2).
   C. But money cannot buy those qualities of the soul which constitute true happiness (523D2-3).

[42] One striking example must suffice. In 526C Plutarch says τοσούτου νόμιζε σεαυτὸν ἄξιον ὅσον ἂν ἔχῃς. Juvenal's version is *quantum quisque sua nummorum servat in arca/tantum habet in fidei*. The Latin seems to be a translation, or at least a paraphrase, of the Greek. Yet the same basic idea appears in Horace (*S.* 1.1.62; 2.6.7-8) and in Lucilius (fr. 119. 4-5). Clearly the expression is a *topos*, and the authors who use it have all been influenced by the Cynics and Stoics.

[43] Several passages in Plutarch's *lib. ed.* and *cohib. ira* closely resemble sections in Juvenal's *Sat.* 14. See the commentary of J. E. B. Mayor, vol. 2, 288-289, etc. A worthwhile study could be made on the many verbal and thematic parallels between these two contemporaries who were influenced by much the same material.

[44] Ziegler, in fact, believes that the composition is incomplete (sec. III.4.h. [cols. 143, 13ff.]), but he is almost certainly wrong. There are a few minor lacunae, but ch. 10 is clearly intended to return the subject to its starting point in ch. 1 and thus round off the whole discussion. Ziegler is not wrong, however, when he says that "Cynic influence is equally strong in the intellectual and stylistic formulation" and "For individual thoughts here and there Aristotle and Theophrastus are used and cited, and Plato and Epicurus are alluded to."

[45] A more detailed summary, however, is needed to explain Plutarch's thoughts, techniques and imagery. This summary appears in the second section of the paper and forms the basis for the discussion of parallel passages in ECL.

[46] Because of a need to pin-point the place where one section ends and another begins, the references here and in the second part of the paper are to the Teubner text. The number which follows the Frankfort page and section refers to the line on the Teubner page, e.g., 526C14 refers to Teubner *Moralia* 3:340, line 14 where a verse of Euripides appears.

II. *Propositio* (chs. 1-3, 523D4-524D12)
  A. Despising wealth is not inherent in being wealthy, nor is the lack of needing luxuries inherent in the possession of luxuries (523D4-5).
  B. Wealth does not relieve the love of wealth (523E6-11).
  C. Wealth worsens the disease, i.e., the love of wealth (523E11-524D12).
    1. One type of sufferer: Those in need of life's necessities who have their appetites diverted to luxuries (523E11-524A10).
    2. Second type of sufferer: Those who spend nothing, have much, and want everything. In the end they lose everything (524A10-D12).

III. *Expositio* (chs. 4-5, 524D13-526A22)
  A. Desire for wealth is "mental poverty" (524D13-E8).
  B. Love of wealth fights against its own fulfillment (524E8-525B11).
  C. Types of love of wealth (525B11-526A22).
    1. Prodigals and misers = ant-like and ass-like love of wealth (525B11-E3).
    2. Bestial love of wealth (525E4-526A22).

IV. *Exhortatio* (chs. 7-9, 526A23-527F20).
  A. Denunciation of misers (526A23-527A12).
  B. Denunciation of prodigals (527A13-F20).

V. *Peroratio* (ch. 10, 527F21-528B3)
  A. The so-called happiness of wealth is one of spectators and witnesses or it is nothing (527F21-22).
  B. How different are self-mastery, philosophy and knowing what is necessary about the gods (527F22-528A9).
  C. With no one to watch, wealth becomes truly blind (528A9-B3).
    1. Example of wealthy man and wife who dine simply when alone but extravagantly when they have guests (528A9-B2).
    2. But self-mastery is necessary whether one dines alone or at a feast (528B2-3).

This outline does not point up Plutarch's use of the canon of faults discussed earlier, but they are here. Greed (πλεονεξία, φιλαργυρία, φιλοπλουτία) is the central idea of the whole treatise, but it occurs specifically in ch. 2 (523E-F); ch. 3 (524C-D); ch. 4 (524D-E); ch. 5 (525B-C) where greed and miserliness are closely associated; ch. 6 (526A); ch. 7 (526C-D).

Miserliness (μικρολογία, ἀνελευθερία) is next. It occurs in ch. 3 (524A-B); ch. 4 (524F-525A); ch. 5 (525B-C) where it is closely associated with Greed; 525E; ch. 7 (526A-527A).

Prodigality, extravagance, ostentation (τρυφή, περιττά, ἄχρηστα) is third. This fault receives more attention and consumes more space than any other item in the canon, and it is the subject which both opens and concludes the treatise. In fact, it occurs in every chapter except 5-6, but the chief passages are ch. 1 (523D-E); ch. 2 (523F-524A); ch. 3 (524B, D); ch. 4 (524D-E); ch. 7 (526E); the whole of chs. 8-10 (527A-528D).

Ambition (φιλοτιμία) is limited to two chapters: ch. 5 (525C-E); ch. 6 (525E-526A). Even in these passages ambition is so closely bound with other faults that one has difficulty in isolating it. Yet it is present as the examples which involve politicians and their motivations for public life clearly demonstrate.

The omission of superstition [47] (δεισιδαιμονία) from the *cup. divit.* cannot alter the fact that Plutarch used certain writings which dealt with the theme of wealth and its effects on people. These writings, as we have said repeatedly, belonged to the Cynic-Stoic tradition. All of the discussion in the past few pages point in this direction. The style of the *cup. divit.*, its language and themes all point to the same conclusion.

Furthermore, the close relationship between the themes of Plutarch and such writers as Bion, Teles, Horace, and Juvenal, each of whom was either a Cynic or under Cynic influence, is significant. Especially significant is the similarity of Plutarch and Juvenal. These men were contemporaries, with Plutarch being a few years older than the satirist.[48] There is no hint that the two men knew one another, but they were in Rome at the same time. Both knew many men of importance in the capitol,[49] and both

---

[47] For a brief discussion of superstition see n. 38 above.

[48] C. P. Jones (*Plutarch and Rome* [Oxford, 1971] 135-137) dates Plutarch's birth between A.D. 40-45 and his death around A.D. 120. G. Highet (*Juvenal the Satirist* [Oxford, 1954] 40-41) puts Juvenal's birth around A.D. 60, but I am inclined to agree with those who prefer an earlier date, sometime between A.D. 50 and 55. Most agree that he was dead by A.D. 131.

[49] Another interesting study could be made on the circles of friends which each man had with a view toward discovering which men, if any, were

had access to the same general sources of information. And Juvenal, for all his expressed hatred of foreigners in general and of Greeks in particular, knew the Greek language well and was acquainted with a vast amount of its literature.

Moreover, in the first and second centuries after Christ, as in earlier eras, the roads that led to Rome brought men and ideas from every corner of the Empire. Indeed, Plutarch himself is representative of this influx. In the capitol, philosophic discussion was a favorite pasttime of the aristocratic society if we can trust the evidence of Plutarch and the younger Pliny. Plutarch describes scenes in his *qu. conv.* which make it apparent that dinner parties offered ample opportunities for discussing any aspect of philosophy that appealed to the host and his guests. And Pliny often refers to similar dinner parties in his letters.[50]

There was another element at work during this period. A revival of Cynicism took place in Rome in the first century after Christ and continued well into the second century.[51] The wandering, and often beggarly, Cynic preachers filled lecture halls and occupied many street-corners as they proclaimed their message of simplicity and self-sufficiency. Yet not all of these messengers of a new morality were ragged and ridiculous, nor was their message accepted only by the non-rich.

Some of them found willing ears among the nobility and drew the attention of the Emperor himself. One of these Cynics was Demetrius, who had the opportunity to scorn Caligula's offer of 200,000 sesterces. More famous than Demetrius is Dio Chrysostom, who fell into disfavor with Domitian but eventually became a friend of Trajan. Then there are those philosophers who are generally classed with the Stoics but who are nearly as much Cynic: Musonius

---

friends of both authors. C. P. Jones, op. cit., 48-64, discusses Plutarch's friends at Rome, and clearly many of them were in positions of authority and were friends of the younger Pliny and Tacitus (cf. Dill, *Roman Society from Nero to Marcus Aurelius*, 402). Juvenal, however, seems not to have been so fortunate. His friends, with certain exceptions, belonged to a lower order. In particular, if Highet's theory (op. cit., 292-294) is correct, the satirist was a bitter foe of Pliny and those associated with him. Thus he could easily have known, or at least known of, Plutarch and disdained him because of his association with Pliny's friends. Perhaps he even had such men as Plutarch in mind when he composed his famous tirade against the whole Greek race (*Sat.* 3. 58ff.).

[50] For an excellent description of the mood and atmosphere of Rome in the period see Dill, op. cit., 401ff.

[51] Cf. D. R. Dudley, *A History of Cynicism*, 125-201.

Rufus, Epictetus, Seneca, and finally Favorinus. This interesting personality was a friend of Dio and Plutarch, a teacher of Herodes Atticus, Gellius and Fronto, who was himself a teacher of the young Marcus Aurelius. He was also on friendly terms with Hadrian and his successor Antoninus Pius.

All of these men were a part of the Cynic-Stoic resurgence which began shortly before Plutarch and Juvenal were born and which continued to gather momentum throughout their lifetime. This movement profoundly influenced the intellectual life of the capitol as well as many centers of culture throughout the Empire. Many people were sceptical of its teachings, for asceticism cannot often be popular among the prosperous. Yet many approved, and many writers used the doctrines in their own works. Two such men were Plutarch and Juvenal, so we need not be surprised that these two authors agree so often. It would be surprising if they did not agree.

The revitalized Cynic-Stoic teachings had a lasting effect on another movement which began at about the same time, i.e., Christianity.[52] For, despite clear evidence that Hellenistic Greek philosophy had already left its mark on Jewish literature,[53] and by this route influenced ECL, the fact remains that the earliest Christian writers and their Jewish compatriots lived in the same regions where the roving pagan teachers were proclaiming their message.

In such places as Alexandria, Antioch, Ephesus, Tarsus, Bithynia, Achaea, even Athens and numerous other centers of commerce and learning, Jews and Christians addressed their message to much the same audience as heard the Cynic and Stoic preachers. One can easily imagine that the audiences could not always discern, from physical appearance, one wandering preacher from another.

To Rome, in particular, many of these men brought their message and met with a similar reception. The Greek philosophers aroused

---

[52] There is no intention here of doing more than identifying the general relationship between the Judeo-Christian tradition and the one special area of Greek philosophy with which this study is concerned. Anything more is quite beyond the plan of the study and the knowledge of the author.

[53] Obvious examples are Sirach, Maccabees and Philo. See Th. Middendorp, *Die Stellung Jesu ben Siras zwischen Judentum und Hellenismus* (Leiden, 1973); H. A. Fischel, *Rabbinic Literature and Greco-Roman Philosophy* (Leiden, 1973); P. Wendland, "Philo und die kynisch-stoische Diatribe," in: P.Wendland and O. Kern, *Beiträge zur Geschichte der griechischen Philosophie* (Berlin, 1895).

the ire of more than one Emperor,[54] and the suspicion which their Jewish and Christian counterparts encountered is well attested.[55] Yet the Cynic-Stoic tradition was already so familiar to the Greeks and Romans that these new teachers could be understood even if their words did not always meet with approval. Such was not the case with the Jews and Christians.

The fervor of their strange religious concepts often repelled the Greeks and Romans. They became suspicious and contemptuous of both Jews and Christians, whom, as often as not, they failed to distinguish. Such suspicion and contempt prevented most Greeks and Romans from learning much about these foreign religons. The result is that the pagan writings of the first century A.D. show very few references to Jewish and Christian matters, and those few are frequently confused and usually hostile.[56]

For their part, the Christians, or at least their leaders, learned a great deal about Greek philosophy. These men soon realized that, while emotional appeal could win converts from the lower classes, something more was needed to gain the attention and respect of the educated upper classes. This realization, whether or not it was as deliberate as these sentences suggest, turned Christian writers to pagan ethics, especially those of the Cynics and Stoics, and caused a fusing of Christian religious teaching and the Greek philosophic tradition.

Still, during the years with which this study is concerned, the fusion was, so to speak, a one-way street. The Christians absorbed much of Greek philosophy, the Greeks learned very little about Christianity. Nor was Plutarch an exception. For all he tells us, he

---

[54] For a brief summary of the relationship between Emperors and philosophers during this period see Dudley, *A History of Cynicism*, 125ff. On the philosophic missionary see Dill, op. cit., 334ff.

[55] See, for example, B. H. Streeter, "The Rise of Christianity," in *CAH*, 11:253ff. and the bibliography listed there. See also A. Momigliano, "Nero," in *CAH*, 10:725ff. and 887-888 for a discussion of the Neronian persecution.

[56] Cf. Dill, *Roman Society from Nero to Marcus Aurelius*, vii: "The pagan world of that age (i.e., from Nero to Marcus Aurelius) seems to have had little communication with the loftier faith which, within a century and a half from the death of M. Aurelius, was destined to seize the sceptre. To Juvenal, Tacitus, and Pliny, to Plutarch, Dio Chrysostom, Lucian, and M. Aurelius, the church is hardly known, or known as an obscure off-shoot of Judaism, a little sect, worshipping a 'crucified Sophist' in somewhat suspicious retirement, or more favorably distinguished by simple-minded charity."

never heard of Christ, or Peter, Paul, or any other Christian for that matter. Yet this cannot have been the case.

He visited many of the cities and regions where Christianity was beginning to exert pressure, and he was in touch with many people who were themselves not unaware of the new movement. In addition, Plutarch was an intellectually curious man. He was interested in the customs and beliefs of many peoples: not only the Greek and Romans, but the Egyptians, Syrians, Persians, etc. He knew about the worship of Mithra, of Isis and Osiris and was interested enough to write about them.

He was himself a priest at Delphi and again was interested enough in Delphic traditions to write several compositions on the subject. He was a deeply religious man, and this fact has affected much of his writing, for he frequently concludes his moral treatises with an application of his theme to religious thought.[57] Yet it is this same Plutarch whose curiosity, for some reason or other, seems not to have extended to Christianity.

We can only speculate on the reasons for this apathy. His training in Greek philosophy, his own aristocratic learning, his friendship with many men from the upper classes of Greek and Roman society, the imperial attitude toward Christianity, even in the reign of Trajan,[58] his constantly looking back into history for moral precepts and guidance—all these things made him, if not blind, at least impervious to the new religion. Whatever the reason for his silence, the fact remains that he is silent. And in this case, silence indicates a lack of knowledge, if not total ignorance.[59]

Thus any point of agreement or even similarity between Plutarch's theology and ethics and those of early Christianity must be either accidental or the result of a common influence. We cannot rule out an occasional coincidence of expression or thought, but the similarities are too numerous to be the result of coincidence alone.

[57] Cf. Betz on *tranq. an.* in this volume, p. 203 and n. 40. Plutarch follows the same pattern here in the *cup. divit.*: cf. ch. 10, 527F-528A.

[58] Cf. Pliny's *Epistle* 10.96. There is no reason to suppose that the situation in Bithynia which Pliny describes was unique or that Pliny was any more hostile and strict than other Roman governors. Indeed, Trajan's reply to Pliny (10.97) shows that the official policy was one of firm control but not aggressive prosecution.

[59] Yet, as Dill (see n. 56) has pointed out, this silence is not unique to Plutarch. Whatever the cause, it was wide-spread among both Greeks and Romans.

Platonic and Aristotelian philosophy had a great influence upon both Plutarch and the early Christian writers, but in the case of the *cup. divit.* Cynic and Stoic influence is, as we have seen, more important and accounts for the largest number of parallels with ECL. Consequently, it is no accident that in the pages that follow we find that Plutarch's treatise has more in common with those compositions of ECL which are themselves most influenced by the Cynics and Stoics: e.g., the Pastoral Epistles, James, Hermas and the epistles of Ignatius. Even in the Gospels, Acts, Paul's epistles, etc. the same common element seems to account for many striking similarities of thought and expression.

II. Plutarch's Treatise and ECL [60]

Exordium A (ch. 1, 523C8-D13)

The trainer Hippomachus, when some people praised a man as being a likely boxer because he was tall and had big hands, said "certainly, if he must take down the crown after it has been hung up." So, too, we may say to those overly impressed by the showy objects of wealth and consider them blessings, "Yes, if it were necessary to buy happiness."

Like many a good writer before and many after him, Plutarch begins the *cup. divit.* with a statement designed to capture the reader's attention. One such opening in the NT is John 1:1. It is brief, provocative and tantalizing. A different type of opening but one that is, in its own way, equally effective appears in Herm Vis 1:1. Here the author presents a brief piece of apparent autobiographical information in such a way that we want to read on, and only later do we begin to understand the importance of the opening sentences to the theme of the whole work.

In the same way, Plutarch opens with the remark of Hippomachus about the outward appearance and inner qualities of a boxer.[61] We see immediately how he uses this idea to introduce

[60] In this part of the discussion the main divisions of the outline (see Introduction) are used, but more detail is given.

[61] Hippomachus appears elsewhere. Plutarch refers to him in *Dio* 958C which is also an introductory passage. He says that the trainer could recognize his pupils from a distance even though they were only carrying meat from the market-place. Plutarch compares this distinctiveness with that of men in public life who had, like Dion and Brutus, been trained in Platonic philosophy and bore witness to the doctrine of their teacher in virtue. Thus, in both passages we have an implied comparison between the demeanor of

his discussion of φιλοπλουτία, but not until we have read the whole treatise can we appreciate the significance of the trainer's words to the theme. In a sense, they are the theme, for the central message of the *cup. divit.* is that the outward show of wealth is nothing compared with the inner worth of a person.

Plutarch's choice of imagery in the opening section is interesting but hardly unique. It appears in compositions of every period and every genre, lending artistic color and providing a basis for moral instruction. Plutarch himself uses athletic imagery some one hundred and twenty-nine times in different contexts and discussions.[62] It is obviously one of his favorite subjects for imagery.

In ECL the situation is somewhat different. With few exceptions (e.g., Luke 13:24; 16:16) only Paul, for whom ἀγών had a special significance, uses athletic imagery.[63] And of all the passages in the Pauline writings, the closest parallel to Plutarch's version is 1 Cor 9:24-27. Not only do vss. 26-27 represent the only reference to boxing in the NT, but, more importantly, the prize is a στέφανος which is compared, or contrasted, to a greater prize.[64] Paul's words seem to lie behind 1 Clem 5, for vs. 5 may be a partial quotation of 1 Cor 9:24, as the use of βραβεῖον suggests.[65] Other passages in ECL which use athletic imagery are 2 Clem 7:1-5; Ign Pol 1:2-3; 2:1-3; Herm Man 12:3.[66]

---

an athlete and the proper conduct of living, and Hippomachus is the example in both cases.

The same trainer appears in a couple of anecdotes reported by Athenaeus in 13, 584C. Despite the frivolous nature of both, it seems clear that Athenaeus found these anecdotes in a context or series of contexts which somehow associated this particular trainer with the proper course of conduct. Thus both Plutarch and Athenaeus use Hippomachus in a similar fashion, one for a serious purpose, one in a light-hearted way. In both passages, the flavor of the narrative is Cynic.

[62] According to Fuhrmann, *Les Images de Plutarque*, 48-49.

[63] Cf. E. Stauffer, *TDNT* 1:134, s.v. ἀγών; Pfitzner, *Paul and the Agon Motif: Traditional Athletic Imagery in the Pauline Literature*.

[64] The style of these verses, from the opening words οὐκ οἴδατε, through the mixed metaphors of running and "shadow-boxing," to the personal application of the theme, is that of the diatribe. Thus Paul's passage belongs to the same tradition as Plutarch's. For a discussion of 1 Cor 9:24-27 see H. Conzelmann, *1 Corinthians* (Philadelphia, 1975) 161-163 and the notes.

[65] This relationship is the more probable because βραβεῖον is used only four times in ECL, according to Bauer. The other two passages are Phil 3:14 and Mart Pol 17:1, both of which use athletic imagery.

[66] The subject of this brief diatribe is ἐπιθυμία, and there will be many occasions in this study to refer to Herm Man 12, for it is one of the most important passages of ECL for a comparison of Plutarch's *cup. divit.* and its relationship with Christian ideas about wealth.

Plutarch's use of χωρία and οἰκίαι as symbols of wealth is a popular one in ECL. The combination of the two words occurs in Acts 4:34, and combinations of comparable terms (e.g., ἀγροὶ καὶ οἰκήσεις, ἀγροὶ καὶ οἰκία) are abundant in Herm Sim 1:1-9. Even alone χωρία is a symbol of wealth in Acts 5:1-11; 28:7.

For examples where people are overly smitten with wealth and possessions cf. Matt 19:16-24//Mark 10:17-25//Luke 18:18-25; and see again Acts 5:1-11. For a similar idea cf. Herm Sim 9:20:1-3, and for a warning against such an attitude cf. Jas 2:2. The notion that outward show brings happiness occurs in ECL more by implication than direct statement, and of course the implied notion is consistently attacked. See, for example, Luke 6:24 (cf. 12:13-21); 16:19-31 with 16:15. See also Matt 13:22//Mark 4:19//Luke 8:14; Herm Sim 1:1-11; 6:2:1-4.

The idea that wealth cannot buy happiness does not, surprisingly, appear in ECL.[67] Even the vocabulary of the phrase is foreign, with only the use of εὐδαιμονέω in Diogn 10:5 being a parallel to the basic idea. In fact, the only example in ECL of anyone attempting to buy an abstraction is the story of Simon the magician, who wants to buy the power of the Holy Spirit: Acts 8:9-24.

A few scattered words of Plutarch's opening and their parallels in ECL need to be listed:

καλός, meaning "fine," "precious," "showy": Matt 13:45; Luke 21:5; Herm Sim 1:10.

μέγας, used to describe a structure in a pejorative way: Mark 13:2.[68] The phrase πύργον μέγαν in Herm Vis 3:2:4 is not a parallel, for it describes the Church which will not be destroyed.

πολύς, in connection with χρῆμα, etc.: Matt 19:22//Mark 10:22; Herm Sim 1:3; cf. τὸ πολύ in 2 Cor 8:15; for the comparative cf. Matt 20:10; Mark 12:43; Luke 7:23; 21:3. For τὸ πλέον cf. Luke 7:43.

ὑπερεκπλήσσω: not in ECL. The simpler verb ἐκπλήσσω is frequent, but it usually expresses a reaction to the teachings of Jesus: e.g., Matt 7:28; 19:25; 22:23; Mark 1:22; 11:18; Luke 4:32; Acts 13:12. Cf. Barn 16:10. See also Luke 9:43; Barn 7:10.

---

[67] Nor, for that matter, is it common in Greek literature. See, however, Democritus, fr. B. 171 (Diels-Kranz II. 179.1-2): εὐδαιμονίη οὐκ ἐν βοσκήμασιν οἰκεῖ οὐδ' ἐν χρυσῷ. With this idea cf. Eccl 6:1-2; Sir 14:5. And see Philo, *spec. leg.* 1.23.

[68] Of the two parallel passages, Matt 24:1 has only τὰς οἰκοδομάς, and Luke 21:5 omits even the noun and uses ταῦτα instead.

μακάριος, in connection with wealth, etc.: cf. perhaps the Beatitudes, esp. Matt 5:3.

εὐδαιμονία: not in ECL, but compare the meanings of ἱλαρότης [69] and χαρά.[70] For ἱλαρότης see Rom 12:8; Herm Man 5:1:2; 10:3:1; Herm Sim 9:15:2. For χαρά see Luke 13:17; 19:6; 24:52; Phil 1:25; Herm Vis 3:13:2. From these passages it is clear that χαρά comes to express joy in suffering (cf. Acts 5:41; Jas 1:2; 1 Pet 1:5-7), and this association with λύπη seems to be a dominant one. For this reason, χαρά may be a logical synonym, or at least a substitute, for ἀλυπία, the term which Plutarch uses to head his catalogue of virtues at the end of the *exordium*.[71]

Exordium B (ch. 1, 523D14-D2)

Yet one can say of many people that they would rather be rich and wretched than spend their money and be happy.

This sentence strikes to the heart of the matter and gives a good description of the miser's attitude. The nearest parallel in ECL to this point of view is the story of the rich young man (ruler) cited earlier: Matt 19:16-24//Mark 10:17-23/Luke 18:8-25. He is the sort of person that Plutarch has in mind. Consider also the injunction against such an attitude in Herm Vis 3:9:6; cf. 6:5-7.

Some of the words used here appear in ECL, some do not. The verb πλουτέω is used absolutely and in its literal sense: e.g., Luke 1:53; 1 Tim 6:9; Herm Vis 3:6:7. More often, however, πλουτέω appears in a figurative sense, to be rich in God or in the sight of God: e.g., Luke 12:21; 1 Tim 6:18. ECL does not use κακοδαιμονέω, and μακάριος means "blessed" rather than "happy." In place of Plutarch's emphasis on the happiness and unhappiness of this world, ECL usually stresses the idea in the eschatological sense.

Exordium C (ch. 1, 523D2-3)

But money cannot buy peace of mind, greatness of spirit, serenity, confidence, and self-sufficiency.

---

[69] Cf. R. Bultmann, *TDNT* 3:297-300, s.v. ἱλαρός, ἱλαρότης.

[70] Cf. H. Conzelmann, *TDNT* 9:359-372, s.v. χαίρω κτλ.

[71] Such blending of these terms and the overlapping of nuances is but one of the problems which we must attempt to solve. This problem exists whether the writings belong to different traditions in the same language or to different languages. For a succinct statement of the problem see, for example, *The New English Bible: New Testament* (Oxford and Cambridge, 1961) viii-ix.

The technique of listing vices and virtues in a catalogue or group is a familiar one in both classical Greek and ECL. One of the longest lists in classical Greek is [Aristotle's] *On Virtues and Vices*, but writers of every period have grouped such related concepts. See, for example, Plutarch's *virt. mor.* 441A where he refers to lists in the writings of Ariston, Zeno, Chrysippus, Plato, and others.

In ECL the catalogues are frequently short but no less significant.[72] They may be divided into three types: vices, virtues, and mixed or double, but the catalogues of vices are in the majority. The following lists do not aim at completeness, but they contain the most significant examples. Vices: Matt 15:19; Mark 7:21-22; Rom 1:29-31; 13:13; 1 Cor 5:10-11; 6:9-10; 2 Cor 12:20-21; Eph 5:3-6; Col 3:5; 3:8; 1 Tim 1:9-10; 2 Tim 3:2-5; Tit 3:3; 1 Pet 2:1; 4:3; 4:15; Rev 21:8; 22:15 (and perhaps 18:11-17); 1 Clem 13:1; 35:5; Pol Phil 2:2; 4:3; Herm Man 5:2:4. Virtues: 1 Tim 6:11; 1 Clem 61:1; Herm Vis 3:8:5-7. Double or mixed: Gal 5:19-23; Eph 4:31-32; 1 Clem 30:7-8; Did 2:1-5:2//Barn 19-20; Herm Man 6:2:2-5; 8:3-10; Herm Sim 9:15:2-3.

Plutarch's list of virtues is perhaps more interesting and instructive for its differences from ECL's concepts than for its similarities. In fact, the basic difference in attitudes toward humanity and the divine appears in this sentence. For Plutarch and most of Greek philosophy man directs his own destiny; in Hellenistic Judaism and Christianity God is in control.

Consequently, one aim of Greek philosophy was to obtain worldly satisfaction and to dispel worldly suffering. Regardless of the philosophic sect, its *summum bonum* was one or both of these concepts. For Christianity worldly satisfaction actually becomes a negative quality, and suffering, deprivation and anguish become positives. These experiences represent man's submission to God, a kind of cleansing that clears the way to eternal joy in the next world. Nowhere is this difference between Greek philosophy and early Christian thought more apparent than in the concept of λύπη.[73]

For Plutarch the opposite of λύπη is ἀλυπία. This noun is not

[72] For a recent study of the subject see M. J. Suggs, "The Christian Two Ways Tradition: Its Antiquity, Form, and Function" in *Studies in the NT and ECL: Essays in Honor of A. P. Wikgren* (Leiden, 1972) 60-74.

[73] R. Bultmann, *TDNT*, s.v. λύπη κτλ.

used in ECL, and the adjective ἄλυπος if formed only in Phil 2:28. Yet the idea of freedom from mental and physical distress as a desirable state is not unknown.[74] See, for example, 2 Clem 19:4; Ign Pol 7:1. As usual, the eschatological concept prevails in both passages as it does in the contrast between λύπη and χαρά (the closest term in ECL to ἀλυπία) in John 16:20-24; Heb 12:11; Jas 1:2. Compare Herm Vis 4:3:4; Herm Man 10:1:1-3. See also the use of μέριμνα in Mark 4:19 (cf. 1 Pet 5:7) and esp. Matt 6:25-34; 1 Cor 7:32-34. For ἀμεριμνία, etc. see 1 Cor 7:32; Ign Pol 7:1 and perhaps Matt 28:14.[75]

The second term in Plutarch's list is μεγαλοφροσύνη. This word does not appear in ECL, and its absence is indicative of some of the basic differences in the ethics of the two traditions. In Greek philosophy the word often designates a vice, but it is also an important virtue, for pride, loftiness of spirit, etc., were desirable qualities for the Greeks.

Such is not the case in ECL. Here the emphasis is rather on meekness and humility,[76] and because of this emphasis the relatively few references to its opposite are naturally pejorative. The closest word in ECL to μεγαλοφροσύνη is ὑψηλοφροσύνη, but it is used only in Hermas: Herm Man 8:3 (a catalogue of vices) and Herm Sim 9:22:3. Hermas also uses ὑψηλόφρων in Herm Sim 8:9:1 and identifies it as a vice of τὰ ἔθνη. Perhaps he had in mind the frequent praise of μεγαλοφροσύνη in Greek philosophic writings. The verb ὑψηλοφρονέω occurs only in 1 Tim 6:17 where the reference is to the haughtiness of the wealthy.[77]

Plutarch's third term is εὐστάθεια. This noun and its related verb and adjective are used only in the Apostolic Fathers: εὐστάθεια in 1 Clem 61:1 (in a list of virtues); 65:1 (an echo of the earlier passage). The verb εὐσταθέω appears in Ign Pol 4:1; Herm Man 5:2:2; Herm Sim 6:2:7; 7:3; and the adjective appears only in Mart Pol 7:2. The absence of these words from the NT is a bit surprising but can perhaps be explained, at least in part, by the

[74] For a discussion of tranquillity see Betz on *tranq. an.* in this volume, pp. 198ff.

[75] Cf. R. Bultmann, *TDNT*, s.v. μεριμνάω κτλ.

[76] Cf. W. Grundmann, *TDNT*, s.v. ταπεινός.

[77] It also appears as a variant reading in Rom 11:20, but even the accepted reading ὑψηλὰ φρόνει expresses the same idea; cf. also Rom 12:16: ὑψηλὰ φρονοῦντες.

similarity of their basic meaning to such words as εἰρήνη, ἡσυχία, and ὑπομονή.[78] Yet none of these words is an exact equivalent of εὐστάθεια.[79]

With Plutarch's fourth term, θαρραλεότης, the difference between the two traditions is even more obvious. This word is a fairly uncommon one in Classical Greek and is not used at all in ECL. Epictetus (3.26.24) defines it as "confidence in what is faithful, free from hindrance, cannot be taken away, that is, in your own moral purpose." Some of Epictetus' meaning seems to lie behind Paul's words in 2 Cor 5:6-8 and cf. Heb 13:6 where the same general notion may be in the author's mind. In both passages the word which conveys the idea of "courage" or "confidence" is θαρρέω,[80] and the thought is surely more than the conventional one of polite encouragement. Rather it expresses the joy, the comfort, and the assurance of a link with the Lord that makes this life bearable and the next life certain. See also the use of θάρσος in Mart Pol 12:1 which describes Polycarp at the moment of his martyrdom as full of θάρσος and χαρά, and this courage and joy is very much like what Paul implies in 2 Cor 5:6-8.

Yet, to repeat what we have said before, the difference between this idea of courage and that in the Greek philosophers is more important than any possible similarity.[81] In the latter, courage belongs to this world and is a quality that is needed to make this life both tolerable and meaningful. For the Christians, courage may make this world tolerable but only because of the assurance the next world alone has any meaning.

The last term in Plutarch's list is αὐτάρκεια, and it stands last

---

[78] Yet each of these words also appear in the Apostolic Fathers, thus weakening the argument.

[79] For a brief discussion of the connection between "steadfastness" and στέφανος cf. *PECL* 1:298.

[80] For the word group around this verb cf. W. Grundmann, *TDNT*, s.v. θαρρέω κτλ.

[81] Plutarch does not make clear what meaning he assigns θαρραλεότης. He may agree with Epictetus or he may have something different in mind, something that bears on the monetary theme of the treatise. For example, Teles twice (4A, p. 35, 2 and 37, 2 in Hense's text) uses the word δυσελπιστία ("despondency") of a man who is illiberal and mean. A similar idea appears in [Aristotle] *VV* 1251b 24-25: "Accompanying small-mindedness is pettiness, querulousness, despondency, self-abasement."

Since δυσελπιστία is clearly the reverse of θαρραλεότης and describes a negative aspect of a miser, Plutarch may well have used the positive term as a desirable attitude of a wealthy man.

as an indication that it is the most important item in the list.[82] From the time of Socrates this word and its underlying concept were basic to Greek philosophic thought. For the Cynics it became an avowed way of life,[83] and for the Stoics the wise man was αὐτάρκης in every respect.[84] Many of the Cynic-Stoic ideas[85] found their way into Hellenistic Judaism[86] and ECL.

The importance of "self-sufficiency" in ECL is actually far greater than the relatively few occurrences of the word-group suggest.[87] The noun αὐτάρκεια is used only four times: 2 Cor 9:8 (but consider the whole of vss. 1-15); 1 Tim 6:6 (where the whole passage, vss. 6-10, is an expression of "self-sufficiency"); Herm Man 6:2:3; and Herm Sim 1:6 which has the curiously redundant τὴν αὐτάρκειαν τὴν ἀρκετήν.

The adjective αὐτάρκης is used only in Phil 4:11, a very significant example of "self-sufficiency" in ECL, where, again, the whole passage (vss. 11-13) must be considered. These words of Paul could just as easily have been uttered by Antisthenes, Diogenes, Crates, or even Teles. The verb ἀρκέω is also used to express the same idea, especially when it governs a pronoun or is passive: e.g., 1 Tim 6:8; Heb 13:5; 2 Cor 12:19. Moreover, many passages express the idea without using the word:[88] e.g., Jas 1:4; Ign Pol 2:2,

---

[82] It has the same position in two catalogues in ECL: Gal 5:19-22; Herm Man 6:2:3. In both passages translators render the word with "self-control," but "self-sufficiency" seems equally accurate.

[83] See Hengel, *Property and Riches in the Early Church*, 9-10, 54-59.

[84] For an extensive list of passages on the wise man's self-sufficiency see *SVF*, III, pp. 146-164. For Plutarch's reference to the wise man see *tranq. an.* ch. 12, 472A and Betz's discussion in this volume, pp. 221ff.

[85] Many critics have pointed out that αὐτάρκεια was "a favorite virtue of the Cynics and Stoics," e.g., Bauer (s.v. αὐτάρκεια, 2); M. Dibelius and H. Conzelmann, *The Pastoral Epistles* (Philadelphia, 1972) 84, n. 6; Hengel, op. cit., 9; and G. Kittel, *TDNT*, s.v. αὐτάρκεια κτλ. For a recent discussion of αὐτάρκεια and its development from ἐγκράτεια see North, *Sophrosyne*, 118, 122, 125-127, 133-135, 219.

[86] Cf. Hengel, op. cit., 10, 54-55 and passages cited on 94, n. 20. See also, for example, such passages as Sir 10:26ff., 29:21ff., 40:18 and perhaps even 1:11ff. where the wisdom and fear of God constitute a kind of self-sufficiency (cf. 2 Cor 9:8), a concept that is very near to the Stoic "sufficiency of virtue" and the wisdom of the truly wise man.

[87] Cf. G. Kittel, *TDNT*, s.v. ἀρκέω κτλ. He seems not, however, to recognize the full implication of the concept, probably because he concentrates on the words rather than on the idea.

[88] One is tempted, for example, to list the Beatitudes (Matt 5:3-12) and even such passages as the Parable of the Lamps (Matt 25:1-13, esp. vs. 9).

for "self-sufficiency" is scarcely less important in Christian ethics than in Greek philosophy.[89]

Both traditions also have their share of men who serve as examples of αὐτάρκεια. Among the Greeks, there is Socrates, Diogenes, Crates, etc.; in ECL, John the Baptist (Matt 3:8) resembles a wandering Cynic teacher, and Paul (1 Cor 4:11-13; 9:15, etc.) proclaims his own self-sufficiency. Consider also Jesus' instructions to the Twelve in Matt 10:8-14//Mark 6:8-11//Luke 9:2-5, and even Jesus himself was a teacher who travelled through the land, subsisting on the hospitality of the local inhabitants and preaching a message which contained a sufficient amount of αὐτάρκεια.[90]

In summary, then, Plutarch's technique of listing virtues in related groups is a part of the philosophic and rhetorical tradition which also found its way into Hellenistic Judaism and ECL. Of the words in Plutarch's list, some are common in ECL, some are rare, some are non-existent. Yet the ideas behind the words, or at least related ideas, are important in Christian ethics, and only the concept of μεγαλοφροσύνη is radically different. Finally, where the ideas of Plutarch and ECL are most alike, the common heritage of Cynic and Stoic ethics is most apparent.

Propositio A (ch. 1, 523D4-5)

Despising wealth is not inherent in being wealthy, nor is the lack of needing luxuries inherent in the possession of luxuries.[91]

The vocabulary of this sentence, the syntax, and even the rhetorically balanced phrases which contain parallel but contrasting ideas (cf. Diogn 5) appear in ECL, but the sum of the elements, the idea itself, is absent.[92]

---

[89] In a sense, Chrysippus expresses the ultimate idea when he says (fr. 685, *SVF*, III, p. 172, 9-10) that ἀρετή is αὐτάρκης πρὸς εὐδαιμονίαν. By setting αὐτάρκεια at the end of his list Plutarch seems to agree with Chrysippus.

[90] Especially in the Sermon on the Mount (Matt 6:25-34). Cf. Teles, fr. 2, p. 7, 4ff. in Hense's text.

[91] The English here is admittedly awkward, but I have tried to express the construction of the Greek as it appears in the Teubner text. Its wording is τῷ πλουτεῖν οὐκ ἔνεστι . . . οὐδὲ τῷ . . . κεκτῆσθαι. The Loeb editors print the less satisfactory reading of a few MSS: τὸ πλουτεῖν οὐκ ἔστι . . . οὐδὲ τὸ . . . κεκτῆσθαι.

[92] This sentence has caused problems for critics. Ziegler (col. 143, 21ff.) uses it as part of his argument that the *cup. divit.* is incomplete by contending that Plutarch never develops the idea. The editors of both the Teubner and

Only one or two words need be discussed here. The meaning of τὸ πλουτεῖν is obvious, and Plutarch does not bother to define it (cf. 523D above). On the other hand, τὰ περιττά can mean several things, so Plutarch later defines the term as he uses it in the *cup. divit.* At the end of ch. 3 (524D) he says the greedy οὐ παύσονται δεόμενοι τῶν περιττῶν, τουτέστιν ἐπιθυμοῦντες ὧν οὐ δέονται.[93] So the term refers to what is "superfluous," "unnecessary," thereby becoming "luxuries."[94] With one exception (τι . . . περιττόν in 527C), Plutarch uses the word in this treatise with the article and in the plural, nor does he ever limit its meaning with a genitive. For him the term is absolute and absolutely perjorative.

In ECL, however, περιττός and related words[95] are usually limited by the genitive: "an abundance of faith, love, hope," etc. In such passages there is no notion of excess, and seldom does the limiting genitive represent material possessions. Yet such a meaning may lie behind Mark 12:44 which contrasts the offerings of the rich and that of the poor widow. In 2 Cor 8:2 also, Paul's metaphor of an overflowing spring is based upon the same idea. This passage displays the same kind of balanced contrasts that we see in Plutarch's sentence. The same device is used in Rom 2:4, and at first glance this verse seems to contain several elements of Plutarch's sentence, esp. τοῦ πλούτου τῆς χρηστότητος αὐτοῦ . . . καταφρονεῖς, but the similarity hardly extends beyond the words themselves.

Loeb editions disagree with the chapter division of the Frankfort edition which included this sentence in ch. 1. By beginning a new paragraph here they indicate that the sentence belongs with what follows, but the matter is admittedly difficult, and the Frankfort edition may have been correct. Plutarch, without being specific, seems to develop the basic idea of the sentence throughout the treatise: e.g., chs. 2-4 dwell on the insatiability of those who want money; chs. 7-9 emphasize their possessions and the reasons for such acquisitions. Thus the sentence looks forward and introduces the themes which follow, and it may either be the end of the introduction or the beginning of the main discussion.

[93] See also ch. 8 (527C-D) and the reference to Scorpas, who based his happiness on τὰ περιττά but not on τὰ ἀναγκαῖα. This attitude of Scorpas was cited with approval by the 19th century historian John Lothrop Motley, whom Oliver Wendell Holmes rebuked in *The Autocrat at the Breakfast Table.*

[94] Bauer cites Plutarch's use of the word here in 523D and puts it in sec. 2.a under the meaning "abundant, profuse." Bauer is incorrect. The juxtaposition of τὸ μὴ δεῖσθαι τῶν περιττῶν anticipates the same idea in 524D where Plutarch defines περιττά. Consequently, Bauer should have cited 524D, and he should have listed the citation in sec. 2.b: "superfluous, unnecessary."

[95] F. Hauck, *TDNT*, s.v. περισσεύω κτλ.

Propositio B (ch. 2, 523E6-11)

From what other evil does wealth give relief, if not from love of wealth? Drink quenches thirst, food satisfies hunger, and a single coat wards off cold.

The thought here is typical of Greek philosophy and of the Cynics and Stoics in particular, but the analogies are alien to the Christian usage despite the fact that much of the vocabulary appears in ECL. For example, ἀπαλλάττω appears several times in the early part of the *cup. divit.* (523E6, 524B16, 23, C5, E1) with the meaning "release, relieve," etc. In each case the word seems to be a medical term, and this usage fits in with the Stoic belief that such vices as greed and miserliness are πάθη. The verb has the same basic meaning in its two appearances in NT: Acts 19:12; Heb 2:15.[96] In the Apostolic Fathers, however, it means simply "depart" (e.g., 2 Clem 17:3), and from this meaning develops the euphemism for dying: 1 Clem 5:7; Mart Pol 3.

Plutarch identifies φιλοπλουτία here as one of the κακά, and this idea is probably Stoic. The closest parallel in ECL to the thought is 1 Tim 6:2-10, esp. vs. 10.[97] Such words as ποτόν and τροφή, as well as many others which refer to food and drink, are common symbols of the appetites, but the idea is almost a cliché in Cynic writings. The only combination of these two words in ECL occurs in Diogn 10:3 where the context is quite different.[98]

The situation with σβέννυμι and ἀκέομαι is similar. The latter verb is not used in ECL, and the former appears only once (1 Thes 5:19) in a figurative sense. Naturally, there are references to hunger and cold, but none uses the vocabulary of Plutarch. His use of ὄρεξις [99] and ἐπιθυμία,[100] however, has some interesting parallels in ECL. In the *cup. divit.* ὄρεξις refers to some physical craving, but when it becomes excessive and illogical, it is ἐπιθυμία. Plutarch's combination here is deliberate.[101] The two related

[96] But cf. also Luke 9:40D; Acts 5:15D.

[97] For a good discussion of this passage and parallels from other writings, see Dibelius and Conzelmann, *The Pastoral Epistles*, 82-86, esp. 85-86.

[98] For similar combinations see Matt 25:35-44; Rom 14:17; 1 Cor 11:30; Ign Trall 2:3; Herm Vis 3:9:3; Herm Man 12:2:1; Diogn 6:9; and esp. 1 Tim 6:8: διατροφαὶ καὶ σκεπάσματα. This passage, as part of a discussion of αὐτάρκεια, is closest in sentiment to Plutarch's sentence.

[99] Cf. H. W. Heidland, *TDNT*, s.v. ὀρέγομαι κτλ.

[100] Cf. F. Büchsel, *TDNT*, s.v. ἐπιθυμία κτλ.

[101] For a similar combination cf. Wis 16:2; Sir 23:5-6.

verbs appear together in 1 Tim 3:1, where the wording may be proverbial,[102] but ὄρεξις is used only in Rom 1:27 in a reference to homosexual desire.[103] The verb ὀρέγω is found alone in Heb 11:16 with a good sense and in 1 Tim 6:10 with a bad sense.

The noun ἐπιθυμία, with its verb ἐπιθυμέω, is more common. The words often represent an impulsive desire and, therefore, a vice. The noun appears in several catalogues of vices: e.g., 1 Pet 4:3; Did 5:1; and see esp. Herm Man 12 which contains the longest treatment of the term in ECL.[104] The closest parallel here to Plutarch's statement is 12:2:1 (cf. 6:2:5 for similar wording).

The verse which Plutarch quotes here comes from a poem by the sixth century Choliambic poet Hipponax (fr. 56 in Knox). It appears with variations in *Stoic. absurd.* 1058D; *adv. Stoic.* 1068D, and a similar line (fr. 59) occurs in Tzetzes' commentary on Lycophron 855. The general context of these fragments indicates that the Cynics and Stoics could easily have used the poem of Hipponax in some discussion of αὐτάρκεια. In particular, the reference to the cloak and its use here would have attracted the Cynics.

Plutarch picks up the same idea. By referring to more than one cloak and by using the phrase πλειόνων ἐπιφερομένων, he plays with the meaning of πλείων in anticipation of his subsequent discussion of πλεονεξία and τὸ πλέον. None of this occurs in ECL, but one may say that those who offer Hipponax more than he asks for exemplify the instructions in Mat 5:40-41//Luke 6:29-30, though the occasion is quite different. For the idea of refusing an offer see, for example, 1 Cor 9:1-18 where Paul proclaims his freedom to act in much the same spirit that a wandering Cynic teacher might have used.[105]

Propositio C. 1 (ch. 2, 523E11-524A10)

Wealth makes the disease (i.e., love of wealth) worse, but it affects different sufferers in different ways: First, it distracts those

[102] Cf. Dibelius and Conzelmann, op. cit., 50-52.

[103] But cf. Heidland, op. cit., 5:448. With this statement of Paul we may compare his words in Gal 5:17.

[104] Other significant passages are Luke 15:16; 16:21 (cf. 22:15); Acts 20:33 (cf. 1 Cor 9:11-15); Jas 4:2; but cf. esp. Jas 1:14-15 for the devastating effect that ἐπιθυμία has upon a person.

[105] Cf. H. Conzelmann, *1 Corinthians* 151-158; Betz, *Paulus*, 100ff. See also the rather effective conclusion of Teles' fr. 4A: "Actually, it is a great and noteworthy thing to take no heed of a wallet, lupines, vegetables, water, but rather to be unkempt and uncompromising."

in need of life's necessities and diverts their appetite to luxuries.

Much of the sentiment expressed in this section is what one expects in such discussions, and the vocabulary is standard. For that reason, most of the words are used in ECL, and even the imagery is not completely missing.

The first important word here is φιλαργυρία. That Plutarch uses it in the original sense "love of silver" as well as its general sense "love of money" or "greed" is obvious from the way in which he constructs his sentence and adds as a deliberate after-thought the words οὐδὲ χρυσίον. In ECL φιλαργυρία always has the general meaning. It is used only once, however, in the NT: 1 Tim 6:10, but it occurs several times in the Apostolic Fathers: 2 Clem 6:4 (cf. 4:3); Pol Phil 2:2; 4:1, 3; 6:1. A related idea is expressed by ἀφιλάργυρος in Heb 13:5, and the same adjective appears in three other passages. In each case it describes part of the character necessary in a church official: 1 Tim 3:3 (Bishop); Pol Phil 5:2 (Deacons); Did 15:1 (Bishop and Deacons).

The next phrase is an important one. Plutarch, despite his playfulness, is actually giving the basic definition of πλεονεξία when he says οὐδὲ πλεονεξία παύεται κτωμένη τὸ πλέον. Thus it is a "grasping for more" which is never satisfied with "the more." [106] In Greek philosophy, esp. among the Cynics and Stoics, πλεονεξία is a very serious fault.[107] The same attitude is held in ECL: e.g., the catalogue of sins in Mark 7:21-22, where πλεονεξία is one of the evils that "come from within and defile a man." [108] See also Rom 1:29; 2 Cor 12:18; 1 Thes 4:6; 1 Clem 35:5; Did 5:1//Barn 20:1; Pol Phil 2:2; Herm Man 6:2:5; 8:5. In Barn 10:4 πλεονεξία is the cause of unrighteous action toward others, a subject which Plutarch takes up in the beginning of ch. 6 of the *cup. divit.*

At this point Plutarch introduces the *topos* of sin and sickness. This concept is especially common in Cynic and Stoic writings and from these sources may have found its way into both the writings of Plutarch and ECL.[109] In the latter the idea is closely associated with demonology, for demonic powers often produce

[106] For a similar play on words see 2 Cor 8:15 (= Exod 16:18).

[107] Among other things it subverts σωφροσύνη. Cf. North, *Sophrosyne*, 106-107, 109, 142, 161, 167.

[108] For a forceful expression of greed and its effects on the person there is no better example than Jas 1:14-15.

[109] A. Oepke, *TDNT*, s.v. ἰάομαι κτλ., νόσος κτλ.

mental as well as physical sickness.[110] These afflictions are often beyond the healing abilities of human physicians, and only Jesus can prevail over the demonic powers and grant healing and forgiveness to those afflicted. This is the implication of Mark 5:26 (cf. Luke 8:43). For other passages on the subject see Matt 13:15//John 12:40//Acts 28:28 (= Isa 6:10); Jas 5:16; 2 Clem 9:7; Herm Vis 1:1:9; 1:3:1; Herm Sim 9:28:5.

By his reference to a ἰατρὸς ἀλαζών Plutarch continues his theme that vain wealth cannot cure the ills which it causes. Neither the idea nor the imagery is found in ECL where most references to ἰατρός are to Jesus, who is the physician of body and soul.[111] In Classical Greek, ἀλαζών repeatedly describes men who pretend to skills which they do not possess: orators, philosophers (esp. sophists), poets, and physicians. In ECL this word may, by implication, refer to anyone who pretends to the healing powers of Jesus.[112] Thus ἀλαζών (and ἀλαζονεία) is a vice and appears in a catalogue in Rom 1:30 (and notice πλεονεξία in vs. 29) and 2 Tim 3:2 (with φιλάργυρος). But the closest parallel to Plutarch's sentence is probably 1 Tim 6:3-4, an excellent description of a man who is ἀλαζών.

In the *topos* of sin and sickness νόσος is a regular term as early as Plato, and the Stoics are fond of the word in this analogy.[113] See, for example, Cicero, *Tusc.* 4.29, a passage which von Arnim has identified as a fragment of Chrysippus (Fr. 425, *SVF* III, p. 104, 7-23). This figurative sense of νόσος is rare in ECL. The one certain example is Herm Sim 6:5:5, in a diatribe against τρυφὴ καὶ ἀπάτη. See also 1 Tim 6:4, where the verb νοσέω conveys the same meaning.

After the verse from an unknown comic poet we return to Plutarch's own words and immediately encounter a textual problem. The text, as both the Teubner and Loeb print it, has ἄρτου δεομένους καὶ οἴκου καὶ σκέπης μετρίας which is the reading of most MSS. Two, however, read οἴνου in place of οἴκου, and this change

---

[110] Cf. *PECL* 1, index, s.v. Demonology, sickness, sin. See also W. Foerster, *TDNT*, s.v. δαίμων, δαιμόνιον, C.3.

[111] Cf. *PECL* 1:193; A. Oepke, *TDNT*, s.v. ἰάομαι κτλ.

[112] Cf. *PECL* 1:267; G. Delling, *TDNT*, s.v. ἀλαζών κτλ.

[113] This word occurs here in a quotation from an unknown comic poet, but its presence is one reason Plutarch quotes the line, and he uses the word later.

seems preferable for two reasons.[114] First, οἴκου is a weak repetition of σκέπης μετρίας. Secondly, οἴνου fits in perfectly with ἄρτου and ὄψου, for it provides the third essential of a normal Greek meal of bread, wine, and meat. See, for example Plato, *Grg.* 518B-C; Thucydides 1.138 (cf. Diodorus Siculus 11.57.7) where the same three nouns appear together.

One may argue that it is reasonable to expect such a combination since the three items are staples of the Greek diet and that Plutarch for this reason tried to insert some novelty. But that is just the point. Plutarch deals here with basics, and he naturally lists those very foods which most Greeks considered essential, and wine was one of them.

The situation in ECL is rather different. The combination οἶνος καὶ κρέας occurs only in Rom 14:21. Yet ἄρτος is a modest necessity in ECL: e.g., Matt 6:11//Luke 11:3 (cf. 1 Tim 6:8); Jas 2:15. On the other hand, there is no reference to οἶνος as a staple. Of course Jesus himself drinks wine (e.g., Matt 11:19; Luke 7:34), and at Cana (John 2:1-11) he turned gallons of water into wine, but in each instant the occasion was special. Wine seems not to have been a common item on the table of the Christians,[115] but consider 1 Tim 5:23. Yet the general sense of this verse makes it clear that the wine is not to be a part of the man's everyday fare.[116]

Plutarch's third necessity, "a modest shelter," is not a subject for discussion in ECL. The only reference to the idea occurs in Matt 8:20//Luke 9:58. Even Plutarch's word σκέπη is used only in Herm Sim 8:1:1; 8:2:2; 9:1:9, where each time it means the shade of a tree.

Plutarch's use of τοῦ τυχόντος ὄψου is more interesting. The phrase refers to "some ordinary tid-bit," for ὄψον is used for a variety of foods: meat in general, sauce, fish, in fact to any prepared dish, and ὁ τυχών means anything one chances upon. This phrase is used in ECL only with a negative to mean "unusual, uncommon, extraordinary" (Acts 19:11; 28:2; 1 Clem 14:2) The noun ὄψον,

---

[114] For some reason the Teubner editors have omitted οἴνου even from their apparatus.

[115] Of course Jesus installed bread and wine in the Eucharist: e.g., Matt 26:27-28//Mark 14:23-24//Luke 22:17-18; cf. John 6:51-56, so in the higher sense both items became necessary to Christians.

[116] Cf. Dibelius and Conzelmann, *The Pastoral Epistles*, 80-81. The Cynics often urged the reverse of this advice and refused to drink wine, preferring water instead. Cf. Teles, fr. 2 (p. 7, 4 Hense): πλήρεις δὲ αἱ κρῆναι ὕδατος and see the so-called Cynic Epistles: Socrates 8, Crates 7, 14, 18.

however, does not appear in ECL. The closest word, etymologically, is ὀψάριον, which John uses to mean "fish."

Because of the general meaning of ὄψον a number of words, in addition to ὀψάριον, serve as synonyms in ECL: τροφή, κρέας, and even σῖτος (on these cf. Bauer). Yet for the essence of Plutarch's meaning perhaps the nearest equivalent is the mysterious τὸν ἄρτον τὸν ἐπιούσιον of the Lord's Prayer (Matt 6:11//Luke 11:3// Did 8:2). Whatever the meaning of ἐπιούσιος may be, the intention is plain: We must pray for the food that is sufficient and necessary to sustain life, and that is very close to Plutarch's meaning of τὸ τυχὸν ὄψον.

When Plutarch gives examples of items which lure a greedy person, he gives almost a catalogue of standard symbols of luxurious and excessive wealth: χρυσός, ἄργυρος, ἐλέφας, σμάραγδοι, κύνες, ἵπποι. For a similar and even longer list see Rev 18:12-13, where all the items appear except σμάραγδοι and κύνες. In place of the former are λίθος τίμιος καὶ μαργαρῖται (cf. Rev 21:19-21 for a long list of precious gems). The κύνες in Plutarch's list are hunting-dogs as their place beside ἵπποι suggests. This bit of luxury was apparently not a part of the Judeo-Christian communities, but it would not have been surprising to find κύνες in Rev 18:12-13 which is a polemic against pagan luxuries.

Plutarch sums up his list of symbols with χαλεπὰ καὶ σπάνια καὶ δυσπόριστα καὶ ἄχρηστα and contrasts with τὰ ἀναγκαῖα. Each word in the first group is, in a sense, a synonym of the others, but each is also stronger than its predecessor and thus builds to a climax. So, the worst quality of these luxuries is "useless," and Plutarch continues to stress this point in the argument that follows.

There is another meaning to the arrangement of these words. By the excessive use of near-synonyms which are balanced with the single antonym τὰ ἀναγκαῖα Plutarch stresses the excessiveness of the luxuries and the unique simplicity of the other. On top of that he casts the simple necessities in the form of a substantive and leaves the elusive qualities of ostentation in a series of less definite adjectives.

Of the four adjectives, only the first and last are used in ECL. The closest parallel to χαλεπά is Pol Phil 4:1 (cf. 1 Tim 6:10), the closest to ἄχρηστα is Did 4:2 [117] (but cf. Herm Vis 3:6:7). The

[117] In Did 4:2 is the combination ἄχρηστα καὶ περισσά which also appears in the last sentence of ch. 2 of the *cup. divit.*

term τὰ ἀναγκαῖα, strangely enough, is not used in ECL. The nearest synonym is χρεία, but it refers to human needs in a practical and tangible way while τὰ ἀναγκαῖα is a generic term of Greek philosophy. The nearest parallel is Tit 3:14: εἰς τὰς ἀναγκαίας χρείας, but even here the emphasis is upon the concrete rather than the abstract.

The *sententia* of the next sentence, "In what is sufficient no one is poor," belongs to the Cynic tradition, and the thought is at the very core of the concept of αὐτάρκεια.[118] Yet Plutarch's version is not quite as stringent as that of Teles (fr. 2, p. 7, 4 Hense): τῶν ἀναγκαίων οὐκ ἐνδεής,[119] though it comes close. The nearest expression in ECL is 2 Cor 6:10, where the last clause in particular resembles the Cynic extreme.

Plutarch's term for "sufficiency" is τὰ ἀρκοῦντα. It is used in ECL only in Herm Sim 5:2:9, where the surface meaning refers to a specific incident, but the underlying thought is not unlike that of the Cynics and Plutarch. The word πένης in Plutarch's expression is an adjective, but is it always a substantive in ECL. The regular adjective is πτωχός (cf. 2 Cor 6:10 again), and it is frequently contrasted to πλούσιος (e.g., Luke 6:20; Jas 2:5-6; Rev 13:16; 1 Clem 38:2; Herm Sim 2:4), so that we may say that πτωχός does the work of πένης.

Plutarch's statement that "no one has ever borrowed money to buy barley meal, cheese, bread, or olives" is aristocratically naive.[120] And it may be for this reason that the idea does not appear in ECL which is primarily concerned with people of a lower social order. For the same reason it is also silent about the purchase of expensive items,[121] and consequently there is little to correspond to Plutarch's list of luxuries with the result that, with few exceptions, the vocabulary here is foreign to ECL.

[118] Consequently, many of the passages cited in the discussion of αὐτάρκεια in ch. 1 should be considered here as well: e.g., Matt 6:25-34; Phil 4:11-12; Heb 13:5.

[119] For Teles' use of ἐνδεής cf. Acts 4:34 (cf. 2:45) and 1 Clem 52:1.

[120] I can remember many a time in my student days and even as a struggling assistant professor when a small loan was the only way to buy milk for the baby and some simple food for her parents. Only the wealthy can praise and condone dire poverty.

[121] The only references to borrowing and lending in ECL are general in nature and without condemnation: Matt 5:42; Luke 6:34-35. See E. Neufeld, "The Rate of Interest and the Text of Nehemiah 5.11," *JQR*, n.s., 44 (1953-54) 194-204.

The exceptions, however, are interesting. Plutarch's χρεωφειλέτης is used in Luke 7:41; 16:5; and cf. χρεώστης in Herm Man 8:10. The more common word, however, is ὀφειλέτης which usually has the added notion of sin: e.g., Matt 6:12; Luke 13:4; Did 8:2; Pol Phil 6:1. Vineyards were, of course, common in most parts of the ancient world, so ἀμπελών occurs frequently in ECL and is a favorite word in parables: e.g., Matt 20:1-16; 21:28-32; 21:33-46// Mark 12:1-12//Luke 20:9-19. The ἵπποι ζυγόφοροι are race-horses and probably the same as those in Rev 18:13: ἵππων καὶ ῥεδῶν.

Plutarch concludes this part of his *propositio* with a comparison of the glutton and the greedy man. This theme is not uncommon in Cynic and Stoic writings,[122] but neither the imagery nor the basic thought is found in ECL. Yet much of the vocabulary is used, probably because several words here are common in the Greek language.

A case in point are πίνω and ἐσθίω which form a natural pair and appear together in such places at Matt 24:49//Luke 21:34; Luke 10:7; 12:19, 45; Acts 10:41. In almost every case an implication of excessiveness is present. See esp. Matt 11:18-19//Luke 7:34 (cf. 5:33). Two other verbs form a natural pair διψάω and πεινάω, but these words are not often used lightly in ECL. Rather they "denote the severest privation" (so Bauer, s.v. διψάω), and they usually have a spiritual meaning not intended by Plutarch.[123] One last verb deserves attention. Although ἐφίημι is not used in ECL, there are synonyms. In particular, see ἐπιζητέω in Matt 6:31-32, which has several elements of Plutarch's sentence and accuses the Gentiles of harboring such desires.

Propositio C. 2 (ch. 3, 524A10-D12)

The second type of sufferer: those who part with nothing, have much, and always want more. If a man has an insatiable desire for food and drink, he consults a physician. Shouldn't the man with an insatiable desire for material possessions seek help? People

[122] Horace, *S.* 2:7, esp. vss. 102-115, is an excellent example. The main theme of the poem is Stoic and deals with the idea that only the wise are free (see the introduction above). The poet sets the scene during the Saturnalia, a time of excessive indulgence, and it is just such an occasion to which Philo refers with disdain in *vit. Mos.* 2.23-24.

[123] J. Behm and G. Bertram, *TDNT*, s.v. διψάω κτλ.; L. Goppelt, *TDNT*, s.v. πεινάω.

with normal desires for drink stop when they have enough, but those who drink on and on without satisfaction need to vomit, for they are sick. So, too, with money-getters: the man in real want will stop acquiring when he has enough; the man with more than enough who wants still more suffers from a disease that must be cured.

Although Plutarch ends the previous section with the words οὗτοι μὲν οὖν τοιοῦτοι as a clear indication that he is changing subject, the break is not complete. He does little more than shift emphasis from the prodigal to the miser and repeats previous ideas in slightly different ways. Even the language is similar, and the opening sentence, with much the same vocabulary as we have already seen, gives a good description of those who are both prodigals and misers.

Nevertheless, there are several words, phrases, and ideas in this section which must be examined. For example, the phrase τοὺς . . . μηδὲν ἀποβάλλοντας is expressive, and while it does not occur in ECL, the verb is used frequently, esp. in Hermas. The closest parallel to Plutarch's idea is probably Herm Vis 3:6:6 (cf. 4:3:4), though the context is different. For those who "have much and always need more" cf. 2 Cor 8:15 (= Exod 16:18), where Paul's idea is a good summary of this whole section in Plutarch; cf. Matt 20:10, but this is a special incident rather than a general maxim.

One word which occurs here for the first time in the *cup. divit.* is πάθος. This word, as everyone knows, represents an important concept in Greek philosophy and especially among the Stoics.[124] In the NT only Paul uses πάθος (Rom 1:26; Col 3:5; 1 Thes 4:5), and in each case it refers to sexual passion. The same meaning occurs in Herm Man 4:1:6, but in Herm Sim 6:5:5 it refers to anger. Probably the word which comes closest to πάθος is νόσος, and the best example is again Herm 6:5:5, where it is used in a summarizing of a catalogue of vices.

The description of the man who wants more beds, more tables, more lands and money, who loses sleep and peace of mind in his insatiable greed is effective and offers some interesting words and ideas for study.[125] Such words as κλίνη and τράπεζα are frequent

[124] Cf. Rist, *Stoic Phil.*, 27-39 and passim; W. Michaelis, *TDNT*, s.v. πάσχω κτλ., esp. 5. 906-907, 926.

[125] For an even more colorful passage on the same subject cf. Teles, fr. 4A, p. 43, 1-7 Hense.

symbols of wealth in Greek literature, but in ECL their symbolism is quite different. For example, κλίνη usually refers to the sick-bed (e.g., Matt 9:2; Mark 7:30; Luke 5:18) and becomes a symbol both for the sickness and for the cure which Jesus effects: e.g., Matt 9:6; and cf. the use of κράβαττος in Mark 2:9, 11-12; John 5:8-9, etc.

The use of τράπεζα is interesting. It can indicate the table on which food is set (e.g., Matt 15:27; Mark 7:28) or the heavenly table (Luke 22:30; cf. 1 Cor 10:21), but more often it designates the table of the money-changers. Consequently it is used in a pejorative sense as a symbol of greed (e.g., Matt 21:12-13; Mark 11:15-17; John 2:14-16). Yet the symbolism is still unlike Plutarch's where the tables themselves are the object of greed. Perhaps the closest parallel to Plutarch's thought is Rom 11:9 (= Ps 69:22), but again the context is different.[126]

The same situation exists for μεστός. Like the other words for "fill" and "full," this adjective is not used with a negative in ECL to express insatiability. Rather it describes people who are full of faults: e.g., Matt 23:28; 2 Clem 13:1; and in Rom 1:29-30 both μεστός and πληρόω are used to describe the godless who are filled with sins of many kinds. See also Acts 2:13, where those speaking in tongues are accused of γλεύκους μεμεστωμένοι.

Plutarch's use of ἀγρυπνέω is derogatory. The implication is that the greedy toss and turn throughout the night in the throes of unrequited passion for gain. In ECL this word usually means "keep alert, care for" and thus describes a virtuous action. The only exception is Did 5:2//Barn 20:2: ἀγρυπνοῦντες . . . ἐπὶ τὸ πονηρόν.

When Plutarch, or rather Aristippus whom he quotes, says that the insatiable man needs someone to diagnose his ailment, the term he used for the physician is ὁ θεραπεύων. This word has an interesting history. Its first appearance in Greek literature is Homer's *Od.* 13.265, where it means "to serve," and this basic meaning continues until long after the period we are considering. Yet as early as Hesiod's *Op.* 135 the word came to mean "do service to the gods," and later (Thucydides 3.12) "to pay court" to someone in authority. Then it acquired the special sense "to treat medically" (e.g. Hippocrates *VM* 9; Thucydides 2.47) and in Plato (e.g. *R.* 3, 403D) "to train, prepare the soul."

[126] For another example of greed and the use of numbers to signify the greed cf. Matt 25:14-30; Luke 19:11-27.

In Plutarch's sentence ὁ θεραπεύων combines the last two meanings, and the same combination seems to lie behind the use of this verb in ECL. There is, however, an important difference. In most cases it is Jesus who heals,[127] for this ability is one of his most important powers: e.g., Matt 9:2-8//Mark 2:3-12//Luke 5:18-26; Mark 2:17. Yet, with all the references to Jesus' healing powers, he is never called ὁ θεραπεύων. This designation, however, is applied to God in 2 Clem 9:7, thus bringing the meaning of the word to the reverse of its usage in Hesiod. There it represents man's service to the gods, in Clement it is God's healing service to man.

As Plutarch leaves Aristippus and continues the medical imagery in his own words, much of the vocabulary is a repetition of earlier terms, but there are a few new words. Most important is κάθαρσις. The concept of physical and spiritual cleansing is important in both Greek and Christian religion.[128] But while κάθαρσις is the regular term in Greek literature, it does not appear in ECL. Instead we find καθαρισμός, καθαρός, etc. Plutarch's term stresses the physical cleansing, though the spiritual is an underlying thought. In ECL the spiritual and cultic concept dominates. Indeed, the only passage where there may be a reference to physical purging is the much disputed Mark 7:18-19. Yet even here, with its background of Jewish food laws, this passage refers to spiritual cleansing.

In his imagery of the man who continues to drink, Plutarch says he is οὐχ ὑπ' ἐνδείας ὀχλούμενον. This idea seems to come from the Cynic Bion, for Teles (fr. 4A, p. 39, 1-5 Hense) uses the same image and much of the same vocabulary and names Bion as his source. One word which appears in both passages is ἔνδεια, a term not used in ECL. The nearest synonym is probably ὑστέρημα, which can refer to a spiritual defect: e.g., 1 Thes 3:10: 1 Clem 2:6; and cf. the association of ὑστέρημα and καθαρίζω in Herm Vis 3:2:2.

The participle ὀχλούμενος appears in ECL only in Acts 5:16, a good parallel which shows both a similarity of vocabulary and a different point of view toward sickness. See also Luke 6:18 where the same words occur except that the participle is ἐνοχλούμενος. In both passages, the people are troubled ὑπὸ πνευμάτων ἀκαθάρτων, while Plutarch puts the blame directly on a physical condition.

The same difference in attitude toward the causes of physical afflictions is apparent in the next few words. Plutarch identifies

[127] Cf. H. Beyer, *TDNT*, s.v. θεραπεύω κτλ.

[128] Cf. F. Hauck and R. Meyer, *TDNT*, s.v. καθαρός κτλ.

the cause as a δριμύτης[129] or a θερμότης. As we have already discussed, ECL usually blames sickness on demons or does not analyze at all. Consequently such technical terms as these are not used. For θερμότης, however, ECL has πυρετός: e.g. Matt 8:14-15//Mark 1:30-31//Luke 4:38-39; John 4:52; Acts 28:8.

Two other elements in Plutarch's sentence deserve notice: παρὰ φύσιν is a common expression in Classical Greek and esp. in Cynic-Stoic writings, for the very basis of αὐτάρκεια is τὰ κατὰ φύσιν, and anything that is παρὰ φύσιν violates αὐτάρκεια. These phrases, however, are used only by Paul in Rom 11:21, 24, where he balances them once in vs. 21 and twice in vs. 24. Yet even here the similarity to Plutarch is only verbal and coincidental, and the contexts are completely different. The other element here is the participle ἐνοῦσα which occurs again at the end of the next clause.[130] This verb is a common one in Greek, but its only occurrence in ECL with the nuance which Plutarch intends is 2 Clem 19:2, though the substantive τὰ ἐνόντα in Luke 11:41 should also be considered.

In the next sentence there are several words which are, for one reason or another, interesting. First he says that a man who is in real want would perhaps be satisfied if he acquired a home (or business or property), found a treasure, or was helped by a friend. For the first item the MSS give ἑστίαν ("hearth, home"). Pohlenz emends this to ἐργασίαν ("business") in the Teubner while De Lacy and Einarson try οὐσίαν ("estate, property" or even "substance"). Of these choices, ἑστία does not appear in ECL; ἐργασία is used with a meaning similar to Plutarch's in Acts 16:16, 19; 19:24-25; and οὐσία occurs only in Luke 15:12-13, where the prodigal son asks for and subsequently squanders his μέρος τῆς οὐσίας.

The next phrase, θησαυρὸν εὑρών, is one of the most interesting expressions in the whole treatise, and it is made all the more so by its strange intrusion into this passage. Every other remark here is practical, concrete, and matter of fact. This phrase, however, seems almost a quotation of some proverb, and in fact it is an old saying with a long and varied history. The idea may have originated in oriental folklore from which it found its way into both Greek and Jewish traditions at an early date.

---

[129] This is an interesting word. It occurs with θέρμη in Hippocrates (*VM* 18) to describe the symptoms of a patient who seems to be suffering from a severe head cold. Plutarch's patient has a more serious ailment.

[130] For a discussion of these sentences see the introduction above.

In Greek literature it occurs several times in the *Fables* of Aesop: 28, 42, 61, 81 and 225. See also the *Fables* of Phaedrus, esp. 1.27.3; 4.214; 5.6.6.[131] In all these passages the theme is either greed or miserliness. Even Aristotle uses the theme and the expression. In *Pol* 5.3.2 (1303b33) he relates a story of two brothers at Hestiaea who began a civil war over the inheritance of θησαυρὸν ὃν εὗρεν ὁ πατήρ. Then, from some Greek source, possibly Menander, the Roman dramatist Plautus borrowed the motif and made it the basis for his comedy *Aulularia* ("Pot of Gold").

In the LXX the same phrase occurs in 4 Kgs 12:19; 16:8; 18:15; 20:13; and cf. Prov 2:4; Deut 33:19. It also appears in 1 Mac 1:23 and esp. Sir 40:18 (but cf. 20:30). And finally, the same idea occurs in Matt 13:44, but now it has acquired a new application.[132] The appearance of the phrase in Plutarch and ECL may be nothing more than coincidence and a result of the wide-spread use of the motif.

Plutarch's third source of help for the man in want is the help of a friend. With this thought he introduces a *topos* from friendship literature, and it is no accident that we find several fragments of his work "On Friendship" referring to money matters: e.g., fr. 160-161, 168-171. Clearly for Plutarch one of the duties of friendship was financial assistance.

Such a duty would seem to be a logical topic in ECL which stresses friendship and charity, but there seems to be no close parallel to Plutarch's idea. Perhaps the closest is Luke 11:5-8, but φίλος is not a common word in ECL. More often we find ἀδελφός (e.g., Matt 12:48-50) or even ὁ πλησίον (e.g., Luke 10:29, which introduces the story of the Good Samaritan). For the idea of helping others see, for example, Matt 5:42; 19:21; Acts 2:45; 4:34; Did 12:2.

In Plutarch's discussion, the friend helps the man pay his debts, and for this idea he uses ἐκτίνω. This verb is not used in ECL where the nearest synonym is ἀποδίδωμι, but for the repayment of debts cf. Matt 5:26; 18:23-25; Luke 7:42; 12:59; Herm Man 3:2. See also Did 1:5 which discusses alms-giving and the mutual responsibility of giver and receiver, and for an even fuller treatment of this idea see Herm Sim 2. Finally, for Plutarch's word for debt, δανειστής, see Luke 7:41.

---

[131] B. E. Perry, ed. Babrius and Phaedrus, LCL, 422ff.

[132] Cf. Aesop *Fable* 61 and Deut 33:19. Is there an echo of the motif in Matt 25:18ff.?

At this point, Plutarch turns from the man whose wants can be satisfied to the man whose greed is insatiable. With the change of direction some few new words and ideas are introduced: This time, instead of repeating τὰ ἀρκοῦντα, he uses τὰ ἱκανά. This word is used frequently in ECL, but it never has the basic notion of "enough," i.e., a modest amount. Rather it has come to mean "much, many" as well as "appropriate," "able," etc. The closest parallel to Plutarch's meaning is probably τὸ ἀρκετόν in Herm Vis 3:9:3.

Among the symbols of wealth which Plutarch gives this time are ἵπποι καὶ πρόβατα καὶ βόες. The horses have already been discussed, and the only appearance of πρόβατα as a symbol of wealth is Rev 18:13. Elsewhere the emphasis is on the helplessness, the submission of sheep, and this idea passes over to the word's most important meaning in ECL: Christ is the shepherd, his followers are the sheep.[133] This image is even further extended with the use of ἀρνίον: Christ becomes τὸ ἀρνίον in Rev 5:6 and repeatedly throughout the work. The symbolism of βόες also differs in ECL, for it is associated more with business than wealth: e.g., Luke 14:19; John 2:14-15. In the latter passage, βόες is combined with πρόβατα, as it is in Did 13:3.

Plutarch concludes this section by summing up the greedy man's problem and suggesting a solution. Then he concludes in an appropriate manner by giving a working definition of περιττά, the object of the man's illogical desires. Most of the words here, including περιττά, have been discussed, and only a very few require attention. First is πενία. Here it is an absolute term, though in the next section Plutarch qualifies and re-defines it. This noun is not used in ECL where the equivalent term is πτωχεία: e.g., 2 Cor 8:2, 9. See also πτωχύτης in Herm Vis 3:12:2.

When Plutarch attempts to analyze the cause of the man's insatiability, he turns to a Stoic phrase: διὰ κρίσιν φαύλην καὶ ἀλόγιστον.[134] In ECL, κρίσις is a frequent word, but it is not used as Plutarch intends, i.e., a person's own moral judgment. Rather it usually has a legal sense: A judge's decision, and God is the final judge. Probably the closest parallel to Plutarch's meaning is Mark 7:19ff.

The case of φαῦλος is similar. It is also used often and with a

---

[133] Cf. H. Preisker and S. Schulz, *TDNT*, s.v. πρόβατον κτλ.

[134] Cf., for example Chrysippus, fr. 456, *SVF*, III, p. 110, 38-41. See also E. V. Arnold, *Roman Stoicism*, 332, n. 4.

moral connotation, but the reference is usually to externals, to the results of a base attitude: e.g., Jas 3:16; 1 Clem 28:1. The last term of the phrase, ἀλόγιστος, is almost a synonym for φαῦλος in Stoic terminology.[135] It is not used in ECL, but see the use of ἄλογος in 2 Pet 2:12; Jude 10.

Plutarch's final opinion about the greedy man is that the fault must be removed, like a tapeworm, from his soul. This is an expressive simile, but, although the tapeworm is discussed by medical writers and by Pliny (*HN* 11.33, 39, 113), I know of no other instance of its figurative use. The closest parallel in ECL is σκώληξ in Mark 9:48 (= Isa 66:24), which is quoted in 2 Clem 7:6; 17:5. See also σκωληκόβρωτος in Acts 12:23.

The noun ψυχή is, of course, an important word in ECL, but as the seat of inner emotions that are wrong see esp. Luke 12:19; Rev 18:14; 2 Clem 16:2; 17:7. And for the verb which Plutarch uses for removing the tapeworm see Matt 5:29, where the general sense is not unlike Plutarch's.

Expositio A (ch. 4, 524D13-E8).

Love of wealth is not a physical disease. It is a kind of mental poverty. For from financial poverty a single friend can bring relief, but mental poverty cannot be cured by all one's friends, alive or dead, because it is boundless.

The medical imagery continues, but a few new words are used. For example, ἐρριμμένος in the sense of "lying prostrate and weak from sickness" is a regular term and occurs in Matt 9:36. See also Matt 15:30 where it is used in the active voice to describe Jesus' casting off a disease. In Herm Sim 2:3-4 the participle describes the ineffectiveness of the vine without the elm. This passage, like Plutarch's combines the idea of sickness and the use of money.

Plutarch's word for "bed" here is the diminutive κλινίδιον instead of his earlier κλίνη. For this word see Luke 5:19, 24; cf. κλινάριον in Acts 5:15. The patient is unwilling to take nourishment: τροφὴν λαβεῖν. According to LSJ (s.v. λαμβάνω, I.8) the verb is rare in this sense, and it cites only medical writers. Obviously LSJ should have added this passage because it is earlier than those cited. Furthermore from its use in such a context we can see that the phrase already had a medical connotation in Plu-

[135] Cf. Philo, *leg. all.* 3.202; Plutarch, *adv. Stoic.* ch. 21, 1068E.

tarch's day. For a similar expression, but without the medical imagery, see Barn 10:3.

The physician, as part of the examination procedure, touches the patient. Plutarch's word is ἅπτομαι which is used either absolutely or with some appropriate object understood. He may imply nothing more than a simple touching of the face or forehead or he may mean what Epictetus (3.22.73) and Galen (19.207) express more fully by saying τῶν σφυγμῶν ἅπτεσθαι: "to feel the pulse." In either case, Plutarch implies that the action is preliminary to any diagnosis and subsequent cure. In ECL the medical use of ἅπτομαι has a stronger meaning, for it is the verb used for "laying on of hands" to effect the cure itself: e.g., Matt 8:3; 17:7 and often.[136]

The physician decides that a ψυχικὴ νόσος rather than a physical ailment is causing the man's distress. This same contrast between mental and physical disorder seems to lie behind many of the passages in which Jesus cures the sick, though it is interesting that he does not cure cases of ψυχικὴ νόσος, or at least the terminology is not used.

When Plutarch applies the analogy of mental disorder to the greedy man who will do anything to acquire more money, he specifies business activities and uses appropriate terminology. Naturally Plutarch does not condemn the business man because he engages in such activity. Rather he deplores the excesses to which the man succumbs and the motivation that drives him on. The same attitude appears several times in ECL: e.g., 2 Cor 4:2-14; Herm Vis 3:9:6; but esp. 1 Tim 6:5-10; Rev 18:3, 11-19; Herm Sim 9:20:1-4.

Among the words in this sentence which have a parallel in ECL are πορισμός in 1 Tim 6:5-6; αἰσχρός in Tit 1:11; and ἀγέλη. Plutarch uses this word to refer back to πρόβατα, βόες, etc. In ECL it is used only of swine and then only in the one incident where Jesus sends demons from two men into the swine: Matt 8:30-32// Mark 5:11-13; Luke 8:32-33.

The phrase πενία ψυχική deserves special attention. Plutarch, of course, equates it with ψυχικὴ νόσος, and he contrasts this poverty to the conventional idea which he calls πενία χρηματική in the next sentence. The phrase πενία (or even πτωχεία) ψυχική is not used in ECL, but one passage comes very close to Plutarch's

[136] This idea appears in healing miracles in pagan religion, esp. in the cult of Asclepius. For a collection of pertinent passages see Bultmann, *HST*, 222.

idea: Herm Sim 2 (esp. vs. 5), where the rich and the poor are compared to the elm and vine. For the reverse of this idea cf. 2 Cor 8:9; Diogn 5:13; and esp. Matt 5:3.

At this point Plutarch quotes Menander's remark that a single friend by his good deeds can bring relief from genuine poverty. As we have seen, Plutarch considers financial responsibility a part of friendship, and this idea is not foreign to ECL. In addition to the passages cited earlier see Luke 10:29-37; Jas 2:8, 14-16; Did 4:5-8; Herm Man 8:7-12; Herm Sim 2:1-10, all of which are concerned in one way or another with the duties of friends.

The verb εὐεργετέω and related words appear often in ECL. Usually they refer to God's benefits to man (e.g., 1 Clem 19:2; 20:11; 21:1; 38:3; 59:3; Diogn 8:11; 9:5) or those of Christ (Acts 10:38), but occasionally they refer to man's good deeds to man (e.g., Acts 4:9; 1 Tim 6:2; but esp. Diogn 10:6 with which compare Gal 6:2).

Plutarch's reference to friends "alive or dead" touches upon a particularly insidious practice among the Greeks and Romans, legacy-hunting. There is also, of course, a veiled reference to inheritance, a subject which he develops more fully in ch. 7. Legacy-hunting seems not to have been a practice or a concern of the early Christians, but there are references to inheritance and to the greed and quarrels of heirs. The passages are discussed in ch. 7.

This section of the *expositio* concludes with a quotation from Solon and a reference to the idea of αὐτάρκεια: that for sensible men need is the boundry of natural wealth. Juvenal (*Sat.* 14. 316-331) offers a brilliant expression and application of this idea which is almost certainly Cynic and Stoic. The closest parallels in ECL occur in those passages where there are instructions or discussions about the needs (χρεία) of brethren: e.g., Acts 2:45; 4:35; 6:1-6 (esp. vs. 3); Rom 12:13; Eph 4:28; Tit 3:13. In a final analysis, of course, God supplies the χρεία: e.g., Matt 6:11; 6:25-33//Luke 12:22-31.

Expositio B (chs. 4-5, 524E8-525B11)

Another peculiarity of the love of money: It is desire fighting against its own fulfillment. Yet other desires even aid in their own satisfaction: i.e., the desire for food, wine, warmth, sex, but not desire for money. It is an ailment that is mad and piteous.

This brief summary fails as usual to reflect Plutarch's colorful language and vivid examples. Yet, he has already used many of the features here, and we can concentrate on new items or changes from the old. Notice first that he shifts his meaning of φιλαργυρία from "love of silver" to the more general "love of money." Then he uses Stoic terminology to define it as one of the ἐπιθυμίαι, of which there are many.[137]

A similar multiplicity of meanings assigned to ἐπιθυμία occurs in Herm Man 12. The term is divided into two broad categories: ἐπιθυμία πονηρά and ἐπιθυμία ἀγαθή. Among the former are "the desire for the wife or husband of another, extravagance of wealth, much needless food and drink, and many other foolish luxuries." Each of these "wicked desires" appears in the *cup. divit.*, but Plutarch makes it clear that for him the worst is the desire for wealth. This is also the opinion in 1 Tim 6:9-10; cf. Pol Phil 4:1. In Hermas, however, all "wicked desires" are equal and they lead to death. In this respect, Hermas is closer to the Stoic point of view than either the author of 1 Tim or Plutarch. The Stoics held that all sins are equal and were forced into all kinds of outlandish arguments to defend their position.[138]

The idea of ἐπιθυμία, or any abstract concept, fighting against itself is quite rare in ECL, but cf. Rom 7:23. The actual construction μάχεσθαι πρός is used only in John 6:52, where the meaning and context are quite different. For the general idea of Plutarch's statement, however, cf. Eph 2:3 and esp. Col 2:23.

At this point, Plutarch returns to the analogy of food, drink, and warm clothing, and much of the vocabulary is necessarily repeated from earlier passages. Some new words, however, appear: ἀπέχομαι echoes the previous φείδομαι, and χρῆσις seems to be a deliberate, concrete allusion to χρεία in the previous section.[139] For parallels to ἀπέχομαι see 1 Thes 5:22; 1 Pet 2:11; 1 Clem 17:3 (= Job 1:1); and esp. Did 1:4; Pol Phil 2:2. With this last passage Plutarch would certainly agree. For parallels to χρῆσις see Diogn 2:2; 4:2, though the context is quite different.

[137] See von Arnim, *SVF* III, pp. 92ff. where many passages on ἐπιθυμία have been identified as fragments of Chrysippus and grouped under the general heading *De Affectibus*.

[138] E. V. Arnold, *Roman Stoicism*, 354ff.; Rist, *Stoic Phil.*, 81-96.

[139] The Loeb editors have translated χρήσεως ὄψου with "good food," but they are obviously confused. The MSS have χρηστός (which should be χρηστοῦ) while χρήσεως is an emendation. De Lacy and Einarson have merely printed one reading and mistranslated the other.

With a typical play on words Plutarch balances ὄψον with φιλοψία and οἶνος with οἰνοφλυγία. Although φιλοψία is not used in ECL, there are discussions of the desire for excessive amounts of food. See, for example, Herm Man 12:2:1 and the passages cited above in the discussion of gluttony. For οἰνοφλυγία, which Plutarch does not use in a pejorative sense,[140] see 1 Pet 4:3 where it clearly has a bad connotation.

In the next sentence Plutarch says that it is μανικόν and οἰκτρόν to abstain from food, warm clothing and the use of wealth because of a love for such things. Neither adjective is used in ECL, nor do the related verbs have the same meaning. In those passages where someone abstains from life's necessities, enemies put the blame on demons: e.g., Matt 11:18//Luke 7:33; Luke 8:27.

In the concluding section of ch. 4 Plutarch quotes Menander and follows up on the idea by continuing the imagery of an erotic desire for money. Some of the erotic vocabulary appears in ECL: e.g., 1 Cor 7:36;[141] Eph 2:3; Ign Pol 4:3.[142] And Plutarch's picture of the greedy man fighting with his servants is somehow a reminder of the roguish steward in Luke 16:1-9, though we see the other side of the picture there.

At this point editors have marked a new chapter, but Plutarch continues his discussion of ἐπιθυμία and retains the erotic imagery. As part of this subject he introduces a statement attributed to Sophocles that old age has freed him from such desires. The use of the phrase γυναικὶ πλησιάζειν is just one of the many euphemisms in the language for sexual intercourse. It does not appear in ECL, but there are equivalents: e.g., γινώσκειν (Matt 1:25; Luke 1:34); ποιεῖν (1 Cor 7:36); ἔχειν (1 Cor 5:1).

By having Sophocles say that he is free, ἐλεύθερος, from sexual desire Plutarch prepares for the double meaning of this word and that of its opposite, ἀνελεύθερος, both of which he uses later. The latter word regularly refers to monetary conditions and attitudes with the notion of "miserly, stingy," etc. Thus the man who is

---

140 If Plutarch had wanted a pejorative term he would probably have used φιλοινία which regularly carries this sense (e.g., Herodotus 3.34; Diodorus Siculus 5.26; Athenaeus 10.430A) and which would have fitted in better with the other compounds of φιλο- in this passage.

141 On this disputed passage see H. Conzelmann, *1 Corinthians*, 134-136.

142 There is at least a hint of eroticism in the midst of a serious discussion in Herm Sim 9:11:3-6, and of course Hermas' experiences began because of his thoughts about Rhoda, cf. Herm Vis 1:1:2, 6-8.

φιλόπλουτος is a slave to his desire and cannot be free, so he is ἀνελεύθερος.

The negative term is not used in ECL, and the positive seems to have no monetary association. Yet Plutarch's contrast and that in ECL between δοῦλος and ἐλεύθερος is part of the traditional philosophic concept,[143] esp. that of the Cynics and Stoics. For them any man not free from desires did not have αὐτάρκεια and was a slave. At the same time, any man without freedom of independent thought and action was also a slave. In Stoic terminology only the wise man is truly free.[144]

An extension of this idea leads to the Christian paradox that only the person who freely elects to become a slave of Christ is truly free. And this paradox, involving a contrast of δοῦλος and ἐλεύθερος, resembles Plutarch's two opposites. See, for example, 1 Cor 7:22; Rom 8:21; Gal 1:10; 5:1, 13, and esp. 24; Ign Rom 4:3; but see esp. Gal 4:1-10.[145]

When Plutarch (or rather Sophocles) terms sexual desires λυττῶντας καὶ ἀγρίους δεσπότας, he uses vivid language. Yet both modifiers have similar meanings in ECL: λυσσάω is used only in Ign Eph 7:1 where it refers to heretical preachers who are likened to vicious dogs; for ἄγριος see Gal 5:13; Herm Man 12:1:2; 12:3:6. The noun δεσπότης, however, is not used in a figurative sense, but see 2 Tim 2:21, where the thought is not unlike that of Sophocles.

The idea that old age frees us from physical desires is not stated explicitedly in ECL, but there are some interesting passages. For example, on the effects of growing old: 1 Clem 23:3-4; on escaping from passions: 2 Pet 1:4 (cf. Herm Man 12 again) and esp. Tit 2:3; and finally, Paul's evaluation of himself and his changing character: 1 Cor 13:11.

This section of the *expositio* concludes with a sentence designed to return the discussion to φιλοπλουτία by drawing a parallel between it and ἐπιθυμία. Plutarch now introduces the idea of ἡδονή which is a central feature throughout most of the remaining sections of the *cup. divit.*

In Greek philosophy ἡδονή and ἐπιθυμία appear together regularly from the time of Plato (e.g., *Phd.* 83B),[146] and the same pair shows

---

143 Cf. H. Schlier, *TDNT*, s.v. ἐλεύθερος κτλ., esp. B.
144 Cf., for example, Arnold, *Roman Stoicism*, 281; Sandbach, *The Stoics*, 22.
145 Cf. Arnold, op. cit., 424ff.
146 Cf. F. Büchsel, *TDNT*, s.v. ἐπιθυμία κτλ.

up in ECL: Tit 3:3; Diogn 9:1; and Jas 4: 1-3, where ἐπιθυμέω is used. That ἡδονή is to be taken in a bad sense is obvious from such passages as Mark 4:19//Luke 8:14 (in the Parable of the Sower) and in the Matthean version (13:22) where ἀπάτη replaces ἡδονή. See also Herm Sim 8:8:5; 8:9:4; Diogn 6:5, where each time ἡδονή may designate sexual pleasure.

Just as Sophocles refers to ἐπιθυμία as a δεσπότης, so Plutarch calls φιλοπλουτία a βαρεῖα καὶ πικρὰ δέσποινα. These adjectives are also used in ECL to modify abstractions: e.g., 1 John 5:3, where the commandments of God are not βαρεῖαι and Herm Man 12:4:6, where those of Satan are πικραί.

Plutarch ends this discussion with an expression that is a *sententia* and virtually an epigram: "Love of wealth is a mistress who forces us to acquire and forbids the use, who arouses desire and removes the pleasure." The erotic language of this statement is missing in ECL, but the play on κτᾶσθαι . . . χρῆσθαι [147] appears in Acts 8:20, where the word order stresses the fact that a verbal pun is intended.

Expositio C. 1 (ch. 5, 525B11-E3)

This section contains a series of six examples in which the emphasis alternates between prodigals and misers:

1. Stratonicus, the Athenian wit, chides the prodigal Rhodians for building as if they will live forever and eating like there is no tomorrow.
2. Lovers of money acquire like prodigals but spend like misers.
3. Demades, the Athenian demagogue and a good example of a miser, visits the statesman Phocion, who typifies self-sufficiency.
4. An apostrophe, in good Cynic fashion,[148] to an unnamed second person who possesses most of the evil attributes of a miser.
5. A Byzantine husband finds an adulterer with his ugly wife and exclaims, "what drives you to it? The dregs are foul!" This

[147] The pairing of κτᾶσθαι and χρῆσθαι, κτῆμα and χρῆμα, etc. is frequent in Greek literature at least from the time of Xenophon. Plutarch uses the pair several times in this treatise, and see Teles, fr. 4A, pp. 37-38 (Hense), where the play on sound can be rendered in English by "cache" and "cash."

[148] For examples of this device cf. Musonius, fr. 9 (Lutz), p. 74, 8 and 21; 76, 2; Teles, fr. 2 (Hense), p. 6, 1-5; 10, 6-11, etc.

episode somehow introduces the main subject of the section: [149] public figures must be prodigals to maintain their power and position.

6. A second apostrophe to the miserly second person who endures every discomfort but gets no good from it, like the bathhouse keeper's ass.

Plutarch opens ch. 6 with the remark that "we have been discussing ass-like and ant-like φιλοπλουτία. Since the sixth example specifically identifies the miser as "ass-like" we see that this designation applies to all the misers, i.e., the even-numbered examples. Consequently, the odd-numbered examples are "ant-like." [150]

No single passage of ECL contains a comparable discussion of prodigals and misers, but the basic ideas are scattered throughout the literature. Consider first the remark of Stratonicus to the Rhodians. As the Loeb editors suggest, it is a *topos* on πολυτέλεια which may be pre-Socratic, but like many other expressions, it found its way into later writings, esp. those of the Cynics and Stoics. It also entered Hellenistic Judaism and, in part at least, Christianity.

The *topos* has, in one form or another, become a part of other topics. It appears in discussions of αὐτάρκεια or ἐγκράτεια which are in a sense the reverse of πολυτέλεια and τρυφή,[151] and it may show up in discussions of exile and eschatology. Indeed, so useful is the *topos* in all types of ethical discussions that hundreds of examples

[149] The textual problems in this section confuse its meaning and purpose. Yet, for two reasons the episode of the Byzantine husband seems to belong to the discussion of public officials: first, as the wording stands, the husband's remarks seem to lead directly into the passage about the officials; secondly, the alternating pattern of the chapter, prodigals vs. misers, is broken if this episode constitutes a separate example.

[150] Plutarch's analogy is interesting. His use of ὀνώδης, especially after his sixth example, is obvious: the "ass-like" love of wealth does the work but has none of the enjoyment. This is the miser. But what about μυρμηκώδης? LSJ defines it as μυρμηκοειδής (which appears only in the 3rd cent. with Cassius Medicus and the 5th century lexicographer Hesychius), but these references are no help. Plutarch uses the word only one other time (*cohib. ira* 458C), where he says "But digging in and biting is μυρμηκῶδες καὶ μυῶδες." The same thought appears in Seneca's *De ira* 2.34.1: "Flies and ants, if you move your hand near, turn their mouths toward you. Weak creatures think they are wounded if they are touched." From these two passages the basic idea of μυρμηκώδης emerges as "stinging, biting," e.g., an aggressive action, and that notion suits the prodigals.

[151] Cf. North, *Sophrosyne*, 134, 227, 245, 312-328.

could be listed which resemble one or both of the basic ideas in Plutarch's sentence, but a very few must suffice.

Consider first the idea of extravagant building.[152] Plutarch himself (*reg. et imp.* 208A) quotes a remark which Augustus made about the elaborate construction of Piso, "you make me happy building like this, as if Rome will be eternal." In Hellenistic Judaism, see Sir 11:14-19, esp. vs. 18; Philo, *conf. ling* 76, p. 416; *agric.* 65, p. 310. In the NT, see Luke 12:15-21 (cf. vss. 22-34) which relates the Parable of the Rich Fool; Gal 4:26; Phil 3:20; and esp. Heb 13:14; and perhaps even John 14:2. In the Apostolic Fathers, see 2 Clem 5:5; 6:6 (where ὀλιγοχρόνιος makes its only two appearances); Herm Man 8:3; 12:2:1, but esp. Herm Vis 3:1-10; Diogn 5:5.

On eating to excess see Sir 31:12-24; Philo *vit. Mos.* 2:23-24; Matt 11:19//Luke 7:34; Luke 12:19; 1 Cor 11:27-34 (cf. Herm Vis 3:9:3); Tit 1:12; Herm Man 6:2:5; 8:3; 12:2:1; and see the earlier discussion of gluttony.

Plutarch's second example is less dramatic but more epigrammatic: "Lovers of money acquire like prodigals, spend like misers; endure the troubles, miss the pleasures." The best example in ECL is again the Parable of the Rich Fool, Luke 12:15-21 (cf. vss. 22-34). See also Sir 8:2; 11:14-19. On the use of πολυτέλεια, etc. see Herm Sim 1:10-11 where πολυτέλεια τῶν ἐθνῶν is contrasted to that of the Christians; Herm Man 8:3; 12:2:1.

For his third example Plutarch turns to two famous models of human conduct: Demades, a notorious demagogue and prodigal, and Phocion, famous for his wisdom and restraint. The emphasis here is on Demades since Plutarch is primarily concerned with faults related to wealth. The virtuous Phocion is merely a foil.[153] For a passage in ECL which reflects Phocion's way of life see Herm Vis 2:3:2 or even, to some extent, the descriptions of John the Baptist Matt 3:4; Luke 7:53.

On the attitude of Demades see, for example, Matt 6:25-33//

---

152 For examples from Greek literature see the list of De Lacy and Einarson in the Loeb, p. 19, n. b.

153 For both of these men see Plutarch's *Life of Phocion*, and for Demades in particular see the old but still very useful article by L. Schmitz in W. Smith's *A Dictionary of Greek and Roman Biography and Mythology* (London, 1844; reprinted New York, 1967) 1:957-958. This article lists the important ancient sources for our knowledge of Demades, and they show that he became a standard example in ethical discussions.

Luke 12:22-31; 2 Pet 2:13-16; and once again Herm Man 12:1:2; 12:2:1-3. For the remark that he was a demagogue εἰς γαστέρα see Tit 1:12. Because of this attitude Plutarch identifies Demades' chief fault as ἀσωτία (i.e., "prodigality" and a close synonym of τρυφή). The word is used three times in the NT, and each time it resembles the meaning in Plutarch's sentence: twice (Eph 5:18; 1 Pet 4:4) it is closely associated with drinking, and in the latter passage it is a Gentile vice. In Tit 1:6 the word has a more general meaning, i.e., "loose living." With this idea cf. ἀσώτως in Luke 15:13.

The description of Demades concludes with a remark of Antipater that in his old age the Athenian demagogue resembled a sacrifical animal when the butchering was done: only the tongue and the belly's cavity remained. The sort of sacrifice referred to here was common among the Greeks, and is a practice to which Paul alludes in 1 Cor 10:14-29, esp. vss. 27-29. He calls it ἱερόθυτος.[154] On the attitude of eating such sacrificial meat cf. Acts 15:29; 21:25; 1 Cor 8:1-13; 10:14-33; Rev 2:14, 20; Did 6:3.

The tongue is regularly used as a symbol of vice. For example, Plutarch refers several times to the story of the sage Bias (or sometimes another sage, Pittacus) who was asked by a king to sacrifice an animal and send him the part that was the best and the worst. In response the sage sent only the tongue (cf. *sept. sap. conv.* 146F-147A and Loeb vol. 2, 352, note a). That the tongue was the worst part of the body lies behind several passages in ECL: e.g., Mark 7:33-35; Luke 1:64; Rom 3:13; Jas 1:26; 1 Clem 15:4-5; Herm Vis 2:2:3.

References to the belly (κοιλία) as a symbol of gluttony are also frequent. In Plutarch's passage, however, κοιλία is not the organ itself but rather the cavity left in the butchered victim after the stomach was removed. Thus Demades' cavity is even larger and more difficult to fill than a mere belly. On the use of κοιλία in ECL as a pejorative term see Mark 7:18-19; Phil 3:19; and for a combination of gluttony and gossip see Rom 16:18.

From this picture of Demades Plutarch abruptly addresses some second person with nothing to mark the transition except σὲ δέ. The denunciation that follows is a characteristic Cynic diatribe

[154] Plutarch uses ἱερόθυτος in *qu. conv.* 729C and quotes (*glor. Ath.* 349C) a fragment of Pindar in which the word appears. He may also allude to this fragment in *reg. et imp.* 192C, but the text is uncertain here.

in miniature form. Its language belongs to the world of business, politics, or at least social activity. Because the concepts and practices to which Plutarch alludes were such a uniquely integral part of Greek aristocratic life, most of the vocabulary and ideas are foreign to ECL, which is generally concerned with different social and cultural strata.

A few terms, however, appear or have equivalents. For example, κακοδαίμων is absent from ECL, but the vocative ἄφρων serves the same purpose: e.g., Luke 11:40; 12:20; Rom 2:20; 1 Cor 15:36; Herm Sim 1:3; and cf. 6:4:3; 6:5:2; 9:14:4. Also missing from ECL are ἀπανθρώπως (but cf. the adjective in Mart Pol 2:3, where it means "inhuman") and ἀμεταδότως. For this word the closest expression is probably Herm Vis 3:9:4, where the key word is ἀσυγκρασία.[155]

Plutarch uses κακοπαθής almost in a neutral sense, i.e. "to suffer hardships." This may be a virtuous course of conduct in other circumstances, but here the emphasis is on the fact that the person suffered the hardships for the wrong reasons and thus suffered in vain. In ECL the idea is a virtue: to suffer misfortune in this life insures a better fortune in the next: e.g., 2 Tim 2:9; 4:5; Jas 5:13; 2 Clem 19:3. See also κακοπάθεια in Jas 5:10, and of course the general idea lies behind the Beatitudes: e.g., Matt 5:4, 6, 10-12.[156]

Both ἀγρυπνέω (see ch. 3) and ἐργολαβέω can have a good sense, but in this passage they are derogatory. Normally ἐργολαβέω is a business term, "to make a profit," but here it also has a political sense and refers to graft: in American jargon it is called "pork-barreling."[157] This verb is not used in ECL, but for a reference to the attitude described here cf. 2 Clem 1:6, and on the proper kinds of work cf. 1 Cor 3:10-15; 1 Clem 34:1-4.

The idea expressed by ὑποπίπτω was particularly loathesome to the Greeks and Romans. It usually means "to cringe, fawn, be a flatterer" and is used of dogs, legacy-hunters,[158] politicians, etc.

---

155 Many texts spell this word ἀσυνκρασία, but why perpetuate the mistake of some ignorant or careless scribe?

156 For references to the virtue of suffering see Bauer, s.v. πάσχω and esp. W. Michaelis, *TDNT*, s.v. πάσχω κτλ., esp. πάσχω, C-D.

157 Plutarch discusses this subject in his *praec. reip.* 806F-809B. See esp. the statement of Themistocles in 807A-B and the attitude of Agesilaüs in 809B.

158 There is a frequent association of ὑποπίπτω and κληρονομέω which is, of course, what Plutarch intends.

In effect, it describes an excessive show of humility in a society where even a moderate amount was viewed with suspicion.[159] In the OT there are many references to "bowing down, making obeisance," but this practice was a mark of respect. The same is true in ECL where the verb ὑπότασσω is used. Here one submits to those whose worth or position merits the submission. Perhaps the closest parallel to Plutarch's meaning of ὑποπίπτω, and it is close only because it stresses the reverse, is 1 Thes 2:5-6. Without the negative, this passage would be a fair description of one who ὑποπίπτει. See, however, Jas 2: 1-7 (esp. vss. 3, 6) for an example of servile flattery.

On the whole, however, the word group which most nearly approaches the meaning of ὑποπίπτω is ὑπόκρισις,[160] etc. See, for example, Matt 6:1-21, where ὑποκρίτης is the central word (vss. 2, 5, 16) and is used of people who make a show of obsequious obedience to God when their real thoughts are quite different. In effect, they are toadies to God. See also Gal 2:11-14, where Paul comes close to accusing Cephas of toadyism;[161] Did 5:1//Barn 20:1, where ὑπόκρισις appears with διπλοκαρδία in a catalogue of vices. Yet the only passage which has a political implication is Gal 2:11-14, which is a clear reference to early church politics.

The episode of the Byzantine husband can be passed over. The textual problems obscure its meaning, and the few ideas and words that can be understood have only remote parallels in ECL. The one exception, perhaps, is ἀνάγκη. In Plutarch it refers both to the sexual urge that drove the man to adultery and, in the general context, it is greed.[162] The basic underlying force is "necessity, compulsion," a meaning that is common in all forms of Greek literature. ECL is no exception, as Bauer demonstrates. The strongest meaning of ἀνάγκη is found in 1 Cor 7:36-37 (cf. 9:16), where it almost means inevitability as some divine pre-ordination.[163] See also Matt 18:7; Rom 13:5 for a similar use of the word.

---

[159] For a brilliant example of this attitude, where the Greeks are the object of ridicule, see Juvenal *Sat.* 3. 73-108. He calls them (vs. 86) *Adulandi gens prudentissima*.

[160] Cf. U. Wilckens, *TDNT*, s.v. ὑποκρίνομαι κτλ.

[161] But cf. Wilckens, ibid., C.2.

[162] For adultery coupled with greed cf. 2 Clem 6:4; Herm Man 12:2:1.

[163] Cf. H. Conzelmann, *1 Corinthians*, 157f., but he does not stress this idea nearly enough. W. Grundmann (*TDNT*, s.v. ἀναγκάζω κτλ., B.2) is much closer to the mark: "he (sc. Paul) is under divine restraint which he cannot escape."

Plutarch's next example involves a special type of prodigal, the politician. This is one of the most important passages for his treatment of ambition as a concept associated with wealth. People seek public offices, Plutarch says, to satisfy their ambition which is a form of greed.[164] The driving force behind the greedy ambition is pretension and self-glorification. This general topic does not appear in ECL, but in 1 Clem 32:2 a similar list of officials appears without reference to their need for money.

Some of the words in Plutarch's discussion are, however, important enough in ECL to merit attention. For example, Plutarch's term for "ambition" is φιλοτιμία. It appears only in Diogn 3:5, where it has a neutral meaning, neither laudatory nor pejorative, though the context leans to the latter. Paul uses φιλοτιμέομαι three times (Rom 15:20; 2 Cor 5:9; 1 Thes 4:11), and in each case it means simply "to aim, to aspire" in a neutral or even laudatory sense.[165] For references to the ambition of officials see, for example, Matt 23:13-36; Luke 11:37-44, since the Pharisees are a type of religious official.

Behind political ambition, says Plutarch, is ἀλαζονεία and ἡ κενὴ δόξα. The first term has already been discussed, but the latter expression deserves study. In ECL δόξα has the same basic meaning which it acquired in the LXX, i.e., "divine splendor" hence "divine honor," etc.[166] Consequently such a concept as κενὴ δόξα is virtually impossible, and the philosophic idea behind the phrase must be expressed by another term. That term is κενοδοξία, which has two basic meanings: "vanity" and "delusion," though the two often come very close to one another. See, for example, Phil 2:3 (cf. κενόδοξοι in Gal 5:26); Herm Sim 8:9:3, where it appears as a Gentile vice. In Did 3:5 κενόδοξος joins φιλάργυρος and ψεύστης, and the three become κλοπαί. In Ign Phld 1:1 the Bishop obtained his office not κατὰ κενοδοξίαν, and in both 1 Clem 35:5 and Herm Man 8:5 κενοδοξία is joined with ἀλαζονεία as it is in Plutarch.

Plutarch concludes his series of examples with another miniature diatribe against, apparently, the same imaginary second person whom he addressed in the fourth example. And as before elements of the Cynic-Stoic style are used, while the language is especially

[164] Cf. Plutarch's discussion of this connection in *praec. reip.* 819F-820F.

[165] For what it is worth, the Vulgate gives three different translations: Rom 15:20: *praedico*; 2 Cor 5:9: *contendo*; 1 Thes 4:11: *operam do*.

[166] Cf. G. Kittel and G. v. Rad, *TDNT*, s.v. δοκέω κτλ.

vigorous as well as flowery with such words as συγχέω, ταράττω, στροβέω and the phrases κοχλίου βίον ζῶν, ὄνος βαλανέως adding to the picturesque details.

Some of these words and expressions offer interesting parallels to ECL. For συγχέω, which Plutarch uses with an inanimate object, cf. Acts 9:22; 21:27, when it has an animate object, and Acts 2:6; Herm Vis 5:4-5; Herm Man 12:4:1, where it is passive with an animate subject. For ταράττω cf. Gal 1:7; 5:10; 1 Pet 3:14 (= Isa 8:12) and John 11:33, where the reflexive construction is used. This idea, however, is more often expressed by the passive: e.g., Matt 2:3; Mark 6:50; Mart Pol 12:1. Yet each of these passages refers to a specific incident or condition that causes the mental disturbance; in Plutarch a style of living produces a complete turmoil of the person's life.

Plutarch's word for "stinginess, meanness" is μικρολογία. This is an extension of the word's basic meaning of "pettiness," i.e. an excessive attention to minute details. The noun is used only in Herm Man 5:2:2 in a discussion of bad temper. Both Bauer and the Loeb translator Lake translate it by "trifle," a meaning which it seems to have nowhere else. Yet, the word seems to refer, not to the small object of attention (i.e., "trifle"), but to the attention itself which is paid to small objects (i.e., "pettiness"). Consequently Bauer and Lake are incorrect, and μικρολογία has one of its regular meanings.

The phrase οὐδὲν εὖ πάσχω is a normal expression in Classical Greek, for πάσχω is basically a neutral verb, though there are numerous passages where it means "suffer." Usually, however, it needs an adverb to specify its meaning, and εὖ and κακῶς are probably the most frequent modifiers. In ECL, πάσχω [167] almost always means "suffer" without the need of an adverb. The two exceptions are Matt 17:15, where κακῶς is added, and Gal 3:4: τοσαῦτα ἐπάθετε εἰκῇ. Contrary to Bauer's remark that τοσαῦτα refers to pleasant experiences and that πάσχω has a good sense, the nuance of the phrase seems neutral. The emphasis of the antecedents of τοσαῦτα is more on their emotional impact than on the pleasure they brought. Consequently, πάσχω here seems to have its classical Greek meaning, simply "experience."

[167] For the meaning and construction of the word Bauer is sufficient; for its place in Christian theology see W. Michaelis, *TDNT*, s.v. πάσχω κτλ., esp. πάσχω, C-D.

Plutarch sums up the lot of the miser, and for that matter each miser in his list of examples, by likening him to the bathhouse-keeper's ass which carries ξύλα καὶ φρύγανα, which is always full of smoke and ashes, but has no share in the bath, the warmth, or the cleanliness. This picturesque description provides an effective conclusion to the passage and offers at least one striking parallel to ECL.

In Mart Pol 13:1, ξύλα καὶ φρύγανα (Plutarch's exact words) are gathered ἔκ τε τῶν ἐργαστηρίων καὶ βαλανείων to feed the fire in which Polycarp is to be burnt. The apparently set phrase and its connection with the baths is both passages indicate that it was a regular term. And from Plutarch's use of the ass in a simile, this animal must have been a regular part of the "equipment" in the baths.[168]

The imagery of the ὄνος βαλανέως is not used in ECL, but its intention resembles the advice "not to muzzle the oxen" in Deut 25:4 [169] which is quoted in 1 Cor 9:9 and, in a slightly different form, in 1 Tim 5:18.

Expositio C. 2 (ch. 6, 525E4-526A22)

With the beginning of ch. 6, Plutarch turns to the third type of φιλοπλουτία which he calls θηριώδης.[170] As he details its characteristics we see that it is little more than a special category of the ὀνώδης in which the emphasis has shifted. This brand of φιλοπλουτία is vicious, destructive and dishonest. It sticks at nothing to acquire wealth, then having amassed the ill-gotten wealth it makes no use of it.

In his description Plutarch continues and even intensifies his use of diatribe elements. The language is vigorous but flowery, the imagery belongs to the animal world of dangerous and deadly insects. And through it all runs a strong current of bitter tirade and cruel invective. Gone is the kindly Plutarch, the gentle adviser of

---

[168] For a good discussion of ancient baths see W. Smith (ed.), *A Dictionary of Greek and Roman Antiquities* (New York, 1843) 143-154; S. Platner and T. Ashby, *A Topographical Dictionary of Ancient Rome* (New York, 1929) 518-536. Neither work, however, mentions a source for the fires that heated the water, nor have I found a reference to this use of an ass. But is it just an interesting coincidence that Polycarp rode to the place of his martyrdom on an ass?

[169] Cf. Josephus *AJ* 4.233; Philo *virt.* 27.145-147.

[170] The first sentence, which serves as a transition by referring back to the previous section, is discussed in ch. 5.

youth. Instead we hear, from whatever source, the voice of an angry man who seems to feel that this θηριώδης φιλοπλουτία is destroying his world.

The wealth of detail and the variety of ideas in this passage prevent a thorough analysis and comparison with ECL. We can only examine those new items which seem most important. For example, he begins by using a series of participles to list the chief characteristics of the θηριώδης φιλοπλουτία: συκοφαντοῦσα, κληρονομοῦσα, παραλογιζομένη, πολυπραγμονοῦσα, φροντίζουσα, and ἀριθμοῦσα τῶν φίλων ἔτι πόσοι ζῶσιν.[171] After this, he pin-points the meaning of θηριώδης by using the analogy of such creatures as vipers, blister-beetles and venomous spiders which, unlike the predatory bears and lions, do not use what they destroy.

Let's take θηριώδης first. It is not used in ECL, but Ign Smyrn 4:1 comes very close. Ignatius says that he guards his brethren in Smyrna ἀπὸ τῶν θηρίων τῶν ἀνθρωπομόρφων, and these beasts in human form are the heretical teachers who deceive and earn money from their teaching. For language similar to Plutarch's see Gal 5:15 and cf. vss. 16-21 which characterize the sort of person Plutarch has in mind and begin with the same imagery.[172]

Among the words that identify the characteristics, συκοφαντέω is used twice: Luke 3:14; 19:17, and the latter passage also has a frequent synonym, ψευδομαρτυρέω. This verb, with its noun ψευδομαρτυρία, is a favorite item in catalogues of vices: e.g., Matt 15:19; Mark 10:19; Luke 18:20; Did 2:3; Pol Phil 2:2; 3:3; Herm Man 8:5. For a similar idea see Herm Sim 9:19:3. The second term, κληρονομέω, is discussed in ch. 7. Next is παραλογίζομαι which has some interesting parallels in ECL, though there is an important difference: Plutarch uses the word absolutely, unless we are expected to supply some personal object. In ECL, this verb always governs a direct object. The nearest parallel to Plutarch's idea is Col 2:4 and cf. Ign Magn 3:2 where the word occurs with ὑπόκρισις, and notice also the development of the verb in λόγος of the next sentence. See also 2 Pet 2:12; Jude 10 for a similar expression with ἄλογος.

---

[171] For comparable lists of vices see such passages as 1 Clem 35:5; Did 5:1-2//Barn 20:1-2; Pol Phil 2:2 (cf. 4:3); Herm Sim 6:2:1-4; 6:4:1-4; and esp. 5:1-7 and many of the catalogues of vices listed in ch. 1.

[172] For perhaps another parallel cf. 1 Cor 15:32 and the article by A. Malherbe, "The Beasts of Ephesus," *JBL* 87 (1968) 71-80.

The verb πολυπραγμονέω does not occur in ECL, and the related noun and adjective are used only once each: Diogn 4:6; 5:3.[173] These words have a regular pejorative meaning in Classical Greek, i.e., "busybody," and "meddlesome," etc., and this is certainly the idea in 4:6. In 5:3, however, the adjective seems to be neutral, i.e., "curious, inquisitive." This passage also associates πολυπράγμων with φροντίς, and notice that Plutarch's next term is φροντίζω. But again, φροντίς and φροντίζω regularly have a good, or at least neutral, sense in ECL (e.g., Tit 3:8; Ign Pol 1:2) while Plutarch's word is clearly pejorative.

The notion of counting how many friends are still alive is an appropriate climax, for they are the targets of the vicious activities listed here. And the insect in the form of a man must know how much prey is available for him to put the bite on. There is no parallel in ECL to this attitude toward friends, though the older brother of the prodigal son may have harbored similar thoughts: cf. Luke 15:29. And for the idea of enjoying or not enjoying vice, sin, etc. see the use of ἀπόλαυσις in Heb 11:25; 2 Clem 10:3; cf. 1 Tim 6:17.

At this point in his discussion, Plutarch makes his analogy of the man who exemplifies θηριώδης φιλοπλουτία with such insects as vipers, blister-beetles, and venomous spiders. Of these three insects only the viper (ἔχιδνα) is mentioned in ECL,[174] and its role as a symbol of rapacity and treachery is amply demonstrated by such passages as Matt 3:7; 23:23; Luke 3:7; but see esp. Matt 12:34. Two other passages should be cited: Barn 10 which discusses the eatable and uneatable animals set forth in Lev and Deut, but cf. esp. 10:4 which offers an interpretation of the injunction against eating the eagle, hawk, kite and crow. This section is remarkably similar to Plutarch's sentence. The same imagery is used in Herm Sim 9:26:7, where the two verbs διαφθείρω and ἀπόλλυμι approximate Plutarch's κτείνω and ἀπόλλυμι.

The symbolic use of bears and lions, which Plutarch contrasts to the vicious insects, has some parallels in ECL. In Rev 13:2 ἄρκτος

---

[173] Diogn 5 is an important passage. It is one which every classical and New Testament scholar should put on a placard and set above his desk, for it gives a forceful and, in the main, accurate evaluation of the unity of ethical ideals in the Greco-Roman, Judeo-Christian world.

[174] Probably the ἀκρίς, mentioned in Lev 11:22 and translated "beetle" by the King James Version in Matt 3:4; Mark 1:6; Rev 9:3 and 7, is a grasshopper. Cf. Bauer, s.v. ἀκρίς.

and λέων appear together: The beast described here resembles a leopard but has the feet of a bear and the mouth of a lion. Then in vss. 5ff. the mouth utters blasphemous words, cf. Rev 4:7; 9:8, 17; 10:3. The bear is used only in Rev 13:2, but the lion appears in 1 Pet 5:8 (= Ps 21:14), where the Devil is likened to a roaring lion; cf. 1 Clem 35:11 (= Ps 49:22); 45:6 (cf. Heb 11:33). Yet the only similarity in any of these examples to Plutarch's passage is the symbolic use of predatory animals.

From the analogy of these animals Plutarch returns to the subject of people driven by θηριώδης φιλοπλουτία, and in doing so he prepares the way for the next major division of the *cup. divit.*, an attack on the real and alleged motives of misers and prodigals. Much of the thought and vocabulary of the section is repeated from earlier discussions, but a few interesting terms appear for the first time: For χρῆσθαι μὴ δύνανται μηδὲ πεφύκασιν see 1 Cor 7:35;[175] 2 Clem 16:1. For ἐν ἀφθόνοις γενόμενοι see 2 Cor 8:2, 14 and perhaps 20 for a similar idea. And for τῆς πονηρίας ... πεπαῦσθαι see 1 Pet 4:1; 1 Clem 8:4 (= Isa 1:16); Herm Vis 3:9:1.

Plutarch concludes the *expositio* with another one of his statements that is almost epigrammatic: For those who use their wealth for nothing pleasant or useful there is no end to greed; they are always empty and still want the whole world.

The idea is very similar to the opening sentence of ch. 3 and to several expressions in that chapter. Consequently, most of the wording and thought has already appeared, but there are some new elements: For the phrase εἰς μηδὲν ἡδὺ μηδὲ χρήσιμον πολιτευόμενοι[176] see the use of ἡδυπάθεια in 2 Clem 16:2; 17:7; ἐπ' οὐδὲν χρήσιμον in 2 Tim 2:14, though the similarity here is only verbal; πολιτεύομαι in Phil 1:27; 1 Clem 6:1; 21:1; Pol Phil 5:2; Herm Sim 5:6:6; and esp. 1 Clem 3:4; 51:2, where it is used, as in Plutarch's phrase, with a prepositional phrase.

The noun ἀνακωχή is a corrupted form of ἀνοχή. In the latter form it occurs in Rom 2:3; 3:26 in the sense of "forbearance, clemency," but in Herm Sim 6:3:1; 9:5:1; 9:14:2 its meaning is closer to

[175] On this difficult passage cf. H. Conzelmann, *1 Corinthians*, 133-134, who aptly cites Epictetus *Diss.* 2.6.28 (the English ed. incorrectly prints 2.16.8, but the German ed. has it correct).

[176] For πολιτευομένοις the Teubner editor prints his own emendation πονηρευομένοις and cites *aer. al.* 829F as a parallel. But the superficial similarity of the two passages is hardly adequate justification for altering the unanimous reading of the MSS.

Plutarch's. For the articular infinitive τοῦ πλεονεκτεῖν see the discussion of πλεονεξία in ch. 2, and for the whole expression here cf. 2 Cor 8:15 (= Exod 16:18); Teles, fr. 4A, p. 40, 6-8 (Hense). For ἀσχολία, which is not used in ECL, cf. ἀνάπαυσις in Rev 4:8; 14:11 as well as καταπαύω in Mart Pol 1:1; 8:1, but the noun κατάπαυσις (e.g., Acts 7:49; Heb 3:11, 18) has a different meaning.

The phrase πρὸς δεομένοις ἁπάντων provides a suitably somber conclusion to this discussion of the greedy. It is also an apt charge against such people for whom there can be no αὐτάρκεια. In ECL, of course, God is αὐτάρκης, for he needs nothing (e.g., Acts 17:25; Diogn 3:3, 4b-5). Rather he provides for men in need: Diogn 3:4a.

Exhortatio A (ch. 7, 526A23-527A12)

In the fourth major section of the *cup. divit.*, Plutarch attacks the real and alleged motives of misers and prodigals. As he has done before, he examines first one group and then the other. Here the misers are first on stage. The excuse that they save their money for heirs is nonsense, for while they are alive they neglect their children. And why save for heirs? Only that they, too, can pass on the hoarded wealth to their heirs and on and on until some outsider grabs it all or the worst member of the line consumes it.

At this point Plutarch turns to the subject of parental training. He points out that by their own actions and attitudes parents train their children to imitate them in their greed and miserliness: [177] the sons of misers are miserable. They are filled with a love of wealth even before they inherit, and instead of loving their parents because they will someday inherit, they hate them because they have not yet received the money. In their impatience they steal from their parents and squander the money on friends.

Then the father dies. The son soon resembles his father: he is morose, a real *agelast*. No more youthful play, no time for study. Instead, all is business and worry, haggling with debtors and stewards, until late at night. So, in conclusion, what has he received from his father compared to the freedom he has lost? He has grown old before his time.

---

[177] It is in this section that Plutarch and Juvenal agree most closely. See the introduction for precise parallels.

The message of this brilliant section is simple. Like begets like, for the sons of misers will become misers and their sons in turn. There can be no other outcome unless such people turn to a philosophy and to a contemplation of the gods. This solution, however, Plutarch postpones until after his discussion of prodigals in chs. 8-9 when he offers it as the answer to both groups and as the climax and message of the whole treatise.

This ultimate resolution must be kept in mind as we examine the final sections, for it draws the whole treatise nearer to the message of ECL even when verbal and thematic similarities are not close in isolated words and phrases. For example, on ch. 7 as a whole compare such passages as Matt 6:19-34; 21:33-46//Mark 12:1-12// Luke 20:9-19; Luke 12:33-34; Gal 4:1-7 (cf. vss. 30-31); 1 Tim 6:17-20. On the duty to provide for heirs see 2 Cor 12:14-15; and for the attitude and, in particular, the impatience of heirs see Luke 15:11-32 (the Parable of the Prodigal Son).

The whole subject of inheritance in ECL is an enormous and important concept, but there is neither the need nor the space to discuss it here.[178] Except in a few places, the terms κληρονομία, κληρονόμος, κληρονομέω and related words have a special religious and eschatological connotation that dominates their usage. And while Plutarch concludes his discussion of the subject with a reference to philosophic and religious contemplation, his advice pales beside the Christian concept of God's inheritance for mankind. Because of this idea the word-group in ECL usually lacks the pejorative sense which the verb, in particular, has in Greek literature and which it certainly has in Plutarch's treatise. In fact, the nearest parallels are Luke 12:13 which prompts the Parable of the Rich Fool and Luke 15:11-32, the Parable of the Prodigal Son. In this parable the older son tries in every way to please his father, seemingly with an eye on the inheritance. His actions (vss. 25-30) resemble, in a sense, those of Plutarch's heir, for he works hard like his father, never engages in youthful frivolity, and is in fact very much an *agelast*.

With the subject of this passage identified, we can now look at individual words and ideas. The two verbs φυλάττω and θησαυρίζω are used frequently in ECL, but the nearest parallel is 1 Tim 6:17-

[178] For the subject of inheritance in ECL cf. W. Foerster and J. Herrmann, *TDNT*, s.v. κλῆρος κτλ., esp. κληρονόμος κτλ., E.

20, esp. vss. 19-20 where both verbs occur.[179] For θησαυρίζω see also Matt 6:19-21; Jas 5:3.

When Plutarch compares miserly parents who do not share their wealth with their children to gold-eating mice which must be killed before the ore can be obtained, he gives one more example of the strange appetites which ancient mice had. They ate pitch (Theocritus *Idyll* 14.51) and iron (Seneca *Apocolocyntosis* 7), licked meal (ibid., 8), and here they eat gold.[180] There are, in fact, several proverbial characteristics of mice in ancient writings, but none appears in ECL.[181] The closest imagery is found in Matt 6:19-20//Mark 10:21//Luke 12:33-34, cf. 1 Tim 6:17-19; Jas 5:1-3.

Another of Plutarch's analogies, the simile of earthen pipes, is clever, expressive and, in the author's society, an apt and logical figure. There is, however, nothing in ECL like it, for the simile of the earthen pots in Rev 2:27 is hardly a parallel. Plutarch's verb κατεσθίω, which echoes ἐσθίω in the simile of the mice, is used several times in ECL. See esp. Mark 12:40; Luke 20:47 (cf. Matt 23:14 t.r.); Gal 5:15. On the idea of saving for the future see Matt 6:19-21//Luke 12:33-34; 1 Tim 6:17-19; Jas 5:1-5; and esp. Luke 12:16-31. On vain inheritance see 1 Pet 1:18.

Plutarch continues his discussion of the sons of misers and compares them with slaves. In doing so, he quotes a verse of Euripides and a saying of the Cynic Diogenes.[182] For a comparison of slaves and heirs (or sons of misers) see Gal 4:1-2 and cf. vs. 7. For a virtuous slave who is made co-heir with the son see Herm Sim 5:2:1-11 (cf. the whole of Sim 5). And for the heir being slain by greedy slaves see Matt 21:33-41//Mark 12: 1-8//Luke 20: 9-15.

[179] The verb here is ἀποθησαυρίζω, but the meaning is the same as the simple verb. For a brief discussion of the terms see F. Hauck, *TDNT*, s.v. θησαυρός, θησαυρίζω, but notice that he omits the use of the compound in 1 Tim 6:19.

[180] Pliny, *HN* 8.67.222 quotes Theophrastus about this peculiar habit of mice among the Chalybes.

[181] The word μῦς appears only in Ker Pet, p. 14, 19 in a list of lowly animals.

[182] Diogenes remarks that it is better to be a Megarian's κρίον ἢ υἱόν. The same words are attributed to him by Diogenes Laertius (6.41) and Aelian (*VH* 12.56). A similar expression, but without the full vocal pun, is found in the LXX version of Ps 28:1: ἐνέγκατε τῷ κρίῳ υἱοὺς κριῶν. These words, however, are not in the Massoretic text. Can the Cynic saying have found its way into the LXX? For a fuller discussion of the idea behind the words see Sir 38:24-26.

When the subject here changes to the parents' training, or rather corruption, of their children, some very interesting parallels with ECL emerge. For a remarkable parallel see John 5:19-20, though even more remarkable is Juvenal *Satire* 14. 107-118, a passage that must be considered in any analysis of either Plutarch's or John's discussion. The passage in Heb 12:7-11 on a father's discipline of his son is only remotely like Plutarch's sentence.

For Plutarch's use of παιδεύω see Acts 22:3; Col 3:21-25 (cf. Eph 6:4); and esp. Rom 2:17-24.[183] For ἀπόλλυμι in the sense of "corrupt, ruin," see Rom 14:15; 1 Cor 1:19 (= Isa 29:14); Herm Man 11:1. The compound προσδιαστρέφω is a Plutarchan combination, but see διαστρέφω in Acts 20:30 and cf. Luke 23:2; 1 Clem 46:8-9; 47:5. The verb ἐμφυτεύω is not used in ECL, but cf. ἔμφυτος in Barn 9:9 (cf. 1:2), and for the image see φυτεύω in 1 Cor 3:6-8 (cf. Diogn 12:6).

An interesting word here is ἐνοικοδομέω:[184] The idea of building a fortress, etc., is common in the OT but very rare in ECL except for the many references in Hermas to the construction of the πυργός. There are important discussions of constructing real buildings, of building the church, etc., but there is no really close parallel to Plutarch's imagery.[185] Yet cf. 1 Tim 1:4, where some ancient sources read οἰκοδομήν in place of οἰκονομίαν.[186] See also Matt 26:61; 27:40; John 2:19; 1 Cor 14:3 and perhaps Gal 2:18. But the context of all these passages differs from Plutarch's.

When he offers his version of the parents' advice to their children as "Get profits and be tight-fisted, and count yourself as good as the amount you have," Plutarch taps some Cynic source.[187] A similar source lies behind Jas 2:1-13, esp. vss. 1-4.[188] And see again the Parable of the Rich Fool in Luke 12:13-21 for more similarities to

[183] On the complicated concept of education in ECL see G. Bertram, *TDNT*, s.v. παιδεύω κτλ.

[184] See O. Michel, *TDNT*, s.v. οἶκος, κτλ. esp. s.v. οἰκοδομέω.

[185] Imagery which is reflected in Juvenal, *Sat.* 14. 115-118. This passage is not unlike Ign Pol 3:1 which is on the same general subject as 1 Tim 1:4.

[186] See M. Dibelius and H. Conzelmann, *The Pastoral Epistles*, 17-18.

[187] A similar statement appears in Lucilius (fr. 1195 Warmington), Horace (*S.* 1.1.62), Petronius (*Satyr.* 77), and above all in Juvenal (*Sat.* 3. 143-144). This combination of authors is a strong indication of Cynic-Stoic influence.

[188] Cf. M. Dibelius and H. Greeven, *James* (Philadelphia, 1976) 124-148. Their argument would have been stronger if they had considered the passages from the Latin authors. They should also have examined the similarity between Jas 2:3-4 and Juvenal *Sat.* 5.132-137.

Cynic expression[189] and for the general meaning of Plutarch's sentence.

Some words here also provide parallels. For παραινέω cf. Ign Smyrn 4:1, and for the combination of διδάσκω with words similar to παραινέω cf. Col 3:16; 1 Tim 4:11; 6:3. For κερδαίνω used absolutely cf. Jas 4:13, and for a meaning similar to Plutarch's cf. 2 Clem 20:4. For συστέλλω cf. perhaps Acts 5:6, where it may mean "wrap up" (but cf. Bauer, s.v.). For βαλλάντιον see Luke 10:4 (cf. 22:35)[190] and esp. 12:33, where an idea similar to Plutarch's seems to lie behind Jesus' urging his disciples not to hoard earthly goods but to count on heavenly treasures. Plutarch's στέγω has a different sense in ECL, but κρύπτω comes close: e.g., Matt 13:44; 25:25; cf. ἀπόκειμαι in Luke 19:20, where the imagery is naturally different. And finally there is εἰσβάλλω. The compound is not used in ECL, but sometimes the simple βάλλω has the same meaning in passages concerned with money: e.g., Mark 12:41-44, where it is used several times to mean "put in, contribute." And cf. John 12:6, where τὰ βαλλόμενα is virtually equivalent to Plutarch's τὸ εἰσβληθέν.

When Plutarch compares the filthy money bag to the sons of misers, he uses words that have already appeared. The one important exception is παραλαμβάνω. In Plutarch it refers to the receptance of a financial inheritance, in ECL to the acceptance of a spiritual inheritance: e.g., 1 Cor 11:33; 15:3; Gal 1:9, 12; 1 Thes 4:1; Herm Vis 1:3:4; Herm Sim 9:25:2.

In his discussion of the sons' feelings for their fathers, Plutarch naturally touches upon the relationship between parents and children. On a proper relationship: Eph 6:1-4; Col 3:20-25. On the role of the heir: Gal 4:1-7, esp. vss. 1-2. For the impatience of the son: Luke 15:11-32, and for a very close parallel see Juvenal *Sat.* 14. 107ff., 250ff. For the son who refuses to support his parents: Mark 7:11-13a.

In this sentence are some new words. For example, διδασκαλία is a frequent word in ECL: cf. esp. Matt 15:9//Mark 7:7 (both based on Isa 29:13); Ign Eph 16:2; 17:1. For the construction μισθοὺς ἄξιος see 2 Clem 1:5; Did 5:2//Barn 20:2. For paying wages, which Plutarch's words imply, see Matt 20:18; cf. Did 4:7; Barn 19:11.

---

[189] Cf. Betz, *Lukian,* 195f. on the *topos* of the foolish rich man.

[190] In the parallel passages, Matt 10:9 and Mark 6:8, πήρα replaces βαλλάντιον, and in Luke 9:3-5 both words are omitted.

A close parallel to ἄξιος is 2 Clem 1:3, and there is the famous Luke 10:7. For the idea of repaying a wrong see Col 3:25.

From their parents the sons learn to admire nothing except wealth and to live only to acquire vast sums. They consider their fathers a hindrance and count their added years as a reduction from their own. For the general thought see again Luke 15:11-32; Col 3:20-25; Eph 6:1-4. See also Matt 10:21, 35-36; Mark 13:12; Luke 21:16. On sin passing from father to son: John 9:3 (but here with a negative). On parents storing up for children: 2 Cor 12:14. On children caring for their parents: 1 Tim 5:3; and the reverse idea in Mark 7:11-13a. On children dishonoring parents: Rom 1:30; 2 Tim 3:2.

In putting their lessons into practice, the sons steal pleasure from their fathers' money and lavish it on friends and on their own desires, even while they are still in school. With this observation Plutarch allows the sons one final fling, and in doing so he reverts to terms which he has used several times before. There are, however, two words which must be singled out: ἡδονή here almost means "use which brings pleasure," a meaning that seems not to occur in ECL though 2 Pet 2:13 comes close. As we have seen, ἡδονή is sometimes joined with ἐπιθυμία: Tit 3:3; Diogn 9:1. For the phrase εἰς ἐπιθυμίας cf. Rom 13:14 and compare ἐν ἐπιθυμίαις in Eph 2:3; 1 Pet 4:3. On youthful ἐπιθυμίαι cf. 2 Tim 2:22 and for ἐπιθυμία in general see again Herm Man 12.

The verb ἀναλίσκω is not used in ECL, and the compound προσαναλίσκω in Luke 8:43 occurs in a clause that is usually deleted. A frequent synonym, however, is δαπανάω: e.g., Mark 5:26//Luke 8:43; Luke 15:14; 2 Cor 12:15; Herm Sim 1:8; but cf. esp. Jas 4:3.

Then the father dies. The son receives the keys and seals—and all the business worries. His face is unsmiling, morose and forbidding, and he has no time for play or school. He spends his days checking servants, examining ledgers, working on accounts with stewards and debtors, and his days extend into the night.

In this gloomy picture of the miser's son Plutarch uses numerous ideas, words and phrases which are interesting: some because of their appearance in ECL, some because of their absence. For example αἱ κλεῖς . . . καὶ αἱ σφραγῖδες: the closest parallel is 1 Clem 43:3 (cf. vs. 5) because of the phrase ἐσφράγισεν τὰς κλεῖδας, but the context is quite different. Elsewhere the two words have a special theological sense (cf. Bauer, s.v.) that bears no resemblance to Plutarch's passage.

On the kind of change in life-style implied in the words ἕτερον βίου σχῆμα, though for an entirely different reason, see Luke 21:34-36; Eph 2:2-5; Jas 4:9. The word σχῆμα is used only once in reference to an inanimate object: 1 Cor 7:31: τὸ σχῆμα τοῦ κόσμου. For parallels to βίος see Luke 8:14 (but the word is not used in the parallels in Matt 13:18-23//Mark 4:13-20) and 2 Clem 1:6.

The words πρόσωπον ἀγέλαστον, αὐστηρόν, ἀνέντευκτον give an excellent description of a miser. The term ἀγέλαστος [191] is not used in ECL, but the older son in the Parable of the Prodigal Son is an *agelast*: cf. Luke 15:25-30. On laughter see Jas 4:9; cf. Luke 6:21 and 25. See also Herm Vis 1:2:3 where three synonyms appear: στυγός, κατηφής, οὐκ ἱλαρός.

Plutarch uses αὐστηρός (with λιτός) in ch. 5 (525C) to describe Phocion's table, but here, in effect, it almost means the opposite. Does Plutarch intend some irony in the contrast? The closest parallel to the present passage is Luke 19:21-22 where the word describes a stern master who is feared by a servant to whom he has entrusted money. The adjective ἀνέντευκτος seems to be a Plutarchan invention; here it means something like "heedless, implacable." In ECL ἔντευξις and the verb ἐντυγχάνω give the opposite idea but both words mean "appeal," "petition," hence "prayer." See Herm Sim 2:5: λίαν μικρὰν ἔχει τὴν ἔντευξιν which is said of the rich man who does not help the poor, i.e., he is ἀνέντευκτος toward the poor: cf. 1 Clem 63:2.

On the business activities of the wealthy which distract them from a meaningful life see Herm Sim 9:20:1-4; cf. Matt 12:22; Herm Vis 3:11:3; Herm Sim 2:5. And cf. esp. Matt 6:25-34 (esp. vs. 32) where Christ directs his message toward just such people as the young man whom Plutarch describes here.

On the business relationship between master and servant [192] see, for example, Matt 25:14-30//Luke 19:12-28; Luke 12:42-48; 16:1-9; 1 Cor 4:2. For a passage dealing with both the master-

---

[191] On the role of the *agelast*, esp. in Roman comedy, see E. Segal, *Roman Laughter* (Harvard, 1968) 70-98, esp. 76: "But the most common trait of the Plautine agelast is greed, an obsession with *lucrum* . . ."

[192] On slavery in the Christian community see K. H. Rengstorf, *TDNT*, s.v. δοῦλος, esp. 2:270ff.

servant and creditor-debtor relationship see Matt 18:23-25. The word χρεοφειλέτης occurs in Luke 7:41; 16:5. The more common word group, however, is ὀφειλέτης, etc.,[193] which is used both in a monetary sense and, more importantly, in a figurative sense where debt equals sin: e.g., Matt 6:12; Luke 13:4.

Plutarch's διαλογισμός is used frequently in ECL but rarely with the meaning intended here, i.e., "quarrel, argument:" e.g., Luke 9:46 (cf. Mark 9:33); 24:38; Phil 2:14; 1 Tim 2:8. The verb διαλογίζομαι may have this meaning in Mark 11:31; Luke 20:14 (though "reason" is equally valid in both verses); and perhaps in Mark 8:16-17. In none of these passages, however, is the quarrel about money. For this idea see perhaps 1 Tim 6:5-6.

The noun φροντίς here refers to the care and concern of a business man. Both the noun and its verb φροντίζω are used in ECL, but it is μέριμνα, etc. that comes closest in meaning to Plutarch's idea: e.g., Luke 8:14; 1 Pet 5:7; Herm Vis 3:11:3; see earlier discussion of this word.

On listening to philosophers cf. Acts 17:16-34. On lack of leisure cf. Sir 38:24, where the subject of the whole passage 38:24-39:11 is the day and night activities of men which deprive them of wisdom and understanding. In ECL σχολάζω has lost its meaning of "to have leisure" and has come to mean "to devote oneself to": e.g., 1 Cor 7:5. Perhaps the closest parallel to Plutarch's meaning is expressed by εὐκαιρέω: e.g., Mark 6:31 and esp. Acts 17:21. See also ἀναπαύω in Luke 12:19.

Plutarch's ταλαίπωρος is used sparingly in ECL: e.g., Rom 7:24; Rev 3:17; Barn 16:1. The passage closest to Plutarch's is Herm Vis 1:3:1-2 which discusses a parent who has allowed his children to be corrupted. The nearest synonym, however, especially in the vocative is ἄφρων which has already been discussed.

With this apostrophe to the young man Plutarch brings to a close his analysis of the miser. The young man has inherited more than his father's wealth. He has grown old before his time, lost his freedom and became a slave to his business and his love of money. We are back where we started in this dreary drama.

Most of the vocabulary has naturally appeared in earlier passages, esp. in this section, and only a very few words merit further study. For the verb μαραίνομαι cf. Jas 1:11; Herm Vis 3:11:2.

[193] Cf. F. Hauck, *TDNT*, s.v. ὀφείλω κτλ., esp. ὀφείλω, B.

For the substantive τὸ γαῦρον see the use of γαυρόω in Herm Vis 3:9:6. Some MSS read γαυριάω here which the Loeb edition prints. See also Herm Vis 1:1:8: γαυριῶντες ἐν τῷ πλούτῳ αὐτῶν.

The word-group around φιλάνθρωπος is rarely used in ECL. The adjective appears in Diogn 8:7; Agr 7; the adverb in Acts 27:3; the noun in Acts 28:2; Tit 3:4; Diogn 9:2. Sometimes φιλάδελφος, etc., is a substitute (e.g., Rom 12:10; 1 Thes 4:9; Heb 13:1-2), but more often ἀγάπη and ἀγαπάω express the idea.[194]

Exhortatio B (chs. 8-9, 527A13-F20)

By considering prodigals after misers, Plutarch prepares the way for the conclusion of the *cup. divit.* From the non-use of wealth and its destructive effect on misers he moves to misuse and its equally harmful results. He contends that prodigals squander their wealth on useless and showy items, and from this idea he progresses in a logical fashion to his conclusion that the outward showiness of wealth is nothing compared to the inner worth of a person. This thought echoes and gives added meaning to the opening statements of the treatise. By returning to his introductory theme Plutarch effectively rounds off the discussion of φιλοπλουτία and, incidentally, disproves the arguments of those who insist that the *cup. divit.* is incomplete.

Despite the length of this section, the basic thought is simple and direct: wealth can be used either for what is sufficient to life or for showy non-essentials, i.e., luxuries. In the first case, the wealthy have no more than people with modest means; in the latter, they have even less, for they are distracted from essentials and resemble those who admire life's pageantry rather than life itself. Plutarch embellishes this message with rich details and colorful examples drawn from Greek life, and it is in these extras that Plutarch differs most from ECL. The message itself is remarkably like that in many passages of the NT and the Apostolic Fathers: e.g., the Parable of the Rich Young Man (Matt 19:16-24//Mark 10:17-23//Luke 18: 18-25);[195] the Parable of the Rich Fool (Luke 12:15-21; cf.

---

[194] Cf. Bauer, s.v. ἀγάπη; and esp. G. Quell and E. Stauffer, *TDNT*, s.v. ἀγαπάω κτλ.

[195] Despite Jesus' statement in this parable about the difficulty for a rich man to enter heaven, one succeeded because he used some of his wealth properly. See the references to Joseph of Arimathea in Matt 27:57-60// Mark 15:43-46//Luke 23:53-60//John 19:38-42.

Rev 3:17); the Parable of the Rich Man and Lazarus (Luke 16:19-31); the Parable of the Talents (Matt 25:14-30//Luke 19:12-28); Zacchaeus (Luke 19:1-10). See also 1 Cor 7:31; 1 Tim 6:17-19; Herm Sim 1:4-11; 2:1-10; 6:2-5.

Plutarch, however, follows Aristotle in ignoring or tacitly rejecting the notion that a man may put his wealth to good use. This omission represents the most important difference between Plutarch and ECL which stresses the proper use of money. In addition to the passages cited above, see Herm Vis 3:6:5-7; 3:9:1-6; Herm Sim 9:30:4-5; cf. 2 Cor 8:9-15; 1 John 3:17-18; 1 Clem 38:2, etc.

Nowhere is this difference in attitude more apparent than in Plutarch's statement that οὐδὲν οὖν πλέον ἔχουσιν οἱ πλούσιοι τῶν μέτρια κεκτημένων. With these words he excludes all consideration of the destitute, thereby putting a vast gulf between the *cup. divit.* and one of the basic themes of ECL.[196]

For his examples Plutarch naturally draws from a tradition and a way of life that, for the most part, are foreign to ECL.[197] Yet there are some interesting parallels: e.g., the reference to Agathon's banquet. Such banquets (συμπόσια in Greek: *convivia* or even *cena* in Latin) were regular social occasions for Greeks and Romans. Their counterpart among early Christians was the Lord's Supper.[198] That these meetings acquired a social significance is clear from such passages as Acts 2:43, 46; Herm Vis 3:9:3; Pliny's *Epistle* 96.7; and above all 1 Cor 10-11, esp. 11:17-34.[199] Paul's remarks to the Corinthians, when he urges them to refrain from externals that obscure the real meaning of the meetings, are not unlike Plutarch's advice to remove the showy and superfluous from the banquet.

The same contrast between simple essentials and showing

[196] For Plutarch aristocratic attitude and its effect on this passage, see the introduction.

[197] On the *symposia* cf. Philo *vit. cont.* 40ff., 64ff. One should perhaps observe that the banquets which Jesus attended in the homes of the tax-collectors seem to be of the pagan Greek type: e.g. Matt 9:10-11//Mark 2:15-16//Luke 5:29-30; Matt 11:19//Luke 7:34.

[198] There is no intention here to discuss the religious significance of the ἀγάπη. For this subject see G. Quell and E. Stauffer, *TDNT*, s.v. ἀγαπάω κτλ.; J. Behm, *TDNT*, s.v. κλάω κτλ.; H. Conzelmann, *TDNT*, s.v. εὐχαριστέω κτλ.

[199] For a different situation but one with similar ideas cf. Luke 14:12-14. For specific instructions on the proper form of the ἀγάπη or εὐχαριστία, see Did 9-10.

extravagance is the basis for other examples in this section. The reference to Scopas emphasizes a contrast of τὰ περιττά and τὰ ἀναγκαῖα, and Plutarch concludes by warning the reader that a person like Scopas praises life's pageant rather than life itself. Similar criticism, in even stronger terms, appears in ECL: e.g., Matt 13:1-9//Mark 4:1-9//Luke 8:4-15 (esp. vs. 14); Matt 23:1-36; Herm Sim 1:10-11; 6:5:3-6 (and, indeed the whole of 6 with its discussion of τρυφὴ καὶ ἀπάτη).[200]

Plutarch's next example is an immediate extension of his remarks about Scopas where he concludes by referring to a pageant and festival. Now he turns to one of the most important festivals on the Greek calendar, the Dionysia. He complains that a once simple and unpretentious religious observance has disappeared beneath the façade of expensive and showy paraphernalia. This criticism of religious practice is frequent in ECL. For attacks on ostentation see Matt 6:1-18; 11:25; Luke 18:10-14; Col 3:23-24; 4:5; cf. also Rom 2:25-29; Gal 6:12-16 for Paul's concept of πεποιθέναι τῇ σαρκί. On pomp vs. real meaning of religion see Matt 23:1-36. Naturally the details of the Dionysia which Plutarch mentions are absent from ECL, for it is this kind of worship, so important to the Greeks, that the Christians abhorred: e.g., Acts 14:11-18: 19:23-41; 1 Cor 8:1-10; Gal 4:8-11.

The whole of ch. 9 is one more example of the idea of praising the pomp rather than life itself. For a representative of this attitude Plutarch uses the youthful and inexperienced Telemachus, who visited both Nestor and Menelaus in search of news about his father Odysseus.[201] In "Sandy Pylos" the naive youth was unimpressed by Nestor's wealth of necessities, but in Sparta he was struck with amazement and awe at the rich appointments of Menelaus' palace.

By setting Telemachus in the middle, flanked by wise old Nestor on one side and luxurious Menelaus and Helen on the other, Plutarch demonstrates his point: it is naive to ignore an abundance of necessities and to admire useless abundance. Nestor represents αὐτάρκεια, Menelaus and Helen a luxurious way of life that once shattered their marriage and destroyed countless Greeks and

---

[200] And when Jesus drove the businessmen from the temple, he was putting into action the same basic lesson: cf. Matt 21:12-13//Mark 11:15-17//Luke 19:45-46//John 2:14-17.

[201] Homer *Od.* 3.385-474; 4.20-112.

Trojans. And after the war, the two resumed their marriage and the same old life of ostentatious splendor. Thus Menelaus is an early example of a rich and foolish ruler, and he has the queen he deserves.[202] Parallels to these ideas have already been discussed and cited several times, e.g., parables of the Rich Fool and Rich Young Ruler, and nothing can be gained by repeating all the references here.

The vocabulary of chs. 8-9 offers some new words that must be examined. For example, προσήκων in the sense of "advantageous" is found in Mart Pol 10:2. For the idea that one's possessions adorn (κοσμέω) see Matt 5:16; 1 Tim 2:9-10. On luxury and its showiness see again Herm Sim 6:2:1-4; 6:4:1-4; 6:5:1-7; and esp. Jas 5:1-5, a brilliant attack on the possessions of the rich with emphasis on items that are visible to others. See also Rev 18:12-14 for a list of luxurious items. And finally, for πλούσιος opposed to πένης[203] see Herm Sim 2:5-7 (cf. 1:8-9); Did 5:2// Barn 20:2.

For Plutarch's reference to various crafts which cater to luxurious tastes see Acts 19:24-41 (esp. vss. 24 and 38), where the harmful influence of the ἀργυροκόπος is obvious. Plutarch's χρυσοχόος is not in ECL, but his products are: i.e., golden trinkets which are a favorite symbol of ostentation and luxury: e.g., 1 Tim 2:9; Jas 2:12; 1 Pet 3:3; Rev 17:4; 18:16; and esp 2 Tim 2:20, where the list of items is very similar to such lists in chs. 8-10 of the *cup. divit.* The other craftsmen on Plutarch's list are not used in ECL, but μύρον is a symbol of wealth and luxury in such passages as Matt 26:6-13//Mark 14:3-9//John 12:1-18; cf. Luke 7:36-38. For the statement that all these craftsmen should be expelled from the state see Herm Sim 1:1-6.

The vocabulary in the rest of ch. 8 is mainly repetition from earlier sections, but a few colorful terms appear for the first time: e.g., σεμνύνω, which describes the emotion felt toward wealth, "to exalt, feel pride in." The word in ECL which comes closest is ὑψηλοφρονέω, etc.: e.g., 1 Tim 6:17 (cf. Rom 11:17-20); Herm Man 8:3, where the noun appears in a catalogue of sins associated with wealth and luxury; Herm Sim 8:9:1, which describes the wealth as ὑψηλόφρονες; and cf. Herm Sim 9:22:3. Not surprisingly, haugh-

[202] On the role of Nestor, Menelaus and Helen in ethical discussions see North, *Sophrosyne*, 1, n. 1-2.

[203] For Plutarch's meaning of πένης, see the introduction.

tiness is a regular attribute of wealth and the wealthy. The use of εὐδαίμων here echoes εὐδαιμονία in ch. 1 (q.v.). This adjective, like κακοδαίμων, is not used in ECL, but the verb εὐδαιμονέω appears in Diogn 10:5, where it refers to happiness in material possessions.

Ch. 9 continues the discussion, but the ideas here are even closer to the concept of ἐγκράτεια and αὐτάρκεια. Consequently, it is no accident that Plutarch finds a way to bring in Socrates and Diogenes. The philosophical importance of ἐγκράτεια began with Socrates, who remained an example of self-control; αὐτάρκεια was first the Cynic and later the Stoic development from self-control to self-sufficiency,[204] and the latter concept, despite the emphasis on φιλοπλουτία, is one of the major themes of the *cup. divit.*

In the final sentences of ch. 9, a few new words appear: e.g., μάταιος. This adjective and related words are used frequently in ECL and in the same general context: e.g., Herm Sim 6:2:2; Man 12:2:1. For κόσμος (cf. κοσμέω above), which has its original meaning of "adornment," see 1 Pet 3:3, a good parallel to Plutarch's word.

At this point, if not before, Plutarch begins to look forward to ch. 10 and his peroration. He attacks Menelaus for adorning his palace like a θέατρον ἢ θυμέλη and identifies this showiness as the use (χρῆσις) for which wealth is admired. The two nouns θέατρον and θυμέλη are virtual synonyms, but only the more general θέατρον is used in ECL: Acts 19:29ff., where it is a meeting place, and 1 Cor 4:9, where the imagery is closer to Plutarch's. These two terms serve to conclude this section by referring back to the pomp and pageantry of the Dionysia and by looking ahead to the philosophical and religious alternatives to a life devoted to the amassing and misuse of wealth.

Peroratio (ch. 10, 527F21-528B3)

This brief section is replete with important words and ideas, as one expects in a passage designed to sum up the argument of the treatise and direct it toward the goal which the author has intended all along the way.

The first sentence picks up the thought of the previous section and repeats it in a way that serves as a foil for the next remark: "The happiness in wealth is one of spectators and witnesses or it

[204] On this development see North, *Sophrosyne*, 118, 122, 125-131.

is nothing." To this statement he immediately contrasts self-mastery, philosophy and proper understanding of the gods. He describes the radiant joy of these activities and identifies them with virtue, truth, and the beauty of mathematics.

These pursuits, he continues, are rewarding whether others see them or not, and this idea allows him to return for a last time to the vain and empty show of wealth. He cites a wealthy husband and wife who dine simply when they are alone and drag out all the finery when guests are present. He terms the latter meal "a spectacle and show," thus echoing the earlier discussion, and he concludes the treatise almost abruptly with the remark that σωφροσύνη is essential whether one dines alone or at a feast.

Some of the vocabulary here has already appeared, but much remains that is important. For example, on wealth needing witnesses see the attitude of the scribes and Pharisees in Matt 23:1-36, though the element of hyprocrisy here is missing from Plutarch's version. For the reaction of witnesses to a show of wealth see Jas 2:2-7. For parallels to τὸ σωφρονεῖν see Tit 2:6; 1 Clem 4:3, but the absence of φιλοσοφέω is more significant. The only passages which use this word-group (Acts 17:18; Col 2:8; Diogn 8:2) refer in a hostile tone to pagan philosophy. The whole concept of a man-oriented philosophy was alien to Christian thinking, and, with these few exceptions, early Christians ignored it. For parallels to τὸ γιγώσκειν ἃ δεῖ περὶ θεῶν see Rom 1:19, 20; 1 Cor 2:11-12; 1 John 2:3.

Twice in this passage Plutarch stresses the satisfaction of philosophic and religious contemplation even if neither men nor gods know about it. Of course nothing can escape the notice of the Hebrew and Christian God, but for references to the secrecy, or at least privacy, of worship see Matt 6:1-18 (and contrast 23:1-36); Ign Eph 15:3. On words in darkness and light see Matt 10:26-27// Luke 12:2-3; cf. Mark 4:22; Eph 5:13. For the idea that such activities have their own inner glow see Matt 5:15-16//Mark 4:21//Luke 11:33; Matt 6:22-23. Plutarch's word φέγγος is not used in a figurative sense in ECL,[205] but cf. φῶς and related words in such passages as John 1:4-5, 9-10; 2 Cor 4:3-6; Eph 1:18.

These contemplations, says Plutarch, also make joy (χαρά) a

[205] Plutarch's expression seems almost Gnostic. See A. Dihle, *TDNT*, s.v. ψυχή κτλ., E.1, on the pairs "light/darkness, good/evil, spirit/matter and soul/body."

fellow inhabitant of the soul as it seeks to grasp the good. Many passages in ECL use χαρά in this sense,[206] but the closest parallels are probably Acts 15:3 (merely a verbal similarity); 1 Clem 63:2; Herm Vis 3:13:2; Diogn 10:3, where knowledge produces χαρά (cf. John 15:11; 17:13; Phil 2:2).

Notice that Plutarch begins this chapter with τοιοῦτος and leads the discussion to the joy that comes from contemplation; then here, where he reverses the process and moves from virtue, truth and knowledge back to examples of ostentatious wealth, he repeats τοιοῦτος. He is fond of using such verbal sign-posts. Of the three abstractions, ἀρετή has a meaning not unlike Plutarch's in Phil 4:8; 2 Pet 1:5; 2 Clem 10:1. For ἀλήθεια see John 1:9; Rom 2:20; Eph 4:24; Ign Phld 2:1; Herm Man 3:1 (cf. 2 Thes 2:10); 10:1:4 and 6. The reference to κάλλος in connection with mathematics has a special significance for Plutarch. We know from such passages as *de E* 387F that he was a keen student of mathematics, and here, where he needs an example of the contemplative life, he looks back to those youthful days before he entered the Academy. This idea does not appear in ECL.

From these abstractions Plutarch turns with disdain to such "trappings of wealth" as περιδέραια καὶ θεάματα[207] κορασιώδη. None of these words is used in ECL, and the closest parallel is Clement *Paedagogus* 3.2.10, which should be read along with the whole of ch. 10. ECL also lacks a parallel to Plutarch's use of the popular *topos* that wealth is blind, but cf. the repeated use of τρυφὴ καὶ ἀπάτη in Herm Sim 6:2-5.

The final sentence of the *cup. divit.* deserves special attention. Plutarch's words are ἀλλὰ σωφροσύνης γε κἂν μόνος δειπνῇ δεῖται κἂν εὐωχῇ.[208] Obviously σωφροσύνη is the key word, and we must consider the possibility that the author places it here to point up

---

[206] Cf. H. Conzelmann and W. Zimmerli, *TDNT*, s.v. χαίρω κτλ., esp. 9:366-372.

[207] The reading of all the MSS is θεάματα which refers to spectacles, shows, etc., not to a person's appearance. Pohlenz emends the word to ἀνθίσματα and cites Clement *Paedagogus* 3.2.10.4, but this word is not in Clement's passage, nor does LSJ list it! Perhaps we should read ἄνθινα, a term that is used for the brightly colored dresses worn by Athenian ἑταῖραι. Notice that in the next sentence, when no guests are present, the wealthy wife is ἄχρυστος καὶ ἀπόρφυρος καὶ ἀφελής. The last adjective expresses the opposite of ἄνθινα.

[208] The MSS, followed by Pohlenz in the Teubner, read εὐωχίας. De Lacy and Einarson emend this to εὐωχῇ, and the verb seems a much better parallel to δειπνῇ, for εὐωχίας is intolerably weak here.

this concept as the logical conclusion to his message in the whole of the *cup. divit.*

As North has clearly demonstrated, Plutarch was especially interested in σωφροσύνη. He sought to identify its effect, or lack of effect, on human conduct not only in his ethical discussions of the *Moralia*, but even in his analyses of the famous men whom he selected for his *Lives*. There is hardly a treatise or a biography in which Plutarch fails to consider the concept, and the *cup. divit.* is no exception.[209]

The interesting point is, however, that he has not used the word until the very last sentence, though he prepares the reader for its appearance with τὸ σωφρονεῖν in the beginning of ch. 10. Yet a close examination of the *exordium* shows that the concept is in his mind from the first. When he says that money cannot buy ἀλυπία, μεγαλοφροσύνη, εὐστάθεια, θαρραλεότης, αὐτάρκεια, he says in effect that money cannot buy σωφροσύνη.

His repeated references and discussions of these concepts and their opposites serve to keep σωφροσύνη in the reader's mind as he is guided from one πάθος to another, from excess to excess, until the final theme of wealth as life's empty πομπὴ καὶ θέατρον. Only then, in his summation of the whole subject, does Plutarch actually use the word, but he has led up to it in such a way that it must apply, not merely to the immediate context of dining alone or with guests, but to the larger subject of wealth and its use and abuse by prodigals and misers. In short, despite its variety of related themes, the *De cupiditate divitiarum* is a study of σωφροσύνη.[210]

---

[209] Surprisingly, North (*Sophrosyne*, 248-249, etc.) has not considered the *cup. divit.* Perhaps it escaped her notice because the actual word appears only the one time. Perhaps, too, it is because Plutarch adds nothing new to the history of the concept. If that is the case, its use in this treatise is all the more important because it sets the *cup. divit.* in the direct philosophical line from the earliest writers to those of late antiquity.

[210] For the role of σωφροσύνη in Christian literature, see North, op. cit., 312-379. See Herm Vis 2:3:2 for an interesting parallel to Plutarch's last remark.

DE INVIDIA ET ODIO (MORALIA 536E - 538E) [1]

BY

DIETER LÜHRMANN
Kirchliche Hochschule Bethel
Bielefeld, Germany

De invidia et odio is a fragment from a larger work that is no longer extant.[2] Since *invid. et od.* was not an independent work, its title does not occur in the Lamprias Catalog. The theme of the fragment is the relationship between envy and hatred. After a description in the first chapter (536E-F) of the similarities between the two πάθη, the subsequent chapters contrast the two:

Ch. 2 (536F-537A): Hatred arises because one considers another evil; envy when one considers another fortunate. Envy, therefore, is without limits, while hatred is limited.

Ch. 3 (537A-B): Hatred can also be directed against animals; envy, however, is only to be found between men.

Ch. 4 (537B-C): Among animals there is no envy, but there is hatred.

Ch. 5 (537C-E): Envy is never proper; hatred, on the other hand, can be praised as μισοπονηρία. Thus there are situations in which one admits one's hatred, but never one's envy.

Ch. 6 (537E-538C): Hatred increases with the πονηρία of the one hated, envy with his ἀρετή. Envy can stop when the one who is envied reaches the pinnacle of fame and fortune, but hatred continues to pursue even the unfortunate.

Ch. 7 (538C-D): Yet hatred can cease if it is proven to be unjustified, while envy has no such possibility.

Ch. 8 (538D-E): Hatred and envy also distinguish themselves in terms of their objectives. The one who hates wants misfortune for the one he hates; the one who envies wants a reduction in the fame of the person he envies.

---

[1] The text used here is Plutarch, *Moralia* 7, ed. P. H. De Lacy and B. Einarson, LCL (1959) 90-107.

[2] Ziegler, sec. III.4.e.

Throughout the essay Plutarch depends on traditional philosophical material, especially Aristotle. E. Milobenski investigated these traditions in his book *Der Neid in der griechischen Philosophie.*[3] It is important for our topic that φθόνος, which Plutarch consistently evaluates as negative, differs from μῖσος, which, depending on the object toward which the hatred is directed, can be viewed as either positive or negative.

The discussion in *invid. et od.* limits itself to the relationship between envy and hatred, but characterizations of envy itself occur in *ex inim. util.* (91B, 92B, C), *tranq. an.* (467E), and *frat. am.* (484C, 485B, C, E, 486E; cf. also *laud. ips.* 540B, 541A, 542F, 544B, D).

In the LXX φθόνος occurs in only four places, all of which are without a Hebrew basis (Wis 2:24; 6:23; 1 Mac 8:16; 3 Mac 6:7). The verb φθονεῖν occurs only in Tob 4:7, 16a, b; the adjective φθονερός only in Sir 14:10 (the extant Hebrew text of this passage is uncertain). Particularly important among these passages is the adoption of the motif "envy of the gods" in Wis 2:24: because of the envy of the devil,[4] death entered into the world through Cain's murder of his brother. As T Benj 7 had already done, 1 Clem 4:7 attributes the responsibility for this murder to *Cain's* envy. The Greek stem μισ- is used throughout the LXX to translate the Hebrew שׂנא. The noun μῖσος is absent from the NT, and the verb is used chiefly to characterize the reaction to the proclamation of the Christian congregation. φθόνος occurs primarily in lists of vices (Rom 1:29; Gal 5:21; 1 Tim 6:4; Tit 3:3; 1 Pet 2:1; cf. φθονεῖν in Gal 5:26), where it can also be found in Jewish as well as Greek literature.[5]

Ch. 1

(536F)

εὔνοια as a contrast to envy (on which cf. Milobenski, 158, n. 80). Phil 1:15 has εὐδοκία as a contrast to φθόνος and ἔρις.

πλησίον is used in the NT primarily on the basis of LXX influence.

φιλέω as a contrast to envy and hatred. In ECL only hatred is so contrasted, chiefly with the stem ἀγαπ- (cf. 1 John 2:9-11, 15; 4:19f.; Did 2:7).

---

[3] (Wiesbaden, 1964) 135-165 on Plutarch, 157-165 on *invid. et od.*

[4] διάβολος. On the relationship between φθόνος and διαβολή, cf. Milobenski, 44f. and n. 33.

[5] Cf. S. Wibbing, *Die Tugend- und Lasterkataloge im Neuen Testament* (Berlin, 1959) 98f.

Ch. 3

(537A)

γαλᾶς . . . ἔνιοι μισοῦσι. Cf. Barn 10:8, καὶ τὴν γαλῆν ἐμίσησεν καλῶς (Μωϋσῆς), which is a reference to Lev 11:29. The Hebrew text actually means the mole, which the LXX translates with "weasel." Hatred of this animal is explained by its veneration among the Egyptians, which Plutarch mentions in *Is. et Os.* 380F (cf. *PECL* 1:79); cf. Clement of Alexandria *prot.* 2. 41. 3; Ker Pet 2 (p. 14, l. 19ff.) in Clement of Alexandria *str.* 6. 5. 40 (veneration in Thebes on account of the transformation of Galanthis into a weasel at the time of the birth of Heracles; *prot.* 2. 39. 6). In *Is. et Os.* 381A Plutarch cites the belief that the weasel conceives through the ear and gives birth through the mouth, a view which Aristotle (*GA* 3. 6. 756b13) already rejected and which is also used in the *Epistle of Aristeas* 144, 163, 165 as support for Lev 11:29. The reversed order in Barn 10:8 (cf. *Physiologus* ch. 21) shows "widernatürliche Unzucht, die mit dem Munde getrieben wurde und die der Vf. auch nur von Hörensagen kennt" (H. Windisch, *Der Barnabasbrief*, HNT Ergänzungsband [Tübingen, 1920] 361). Cf. Th. S. Duncan, "The Weasel in Myths, Superstition and Religion," *Washington University Studies*, Humanistic Series, 12 (1924): 33-66; Riegler, *Handwörterbuch des deutschen Aberglaubens*, s.v. Wiesel; B. E. Perry, "Physiologus," PW 20.1 (1941): 1074-1129, esp. 1087.

οἱ δὲ Περσῶν μάγοι. Cf. *PECL* 1:65.

Ch. 5

(537D)

μισοπονηρία. Cf. Barn 4:10: μισήσωμεν τελείως τὰ ἔργα τῆς πονηρᾶς ὁδοῦ, Herm Man 12:1:1: μισήσεις τὴν πονηρὰν ἐπιθυμίαν.

ἐπιεικῆ . . . καὶ πρᾶον. Cf. 2 Cor 10:1; Tit 3:2; 1 Clem 30:8.

Ch. 6

(537F)

συκοφαντέω. Cf. Luke 3:14; 19:8.

(538A)

ἀπάγχω. Cf. Matt 27:5. Judas hanged himself (differently in Acts 1:18) like those who slandered Socrates.

(538B)

μισοῦσι . . . τοὺς ἐχθρούς. Contrasting with this natural conduct is the command to love one's enemies (Luke 6:27-36//Matt 5:39-48; Did 1:3; 2 Clem 13:4). This passage in Plutarch stands closest to Matthew's polemical interpretation of the OT command for love of one's neighbor: μισήσεις τὸν ἐχθρόν σου (5:43). Cf. D. Lührmann, "Liebet eure Feinde (Lk 6, 27-36/Mt 5, 39-48)," *ZTK* 69 (1972) 412-38. On the other hand, to be hated like an enemy is the fate of Jesus' disciples, as it was the fate of the OT prophets and even of Jesus himself (cf. Mark 13:13//Matt 24:9//Luke 21:17, John 15:18f. and often).

DE LAUDE IPSIUS (MORALIA 539A - 547F)

BY

HANS DIETER BETZ

Claremont Graduate School and School of Theology
Claremont, California

I. INTRODUCTION

The catalogue of Lamprias (LCL 15:16, no. 85) gives the title of this treatise as πῶς ἄν τις ἑαυτὸν ἐπαινέσειεν ἀνεπιφθόνως. It describes its contents precisely. But the MSS formulate the title as Περὶ τοῦ ἑαυτὸν ἐπαινεῖν ἀνεπιφθόνως, a formulation indicating a treatise in the diatribe style. Self-praise (περιαυτολογία) as a form of the *encomium*, common as it was, presented problems both for rhetorical theory and ethics. For this reason the idea had long been a topic of discussion by rhetoricians, and L. Radermacher and M. Pohlenz have demonstrated that Plutarch had access to these earlier discussions of the subject. It was, however, the ethical implications of the historical problem in which Plutarch was primarily interested.[1]

The composition of the work is clear. Addressed to one individual, Herculanus,[2] the essay is arranged along the lines of a speech, with the traditional parts of *exordium*, *propositio*, *argumentum*, *exhortatio*, *conclusio*. Yet, its primary purpose is not epideictic, but moral instruction. This paraenetical purpose of the treatise is evident from the usage of the first person plural in the *exordium* (ch. 1, 539A-E) and in the last part containing the *exhortatio*

[1] Bibliography: L. Radermacher, "Studien zur Geschichte der griechischen Rhetorik, II: Plutarchs Schrift *De se ipso citra invidiam laudando*," *RhM* 52 (1897) 419-424; M. Pohlenz, "Eine byzantinische Recension Plutarchischer Schriften," *Nachrichten von der Kgl. Gesellschaft der Wissenschaften zu Göttingen* (1913) 358f.; R. Jeuckens, *Plutarch von Chaeronea und die Rhetorik*, Dissertationes philologicae Argentoratenses selectae, XII:4 (Strassburg, 1907 [1908]); cf. the review by G. Lehnert, *PhW* 32 (1912) 1241-1245; Ziegler, sec. III.4.1; H. G. Ingenkamp, *Plutarchs Schriften über die Heilung der Seele* (Göttingen, 1971); Betz, *Paulus*, 75ff.

The edition used here is that of Ph. H. De Lacy & B. Einarson, *Plutarch's Moralia*, LCL, vol. 7 (1959); cf. also the BT edition of M. Pohlenz & W. Sieveking, *Plutarchi Moralia* 3 (1929).

[2] Cf. Ziegler, sec. I.8 (col. 40); De Lacy & Einarson, LCL 7:113.

(chs. 18-22, 546B-547F).[3] This means that in composing the treatise in this way Plutarch has actually carried out his recommendation in the treatise, to make rhetoric a useful tool for ethics.[4]

The composition shows the following structure: [5]

539A-E I. *Exordium*

A. presentation of the problem as a conflict between λόγος and ἔργον — Ch. 1

539A 1. the popular agreement: Τὸ περὶ ἑαυτοῦ λέγειν ὥς τι ὄντος ἢ δυναμένου πρὸς ἑτέρους . . . λόγῳ μὲν ἐπαχθὲς ἀποφαίνουσιν

539B 2. the actual practice: ἔργῳ δὲ οὐ πολλοὶ τὴν ἀηδίαν αὐτοῦ διαπεφεύγασιν οὐδὲ τῶν ψεγόντων

B. address: ὦ Ἡρκυλανέ

539 B-C C. examples illustrating the conflict: the poets Euripides, Pindar, and Timothy

D. restatement of the popular opinion

539D 1. formulated by Xenophon

539D-E 2. list of commonly accepted reasons

a. a self-praiser should be embarrassed even if he is praised by others; if he praises himself, he reveals his indecency

b. a self-praiser is ἄδικος because he encroaches upon the right of others to praise him

c. the impact of the self-praiser upon the listener is detrimental

1) if the listener is silent, he appears to feel disgust and envy (ἄχθεσθαι καὶ φθονεῖν)

---

[3] Cf. De Lacy & Einarson, LCL 7:111, n. b. By contrast, the middle part (chs. 2-17, 539E-546B) speaks about the πολιτικὸς ἀνήρ (cf. 539E, F; 541C; 542E; 545D, E; and De Lacy & Einarson, ibid., n. a).

[4] See 539F; 547F.

[5] I have used to some extent the analyses by Jeuckens, *Plutarch*, 142ff., and Ingenkamp, *Schriften*, 62ff.

2) if the listener is compelled to join in the self-praise to confirm it against his better judgment, the praise is spoiled, becoming a matter of "flattery" (κολακεία) rather than praise

539E-540C II. *Propositio*

539E A. thesis: in spite of the common agreement to reject self-praise, its use may be recommendable in certain circumstances. Ch. 2

539E-F B. presuppositions underlying use and rejection of self-praise

1. accepted usefulness of self-praise (practice of the πολιτικὸς ἀνήρ)
   a. if self-glorification is not done for personal glory or pleasure, but because the moment or circumstances demand the person to speak about himself
   b. if self-praise consists of listing achievements and good deeds which may inspire others to achieve similar good deeds
   c. if self-praise does not lead to rewards for past achievement, but to new opportunities for further good achievements
   d. if self-praise creates a climate of confidence in which useful things can be done easily

540A-C 2. description of "empty praise" (κενὸς ἔπαινος) as it is commonly despised Ch. 3

540C-546B III. *Argumentum*: situations exist in which self-praise becomes ethically acceptable [6]

[6] The section is ended by the phrase καλὸς γὰρ ὁ τοιοῦτος ἔπαινος . . . (546B), which occurs also at the beginning (539E).

	A. cases with "external antidotes" (544C: . . .ταῦτα μὲν ἔξωθέν ἐστιν ἐπεισάγεσθαι φάρμακα τῆς περιαυτολογίας.)	
540C-543A	1. against opponents who are χαλεποὶ καὶ βάσκανοι (543A) self-praise may be used in the following cases:	
540C-541A	a. when one clears one's good name against a charge	Ch. 4
541A-C	b. when the *un*fortunate praises himself	Ch. 5
541C-E	c. when it is part of παρρησία in a case of affront	Ch. 6
541E-F	d. when a defendant employs the tactic of reversing the charges against him and calling them triumphs instead	Ch. 7
541F-542A	e. when the device of *antithesis* is used, i.e., when one implicitly admits past action, but shows the opposite of what one has done would have been shameful	Ch. 8
542B-C	f. if the self-praise is blended with praise of the audience	Ch. 9
542C-D	g. when one praises others whose aims and deeds are the same as one's own	Ch. 10
542E-543A	h. when in praising oneself not everything is claimed, but part of the success is attributed to "Chance" or god	Ch. 11
543A-544C	2. against opponents who are μέτριοι (543A) self-praise is permissible in the following cases:	Ch. 12
543A-F	a. when the device of *metathesis* is used, i.e., when excessive claims are avoided or replaced by things humanly praiseworthy; Plutarch includes here a polemic against rulers and "sophists" accepting deification by the audience	

543F-544C	b. when minor shortcomings and failures are thrown in, so as to avoid the appearance of perfection	Ch. 13
544C-546B	B. cases with "inherent antidotes" (544C: ἕτερα δὲ αὐτοῖς τρόπον τινὰ τοῖς ἐπαινουμένοις ἔνεστιν.)	Ch. 14
544C-D	1. when the enormous hardships and costs are emphasized in self-praise	
544D-546A	2. when self-praise is employed as a pedagogical device to stimulate emulation	Ch. 15
544E	a. giving hope (ἐλπίδες) that the task can be attained and is not impossible	
544F-545D	b. creating fear (κατάπληξις) in the overconfident and overbold	Ch. 16
544F-545A	1) when used against enemies	
545B-D	2) when used among friends	
545D-546A	c. when, for the benefit of others, true self-praise is put side-by-side with false self-praise in order to destroy the impact of the latter	Ch. 17
546B-547F	IV. *Exhortatio*:[7] ὅπως ἂν ἕκαστος ἐκφύγοι τὸ ἐπαινεῖν ἀκαίρως ἑαυτόν (546B)	
546B	A. principal statement about "self-love" (φιλαυτία) as the source of self-praise	Ch. 18
546C	B. general exhortation: avoid treacherous situations (καιροὶ καὶ λόγοι) which are known as leading to self-praise	
546C-547C	C. description of four such situations	
546C-D	1. when others are praised, a situation of rivalry is created in which "jealousy" takes possession of oneself	

[7] The beginning of this section is indicated by the words in 546B: Λείπεται δὲ ἡμῖν, τοῦ λόγου τὸ ἐφεξῆς ἀπαιτοῦντος καὶ παρακαλοῦντος . . .

546D-F	2. when one tells about one's own good luck, out of joy one easily drifts into vainglorious boasting (κόμπος)	Ch. 19
546F-547A	3. in exercising censure and reproof one easily recommends oneself as a good example and thus praises oneself at the expense of others	Ch. 20
547B-C	4. in being praised by others one is tempted to take over, push for more, fish for compliments; this destroys the praise by others	Ch. 21
547D-F	D. statement of ethical advice (εὐλάβεια καὶ φυλακή)	Ch. 22
547D	1. negatively: μήτε συνεκπίπτοντα τοῖς ἐπαίνοις μήτε ταῖς ἐρωτήσεσιν ἑαυτὸν προϊέμενον.	
547D-E	2. positively: the best methods are:	
	a. to pay attention to others when they praise themselves	
	b. to remember the embarrassment of the acts, the unpleasant experiences of witnessing others praising themselves	
547F	c. to realize the inevitable bad consequences of ἀδοξία, κενοδοξία, τὸ λυπεῖν τοὺς ἀκούοντας	

V. *Conclusio*: we should avoid speaking about ourselves unless it is beneficial either to ourselves or to our hearers

II. Plutarch's Treatise and Early Christian Literature

The relationship between Plutarch's treatise and ECL involves several aspects. First, there is a clear relationship between Plutarch and the Christian writers in regard to the main subject of Plutarch's treatise. This is the most important part of the comparison. Second, there are a considerable number of minor points of comparison, some related to the major issue, some not.

A. *Self-praise as an Ethical Problem*

In Plutarch's view there are several reasons why self-praise as a rhetorical exercise presents a problem for ethics. On one level, there are two conflicting traditions: although there is general agreement in the Greco-Roman culture that self-praise is to be rejected, great poets like Euripides, Pindar and Timotheus unashamedly indulge in it; [8] there is also the clear precept that in the athletic games the victory should not be proclaimed by the winner himself, but by another; [9] finally, Xenophon [10] declares that the acceptable *encomium* is one delivered by someone else. This conflict in popular morality is, however, only the surface. The underlying problems are religious and ethical in the stricter sense, i.e., those of psychology and interpersonal relationships.

1. *The religious problem.* As Plutarch presents the matter, self-praise becomes self-deification, unless it is restrained by some kind of "antidote." Self-deification, however, must be rejected as blasphemy. It is part of the old doctrine of "hybris-nemesis" that claiming things which are beyond human limits is an improper over-extension which will bring down catastrophe upon the self-praiser. Plutarch, it is noteworthy, does not devote much space to this religious issue, but it is the background for everything he has to say. He can assume that this background, even if it is largely unexplained, is shared and agreed upon by every reader as part of Greco-Roman popular religion.[11] Therefore, Plutarch can restrict himself to simply denouncing self-deification at several points of the argument.

In discussing the device of *metathesis* [12] he recommends the citation of Homer (*Od.* 16. 187) as a proper reply to the "flatterers": οὔ τίς τοι θεός εἰμι· τί μ' ἀθανάτοισιν ἐίσκεις; In the following section Plutarch refers to three examples for implementing his advice:

---

[8] 539A-C.

[9] 539C.

[10] 539D, referring to Xenophon *Mem.* 2. 1. 31.

[11] For the doctrine of "hybris-nemesis" see M. P. Nilsson, *Greek Folk Religion* (New York, 1961) 108f.; Id., *GGR*, 3d ed. (Munich, 1967) 1:735ff.; E. R. Dodds, *The Greeks and the Irrational* (Berkeley & Los Angeles, 1957) 28ff.; G. Bertram, *TDNT*, s.v. ὕβρις (further literature).

[12] 543D. The verse from Homer seems to have become a popular denial of deification. It is also quoted in *prof. virt.* 81D; Lucian *Icar.* 13. Cf. *adul. et am.* 48E-49B.

Referring to the ruler-cult, he approves of those rulers who adopt names which are highly respectable, but still human (ταῖς καλαῖς μὲν ἀνθρωπικαῖς. . . προσηγορίαις) like Philadelphos, Philomētor, Euergetēs or Theophilēs, instead of allowing themselves to be proclaimed "gods" or "sons of gods": τοὺς μὴ θεοὺς μηδὲ παῖδας θεῶν ἀναγορεύεσθαι θέλοντας.[13] These examples show that Plutarch is critical of the ruler-cult of his day, but it is perhaps intentional that he overlooks the Roman ruler-worship and confines himself to the past.[14]

Equally reprehensible are those writers and speakers who claim for themselves the name of "wisdom" (τοὺς τὸ τῆς σοφίας ἐπιγραφομένους ὄνομα), while those are delightful who inoffensively and moderately claim no more than to love wisdom, or to make progress in it, or some such remark: χαίρουσι τοῖς φιλοσοφεῖν ἢ προκόπτειν ἤ τι τοιοῦτο περὶ αὑτῶν ἀνεπίφθονον καὶ μέτριον λέγουσιν.[15] By contrast, during their speeches, the "rhetorical sophists"[16] accept from the audience praising shouts like θείως or δαιμονίως. They thereby miss what would be proper commendations, like μετρίως and ἀνθρωπίνως.[17]

For the same reason Plutarch advises that those who are compelled to praise themselves under certain circumstances do so by putting in a disclaimer, to the effect that they do not claim everything to be their achievement, but attribute part of their success to Tyche or god: τὸ μὴ πάντα προσποιεῖν ἑαυτοῖς, ἀλλ' ὥσπερ φορτίου τῆς δόξης τὸ μὲν εἰς τὴν τύχην τὸ δὲ εἰς τὸν θεὸν ἀποτίθεσθαι.[18]

2. *The ethical problem.* When we discuss the ethical problems Plutarch sees connected with self-praise, we can distinguish between the level of popular morality and that of philosophical doctrine, which leans heavily upon psychological observations.

For the most part Plutarch presupposes the popular morality and does not explicitly discuss it. It does, however, provide the background for most of what he says, and the philosophical doc-

---

[13] 543E.

[14] For a sizable collection of passages from Plutarch, see K. Scott, "Plutarch and the Ruler Cult," *TAPhA* 60 (1929) 117-35; A. D. Nock, *Essays on Religion and the Ancient World* (Cambridge, Mass., 1972) 2:726; C. P. Jones, *Plutarch and Rome* (Oxford, 1971) 123f.

[15] 543E. On the subject of progress in virtue, see *prof. virt.*, passim.

[16] Cf. the parallel passage in *aud.* 45F.

[17] 543E-F. On the notion of σοφιστής, see Jeuckens, *Plutarch,* 39, 47ff.

[18] 542E. Examples are provided in 542E-543A.

trines only provide a rationale for what popular morality knows anyway. The primary problem of self-praise is its flat contradiction of the Delphic maxims, especially the μηδὲν ἄγαν. It is not accidental that Plutarch quotes in the beginning from Pindar (*O.* 9. 41f.): καὶ τὸ καυχᾶσθαι παρὰ καιρὸν μανίαις ὑποκρέκειν. This verse is clearly an expression of the Delphic piety and may even be a reflection of another of the maxims: ἐπὶ ῥώμηι μὴ καυχῶ.[19] For some reason Plutarch never uses the term καυχᾶσθαι himself,[20] but he has other terms to describe the offense, e.g., μεγαλαυχία, μεγαληγορία, etc.[21] People who indulge in this easily lose control and go too far: οὐ κρατοῦσιν οὐδὲ μετριάζουσιν.[22] The terms μέτριος and μετρίως, etc., are used by Plutarch [23] to describe in a positive way what is meant by the μηδὲν ἄγαν.[24]

Plutarch has summarized the more philosophical doctrines in the *Exordium* and in the *Conclusio*. At the end of the *Exordium* (539D-E) he gives three basic reasons why self-praise creates distress on the part of the listener.[25]

The first of these reasons has to do with "decency." If we expect a decent person to feel embarrassed even when praised by others, a self-praiser must be utterly "without decency": πρῶτον μὲν γὰρ

---

[19] *SIG,* III, no. 1268. On Pindar's religion see H. Strohm, *Tyche: Zur Schicksalsauffassung bei Pindar und den frühgriechischen Dichtern* (Stuttgart, 1944) 55ff.; C. M. Bowra, *Pindar* (Oxford, 1964) 42-98, 226. On the Delphic maxim see *PECL* 1: 76, 85-102, 128, 145, 147; P. Courcelle, *Connais-toi toi-même de Socrate à saint Bernard,* vol. 1 (Paris, 1974).

[20] See *Index Verborum Plutarcheus,* s.v.; Bultmann, *TDNT,* s.v., B.4.

[21] See *Index Verborum Plutarcheus,* s.v.

[22] 546D.

[23] See *Index Verborum Plutarcheus,* s.v. On Plutarch's rejection of Asianism as a violation of the μηδὲν ἄγαν, see Jeuckens, *Plutarch,* 55ff.; on μέτριος κτλ., see M. Pinnoy, "Het begrip 'Midden' in de ethica van Plutarchus," in: *Zetesis, Album amicorum . . . aangeboden aan . . . E. de Strycker* (Antwerpen, Utrecht, 1973) 224-33.

[24] One would expect Plutarch to cite the μηδὲν ἄγαν here, but he does not. He is, however, familiar with this maxim, as the following passages (collected by E. O'Neil) show: *cons. Apoll.* 116C, D (there also in a quotation from Pindar); cf. the interpretation in 116E; *sept. sap. conv.* 163D; 164B, C; *de E* 385D; 387F; *garrul.* 511B. Since Plutarch often joins together the μηδὲν ἄγαν and the γνῶθι σαυτόν, we may assume that he treated both in his lost treatise on the γνῶθι σαυτόν (cf. Lamprias Cat. 177); for the γνῶθι σαυτόν see *aud. poet.* 36A; *adul. et am.* 49B; 65F; *ex inim. util.* 89A; *cons. Apoll.* 116C, D; *sept. sap. conv.* 164B; *de E* 385D; 392A; 394C; *garrul.* 511B; *adv. Col.* 1118C.

[25] 539D: ὁ παρ' ἄλλων ἔπαινος ἥδιστον ἀκουσμάτων ἐστιν, . . . ἑτέροις δὲ ὁ περὶ αὑτοῦ λυπηρότατον. Cf. 547D.

ἀναισχύντους ἡγούμεθα τοὺς ἑαυτοὺς ἐπαινοῦντας, αἰδεῖσθαι προσῆκον αὐτοῖς κἂν ὑπ' ἄλλων ἐπαινῶνται. This means that his healthy relationship with himself is destroyed.

Secondly, because of the rule that praise be expressed properly by others, one who does it himself is ἄδικος: he usurps what others ought to bestow and thereby deprives them of their proper rights: ἃ λαμβάνειν ἔδει παρ' ἑτέρων αὐτοὺς αὐτοῖς διδόντας.[26]

The third reason has to do with the impact of the self-praise upon the listener. If the listener remains silent, simply observing the self-praise of another, it creates in him bad feelings of ἄχθεσθαι καὶ φθονεῖν. Plutarch points out [27] again and again that this "envy" destroys the good relationships between people and makes life unbearable. If, however, the listener fears those ill-feelings, he feels compelled to join in the praises, thus confirming them. But then the matter becomes one of "flattery" (κολακεία), quite unfit for a free man and certainly no longer a proper way of praising someone.[28]

In the *Conclusio* (547D) he adds another argument which comes from the theory of rhetoric itself. In general Plutarch is very critical of rhetoric if it does not serve the goals and purposes of ethics, but is exclusively preoccupied with "form" (περιεργία) and techniques.[29] Put in its proper place rhetoric becomes acceptable and even useful. This is the case when rhetoric, which is merely a τέχνη by itself, assumes the role of πειθοῦς συνεργός and becomes beneficial (547F: ὠφελεῖν . . . τοὺς ἀκούοντας) to the listener in the sense of guiding him towards ἀρετή.[30] Then rhetoric also becomes an important "tool" of the philosopher.[31]

In this context, Plutarch observes, self-praise impresses the

---

[26] On the use of a proverb at this point, see above, pp. 373, 384.

[27] See the *Index Verborum Plutarcheus*, s.v. ἄχθομαι, φθονέω, φθόνος, ἐπίφθονος, ἀνεπίφθονος, ἀνεπιφθόνως. On the subject see E. Milobenski, *Der Neid in der griechischen Philosophie* (Wiesbaden, 1964), which deals with Plutarch specifically in ch. 8 (135-65).

[28] On the "flatterer," see *adul. et am.*, passim.

[29] On the relationship of Plutarch and rhetoric, see Jeuckens, *Plutarch*, passim.

[30] Cf. the reference to the politician using virtue, 539F (χρήσασθαι τῇ ἀρετῇ).

[31] Cf. Jeuckens, *Plutarch*, 30, who tries to describe rhetoric as Plutarch sees it: "die ῥητορική ist eine τέχνη, die als πειθοῦς συνεργός neben dem ἦθος vom Redner angewendet werden muss, deren Hauptaufgabe die richtige Behandlung der ἤθη und πάθη der Zuhörer ist, die aber auch durch ihre natürliche χάρις diesen für sich einnehmen will, deren Gesamtzweck das πείθειν mit ethischen und logischen Beweisgründen bildet."

listeners in a negative way and, hence, becomes a hindrance for the orator himself. Apparently drawing on older rhetorical theory,[32] Plutarch describes self-praise as the most sickening form of speech: ... καὶ λόγος ἄλλος οὐδεὶς οὕτως ἐπαχθὴς οὐδὲ βαρύς. οὐδὲ γὰρ ἔχοντες εἰπεῖν ὅ τι πάσχομεν ἄλλο κακὸν ὑπὸ τῶν αὑτοὺς ἐπαινούντων ὥσπερ φύσει βαρυνόμενοι τὸ πρᾶγμα καὶ φεύγοντες ἀπαλλαγῆναι καὶ ἀναπνεῦσαι σπεύδομεν (547D). Therefore, removing the offense in self-praise is not only required because of religious and ethical concerns, but also for rhetorical reasons. A rhetorician who stands in the way of his own persuasiveness is a bad rhetorician, while the primary concern with ἀρετή helps rhetoric itself. At this point it becomes understandable why for Plutarch there is no division between the problems of ethics and of rhetoric.

Both the rhetorical and ethical consequences of this self-praise are then fairly obvious: "self-praise" always results in "dispraise" from others, and the end of this "vainglory" is no glory at all: ... τοῖς ἰδίοις ἐπαίνοις ἀλλότριος ἕπεται ψόγος ἀεὶ καὶ γίνεται τέλος ἀδοξία τῆς κενοδοξίας ταύτης...[33] In other words: self-praise defeats itself, unless the offensive element is taken out and the ethical concern is put in. It is noteworthy that Plutarch ends his treatise on this rather negative note. The ending shows that the author is primarily concerned with the *ethical* problem of the offensiveness of self-praise, while the rhetorical possibilities for inoffensive self-praise are only used for argumentative purposes. His intention is not to recommend inoffensive self-praise, but to avoid its offensiveness. In effect this means for him the avoidance, if possible, of open self-praise altogether.

B. *Self-praise in Plutarch and in early Christianity*

In general Plutarch and the early Christian writers share the critical sensitivity toward self-praise as well as many of the concerns expressed in connection with it. This is true in spite of the fact that the theological presuppositions, as well as the terminology, of both sides are very different. The early Christian authors are also different from Plutarch in that they had no interest in theoretical reflection. In addition, the early Christian writers were informed

---

[32] Similar ideas are found in Hermogenes and Quintilian, see Radermacher, *RhM* 52 (1897) 420ff.

[33] 547E.

foremostly by the Jewish (OT) tradition. The agreement is largely due, it seems, to the level of popular religion and morality which Greek philosophical tradition and early Christianity, together with Judaism, share. Another link of agreement is provided by diatribe material which all sides have taken up.

The rejection of self-praise figures prominently in connection with Jesus' claim to be the "Son of God." [34] For the Jewish ear such a claim is βλασφημία. In John 5:18, the Jewish interpretation is this: . . .ἴσον ἑαυτὸν ποιῶν τῷ θεῷ.[35] The mocking of the crucified Jesus by the crowds and the soldiers shows that this is a reflection of popular sentiment.[36] In substance Plutarch would agree with the Jews, saying that self-deification goes beyond the limits for man and amounts to ἀλαζονεία.[37] For the Christians, however, Jesus' claim is not blasphemy, because he is not merely a human being, but the divine redeemer.[38]

Self-deification of human beings is strictly rejected in ECL. This concern is especially expressed by Acts: 5:36 (Theudas): 8:9 (Simon Magus); 12:21-23 (Herod); Arist Apol 7; but also by 2 Thes 2:4. Affirmations of the apostles' "humanity" serve the same purpose: Acts 3:12; 10:26; 14:15.

In the NT Paul especially is very sensitive with regard to self-praise. In this connection his entire doctrine of καυχᾶσθαι must be mentioned. The term καυχᾶσθαι is never used by Plutarch, except in the quotation from Pindar (539C). Paul, however, uses it often, also Eph 2:9; Jas 1:9; 4:16; 1 Clem 13:1; 34:5; Ign Phld 6:3; Ign Pol 5:2; Ign Eph 18:1; Ign Trall 4:1; Herm Man 8:3.[39] For Paul improper καυχᾶσθαι includes every kind of self-claim

---

[34] See, esp. Matt 26:63-66//Mark 14:61-64//Luke 22:67-71.

[35] Cf. also John 10:33, 36-38; 19:7. See R. Bultmann, *The Gospel of John* (Philadelphia, 1971) 244, n. 6.

[36] See Matt 26:61//Mark 14:58; Matt 27:40//Mark 15:29; Matt 26:67f.// Mark 14:65; Matt 27:27-31//Mark 15:16-20; Barn 7:9f.; Gos Pet 9.

[37] See on 543D-E; also *cons. Apoll.* 116D-E.

[38] Cf. Phil 2:6: ὃς ἐν μορφῇ θεοῦ ὑπάρχων οὐχ ἁρπαγμὸν ἡγήσατο τὸ εἶναι ἴσα θεῷ. See also Mart Matt 2:1; Epist Apos 21 (Copt.). Differently, in the Odes of Solomon, the Redeemer himself praises God for his redemption (see, esp., Odes Sol 17; 22); in Odes Sol 42 the orant takes the role of the redeemer in praising himself.

[39] See Bauer, s.v.; R. Bultmann, *TNT*, s.v. καυχάομαι; J. S. Bosch, *"Gloriarse" ségun San Pablo: Sentido y teologia de καυχάομαι*, AnBib 40 and Colectanea San Paciano, 16 (Rome, 1970); cf. the review by R. J. Karris, *JBL* 92 (1973) 144-46.

before God, cf. 1 Cor 1:29: ὅπως μὴ καυχήσηται πᾶσα σάρξ ἐνώπιον τοῦ θεοῦ. This amounts to more than just the Jewish concept of ἔργα νόμου (cf. esp. Gal 6:13f.; Rom 2:17ff.); it also includes any kind of spiritual claims made by Christians on behalf of themselves: claims to do miracles, to have the power of prophecy, of speaking with tongues, wisdom, etc. But, like Plutarch, Paul also knows of a proper form of boasting for which he states the rule in 1 Cor 1:31; 2 Cor 10:18: ὁ καυχώμενος ἐν κυρίῳ καυχάσθω. The application of this rule is the basis of all Pauline theology, especially his doctrine of "justification by faith." [40]

It is in this frame-work that we must discuss those passages in which Paul does in fact praise himself. As Bultmann [41] points out in his excellent article: "The basic rejection of self-glorying is not contradicted by passages in which Paul boasts of his work." Whenever he glorifies himself, he does so indirectly and with the addition of the necessary "antidote." In speaking about himself, he praises God's grace: χάριτι δὲ θεοῦ εἰμι ὅ εἰμι (1 Cor 15:10).[42] It is with the same intent that he states: οὐ γὰρ ἐπαισχύνομαι τὸ εὐαγγέλιον (Rom 1:16). Other forms of boasting include the praise of his churches, of his work, of his "weaknesses" and "tribulation," or he unashamedly brags in the form of a "foolish discourse." [43]

Paul sees the dangers of self-glorification inherent in any kind of expression of human self-understanding. Especially noteworthy is the "macarism" in Rom 14:22b: μακάριος ὁ μὴ κρίνων ἑαυτὸν ἐν ᾧ δοκιμάζει. Often Paul expresses his caution in regard to self-evaluation in the form of gnomic sentences. These are sometimes very similar to those found in the Greek diatribe literature, where they are an application of the Delphic maxim γνῶθι σαυτόν. Paul, to be sure, never quotes the Delphic maxim. For him, human self-glorification violates the principle stated in 1 Cor 1:29: ὅπως μὴ καυχήσηται πᾶσα σάρξ ἐνώπιον τοῦ θεοῦ.[44] Both the Delphic maxim and Paul's principle agree that man must not transcend the limits set for him. This excludes any kind of "boasting" before

[40] See Bultmann, *TDNT*, s.v. καυχάομαι, C.1, with the collection of passages; also W. Beardslee, *Human Achievement and Divine Vocation in the Message of Paul* (Naperville, Ill., 1961).

[41] Bultmann, *TDNT* 3:650.

[42] Cf. also Gal 2:19f. and passim; Odes Sol 7:1-25, and often.

[43] See Betz, *Paulus*, 70ff. Paul's "self-presentation" in his letters is a literary problem which needs further investigation.

[44] Cf. above.

the deity.[45] Even if Paul uses Jewish terms,[46] he comes very close to what the Delphic maxim also intends to say, so that it is understandable why he can take over or imitate gnomic sentences as we find them in the Greek diatribe literature.[47] The closest parallels are:

1 Cor 3:18: Μηδεὶς ἑαυτὸν ἐξαπατάτω· εἴ τις δοκεῖ σοφὸς εἶναι ἐν ὑμῖν ἐν τῷ αἰῶνι τούτῳ, μωρὸς γενέσθω, ἵνα γένηται σοφός.
1 Cor 11:28a: δοκιμαζέτω δὲ ἄνθρωπος ἑαυτόν,. . .
1 Cor 11:31: εἰ δὲ ἑαυτοὺς διεκρίνομεν, οὐκ ἂν ἐκρινόμεθα, . . . ἵνα σὺν τῷ κόσμῳ κατακριθῶμεν.
2 Cor 13:5: ἑαυτοὺς πειράζετε εἰ ἐστὲ ἐν τῇ πίστει, ἑαυτοὺς δοκιμάζετε.
Gal 6:3: εἰ γὰρ δοκεῖ τις εἶναί τι μηδὲν ὤν, φρεναπατᾷ ἑαυτόν.
Gal 6:4: τὸ δὲ ἔργον ἑαυτοῦ δοκιμαζέτω ἕκαστος, καὶ τότε εἰς ἑαυτὸν μόνον τὸ καύχημα ἕξει καὶ οὐκ εἰς τὸν ἕτερον.

Related to these are the warnings against judging other people in comparison with oneself,[48] against pleasing oneself, and against self-confidence: Rom 2:1ff.; 15:1 (μὴ ἑαυτοῖς ἀρέσκειν); 1 Cor 4:6-8; 2 Cor 1:9 (μὴ πεποιθότες ὦμεν ἐφ' ἑαυτοῖς).[49] In this connection his warnings against τὰ ὑψηλὰ φρονεῖν[50] and ὑπαίρειν[51] must also be mentioned.

Positively speaking, self-evaluation is impossible, according to Paul, because man does not by himself know who he is. What the

---

[45] For Plutarch, see esp. *de E* 394C; also H. D. Betz, "The Delphic Maxim ΓΝΩΘΙ ΣΑΥΤΟΝ in Hermetic Interpretation," *HTR* 63 (1970) 465-83.

[46] For the OT Judaism, self-praise is the mark of foolishness and godlessness; it expresses man's desire to be independent from God. See for the passages Bultmann, *TDNT*, s.v. καυχάομαι κτλ., B.1-4; J. Schreiner, "Jeremia 9, 22.23 als Hintergrund des paulinischen 'Sich-Rühmens,'" in *Neues Testament und Kirche: Festschrift für R. Schnackenburg* (Freiburg, 1974) 530-42.

[47] The same is true for Philo; see Bultmann, ibid., B.4; P. Courcelle, "Philon d'Alexandrie et le précepte delphique," *Philomathes, Studies and Essays in the Humanities in Memory of P. Merlan* (The Hague, 1971) 245-50; Id., *Connais-toi toi-même*, 39-48; J.-G. Kahn, "'Connais-toi toi-même' à la manière de Philon," *RHPhR* 53 (1973) 293-307.

[48] See Betz, *Paulus*, 118ff.

[49] See also Rom 2:19; Phil 3:3f.; 1 Cor 3:1, 5; 4:2, 5; 5:12; 6:4; 10:7, 12, 14, 18; 12:6f.; etc.

[50] Rom 11:20; 12:16; cf. 1 Tim 6:17; and often in the Apostolic Fathers (see Kraft, *Clavis Patrum Apostolicorum*, s.v. ὑψηλός, ὑψηλόφρων, ὑψηλοφροσύνη, ὕψος, ὑψόω).

[51] 2 Cor 12:7: . . . ἵνα μὴ ὑπεραίρωμαι, . . . Cf. 2 Thes 2:4.

Christian knows about himself, has been revealed to him by the Spirit (Rom 8:15f.; Gal 4:6, cf. 4:8f.). Therefore, the proper self-evaluation is the praise of what God has revealed about man. The greatest example of this in Paul is found in Rom 8:31-39.[52] By comparison, Plutarch comes close to this, although he seems to be content with the traditional Platonic belief that all man needs for understanding himself is given to him: reason and philosophical contemplation. But at this point Plutarch reflects an underlying tension within Platonism. He can be very skeptical in regard to human rational abilities.[53] On the other hand, for him the god Apollo is identical with Reason,[54] and it is Apollo who calls upon man to recognize himself.[55]

This paraenesis, however, extends well beyond Paul. We can assume that it belonged to popular wisdom when the rich man who praises his good fortunes is called a fool (Luke 12:19f.). It is Luke's theology when he evaluates the Jews as self-righteous before men.[56] Common to the synoptic tradition is the Jewish saying in Matt 23:12: ὅστις δὲ ὑψώσει ἑαυτὸν ταπεινωθήσεται καὶ ὅστις ταπεινώσει ἑαυτὸν ὑψωθήσεται,[57] and the saying in Mark 10:34 is similar.[58] In addition to these sayings we have examples of the attitude to be rejected: the caricature of the Pharisee in Luke 18:9-14, and of Christians in Matt 7:21-23//Luke 6:46.[59]

Similar to Paul is the material in the Apostolic Fathers. There we find the same rule Paul refers to in 1 Cor 1:31; 2 Cor 10:18, but in its fuller text based upon Jer 9:22f. (cf. 1 Kgs 2:10) in 1 Clem 13:1:

---

[52] The nature of this text becomes clearer in comparison with the Odes of Solomon, where we have hymnic self-praises of the Redeemer (10:4-6; 17; 22; 42) and the redeemed (11; 12; 15; 18; 21; 25; 28; 35; 36; 38). In these hymns the frequent statements in the first person singular are always coupled with praises of God or the Redeemer. See also Christ's hymn in Acts of John 94-96.

[53] See my article "Observations on Some Gnosticizing Passages in Plutarch," *Proceedings of the International Colloquium on Gnosticism, Stockholm, August 20-25 1973* (Stockholm, 1977) 169-78.

[54] For the doctrine of "revelation" of Apollo, see *PECL* 1:86-88 on *de E* 384F-385A.

[55] *De E* 392A; 394C.

[56] Luke 10:29; 16:15: ὑμεῖς ἐστε οἱ δικαιοῦντες ἑαυτοὺς ἐνώπιον τῶν ἀνθρώπων. Cf. 1 Cor 3:21.

[57] Cf. Matt 18:4; Luke 18:14; 2 Cor 11:7; Jas 4:6, 10; 1 Pet 5:5f.; 1 Clem 59:3; Did 3:9; Barn 19:3; Herm Sim 9:22:3; Odes Sol 41:12; etc. See G. Bertram, *TDNT*, s.v. ὑψόω κτλ., D.1-2.

[58] Matt 20:26f.//Mark 10:43f.//Luke 22:26.

[59] Cf. also 2 Clem 4:1-2, 5; Matt 25:10-12, 41; Luke 13:25-27.

μὴ καυχάσθω ὁ σοφὸς ἐν τῇ σοφίᾳ αὐτοῦ μηδὲ ὁ ἰσχυρὸς ἐν τῇ ἰσχύϊ αὐτοῦ μηδὲ ὁ πλούσιος ἐν τῷ πλούτῳ αὐτοῦ, ἀλλ' ὁ καυχώμενος ἐν κυρίῳ καυχάσθω. . .

An "antisophistic" polemic is included in 1 Clem 21:5:

μᾶλλον ἀνθρώποις ἄφροσι καὶ ἀνοήτοις καὶ ἐπαιρομένοις καὶ ἐγκαυχωμένοις ἐν ἀλαζονείᾳ τοῦ λόγου αὐτῶν προσκόψωμεν ἢ τῷ θεῷ.

Common Hellenistic religion is reflected in 1 Clem 30:6-8:[60]

ὁ ἔπαινος ἡμῶν ἔστω ἐν θεῷ καὶ μὴ ἐξ αὐτῶν· αὐτεπαινέτους γὰρ μισεῖ ὁ θεός. ἡ μαρτυρία τῆς ἀγαθῆς πράξεως ἡμῶν διδόσθω ὕπ' ἄλλων, καθὼς ἐδόθη τοῖς πατράσιν ἡμῶν τοῖς δικαίοις. θράσος καὶ αὐθάδεια καὶ τόλμα τοῖς κατηραμένοις ὑπὸ τοῦ θεοῦ. ἐπιείκεια καὶ ταπεινοφροσύνη καὶ πραΰτης παρὰ τοῖς ηὐλογημένοις ὑπὸ τοῦ θεοῦ.

It is interesting that the same paraenetical material can be applied in a polemic against the gnostics in Herm Sim 9:22.[61]

III. Other Parallels

Ch. 1

(539A)

ὥς τι ὄντος. For this expression, see Acts 5:36, where it is said of Theudas: λέγων εἶναί τινα ἑαυτόν. See also 1 Cor 3:7; Gal 2:6a; Ign Eph 3:1. Quite close to Plutarch is the gnome Gal 6:3: εἰ γὰρ δοκεῖ τις εἶναί τι μηδὲν ὤν, φρεναπατᾷ ἑαυτόν.

ἢ δυναμένου. Boasting because of one's powerful deeds is rejected or restricted also in ECL, where it often includes miraculous deeds. See esp. Gal 6:5; 1 Cor 1:18-31; 2 Cor 12:9f.; Matt 7:21-23; Acts 4:7-9; Barn 20:1, where ὕψος δυνάμεως appears in a list of vices. Most impressive is 1 Cor 4:7: τί δὲ ἔχεις ὃ οὐκ ἔλαβες; εἰ δὲ καὶ ἔλαβες, τί καυχᾶσαι ὡς μὴ λαβών; cf. 1 Clem 38:1-4; Just Dial 101:1.

---

[60] See also 1 Clem 38:1-4; 39:1; Ign Magn 12:1; Ign Smyrn 5:2; Just Dial 101:1; Didasc (Gibson, 2:14, 21). For further texts see Bultmann, *TDNT*, s.v. καυχάομαι, C.2.

[61] See on this point, J. Reiling, *Hermas and Christian Prophecy* (Leiden, 1973) 51, 66.

πρὸς ἑτέρους. The remark points to the *syncrisis* motif, which underlies all self-praise. Cf. Luke 18:9-14; Ign Magn 12:1; 2 Cor 10:12, and on the subject Betz, *Paulus*, 118ff.

ἐπαχθές. The term often describes the negative effect of self-praise in *laud. ips.*; it is popular in Greek philosophical ethics (see LSJ, s.v.), but is absent from ECL.

(539B)

λόγῳ-ἔργῳ. This familiar contrast is found also in Rom 15:18; 2 Cor 10:11; Col 3:17; 1 John 3:18; etc. For the reverse order see Luke 24:19; Acts 7:22; 2 Thes 2:17. See Bauer, s.v. ἔργον, 1.a.

ἀηδία. The Greek ethical concept occurs often in the treatise, but in ECL only in Luke 23:12 v.l. (D,c). See Bauer, s.v.

(539C)

μεγαλαυχία. Although this term occurs frequently in Hellenistic literature, it is not found in ECL, except as a verb μεγάλα αὐχέω in Jas 3:5.

οὐ παύεται, with present active participle. The construction occurs also in Acts 5:42; 6:13; 13:10; 20:31; Eph 1:16; Col 1:9; Herm Vis 3:3:2.

ἀξίας ἐγκωμίων οὔσης. Cf. Phil 4:8: εἴ τις ἔπαινος... Acts 13:46: οὐκ ἀξίους κρίνετε ἑαυτοὺς τῆς αἰωνίου ζωῆς...

τοὺς στεφανουμένους ἐν τοῖς ἀγῶσιν ἕτεροι νικῶντας ἀναγορεύουσι. Plutarch recalls the practice at the athletic games, where the victor is proclaimed by someone other than himself. Cf. 2 Cor 12:2, 4 where Paul avoids referring to himself (οἶδα ἄνθρωπον); see on this Betz, *Paulus*, 95. ECL has no miracle-stories told in the first person singular by the Christians who performed them; that this is intentional is shown by the inherent polemics in Matt 7:21-23; 2 Cor 12:7-10 (see Betz, *Paulus*, 92ff.). Cf. also Ign Smyrn 5:2: τί γάρ με ὠφελεῖ τις, εἰ ἐμὲ ἐπαινεῖ, ...

περιαυτολογία. This important rhetorical term is found often in Plutarch's treatise (see 539C, E, 540B, F, 544C, 546B, C [2x], D, F, 547C; also *aud. poet.* 29B; *aud.* 41B; 44A; Cicero 887A (these references are from *Index Verborum Plutarcheus*, s.v.). In ECL, the expression is not found prior to Origen (see Lampe, s.v.). It is noteworthy that the synonymous αὐτεπαινετός (1 Clem 30:6) is a hapax legomenon; cf. LSJ, s.v. αὐτέπαινος.

(539D)

τὴν ἑαυτοῦ νίκην. Cf. the proclamation by Christ of his victory, a proclamation which is not considered offensive since it is done by the redeemer, John 16:33: θαρσεῖτε, ἐγὼ νενίκηκα τὸν κόσμον (see also Odes Sol 10:4-6; 17; 22; 42). The Christian's proclamation in 1 John 5:4: ἡ νίκη ἡ νικήσασα τὸν κόσμον, ἡ πίστις ἡμῶν is carefully interpreted in 5:5-12 to make sure that the μαρτυρία is by God. Paul in interpreting ὑπερνικῶμεν in Rom 8:37 is very cautious to attribute every glory to God: διὰ τοῦ ἀγαπήσαντος ἡμᾶς, cf. 1 Cor 15:54-57; 4:8; Odes Sol 5; 6; 15:8f.; etc. Differently, the victorious athlete is used as a comparison in the struggle against heresy in Ign Pol 3:1.

ὁ παρ' ἄλλων ἔπαινος ἥδιστον ἀκουσμάτων. Plutarch attributes the statement to Xenophon (*Mem.* 2. 1. 31), but it is certainly common opinion. For a psychological explanation of the phenomenon, see 542C. The same view is found in 1 Clem 30:7: ἡ μαρτυρία τῆς ἀγαθῆς πράξεως ἡμῶν διδόσθω ὑπ' ἄλλων. Similarly 38:2: ὁ ταπεινοφρονῶν μὴ ἑαυτῷ μαρτυρείτω, ἀλλ' ἐάτω ὑφ' ἑτέρου ἑαυτὸν μαρτυρεῖσθαι. See also Rom 13:3; 2 Cor 8:18; 1 Pet 2:14; Ign Magn 12:1; Ign Smyrn 5:2. Only the ἔπαινος coming from God is important: see Rom 2:29; 1 Cor 4:5; 1 Pet 1:17; 1 Clem 30:6; etc.

ἑτέροις δὲ ὁ περὶ αὑτοῦ λυπηρότατον. That self-praise always puts the burden upon those who are witnesses is exemplified by the contrasts between the Pharisee and the tax-collector in Luke 18:9-14; the two brothers in Luke 15:29; the contrast is presented in reversed form in Matt 25:31-46.

ἀναισχύντους ἡγούμεθα τοὺς ἑαυτοὺς ἐπαινοῦντας. For the same views, see 1 Clem 30:6; Herm Sim 9:22:2. See the Pharisee in Luke 18:11: πρὸς ἑαυτόν. Cf. Paul's "foolish discourse," 2 Cor 11:16ff.: Paul engages in self-praise only by playing the "fool" (see Betz, *Paulus*, 79ff.).

ἀδίκους, ἃ λαμβάνειν ἔδει παρ' ἑτέρων αὑτοὺς αὑτοῖς διδόντας. Cf. 1 Cor 4:7 (quoted above on 539A: ἡ δυναμένου). Cf. also the proverb in Acts 20:35; 1 Clem 2:1 (in the same context!); Did 4:5; Herm Man 2:4-7; also Matt 10:8: δωρεὰν ἐλάβετε, δωρεὰν δότε (cf. Acts 8:20).

ἄχθεσθαι καὶ φθονεῖν. The terms describe the negative effect of self-praise. Only the latter concept is found in ECL, always in the negative sense. See esp. Gal 5:26, and Bauer, s.v. (*TDNT* 9 has no article!).

(539E)

συνεπιμαρτυρέω. Cf. the usage of the term in Heb 2:4; 1 Clem 23:5; 43:1.

Ch. 2

καιροῦ καὶ πράξεως ἀπαιτούσης. Cf. Ign Pol 2:3: ὁ καιρὸς ἀπαιτεῖ σε. See Bauer, s.v. ἀπαιτέω, 2.

ἐκφέρει καρπόν. This ethical terminology is found also in 1 Clem 24:5. καρπός is used, as an ethical term, Gal 5:22; Eph 5:9; Odes Sol 1:5; 4:4; 7:1; 10:2; etc. See Bauer, s.v., 2.a.

(539F)

ὥσπερ ἀπὸ σπέρματος πλειόνων ἑτέρων ἀπ' αὐτοῦ καὶ κρειττόνων φυομένων ἐπαίνων. The figure of the seed producing a great harvest was very popular in Hellenistic literature. Cf. the Parable of the Mustard Seed (Matt 13:31-32//Mark 4:30-32// Luke 13:18-19); 2 Cor 9:6; Gal 3:16; etc. See S. Schulz, *TWNT*, s.v. σπέρμα κτλ., A, D.

ἀφορμὰς δίδωσι. Cf. this expression in 2 Cor 5:12; 1 Tim 5:14; Ign Trall 8:2; Herm Man 4:1:11; 4:3:3; also Gal 5:13.

πειθομένους γὰρ ἅμα καὶ φιλοῦντας ἡδὺ καὶ ῥᾴδιον ὠφελεῖν. . . The statement contains Plutarch's main interest: to lead the listener towards ἀρετή (see above p. 376). The terms ὠφέλεια, ὠφελέω, ὠφέλιμος figure prominently in Paul: cf. Rom 2:25; 3:1; 1 Cor 13:3; 14:6; Gal 5:2; also 1 Tim 4:8; Tit 3:8; etc. See Bauer, s.v. (no article in *TWNT*!).

Ch. 3

(540A)

δόξης ἀκαίρου. Cf. the proverbial εὔνοια ἄκαιρος in Ign Rom 4:1. See Bauer, s.v. ἄκαιρος.

ὡς. . .οὕτως. . . Plutarch compares those "who hunger for praises" with those who at the height of starvation feed on their own bodies. This type of absurd comparison was especially popular in the diatribe material. Cf., e.g., Gal 5:15.

πεινῶντες ἐπαίνων. For the figurative use of πεινάω cf. Matt 5:6; John 6:35.

(540B)

ἁμιλλώμενοι πρὸς ἀλλοτρίους ἐπαίνους ἔργα καὶ πράξεις ἀντιπαραβάλλωσιν αὐτῶν ὡς ἀμαυρώσοντες ἑτέρους. . . Plutarch refers to the *syncrisis*-motif which belongs to the tools of self-praise: the self-praiser compares himself favorably with others, at their expense. A typical example is found in Luke 18:9-14; also 2 Cor 10:12 (and the interpretation by Betz, *Paulus*, 118ff.); Gal 5:26. Paul's concern about καυχᾶσθαι ἐν ἀλλοτρίοις κόποις in 2 Cor 10:15f. is also related.

τὴν δὲ ἀλλοτρίοις ἐπαίνοις εἰς μέσον ὑπὸ φθόνου καὶ ζηλοτυπίας ἐξωθουμένην περιαυτολογίαν εὖ μάλα δεῖ φυλάξεσθαι. Plutarch formulated this as a kind of rule of ethics. Is there any connection between this and the missionary rule in Rom 15:20; 1 Cor 3:10; 2 Cor 10:13-16?

(540C)

παραχωρεῖν τοῖς τιμωμένοις ἀξίοις οὖσιν. This general rule is also referred to by Paul in Rom 13:7: . . .τῷ τὴν τιμὴν τὴν τιμήν. Cf. also Rom 12:10; 1 Tim 5:17; 6:1; 1 Pet 2:17; Rev 4:11; 5:12.

ἂν δὲ ἀνάξιοι καὶ φαῦλοι δόξωσιν εἶναι, μὴ τοῖς ἰδίοις ἐπαίνοις ἀφαιρώμεθα τοὺς ἐκείνων, ἀλλ' ἄντικρυς ἐλέγχοντες καὶ δεικνύντες οὐ προσηκόντως εὐδοκιμοῦντας. Presisely this strategy is followed by Paul in 2 Cor 10-13, esp. in the "foolish discourse." Cf. 2 Cor 12:11 (οὐδὲν . . . ὑστέρησα) and the interpretation in Betz, *Paulus*, 77, 121f.

Ch. 4

ἂν ἀπολογούμενος . . . πρὸς διαβολὴν ἢ κατηγορίαν. Self-praise is allowed as a means of defense against slander and accusation. This view is shared by Paul in 1 Cor 9:3ff.; 2 Cor 12:19 (on this, see Betz, *Paulus*, 14ff.); Gal 1-2; and Luke (Acts 24:10ff.: περὶ ἐμαυτοῦ ἀπολογοῦμαι, 22:1; 25:8, 16; 26:1, 2, 24). Actually, Paul never glorifies himself, except ironically in 2 Cor 11:21ff.; Phil 3:5ff. Cf. 541E infra.

(540D)

ὡς ἐπιμαρτυρεῖ τὰ γινόμενα, The reference points to the examples from history which Plutarch adduces as support. Also Paul points to "facts" to support his arguments. He does not, however, take them only from history, and he does not use them in the same way Plutarch does, but he includes "allegory" and even "facts" from the "history" of the addressees of the letters. Cf. 1 Cor 10:1ff.; Gal 3:6ff.; 4:21ff.; Rom 4:3ff.; see also 1 Cor

1:26; 10:18; 2 Cor 10:7; 12:6, etc. On this point, see Betz, *Paulus*, 132ff.

(540E)

ὡς ἕτοιμός ἐστιν ἀποθνήσκειν. This rhetorical phrase has parallels in Luke 22:33: μετά σου ἕτοιμός εἰμι καὶ εἰς φυλακὴν καὶ εἰς θάνατον πορεύεσθαι. See also Acts 21:13; 23:15.

τὴν Μεσσήνην ᾤκισε. One of the deeds by which Epameinondas glorifies himself is that he founded Messene. The story is found also in *reg. et. imp.* 194A-C; *praec. reip.* 799E; see F. C. Babbitt, LCL, vol. 3:150 n. a. Cf. Paul who takes the founding of a church as part of his καύχησις (2 Cor 10:13-18; 1:14; etc.). See Betz, *Paulus*, 130f.

τὴν Λακωνικὴν διεπόρθησε. Cf. Paul who before his conversion had regarded the persecution of the church as part of his "achievements" (πορθέω Gal 1:13, 23; cf. Acts 9:21).

θαυμάζοντες τὸν ἄνδρα. In Plutarch, this is the proper reaction to proper self-praise. Cf. θαυμάζειν as the reaction to the miracle-worker. See Bultmann, *HST*, 225f. Cf. also 542B infra.

(540F)

Ῥωμαῖοι Κικέρωνι μὲν ἐδυσχέραινον ἐγκωμιάζοντι πολλάκις ἑαυτοῦ... Plutarch shares the well-known criticism of Cicero (see Quintilian *Inst.* 11. 1. 17; Jeuckens, *Plutarch*, passim): Cicero praised himself οὐκ ἀναγκαίως ἀλλ' ὑπὲρ δόξης (541A). Cf. 1 Cor 3:21: ὥστε μηδεὶς καυχάσθω ἐν ἀνθρώποις. Cf. also 2 Cor 11:18; Gal 6:13.

Σκιπίωνι δὲ εἰπόντι μὴ πρέπειν αὐτοῖς κρίνειν περὶ Σκιπίωνος. Cf. Paul's refusal to be judged by the Corinthians: 1 Cor 4:1ff.; cf. also 2:14f.; 9:3ff.; Rom 14:4; Jas 4:11f.

τὸ κρίνειν πᾶσιν ἀνθρώποις. Cf. 1 Cor 6:3: ἀγγέλους κρινοῦμεν.

Ch. 5

(541A-B)

δυστυχοῦσι μᾶλλον ἁρμόζει μεγαλαυχία καὶ κόμπος ἢ εὐτυχοῦσιν. Plutarch discusses in this section the interesting theory that the self-praise of those in difficult circumstances is more believable than that of the successful. While the latter raises the suspicion of φιλοτιμία, the boasting of the unfortunate is usually met with admiration. This is true because no one would think of them as having φιλοτιμία, and their boasting is taken as a heroic witness of man's struggle against Tyche. The idea of man vs. Tyche is also predominant in *Alex. fort.*, where the case is made that Alexander's achievements were not given to him ready-made, but only after terrible struggles (cf. esp. the descriptions of the struggles in 326E-F; 327B-E). In *fort. Rom.*, Plutarch applies the idea to a whole nation. Perhaps following Polybius, Plutarch sees the power of Rome as a result of a contest between Arete and Tyche; see on this point Jones, *Plutarch and Rome*, 67ff. In *laud. ips.* Plutarch argues that men fighting Tyche are admired for propping up courage and for overcoming self-pity, lamenting, and self-abasement. After an illustration from boxing (see below) Plutarch concludes: . . .ἐκ τοῦ ταπεινοῦ καὶ οἰκτροῦ τῇ μεγαλαυχίᾳ μεταφέρων εἰς τὸ γαῦρον καὶ ὑψηλόν, οὐκ ἐπαχθὴς οὐδὲ θρασὺς ἀλλὰ μέγας εἶναι δοκεῖ καὶ ἀήττητος. . . (541B). Thus Paul's concept of καυχᾶσθαι ἐν ταῖς ἀσθενείαις (2 Cor 11:30; 12:9; Rom 5:3), although based upon his christology of "Christ crucified," was by no means alien to the culture. The catalogs of περιστάσεις (1 Cor 4:10ff.; 2 Cor 4:7ff.; 6:4ff.; 11:23ff.; 12:10) are, of course, a traditional form of this kind of self-praise. See Betz, *Paulus*, 97ff.; W. Schrage, "Leid, Kreuz und Eschaton: Die Peristasenkataloge als Merkmale paulinischer Theologia crucis und Eschatologie," *EvT* 34 (1974) 141-175.

πυκτεύοντες. Boxing is also used as an illustration by Paul in 1 Cor 9:26.

(541C)

συναποθνήσκειν. This term occurs also in Mark 14:31; 2 Cor 7:3; 2 Tim 2:11. Cf. also the two thieves dying on the cross with Jesus, esp. the version in Luke 23:39-43 (cf. Gos Pet 10-14). Here the differences are more interesting than the similarities: the two who die with Jesus are not his friends but criminals; he does not take a heroic attitude towards his death, nor does he expect heroism of the thieves; he does not say as Phocion: τί λέγετε; οὐκ ἀγαπᾶτε ἀποθνήσκων μετ' ἐμοῦ;

οὐκ ἀγαπᾷς ἀποθνήσκειν μετὰ Φωκίωνος; The story of Phocion illustrates the heroic *topos* of "dying together." The man apparently belonged to Phocion's party. Phocion expected the man to die with him instead of lamenting like a coward; cf. also *reg. et imp.* 189A; *Phoc.* 36. 3. G. Stählin has collected passages from ancient literature, among them *Ant.* 71. 3; *par. min.* 312C-D, and compares the material with 2 Cor 7:3 and other NT passages ("'Um mitzusterben und mitzuleben'; Bemerkungen zu 2 Kor 7, 3," in *Neues Testament und christliche Existenz: Festschrift für H. Braun zum 70. Geburtstag* [Tübingen, 1973] 503-21); cf. 2 Tim 2:11. According to the synoptic tradition (Matt 26:35//Mark 14:31//Luke 22:33; cf. John 13:37; 11:16) the disciples of Jesus declare themselves ready to die with him, but instead they all flee (Matt 26:56//Mark 14:50-52).

Ch. 6

ὑφίετο τῷ θείῳ τῆς δόξης καὶ μέτριος ἦν. . . To yield the honor to the deity is a way of avoiding improper self-glorification; see above, p. 374. Cf. the phrase δόξαν δίδωμι θεῷ, Luke 17:18; John 9:24; Acts 12:23, etc. τὸ θεῖον occurs only in Acts 17:29.

(541D, E)

ἡ παρρησία, μέρος οὖσα τῆς δικαιολογίας. Plutarch remarks that in a defense speech self-praise may be allowed as part of παρρησία. His example, an apophthegm of Themistocles, uses *ironic* self-praise. Cf., esp., 2 Cor 11:7ff.; 12:13.

Ch. 7

οὐκ ὀνειδίζειν ἀλλ' ἀπολογεῖσθαι. Plutarch cites Demosthenes, *De corona*, as an example that one may recount one's "record" if the public fails to appreciate it. Cf. above 540C. A case of this is also Paul's "record," esp. 1 Cor 15:9-10; Gal 1-2.

Ch. 8

(541F)

ὅταν ἐφ' ᾧ τις ἐγκαλεῖται τούτου τοὐναντίον αἰσχρὸν ἀποδεικνύῃ καὶ φαῦλον. Discussing in this chapter the device of *antithesis*, Plutarch provides this definition. See De Lacy and Einarson, LCL 7:131 ad loc., and on *antithesis* H. Lausberg, *Handbuch der literarischen Rhetorik* (Munich, 1960) secs. 181-182, who cites as an example John 11:50: συμφέρει ὑμῖν ἵνα εἷς ἄνθρωπος ἀποθάνῃ ὑπὲρ τοῦ λαοῦ καὶ μὴ ὅλον τὸ ἔθνος ἀπόληται. Cf. also John 18:14. In Plutarch's example it is the Athenian orator Lycurgus who defends himself by asking what the Athenians think of a citizen who after so many years in office gives away money illegally instead of taking it (cf. also *or. vit.* 842A-B, and H. N. Fowler, LCL 10:402 n. a). A similar argument is made by Paul, also ironically, in 2 Cor 11:7ff.; 12:13ff. See Betz, *Paulus*, 100ff.

διδοὺς μᾶλλον ἀδίκως ἢ λαμβάνων... Again, the popular proverb is used; see on 539D.

(542A)

"τίς δέ," εἶπεν, "οὔ φησιν ἐν ἐμοὶ πλέον εἶναι πίστεως ἢ δεινότητος;" In this example Cicero defends himself by saying that he is more trustworthy than eloquent. Cf. 2 Cor 10:10; 11:6 (ἰδιώτης τῷ λόγῳ); 13:8, and the interpretation by Betz, *Paulus*, 57ff.

Ch. 11

(542E)

τοὺς δὲ ἀναγκασθέντας ἐπαινεῖν αὑτούς. If one is forced, self-praise is allowed. Cf. Paul who concludes his "foolish discourse," 2 Cor 12:11, by saying: ὑμεῖς με ἠναγκάσατε. See Betz, *Paulus*, 72.

τὸ μὴ πάντα προσποιεῖν ἑαυτοῖς, ἀλλ' ὥσπερ φορτίου τῆς δόξης τὸ μὲν εἰς τὴν τύχην τὸ δὲ εἰς τὸν θεὸν ἀποτίθεσθαι. See supra, on 539A and p. 374. Cf. by contrast Acts 12:23: Herod is killed by an angel of God because οὐκ ἔδωκεν τὴν δόξαν τῷ θεῷ.

Αὐτοματίας βωμὸν ἱδρυσάμενος. This name of the goddess of "Chance" —typical for Hellenistic religious sentiment—is mentioned several times by Plutarch (also 816E; *Tim.* 36. 2; see Nilsson, *GGR*, 2:203f.). Mart Pol 9:2; 10:1 recognizes as typically pagan: ὀμνύναι τὴν Καίσαρος τύχην.

Ἀγαθῷ Δαίμονι. This name for Tyche is not mentioned in ECL (see Nilsson, *GGR*, 2:203; 213-218). But the dative is typical for honoring a "nameless" deity, as is also reflected in Acts 17:23 in the inscription Ἀγνώστῳ Θεῷ.

(542F)

"ταῦτα," εἶπεν, "ἄνδρες Ἀθηναῖοι, θεός τις ἔπραξεν. ἡμεῖς δὲ τὰς χεῖρας ἐχρήσαμεν." On the background of this statement, see above p. 374, and on 539A. Cf. esp. Luke 11:20: ...ἐν δακτύλῳ θεοῦ [ἐγὼ] ἐκβάλλω τὰ δαιμόνια, a statement of Jesus summing up his activity as an exorcist. See also Acts 3:12; Mark 6:2: αἱ δυνάμεις... διὰ τῶν χειρῶν αὐτοῦ... See furthermore E. Lohse, *TDNT*, s.v. χείρ, C.2.b, and passim.

Ἐπαφρόδιτον ἑαυτὸν ἀνηγόρευσε. Sulla went so far to attribute all his accomplishments to "Chance" and named himself Epaphroditus (Lat. *Felix*). This explanation agrees with *Sull.* 34. 2-3 (473D-E), but according to *fort. Rom.* 318C-D, his appropriation of the name is almost an act of "hybris." Both names were popular and appear in ECL: Phil 2:25; 4:18; Acts 23:24, 26; 24:3, 22, 24f., 27; 25:14.

(543A)

τὴν 'Αθηνᾶν ἔφασκεν αὐτῷ φοιτῶσιν εἰς ὄψιν ἑκάστοτε τοὺς νόμους ὑφηγεῖσθαι καὶ διδάσκειν. Plutarch reports on the widespread belief in antiquity that famous law-codes were revealed by deities through their appearances. The example given is that of Zaleucus, law-giver of the Locrians. It may be noteworthy that Plutarch does not attribute the same idea to Numa (cf. *Num.* 4. 1-2; 8. 6; *comp. Lyc. et Num.* 1. 4-5). ECL frequently mentions God's revelation of the Torah to Moses (e.g., John 1:17; 9:29, but cf. Gal 3:19f.). Also the resurrection-appearances of Jesus must be mentioned because in these appearances Christ reveals the fundamental doctrines and regulations for the church: Matt 28:16-20; Mark 16:9-18; Luke 24; Acts 1:6-8; John 20:19-23; 21:1-23. Paul bases his entire mission and message upon a vision of Christ; see esp. his self-defense in Gal 1-2; 1 Cor 15:1ff.; Acts 22:3ff.; 26:9ff.; etc.

αὐτοῦ δὲ μηδὲν διανόημα μηδὲ βούλευμα τῶν εἰσφερομένων. Cf. Gal 1:1: οὐκ ἀπ' ἀνθρώπων οὐδὲ δι' ἀνθρώπου..., also 1:11, 12; Acts 20:23; 21:4, 11; 26:22; furthermore 1 Cor 2:9; etc.

Ch. 12

(543D)

τὸ ἀδωροδόκητον ἢ τὸ σῶφρον ἢ τὸ εὔγνωμον ἢ τὸ φιλάνθρωπον. This short catalog of virtues has parallels in ECL as far as the "form" is concerned; cf. Rom 1:29ff., and H. Lietzmann, *An die Römer* (Tübingen, 1971) ad loc.; Betz, *Lukian*, 206ff.

(543E)

βαρυνόμενοι τοὺς τὸ τῆς σοφίας ἐπιγραφομένους ὄνομα. It is offensive just to call someone "wise." ECL agrees; cf. Matt 11:25//Luke 10:21; Rom 1:14, 22; 16:27; 1 Cor 1:18-31; 2:1-13; 3:19; 6:5; 2 Cor 1:12; etc. On this point Jewish wisdom (cf. esp. Jer 9:22f.) and Hellenistic philosophy converge. See G. Fohrer, *TDNT*, s.v. σοφία, B.VI.2; U. Wilckens, ibid., C-F.

Ch. 13

(544B)

δυσγενείας ἐξομολόγησιν. One of the devices to make self-praise acceptable is to throw in a confession of low birth. The example (544B-C) shows that the praise points to the career, e.g., from low birth to kingship. This idea is almost proverbial; cf. Hesiod, *Op.*, in the beginning; Luke 1:52: ὕψωσεν ταπεινούς (cf. 1 Sam 2:7f.; Sir 10:14; Job 5:11; 12:19; Ezek 21:31; etc.; see G. Bertram, *TDNT*, s.v. ὑψόω, C). The stories about Christ's low birth in a manger show that christology has adopted the idea (Matt 1-2//Luke 1-2); cf. 1 Cor 1:26: οὐ πολλοὶ εὐγενεῖς (cf. 4:8); Jas 2:1-5; 1 Clem 59:3.

Ch. 14

(544C)

τῶν ἰδίων ἀμελεῖ καὶ τὰς νύκτας ἀγρυπνεῖ διὰ τὴν πατρίδα. Cato praised himself ironically by saying that he was envied for neglecting his own affairs and having sleepless nights because of the fatherland. Cf. Paul's statement νυκτὸς καὶ ἡμέρας ἐργαζόμενοι (1 Thes 2:9; cf. 3:10; 2 Thes 3:8; 1 Tim 5:5; 2 Tim 1:3; Acts 20:31). Cf. also Paul's catalogs of περιστάσεις (see on 541A-B), esp. 2 Cor 11:28; 12:15; Phil 2:17; 1 Cor 4:10-13. On ἀγρυπνία cf. 2 Cor 6:5; 11:27.

(544D)

οὐ τοῖς πριαμένοις πόνων πολλῶν καὶ κινδύνων. Cf. 1 Cor 6:20: ἠγοράσθητε γὰρ τιμῆς; 7:23; etc. See Bauer, s.v. ἀγοράζω, 2. De Lacy and Einarson, LCL, ad loc., n. c, refer to Cicero, *De orat.* 2, 52. 210.

Ch. 16

(544F)

κατάπληξις. The ch. discusses self-praise as a device τοῦ ταπεινοῦ καὶ λαβεῖν ὑποχείριον τὸν αὐθάδη. . . . Paul uses the same device *ironically* in 2 Cor 10-13. Cf. esp. 2 Cor 11:7: ἐμαυτὸν ταπεινῶν ἵνα ὑμεῖς ὑψωθῆτε. See also 1 Cor 9:19-23; 15:10.

(545C)

θαρρεῖν τοῖς φίλοις. Boasting is permitted as a device of leadership in a moment of danger. Cf., esp., John 16:33: θαρσεῖτε, ἐγὼ νενίκηκα τὸν κόσμον. But cf. also Matt 26:53; John 18:36; Matt

14:27; Acts 23:11; Heb 13:6. The view is held by the OT (see passages in W. Grundmann, *TDNT* 3: 26, lines 18ff.)

Ch. 19

(546D)

τὸ αὐλικὸν. . . καὶ στρατιωτικόν. Plutarch observes that certain people easily succumb to vainglory, esp. the courtiers and the military. Cf. the MSS variant ναυλιτικόν and, for the readiness of travellers and sailers to tell stories, *qu. conv.* 630C. The boasting of soldiers has examples in ECL, see Matt 8:9//Luke 7:8; John 19:10; cf. Acts 23:3-5.

(546E)

βασιλέων καὶ αὐτοκρατόρων δεξιώσεις. Reports of being greated by kings and commanders are a form of self-praise. Cf. Phil 4:22.

Ch. 22

(547F)

ἀφεξόμεθα τοῦ λέγειν περὶ αὑτῶν, ἂν μή τι μεγάλα μέλλωμεν ὠφελεῖν ἑαντοὺς ἢ τοὺς ἀκούοντας. This conclusion again states Plutarch's position that self-praise is allowed only if an ethical "benefit" can be gained from it. Paul agrees and ironically rejects self-praise, in order then to do it anyway in the "foolish discourse"; cf. 2 Cor 12:1: οὐ συμφέρον, also 1 Cor 6:12; 10:23; 12:7. See Betz, *Paulus*, 72ff.

CONSOLATIO AD UXOREM (MORALIA 608A - 612B)

BY

HUBERT MARTIN, JR. and JANE E. PHILLIPS*

University of Kentucky
Lexington, Kentucky

I. CIRCUMSTANCES AND COMPOSITION

This essay, no. 112 in the Lamprias Catalogue,[1] is cast in the form of a letter of consolation, which Plutarch wrote to his wife on the occasion of the death of their infant daughter Timoxena. According to Ch. 1, Plutarch was away from Chaeronea when the little girl died and learned of her death only from a relative after he reached Tanagra, the messenger sent to inform him having missed him on the road to Athens.[2] All this creates the impression that Plutarch composed the document we possess at Tanagra and then dispatched it to his wife at Chaeronea.[3] Plutarch, however, does not explicitly state that he did so, and there are reasons for thinking that the facts of the matter are otherwise. Tanagra is approximately fifty miles, a journey of one to two days,[4] from Chaeronea; and we may presume that Plutarch would have wanted to leave for home as soon as possible after learning of his daughter's death. If so, why would he have taken time to compose a formal essay of nine or so pages, especially since he himself could reach Chaeronea as quickly, or almost as quickly, as it would? It seems likely, therefore, that *Consolatio ad uxorem* was entirely composed at leisure after the event, or else that Plutarch immediately dis-

---

* Although the authors have regularly consulted with each other, Phillips is responsible for sections III and IV of the introduction, Martin for the commentary and the remainder of the introduction.

[1] On the Lamprias Catalogue, see my *amat.* commentary in this volume, Intro. I, p. 442, n. 1.

[2] Tanagra is located on the road running from Chaeronea to Athens, roughly midway between the two cities.

[3] Cf., e.g., Ziegler, sec. III.4.q; M. Hadas, *On Love, the Family, and the Good Life: Selected Essays of Plutarch* (New York, 1957) 93; P. H. De Lacy and B. Einarson, *Plutarch's Moralia*, LCL vol. 7 (1959) 576.

[4] E. Badian (*OCD*, s.v. "Travel") remarks that "40 Roman miles seems to have been a very good day's journey at the best."

patched a short letter to his wife, which he later elaborated into the present essay. In either event, the main purpose of Ch. 1 would have been to provide the requisite factual information, and to lend verisimilitude to the literary form in which Plutarch chose to express himself. As will be illustrated below (III.A), classical authors often selected an epistolary form for consolations, even those that were obviously works of chiefly literary aspiration. So to observe, and to explain *Consolatio ad uxorem* as I have just done, is in no way to question either Plutarch's sincerity or the reliability of the factual information included in this essay.

Consolatio ad uxorem furnishes an unusual glimpse into Plutarch's domestic life. And from it we learn that Timoxena, who was two when she died, was named after her mother and was the youngest of five children (608C, 610D-E, 611D); that the other four were sons (608C), two of whom had already died (609D); that Plutarch's wife had undergone some sort of breast surgery to treat a lesion caused by nursing one of the boys (609E); and that Plutarch and his wife had been initiated into the Dionysiac mysteries (611D).[5] No information is given, however, that would enable us to assign a date to Timoxena's death.[6]

II. Summary

608B: ὃν . . . μέτεστι. General information and practical instruction.

Plutarch explains to his wife the circumstances under which he received the news of their daughter's death and recommends to her whatever measures she thinks will diminish her grief, provided they do not involve any superstitious display.

608C-D: μόνον . . . αὑτήν. Their need to restrain their grief. Its intensifying factors.

---

[5] At 608B, Plutarch refers to his θυγατριδῇ who lives in Tanagra. Whatever the precise meaning of this word in its present context, the evidence is strongly against translating it as "grand-daughter" (so De Lacy-Einarson, 581 and R. Warner, *Plutarch: Moral Essays* [Baltimore, 1971] 176) and interpreting it as "daughter's daughter" (so De Lacy-Einarson, 575f., 578). See R. Volkmann, *Leben, Schriften, und Philosophie des Plutarch von Chaeronea* (Berlin, 1869) 1:28-29; U. v. Wilamowitz-Moellendorff, "Commentariolum Grammaticum III (1889)" 23f., *Kleine Schriften* (Berlin, 1962) 4:648f.; W. v. Christ et al., *Geschichte der griechischen Literatur* (Munich, 1920) 2.1:486; Ziegler, sec. I.2 *fin.*

[6] C. P. Jones, *Plutarch and Rome* (Oxford, 1971) 136 dates *cons. ux.* to "between *c.* 85 and *c.* 95."

Let us maintain control over our grief, as overwhelming as it is because of our closeness to our children, our daughter's special place among them, her tender age, and her loving disposition and behavior.

608D-F: ἀλλ' . . . ἀνταποδιδόντας. An error to be avoided.

Let us not, in trying to assuage our grief, stifle the remembrance of her disposition and behavior; for such remembrance brings with it more of joy than of pain.

608F-609E: καὶ . . . διδόντι. Your exemplary behavior.

Reports disclose that you have maintained a proper restraint in your mourning and in the manner of the funeral. This does not surprise me, since restraint and simplicity have always characterized your public behavior (ἐγὼ . . . λιτόν [609A], ἀλλὰ . . . ἀφέλειαν [609C-D]), even at the deaths of our two sons (ἤδη . . . διδόντι [609D-E]). Behavior such as yours is universally commendable (οὐ . . . δεομέναις [609A-C]).

609E-F: καίτοι . . . θέλουσιν. The emotional basis of your stability.

You expressed your affection for your children while they were alive and did not need to imitate those mothers who compensate for their lack of natural affection for their children by making a great display of grief when they die. Such grief is self-imposed.

609F-610D: ἐν . . . φυλάξῃ. A pathology of grief (πένθος).

We impose grief on ourselves, and its chronic display corrupts the mind. The ensuing neglect of the body leads to disorders within the soul, which with difficulty is restored to a sound condition. And then there is that gang of shrieking women who crave to keep one's grief active and one's soul in disorder as long as possible. Your past behavior assures me that you are not susceptible to their pernicious influence.

610D-611A: πειρῶ . . . ἄλλοις. Remembrance as a source of consolation.

Blot out from your memory for the moment the two years she was with us. Do you not see that to seek consolation in this fashion is actually to reject one of its major sources, the remembrance of a past blessing? Let us rather accept fortune's bad along with her good, and fix our thoughts upon those two joyful years, that they may dispel our present grief.

611A-C: ὅτι . . . ἀπολομένων. Consolation from comparison.

If we accept the materialistic standards whereby the many judge happiness, we will discover that our present blessings far outweigh our misfortune. It would be terrible for us to allow our misfortune to devastate the enjoyment of these blessings.

611C-D: εἰ . . . λέγοιτο. Consolation from Timoxena's present state.

To pity her for having been deprived of marriage and children is to give yourself grounds for taking pleasure in the fact that you have enjoyed both. Yet we have no real reason to feel pain on her behalf, since she herself is now beyond pain; and it actually is illogical to say that she has been deprived of what she never had.

611D-612A: καὶ . . . μεθεστηκότας. A special consolation.

Our belief in the immortality of the soul leads to the awareness that hers did not have time to become inured to the body and the things of this world and that it has quickly made the journey to the world beyond. This awareness is enshrined in custom and law, which forbid memorial rites or even elaborate mourning in the case of the deaths of infants.

612A-B: ἐπεὶ . . . . Peroration.

Let us behave as the laws enjoin and keep ourselves free from the pollution of grief.

III. The Consolation of Death and Bereavement in Classical Literature

Plutarch's *consolatio ad uxorem* belongs to a well developed tradition in classical literature. Consolatory themes, dealing with a wide range of human ills, were present from the beginning in Greek and Roman literary works, and consolation as a genre was not long in emerging. In order to set Plutarch's work in the perspective of this tradition, the following essay is a short review of the consolation genre as it concerns the archetypical human misfortune, death and bereavement.[7]

---

[7] A collection of references to all Greek and Roman consolation material, with now outdated discussions of sources and authorships: C. Buresch, "Consolationum a Graecis Romanisque scriptarum historia critica," *Leipziger Studien zur classischen Philologie* 9:1 (1886) 3-170. A more analytical treat-

A. *Forms*

Epic and tragedy, in their involvement with universal human problems, necessarily present circumstances which evoke words of consolation from one character to another. A few of the more obvious examples are Achilles' comforting words to Priam at the ransoming of Hector's body (*Il.* 24.518ff.), the remarks of the Chorus (416-419, 872ff.) and of his father (614-628) to Admetus in Euripides' *Alcestis*, and Adrastus' eulogy of the dead in the same author's *Suppliants* (857-917). Early Roman epic and tragedy is lost, of course, but its subject matter was like the Greek, and there is no reason to doubt that consolatory speeches were found there too.[8] In these genres the consolation is subsidiary to the working out of the author's main narrative or dramatic intention.

Consolation is one of the standard formal parts of speeches written for the public funerals for the Athenian war dead, though such speeches have praise of the dead as their chief purpose.[9] Consolatory remarks are found in the funeral orations of Pericles (Thucydides 2.44), Socrates (Plato *Mx.* 247C-248C), Hyperides (*Epit.* 41-42), pseudo-Demosthenes (60.32-37), and pseudo-Lysias (2.77-81), all from the later fifth and the fourth centuries B.C. Later, speeches at the funerals of private individuals became common, and in these the consolatory element was more prominent. Discourse 29 of Dio Chrysostom (born in A.D. 40) takes the form of such a speech for a dead athlete and may have been actually delivered. A mid-second century A.D. writer, Aelius Aristides, has two such speeches (11 and 12, W. Dindorf, *Aristides*, 3 vols. [Leipzig, 1829]). The Romans also made a practice of eulogizing the dead person at his funeral, but the content of such speeches is only sketchily known, and it is not certain that they contained any consolatory words for the survivors (Polybius 6.53-54).[10]

---

ment of the material, and further bibliography, in R. Kassel, *Untersuchungen zur griechischen und römischen Konsolationsliteratur*, Zetemata 18 (Munich, 1958) [hereafter cited as Kassel]. The author has benefited greatly in the preparation of this essay from consultation with Robert J. Rabel.

[8] While *cons. Apoll.* quotes the Greek tragedians for illustrative purposes, Cicero, in his discussion of consolatory themes in *Tusc.* 1 and 3, quotes Ennius, Caecilius, Pacuvius, and so on.

[9] For praise as the main constituent of the public funeral orations, see the passages cited from the rhetoricians in Section B, below.

[10] See Kassel, 45 and n. 1. It is hard to imagine, however, that there was not some element of consolation in the *laudatio funebris*.

Another occasion on which consolation is offered in the form of a speech is found in Plato's *Apology*. After passing judgment in his turn on the jurors who voted for his condemnation, Socrates addresses himself to those who voted to acquit, explaining why he does not regard death as an evil (39E-42A, especially 39E-40A and 41C-D). Though he does not directly say so, his purpose is clearly to reconcile them to his death; that is, to console them.

The other two dialogues connected with Socrates' death, the *Crito* and the *Phaedo*, also present him as consoling his friends but this time in the form of philosophic conversations in his usual style. In the first, Crito's dismay at the impending death has led him to make plans for Socrates' escape. Socrates justifies his obedience to the state in order to make Crito accept the fact that he declines the opportunity and intends to die as ordered. In the second, Socrates is shown spending his last day of life in conversation with some of his friends. Circumstances dictate the topic, the nature of death, reality, and the soul. At the close of the discussion Socrates himself describes the conversation as a consolation for both his friends and himself (115D).[11] Consolation as philosophic discourse appears again in the pseudo-Platonic *Axiochus*, in which Socrates is summoned to a sickbed to prepare its occupant to face death. Also of the conversational type, but with rather less of philosophy, is Dio Chrysostom's discourse 28, which is on the death of the young athlete who is also the subject of 29, mentioned above. In 28, Dio represents himself as consoling one of the athlete's mourning admirers in what begins as a casual conversation struck up at a sports event.

In all of the works mentioned so far the consolations proper are oral, not written; the written works only record or purport to record what was said or might have been said by the consoler to the mourners on some specific occasion. The form, therefore, was limited to the range from conversation to formal oration. In the case of written consolations, the document itself does not merely represent but actually is the consolation. Yet the importance of the difference must not be exaggerated, for in Graeco-Roman literature the written word was nearly always either a representative of

[11] It is true that Plato's philosophic purpose in these three dialogues is far from consolatory, as Kassel, 33-34, points out, but in their dramatic setting the speech and conversations referred to are certainly consolatory in intent.

or a substitute for the spoken work; the conventions of written literature in organization, style, and diction rarely departed from those of spoken literature.[12] It is likely enough that written consolations began when letterwriting became the means of communication between individuals who could not meet face-to-face, and if that is so they came to exist in an area where the distinction between literature and life is particularly hard to draw. The letter form quickly became a literary convention itself, with the result that we cannot always be sure whether a given consolation, once written, was immediately handed to a messenger for delivery to the addressee or to a copyist for reproduction and circulation among the writer's literary audience.

On the Greek side it is almost impossible to find genuine examples of private epistolary consolations. The lost consolation of Crantor the Academic, who lived through the second half of the fourth century and into the third, was addressed to one Hippocles on the occasion of the death of his children (ps.-Plutarch *cons. Apoll.* 104C), but whether it was in letter form or simply conformed to the widespread ancient practice of giving all sorts of literary compositions an addressee, there is no way of knowing. His contemporary Epicurus apparently had an extensive private correspondence, to judge from the references to and quotations from his letters, and from the mention of letters among his collected works;[13] one of the letters evidently was one of consolation to the father and brother of Hegesianax (Plutarch *non posse* 1101B), but again we cannot tell whether it was a private letter or more like the three philosophical essays in epistolary form quoted by Diogenes Laertius (10.35-135). Seneca twice quotes from a letter by Epicurus' companion Metrodorus to his sister on the death of her son (*Ep.* 98.9, 99.25). Dio Chrysostom's discourse 30 is largely made up of a consolation composed by a dying man for his father; the form seems to be a speech but it was never intended for delivery.[14] The form of Plutarch's consolation to his wife and of the *Consolatio ad Apollonium* ascribed to him is a letter, but in length alone both are more like epistolary essays.

---

[12] G. Kennedy, *The Art of Persuasion in Greece* (Princeton, 1963) 3-7.

[13] C. Bailey, *Epicurus: The Extant Remains* (Oxford, 1926) 125-32; Diogenes Laertius 10.28.

[14] Dio describes the speech as a παράκλησις (6). For this word in ECL see Bauer, s.v., and O. Schmitz, *TDNT*, s.v. παρακαλέω, F.3-4.

In Latin there are examples of consolations in letter form that were written and actually sent to bereaved persons: the famous letter of Servius Sulpicius to Cicero on the death of Tullia (Cicero *Fam.* 4.5), and letters by Cicero himself, to Brutus on the death of his wife (*Ad Brut.* 1.9), to an unknown Titius on the death of his children (*Fam.* 5.16), and a brief note to Atticus on the death of (apparently) a favorite slave (*Att.* 12.10). Cicero's lost *Consolatio* to himself on the death of his daughter was perhaps an essay in dialogue form like his other philosophical works, or it may have followed Crantor, its professed model in content (Pliny *Nat. praef.* 22), in form as well. At the end of the first century A.D. the younger Pliny addresses a letter of consolation to Colonus on the death of a friend (*Ep.* 9.9). Other letters, which are not extant, are mentioned by both Cicero and Pliny.[15] In the generation before Pliny, several of Seneca's letters to Lucilius are consolations on the deaths of friends or acquaintances of his correspondent (*Ep.* 63, 93, 99); but Seneca's letters are far different from those of Cicero, where correspondence and not psychagogy is the object, and almost equally different from Pliny's somewhat more consciously literary productions. Each letter in the entire collection is the occasion for the development of some philosophical subject almost in an essay manner. The consolations provide a formal bridge to Seneca's consolatory essays, *Dialogus* 6, *ad Marciam*, and 11, *ad Polybium*, on death (and 12, *ad Helviam*, on exile), in which the author addresses a particular person about a particular event, but with only the merest fiction that the work is a letter.[16]

B. *Themes*

One of the chief concerns of Greek and Roman thought was the relation of man to the seemingly indifferent, if not hostile, universal forces which inflict unhappiness, suffering, reversals, and finally annihilation on the human race. Since humans are almost entirely helpless to control or influence the occurrence of misfortune, the problem resolved itself into a question of understanding the meaning of misfortune, defining the degree of human liability, and

[15] For instance, Cicero *Att.* 12.14.4, 13.20.1; *Fam.* 5.13, 9.11; Pliny *Ep.* 5.16.

[16] Poems of consolation are found in Latin: Catullus 96, Horace *Carm.* 1.24, Propertius 4.11, Ovid *Pont.* 4.11, the anonymous *Consolatio ad Liviam*, Statius 2.1, 2.6, 3.3.

cultivating the correct attitude towards the inevitable, either in anticipation of it or after it has happened. In one form or another this question pervades the whole of classical literature. Almost without exception the recommended solution was to accept with fortitude and cautious pessimism all that is beyond human power to alter, neither rejoicing nor grieving too much and remembering that only death is assured. The writings on consolation, both the consolations proper just reviewed and the more theoretical works to be mentioned shortly, are directly connected to this general problem, for the task of the consoler is to reconcile the bereaved or dying person to the immutable and inevitable.

The themes and topics used by the consolatory writers mentioned in Section A illustrate these observations in almost wearying detail.[17] Their material is not unique to their purpose but is common to and drawn from the whole spectrum of classical thought and literature; the only difference is that it is focused on the particular matter at hand, the relief of the mourner's mental anguish. It can be roughly sorted into two categories, the first of material relating to the idea that the mourner has no cause to grieve because nothing bad has happened or is happening to the dead, and the second of material concerning the ill effects of grief and ways to alleviate or avoid them. Under the first division are included such commonplaces as these: Death is not evil or is even positively good; life is misery and death is the escape from present or future ills. Our state after death is like that before our birth. Either there is no sensation, or no existence, after death and hence no suffering, or the soul is immortal, freed from its bodily prison, and enjoying a blessed existence in the traditional underworld or in some more mystically conceived union with the divine. The threats of punishment after death are just the inventions of poets and story-tellers. The dead, whatever their state, have no need or desire for the goods of this life. Death is the fate of all men; it does not matter whether it comes early or late, for the longest lifetime is a moment when compared with the eternity of death. The virtuous life, not the long one, is to be desired. There is no such thing as an untimely death; early death means the avoidance of ills and an earlier reunion with the divine. That this is the general opinion of mankind

[17] The lists of themes are drawn from the consolations mentioned in Section A, with the exception of the *cons. ux.* Each theme appears in at least two consolations.

is shown by the fact that the deaths of young children go unmourned. It is best never to have been born, but an early death is second best. The gods' judgment about the relative values of life and death is shown by the stories of their awarding death to men for great virtue. Death is like sleep or like a journey; life is a loan. Death matters to neither the living nor the dead.

The subject of grief is treated as follows: Grief is like a physical pain which must be allowed to subside somewhat on its own before medical treatment is applied. Grief arises from a decision to grieve or a belief that it is obligatory, and can be eased by the realization that we do not have to grieve. Grief becomes a habit from overindulgence. The loss of the companionship of the deceased is a cause of grief. Ideally we would suffer no anguish from grief. Grief is natural; the absence of all feeling is undesirable, but moderation in grief should be observed, as in the face of all good or evil. Moderate behavior is especially called for from those who occupy prominent public positions. Immoderate grief is selfish, harmful, brings no advantage to either the mourner or the mourned, and dishonors the dead. The passage of time eases grief. Training the mind in the thought that nothing is unexpected makes grief easier to bear when it comes. Above all, reason eases or completely removes grief. Lamentation for the dead is either to be allowed or forbidden. The dead would not want survivors to grieve. Recalling the virtues of the dead does them honor; remembering the happy times when they were alive eases the pain of their absence. Loss of the deceased one is outweighed by the goods the survivors still enjoy. Others have had worse to bear and have behaved nobly, as shown by literary and historical examples. Other typical themes are a laudatory description of the deceased, the participation of the consoler in the sense of bereavement, and the suggestion that the mourner apply to himself the good advice with which he has comforted others.

Contributions to this miscellany of consolatory themes came from several sources. The most obvious is the common cultural heritage, the accumulated folk wisdom that spoke to generation after generation through the old poets and tragedians on the one hand and through proverbs and wise sayings on the other. But there were two other important sources of influence, each of which in its own way imparted some degree of development and systematization on the material.

One influence arose from the philosophical schools. The major schools had in common the goal of subjecting man's emotional life, uncontrolled, unpredictable, and unconstructive, to the rule of reason, although they differed in their opinions about the nature of the soul, of emotions, and of reason, and in the methods to be used to achieve the goal. For Plato, the immortal soul's task both while it had separate existence and when it was incarnate was to be the attempt of its reasoning constituent to gain control over its emotional constituent and to direct the attention of the whole soul, the emotional part included, to the perception of the eternal forms, the perfect vision of which could only be achieved after death.[18] From this point of view death is a good, as long as life has been spent in the service of philosophy, and the emotions have a necessary but subservient part to play in the philosopher's existence. Aristotle refined the conception of the relationship between emotion and reason by asserting that emotion was a product of the operation of the cognitive element of the mind, thus allowing for an explanation of the capacity of the reason to influence or alter emotional states.[19]

The Stoics took a stern position against the upheaval produced in the human soul by the unregulated action of the emotions. Following a line of thinking like that of Aristotle's, they defined emotions as judgments, though mistaken ones, which could be appealed to by reason.[20] The wise man's reasoned attitude towards the universe is not susceptible to disturbance from emotions; all that happens has to happen and no event is cause for either sorrow or rejoicing. Souls are composed of the same fiery matter as the divine soul and will disappear in the conflagrations that periodically consume the universe, but in the intervals between conflagrations they may be reabsorbed after death into the divine. Reason prevails to produce the Stoic apathy, freedom from mental distress, and death is viewed as no evil, not least because it is in accordance with nature.

For the Epicureans reason led not to the Platonic forms or the

---

[18] This is certainly Plato's own position in, e.g., *Phaedo* and *Phaedrus*. In the *Apology* he represents Socrates as less willing to commit himself to belief in the immortality of the soul (40C and ff.), which may have been the attitude of the historical Socrates.

[19] Aristotle *Top.* 150 b27-151 a19 and 156 a32-33, *Rh.* 1378 a30-32; W. W. Fortenbaugh, *Aristotle on Emotion* (New York, 1975) 9-12.

[20] *SVF*, III, 378, 384, 461; Rist, *Stoic Phil.*, 22-36.

Stoic divine necessity but to an understanding of the completely mechanical nature of the universe and all that it contains. The atomic physics of the Epicureans meant that death is nothing more than the dissolution of the constituent elements of the person, body and soul, and therefore not to be feared. It is neither good nor evil; it is something which does not affect us while we are alive and which cannot affect us after death because "we" do not exist. Emotions in the Epicurean system consist of pleasures and pains, the one to be sought for and the other avoided in the interest of maintaining philosophical equanimity.[21] A sympathetic attitude towards grief at bereavement is suggested by the high value placed on friendship and by Metrodorus' remark that there is some pleasure related to the experience of grief (Seneca *Ep.* 99.25).[22] Grief is removed by removing the fear of death and by withdrawing the mourner's attention from the pain of the loss to the remembered pleasures of the time before the death.

The schools found spokesmen for their theoretical positions in those writers who produced general works on the emotions, the soul, or consolation. Plato's *Phaedo* has already been mentioned, and other Platonic works, such as the *Phaedrus*, would also be applicable. Aristotle's lost *Eudemus de anima* and Theophrastus' work on grief, *Callisthenes*, supplied material. The Academic Crantor's consolation to Hippocles, mentioned in Section A, while it may have been intended as a private letter, was admired for its general consolatory principles by the Stoic Panaetius (Cicero *Luc.* 135), and Cicero claimed to have used it as his model in his own *Consolatio* (Pliny *Nat. praef.* 22). Cicero and pseudo-Plutarch cited Crantor particularly for his opinion that emotions were not to be entirely suppressed (*Tusc.* 3.12; *cons. Apoll.* 102D-E). Much of Epicurus' own writings and those of his followers pertained to those consolatory themes that sought to relieve the fear of death. The Epicurean view is most elaborately stated, and ornamented by typical consolatory *exempla* and topics, by Lucretius in the *De rerum natura* 3, especially from line 830 to the end.

In this connection the third book of Cicero's *Tusculanae disputationes* is of special interest. Cicero's purpose is to discuss the

[21] E.g., Epicurus' letters to Herodotus, Diogenes Laertius 10.35-83, and to Menoeceus, Diogenes Laertius 10.122-135.

[22] J. Rist, *Epicurus: An Introduction* (Cambridge, 1972) 127-39; Diogenes Laertius 10.120.

overcoming of mental distress, which interferes with the achievement of a philosophic outlook (3.12-13). Taking grief as the typical case, he reviews the explanations of the cause of mental distress put forward by the various schools, Stoics, Epicureans, Cyrenaics, and Peripatetics, and describes what each one advises as the method of easing it (3.14-75). The summary at 3.76, coupled with what Cicero had said about the schools earlier in the book, shows that each school cultivated an individualistic approach to the theory of mental distress. But Cicero's next words betray what happens when real consolation is called for: *sunt etiam qui haec omnia genera consolandi colligant—alius enim alio modo movetur—ut fere nos in Consolatione omnia in consolationem unam coniecimus*. In the surviving consolations there are almost no examples of an approach strictly based on the doctrines of any one school.[23] The philosophers certainly elaborated the ways in which consolation could be approached, especially through their interest in understanding the emotions and through their concern with what happens after death. But any real innovation tended to become quickly obscured by the eclectic attitudes of late Hellenistic and Roman students of philosophy; little attention was paid to the rigors of definition and logic required by each school—the widespread misconceptions about Epicureanism are notorious—and philosophical catchwords and clichés were dumped back into the common pool—*omnia in consolationem unam coniecimus*. It would be fair to say that while the greatest benefit from philosophy to writers of consolations was in the various doctrines concerning the fate of the soul after death, the next greatest was the expansion of carefully thought out techniques for achieving consolatory goals, as Cicero demonstrates in *Tusc*. 3.

The Epicureans provide an example of a case in which a philosophical theory is explicitly rejected by those hostile to the school at the same time that a technique recommended by the Epicureans is applied and promoted. One Epicurean method of relief from pain was to turn the attention to pleasures, remembered, present, and anticipated, and thus distract the soul from the source of distress (Cicero *Tusc*. 3.33). Cicero enjoys refuting the philosophical correctness of this technique (3.35-51); yet in the summary passage

[23] An exception is a consolatory letter filled with neo-Pythagorean esoterica by Apollonius of Tyana, 58 (R. Hercher, *Epistolographi Graeci* [Paris, 1873]).

quoted above he includes it as a method of consolation—*sunt qui abducant a malis ad bona, ut Epicurus*—though he will not quite give it his approval (3.78). Seneca, professedly a Stoic and one who tendentiously quotes the Epicurean Metrodorus to Metrodorus' detriment (*Ep.* 99.25-29),[24] urges the pleasures of happy memories of the dead on Marcia (*Dial.* 6.12.1-4) and Polybius (*Dial.* 11. 10.1-6), and admits that pleasant memories may bring pains with them (*Ep.* 63.5-7). Even Plutarch, while rejecting the Epicurean interpretation of what happens at death (*cons. ux.* 611D), recommends the Epicurean remedy of remembered pleasures to ease grief (*cons. ux.* 610E-F). The explanation for this apparent ambivalence lies in the fact that a remedy which under one aspect is the logical development of a particular philosophical system's theory of emotions is, under another aspect, simply one more of a series of pragmatic approaches to a problem of human psychology. In terms of the part of grief which arises from the experience of bereavement the schools do not differ so very much from each other or from the precepts of practical wisdom. It tends to be a case of philosophy's being used to justify a particular consolatory approach more than one of philosophy's supplying what the untrained mind could not have discovered on its own.

The other influence on the consolatory genre is that of the rhetoricians. Cicero was familiar with Greek rhetorical works which alluded to consolatory themes (though they probably had more to do with funeral orations, as do the extant rhetorical treatments of the subject, than with written consolations as such). Near the end of the first book of the *Tusculanae disputationes,* after demonstrating that death is no evil, he declares that that fact is the greatest comfort in time of grief (1.112; it is the *prima medicina* of grief at 3.77) and then asks the interlocutor whether he should add the *rhetorum epilogus* to what has been said (1.112). The answer is of course yes, and Cicero proceeds to give examples which he says are used in the rhetorical schools to illustrate the judgment of the gods that death is no evil (1.113-116). He concludes with further examples used by the rhetoricians to prove that dying for one's country is blessed (1.116-117), and urges that the resources of

[24] Metrodorus says that there is a certain pleasure related to pain, which ought to be pursued; it is easy to see in this statement a reference to the Epicurean pleasure of memory, instead of taking it, as Seneca does, to mean that suffering feels good.

eloquence be put to use to rid men of the fear of death (1.117). The influence of his rhetorical training and, surely, of his familiarity with Greek rhetorical treatises can also be seen in his discussion of consolatory techniques at the end of *Tusc.* 3, mentioned above. Having summarized the techniques suggested by the philosophers, closing with his own eclectic approach, he points out that the arguments should be presented in a certain order according to how recent the occasion of grief is (76-77), and that the circumstances of the mourner affect the choice and presentation of the arguments (77-79). He ends with a comparison between the adjustment of arguments to fit the situation in court cases and in consolations: *ut in causis non semper utimur eodem statu—sic enim appellamus controversiarum genera—sed ad tempus, ad controversiae naturam, ad personam accommodamus sic in aegritudine lenienda quam quisque curationem recipere possit videndum est* (79).

Examples of the rhetoricians to whom Cicero was referring have not survived, but there are some discussions of consolatory themes in works by Greek rhetoricians under the Empire. In the *Progymnastica* of a first century A.D. writer, Theon, under the discussion of prosopopoeia, speeches composed in the person of some mythological, historical, or typical character as an exercise in appropriateness, there is a list of suitable topics for consolatory prosopopoeia (apparently referring to public funeral orations; there is a gap in the text at the beginning of the passage): the common lot of mankind, the endurance of those who have suffered greater misfortune, that the death was glorious and honorable, the utility (or lack of it) or grief. The list ends with the observation that the subject calls for the inclusion of a certain amount of lamenting, in order to win the sympathy of the mourners and make them receptive to the reasoned arguments and admonitions of the consoler (2.117.6-24, L. Spengel, *Rhetores Graeci*, 3 vols. [Leipzig, 1853-56]).

Two later rhetoricians discuss funeral orations, both for the mass public funerals and for private funerals for individuals, the second of which is more applicable to the written consolation.[25]

[25] Menander's work is third century A.D. The pseudo-Dionysius *Rhetoric* is not the work of a single author; the section on funeral orations is probably no later than the Antonine period (Hermann Usener and Ludwig Radermacher, *Dionysii Halicarnasei Quae Extant*, vol. 6: *Opusculorum volumen secundum* [Leipzig, 1929] xxii-xxvi, esp. xxiv).

Menander says that the first part of the funeral oration, public or private, should follow the standard outline of the encomiastic speech: forebears, birth, upbringing, accomplishments, and good fortune, with all turned to the pathetic. Then follows a section of lamentation to provoke the tears of the hearers, and then a section of consolation on the theme that the deceased is dwelling happily in the other world. Private orations should end with admonitions to the wife and children of the deceased, and praise of the family for their attention to the funeral arrangements and the memory of the deceased (3.418-422 Spengel). In another section (3.413-414 Spengel) Menander runs through the topics of the purely consolatory speech (presumably not given at the funeral), again making the connection with encomium. The first part will follow the encomiastic outline with the slant towards the pathetic, so as to inflame the hearers' grief. The second part, which is properly consolatory, will include a quotation from Euripides (fr. 452, A. Nauck, *Euripidis Tragoediae*, vol. 3: *Perditarum Tragoediarum Fragmenta*, BT [1885]) on the nature of life and death, the story of Cleobis and Biton, some remarks on the divine law that all men must die, lessons drawn from the decline of cities and nations, mention of the ills and misfortunes that the dead has escaped, an expression of confidence about the released soul's happy existence either in the underworld or above the heavens, and remarks on the affinity of the soul with the divine. It is interesting that the quotation from Euripides and the story of Cleobis and Biton appear in Cicero (*Tusc.* 1.115 and 113 respectively), and Cleobis and Biton also in the *Axiochus* (367C) and the *Consolatio ad Apollonium* (108F).

The author of the *Rhetoric* incorrectly attributed to Dionysius of Halicarnassus also classes the first part of public and private funeral orations with encomium, but prefers to follow this with a section of admonition to the survivors to follow the good example set by the deceased, except of course when the deceased are children. He goes on to the consolatory part, where, in contrast to Menander and Theon, he advises avoidance of any lamentation as not having a comforting effect. The topics of consolation are organized by this author according to the age of the deceased when he died and the circumstances of the death, but they are essentially the familiar ones: the dead person is spared present or future suffering, he died a noble death, he was a paradigm of virtue, he enjoyed the blessings of a long life; or else, the writer suggests, the individual characteristics of the deceased will offer the orator topics on which to speak. He should conclude in any case with remarks on the blessed state of the soul, in a style like that of Plato (*Rh.* 6, in Dionysius of Halicarnassus 6.2.277-283 Usener-Radermacher).

Although these rhetoricians were primarily concerned with the composition of speeches for delivery, the close connection between the spoken and the written word in classical antiquity made them also useful for writers of consolations. The authors of the extant consolations were educated men, and education meant above all rhetorical training. Theon, Menander, and the pseudo-Dionysius show what sort of help rhetorical theory offered to the would-be consoler: handy lists of commonplaces, solidly based on traditional consolatory themes and treated with the same eclecticism already pointed out in the philosophical material—Menander even gives the speaker a choice in describing the state of the dead man's soul between the traditional Homeric underworld and the mystical-philosophical dwelling-place of the gods. (None of the rhetoricians even alludes to the Epicurean view that the soul does not exist after death, perhaps recognizing that the limited consolatory effect of that view made it unsuitable for the ordinary audience.) But the rhetoricians' provision of material for consolations was perhaps not as important as the other kind of help they supplied, the treatment of organization, the definition of the parts of a consolatory or funeral discourse, and the concentration of the speaker's efforts on the achievement of his purpose. For in the matter of purpose all consolers are more closely aligned with rhetoric than with philosophy: they are more concerned with changing the mourners' mental state than with the pursuit of objective truth. Philosophical truth in consolation is a means to a rhetorical end, as had been true of rhetoric's attitude to philosophy in general from the time when the two emerged as separate fields of study.[26]

IV. Plutarch and the Consolatory Tradition

The *cons. ux.* uses many of the standard consolatory themes. Plutarch devotes much of the letter to urging moderate behavior

[26] Cf., for instance, the whole discussion of the relationship between truth and rhetoric in the second part of the *Phaedrus*, 259E and ff.

in her grief on his wife and commending her for the moderation she has already displayed (608C, 608F-610D). Moderation in grief is as important as moderation in pleasure (608F-609B). Excessive displays of grief are shameful and harmful to the mourner (609B, 610A-B). Grief becomes a habit from overindulgence (609F-610A) and is mistakenly believed to be obligatory (609F, 611B). Grief subsides with time (by itself) (610C); it can be eased or removed by reason (611A), by happy memories of the dead child (608E-F, 610E), by the thought that she is free from suffering and desires for earthly goods (611C-D), and by remembering the blessings the survivors still enjoy (611B-C). Plutarch uses as an *exemplum* of moderate behavior in grief his wife herself, at the time of the death of their oldest child, contrasts her behavior with that of other mothers who love their children less and are less influenced by reason and philosophy, and repeats a fable concerning the honors granted to Grief by Zeus (609D-F). He describes the character and behavior of the dead child (608C), advises that he and his wife console themselves with the same thoughts that they have used to comfort others (608F), and compares the pain of grief to a physical affliction (610D). In a variation on a common theme he says that the state of the survivors after the child's death is like their state before her birth (610D). Finally he asserts the child's return to the soul's natural dwelling place and strengthens this assertion by reference to the laws and customs forbidding mourning for children (611E-612A).

Besides basing his material on traditional themes, Plutarch gives it a rhetorical arrangement much like that recommended for private funeral speeches by the pseudo-Dionysius *Rhetoric* (III.B above). The *Rhetoric* advises encomium first, on the topics of forebears, birth, upbringing, character and usual behavior (6.2.278.15-280.8 Usener-Radermacher); Plutarch speaks of his and his wife's happiness at having a girl after four boys, describes the child's pleasant personality, and recalls deeds of hers that evidenced her generous nature (608C-D), fitting the encomiastic organization to the circumstances of his audience and his subject. In the *Rhetoric* the next section of a funeral speech is to be protreptic, although the author has no recommendations for the material of the protreptic part in private speeches for dead children (6.2.280.15-17 Usener-Radermacher). A large part of the *cons. ux.* is devoted to Plutarch's advice to his wife about her behavior in grief—much of it disguised as praise of the behavior she has previously practiced and is now practicing, but certainly aimed at encouraging her to continue in the same way (608F-610D). The last section of a funeral speech, according to the *Rhetoric*, will be the consolation proper. It will not include lamentation, since that has an effect opposite to consolation, but will show sympathy with the bereaved (6.2.281.2-11 Usener-Radermacher). Plutarch advises his wife against lamentation (609B, 610B-C) and does not indulge in it himself. The *Rhetoric* suggests topics of consolation according to the circumstances of the death (6.2. 281.21-282.6 Usener-Radermacher), which Plutarch does not use at all, and according to the age of the deceased: if the deceased was young, then the recommended consolation is that he was beloved of the gods, who have not wanted him to suffer earthly ills but to be free (6.2.282.6-18 Usener-Radermacher). Plutarch does not dwell on the sufferings his daughter has avoided, though he mentions them in passing (611C, E), but he does make much of the early release of her soul from the body (611D-612A). The *Rhetoric* says that at the end of the speech the immortal nature of the soul must be discussed (6.2.283.8-10); Plutarch puts his treatment of the soul, which is in the passage just mentioned, at the end of the consolation.

In thematic material and general rhetorical approach, then, Plutarch follows the classical consolation tradition. But he does not do so mechanically or slavishly; he puts into practice the advice of Cicero (above, III.B) to suit the consolation to the particular situation. He shares with his wife the grief at their child's death and the happy memories of the little girl when she was still alive. His advice concerns itself largely with customary manifestations of grief in outward behavior and dress, probably because such manifestations were more common among grief stricken women than among men. He displays particular tact by cloaking his admonitions in a positive form, as praise for the self-restraint and moderation his wife has already shown. When he offers comfort, the emphasis is not on the achievement of any sort of philosophical indifference but on pleasure—the pleasure of remembering their daughter, the other pleasures life still holds, the pleasure, if it can be called that, of viewing the early death as a blessing for the child. The consolation as a whole is a successful combination of learning and humanity.

V. Consolatio ad uxorem and ECL

Plutarch's letter of consolation to his wife is representative of a definable and traditional classical literary form that is without generic parallel in ECL. Moreover, the most crucial element in ECL's vocabulary of consolation, παρακαλέω and cognates, is completely missing from *Consolatio ad uxorem*, together with the concepts that go with it. And Plutarch's conviction that grief can be suppressed, and thereby eliminated as a destructive emotional factor, by discursive reasoning and force of will (608D-611D) is as classical in spirit and in the manner in which it is expressed as it is foreign to the intellectual and emotional fabric of OT and ECL.

Plutarch moves nearest to the grief and consolation temperament of ECL when he designates the grief of bereavement as λύπη and as πένθος,[27] and when he seeks consolation in his *religious* belief in the immortality of the soul (611 D-612B). This consolation is at least reminiscent of 1 Thes 4:13-18, where Paul urges the Thessalonians not to grieve (μὴ λυπῆσθε) for the dead in Christ since they will rise from their graves at the Parousia.[28] Conversely, Mart Pol shows some traces of resemblance to *Consolatio ad uxorem*, since it too is cast in the form of a letter, is consolatory in spirit (especially at 2:1, 14-16, 19), and stresses towards its conclusion the immortality that Polycarp has gained (14-16, 19).

VI. Some Notes on the Commentary

1. The commentary is keyed to P. H. De Lacy and B. Einarson's Loeb edition (*Plutarch's Moralia*, vol. 7 [1959] 573-605). The textual condition of *cons. ux.*, however, is poor and I have received constant assistance from W. Sieveking's Teubner edition (*Plutarchi Moralia*, vol. 3 [1929] 533-42). I have also occasionally consulted the translations of M. Hadas (*On Love, the Family, and the Good Life: Selected Essays of Plutarch* [New York, 1957] 93-100) and of R. Warner (*Plutarch: Moral Essays* [Baltimore, 1971] 176-85). All of these works are cited merely by the names of the editors and/or translators.

2. My *amat.* commentary (pp. 452ff. in this volume) was written

[27] See my comments on 608B (references to λύπη), 608D-F, 609E-610A, 610A, 610B (first comment), 611C.

[28] Cf. 1 Cor 15:12-54 and my comment on 611D-E.

before the present one. Cross-references between the two are, therefore, from the *cons. ux.* to the *amat.* commentary, but never vice versa. A reference such as "cf. on 766B" is to the *amat.* commentary, "see 766B" would be to the Greek text.

3. On what is meant by "classical Greek" and related terms and on the distinction I make between "cf." and "see," the reader is referred to the Introduction to my *amat.* commentary, VI. 3-4.

Ch. 1

(608A)

Πλούταρχος τῇ γυναικὶ εὖ πράττειν. The (elliptical) salutatory infinitive, when used in ECL (Acts 15:23, 23:26, Jas 1:1, Ign Eph inscr., Ign Rom inscr., Ign Smyrn inscr., Ign Pol inscr.), is always χαίρειν, which was regular at all periods and in all linguistic varieties of the language (see, e.g., Plato *Ep.* 315A-B, Diogenes Laertius 10.14, Xenophon *Cyr.* 4.5.27, Theocritus 14.1, and the many examples collected by F.X.J. Exler, *A Study in Greek Epistolography* [Washington, 1923] 23-68). The present formula of salutation (writer's name or identifying title in the nominative case + recipient's name or identifying title in the dative case + εὖ πράττειν) is the only one Plutarch ever employs (see *conj. praec.* 138A, *tranq. an.* 464E, *an. proc.* 1012A), and is that of the Platonic *Epistles* (see the remarks at the beginning of *Ep.* 3 and the salutations of the rest; Diogenes Laertius 10.14 states that Epicurus often chose εὖ πράττειν in his salutations). ECL salutations tend to be more, often far more, elaborate; and only those at Acts 15:23 and 23:26 match Plutarch's in simplicity. On such matters, one may begin with K. Dziatzko, PW 3.1 (1897), s.v. "Brief," 839; Exler, *ibid.* 23-68, 102-113, 133-35; J. Sykutris, PW Suppl. 5 (1931), s.v. "Epistolographie," 191 (B.3), 195 (B.8); De Lacy-Einarson, 581, n. a; H. Conzelmann, *TDNT*, s.v. χαίρω, A.1.b (esp. n. 9), D.1; LSJ, s.v. χαίρω, III.1.c; Bauer, s.v. χαίρω, 2.b; BDF, secs. 389, 480.5.

(608B)

ὃν ἔπεμψας ἀπαγγελοῦντα περὶ τῆς τοῦ παιδίου τελευτῆς. The future participle expressing purpose after verbs involving motion is a regular construction in classical Greek, but in ECL is confined to Acts (8:27, 22:5, 24:11, 24:17, 25:13 [v.l.]) and Matt 27:49.

See Goodwin-Gulick, sec. 1566.d; Smyth-Messing, sec. 2065; BDF, secs. 65.1, 351.1, 390.1, 418.4; cf. on 749B (θύσων), 750A (πολεμήσων). τελευτή appears in ECL only at Matt 2:15, where it is also a euphemism for death; cf. on 766B.

τὰ ... περὶ τὴν ταφὴν ... ἐχέτω ὥς σοι μέλλει καὶ νῦν ἀλυπότατα καὶ πρὸς τὸ λοιπὸν ἕξειν. The adverb-ἔχω idiom (here represented twice: ἐχέτω ὥς, ἀλυπότατα ἕξειν ["to cause the smallest amount of pain"]) is typical of classical Greek and moderately common in ECL: see Goodwin-Gulick, sec. 1092; LSJ, s.v. ἔχω, B.II.2; Smyth-Messing, secs. 1438, 1441, 1709.b; Bauer, s.v. ἔχω, II; BDF, secs. 308, 393.4, 434.1. I take ἀλυπότατα as a relative or genuine superlative (so, apparently, Hadas, De Lacy-Einarson, and Warner), as against an absolute or elative one (on the distinction, see Smyth-Messing, sec. 1085); most superlatives in NT have the latter force (see BDF, secs. 60, 244). Morphologically, Plutarch shares with ECL a penchant for compounding with alpha-privative (cf. ἀλυπότερος [Phil 2:28] and ἀλύπητον [2 Clem 19:4] and see B. Weissenberger, *Die Sprache Plutarchs von Chaeronea und die pseudo-plutarchischen Schriften*, I. Teil [Straubing, 1895] 10 [under "die Form des Oxymorons"], hereafter cited as Weissenberger; Griffiths, 14; BDF, secs. 117.1, 120.2, 124 [at end]; and on 751B), but NT shows a preference for the -ιστ- over the -τατ- variety of superlative (see BDF, sec. 60; cf. Goodwin-Gulick, secs. 346-56; Smyth -Messing, secs. 313-18). The infinitive characteristically accompanies μέλλω in ECL as well as classical Greek (see Goodwin-Gulick, sec. 1254; LSJ, s.v. μέλλω, I-III; Smyth-Messing, sec. 1959; Bauer, s.v. μέλλω, 1; BDF, secs. 338.3, 350, 356), though the two bodies of literature differ noticeably in regard to the tense of this infinitive: in classical Greek, the present and the future are equally regular, with the future somewhat in the majority (note Plutarch's ἕξειν) and the aorist rare; in ECL, the future is rare (e.g., in NT it is confined to Acts), the aorist not unexpected, and the present regular. The position of ἀλυπότατα near the beginning of *cons. ux.* takes on special significance when one notes that Plutarch frequently chooses λύπη or a cognate when he refers to the painful emotion(s) he is urging his wife to suppress: λύπη or λύπαι (608E, 608F, 610B, 610B-C), τὸ λυποῦν (608D-E, 608E-F, 610A-B, 610E-F), τὸ λυπηρόν (609B), λυπεῖν (611C). In both classical literature and ECL, λύπη and cognates are less likely to refer to physical than to emotional or spiritual pain (see R. Bultmann, *TDNT*, s.v. λύπη and the appropriate entries in LSJ and Bauer). Moreover, Paul uses λύπη to designate the grief he would have felt had Epaphroditus died (Phil 2:27), and at John 16:6 and 16:20-22 Jesus speaks of the λύπη his disciples are experiencing at the prospect of and will experience after his death-departure.

εἰ δέ τι βουλομένη μὴ πεποίηκας ἀλλὰ μένεις τὴν ἐμὴν γνώμην, οἴει δὲ κουφότερον οἴσειν γενομένου . . . "Approval" or "consent," in a somewhat similar verbal context, is also the sense of γνώμη at Phlm 14 (χωρὶς . . . τῆς σῆς γνώμης οὐδὲν . . . ποιῆσαι) and Ign Pol 4:1 (μηδὲν ἄνευ γνώμης σου γινέσθω μηδὲ σὺ ἄνευ θεοῦ τι πρᾶσσε); cf. Ign Pol 5:2 ("with the consent [γνώμη] of the bishop") and see Bauer, s.v., 3 and R. Bultmann, *TDNT*, s.v. (under γινώσκω), 1 (near end). φέρω has the sense "endure" in several ECL passages (see Bauer, s.v., 1.c), but none of them offers a true parallel to its present use with an adverb. The genitive absolute (here γενομένου) is characteristic of both classical Greek and ECL (cf. on 771D and see Goodwin-Gulick, secs. 1156, 1570, 1595.b; Smyth-Messing, secs. 2032.f, 2058, 2070-75; BDF, secs. 417, 423); as here and at 608D (ζώσης), its substantive, if implicit, is sometimes omitted in either body of literature (see Goodwin-Gulick, sec. 1570.a; Smyth-Messing, sec. 2072.a-b; BDF, sec. 423.6; and, for some ECL examples, Matt 17:14 [ἐλθόντων; for contrast, cf. ἐλθόντων . . . αὐτῶν at 17:24], 17:26 [εἰπόντος], Luke 12:36 [ἐλθόντος καὶ κρούσαντος], Acts 21:10 [ἐπιμενόντων], 21:31 [ζητούντων]).

Plutarch approves of any measures his wife wishes to take to diminish her grief, provided they do not involve περιεργία καὶ δεισιδαιμονία. For the attitudes and behavior Plutarch is warning against, see *superst.* (esp. 166A, 168A-D). If περιεργία here connotes superstitious behavior (cf. the force of its cognate adjective at *Alex.* 2.8 and its coordination again with δεισιδαιμονία at *Is. et Os.* 352B), cf. at Acts 19:19 the reference to those who practice "magic" (τὰ περίεργα). For Plutarch, δεισιδαιμονία is a thoroughly pejorative word: see, e.g., *superst.* (passim), *Alex.* 75.2, *adul. et am.* 66C, *amat.* 756C, and *PECL* 1:41 (352B), 44 (353E), 47 (355D), 75 (378A), 77 (379E), 78 (380A), 206 (555A), 209 (556B), 254 (579F), 255 (580A), 257 (580C); cf. on 756C. In ECL, δεισιδαιμονία is pejorative in two of its three occurrences (Diogn 1, 4:1) and neutral in the other (Acts 25:19; the procurator Festus uses it in the sense "religion"); the adjectival cognate displays favorable connotations in its single occurrence at Acts 17:22, where Paul opens his sermon on the Areopagus with ... κατὰ πάντα ὡς δεισιδαιμονεστέρους ὑμᾶς θεωρῶ.

Ch. 2

(608C)

In ECL, πάθος is not used of grief, as it is here and at 609A, 609C, 610B, and 610C-D (cf. the force of the cognate πάσχειν at 611B-C). Cf. on 750F.

At the beginning of Ch. 2, Plutarch thrice employs neuter singular participles as abstract substantives (τοῦ καθεστῶτος, τό συμβεβηκός, τοῦ γεγονότος), and appears to make greater use of such substantives in *cons. ux.* and elsewhere than either ECL (but cf. τὸ γεγονός at Luke 8:56) or earlier classical writers, with the exception of Thucydides: cf. on 758E and see Weissenberger, 27-28; Goodwin-Gulick, secs. 932, 1565; Smyth-Messing, secs. 1025, 1153.b (N.2), 2050-51; BDF, sec. 413.3. Most striking, and most reminiscent of Thucydides, is Plutarch's use of these participles in circumstances in which a cognate noun or articular infinitive would have been semantically convenient, e.g., τῷ λυποῦντι (*cons. ux.* 608D-E) instead of τῇ λύπῃ or τῷ λυπεῖν. Cf., e.g., *cons. ux.* 608C (τὸ εὐφραῖνον), 608D (τὸ ἀντιφιλοῦν καὶ χαριζόμενον αὐτῆς), 608E (τὸ δυσχεραινόμενον), 608F (τὸ εὐφραῖνον ἢ τὸ λυποῦν), 610A-B (τοῦ λυποῦντος), 610D (ἐκ μικροῦ τοῦ γαργαλίζοντος), 610E-F (τὸ λυποῦν ... μικρὸν καὶ ἀμαυρὸν), 611B (τοῦ δάκνοντος), 611C-D (τὸ λυποῦν), *virt. mor.* 447C (τὸ βουλευόμενον τοῦ ἀνθρώπου), 447D (τῆς ψυχῆς τὸ φρονοῦν), 447 F (μάχην ποιεῖ ... τὸ ἡδόμενον καὶ τὸ ἀλγοῦν πρὸς τὸ κρῖνον καὶ τὸ βουλευόμενον), *frat. am.* 478B (τὸ χαῖρον ὑμῶν), *num. vind.* 548E (τὸ παρηγοροῦν τοὺς πεπονθότας), *amat.* 758E (παρατροπὴ τοῦ λογιζομένου καὶ φρονοῦντος), *Marc.* 23.4 (τὸ πεποιθὸς τοῦ ἀνδρός). Cf. also, e.g., Thucydides 1.36.1 (τὸ μὲν δεδιὸς αὐτοῦ ... τὸ δὲ θαρσοῦν), 1.142.8 (ἐν τῷ μὴ μελετῶντι), 2.59.5 (τὸ ὀργιζόμενον τῆς γνώμης), 2.63.1 (τῆς ... πόλεως τῷ τιμωμένῳ).

ἂν δὲ σὲ τῷ δυσφορεῖν ὑπερβάλλουσαν εὕρω, τοῦτό μοι μᾶλλον ἐνοχλήσει τοῦ γεγονότος. This conditional sentence displays throughout linguistic qualities that bear comparison with their ECL counterparts. Its future-more-vivid form (subjunctive in the protasis, future indicative in the apodosis) is typical of both classical and early Christian writers (cf., for Plutarch, Weissenberger, 33-5 [Hypothetische Sätze] and see Goodwin-Gulick, secs. 1398.III, 1413; Smyth-Messing, secs. 2291.3.a, 2297 [under Future], 2323-25, 2326.a; Bauer, s.v. ἐάν, 1.a [Luke 10:6, Matt 15:4], 1.b [Matt 6:14, 9:21, 12:11, 24:48-51, Mark 8:3, Luke 4:7, 14:34, John 15:10], 1.c [1 Cor 14:23, Matt 21:21], 1.d [John 12:32, 14:3]; BDF, secs. 371, 373). ἄν = ἐάν, however, is as rare in ECL as it is frequent in Plutarch and classical Greek: see D. Wyttenbach, *Lexicon Plutarcheum* 1 (1830), s.v. ἄν (passim); LSJ, s.v. ἄν (B); Smyth-Messing, secs. 1768.a, 2283.a, 2323, 2337, 2852.a; Bauer, s.v. ἄν (second entry); BDF, sec. 107; on 765C-D (cf. ἂν μὴ τύχῃ at 764F). Though the articular infinitive (here τῷ δυσφορεῖν; cf. on 749D [ἐκ τοῦ συμπαρεῖναι καὶ διαλέγεσθαι], 749D-E [εἰς τὸ ἐρᾶν]) is exceedingly common in ECL (see Bauer, s.v. ὁ, ἡ, τό, 4; BDF, secs. 398-404), as it is in classical Greek (see Goodwin-Gulick, secs. 953.a, 1520.b, 1544-58; Smyth-Messing, secs 1153.f., 1322, 2025-2038, 2238, 2712, 2744 [passim], 2749), its use in ECL in the dative case without a governing preposition is confined to 2 Cor 2:13 (see BDF, sec. 401); independent datives of the articular infinitive are moderately common in classical literature (see Goodwin-Gulick, sec. 1550; Smyth-Messing, sec. 2033). In ECL, the dative of respect, often with adjectives or participles as here (τῷ δυσφορεῖν ὑπερβάλλουσαν), is far more common than its accusative counterpart (see BDF, secs. 160, 197; cf. Goodwin-Gulick, secs. 1182, 1056-57 and Smyth-Messing, secs. 1516, 1600-1605); Plutarch is at least comfortable with either case in his respect constructions (see on 749D [γυνὴ πλούτῳ καὶ γένει λαμπρὰ καὶ . . . εὔτακτος βίον and καίπερ . . . ἱκανὴ τὸ εἶδος], 760E [ἄνδρα λαμπρὸν . . . ψυχήν]; cf. γένει λαμπρός at 766D). δυσφορέω and cognates do not appear in ECL; cf. on δυσχεραίνω at 608E. The genitive of comparison (here τοῦ γεγονότος) is typical of classical and ECL syntax: see Goodwin-Gulick, sec. 1147; Smyth-Messing, secs. 1069, 1077, 1431; BDF, sec. 185. On τοῦ γεγονότος as a substantival participle, see the preceding comment.

Plutarch here quotes a portion of a Homeric verse (*Il.* 22.126 = *Od.* 19.163). At various points later in the essay, he quotes Theognis (427; 611F) and from three of Euripides' plays (608E, 609A, 610B; see De Lacy-Einarson, 585 [nn. a-b], 587 [n. b],

593 [n. a]), and briefly summarizes a story he attributes to Aesop (609F). Such use of antecedent literature for quotation and reference bears a general resemblence to the use made of OT by the authors of NT. For more on all this, see my first comment to 749A.

Plutarch speaks of his wife as τοσούτων μοι τέκνων ἀνατροφῆς κοινωνοῦσα (κοινωνήσασα Sieveking), πάντων ἐκτεθραμμένων οἴκοι δι' αὐτῶν ἡμῶν. ἀνατροφή does not appear in ECL, but ἀνατρέφω is used of the nurture or rearing of children at Acts 7:20, 7:21, 22:3, Luke 4:16 (v.l.) and ἐκτρέφω at Eph 6:4, Herm Vis 3:9:1 (the τέκνα here, however, are metaphorical children); cf. my remarks at 749D-E (second entry) about compounding with prepositional prefixes in Plutarch and ECL. διά may govern a genitive of the agent in both classical and early Christian writers (see LSJ, s.v., A.III.a; Bauer, s.v., A.III.2; Goodwin-Gulick, sec. 1208; Smyth-Messing, secs. 1678, 1685.d, 1755; A. Oepke, *TDNT*, s.v., A.4); ECL appears to exhibit the more fully developed usage in this regard. Hovering behind Plutarch's present use of κοινωνέω are, I suspect, the notions of erotic κοινωνία one encounters in *amat*. On these notions vis-à-vis ECL, see on 757C-D, 763F (first entry), 769A, 769F, 770C. Significantly, ECL does not, as Plutarch and other classical authors sometimes do, speak of marriage as a κοινωνία.

Plutarch's ἀγαπητόν (neuter singular) apparently (the textual condition of its sentence is poor) has no emphatic or distinctive significance.

πρόσεστι . . . δριμύτης . . . τῷ πρὸς τὰ τηλικαῦτα (children as young as their daughter) φιλοστόργῳ, τὸ εὐφραῖνον (sc. ἡμᾶς) αὐτῆς (MSS except C[1]; αὐτῶν Sieveking; αὐτοῦ De Lacy-Einarson) καθαρόν τε ὂν . . . καὶ πάσης ἀμιγὲς ὀργῆς καὶ μέμψεως. In its single ECL occurrence, πρόσειμι (the second element is εἰμί) also has an abstract noun as its subject and governs a dative (Diogn 7:4). Plutarch is likely to employ the φιλοστοργ- word group when referring to deep and sincere affection, both in *cons. ux.* (see, in addition to the present passage, 609A [twice], 609E) and elsewhere (see D. Wyttenbach, *Lexicon Plutarcheum* 2 [1830], s.v. φιλοστοργέω ff.). In contrast, this word group is represented only twice in ECL, though in each instance under circumstances that are semantically and syntactically reminiscent of Plutarch's τῷ πρὸς . . . φιλοστόργῳ: φιλοστοργίαν . . . πρὸς ἀλλήλους (Diogn 1;

in reference to the affection Christians have for one another), φιλαδελφίᾳ εἰς ἀλλήλους φιλόστοργοι (Rom 12:10). Despite the fact that it is not an impersonal expression (but cf. Smyth-Messing, secs. 2076.C, 2078), τὸ εὐφραῖνον . . . καθαρόν τε ὂν . . . καὶ . . . ἀμιγές, if this is the correct text, must be an accusative absolute. I would translate, "the joy she gave us being absolutely pure and free from all anger and resentment." εὐφραίνω is also active at *cons. ux.* 608D (τοῖς εὐφραίνουσιν αὐτήν), 608F (τὸ εὐφραῖνον [sc. ἡμᾶς]) and 610F (μύρον . . . εὐφραίνει τὴν ὄσφρησιν) and, in ECL, at 2 Cor 2:2, Barn 21:9, and Herm Man 12:3:4; it is, however, usually passive in ECL; cf. R. Bultmann, *TDNT*, s.v. The accusative absolute, moderately common in classical Greek (see Goodwin-Gulick, secs. 1571-72; Smyth-Messing, secs. 2059, 2076-78), is virtually non-existent in ECL (see BDF, sec. 424). καθαρός as here used has moral connotations that bring it into loose, but very loose, connection with Bauer, s.v., 3; for more on this term, see on 765A (first entry).

(608D)

. . . φύσει θαυμαστὴν ἔσχεν (their daughter) εὐκολίαν καὶ πραότητα. This statement would be generally out of place in ECL, where the εὐκολ- word group is represented only by an adverb as v.l. at Herm Man 12:3:5 and the adjective θαυμαστός is applied once to God (1 Clem 60:1) and otherwise almost exclusively to what is in some fashion related to God or Christ (see Bauer, s.v. θαυμαστός; cf. on 762D [last entry]). Also, the only thing in the way of an ECL parallel to Plutarch's use of φύσει in reference to an innate, *individual* character trait is at Ign Trall 1:1, where Ignatius speaks of the Trallians as possessing οὐ κατὰ χρῆσιν ἀλλὰ κατὰ φύσιν a commendable διάνοια. On the concept of φύσις behind Plutarch's present usage, cf. on 755D (first entry) and see A. Dihle, *Studien zur griechischen Biographie* (Göttingen, 1956) passim (s.v. φύσις in Register 3); H. Martin, "The Character of Plutarch's Themistocles," *TAPhA* 92 (1961) 326-36; H. Köster, *TDNT*, s.v. φύσις, A.2.a, A.4.b. πραότης (predominantly πραΰτης in NT), however, is a significant ECL, and Hellenistic, virtue (see on 762D [first entry]).

Their daughter's loving behavior, an expression of τὸ φιλάνθρωπον (substantivized neuter singular adjectives are common in both classical Greek and ECL; see on 759E), gave them ἡδονή; and in her childish attempts to entertain other infants and even her playthings, she was motivated by φιλανθρωπία. Cf. Acts 27:3 and 28:2, where, respectively, φιλανθρώπως and φιλανθρωπία are used to describe deeds of hospitality and kindness; for more on φιλανθρωπία in both pagan and Christian literature, see the Introduction to my *amat.* commentary (V.4 and n. 16) and on 758A, 762D, 767A. The present use of ἡδονή in a favorable sense has parallels at 2 Clem 15:5 and Herm Sim 6:5:7; though often used in a favorable sense by classical authors, this term is infrequent and customarily pejorative in ECL (see on 750C-D).

Their daughter is described as τὰ ἥδιστα κοινουμένη τοῖς εὐφραίνουσιν αὐτήν. In its ten or so ECL occurrences, κοινόω always has a far different meaning, signifying to "defile," "profane," or "consider unclean": see Bauer, s.v.; F. Hauck, *TDNT*, s.v. (under κοινός).

Ch. 3

(608D-F)

In Ch. 3, Plutarch argues that he and his wife must not, in attempting to drive away their grief (τὸ λυποῦν [608D, 608F] or, by inference from the reference to Clymene, λύπη [608E]), let themselves forget their daughter, since the memory of her can, and should, bring with it more τὸ εὐφραῖνον than τὸ λυποῦν (608F), more ἡδοναί than λύπαι (608F). Plutarch's λυπῶ-εὐφραίνω antithesis has parallels at 2 Cor 2:2-3 and 2 Clem 19:4. His λύπη-ἡδονή antithesis, however, is missing from ECL (see R. Bultmann, *TDNT*, s.v. λύπη, C.1). Cf. on λύπη at 608B and on abstract substantives at 608C.

(608D)

Plutarch uses ἐπίνοια as a virtual synonym of μνήμη here (cf. μνήμην and ὑπόμνησιν τοῦ παιδός in the following sentence) and later at 608E-F (note its contextual association with the μνήμην at 608D-E), 610D (cf. μνήμης in the first sentence of 610E), and 610F (ἐπίνοια τῶν ἀγαθῶν; cf. from the same context μνήμης τῶν ἀγαθῶν [610E] and τὸ μεμνῆσθαι τῶν χρηστῶν [610F]). The term does not have such force in its three ECL occurrences (see Bauer, s.v.), and is perhaps seldom so used by other classical writers (see LSJ, s.v. ἐπίνοια). The text at 611D (Ch.9) is too problematic to admit, in this regard, consideration of its one *or* two occurrences there.

(608D-E)

δέδια . . . μὴ συνεκβάλωμεν τῷ λυποῦντι τὴν μνήμην (sc. of her delightful behavior). Plutarch's verb of fearing is followed by an object clause with μή as its introductory conjunction and an aorist subjunctive as its verb. This syntactical pattern is typical of classical Greek and has ECL parallels at, e.g., Acts 23:10 (φοβηθεὶς . . . μὴ διασπασθῇ), 27:17 (φοβούμενοι . . . μὴ . . . ἐκπέσωσιν), 2 Cor 11:3 (φοβοῦμαι . . . μή . . . φθαρῇ). On object clauses after verbs of fearing, which exhibit far more variety in classical Greek than in ECL, see Smyth-Messing, secs. 2207, 2221-33; Bauer, s.v. μή, B.1; BDF, secs. 370, 364.3. Note that Bauer and BDF disagree in their syntactical analysis of such phrases as βλέπετε . . . μὴ ἐπέλθῃ (Acts 13:40) and ὁρᾶτε μὴ καταφρονήσητε (Matt 18:10); cf. Smyth-Messing, sec. 2224.a. μνήμη, limited to four occurrences in ECL, has the same basic sense as here at 2 Pet 1:15 and Mart Pol 18:3; on this term in ECL, see Bauer, s.v. and O. Michel, *TDNT*, s.v. (under μιμνήσκομαι).

(608E)

Clymene tried to avoid what reminded her of her dead son because of the λύπη it aroused, πᾶν γὰρ ἡ φύσις φεύγει τὸ δυσχεραινόμενον. Plutarch thus uses φύσις in the sense of "human nature." Cf. Diogn 9:6 (τὸ ἀδύνατον τῆς ἡμετέρας φύσεως εἰς τὸ τυχεῖν ζωῆς) and, possibly, Jas 3:7 (τῇ φύσει τῇ ἀνθρωπίνῃ) and Rom 2:14 (ὅταν . . . ἔθνη τὰ μὴ νόμον ἔχοντα φύσει τὰ τοῦ νόμου ποιῶσιν). On the exegetical problems attendant on the latter two passages, see Bauer, s.v. φύσις, 2-3 and H. Köster, *TDNT*, s.v. φύσις, C.2.b, C.3.a. δυσχεραίνω is missing from ECL; and of the thirteen or so ECL vocables with δυσ- as a compounding prefix, only a couple appear with even moderate frequency. Cf. my comments at 608C on neuter singular participles as abstract substantives and on δυσφορέω. Plutarch's thought and vocabulary here is perhaps influenced by Aristotle *EN* 1172.a.25f. (τὰ μὲν . . . ἡδέα προαιροῦνται, τὰ δὲ λυπηρὰ φεύγουσιν), 1172.b.18-20 (. . . ᾤετ' [Eudoxus] . . . τὴν . . . λύπην καθ' αὑτὸ πᾶσι φευκτὸν εἶναι . . .); cf. Plutarch's ἡδοναί-λῦπαι antithesis at 608F.

(608E-F)

δεῖ (sc. ἡμᾶς) . . . μὴ καθῆσθαι μηδ' ἐγκαλεῖσθαι (MSS except LC[1], which offer the ἐγκεκλεῖσθαι chosen by Sieveking and De Lacy-

Einarson) πολλαπλασίας (Sieveking and De Lacy-Einarson; πολλαπλασίαις LC[1]) ταῖς ἡδοναῖς ἐκείναις λύπας ἀνταποδιδόντας. I render ἐγκαλεῖσθαι as "to be liable to the charge of" (cf. LSJ, s.v. ἐγκαλέω, II.1) and construe it with ἀνταποδιδόντας as a supplementary participle. Sieveking punctuates so as to have the infinitives governed by εἰκός ἐστι rather than δεῖ.

Ch. 4

(608F)

Plutarch commends his wife because she did not put on a mourning garment (ἱμάτιον πένθιμον) or impose any αἰκία on herself or her attendants, because the funeral was conducted without extravagance (πολυτέλεια), and because ἐπράττετο κοσμίως πάντα καὶ σιωπῇ μετὰ τῶν ἀναγκαίων. Cf. 1 Tim 2:8-11 (βούλομαι . . . γυναῖκας ἐν καταστολῇ κοσμίῳ . . . κοσμεῖν ἑαυτάς, μὴ ἐν . . . ἱματισμῷ πολυτελεῖ . . . γυνὴ ἐν ἡσυχίᾳ μανθανέτω . . .), *PECL* 1:44 (354A), and on 753B, 767E-F. Cf. also the similar sense of ἀναγκαῖος at Acts 10:24 (τοὺς συγγενεῖς αὐτοῦ καὶ τοὺς ἀναγκαίους φίλους). In ECL, αἰκία and cognates are limited to five appearances in 1 Clem (6:1, 6:2, 11:1, 45:7, 51:2).

(609A)

There is a peculiarly Greek ring to Plutarch's mention of his wife's manner of dress περὶ θέατρον ἢ πομπήν. In ECL, πομπή does not appear; and θέατρον is used three times, once metaphorically (1 Cor 4:9) and twice of the theater at Ephesus (Acts 19:29-31). Cf. on 749C (first entry).

Plutarch refers to his wife as being ἐν τοῖς σκυθρωποῖς (because of the death of their daughter). σκυθρωπός is used of persons in its two ECL occurrences (Matt 6:16, Luke 24:17), but in the second it is Jesus' two followers on the road to Emmaus who are so described.

δεῖ . . . "τὴν σώφρονα" (quoted from Euripides *Ba.* 318; cf. De Lacy-Einarson, 587, n. b) . . . οἴεσθαι τὸν ἐν πένθεσι σάλον . . . ἐγκρατείας δεῖσθαι διαμαχομένης οὐ πρὸς τὸ φιλόστοργον . . . ἀλλὰ πρὸς τὸ ἀκόλαστον τῆς ψυχῆς. For discussion of σωφροσύνη in Plutarch, other classical authors, and ECL, see on 752A, 752C, 753B; it is presented as a virtue especially appropriate to women at 1 Tim 2:9, 2:15, Tit 2:5, 1 Clem 1:3, Pol Phil 4:3. On ἐγκράτεια, see on 753B (last entry), 754B; though generally much more significant in Greek philosophical literature than in ECL, Paul includes it among the fruit of the Spirit (Gal 5:23) and Hermas classifies it as one of the four cardinal Christian virtues (Sim 9:15:1-3) and treats it prominently at Man 8. In its single ECL occurrence (Acts 23:9), διαμάχομαι is also used figuratively; cf. on 750B, 763C (figurative usage of μάχομαι). On τὸ φιλόστοργον, see on 608C; on substantivized neuter singular adjectives, on 608D, 759E. Behind Plutarch's reference to ψυχή is undoubtedly the dichotomous σῶμα-ψυχή anthropology that reveals itself more fully later in *cons. ux.* (610A-B, 611D-F) and often in *amat.*; on this anthropology and on its relation to ECL, see on 758D-759D, 764D-E, 764E-765D.

τὸ ποθεῖν καὶ τὸ τιμᾶν καὶ τὸ μεμνῆσθαι τῶν ἀπογενομένων (the dead). On the articular infinitive, see on 608C (τῷ δυσφορεῖν). Cf. ἁμαρτίαις ἀπογενόμενοι (1 Pet 2:24); this is the only ECL occurrence of a form of this verb.

(609B)

Plutarch condemns the insatiable desire for lamentations (θρῆνοι) that leads to beating the breast (κοπετοί) as no less disgraceful than ἡ περὶ τὰς ἡδονὰς ἀκρασία. Cf. at Luke 23:27 the reference to the women αἳ ἐκόπτοντο καὶ ἐθρήνουν αὐτόν. ἀκρασία is insignificant in ECL, except at Herm Sim 9:15:1-3, where it appears among the four cardinal vices that contrast to the four cardinal Christian virtues; cf. on 753B (last entry).

κλαυθμῶν καὶ ὀδυρμῶν. Cf. at Matt 2:18 (Jer 31:15) κλαυθμὸς καὶ ὀδυρμός.

Plutarch speaks of the common πηγή ("spring," "source") of both laughter and tears. πηγή is a significant term in the figurative language of both classical literature and ECL: see LSJ, s.v.; Bauer, s.v.; W. Michaelis, *TDNT*, s.v., A.1, B.2. In its non-literal usage in ECL, it is always truly metaphorical (the author is consciously making a metaphor and a translation such as "spring" or "fountain" is required), and never merely figurative (its metaphor is inherent within it and it may be translated "source," "origin"); on this distinction, sometimes difficult to make, cf. VI.6 in the Introduction to my *amat.* commentary.

διαμάχεσθαι ταῖς γυναιξί. On the figure and syntax, see on 609A (διαμαχομένης), 750B, 763C.

(609C)

Those overwelmed by grief at the death of a loved one are described as being ἐν πάθεσι καὶ τύχαις ῥᾳστώνης καὶ φιλανθρωπίας δεομέναις. This phrase clashes with the vocabular usage of ECL, from which ῥᾳστώνη is fully and τύχη virtually absent and in which πάθος and δέομαι lack their present sense (see, respectively, on 608C and 749A). φιλανθρωπία, however, establishes a small point of semantic contact, especially in relation to Acts 27:3 and 28:2, where, respectively, φιλανθρώπως and φιλανθρωπία are used in description of acts of kindness by *human* beings; cf. on 608D, where I list my other discussions of φιλανθρωπία. Plutarch is perhaps using τύχαι in the loose and popular sense of "misfortunes," without implying any overriding concept of τύχη; but cf. 610E, where we encounter such a concept.

Ch. 5

ἡμῖν . . . πρὸς ἀλλήλους οὔτ' ἐκείνης ἐδέησε τῆς μάχης οὔτε ταύτης . . . δεήσειν. On the battle figure, see on 609A (διαμαχομένης), 763C. ECL employs only the present and imperfect tenses of impersonal δεῖ, and it appears that ECL also eschews the classical practice of sometimes allowing it to govern either a genitive of the thing or, as here, a genitive of the thing plus a dative of the person (see LSJ, s.v. δεῖ, II.1-2; Goodwin-Gulick, secs. 1115, 1116.a, 1161; Smyth-Messing, secs. 1399, 1400, 1467; Bauer, s.v. δεῖ, 6; BDF, secs. 393.1, 405, 407, 408).

(609C-D)

Plutarch again (εὐτελείᾳ . . . προλιπόντος) takes us into a terminological and cultural environment that shares little with ECL. Most significantly, the ethical terms he applies to his wife's commendable behavior (εὐτέλεια, ἀθρυψία, ἀφέλεια, εὐστάθεια) are either missing or extremely rare in ECL, and the mention of φιλόσοφοι and of her conduct and appearance ἐν ἱεροῖς καὶ θυσίαις καὶ θεάτροις gives the passage a strikingly Greek tone. θέατρον appears only thrice in ECL (see on 609A, 749C [first entry]); and φιλοσοφία/φιλόσοφος is just as rare, being used twice (Col 2:8, Diogn 8:2) with pejorative and once (Acts 17:18) with probably neutral force (cf. on 749C [first entry], 752A). In the case of ἱερός and θυσία, however, Plutarch participates in the vocabulary, though not the concepts, of ECL: see on 749B (θύσων, θυσία), 760C.

(609D)

Plutarch remembers that, when he was previously summoned home because of the death of one of their sons, ξένοι accompanied him from the coast up to Chaeronea. ξένος is probably being used in the sense of "guest-friend" or "friend from abroad" and as such has no parallel in ECL; see my comment on this term at 749B.

(609D-E)

When our son died, Plutarch continues, visitors at our house (οἰκία) were amazed at the κατάστασις and ἡσυχία; οὕτω σωφρόνως κατεκόσμησας τὸν οἶκον ἐν καιρῷ πολλὴν ἀκοσμίας ἐξουσίαν διδόντι. This vocabular complex calls to mind the prescriptions at 1 Tim 2:8-15 (βούλομαι ... γυναῖκας ἐν καταστολῇ κοσμίῳ, μετὰ ... σωφροσύνης κοσμεῖν ἑαυτάς .... γυνὴ ἐν ἡσυχίᾳ μανθανέτω .... γυναικὶ ... ἐπιτρέπω ... εἶναι ἐν ἡσυχίᾳ .... ἐὰν μείνωσιν [women] ... μετὰ σωφροσύνης.), Tit 2:5 (the older are to teach the younger women to be, among other things, σώφρονες and οἰκουργοί), 1 Clem 1:3 (the Corinthians are praised because they taught their women τὰ κατὰ τὸν οἶκον ... οἰκουργεῖν ... σωφρονούσας), 1 Tim 3:2-5 (in addition to much else, a bishop must be σώφρων and κόσμιος and properly oversee his own οἶκος); cf. Pol Phil 4:3 (χήρας σωφρονούσας) and on 608F, 609A ("τὴν σώφρονα"), 753B, 767E-F. Moreover, καιρός (often in the phrase ἐν καιρῷ; see Bauer, s.v., passim) and ἐξουσία are common throughout ECL. κατάστασις, however, is limited to one ECL occurrence (Diogn 5:4) in a quite different sense. And though ἐξουσία may appear in ECL as the direct object of δίδωμι (Mark 13:34, Ker Pet 2 [p. 14], 2 Cor 10:8, 13:10; cf. ἐδόθη ... ἐξουσία at Matt 28:18), to my knowledge ECL uses this term neither with an objective genitive (here ἀκοσμίας) nor in its present sense ("opportunity, occasion [for]"); for classical antecedents to Plutarch's present usage of ἐξουσία, see LSJ, s.v., 1.

(609E)

And yet, Plutarch adds, you nursed this child yourself (instead of giving him to a wet nurse) and even had to endure surgery when your nipple became infected. γενναῖα γὰρ ταῦτα καὶ φιλόστοργα. γενναῖος and γενναιότης appear with a high degree of relative frequency in 1 Clem and Mart Pol (see Bauer, s.v.), but nowhere else in ECL. On φιλόστοργος, see on 608C (last entry);

ἄστοργος occurs twice in ECL (Rom 1:31, 2 Tim 3:3), each time in a catalogue of vices.

Ch. 6

(609E-610A)

In this section (Ch. 6: τὰς ... ἐρρωμένου), Plutarch chooses πένθος as the denotation for the emotion he is combatting. This is the most precise of his several designations for it (see R. Bultmann, *TDNT*, s.v. πένθος, A; *TDNT*, s.v. λύπη, A.1-2; W. Michaelis, *TDNT*, s.v. πάθος, 1; LSJ, s.v. πένθος [2], πενθέω [1]; cf. on 608B [λύπη], 608C [πάθος]); and in the case of all *cons. ux.* occurrences of πένθος (four in this section) and its cognates (608F [ἱμάτιον ... πένθιμον], 609B [κουρὰς ... πενθίμους], 610C-D [ὁ πενθῶν]), the referent is simultaneously grief occasioned by death and, explicitly or implicitly, the emotion he wants his wife to suppress. In ECL, πένθος/πενθέω is not so narrowly and exclusively associated with grieving for the dead (see Bauer, s.v. and R. Bultmann, *TDNT*, s.v. πένθος, C); but note Matt 9:14-15, Mark 16:10, Gos Pet 7:27, Rev 18:7-8.

(609E-F)

Many mothers leave the care of their children to others and then, if they die, abandon themselves εἰς κενὸν καὶ ἀχάριστον πένθος, οὐχ ὑπ' εὐνοίας (εὐλόγιστον γὰρ εὔνοια καὶ καλόν). In at least four (1 Cor 7:3 [t.r.], Ign Rom 4:1, Ign Trall 1:2, Mart Pol 17:3), and possibly all, of its five ECL occurrences (the fifth one is at Eph 6:7), εὔνοια has the same general sense as here ("affection"). And ECL offers a number of examples of κενός (here, "vain, [figuratively] empty") and καλός (here simply "good") in roughly their present sense: see Bauer, s.v. κενός (2.a), καλός (2); A. Oepke, *TDNT*, s.v. κενός, B.2; and W. Grundmann, *TDNT*, s.v. καλός, E.5, who finds similarity between Plutarch and the Pastorals in the usage of καλός (but see on 759E [τὸ καλόν]). Whatever the meaning of Plutarch's ἀχάριστον ("unbecoming" and "thankless" strike me as the best possibilities), this adjective describes *persons* in both of its ECL occurrences (Luke 6:35, 2 Tim 3:2). Though εὐλόγιστος is absent from ECL, cf. the implicit coordination of εὔλογόν ἐστιν and καλῶς ἔχει at Ign Smyrn 9:1.

Plutarch next explains why such mothers are not motivated by εὔνοια (or τὸ φιλόστοργον; note that Plutarch is using these two terms synonymously, as is evident from the φιλόστοργα/οὐχ ὑπ' εὐνοίας antithesis in 609E; cf. the preceding comment and on τῷ φιλοστόργῳ at 608C): μικρῷ τῷ φυσικῷ πάθει (=εὔνοια/τὸ φιλόστοργον; note that Aristotle *EN* 1105.b.21-23 classifies φιλία as a πάθος) πολὺ συγκεραννύμενον τὸ πρὸς κενὴν δόξαν (sc. πάθος) ἄγρια ποιεῖ καὶ μανικὰ . . . πένθη. My interpretation of this passage is summed up in the parenthetical insertions into the Greek text; I would translate τὸ πρὸς κενὴν δόξαν (πάθος [cf. Aristotle's classification of ἐπιθυμία and πόθος as πάθη at *EN* 1105b.21-23]) as "vainglorious passion," i.e., a yearning to gain the reputation of being a mother who loved her child. Plutarch is obviously using φυσικός with reference to *human* nature; cf. on 608E. For a subtle parallel, cf. with Plutarch's ἄγρια πένθη Hermas' description of ἡ ἐπιθυμία ἡ πονηρά as ἀγρία (Man 12:1:2). Though the adjective μανικός does not appear in ECL, the μανία-σωφροσύνη antithesis at Acts 26:24-25 is certainly within Plutarch's conceptual framework (cf. on 609A ["τὴν σώφρονα"], 609D-E); with σωφροσύνη, Paul is apparently answering his pagan examiner Festus in the man's own terms (cf. on 758D-759D). Plutarch here uses the plural of an abstract noun (πένθη) to stress the occasions and particularly the expressions of what is denoted by its singular; such usage is perhaps more common in classical Greek than in ECL (see Smyth-Messing, secs. 1000 [3], 1001; BDF, sec. 142).

(609F)

Plutarch writes of Zeus' assigning τιμαί to the gods. Cf. Diogn 2:8 and 3:5; in these instances, however, the τιμαί are conferred on deity by *men* and are of an order different from that Plutarch has in mind. Cf. on 752B, 761D.

(609F-610B)

In the remainder of Ch. 6, Plutarch sets out a pathology of grief. First, he claims, its expressions corrupt the διάνοια. This leads to extreme neglect of the σῶμα, whose strength is needed to keep the ψυχή healthy. Instead, the ψυχή is infected by the expressions of grief emanating from the σῶμα. On Plutarch's ψυχή-σῶμα anthropology, see on his reference to ψυχή at 609A and on 758D-759D, 764D-E, 764E-765D. My impression is that Plutarch is using διάνοια ("mind") in a popular, non-philosophical sense (the sense it has throughout ECL; see J. Behm, *TDNT*, s.v. διάνοια [under νοέω], 2 and cf. on διάνοια at 759C), and is not presently dealing in any tripartite, but of course still dualistic, anthropology of the sort we encounter at *fac. lun.* 943Aff., where two separate metaphysical entities hierarchically related (νοῦς the superior, ψυχή the inferior) are conceived of as combining with σῶμα to produce what we in the phenomenal world recognize as a human being. In other words, διάνοια here has, as in ECL, the purely analytical function of defining an aspect of the inner life, and derives its metaphysical implications solely from its contextual association with ψυχή.

(609F)

Plutarch speaks of the dangers of allowing πένθος to become σύντροφον καὶ σύνοικον. Each of these two terms has a single, literal (and not as here, metaphorical) representative in ECL (Acts 13:1, 1 Pet 3:7).

(610A)

μικρὰν καὶ στενὴν καὶ ἀνέξοδον καὶ ἀμείλικτον καὶ ψοφοδεῆ ποιεῖ (expressions of grief such as mourning attire and cropped hair) τὴν διάνοιαν, ὡς οὔτε γέλωτος αὐτῇ μετὸν . . . οὔτε φιλανθρώπου τραπέζης τοιαῦτα περικειμένῃ . . . διὰ τὸ πένθος. Of the adjectives used to describe the διάνοια corrupted by grief, only μικρός has any currency in ECL, where, however, it lacks an ethical sense, which it obviously has here (cf. on 762E). Plutarch's μετόν is a typically classical accusative absolute, a construction virtually not existing in ECL: see on 608C (last entry). His περίκειμαί (τι) has syntactical parallels in both classical and early Christian writers (see LSJ, s.v., II; Bauer, s.v., 2). On φιλάνθρωπος, whose meaning here is moderately weak ("friendly," "pleasant") but with implications of hospitality, see on 608D (τὸ φιλάνθρωπον), 749D (λόγους φιλανθρώπους). γέλως in its single ECL appearance is associated with πένθος (Jas 4:9-10), but there the writer is exhorting his readers to abandon laughter for grief and tears, a notion that would be abhorrent to Plutarch.

τὴν ψυχὴν πονοῦσαν (sc. because of πένθος). Cf. POxy 1, lines 17-18 (πονεῖ ἡ ψυχή μου), 1 Clem 16:12 (ἀφελεῖν ἀπὸ τοῦ πόνου τῆς ψυχῆς αὐτοῦ), and the coordination of πένθος and πόνος at Rev 21:4.

(610A-B)

Plutarch avers that grief is dissipated, ὥσπερ ἐν εὐδίᾳ κῦμα, τῇ γαλήνῃ τοῦ σώματος. With Plutarch's marine simile-metaphor, cf. the metaphorical κύματα of Jude 13 and εὐδία of Ign Smyrn 11:3. εὐδία, κῦμα, and γαλήνη, however, are rare in ECL; and the last is literal in its three occurrences (Matt 8:26//Mark 4:39// Luke 8:24). For more on nautical and marine figures in classical literature and ECL, see on 751E, 754C (last comment).

(610B)

The body that is neglected because of grief sends up to the soul μηδὲν εὐμενὲς μηδὲ χρηστὸν . . . πλὴν ὀδύνας καὶ λύπας. εὐμενής and cognates are absent from ECL (cf. on 762B [first comment], 766C), and ECL offers only some general semantic parallels to Plutarch's χρηστός ("benevolent, kind," as is shown by its coordination with εὐμενής; see Bauer, s.v. χρηστός [1.b.2], χρηστότης [2] and K. Weiss, *TDNT*, s.v. χρηστός [C.2-3, D.1], χρηστότης [3.b-c, 4]). But cf. at Rom 9:2, λύπη μοί ἐστιν . . . καὶ . . . ὀδύνη τῇ καρδίᾳ μου. On the two abstract plurals, see on 609E-F, where πένθη is so used.

τοιαῦτα λαμβάνει πάθη τὴν ψυχὴν οὕτω κακωθεῖσαν. For a verbal parallel, if nothing more, cf. ἐκάκωσαν τὰς ψυχὰς . . . (Acts 14:2).

Ch. 7

οὐκ ἂν φοβηθείην. φόβος and cognates are extremely common in ECL (cf. *PECL* 1:8-14, 22, 50 [358A], 189, 300, 323). For comments on the potential optative, see on 750A (ἂν . . . προσδοκήσειεν).

(610C)

ποίους . . . ἀγῶνας ἠγωνίσω. The same figure, together with the cognate accusative, occurs at 1 Tim 6:12 (ἀγωνίζου τὸν καλὸν ἀγῶνα) and 2 Tim 4:7 (τὸν καλὸν ἀγῶνα ἠγώνισμαι). The cognate accusative is a feature of Plutarchan-classical and ECL usage: see Weissenberger, 25; Goodwin-Gulick, secs. 1049-55, 1074; Smyth-Messing, secs. 1563-77, 1620; BDF, secs. 153-54, 156.

Plutarch mentions the time when a death occurred in the family of a friend and his wife commendably opposed the pernicious women who came μετὰ ὀλοφυρμῶν καὶ ἀλαλαγμῶν, bringing as it were πῦρ ἐπὶ πῦρ. The two nouns of lamentation do not appear in ECL, but a cognate of the second is used of lamenting over the dead at Mark 5:38 (κλαίοντας καὶ ἀλαλάζοντας πολλά). Though πῦρ and its cognate verb occur in some ECL metaphors (cf. on 752D [first comment] and see Bauer, s.v. πῦρ, 2 and πυρόω, 1.b; F. Lang, *TDNT*, s.v. πῦρ, D.II and πυρόω [under πῦρ], C-D), ECL offers no true parallel to Plutarch's fire figure, which is proverbial (see Sieveking's testimonium, p. 538 and De Lacy-Einarson, 594f., n. a) and can be traced as far back as Plato *Lg.* 666A.

τὰς δέ ψυχὰς φλεγομένοις αὐτοῖς (De Lacy-Einarson; ταῖς δέ ψυχαῖς φλεγομέναις αὐτοὶ Sieveking) προσφέρουσιν ὑπεκκαύματα. I prefer the text of De Lacy-Einarson; cf. at Plato *Lg.* 716A τις . . . φλέγεται τὴν ψυχὴν μεθ' ὕβρεως, which also exhibits the accusative of respect. At any rate, Plutarch's φλέγομαι is metaphorical, as in one of its two ECL occurrences (Gos Pet 12:50).

(610D)

Plutarch compares the mourner's grief to an open sore (ῥεῦμα). I find no similar figure in ECL, though ῥέω is used metaphorically in each of its few ECL occurrences (see Bauer, s.v.).

ταῦτα . . . οἶδ' ὅτι φυλάξῃ. The middle of φυλάσσω regularly has this sense ("guard against, avoid") in ECL (see Bauer, s.v., 2).

Ch. 8

τὴν γένεσιν . . . τοῦ τέκνου. γένεσις, very rare in ECL, also means "birth" at Matt 1:18 and Luke 1:14. Plutarch again uses the term in this sense at 611E (διὰ τῶν γενέσεων).

πρὶν ἐκείνην (their daughter) γενέσθαι. For ECL parallels and comments on the construction, see on 749B (πρὶν ἡμᾶς γενέσθαι).

(610E)

Plutarch urges his wife "to regard with pleasure" (ἐν ἡδονῇ τίθεσθαι; my translation is based on LSJ, s.v. τίθημι, B.II.3 and such phrases as τοῦτο . . . τὸ αἰσχρὸν οὐκ ἐν γέλωτι θήσεσθαι [*TG* 17.6], ἐν ἐπαίνῳ . . . μείζονι τίθεσθαι . . . [*Cat. Ma.* 20.3]) the two years they had with their daughter, since they afforded "delight and enjoyment" (χάριν καὶ ἀπόλαυσιν). Again, ἡδονή with (highly) favorable force; cf. on this term at 608D and at 608D-F. It would scarcely have occurred to an ECL writer to couple ἀπόλαυσις with χάρις, which never means "delight" or anything similar in its host of ECL occurrences, except *possibly* at 2 Cor 1:15 (the possibility is slight, though Bauer entertains it, s.v. χάρις, 3; it is ignored by H. Conzelmann, *TDNT*, s.v. χάρις [under χαίρω], D.2.d).

ἡ περὶ τὸ θεῖον εὐφημία καὶ τὸ πρὸς τὴν τύχην ἵλεων καὶ ἀμεμφὲς καλὸν καὶ ἡδὺν ἀποδίδωσι καρπόν (note Plutarch's two references earlier in Ch. 8 to their treatment at the hands of τύχη). ECL parallelism to this matter is more or less confined to its frequent use of καλός, ἀποδίδωμι, and καρπός (the last commonly, as here and throughout classical literature, in a figurative sense; see on καρπὸν ἤθους at 750E), and to the occurrence of Plutarch's καρπός idiom at Heb 12:11 (παιδεία ... καρπὸν ... ἀποδίδωσιν; note the figurative usage) and at Rev 22:2 (ξύλον ζωῆς ... ἀποδιδοῦν τὸν καρπόν; cf. Ezek 47:12). τὸ θεῖον, a common enough expression for deity in Plutarch and other classical writers (see LSJ, s.v. θεῖος, II. 1-2 and on τὸ θεῖον at 758A), appears in ECL only at Acts 17:29, where Paul so designates God while speaking to his Athenian audience in their own terms (cf. *PECL* 1:22). εὐφημία (here "religious silence" or "abstinence from inauspicious utterance") means "good repute" in its one occurrence in ECL (2 Cor 6:8); a cognate, εὔφημος, also appears once, in an uncertain sense at Phil 4:8. ἵλεως is never used with reference to human beings in ECL, and is descriptive of God in at least six of its seven occurrences (for the possible exception of Matt 16:22, see BDF, sec. 128.5; cf. on 749A [last comment]). ἡδύς is virtually (cf. 762D) and ἀμεμφής (here carrying its active sense of "not blaming") actually missing from ECL, and the latter's synonym ἄμεμπτος always has the passive meaning "blameless" in ECL. One has only to examine the vast τύχη entry in LSJ and then note that the use of this word in ECL is limited to three references within the same context (Mart Pol 9:2-10:1) to swearing by ἡ Καίσαρος τύχη, to become quickly aware that the term τύχη and the notions associated with it constitute a monumental element of Greek thought and feeling that is fully extrinsic of the conceptual framework of ECL. A comprehensive treatment of τύχη is beyond the scope of this commentary, but it is notable for present interests that, as in the Plutarchan passage under scrutiny, τύχη is often brought into conjunction with the divine in classical literature and that during the Hellenistic Age τύχη became a common object of cultic veneration, if you will, an idol of pagan despair. It comes as no surprise that early

Christian writers, with their firm belief in a god who was personal, benign, and providential, and in view of the positive terms in which they presented this belief to the world, would exclude from their vocabulary a word denoting a blind, impersonal force popularly regarded as a deity, or that martyrs such as Polycarp would refuse to swear by Caesar's τύχη. (The use of the verb τυγχάνω was another matter, for it was so much a part of the Greek idiom, classical, Hellenistic, and Koine, that one could scarcely speak or write Greek without using it.) Plutarch devotes much attention to τύχη at *cons. ux.* 610D-611B, where the term itself appears no less than seven times (cf. πάθεσι καὶ τύχαις at 609C and 611E). In so doing (cf. his treatises *fort.*, *fort. Rom.*, and *Alex. fort.*), he is very much a child of his age and of his Hellenic past. He is equally a child of this age and past when he seeks consolation, amid the turns of fortune (αἱ ἀπὸ τῆς τύχης τροπαί, 611A), in rhetorical and philosophical arguments (throughout *cons. ux.*) and in the religious conviction of the immortality of the soul (611D-end). On τύχη, see, e.g., LSJ, s.v; W. C. Greene, *Moira* (Cambridge, Mass., 1944) passim (s.v. "Chance" and "*Tyche*" in Index of Names and Subjects); M. P. Nilsson, *Greek Piety* (Oxford, 1948) 84-91; E. R. Dodds, *The Greeks and the Irrational* (Berkeley and Los Angeles, 1951) 42, 58 (n. 80), 242, 259 (n. 37); G. Murray, *Five Stages of Greek Religion* (New York, 1951) 87, 126-31, 141, 201-202; U.v. Wilamowitz-Moellendorff, *Der Glaube der Hellenen* (Tübingen, 1955) 2:294-305; N. Robertson, *OCD*, s.v. "Tyche."

Plutarch recommends that they concentrate on remembering τὰ ἀγαθά (cf. the similar reference to τὰ ἀγαθά at 610F). ECL uses τὰ ἀγαθά in the same general sense: see Bauer, s.v. ἀγαθός, 2.b; cf. on 762B (first comment).

(610E-F)

Plutarch further recommends turning τοῦ βίου πρὸς τὰ φωτεινὰ καὶ λαμπρὰ ... ἐκ τῶν σκοτεινῶν καὶ ταρακτικῶν τὴν διάνοιαν. ECL offers a number of rather striking parallels in the area of verbal association: μηδὲ ἐκεῖνο τὴν διάνοιαν ὑμῶν ταρασσέτω (2 Clem 20:1; cf. on 769E-F); ἐσκοτωμένοι τῇ διανοίᾳ (Eph 4:18); ἐσκοτίσμεθα τὴν διάνοιαν (2 Clem 19:2); ἡ ... ἐσκοτωμένη διάνοια ... ἀναθάλλει εἰς τὸ φῶς (1 Clem 36:2); the φωτεινός-σκοτεινός antithesis at Matt 6:22-23//Luke 11:34, Luke 11:35-36; the φῶςσκοτία/σκότος antithesis at Matt 4:16 (Isa 9:2), 6:23, John 3:19, Acts 26:18 (Isa 42:7, 42:16), Rom 2:19, 2 Cor 6:14, 1 Thes 5:4-5, 1 Pet 2:9, 1 John 1:5-7, 1 Clem 59:2 (cf. Acts 26:18), Barn 14:7 (Isa 42:6-7), 18:1. Light and darkness imagery and metaphor runs throughout Greek and Jewish literature and permeates the Johannine writings: see on 748F (λαμπρῶς), 751F, 762A (φῶς), 766D (ἐκ . . . λαμπρῶν).

(610F)

The procedure just recommended either "extinguishes grief" (ἔσβεσε τὸ λυποῦν) or diminishes it. Cf. the figurative τὸ πνεῦμα μὴ σβέννυτε (1 Thes 5:19) and on 765B (σβεννύναι . . . τὸ πάθος). Plutarch's ἔσβεσε is gnomic, as is the aorist coordinated with it (ἐποίησεν). The gnomic aorist is common in classical Greek but infrequent in ECL (see Goodwin-Gulick, secs. 1293-94; Smyth-Messing, secs. 1931-32; BDF, sec. 333.1; cf. on ἐποίησεν at 759F).

Perfume is a φάρμακον ("medicine") against foul odors. φάρμακον has this sense in ECL only at Ign Eph 20:2, where Ignatius, also speaking metaphorically, calls the eucharistic bread the φάρμακον ἀθανασίας.

Ch. 9

(611A)

Plutarch speaks of the doctrine that "happiness depends on right reasoning that results in a stable disposition" (ἐξ ὀρθῶν ἐπιλογισμῶν εἰς εὐσταθῆ διάθεσιν τελευτώντων ἤρτηται τὸ μακάριον. μακάριος is of course an important concept word in ECL (see Bauer, s.v. and F. Hauck, *TDNT*, s.v., D), and εὐσταθής and cognates have the same basic sense as Plutarch's adjective in their few ECL occurrences. But ECL lacks ἐπιλογισμός (λογισμός is used a few times) and διάθεσις, and always uses τελευτάω in the sense "die, come to an end." ὀρθός is infrequent in ECL, and only at Epil Mosq 1 does it have its present meaning.

τοῖς ἔξωθεν κυβερνᾶσθαι πράγμασι. κυβερνάω, here used figuratively, is absent from ECL; but its cognates κυβέρνησις and κυβερνήτης make a figurative appearance apiece (1 Cor 12:28, Mart Pol 19:2). Cf. on 754C-D, 758D.

Plutarch claims that there is consolation in the popular judgment about εὐδαιμονία ("happiness;" the term is synonymous with τὸ μακάριον of the previous sentence). εὐδαιμονία, represented in

ECL by a single occurrence of a cognate (Diogn 10:5), is a significant term in Greek ethical thought, whether on a popular or a philosophical level: see, e.g., the appropriate entries in LSJ; W. C. Greene, *Moira*, 84-85, 324-27, 335-36; U.v. Wilamowitz-Moellendorff, *Der Glaube der Hellenen*, 2:275 and n. 1; Aristotle *EN* 1095.a.18ff. (... περὶ δὲ τῆς εὐδαιμονίας, τί ἐστιν, ἀμφισβητοῦσι καὶ οὐχ ὁμοίως οἱ πολλοὶ τοῖς σοφοῖς ἀποδιδόασιν.).

(611B)

Plutarch speaks of the lamentations of visitors, which get at the bereaved ἔθει τινὶ φαύλῳ. Both ἔθος and φαῦλος exhibit a modest frequency within the vocabulary of ECL (see Bauer, s.v. and H. Preisker, *TDNT*, s.v. ἔθος), and the latter can modify such abstracts at πρᾶγμα (Jas 3:16) and ἔργον (1 Clem 28:1). Cf. *PECL* 1:201 (ἔθος) and on the use of φαῦλος at 753F, 769B.

ζηλουμένη διατελεῖς ὑπὸ τούτων (people in general, but especially mourners who come to her with lamentations) ἐπὶ τέκνοις καὶ οἴκῳ καὶ βίῳ. The supplementary participle not in indirect discourse (here ζηλουμένη) is far less common in ECL than in classical Greek (see Goodwin-Gulick, secs. 1580-89 [διατελέω at secs. 1582, 1589]; Smyth-Messing, secs. 2094-2105 [διατελέω at sec. 2097]; BDF, secs. 414-15; cf. on 760C [last comment]), and διατελέω in its one ECL occurrence *perhaps* takes a supplementary adjective rather than participle (see Bauer, s.v. and BDF, sec. 414.1). Too, ζηλόω in my judgment lacks its present sense in ECL. The rest of Plutarch's statement would be at home in ECL by any criterion, whether it be that of syntax, semantics, or vocabulary. On ὑπό plus the genitive of agent in classical and early Christian writers, see Goodwin-Gulick, secs. 1208, 1236; Smyth-Messing, secs. 1491-94, 1678, 1698.1, 1755; BDF, secs. 232.2, 210.2.

δεινόν ἐστιν ἑτέρους ... ἂν ἑλέσθαι τὴν σὴν τύχην. Plutarch's aorist infinitive with ἄν represents either an aorist optative with ἄν and is potential in character, or else an aorist indicative with ἄν and is contrary-to-fact in character. Cf. Goodwin-Gulick, secs. 1308, 1509; Smyth-Messing, secs. 1845-48, 2023, 2270. This construction occurs certainly in ECL only at Diogn 1 (ἂν ... γενέσθαι), and is a remote possibility at 2 Cor 10:9. See Bauer, s.v. ἄν, 6; BDF, secs. 396 (at end), 453.3.

δεινόν ἐστιν ... μηδὲ ἀπ' αὐτοῦ τοῦ δάκνοντος αἰσθάνεσθαι πηλίκας ἔχει τὰ σῳζόμενα χάριτας ἡμῖν. Plutarch uses τὸ δάκνον figuratively to designate the pain of bereavement; cf. Paul's metaphorical use of this verb at Gal 5:15. But χάρις does not mean "delight" in ECL (cf. on 610E [first comment]); and, so it seems to me, ECL does not employ σῴζω in so weak a sense as it has here.

(611B-C)

Plutarch deprecates the behavior of οἱ ἀνελεύθεροι καὶ φιλάργυροι. ἀνελεύθερος and cognates are missing from ECL, but φιλαργυρία is a more significant vice in ECL than its absence from *TDNT* would indicate (see Bauer and on 762B-C).

(611C)

Our daughter has gone εἰς τὸ ἄλυπον, where there is now nothing λυπηρόν to her. Although ECL may describe the Christian afterlife as being free from grief and pain (e.g., Matt 5:4, Luke 6:21, Rev 7:16-17, 21:4), to my knowledge only in the brief description at 2 Clem 19:4 do we find a verbal parallel to the present passage (ὁ εὐσεβής ... εὐφρανθήσεται εἰς τὸν ἀλύπητον αἰῶνα). In the generation after Plutarch, Justin Martyr lists ἀλυπία as one of the features of blessedness (Dial 45:4) and applies the adjectives ἀλύπητος (Dial 69:7) and ἄλυπος (117:3) to the blessed. Since Plutarch is here thinking "gnostically" in terms of the state of his daughter's ψυχή, which has by death been freed from the corrupting influence of the σῶμα (see Chs. 10-11), a passage in the gnostic Acts Thom provides an interesting parallel (142, p. 249.5ff. [*Acta Apostolorum Apocrypha*, ed. Lipsius and Bonnet]). There, Judas Thomas, identifying himself with his soul just as Plutarch identified his daughter with her soul, speaks as follows of entering his state of Christian blessedness: ἰδοὺ ἀπαλλάττομαι λύπης .... ἰδοὺ γίνομαι ... ἄλυπος ... Plutarch above, as in the next sentence (τὸ λυποῦν) and in the first sentence of Ch. 10 (οὐδὲν ... κακὸν οὐδὲ λυπηρόν), uses his λυπ- words in their broadest sense to refer to pain of every variety, whether physical or emotional; elsewhere in *cons. ux.* the referent of these words is always the grief of bereavement.

(611D)

πῶς ἂν ... λέγοιτο; πῶς is of course regularly followed by the indicative or the subjunctive in ECL. Bauer in fact lists (s.v., 1.d) only one syntactical parallel to the present optative usage: πῶς ... ἂν δυναίμην ...; (Acts 8:31).

Ch. 10

I know, Plutarch observes, that ὁ πάτριος λόγος καὶ τὰ μυστικὰ σύμβολα τῶν περὶ τὸν Διόνυσον ὀργιασμῶν prevent you from believing (πιστεύειν) the (Epicurean [see Intro. III.B and De Lacy-Einarson, 600-601, nn. d-e]) doctrine that there is no afterlife. Plutarch then goes on to apply their shared belief in the immortality of the ψυχή to their daughter's circumstances. Along with Hadas (99), De Lacy-Einarson, and Warner (184), I take λόγος in the non-philosophical sense of "teaching, doctrine," and would place it semantically among those seventeen ECL uses of the term grouped by Bauer, s.v., 1.a.β under the translation complex "proclamation, instruction, teaching, message." ὁ πάτριος λόγος is basically synonymous with ἡ πάτριος καὶ παλαιὰ πίστις, which Plutarch extols at *amat.* 756A-B, and bears comparison with Gal 1:14 (ζηλωτὴς . . . τῶν πατρικῶν μου παραδόσεων), Acts 22:3 (τοῦ πατρῴου νόμου), 24:14 (τῷ πατρῴῳ θεῷ), 28:17 (τοῖς ἔθεσι τοῖς πατρῴοις); cf. *PECL* 1:192 (549E), 318 (Frag. 157) and on 756A-B. μυστικός, σύμβολον, and ὀργιασμός do not appear in ECL. But Plutarch's πιστεύειν is fully consistent with ECL usage; and the concept of σύμβολον, if not the word itself, occurs throughout Barn (see *PECL* 1:154 [417B] and, e.g., 7-8). Moreover, μυστήριον is a significant, though not frequent, concept word in ECL, where it is used in reference to the secret things of God that are imparted to men through revelation (see Bauer, s.v., and G. Bornkamm, *TDNT*, s.v., C, D.1); it is, however, not until the Apologists that the term is applied to pagan mystery cults (see Bornkamm, ibid., D.2.a). On the rites of Dionysus, a god of souls and of immortality, and on their relation to ECL, one may begin with J. Harrison, *Prolegomena to the Study of Greek Religion* (Cambridge, 1922) 556-64, 567-71; A. D. Nock, "Hellenistic Mysteries and Christian Sacraments," *Mnemosyne* 5 (1952) 177-213 (passim)=Nock, *Early Gentile Christianity and its Hellenistic Background* (New York, 1964) 109-145 (passim)= Z. Stewart (ed.), A. D. Nock: *Essays on Religion and the Ancient World* (Cambridge, Mass., 1972) 2:791-820 (passim); M. P. Nilsson, *The Dionysiac Mysteries of the Hellenistic and Roman Age* (Lund, 1957); Nilsson, *GGR*, 2:99f., 358-67; Griffiths, 429-36; Nilsson *et alii*, *OCD* (1970), s.v. "Dionysus;" G. Bornkamm, *TDNT*, s.v. μυστήριον, A.1; *PECL* 1:59-60 (Ch. 35).

Plutarch mentions, in reference to the rites of Dionysus, τὰ μυστικὰ σύμβολα . . ., ἃ σύνισμεν ἀλλήλοις οἱ κοινωνοῦντες. This is about as close as Plutarch is going to come to the ECL concept of κοινωνία; cf. Rom 15:27 (the gentile Christians "shared in" [ἐκοινώνησαν] the spiritual blessings of the saints at Jerusalem) and on 757C-D, 758D-759D (at end), 763F, 769F, 770C. Though it was of another sort, Ananias also shared secret knowledge with his wife (συνειδυίης καὶ τῆς γυναικός, Acts 5:2). That Plutarch was both priest of Apollo at Delphi and an initiate into the mysteries of Dionysus would have surprised or offended no one in the age of religious syncretism in which he lived (cf., e.g., *Is. et Os.* 364D-E and Griffiths' comments on this passage).

(611D-E)

As we have learned from the rites of Dionysus, Plutarch stresses, the ψυχή is "immortal" (ἄφθαρτος). ECL often uses ἀφθαρσία of the "immortality" that believers are heir to (see Bauer, s.v.); and Paul, when revealing to the Corinthians the μυστήριον of the day of resurrection (1 Cor 15:50-54), informs them that οἱ νεκροὶ ἐγερθήσονται ἄφθαρτοι (cf. the occurrences of ἄφθαρτος at 1 Cor 9:25, 1 Pet 1:4, 1:23, 3:4, 2 Clem 7:3, Barn 16:9). Cf. *PECL* 1:51 (358E, 359C), 70 (373A), 95 (388F), 99 (392E), 161 (420E). Plutarch here traces his belief in the immortality of the soul to the Dionysiac mysteries; it also inheres in his Platonic philosophy (see J. Harrison, *Prolegomena to the Study of Greek Religion*, 570f., and on 758D-759D, 764D-E, 764E-765D).

(611E)

The experience of the soul when it enters a human body, Plutarch asserts, is like that of a bird being raised in captivity. Cf. the statement at Mart Pol 16:1 that a dove emerged from the dagger wound which brought death to Polycarp; note the textual comment on this statement by Bauer, s.v. περιστερά, who observes that the "concept of the dove as representing the soul underlies this." Cf. also the gospel accounts that the Spirit descended on Jesus as a dove (Matt 3:16//Mark 1:10//Luke 3:21-22, John 1:32-34). These accounts, however, are completely without the pejorative and dualistic connotations of Plutarch's comparison. In a context quite different from Plutarch's, Plato likens the soul to a bird at *Phdr.* 249D.

ἂν (=ECL ἐάν; see on the conditional sentence beginning with ἄν at 608C) . . . πολὺν ἐντραφῇ (the soul) τῷ σώματι χρόνον . . ., . . . πάλιν ἐνδύεται. Present-general conditions such as this (subjunctive in the protasis, present indicative in the apodosis) characterize both classical and ECL syntax: cf. on 608C and see Goodwin-Gulick, secs. 1398.I, 1403; Smyth-Messing, secs. 2295.1, 2297 (under Present), 2335-39; Bauer, s.v. ἐάν, I. 1; BDF, secs. 371, 373. Plutarch follows classical practice in using the accusative case to express duration of time (πολὺν . . . χρόνον; see Goodwin-Gulick, sec. 1061; Smyth-Messing, secs. 1447, 1582-87); in ECL, the dative competes with the accusative in this construction (see BDF, secs. 161.2, 201). Cf. on 749D (οὐκ ὀλίγον χρόνον).

μὴ . . . οἴου λοιδορεῖσθαι καὶ κακῶς ἀκούειν τὸ γῆρας διὰ . . . τὴν ἀσθένειαν τοῦ σώματος. Cf. Acts 23:4-5, where λοιδορεῖς and ἐρεῖς κακῶς function synonymously, and on 750A (ἔλεγε κακῶς). ECL can speak in terms of either ἀσθένεια τῆς σαρκός (Gal 4:13, Matt 26:41//Mark 14:38//Pol Phil 7:2, Herm Vis 3:9:3, Sim 9:1:2) or ἀσθένεια τοῦ σώματος (2 Cor 10:10, 1 Clem 6:2, Herm Vis 3:11:4); cf. on 767E (first comment).

(611E-F)

τὴν ψυχὴν . . . κάμπτει (old age). Cf. the slightly similar metaphor at 1 Clem 57:2 (κάμψαντες τὰ γόνατα τῆς καρδίας).

(611F)

Though the text is very poor, it appears that Plutarch introduces a simile in which he compares the soul to πῦρ, which is used in ECL similes at Acts 2:3, 1 Cor 3:15, Rev 1:14, 2:18. Cf. on 752D (first comment), 753A.

Our daughter's soul left her body when she was very young πρὶν ἔρωτα πολὺν ἐγγενέσθαι τῶν αὐτόθι πραγμάτων καὶ μαλαχθῆναι πρὸς τὸ σῶμα. Cf. Herm Vis 3:11:3 (just as old people with no hope of becoming young again merely await death, so you μαλακισθέντες ἀπὸ τῶν βιωτικῶν πραγμάτων have given yourselves over to despair) and, perhaps, at Ign Rom 7:2 ὁ ἐμὸς ἔρως ἐσταύρωται, which Bauer, s.v. ἔρως, renders as "my passionate love (for the world) has been crucified" (Bauer's rendering is in harmony with the exegesis of A. von Harnack, "Der 'Eros' in der alten christlichen Literatur," *Sitzungsberichte der preussischen Akademie der Wissen-*

schaften zu Berlin [1918] 84 and A. Nygren, *Agape and Eros* [Philadelphia, 1953] 390). Cf. Plato *Phd.* 80E-84B, where Socrates discusses the corrupting influence of σῶμα on ψυχή.

Ch. 11

(612A)

τοῖς δὲ πατρίοις καὶ παλαιοῖς ἔθεσι καὶ νόμοις ἐμφαίνεται μᾶλλον ἡ περὶ τούτων (the fact that the souls of those who die young depart this world uncorrupted by it) ἀλήθεια. Striking verbal-conceptual parallels exist at Acts 22:3 (τοῦ πατρῴου νόμου), 28:17 (τοῖς ἔθεσι τοῖς πατρῴοις), 24:14 (λατρεύω τῷ πατρῴῳ θεῷ, πιστεύων πᾶσι τοῖς κατὰ τὸν νόμον ...), Gal 1:14 (ζηλωτὴς ... τῶν πατρικῶν μου παραδόσεων), 1 John 2:7 (γράφω ὑμῖν ... ἐντολὴν παλαιὰν ἣν εἴχετε ἀπ' ἀρχῆς· ἡ ἐντολὴ ἡ παλαιά ἐστιν ὁ λόγος ὃν ἠκούσατε.), 2 Cor 3:14 (τῆς παλαιᾶς διαθήκης); cf. Herm Sim 9:2:2, 9:12:1, *PECL* 1:151 (on κατὰ νόμον πατέρων at 416C), 192 (549E) and on 611D (ὁ πάτριος λόγος), 756A-B (ἡ πάτριος καὶ παλαιὰ πίστις), 756B. Also, there are generally similar uses of ἀλήθεια as "truth" throughout ECL (cf. on 762A [last comment] and see Bauer, s.v., 2.b; R. Bultmann, *TDNT*, s.v., D). A glance through Bauer, s.v. νόμος, however, indicates that νόμος in the plural (as at Heb 8:10, 10:16, Herm Sim 1:3, Diogn 5:10) is relatively infrequent in ECL.

οὐ γὰρ μέτεστι γῆς οὐδὲν οὐδὲ τῶν περὶ γῆν αὐτοῖς (those who die in infancy and whose souls, therefore, go on to the other world untainted by this one). Cf. Col 1:16 (τὰ πάντα ἐν τοῖς οὐρανοῖς καὶ ἐπὶ τῆς γῆς), 3:2 (τὰ ἄνω φρονεῖτε, μὴ τὰ ἐπὶ τῆς γῆς), 2 Pet 3:10 (οἱ οὐρανοὶ ... καὶ γῆ καὶ τὰ ἐν αὐτῇ), and the many other ECL passages where γῆ is contrasted with heaven (see Bauer, s.v. γῆ [5], ἐπίγειος and H. Sasse, *TDNT*, s.v. γῆ [3], ἐπίγειος [under γῆ]). Sasse, s.v. γῆ, 3, contends that "γῆ and οὐρανός ... are almost understood dualistically as two different worlds, particularly in the Pauline Epistles and John." Cf. R. Bultmann, *TNT*, secs. 15 (Gnostic Motifs), 26 (The Term "World" [Cosmos]) and *PECL* 1:142 (οἴχεται), 143-44 (413C), 173 (433F).

When infants die, it is our ancestral custom not to linger περὶ ταφὰς καὶ μνήματα καὶ προθέσεις νεκρῶν. ταφή/τάφος and μνῆμα/μνημεῖον are common enough in ECL, and in their present sense. It is the reference to laying out their bodies for mourning that gives this prepositional phrase its peculiarly Greek tone, for the present sense of πρόθεσις/προτίθημι is exclusively classical (see LSJ, s.v. πρόθεσις [I.1], προτίθημι [II.1]) and not recognized by either Bauer or Lampe.

Our laws forbid us to mourn for infants on the grounds that their souls have gone to a better and more godly μοῖρα and country. (This is apparently the general sense of a sentence marred by a serious lacuna.) μοῖρα, so significant and prominent a concept term among classical authors that W. C. Greene could use it as the basic title of his book on fate in Greek thought (Cambridge, Mass., 1944), appears in ECL only at Apoc Pet, fr. 2. Its virtual absence from ECL is attributable *mutatis mutandis* to the same factors that were adduced on 610E to account for the similar state of the kindred term τύχη; cf. *PECL* 1:223 (on μοίρα τινὶ θεῶν at 564C). Wyttenbach's *Lexicon Plutarcheum* 2 (Oxford, 1830), s.v. μοῖρα would lead us to conclude that μοῖρα appears with moderate frequency throughout the Plutarchan corpus.

(612A-B)

τὰ μὲν ἐκτὸς οὕτως ὡς οἱ νόμοι προστάσσουσιν ἔχωμεν, τὰ δὲ ἐντὸς ἔτι μᾶλλον ἀμίαντα καὶ καθαρὰ καὶ σώφρονα. Cf. Matt 23:26 (τὸ ἐντὸς τοῦ ποτηρίου . . . τὸ ἐκτὸς αὐτοῦ), Herm Man 2:7 (keep this commandment ἵνα . . . εὑρεθῇ . . . ἡ καρδία καθαρὰ καὶ ἀμίαντος), Jas 1:27 (θρησκεία καθαρὰ καὶ ἀμίαντος), Herm Sim 5:7:1 (keep this σάρξ of yours καθαρὰ καὶ ἀμίαντος); cf. on 756A (καθαρός). On σωφροσύνη in classical authors and ECL, see on 752A (φιλοσοφεῖν . . . καὶ σωφρονεῖν). Hortatory subjunctives such as ἔχωμεν are common in both classical Greek and ECL: cf. on εὐχώμεθα at 749A and see Goodwin-Gulick, sec. 1343; Smyth-Messing, secs. 1797-99; BDF, sec. 364.

AMATORIUS (MORALIA 748E - 771E)

BY

HUBERT MARTIN, JR.
University of Kentucky
Lexington, Kentucky

I. GENERAL INFORMATION*

This dialogue is no. 107 in the antique list of Plutarch's works known as the Lamprias Catalogue,[1] and its Plutarchan authorship has never been effectively challenged.[2] Its text is preserved in two imperfect MSS, E (*Parisinus* 1672) and B (*Parisinus* 1675), and is marred throughout by cruces and lacunae (the longest and, for interpretive purposes, most troublesome lacuna is at the end of Ch. 20 [766D]).[3] My introductory essay and commentary are based on the most recent edition of the *Amatorius*, that by W. C. Helmbold in the Loeb Classical Library (*Plutarch's Moralia*, vol. 9 [1961]), but with frequent consultation of C. Hubert's Teubner edition (*Plutarchi Moralia*, vol. 4 [1938]) and the edition, with French translation, by R. Flacelière (*Plutarque: Dialogue sur l'amour* [Paris, 1953]). Flacelière's edition is particularly valuable for its

* For assistance in checking references, I am indebted to Ricky Ezell; for typing, to Sharon S. Gill.

[1] On the Lamprias Catalogue, compiled perhaps during the third or fourth century, see M. Treu, *Der sogenannte Lampriaskatalog der Plutarch-Schriften* (Progr. Waldenburg, 1873); Ziegler, sec. II.1; R. H. Barrow, *Plutarch and His Times* (Bloomington and London, 1967) 193-94; F. H. Sandbach, *Plutarchi Moralia*, BT (1967) 7:xii-xiii, 1-10; Sandbach, *Plutarch's Moralia*, LCL (1969) 15:3-29.

[2] *Pace* E. Graf, *Commentationes Philologae für O. Ribbeck* (Leipzig, 1887) 68-70; R. Hirzel, *Der Dialog* (Leipzig, 1895) 2:234-36; C. Cichorius, *Römische Studien* (Leipzig, 1922) 406-11. On Plutarch as the author, see C. Hubert, *De Plutarchi Amatorio* (Diss. Berlin, 1903); Ziegler, sec. III.4.s (cols. 159-60); Sandbach, "Rhythm and Authenticity in Plutarch's *Moralia*," *ClQ* 33 (1939) 197-98; Flacelière, *Plutarque: Dialogue sur l'amour*, 11 (n. 2), 28ff. I do not, however, endorse Hubert's thesis that Plutarch left *amat.* unfinished.

[3] On the text of *amat.*, see Flacelière, 34-38; H. Cherniss, *Plutarch's Moralia*, LCL (1957) 12:26-29; Helmbold, 304-5. Though posed by Flacelière, 36, n. 1, the question of whether the frr. of the περὶ Ἔρωτος (Sandbach, BT *Mor.* 7 and LCL *Mor.* 15, nos. 134-38) derive from *amat.* and originally helped fill the lacuna at 766D has to my knowledge never been adequately investigated.

Introduction and Hubert's for the *testimonia* listed on each page.

A reference in Ch. 25 (771C) to the demise of the Flavian dynasty places the composition of the *Amatorius* sometime after the death of Domitian, the last of the Flavians, in A.D. 96. A more precise composition date cannot be assigned the dialogue with any certainty.[4] Its dramatic date is soon after Plutarch's marriage (Ch. 2:749B), whenever that was.

The dialogue proper is narrated by Plutarch's son Autobulus to one Flavian and a group of silent and anonymous auditors (Ch. 1:748E-F), and Plutarch himself is the chief speaker. Plutarch also appears as a speaker in *de E*, *num. vind.*, *qu. conv.*, *non posse*, and *adv. Col.* (cf. *sanit. praec.* Ch. 2-3:122F-123B and Ch. 5:124C). Of Plutarch's dialogues, *cohib. ira*, *soll. an.*, *brut. an.*, and *adv. Stoic.* have no narrator; the rest are in some fashion narrated: *sanit. praec.*, *sept. sap. conv.*, *de E*, *Pyth. or.*, *def. or.*, *num. vind.*, *gen. Soc.*, *qu. conv.*, *amat.*, *fac. lun.*, *non posse*, and *adv. Col.*[5] Despite the roles played by Plutarch and Autobulus in the *Amatorius* and the personal details about Plutarch's marriage given by Autobulus (Ch. 2:749B), the reader should bear in mind that the work is a dramatic essay, not a historical document. To say this is not to deny that its setting and circumstances may include factual elements and that it reflects the conversation and behavior of Plutarch and his circle; it is merely to insist that there is to the *Amatorius* a basically fictional quality, that there are no means for accurately segregating its fact from its fiction, and that we have no grounds for assuming that either the prefatory conversation between Flavian and Autobulus or the dialogue proper occurred, if at all, in anything like their present form.[6]

The Latin title by which this dialogue is customarily cited is an adjective rendering the Greek adjective Ἐρωτικός, the title assigned

[4] On the composition date, see Ziegler, sec. II.3 (cols. 78-79); Flacelière, 10-12; C. P. Jones, "Towards a Chronology of Plutarch's Works," *JRS* 56 (1966) 66, 72.

[5] For a brief statement as to how Plutarch's narrated dialogues begin, see my article "Plutarch's *De facie*: the Recapitulations and the Lost Beginning," *GRBS* 15 (1974) 85-88.

[6] Cf. Ziegler, sec. II.3 (cols. 78-79); Flacelière, 12-13, 14-15, 27-31; D. A. Russell, "On Reading Plutarch's Moralia," *G & R* 15 (1968) 135-37, 140-46; F. Fuhrmann, *Plutarque: Oeuvres morales*, Budé ed. (1972) 9.1:vii-xx; D. A. Russell, *Plutarch* (New York, 1973) 5, 35. My remarks about the fictional quality of *amat.* could be applied, *mutatis mutandis*, to all of Plutarch's dialogues.

the work in the MSS and the Lamprias Catalogue. The implied noun is probably λόγος;[7] and, as the following summary will show, an appropriate English translation of the Greek title would be *The Conversation about Eros*.[8]

II. Summary of the Amatorius

1. *Prologue* (Ch. 1:748E-Ch. 3:750A)

The *Amatorius* opens with a prefatory conversation between Autobulus, Plutarch's son and the narrator of the dialogue proper, and Flavian. Prior to this conversation, Autobulus has agreed to narrate a discussion about Eros, which took place before his birth and of which he learned from his father (Ch. 1:748E-F, Ch. 2:749 B). He now explains the circumstances of the discussion. Plutarch had rescued his bride, Autobulus' mother, from a squabble involving in-laws and had brought her to Thespiae in Boeotia that they might sacrifice to the god Eros, in whose honor the Thespians were celebrating a festival (Ch. 1:748F, Ch. 2:749B). The turmoil of the festival drives Plutarch and his company to a near-by sanctuary of the Muses (Ch. 2:749C), where they are sought out by two Thespians, Anthemion and Pisias, the former a kinsman, the latter a lover (ἐραστής), of a local youth named Bacchon, whom a wealthy widow, Ismenodora, is determined to marry (Ch. 2:749 C-E). Anthemion, who favors the marriage, and Pisias, who opposes it, ask Plutarch and his friends to act as arbitrators and decide the fate of the youth (Ch. 2:749F-Ch. 3:750A); and each gains a supporter among Plutarch's circle, Protogenes siding with Pisias and Daphnaeus with Anthemion (Ch. 3:750A).

2. *The Debate* (Ch. 3:750A-Ch. 9:754E)

First Part

Protogenes' abuse of Ismenodora prompts Daphnaeus to accuse him of waging war against Eros (Ch. 3:750A-B), and Protogenes responds with a defense of pederastic love as the only true love (Ch. 4:750A-751B). Daphnaeus then delivers an apology for mar-

[7] Note τοὺς περὶ Ἔρωτος λόγους (Ch. 1:748E) and τὸν περὶ Ἔρωτος ... λόγον (Ch. 26:771D). Cf. τῶν ἐρωτικῶν λόγων in Plato *Smp*. 172B.2.

[8] On the speakers, see Flacelière, 13-19.

ried love (Ch. 5:751B-752B), and receives support from Plutarch (Ch. 6:752B-D).

Second Part

Pisias recalls the debate to the question of whether Bacchon should be allowed to marry Ismenodora (Ch. 6:752D-E); and he and Protogenes argue the case against the marriage (Ch. 7:752E-Ch. 8:753B), contending that Ismenodora is too wealthy and too old for Bacchon and is behaving indecently by displaying her love. Plutarch himself comes forward as the advocate for the marriage and attacks each of these three arguments (Ch. 9:753B-754E).

3. *The Interruption* (Ch. 10:754E-Ch. 13:756A)

News arrives that Ismenodora has kidnapped Bacchon and is making preparations for a wedding (Ch. 10:754E-755B). Pisias and Protogenes rush off for Thespiae (Ch. 11:755B-C), and Anthemion is soon summoned by Ismenodora (Ch. 13:756A).

4. *Plutarch's Assertion of Eros' Divinity* (Ch. 13:756 A-Ch. 18:763F)

The arbitrants removed, Plutarch replies to a request just lodged by Pemptides (Ch. 12:756A): "I should like to hear from you on what those who first declared Eros a god (θεός) based their declaration." Plutarch's immediate reaction (Ch. 13:756B) is to appeal to "our ancient and ancestral faith (πίστις)," which he regards as the common foundation of piety and according to which Eros is a primal deity (756B-F), and to brand as atheism attempts to rationalize the gods into emotions, faculties, and virtues (757 B-C). Eros is then defined as the god who superintends the erotic impulse toward friendship, fellowship, and marriage (Ch. 14:757 C-E, Ch. 16:759A-D) and who guides fair youths toward virtue and lovers in their devotion to such youths and to virtuous women (Ch. 15:757F-758C, Ch. 16:759A-D). At Ch. 16:759D-E the assertion of Eros' godhead shifts to a eulogy of the god for his power and benevolence, the former attribute being demonstrated chiefly by the fact that he is stronger than either Aphrodite or Ares (Ch. 16:759E-Ch. 17:762B) and the latter by a catalogue of the virtues he bestows on lovers (Ch. 17:762B-Ch. 18:762E). There is a subtle return to the assertion of godhead at Ch. 18:762E-763A, and Plutarch rests his case with an appeal to the "possessed" behavior of lovers (762E-763B), and to the agreement among poets, lawgivers, and philosophers that Eros is a god (763B-F).

5. *Plutarch on Egyptian and Platonic Doctrines of Eros* (Ch. 19: 764A-Ch. 20:766B; cf. Ch. 17:762A)

Plutarch delivers this excursus at the insistence of Soclarus (Ch. 19:764A-B). Its Egyptian section involves a comparison of Eros and the sun, alike in some respects but different in others (Ch. 19:764B-E). In the Platonic section, Plutarch explains the ultimate function of Eros: to educate the soul of the lover to perceive and appreciate that metaphysical beauty of which the beauty of youths and women is only a reflection (Ch. 19:764E-Ch. 20:766B).

6. *Plutarch on Eros as Avenger* (Ch. 20:766C-D)

Plutarch eschews further metaphysical inquiry to begin depicting Eros as the avenger of abused lovers, only to be cut short by the great lacuna at 766D.

7. *Plutarch's Defense of Married Love* (Ch. 21:766D-Ch. 25:771C)

When the MSS resume, the company has left the sanctuary of the Muses and is continuing the conversation as it returns to Thespiae (see Ch. 26:771D). Plutarch is well into his final discourse, probably begun in response to Zeuxippus' suggestion, with implied calumniation of married love, that Eros is a soul-corrupting passion (Ch. 21:767C-D). Yet only Plutarch's statement at Ch. 21: 767 E-Ch. 22:768D as to the virtuous behavior Eros inspires, especially in married women, seems aimed explicitly at Zeuxippus' suggestion, which Plutarch apparently used as a springboard for a full-scale apology on behalf of married love. His conclusion that conjugal φιλία is Eros' finest creation (Ch. 24:769F-Ch. 25:771C) derives from the preceding vindications of conjugal sex (Ch. 23:768D-769B) and of the moral and emotional capacities of women (Ch. 21:766D-767B, Ch. 23:769B-E).

8. *Epilogue* (Ch. 26:771D-E)

News arrives from Thespiae that the wedding of Bacchon and Ismenodora is underway and that Pisias himself, formerly Bacchon's lover and an ardent champion of the pederastic Eros (Ch.

2:749E-F, Ch. 6:752B-Ch. 7:752E), is now ready to lead the wedding procession. The dialogue ends with Plutarch's exhortation that the company go have a laugh at Pisias and pay homage to Eros.

III. The Interpretations of Eros

The formal subject of the *Amatorius* is Eros, as is clear both from its substance and from explicit statements at the beginning (Ch. 1:748E) and the end (Ch. 26:771D). Three different interpretations of this subject are presented: in the debate, those of Protogenes, the advocate of the pederastic Eros, and of Daphnaeus, the advocate of the heterosexual (especially conjugal) Eros and, in the subsequent chapters, that of Plutarch, which amalgamates both Erotes into one. Neither Daphnaeus nor Plutarch make an explicit distinction between heterosexual and conjugal love, though Plutarch seems to have in mind chiefly the latter when speaking of the heterosexual Eros and Daphnaeus to assume that heterosexual love naturally leads to marriage.

For Protogenes (Ch. 4), only the pederastic Eros is true and legitimate (750C, 750F-751A). It does not express itself in the form of sexual acts (750B-C, 751A-B), and is inspired by a youth capable of ἀρετή (750D-E, 751A). Its consummation is φιλία between the lover and the youth and, ultimately, the quickening of the youth's native ἀρετή by means of this φιλία (750D-E, 751A). The passion men feel for women is not Eros, merely ἐπιθυμία (750C-D), whose sole fulfillment is the ἡδονή occasioned by acts of lust and unions devoid of φιλία and the possibility of ἀρετή (750B-E, 751A-B). The presumptions are that sexual acts and desires subvert φιλία and that women lack the capacity for either φιλία or ἀρετή.

Daphnaeus previously asserted that there was no holier union than that between man and wife (Ch. 4:750C). Though he now (Ch. 5) makes concessions to Protogenes at 751C, 751E-F, and 752A-B, his convictions remain obvious: homosexual intercourse is loathsome and inherent in pederasty (751D-E, 752A); only the heterosexual-conjugal Eros is natural and legitimate (751C-752A); and Eros is totally dependent on Aphrodite, the deity of sexual union (752A-B). For Protogenes' formulation that (pederastic) Eros finds fulfillment in virtue inspired by friendship (εἰς ἀρετὴν διὰ φιλίας τελευτᾷ, Ch. 4:750D), Daphnaeus substitutes his own, that (heterosexual) Eros results in friendship inspired by sexual intercourse (εἰς φιλίαν διὰ χάριτος ἐξικνεῖσθαι, 751D).[9] He thereby skirts the question whether women have a capacity for ἀρετή.

Plutarch's treatment of Eros vastly extends the conceptual framework set up by Protogenes and Daphnaeus and discloses fundamental disagreements, as well as areas of agreement, with each. They ignored the questions of whether Eros is a deity or an emotion and whether he (it) has a metaphysical purpose. Plutarch's answer to the former is that he is a god who superintends an emotion (Ch. 13:756A-Ch. 18:763F) and, to the latter, that his ultimate function is to guide men's souls anamnestically to a vision of eternal beauty (Ch. 19:764E-Ch. 20:766B). Protogenes denied women the capacity for both φιλία and ἀρετή. Plutarch, while recognizing the validity of pederastic φιλία and its goal of ἀρετή (Ch. 15:757F-758C, Ch. 16:759A, Ch. 19:764E-Ch. 20:766B, Ch. 24:770C), contends that women are eminently capable not only of φιλία, as did Daphnaeus, but also of ἀρετή (Ch. 16:759A, Ch. 21:766D-Ch. 25:771C). Daphnaeus' conviction that Eros is dependent on Aphrodite and φιλία on sexual union is balanced against Protogenes' that φιλία and sexual union are incompatible. Plutarch believes in one Eros as the god of love, whether pederastic or heterosexual (Ch. 13:756A-Ch. 26:771E passim), and regards Aphrodite as no more than the patron of carnal desire, whose sole fulfillment is ἡδονή (Ch. 13:756E-F, Ch. 16:759E-F, Ch. 19:764D, Ch. 23:769A-B). Though her presence vitiates pederastic φιλία, it vitally assists Eros in the creation of its conjugal variety (Ch. 23:768E-769B). And it is in marriage that both carnal desire and erotic passion can be most fully satisfied (Ch. 24:769F-770A).

IV. Influences on the Amatorius

The *Amatorius* is Plutarch's own comprehensive statement about the nature of Eros and φιλία; and as such its conception, form, and manner are fully his own. It is also a synthesis of contemporary and antecedent Greek thought on these subjects; and in composing it Plutarch has in his customary fashion drawn abundantly from his vast philosophical, literary, and historical knowledge for ideas, quotations, and anecdotes, though derivative ideas

[9] As background to the blatantly sexual meaning here forced on χάρις, see LSJ, s.v. χαρίζω, I.3 and χάρις, III.2.

flow into the dialogue, not directly from their sources, but through Plutarch's own intellectual crucible.[10] The most profound influences on the concepts and vocabulary of the *Amatorius* are those of Plato, especially the *Symposium* and *Phaedrus*, and, as a distant second, of the Stoics. Plato is cited by name at Ch. 1:749A, Ch. 5:751D-E, Ch. 16:758D, Ch. 16:759E, Ch. 17:762A, Ch. 18:763E, Ch. 19:764A, Ch. 21:767D, and Ch. 23:769D and, in addition, has exerted influence at least at Ch. 2:749F-750A, Ch. 3:750A(?), Ch. 6:752C, Ch. 13:756E-F, Ch. 14:757D-E, Ch. 16:758E-759A, Ch. 16:759C-D (?), Ch. 16:760B-C, Ch. 17:760D, Ch. 17:761E-762A, Ch. 17:762B, Ch. 18:762E, Ch. 18:763C, Ch. 18:763F, Ch. 19:764B, Ch. 19:764D-765D, Ch. 20:765F-766B, Ch. 21:766E-F, Ch. 21:767D-E, Ch. 24: 769E (?), Ch. 24:770B, and Ch. 26:771D.[11] Though the only Stoic writers mentioned by name are Chrysippus (Ch. 13:757B) and (probably) Ariston of Chios (Ch. 21:766F), the consultation of Stoic literature is apparent also at Ch. 21:767B and Ch. 24:769F.[12]

Much has been made of a seeming discrepancy between Plutarch and Plato:[13] Plutarch asserts that Eros is a θεός (Ch. 12:756A-Ch. 16:758D); while in the *Symposium* (202D-204A) Socrates depicts Eros as a δαίμων, a being neither θεός nor θνητός but midway between the two. Actually, Plutarch is no more at odds with Plato than Plato is with himself, for in the later *Phaedrus* (from which, as a glance through the passages of Platonic influence listed above will reveal, Plutarch has borrowed even more than from the *Symposium*) Socrates insists that Eros is θεὸς ἤ τι θεῖον (242D-E).[14]

---

[10] On Plutarch's manner with his sources, see my articles "*Amatorius*, 756E-F: Plutarch's Citation of Parmenides and Hesiod," *AJPh* 90 (1969) 184-86, 197-200 and "Plutarch's Citation of Empedocles at *Amatorius* 756D," *GRBS* 10 (1969) 59, 67-70.

[11] In compiling this list of Platonic citations and influences, I have consulted simultaneously Hirzel (above, n. 2), 232-33; Hubert's *testimonia* (passim); Flacelière, 20, 25-26, 127-35 (passim), 139; Helmbold's notes (passim); Helmbold and O'Neil, 59, 61.

[12] On these Stoic influences, see, in addition to Flacelière's and Helmbold's notes to the passages listed, Flacelière, 22-24 and D. Babut, *Plutarque et le Stoïcisme* (Paris, 1969) 108-15.

[13] Esp. by Hirzel (above, n. 2) 233 and n. 4 and Flacelière, 26-27.

[14] R. Hackforth (*Plato's Phaedrus* [Cambridge, 1952] 54-55) mediates the discrepancy between *Smp.* and *Phdr.*

V. The Amatorius and ECL

Exclusive of purely grammatical and stylistic considerations, the *Amatorius* impresses this writer as of special interest to students of ECL for the following reasons.

1. It offers a synthesis of contemporary and antecedent Greek thought about love, sex, friendship, virtue, youths, women, and marriage, a complex of subjects curiously interrelated in the Hellenic mind. As such, it is valuable for pinpointing similarities and differences between Greek and ECL sentiment on these subjects.

2. It illustrates the gulf separating Greek and Plutarchan from ECL thought and vocabulary on the subject of ἔρως. The very notion of Eros as a god clashes sharply with the whole of ECL, in which there is, in fact, no concept of ἔρως at all. The terms ἐραστής and ἐρωτικός are absent from ECL; and the only ECL writer to use ἔρως/ἐράω is Ignatius, but only four times (Rom 2:1, 7:2 [twice], and Pol 4:3) and never conceptually or of a personal relationship.[15]

3. It demonstrates that Plutarch saw no inherent conflict among practical morality, traditional religious belief, and Platonic metaphysics; the intellectual fiber of the *Amatorius* is an amalgam of the three. And especially in the case of the last two, numerous passages offer us the material for discriminating between Greek and early Christian vocabulary and modes of thought.

4. It reveals that the φιλανθρωπία ethical tradition has had no more than incidental effect on the ἔρως-φιλία tradition enshrined in the *Amatorius*. The former, sprung perhaps from Hesiod's and Aeschylus' characterization of Prometheus, is present in low relief throughout Plutarch and reaches its apogee in the fourth century, when Julian the Apostate treats φιλανθρωπία as a (if not the) supreme pagan virtue and as the antidote to Christian ἀγάπη.[16]

[15] Cf. R. Bultmann, *Primitive Christianity* (New York, 1956) 47, 130-31. The lack of a concept or even vocabulary of ἔρως in ECL caused later Platonizing Christians much difficulty. Origen, e.g., arguing that ἔρως and ἀγάπη are synonyms (*Cant.* [surviving only in Rufinus' Latin rendering], proem.), is forced to press into service Ignatius' ὁ ἐμὸς ἔρως (= "my love for the world"; see Bauer, s.v. ἔρως) ἐσταύρωται (Rom 7:2) and to misconstrue it as "meus autem amor [= Christus] crucifixus est" (*PG* 13:70D). On Origen's argument, see A. von Harnack, "Der Eros in der alten christlichen Literatur," *Sitzungsberichte der preussischen Akademie der Wissenschaften zu Berlin* (1918) 81-94; A. Nygren, *Agape and Eros* (Philadelphia, 1953) 387-92 (hereafter cited as Nygren); Lampe, s.v. ἔρως, A.

[16] On Prometheus, see Hesiod *Th.* 507-616, *Op.* 42-105 and Aeschylus *Pr.*, esp. 8-11, 28, 123. On φιλανθρωπία, see Bauer, s.v. φιλανθρωπία, φιλάνθρω-

VI. Some Notes on the Commentary

1. Plutarch's syntax is fundamentally that of classical Attic, and as such it provides a convenient base for the comparison of the syntactical features of classical Greek with those of ECL. Plutarch's vocabulary, however, is enormous (three times that of Demosthenes, for example), and every chapter of a Plutarchan treatise confronts the reader with a fusillade of words that either do not exist or are rare in ECL; at the same time, both Plutarch and ECL along with their respective higher linguistic units, Hellenistic Greek and the Koine, exhibit a free use of compounds, often verbs with a double prepositional prefix such as συνανα-.[17] For the first two chapters of the *Amatorius*, I have commented regularly on quite ordinary items of Plutarchan syntax and vocabulary vis-à-vis ECL, in the belief that a series of comments on such items would contribute to an understanding of the general nature of the linguistic agreements and discrepancies between the two bodies of literature under scrutiny. To have continued this practice, however, would have entailed much redundancy and added inordinately to the bulk of the commentary. Beyond Ch. 2, I have, therefore, usually confined my comments on syntax and vocabulary to items that impressed me as being of more than ordinary significance.

2. Except for some observations about compounds, I have eschewed morphological comments. And I seldom comment on textual conjectures.

3. By "classical Greek," "classical [Greek] authors," and related terms, I refer to that body of non-Jewish, non-Christian literature written in Greek over a period extending roughly from Homer to Plutarch.

πος, φιλανθρώπως; J. Kabiersch, *Untersuchungen zum Begriff der Philanthropia bei dem Kaiser Julian* (Wiesbaden, 1960), together with my review (*AJPh* 83 [1962] 329-30); my article "The Concept of *Philanthropia* in Plutarch's *Lives*," *AJPh* 82 (1961) 164-75; J. H. Oliver, *The Civilizing Power* (*TAPhS* 58, pt. 1 [1968]) 92-93 (on sec. 4), 105-6 (on sec. 44); U. Luck, *TDNT*, s.v. φιλανθρωπία. Forms of the word occur in *amat.* only at Chs. 2:749D, 14:758A, 17:762C, 18:762D, 21:767A.

[17] On Plutarch's syntax and vocabulary, see B. Weissenberger, *Die Sprache Plutarchs von Chaeronea und die pseudo-plutarchischen Schriften*, I. Teil (Straubing, 1895) [hereafter cited as Weissenberger]; A. Hein, *De Optativi apud Plutarchum Usu* (Trebnitz, 1914) [hereafter cited as Hein]; Griffiths, 10-16; Russell, *Plutarch*, 21-22.

4. In my references, I strive to maintain a distinction between "cf." and "see." "Cf." merely calls attention to parallelism, while "see" refers the reader to discussions of particular items (e.g., "On Eros, see Intro. V. 2.") and to documentary proof or illustration.

5. The cross-references to my own commentary are generally cumulative backwards; e.g., at 757E I cite my earlier comments on φιλία, but not those that will follow. A reference such as "see on 757E" is to the commentary, "see 757E" would be to the Greek text.

6. I had written approximately half of the commentary before I read Owen Barfield's *Poetic Diction* (London, 1952) and became aware that, when discussing figurative language, one must distinguish between a metaphor that is inherent in a word (e.g., καρπός in the sense of "profit") and a metaphor that is the result of conscious effort by an author. Despite some revising, time has not always permitted me to take full account of what I learned from Barfield.

7. F. Rehkopf's revision (Göttingen, 1976) of F. Blass and A. Debrunner's *Grammatik des neutestamentlichen Griechisch* appeared too late for me to make use of it, except on one occasion (in my last comment to 760C).

Ch. 1

(748E)

ὦ Αὐτόβουλε. Note, also in the prefatory conversation (Ch. 1), ὦ Φλαουιανέ (748F) and ὦ ἄριστε Φλαουιανέ (749A) and cf. ὦ Θεόφιλε (Acts 1:1) and κράτιστε Θεόφιλε (Luke 1:3). Autobulus, narrator of the dialogue, is Plutarch's son; Luke's Theophilus and Plutarch's Flavian are otherwise unknown. The roles Plutarch assigns Autobulus and Flavian are dedicatory in spirit; but Luke's dedicatory vocatives, without parallel in the other gospels, have more exact Plutarchan counterparts elsewhere, in numerous works dedicated by Plutarch in his own person as author to someone addressed in the vocative: e.g., *Thes.* 1.1, *Dem.* 1.1, *Dio* 1.1, *aud.* 37B-C, *adul. et am.* 48E, *Is. et Os.* 351C, *de E* 384D, *adv. Col.* 1107E. On the polite ὦ, see Bauer, s.v., 2, and BDF, sec. 146.1.a.

τοὺς περὶ Ἔρωτος λόγους. On this and all future occurrences of ἔρως and its cognates, see Intro. V. 2. λόγοι also means "conversation" or "discussion" at 749A below and at Luke 24:17. On the pl. λόγοι in ECL, see Bauer, s.v. λόγος. 1.δ.

(748E-F)

τῷ πολλάκις ἐπανερέσθαι. The articular infinitive in the dative case occurs in ECL without a preposition only at 2 Cor 2:13: τῷ μὴ εὑρεῖν (for which, however, D E offer ἐν τῷ). Elsewhere in ECL, ἐν always introduces this construction. See BDF, secs. 401, 404.

(748F)

παρὰ ταῖς Μούσαις. The Muses are never mentioned in ECL; the cognate μουσικός occurs once, as a substantive at Rev 18:22. Cf. *PECL* 1:21 (n. 1), 107 (396C).

τὰ Ἐρωτίδεια Θεσπιέων ἀγόντων· ἄγουσι γὰρ ἀγῶνα πενταετηρικόν. ἄγω is rare in ECL in the sense of celebrating or observing a festival; but note the exceptions at Ker Pet 2, p. 14, 28-29 (twice) and Matt 14:6 (v.l.). ἀγών never, as here, bears the meaning "festival" in ECL. Cf. *PECL* 1:243.

Ἔρωτι. See Intro. V.2.

φιλοτίμως πάνυ καὶ λαμπρῶς. On φιλοτιμία, common in Plutarch and many Greek writers, see H. Bolkestein, *Wohltätigkeit und Armenpflege im vorchristlichen Altertum* (Utrecht, 1939) 152-56 and passim (see index, s.v.); A.D. Nock, "Religious Attitudes of the Ancient Greeks," *TAPhS* 85 (1942) 79 = Z. Stewart (ed.), A. D. Nock: *Essays on Religion and the Ancient World* (Cambridge, Mass., 1972) 2:545-46; my article "The Character of Plutarch's Themistocles," *TAPhA* 92 (1961) 327 and n. 4, 331-37; J. H. Oliver, *The Civilizing Power* (*TAPhS* 58, pt. 1 [1968]) 138 (on sec. 214). φιλοτιμία and its cognates are rare in ECL: φιλότιμος and φιλοτίμως are absent, φιλοτιμία (to designate the honor or respect shown idols) occurs once (Diogn 3:5), and φιλοτιμέομαι thrice (Rom 15:20, 2 Cor 5:9, 1 Thes 4:11). The instance of φιλοτιμία, however, bears comparison with Plutarch's φιλοτίμως here, since both are associated with the worship of pagan deities. While the figurative quality of Plutarch's λαμπρῶς has parallels at Luke 16:19 (λαμπρῶς), Rev 18:14 (τὰ λαμπρά), and 1 Clem 35:2 (λαμπρότης), never in ECL is λαμπρότης or its adjectival-adverbial cognate used to describe an act of worship.

οἱ πρὸς τὴν ἀκρόασιν ἥκοντες. ἀκρόασις is missing from ECL, though ἀκροατήριον appears once (Acts 25:23) and ἀκροατής several times (see Bauer, s.v.).

(749A)

τὸν Πλάτωνος Ἰλισσὸν . . . πεφυκυῖαν. The reference, with the reproduction of some of Plato's vocabulary, is to *Phdr.* 229 A-B, 230B-C. A hallmark of Plutarch's literary technique in *amat.*, and throughout *Mor.*, is the continuous use of antecedent Greek literature for quotation, paraphrase, reference, and allusion. This practice bears a general similarity to the use made of OT, and to a much lesser degree of apocryphal and pseudepigraphical Jewish literature, by the writers of NT (cf. *PECL* 1:24 [167F]). Frequently, as here, Plutarch's purpose is chiefly or exclusively stylistic adornment. On Plutarch's quotations, etc., see Intro. IV and n. 10; H. Schläpfer, *Plutarch und die klassischen Dichter* (Zürich, 1950); Ziegler, sec. V; Helmbold and O'Neil; Russell, *Plutarch*, 42-54; *PECL* 1:304. On quotations within NT, see F. H. Woods, *A Dictionary of the Bible*, ed. J. Hastings (1902), s.v. "Quotations"; Bultmann, *Der Stil*, 94-96; F. B. Denio, *A Dictionary of Christ and the Gospels*, ed. J. Hastings (1917), s.v. "Quotations"; A. R. Gordon, *Dictionary of the Apostolic Church*, ed. J. Hastings (1919), s.v. "Quotations"; *PECL* 1:304 f. Cf. *PECL* 1:200 (551D).

ἄφελε τοῦ λόγου. λόγος occasionally bears the meaning "report," "account," or "story" also in ECL (e.g., at Matt 28:15, Mark 1:45//Luke 5:15, John 21:23, Acts 11:22). See Bauer, s.v., 1.β and G. Kittel, *TDNT*, s.v. λέγω, D.1.

Flavian speaks of authors who strive "to appropriate" or "to enlist the help of" (ἐπιγράφεσθαι) certain Platonic images (cf. my first comment to 749A) by introducing rhetorical commonplaces derived from them. Ignatius perhaps uses this verb in a somewhat similar figurative sense at Rom 2:1 (cf. Bauer, s.v. ἐπιγράφω, 2).

τί δὲ δεῖται τοιούτων . . . προοιμίων ἡ διήγησις; This question varies from ECL semantically and terminologically. προοίμιον is absent from ECL; διήγησις appears only once (Luke 1:1); and in ECL δέομαι always means "ask" (see Bauer, s.v.), never, as here and probably below (749A) in σκηνῆς δεῖται, "need" or "want."

οἱ λόγοι. See on 748E.

χορὸν αἰτεῖ . . . σκηνῆς δεῖται, τά τ' ἄλλα δράματος οὐδὲν ἐλλείπει. The theatrical terminology whereby Plutarch compares his dialogue to a play contrasts somewhat with ECL vocabulary. In ECL, δρᾶμα does not occur, χορός never literally designates the chorus of a play (cf. *PECL* 1:167 [426A]), and σκηνή is not used in a theatrical sense. See Bauer, s.v. χορός, σκηνή and W. Michaelis, *TDNT*, s.v. σκηνή, D-E.

μόνον εὐχώμεθα τῇ μητρὶ τῶν Μουσῶν ἵλεω παρεῖναι καὶ συνανασῴζειν τὸν μῦθον. This sentence is an interesting mixture of affinities and contrasts to ECL usage. The adverb μόνον and πάρειμι are extremely common in ECL. The dative of the person and the accusative with infinitive (Plutarch's ἵλεω is accusative; cf., e.g, ἕω, the normal accusative singular of ἕως) appear separately after εὔχομαι in ECL, and in combination, as here, at Acts 26:29 (εὐξαίμην ἂν τῷ θεῷ . . . οὐ μόνον σὲ ἀλλὰ καὶ πάντας . . . γενέσθαι τοιούτους . . .). See Bauer, s.v. εὔχομαι and BDF, secs. 187.4, 392.1.c. The hortatory subjunctive is characteristic of ECL (see, e.g., Gal 5:26 [μὴ γινώμεθα], 1 Clem 48:1 [ἐξάρωμεν, . . . καὶ προσπέσωμεν . . . καὶ κλαύσωμεν . . .]) but is frequently accompanied by a supplementary imperative, as at John 14:31 (ἐγείρεσθε ἄγωμεν ἐντεῦθεν), Matt 27:49 (ἄφες ἴδωμεν)//Mark 15:36 (ἄφετε ἴδωμεν). (The treatment of the hortatory subjunctive in BDF, sec. 364 is misleading; for one thing, it is the imperative rather than the subjunctive that is supplementary, since the subjunctive carries the main thought whether or not the imperative is present.) The mother of the Muses is Μνημοσύνη, and the appeal to her in this capacity is typically and strictly classical (cf. *h. Merc.* 429-30, Hesiod *Th.* 50-54, Plato *Tht.* 191D); μοῦσα is absent from ECL (cf. on 748F), and μνημοσύνη (occurring once, at Gos Pet 12:54) and μνημόσυνον (see Bauer, s.v.) are never personified in ECL. ἵλεως is descriptive of God in the basic sense of "merciful" in its seven ECL occurrences (Matt 16:22, Heb 8:12 [Jer 31:34], 1 Clem 2:3, 48:1, 61:2, Herm Sim 9:23:4, Vis 2:2:8), with the possible exception of that at Matt 16:22 (for which, see Bauer, s.v. ἵλεως and BDF, sec. 128.5); here, though descriptive of deity, it means "propitious" or "favorable." Fr. Büchsel, *TDNT*, s.v. is only useful for ἵλεως outside ECL. Though συνανασῴζω is not attested in ECL, Bauer lists six verbs beginning with the compound prefix συνανα-. μῦθος, as often in classical literature (see LSJ, s.v.), here lacks the pejorative connotation of falsity which it regularly exhibits in ECL (1 Tim 1:4, 4:7, 2 Tim 4:4, Tit 1:14, 2 Pet 1:16, 2 Clem 13:3). See Bauer, s.v. μῦθος and G. Stählin, *TDNT*, s.v. μῦθος, E-F. For μῦθος in *Mor.* in the sense of "myth" or with implications, sometimes emphatic ones, of falsity, see *Is. et Os.* 358E; *def. or.* 420B; *PECL* 1:47 (355B), 51 (358E), 106 (395C), 113 (398D), 135 (409E), 176 (435D), 181-82, 210 (557F), 216 (561B), 257 (580C), 272 (589F), 279-80 (592F), 292 (940F), 319 (Frag. 157).

Ch. 2

(749B)

πρὶν ἡμᾶς γενέσθαι. Cf. πρὶν 'Αβραὰμ γενέσθαι (John 8:58), πρὶν ἡμᾶς γεννηθῆναι (1 Clem 38:3), πρὶν αὐτὸν ἐλθεῖν (Diogn 8:1; "before the Lord came into the world," "before Jesus was born"). πρίν or πρὶν ἤ followed by the accusative and an aorist infinitive describing a past event is characteristic of ECL. In this construction in classical Greek, Attic almost invariably offers πρίν, Ionic either πρίν (e.g., at Herodotus 1.46.1) or πρὶν ἤ (e.g., at Herodotus 2.2.1). See Smyth-Messing, secs. 2453-54, 2460; Bauer, s.v. πρίν, 1, 1.b; BDF, sec. 395.

ἀφίκετο τῷ Ἔρωτι θύσων. On Eros, see Intro. V. 2. In ECL, the dative after θύω occurs only at Acts 14:18, 1 Cor 10:20 (Deut 32:17), 2 Clem 3:1 (τοῖς νεκροῖς θεοῖς οὐ θύομεν); see Bauer, s.v. θύω. In NT, θύω is used only of pagan sacrifices (see J. Behm, *TDNT*, s.v. θύω, A.1.a). On θύω, cf. *PECL* 1:140 (412D), 154 (417B). The future participle expressing purpose after verbs involving motion, a regular construction in classical Greek (see Smyth-Messing, sec. 2065), excepting Acts 8:27 (ἐληλύθει προσκυνήσων εἰς 'Ιερουσαλήμ), 22:5, 24:11, 24:17, appears in ECL only at Matt 27:49 (but note v.l.) and as v.l. at Acts 25:13. See BDF, secs. 65.1.c, 351.1, 390.1, 418.4.

ἑορτήν. Frequent in ECL for a Jewish religious festival. See Bauer, s.v. and cf. *PECL* 1:43 (352E), 154 (417C).

καὶ γὰρ ἦν ἐκείνης ἡ εὐχὴ καὶ ἡ θυσία. "In fact she herself was to make the prayer and the sacrifice" (Helmbold); "parce que c'était elle qui devait faire la prière et le sacrifice" (Flacelière). I prefer "in fact she was responsible for the vow and sacrifice" or, better still, "in fact she was the one who had vowed to make the sacrifice," i.e., she had vowed to sacrifice to Eros if, as he did, he restored her to her husband. εὐχή means either "prayer" or "vow" in both classical Greek (see LSJ, s.v.) and ECL (see Bauer, s.v. and H. Greeven, *TDNT*, s.v. εὔχομαι, A.1-2). By my interpretation, ἡ εὐχὴ καὶ ἡ θυσία is akin to θυσίαι . . . εὐχῶν ("votice offerings"; see Bauer, s.v. εὐχή) at 1 Clem 41:2. On θυσία, common in ECL, see Bauer, s.v.; J. Behm, *TDNT*, s.v. θύω; *PECL* 1:154 (417B). Cf. on θύσων above (749B).

τῶν δὲ φίλων . . . οἱ συνήθεις. φίλος is common in the sense of "friend" also in ECL (see Bauer, s.v. and G. Stählin, *TDNT*, s.v. φίλος [under φιλέω], A.I.1, B.I.1, C.1-4, D.I.1-5; cf. *PECL* 1:86 [on 384E]), but in neither of its two ECL occurrences (Mart Pol 5:1, 7:1) does συνήθης refer to persons.

ἐρῶντα. See Intro. V. 2.

Plutarch's nominal formula in Δαφναῖον τὸν 'Αρχιδάμου, Λυσάνδρας . . . τῆς Σίμωνος, and Σώκλαρον . . . τὸν 'Αριστίωνος is consistent with ECL usage, which, however, frequently includes either υἱός (e.g., 'Ιωάννην τὸν Ζαχαρίου υἱόν, Luke 3:2) or another article in the genitive case (e.g., 'Ιάκωβον τὸν τοῦ Ζεβεδαίου, Matt 4:21). See BDF, sec. 162.1-2.

μάλιστα τῶν μνωμένων αὐτὴν εὐημεροῦντα. The general decline of the superlative in Koine did not affect μάλιστα (see Bauer, s.v. and BDF, sec. 60), though in ECL it is not used, as it is here and often in classical authors (see LSJ, s.v. μάλα, III), with the partitive genitive, itself moribund in Koine (see BDF, sec. 164). εὐημερέω is absent from ECL, and μνάομαι occurs only as v.l. (D) at Luke 1:27.

Πρωτογένης ὁ Ταρσεύς. On this man of Tarsus, see Intro. II. 1-3, III and Flacelière, 15-16. This Protogenes is mentioned at *num. vind.* 563B-C, and probably is to be identified with Protogenes the grammarian of *qu. conv.* 7.1, 8.4, 9.2, 9.12, 9.13. On Tarsus, capital of Cilicia and a seat of Greek learning, see Bauer, s.v. Ταρσός, and the bibliography there cited. Paul is the only Ταρσεύς in ECL (Acts 9:11, 21:39; cf. 22:3).

ξένοι. "Friends of his from abroad" (Helmbold), "guest-friends." ξένος does not bear this meaning in ECL. On the Greek institution of guest-friendship, see W. K. Lacey, *The Family in Classical Greece* (Ithaca, 1968) 30-32, 48-50, 68, 231-32, 263, n. 77 (hereafter cited as Lacey). On Plutarch's friends, see Ziegler, sec. I.8; R. H. Barrow, *Plutarch and his Times* (Bloommington and London, 1967) 21-29; C. P. Jones, *Plutarch and Rome* (Oxford, 1971) 39-64.

(749B-C)

τῶν γνωρίμων τοὺς πλείστους. γνώριμος occurs in ECL only as v.l. at John 18:16. On the superlative with partitive genitive, cf. on μάλιστα above (749B).

(749C)

φιλοσοφοῦντες ἐν ταῖς παλαίστραις καὶ διὰ τῶν θεάτρων. This phrase has a peculiarly Greek ring to it. In ECL, θέατρον occurs merely thrice (Acts 19:29, 31 [the theatre at Ephesus], 1 Cor 4:9 [figuratively]), and φιλοσοφέω and παλαίστρα not at all; φιλοσοφία appears once with pejorative force (Col 2:8), and φιλόσοφος once with pejorative force (Diogn 8:2) and once of the Epicureans and Stoics (Acts 17:18). See Bauer, s.v. φιλοσοφία, φιλόσοφος and O. Michel, *TDNT*, s.v. φιλοσοφία, D; cf. *PECL* 1:87 (384F). For διὰ τῶν θεάτρων, I prefer Flacelière ("dans . . . les théâtres") to Helmbold ("between spectacles").

κιθαρῳδῶν. In ECL, κιθαρῳδοί appear only at Rev 14:2, 18:22.

ἀνέζευξαν . . . ὥσπερ ἐκ πολεμίας . . . καὶ κατηυλίσαντο. Although ἀναζεύγνυμι, πολέμιος, and καταυλίζομαι are absent from ECL (αὐλίζομαι is occasionally used, but in a non-military sense; see Bauer, s.v.), military metaphor abounds. See, e.g., Rom 13:12, 2 Cor 6:7, 10:4, Eph 6:11-13, Jas 4:1, 1 Pet 4:1, Diogn 6:5, Herm Man 12:2:4, Ign Trall 4:2, Pol Phil 4:1; Bauer, s.v. ὁπλίζω, ὅπλον (2.b), πανοπλία (2), πολεμέω (2), and πόλεμος (2); Bultmann, *Der Stil*, 104 (item 8); L. D. Agate, *Dictionary of the Apostolic Church*, ed. Hastings *et alii* (1919) s.v. "Metaphor," I.2(3), II.2.

παρὰ ταῖς Μούσαις. See on the same phrase at 748F.

ἄνδρες ἔνδοξοι. ἔνδοξος in this sense has close ECL parallels at Matt 20:28D (= Agr 22), 1 Clem 3:3, Mart Pol 8:1. Cf. 1 Cor 4:10 and Bauer, s.v., 1.

Βάκχωνι δὲ τῷ καλῷ λεγομένῳ. This usage of καλός is peculiarly Greek and without parallel in ECL. The epithet ὁ καλός, when applied to a youth such as Bacchon (as an ἔφηβος [749E] he was between 15 and 20; see Helmbold, p. 311, n.a and F. A. G. Beck, *OCD*, s.v. "Epheboi"), means that he is regarded as "beautiful" and is being courted by male lovers (ἐρασταί) who are his senior. Bacchon's counsellor Pisias is soon (749E-F) to be characterized as "the most austere of his lovers" (αὐστηρότατος τῶν ἐραστῶν) and to be charged by Anthemion with imitating base lovers by trying to prevent Bacchon from getting married. On this usage of καλός, see LSJ, s.v., 2.a and H. Licht, *Sexual Life in Ancient Greece* (London, 1932) 428-30 (hereafter cited as Licht); cf. 'Αλκιβιάδης ὁ καλός (Plato *Alc.*1, 113B) and the vast quantity of vase inscriptions saying that such-and-such a youth is καλός (for examples, see R. Flacelière, *Love in Ancient Greece* [New York, 1962] 72-73 [hereafter cited as Flacelière, *Love*]; Lacey, 61, pl. 15; and the vases and plate cited by H. R. Immerwahr, "Stesagoras II," *TAPhA* 103 [1972] 180, n. 2 and 185, n. 13). On Greek pederasty, see, e.g., Plato's *Smp.* and *Phdr.*; pseudo-Lucian's *Am.*; the summary of *amat.* in my introduction; W. Kroll, PW 11.1 (1921), s.v. "Knabenliebe"; Licht, 441-98; H. I. Marrou, *A History of Education in Antiquity* (New York, 1956) 50-62 (hereafter cited as Marrou); Flacelière, *Love*, 62-100; Lacey, 60-63 (pls. 13, 15, 17), 157-58, 211-12, 229. For contrast, note Paul's castigation of pagan homosexuality at Rom 1:26-27 and the commandment οὐ παιδοφθορήσεις at Barn 19:4 and again at Did 2:2 (cf. 1 Cor 6:9, 1 Tim 1:10, Pol Phil 5:3). Plutarch's sentiments about παιδεραστία in *amat.* are, to a degree, ambivalent: he sternly condemns its sexual expression (Ch. 23:768E), but demonstrates a wryly tolerant, sometimes admiring, attitude toward it as a social or philosophical institution at Chs. 15:757F-758C, 16:759 A-D, 17:762B-18:762E, 19:765B-D, 24:770B-C.

προσήκοντες. In ECL, this verb is rare and apparently never means "be attached to" or "be related to," though its meaning at Ign Rom 9:3 is not beyond dispute.

τρόπον τινά. Cf. τίνα τρόπον ("in what manner," 1 Clem 24:4), παντὶ τρόπῳ ("in every way," Phil 1:18), and the many adverbial uses (with and without a preposition) listed by Bauer, s.v. τρόπος, 1.

εὔνοιαν. This word is rare in ECL, but it has the same basic sense as here ("affection," "benevolence") at 1 Cor 7:3 (t.r.), Ign Rom 4:1, Ign Trall 1:2, Mart Pol 17:3.

(749D)

διαφερόμενοι πρὸς ἀλλήλους. διαφέρομαι in the sense of "quarrel" or "be at variance with," common in classical Greek (see LSJ, s.v. διαφέρω, IV), is unknown to ECL.

γυνὴ πλούτῳ καὶ γένει λαμπρὰ καὶ . . . εὔτακτος βίον. εὔτακτος does not appear in ECL (the adverb occurs a few times); and λαμπρός, though moderately common, modifies only objects, never persons. In ECL, the dative of respect (note Plutarch's πλούτῳ and γένει), often with adjectives as at Acts 4:36 (Κύπριος τῷ γένει), is far more common than its accusative counterpart (note Plutarch's βίον). In classical Greek, the ratio is reversed. See BDF, secs. 160, 197 and Smyth-Messing, secs. 1516, 1600.

νὴ Δία. A strikingly classical expression. In ECL, νή is limited to 1 Cor 15:31 (νὴ τὴν ὑμετέραν καύχησιν), and Zeus is mentioned only at Acts 14:13.

ἐχήρευσε (ἐχήρωσε E B, for which see LSJ, s.v. χηρόω, II). χήρα, the regular ECL word for "widow," surprisingly lacks a verb cognate in ECL.

οὐκ ὀλίγον χρόνον. Cf., e.g., ἀπεδήμησεν χρόνους ἱκανούς (Luke 20:9) and, also with litotes, ἔμειναν οὐ πολλὰς ἡμέρας (John 2:12). Litotes is frequent in both Plutarch (see Weissenberger, 10) and, often involving οὐκ and ὀλίγος, ECL (see Bauer, s.v. οὐ, 2.b). In classical Greek, as here, the accusative is the proper case for expressing duration of time (see Smyth-Messing, secs. 1447, 1582-87); in ECL, however, the dative competes with the accusative in this construction (see BDF, secs. 161.2, 201).

ἄνευ ψόγου. The noun does not appear in ECL, but ἄνευ is fairly common (note, e.g., ἄνευ λόγου at 1 Pet 3:1).

καίπερ οὖσα νέα καὶ ἱκανὴ τὸ εἶδος. This expression would appear natural in ECL, excepting the accusative of respect, which would probably be replaced by a dative. On the dative and the accusative of respect, see on γυνὴ . . . βίον (749D).

φίλης . . . καὶ συνήθους γυναικός. See on τῶν δὲ φίλων . . . οἱ συνήθεις (749B).

κόρης . . . προσηκούσης. Both words are rare in ECL and without this meaning. See Bauer, s.v. κόρη, προσήκω and on προσήκοντες (749C).

ἐκ τοῦ συμπαρεῖναι καὶ διαλέγεσθαι. Cf., e.g., ἐκ τοῦ ἔχειν (2 Cor 8:11). The genitive of the articular infinitive after prepositions is common in ECL (see BDF, sec. 403).

ἔπαθε πρὸς τὸ μειράκιον. πάσχω πρός (or εἰς), a common enough expression in classical Greek (see LSJ, s.v. πάσχω, II.2), is missing from ECL, as is μειράκιον.

λόγους φιλανθρώπους. This weakened meaning of φιλάνθρωπος ("favorable," "pleasant") is foreign to ECL, where it occurs twice, at Diogn 8:7 (descriptive of God) and Agr 7 (descriptive of ἀγάπη). φιλανθρωπία and φιλανθρώπως are also rare in ECL. On φιλανθρωπία and cognates, see Intro. V. 4 and n. 16.

(749D-E)

πλῆθος ὁρῶσα γενναίων ἐραστῶν εἰς τὸ ἐρᾶν προήχθη καὶ διενοεῖτο μηδὲν ποιεῖν ἀγεννές, ἀλλὰ γημαμένη φανερῶς συγκαταζῆν τῷ Βάκχωνι. On ἐραστής and ἐράω, see Intro. V. 2 and on 749C (καλός). Whether γενναῖοι here refers to birth or character (in ECL it would undoubtedly be the latter; see Bauer, s.v. γενναῖος, γενναιότης), the very notion that a woman would fall in love with a youth in part because of the quantity and quality of his male lovers is foreign to ECL and would be offensive to Paul (see Rom 1:26-27, 1 Cor 6:9; cf. Pol Phil 5:3, 1 Tim 1:10). Yet he would surely have approved of Ismenodora's decision to do nothing dishonorable but to seek marriage, in view of the advice he gives the unmarried and widows at 1 Cor 7:8 (εἰ δὲ οὐκ ἐγκρατεύονται, γαμησάτωσαν· κρεῖττον γάρ ἐστιν γαμεῖν ἢ πυροῦσθαι; cf. 7:25-28). In view of its rarity in ECL, however, it is unlikely that Paul would have used ἀγενής in a description of Ismenodora's behavior.

εἰς τὸ ἐρᾶν προήχθη . . . διενοεῖτο . . . ποιεῖν . . . ἀλλὰ . . . συγκαταζῆν. Both the accusative of the articular infinitive after εἰς and the complementary infinitive are characteristic of ECL (see BDF, secs. 402.2, 392), though συγκαταζάω is absent and διανοέομαι (common in classical Greek) is limited to a single occurrence in a different sense at Gos Pet 11:44. Plutarch and ECL, however, share a penchant for verbs compounded with a prepositional prefix, often as here a double one. Cf. on συνανασώζειν (749A) and see Weissenberger, 12; Griffiths, 14; Russell, *Plutarch*, 22; BDF, sec. 116; Bauer, s.v. (e.g.) ἐγκατα-, προσανα-, συγκατα-, συνανα-, συνεπι-.

(749E)

παραδόξου δὲ τοῦ πράγματος . . . φανέντος. The genitive absolute is characteristic of both classical Greek and ECL. See Smyth-Messing, secs. 2070-75 and BDF, secs. 417, 423.

τινὲς . . . συγκυνηγοὶ . . . δεδιττόμενοι τὸν Βάκχωνα καὶ σκώπτοντες. The mention of the banter of hunting companions creates an atmosphere foreign to anything in ECL. Hunting was a Greek institution and a favorite pastime among young men of Plutarch's social class (see Xenophon *Cyn.*; Plutarch *soll. an.* 959A-D; Orth, PW 9.1 [1914], s.v. "Jagd;" D.B. Hull, *Hounds and Hunting in Ancient Greece* [Chicago and London, 1964]; F. A.

Wright, *OCD*, s.v. "Hunting"). Plutarch assuredly does not here have in mind the type of animal hunts (κυνηγέσια) authorized by public officials and mentioned at Mart Pol 12:2.

ἐργωδέστεροι τῶν ἀπὸ σπουδῆς ἐνισταμένων. The genitive of comparison after adjectives and adverbs of the comparative degree is typical of both classical Greek and ECL. See Goodwin-Gulick, secs. 1147-50; Smyth-Messing, secs. 1431, 1437; BDF, sec. 185.

ἔφηβος ἔτ' ὤν. On the ephebia, a thoroughly Greek institution for the educating of young men, see Marrou, 151-59, 256-60 and F. A. G. Beck, *OCD*, s.v. "Education" (IV), "Epheboi." Even if with Helmbold we take ἔφηβος in the sense of "a minor" rather than as a designation for a youth at a certain stage in his education, the connotations of the term are entirely classical; for neither the word ἔφηβος (except once as a person's name at 1 Clem 65:1) nor any reference to the institution appear in ECL.

τὸ συμφέρον. Frequent also in ECL in the sense of "what is to one's advantage." See Bauer, s.v. συμφέρω, 2.γ.

(749E-F)

αὐστηρότατος τῶν ἐραστῶν . . . τοὺς φαύλους ἐραστάς. On ἐραστής, see Intro. V.2 and on 749C (καλός). In ECL, αὐστηρός appears only in the two occurrences of the phrase ἄνθρωπος αὐστηρός at Luke 19:21-22.

(749F)

τὸν φίλον. Here to designate the youth in a pederastic relationship, a usage foreign to ECL. Cf. on Βάκχωνι τῷ καλῷ (749C).

ἄθικτος καὶ νεαρός. The former adjective appears once in ECL (Ign Phld 8:2) and the latter not at all.

(749F-750A)

ὅπως . . . ἀποδύοιτο. Here and in the clause opening Ch. 3 (ἵνα . . . προαγάγοιεν) Plutarch uses an optative (without ἄν) in a purpose clause after a secondary tense (ἔλεγε, 749F and παρεγένοντο, 750A). This is standard Attic and Plutarchan practice (see Hein, 98-102 and Smyth-Messing, secs. 2193-2206). In ECL, the optative is moribund and is not used in purpose clauses following a secondary tense (see BDF, secs. 65.2, 357, 369; the passages listed by Bauer, s.v. ἵνα, I and ὅπως, 2.a; and, e.g., Acts 9:24 [παρετηροῦντο . . . ὅπως αὐτὸν ἀνέλωσιν], Matt 19:13 [προσηνέχθησαν αὐτῷ παιδία, ἵνα τὰς χεῖρας ἐπιθῇ αὐτοῖς καὶ προσεύξηται]). Plutarch regularly chooses ὅπως or ὡς, rarely ἵνα, to introduce such clauses (see Hein, 98-102); in ECL, the normal final conjunctions are ἵνα and ὅπως (see BDF, sec. 369), with ὡς being used once (Acts 20:24). For a brief, general statement about Plutarch's use of the optative, see Ziegler, sec. VI.2.a.

(750A)

ἐν ταῖς παλαίστραις. Cf. my first comment to 749C. The παλαίστρα (lit. "wrestling ground," but regularly used in a broader sense to designate the athletic field with its adjacent buildings), *never* mentioned in ECL, was a standard feature of Greek education and, by Plutarch's day, of intellectual as well as physical activity (see Marrou, 69, 172-73, 180-83 and F. A. Wright, *OCD*, s.v. "Gymnasium," "Palaestra"). On the palaestra as a scene for pederastic encounters, see, in addition to the present passage, Protogenes' remarks at Ch. 4:751A; Licht, 90-96; Flacelière, *Love*, 64-67; Lacey, 62 (pl. 17).

Ch. 3

On Eros, mentioned by name four times in Ch. 3, see Intro. V. 2.

τῶν ἄλλων φίλων. On φίλος as "friend," see on τῶν φίλων (749B).

ἔλεγε κακῶς τὴν Ἰσμηνοδώραν. Cf. Ἄρχοντα τοῦ λαοῦ σου οὐκ ἐρεῖς κακῶς (Acts 23:5 [Exod 22:28]) and ὅταν καλῶς ὑμᾶς (ὑμῖν D) εἴπωσιν πάντες οἱ ἄνθρωποι (Luke 6:26). The normal ECL expressions, however, are κακολογεῖν τινα and εὐλογεῖν τινα (see Bauer, s.v. εὐλογέω [1], κακολογέω and BDF, sec. 151.1).

τί οὐκ ἄν τις προσδοκήσειεν, εἰ ...; Cf. τί ἂν θέλοι ... οὗτος λέγειν; (Acts 17:18; cf. v.l. at 17:20) and πῶς γὰρ ἂν δυναίμην ἐὰν ...; (Acts 8:31). The optative, however, is generally moribund in ECL, and the potential optative is used only in Acts (see BDF, secs. 65.2, 385; cf. on Plutarch's use of the optative in purpose clauses [749F-750A]). The potential optative abounds in Plutarch and throughout classical Greek (see Hein, 58-78, 126-27, 135-37 and Smyth-Messing, esp. secs. 1824-34, 2300.e, 2329-34, 2356).

Ἔρωτι πολεμήσων. Cf. Ἔρωτι νῦν πολεμεῖν (Ch. 4:750B). Military metaphor is characteristic of ECL (see on ἀνέζευξαν ... κατηυλίσαντο [749C]); but the use of the future participle to express purpose, with probably one exception, is confined to Acts (see on θύσων [749B]). The dative of (hostile) association with πολεμέω, a construction typical of classical Greek (see Goodwin-Gulick, secs. 1188-89; Smyth-Messing, sec. 1523; LSJ, s.v. πολεμέω, I), is unknown to ECL. In fact, in ECL πολεμέω is customarily not accompanied by any syntactical construction expressive of hostile association, except in Rev, where μετά (in the sense of "against") with a genitive object frequently accompanies πολεμέω (2:16, 12:7, 13:4, 17:14) and πόλεμον ποιέω (11:7, 12:17, 13:7 [cf. Dan 7:21], 19:19); in a few irregular passages, however, the accusative alone either functions or seems to function as an object of πολεμέω in the sense of "to wage war against": as v.l. (G) at Gal 1:13 and 23, perhaps by inference at Diogn 6:5, and at Ign Trall 4:2 in a sentence of difficult exegesis. In Plutarch or any classical author, πολεμέω μετά τινος would mean "wage war as an ally with someone" (see Smyth-Messing, sec. 1523.b [N.1] and BDF, sec. 193.4).

πέντε μόνον ἡμερῶν ἀπέχοντι τῆς πατρίδος. Cf. BDF, sec. 186.2 and the similar uses of the temporal genitive at Rev 2:10 (ἕξετε θλῖψιν ἡμερῶν δέκα [cf. Dan 1:12 and 14]) and Acts 1:3 (δι' ἡμερῶν τεσσεράκοντα [τεσσεράκοντα ἡμερῶν D*]).

(750B)

τοὺς καλοὺς ἐφορῶν. On ὁ καλός as a pederastic term, see on 749C.

Ch. 4

(750B-751B)

Protogenes' concept of Eros is absolutely foreign to ECL, would certainly have offended Paul (see Rom 1:26-27), and is out of harmony with the commandment οὐ παιδοφθορήσεις (Barn 19:4, Did 2:2). On this concept, see Intro. II. 2 (First Part), III, and V. 2 and cf. on Βάκχωνι τῷ καλῷ (749C), πλῆθος . . . Βάκχωνι (749D-E), αὐστηρότατος τῶν ἐραστῶν (749E-F), τὸν φίλον (749F), ἐν ταῖς παλαίστραις (750A), and τοὺς καλοὺς ἐφορῶν (750B). It should be kept in mind, however, that Protogenes is extolling a form of pederastic love sublimated beyond physical expression into an educative and moral force that yields φιλία and ἀρετή. It is, nevertheless, φιλία between a youth and an older man and is instigated by Eros. As such, it remains essentially pederastic and is so proclaimed by Protogenes: εἷς Ἔρως γνήσιος ὁ παιδικός ἐστιν. On the role of pederasty in Greek education, see Marrou, 50-61 and Flacelière, *Love*, 68, 77-78, 84-92.

(750B)

διαμάχεσθαι πρὸς ἀκολασίαν καὶ ὕβριν. Neither ἀκολασία nor any of its cognates appears in ECL (cf. *PECL* 1:140 [351F]), and ὕβρις and its cognates (ὑβρίζω and ὑβριστής) are of no more than modest importance as pejorative ethical terms (see Bauer, s.v. and G. Bertram, *TDNT*, s.v. ὕβρις, D-E; cf. *PECL* 1:33 [170D-F]). Throughout classical Greek literature, however, ὕβρις ("arrogance," "presumption," "insolence") is a key term in the expression of moral concepts: see, e.g., M. P. Nilsson, *Greek Folk Religion* (New York, 1940) 108-10; W. C. Greene, *Moira* (Cambridge, Mass., 1944), passim (s.v. "*Hybris*" in Index of Names and Subjects); E. R. Dodds, *The Greeks and the Irrational* (Berkeley and Los Angeles, 1951) 31, 38-39, 48, 52, n. 13 (hereafter cited as Dodds); V. Ehrenberg, *The Greek State* (London, 1960) 51, 79, 178; North, *Sophrosyne*, passim (s.v. "Hybris" in Subject Index); G. Bertram, *TDNT*, s.v. ὕβρις, A.

(750C)

ἀναγκαῖα πρὸς γένεσιν ὄντα σεμνύνουσιν οὐ φαύλως οἱ νομοθέται. Protogenes grants that marriage is necessary for the preservation of the race, a concern precluded from ECL by the expectation of the immediate end of the world. Cf. *PECL* 1: 146 (413F) and, on this expectation, see, e.g., 1 Cor 7 (where, in view of the approaching end [26-31], Paul extols celibacy and commends marriage solely as a prophylactic against lust); 1 Thes 4-5:11; 2 Thes 1:6-2:12; Barn 4; Bultmann, *Primitive Christianity*, 86-93, 175-79, 186.

οὐδ' ἐρᾶν ὑμᾶς ἔγωγέ φημι . . . ὥσπερ οὐδὲ μυῖαι γάλακτος οὐδὲ μέλιτται κηρίων ἐρῶσιν οὐδὲ σιτευταὶ καὶ μάγειροι φίλα φρονοῦσι πιαίνοντες . . . μόσχους καὶ ὄρνιθας. Cf. ἐκύκλωσάν με ὡσεὶ μέλισσαι κηρίον (Barn 6:6 [Ps 117(118):12]); the metaphoric use of γάλα καὶ μέλι at Barn 6:8-17 (Exod 33:3); and the ECL comparisons and parables involving μέλι (Rev 10:9, Herm Man 5:1:5-6), μόσχος (Barn 8:2), ὁ σιτευτὸς μόσχος (Luke 15:11-32), οἱ ταῦροί μου καὶ τὰ σιτιστά (Matt 22:4), and ὄρνις (Matt 23:37//Luke 13:34). μυῖα, at home in classical comparisons from Homer to Lucian (see the passages cited by LSJ, s.v. μυῖα), never appears in ECL.

(750C-D)

ὥσπερ . . . ἡ φύσις, οὕτως ἔνεστι τῇ φύσει τὸ δεῖσθαι τῆς ἀπ' ἀλλήλων ἡδονῆς γυναῖκας καὶ ἄνδρας. Protogenes' argument from nature has parallels at Rom 1:26 (where the condemnation of homosexuality hinges on its being contrary to nature [παρὰ φύσιν]) and 1 Cor 11:14-15 (φύσις teaches that long hair, a woman's glory, is a disgrace to a man). Aune (PECL 1:306f. [993A], 312 [994F]), on the grounds that "the functional equivalent of this argument in early Christianity is the laws inherent in the created order," cites several other parallels that lack the term φύσις. In classical authors, we encounter φύσις as an important concept word on the philosophical level (e.g., in the Pre-Socratics, Aristotle, and the Stoics) as well as on a more popular and rhetorical level (e.g, in Herodotus and Plutarch's *Lives*); we find only the latter in ECL. On φύσις in classical authors, see, e.g., W. Jaeger, *The Theology of the Early Greek Philosophers* (Oxford, 1947) passim (s.v. "Physis," φύσει θεός, φυσικά in Indexes); Bultmann, *Primitive Christianity*, 119-123, 135-45; A. Dihle, *Studien zur griechischen Biographie* (Göttingen, 1956) passim (s.v. φύσις in Register 3); H. Köster, *TDNT*, s.v. φύσις, A. On the term in ECL, see Bauer, s.v.; Köster, *TDNT*, s.v., C-D; *PECL* 1:289 (923E), 306f. (993A), 311 (993E), 312 (994F). ἡδονή as used by Protogenes here and below (ἡδονήν [750D], ἡδέως. . . χρῆται [750D-E], ἡδονή [750E]; cf. ἡδονάς at *num. vind.* 556F [Ch. 27]) is ethically at least neutral and accordingly has general parallels at 2 Clem 15:5 and Herm Sim 6:5:7. This term, however, though often used in a neutral or a positive sense by classical writers, is infrequent and customarily pejorative in ECL (see Bauer, s.v.; G. Stählin, *TDNT*, s.v., A-B, E; *PECL* 1:217 [561F], 229 [565F]).

(750D)

εἰς ἀρετὴν διὰ φιλίας (cf. εἰς φιλίαν καὶ ἀρετήν at 750E). A strikingly Greek expression. In ECL, the noun φιλία occurs only twice (note Bauer, s.v.; G. Stählin, *TDNT*, s.v. φίλος, C.1, D.4; *PECL* 1:166 [423D]); and ἀρετή, though customarily in the sense of "moral excellence" or "virtue," is an incidental moral term (esp. in view of its prominence in classical literature), except perhaps for Hermas, who brings it into association with δικαιοσύνη at Man 1:2, 6:2:3, 12:3:1, Sim 6:1:4, 8:10:3. On ἀρετή in

Plutarch and in ECL, see Bauer, s.v.; O. Bauernfeind, *TDNT*, s.v., B; *PECL* 1:30 (169B-C), 149 (415C), 200 (551D), 237-44, 259 (581C), 264 (584F), 282 (593E, 593F), 283 (594B), 284 (595D). On the importance of the term throughout Greek literature, see, e.g., W. C. Greene, *Moira*, passim (s.v. "*Arete*" in Index of Names and Subjects, ἀρετή in Index of Greek Words and Phrases); W. Jaeger, *Paideia* (New York, 1945) vol. 1, passim (s.v. "Areté" in Index); B. Snell, *The Discovery of the Mind* (Cambridge, Mass., 1953) 153-90; Marrou, passim (s.v. "*arete*" in Analytical Index II); North, *Sophrosyne*, passim (s.v. "*Aretê politikê*" in Subject Index).

ταῖς δὲ πρὸς γυναῖκας ἐπιθυμίαις ταύταις. The singular ἐπιθυμία at 750E also is morally neutral and designates sexual desire. Though certainly not morally neutral, ἐπιθυμία is used of sexual desire at 1 Thes 4:5, Did 3:3, Herm Man 6:2:5 (in the plural), Ign Pol 5:2 (see Bauer, s.v., 3). On ἐπιθυμία in general, see F. Büchsel, *TDNT*, s.v. θυμός, A-B; *PECL* 1:263 (584D), 300 (944F).

(750E)

τέλος γὰρ ἐπιθυμίας ἡδονὴ καὶ ἀπόλαυσις. Note Ἔρως ... εἰς ἀρετὴν διὰ φιλίας τελευτᾷ at 750D and cf. τέλος γὰρ νόμου Χριστὸς (Rom 10:4), τὸ δὲ τέλος τῆς παραγγελίας ἐστὶν ἀγάπη (1 Tim 1:5), κομιζόμενοι τὸ τέλος τῆς πίστεως ὑμῶν σωτηρίαν ψυχῶν (1 Pet 1:9). On τέλος as "goal," "purpose," "outcome," or "final cause," see LSJ, s.v., III.3.b; Bauer, s.v., 1.c; G. Delling, *TDNT*, s.v., D.2.a. Betz and E. W. Smith (*PECL* 1:40, on ὧν τέλος ἐστὶν ἡ τοῦ πρώτου καὶ κυρίου καὶ νοητοῦ γνῶσις at 352A), however, would probably reject the parallelism I find between Plutarch and NT in the passages above.

καρπὸν ἤθους. Note τῆς ἀδικίας τὸν μὲν καρπόν (*num. vind.* 549B) and the figurative use of καρποῦσθαι at 750D. Cf., e.g., καρπὸς τοῦ πνεύματος (Gal 5:22), καρπὸν δικαιοσύνης (Herm Sim 9:19:2). In both classical authors and ECL, καρπός is probably more common in a figurative than a literal sense (see LSJ, s.v., II-III; Bultmann, *Der Stil*, 89; Bauer, s.v., 2; F. Hauck, *TDNT*, s.v.; *PECL* 1:190 [549B]). ἦθος is not represented in *TDNT*, and apparently never, as here, bears the meaning "character" in ECL (see Bauer, s.v.).

(750F)

εἰ ... τοῦτο τὸ πάθος δεῖ καλεῖν Ἔρωτα. With this remark by Protogenes, cf. Daphnaeus' statement at 751F (Ch. 5): ἓν καὶ ταὐτόν ἐστι πρὸς παῖδας καὶ γυναῖκας πάθος τὸ τῶν Ἐρώτων (appositive genitive; see Helmbold's translation). Though not explicit on the point, both Protogenes and Daphnaeus appear to personify Eros merely figuratively and to regard ἔρως as a πάθος ("passion," "emotion") rather than a deity that superintends a πάθος (cf. Intro. III). In ECL, πάθος is used of erotic or sexual passion at Rom 1:26, Col 3:5, 1 Thes 4:5, Herm Man 4:1:6. On πάθος in the sense of passion (not necessarily erotic) in Plutarch and in ECL, see Bauer, s.v., 2; W. Michaelis, *TDNT*, s.v. πάθος (under πάσχω), 4; *PECL* 1:2, 14, 34, 187 (548D), 243f., 248 (575C), 253 (579D), 277 (591D), 278 (592B).

(750F-751A)

ὥσπερ ἀετόν τινα λέγουσι γνήσιον καὶ ὀρεινόν ... ἄλλα δὲ γένη νόθων ... οὕτως εἷς Ἔρως γνήσιος ... ἐστιν. With Protogenes' simile, cf. at Rev 12:14 ἐδόθησαν τῇ γυναικὶ αἱ δύο πτέρυγες τοῦ ἀετοῦ τοῦ μεγάλου, which I take as containing an implied comparison involving ἀετός ("there were given to the woman two wings *like those of the great eagle*"). Perhaps Protogenes and the author of Rev have the same species of eagle in mind.

(751A)

ἐν σχολαῖς φιλοσόφοις ἤ που περὶ γυμνάσια καὶ παλαίστρας. These were the haunts of pederastic encounters. Cf. on 750A (Ch. 2) and see Licht, 91-92, 254; Marrou, 58-59; Flacelière, *Love*, 64-67, 80-81, 84, 90-92; Lacey, 62 (pl. 17).

ἐγκελευόμενον πρὸς ἀρετὴν τοῖς ἀξίοις ἐπιμελείας. See my first comment to Ch. 4 and on 750D, E.

(751B)

θρυπτόμενον ἡδοναῖς ἀνάνδροις καὶ ἀφίλοις καὶ ἀνενθουσιάστοις ... καλὸν γὰρ ἡ φιλία ... ἡ δ' ἡδονὴ κοινὸν καὶ ἀνελεύθερον. Plutarch and ECL share a penchant for compounds beginning with alpha-privative (cf. my remarks on the compounds at 749A, 749D-E and see Weissenberger, 10 [under "die Form des Oxymorons"]; Griffiths, 14; BDF, secs. 117.1, 120.2, 124 [at end]). On ἡδονή, which here, as customarily in ECL, has pejorative connotations, see on 750C-D. On Protogenes' notion that women are incapable of φιλία, see Intro. III.

Ch. 5

(751B-752B)

On Daphnaeus' concept of ἔρως and φιλία, which is a bit closer than Protogenes' to early Christian thinking about the proper relationship between the sexes, see Intro. II.1-2, III.

(751C)

καθάπερ θύτας καὶ μάντεις. In this simile, ἐρασταί are likened to sacrificing priests and diviners. Vaguely parallel is the simile at Herm Man 11:2: some Christians go to the false-prophet ὡς ἐπὶ μάντιν. μάντις and related terminology, common in Plutarch, are rare in ECL; see *PECL* 1:88 (385B), 163 (421B), 248 (576D), 257 (580C [Ch. 10]), 258 (580D), 258f. (580F [Ch. 11]), 266 (586F), 281 (593C), 293 (942A).

(751C-D)

εἰ γὰρ ἡ παρὰ φύσιν ὁμιλία πρὸς ἄρρενας οὐκ ἀναιρεῖ τὴν ἐρωτικὴν εὔνοιαν οὐδὲ βλάπτει, πολὺ μᾶλλον εἰκός ἐστι τὸν γυναικῶν καὶ ἀνδρῶν ἔρωτα τῇ φύσει χρώμενον εἰς φιλίαν διὰ χάριτος ἐξικνεῖσνθαι. Paul would scarcely have made such concessions concerning homosexuality (see Rom 1:26). On φύσις and the argument from nature, see on 750C-D.

(751D)

χάρις . . . ἡ τοῦ θήλεος ὕπειξις τῷ ἄρρενι κέκληται πρὸς τῶν παλαιῶν. On χάρις in the sense of "sexual favors," a sense it never bears in ECL, see LSJ, s.v., A.III.2 and H. Conzelmann, *TDNT*, s.v. χάρις (under χαίρω), A.1.a. Daphnaeus' statement indicates that in classical Greek χάρις had lost this sense by Plutarch's time.

(751E)

παρὰ φύσιν. Daphnaeus again employs the argument from nature. Cf. on 750C-D, 751C-D.

ἄχαρις ⟨χάρις⟩ . . . καὶ ἀσχήμων καὶ ἀναφρόδιτος. I see no reason to accept Winckelmann's χάρις, as do Hubert, Flacelière, and Helmbold, since the word is to be mentally supplied from above. Whether or not it is accepted, Daphnaeus apparently intends for the adjective ἄχαρις to carry the meaning "that is not true sexual intercourse." On compounds beginning with alpha-privative, see on 751B.

ὥσπερ ἐκ ζάλης καὶ χειμῶνος τῶν παιδικῶν ἐρώτων ἔν τινι γαλήνῃ τῇ περὶ γάμον καὶ φιλοσοφίαν θέμενος τὸν βίον. Nautical simile, metaphor, and allegory of this sort is a feature of classical literature (see M. Hadas [ed. and tr.], *The Third and Fourth Books of Maccabees* [New York, 1953], on 4 Mac 7:1-3; D. Page, *Sappho and Alcaeus* [Oxford, 1955] 182 [n. 1], 181-197; H. Martin, *Alcaeus* [New York, 1972] 53-63). Though they are less frequent than military metaphors in ECL and never involve the vocabulary employed by Daphnaeus, one does encounter nautical and marine figures at, e.g., 1 Cor 12:28, Eph 4:14, 1 Tim 1:19, Jas 1:6, 3:4-5, Jude 13, Mart Pol 19:2. For a later example of metaphor of this type, see M. Ign. Ant. I.A. (*PG* 5:980), where Daphnaeus' χειμών and ζάλη are used. Though Daphnaeus is the speaker, the associating of marriage with philosophy is especially Plutarchan (see *conjug. praec.* 138B-D [Ch. 1], 145B-D [Ch. 48] and L. Goessler, *Plutarchs Gedanken über die Ehe* [Zürich, 1962] 40-43, 44-47, 60-61, 134-38, 148-51).

(751F)

εἰ δὲ βούλοιο . . . ⟨ἂν⟩ δόξειε. A typical future less vivid condition, with the optative in both protasis and apodosis. This conditional pattern is common in Plutarch and all classical Greek (see Hein, 126-27 [C.1]; Goodwin-Gulick, secs. 1418-1422; Smyth-Messing, secs. 2329-2334) but never appears in NT (see BDF, secs. 371, 385.2). Cf. on 749F-750A (Ch. 2), 750A (Ch. 3) for other comments about the optative.

ὁ παιδικὸς οὗτος . . . ὥσπερ ὀψὲ γεγονὼς καὶ παρ' ὥραν τῷ βίῳ νόθος καὶ σκότιος ἐξελαύνει (Flacelière and the MSS; Hubert and Helmbold accept Meziriacus' ἐξελαύνειν, to be construed with δόξειε above) τὸν γνήσιον Ἔρωτα καὶ πρεσβύτερον. This combination simile-metaphor, in which the pederastic Eros is likened to a bastard son of darkness who is trying to deprive the legitimate heir, the heterosexual Eros, of his birthright, bears comparison with several ECL passages, in which similar figures are used. At Heb 12:8, those who reject God's παιδεία are metaphorically designated νόθοι καὶ οὐχ υἱοί. And at Gal 4:29-30, the Christians are by simile likened to Abraham's legitimate son, Isaac, and their persecutors to Ishmael, his son by the concubine Hagar who was not allowed to be his heir (note esp. ὥσπερ τότε ὁ κατὰ σάρκα γεννηθεὶς ἐδίωκεν τὸν κατὰ πνεῦμα, οὕτως καὶ νῦν); Paul then (4:31) adds the metaphor, οὐκ ἐσμὲν παιδίσκης (= Hagar) τέκνα ἀλλὰ τῆς ἐλευθέρας (= Sarah). Darkness imagery and metaphor runs throughout all Greek and Jewish literature, and permeates the Johannine writings: see, e.g., Bauer, s.v. σκοτία (2), σκοτίζω (2), σκότος (2); H. Conzelmann, *TDNT*, s.v. σκότος; *PECL* 1:19, 65 (369E), 71 (373C), 81 (382C [Ch. 77]), 102 (394A), 211 (558D), 230 (566C), 275 (590F), 298 (944B). Cf. perhaps τὸ τῆς ὑμετέρας ἀγάπης γνήσιον (2 Cor 8:8) and περὶ . . . γνησίας ἀγάπης (1 Clem 62:2).

(751F-752A)

εἰς τὰ γυμνάσια . . . ἐν ταῖς παλαίστραις. Cf. on 750A (Ch. 2), 751A.

(752A)

ἀρνεῖται [ὁ παιδικὸς Ἔρως] τὴν ἡδονήν. Cf. on 750C-D, 751B.

καλῶν καὶ ὡραίων. Cf. on 750B (Ch. 3), 749C (καλός).

φιλία καὶ ἀρετή. Cf. on 750B-751B (Ch. 4), 750D, 751A.

φιλοσοφεῖν φησι [ὁ παιδικὸς Ἔρως] καὶ σωφρονεῖν. Daphnaeus' vocabulary here is Greek to the core. φιλοσοφία and its cognates are extremely rare in ECL (see on φιλοσοφοῦντες at 749C); and σωφροσύνη, one of the cardinal Platonic virtues and a constant subject in Greek philosophical and ethical literature, is no more than an incidental ethical quality in ECL, except in the Pastorals, which are noticeably influenced by Hellenistic ethical traditions (see North, *Sophrosyne,* who discusses Plutarch's notion of σωφροσύνη on 248-49, 385; U. Luck, *TDNT*, s.v. σώφρων; PECL 1:202 [552A]). If Daphnaeus' σωφρονεῖν is to be rendered "that he is chaste," as I think it is, there are implicit parallels at 1 Tim 2:9, Tit 2:5, 1 Clem 1:3, Pol Phil 4:3. On σωφροσύνη as "chastity" in the Apologists, see U. Luck, *TDNT*, s.v. σώφρων, D.

(752B)

τιμῆς . . . μετέχειν καὶ δυνάμεως. With Daphnaeus' claim that Eros can receive only so much τιμή and δύναμις as Aphrodite grants, cf. *def. or.* 421E (a similar remark about δαίμονες). In Rev these terms twice occur together in lists of appropriate tokens of godhead (4:11, 5:12).

ὥσπερ μέθη χωρὶς οἴνου πρὸς σύκινον πόμα καὶ κρίθινον. Though there is no parallel in ECL to Daphnaeus' simile, there are, esp. in NT, numerous occurrences in a metaphoric sense of οἶνος (see Matt 9:17//Mark 2:22//Luke 5:37-39 and Bauer, s.v., 2), πίνω (see Luke 5:39 and Bauer, s.v., 2), and ποτήριον (see Bauer, s.v., 2).

ἄκαρπον . . . ἀτελές. Cf. on 750E, 751B, 751E.

Ch. 6

ὦ Ἡράκλεις . . . τῆς εὐχερείας καὶ θρασύτητος. In classical Greek, the exclamatory genitive is often preceded by the interjection ὦ plus the name of a deity (see Goodwin-Gulick, sec. 1124). Though rare in ECL (see BDF, sec. 176.1), this construction, with ὤ (= ὦ) alone as the introductory word, is employed as a stylistic device at 1 Clem 53:5 (twice), Diogn 9:2, 9:5 (3 times).

ἀνθρώπους . . . μεθιστάναι καὶ μετοικίζειν. On the exclamatory infinitive, a construction not represented in ECL, see Goodwin-Gulick, sec. 1558 and Smyth-Messing, sec. 2015.

ὥσπερ οἱ κύνες. With this pejorative simile, cf. οὓς δεῖ ὑμᾶς ὡς θηρία ἐκκλίνειν· εἰσὶν γὰρ κύνες . . . (Ign Eph 7:1); the metaphoric use of κύνες and κυνάρια at Matt 7:6//Did 9:5, Matt 15:26-27//Mark 7:27-28, Phil 3:2, Rev 22:15; and *PECL* 1:63 (368F).

(752C)

ἐκ γυμνασίων καὶ περιπάτων . . . Cf. on 750A (Ch. 2), 751A, 751F-752A.

ἀκολάστων γυναικῶν. On ἀκόλαστος, absent from ECL, cf. on 750B and see *PECL* 1:40 (351F).

ταῖς γε σώφροσιν οὔτ' ἐρᾶν οὔτ' ἐρᾶσθαι . . . προσῆκόν ἐστιν. σωφροσύνη is presented as a virtue especially appropriate to women at 1 Tim 2:9, 2:15, Tit 2:5, 1 Clem 1:3, Pol Phil 4:3, though it is never claimed, as it is by Pisias here, that this virtue entails their not feeling erotic emotion toward their husbands. In fact, in Titus αἱ σώφρονες are to be also φίλανδροι; and though Paul does not go so far as Plutarch, who at 752C and elsewhere in *amat.* extolls erotic emotion toward husbands on the part of women (see Intro. II.2 and 7, III), he is fully accepting and tolerant of such emotion (see esp. 1 Cor 7:2-9). On σωφροσύνη, see on 752A.

(752C-D)

Plutarch's vocabulary here, excepting his figurative use of ζυγά and χαλινοί, contains no noteworthy parallels to that of ECL. But his present defense of conjugal φιλία against Pisias and the pederastic tradition he represents, as well as what Plutarch says about married love later in *amat.* (for which, see Intro. II.2 and 7, III) and in *conjug. praec.*, offers some general affinities to the views of marriage we encounter at, e.g., Matt 19:4-6// Mark 10:3-9, Eph 5:22-23, Col 3:18-19. Tit 2:5, Heb 13:4, 1 Clem 1:3, Ign. Pol 5:1. Cf. J. Vogt, *Von der Gleichwertigkeit der Geschlechter in der bürgerlichen Gesellschaft der Griechen* (Wiesbaden, 1960) 43-45; Flacelière, *Love*, 179-86; and L. Goessler, *Plutarchs Gedanken über die Ehe.*

κοινωνίαν . . . ζυγοῖς καὶ χαλινοῖς ὑπ' αἰσχύνης καὶ φόβου . . . συνεχομένην. Cf. in ECL the figurative uses of ζυγός (see Bauer, s.v., 1), χαλιναγωγέω (Jas 1:26, 3:2, Herm Man 12:1:1, Pol Phil 5:3), and χαλινός (Jas 3:3); also, though the context is quite different from Plutarch's, ἐν αἰσχύνῃ καὶ φόβῳ (Barn 19:7, Did 4:11) and αἰσχυνθῶμεν, φοβηθῶμεν (Ign Eph 11:1).

(752D)

As I interpret Pisias' simile-metaphor, Daphnaeus corresponds to χαλκός, Plutarch to molten χαλκός, and πῦρ to erotic passion. It is Daphnaeus' nearness to the blazing and molten Plutarch that is inflamming him with erotic passion. Cf. γέγονα χαλκὸς ἠχῶν (1 Cor 13:1), Jesus' remark at Agr 3 (ὁ ἐγγύς μου ἐγγὺς τοῦ πυρός. ὁ δὲ μακρὰν ἀπ' ἐμοῦ μακρὰν ἀπὸ τῆς βασιλείας.), and at 1 Cor 7:9 Paul's metaphoric use of πῦρ to represent sexual passion (κρεῖττον γάρ ἐστιν γαμεῖν ἢ πυροῦσθαι.). πῦρ is common in the figurative language of classical writers, OT, and NT (see LSJ, s.v., II; F. Lang, *TDNT*, s.v. πῦρ, A.I.2, C.I.3, D.II and πυρόω [under πῦρ], A.2, B.1-2, C, D).

συνεξυγραινόμενος . . . συνδιακεκαυμένῳ. Cf. my comments about verbs compounded with a prepositional prefix (on 749A, 749D-E).

δῆλός ἐστιν, εἰ μὴ . . . φύγοι . . . , συντακησόμενος. This conditional pattern (optative in the protasis, future indicative in the apodosis) is moderately common in Plutarch and classical Greek (see Hein, 127 and Smyth-Messing, sec. 2361) but to my knowledge represented in ECL only at Herm Sim 9:12:4 (οὐδεὶς εἰσελεύσεται, εἰ μὴ λάβοι . . .) and, by implication, 1 Pet 3:14

(εἰ . . . πάσχοιτε . . . , μακάριοι.) In ECL, the optative in hypothetical protases is very rare, no matter what the form of the apodosis (see BDF, secs. 371, 385.2; cf. on 749F-750A [Ch. 2], 750A [Ch. 3], 751F).

ἂν . . . σπουδάσειεν. Cf. the preceding comment and on 749F-750A (Ch. 2), 750A (Ch. 3), 751F.

Ch. 7

(752E)

ὥσπερ ἐν χαλκῷ κασσίτερον. Though κασσίτερος does not appear in ECL, cf. on 752D, where Pisias also uses χαλκός in a simile.

οἴνου δίκην. Cf. on the simile at 752B.

οὐ γὰρ ἂν . . . ἐμνᾶτο. An unreal or potential indicative (see Goodwin-Gulick, secs. 1304, 1334-40, 1407-12 and Smyth-Messing, secs. 1784-94, 2302-20). Cf., e.g., ἐλθὼν . . . ἂν . . . ἔπραξα (Luke 19:23) and ἐπεὶ (having the same syntactical force as Plutarch's γάρ) οὐκ ἂν ἐπαύσαντο . . . (Heb 10:2). ECL employs the unreal or potential indicative in the classical manner, and its contrary-to-fact conditions follow classical patterns (see BDF, secs. 360, 371.3).

(752F)

περικόπτουσιν ὥσπερ ὠκύπτερα τῶν γυναικῶν τὰ περιττὰ χρήματα . . . ὑφ' ὧν ἐπαιρόμεναι . . . ἀποπέτονται (cf. at 751F Daphnaeus' description of the personified pederastic Eros as "having sprouted wings," πτεροφυήσας). For bird imagery in ECL, see Barn 5:4 and cf. on 750C, 750F-751A. There are, however, in ECL no parallels to Pisias' simile-metaphor.

Ch. 8

(753A)

ἐρᾶται . . . καὶ κάεται. Protogenes metaphorically likens Ismenodora's erotic passion to fire (cf. on 752D). In a similar metaphor, Paul chooses πυροῦμαι (1 Cor 7:9). The metaphoric use of καίομαι at Luke 24:32 does not involve erotic or sexual passion.

(753B)

ταῦτα . . . ἐρωτικά. This prospective behavior on the part of Ismenodora is strictly Greek and like nothing in ECL.

On πάθος as erotic or sexual passion, see on 750F.

εἰ δ' αἰσχύνεται καὶ σωφρονεῖ, κοσμίως οἴκοι καθήσθω. Protogenes is prescribing what he considers proper behavior for the widow Ismenodora. Note the prescriptions with similar vocabulary at 1 Tim 2:8-9 (βούλομαι ... γυναῖκας ἐν καταστολῇ κοσμίῳ, μετὰ αἰδοῦς καὶ σωφροσύνης κοσμεῖν ἑαυτάς), 1 Tim 3:2-5 (δεῖ ... τὸν ἐπίσκοπον ... εἶναι ... σώφρονα, κόσμιον and to properly oversee his own οἶκος), Tit 2:5 (the older are to teach the younger women to be, among other things, σώφρονες and οἰκουργοί), 1 Clem 1:3 (Clement praises the Corinthians because they taught their women to manage obediently τὰ κατὰ τὸν οἶκον with σωφροσύνη), and Pol Phil 4:3 (σωφροσύνη is enjoined on widows). κοσμιότης is often associated with σωφροσύνη in classical literature (see North, *Sophrosyne*, 94-95, 162-63, 205, 219 and H. Sasse, *TDNT*, s.v. κόσμιος [under κοσμέω]). On σωφροσύνη in general, see on 752A, 752C.

ἐρᾶν ... φάσκουσαν γυναῖκα φυγεῖν τις ἂν ἔχοι καὶ βδελυχθείη. Cf. on 752C, where Pisias expresses a similar attitude about women; for the potential optative, see on 750A (Ch. 3), 751 F and cf. on 749F-750A (Ch. 2), 752D.

With Protogenes' imputing of ἀκρασία ("lust") to Ismenodora, cf. Paul's use of the term in this sense at 1 Cor 7:5; it designates a more general vice at Matt 23:25 and 2 Tim 3:3. ἀκρασία is thus a very modest ECL vice, except for Hermas, who places it among the four cardinal vices which he contrasts to the four cardinal Christian virtues (Sim 9:15:1-3); the significance for Hermas of ἀκρασία and its virtuous analogue ἐγκράτεια becomes apparent when one notices that he lists ἀγάπη among the eight lesser virtues. Cf. *PECL* 1: 116 (401A), 198 (550F), 217 (561D), 315 (997B).

Ch. 9

(753B-C)

ἡμῖν (the speaker Plutarch, Daphnaeus, and Anthemion) τοῖς οὐκ ἀρνουμένοις οὐδὲ φεύγουσι τοῦ περὶ γάμον Ἔρωτος εἶναι χορευταῖς. See on 752C and 753C-D, where I discuss the sentiments one encounters in *amat.* and ECL about erotic passion on the part of wives. On Plutarch's choral metaphor (χορευτής = choral dancer), which is perhaps derived from Plato (*Phdr.* 252C-D), cf. on 749A; Ignatius' choral metaphor at Eph 4:2 and Rom 2:2 involves a χορός of singers rather than of dancers.

(753C-D)

Plutarch here contends that a wife's σωφροσύνη needs to be tempered with erotic passion for her husband. No ECL writer so extolls such emotion by wives, esp. at the expense of σωφροσύνη (see on 752C, 753B [Ch. 8]).

(753D-F)

Plutarch drives home his point that women of the lowest birth can dominate great and wealthy men if they are of weak character by citing the examples of Aristonica, Oenanthe, Agathoclea, Belestiche, Phryne (on her identification, see Helmbold, 335, nn. b, c), and Semiramis, whose story is told in some detail. Such use of "historical" reference and anecdote for illustration and proof characterizes Plutarch's argumentation in *amat.* and throughout *Mor.* (see Russell, *Plutarch,* 23-34 and, for an extreme example of the practice, *mul. virt.*, whose thesis that the ἀρετή of women does not differ from that of men is supported by twenty-seven separate accounts of ἀρετή exhibited by women), and invites comparison with, e.g., Acts 7, Heb 11:1-12:2, 1 Clem 4-12, 45, 51-55, where illustrative material is drawn from OT and the history of the early Church; though the story of Ananias and Sapphira at Acts 5:1-11 is not cast in the form of an illustrative anecdote, it seems to serve that purpose. There is, however, a directly hortatory quality to the "historical" references and exempla in these ECL passages that is lacking in Plutarch, who introduces his illustrations primarily as a means of proof and only by inference on the part of his reader as a paraenetic device (but note his statements at *Aem.* 1 and *Demetr.* 1). Also, a Plutarchan anecdote often culminates in a witty remark by one of its personae, as at *amat.* 750D-E, 760A, 762C. Cf. *PECL* 1:198 (551A), 202 (551F).

(753E)

ἐπεὶ δ' ἑώρα μηδὲν ἀντιλέγοντας μηδ' ὀκνοῦντας. This use of μή as the negative with the supplementary participle in indirect discourse is not characteristic of Attic Greek, which chooses οὐ (see Smyth-Messing, sec. 2729). In such a construction, μή is normal for Plutarch, who shares with Koine and ECL a penchant for μή in many syntactical circumstances where οὐ would be regular in Attic (see Weissenberger, 29-30; Russell, *Plutarch,* 22, n. 7; BDF, sec. 430).

(753F)

δι' ἀσθένειαν ἑαυτῶν καὶ μαλακίαν. ECL also employs these terms and their cognates with reference to moral and spiritual weakness: see Bauer, s.v. ἀσθένεια (2), ἀσθενέω (2), ἀσθένημα, ἀσθενής (2.b), μαλακία (2), μαλακός (2); G. Stählin, *TDNT*, s.v. ἀσθενής (B.1.c-d), *PECL* 1:108 (396F).

φαύλων γενόμενοι λεία γυναικῶν. In ECL, φαῦλος is an occasional moral term (see Bauer, s.v.), but there is no parallel to Plutarch's booty metaphor.

(753F-754A)

ἄδοξοι καὶ πένητες . . . πλουσίαις γυναιξὶ καὶ λαμπραῖς συνελθόντες. On ἄδοξος and λαμπρός, cf. on 749C, 749D.

(754A)

μετ' εὐνοίας. Cf. on 749C.

συγκατεβίωσαν. On compounds of this sort, see on 749A, 749 D-E, 752D.

Though ECL offers no parallel to Plutarch's simile involving mares, there is a horse simile at Jas 3:2-3; and horses figure prominently in the imagery of Rev. See Bauer, s.v. ἵππος and O. Michel, *TDNT*, s.v. ἵππος, 2.

πλοῦτον δὲ γυναικὸς αἱρεῖσθαι μὲν πρὸ ἀρετῆς ἢ γένους ἀφιλότιμον καὶ ἀνελεύθερον, ἀρετῇ δὲ καὶ γένει προσόντα φεύγειν ἀβέλτερον. See, for ἀρετή, Intro. III and on 750 B-751B, 750D; for φιλοτιμία, on 748F; for forms compounded with alpha-privative, on 751B, 751E.

(754B)

Plutarch ascribes to Antigonus Gonatas the metaphor involving the dog and its collar. There is no ECL parallel, but cf. on 752B.

ἑαυτὸν ἐγκρατείᾳ καὶ φρονήσει . . . ἴσον παρέχειν καὶ ἀδούλωτον. ἐγκράτεια is far more prominent in Greek philosophical literature than in ECL (cf. *PECL* 1:264 [584F], 315 [997B] and on ἀκρασία at 753B; see, e.g., North, *Sophrosyne*, passim [s.v. "*Enkrateia*" in Subject Index] and W. Grundmann, *TDNT*, s.v. ἐγκράτεια, 2-4), except for Hermas, who at Sim 9:15:1-3 classifies it as one of the four cardinal Christian virtues (cf. Man 8 and on 753B; see North, *Sophrosyne*, 320, n. 15 and Grundmann, *TDNT*, s.v., 4), and perhaps at Gal 5:23, where ἐγκράτεια is included among the fruit (καρπός; cf. on 750E) of the Spirit. φρόνησις also is a term more significant in Greek philosophical literature than in ECL (see North, *Sophrosyne*, passim [s.v. "*Phronêsis*" in Subject Index]; G. Bertram, *TDNT*, s.v. φρήν, A.3, C.2. a-b, D. 4-5, E.1; *PECL* 1:38 [351D], 318 [Frag. 23]), though Paul uses φρόνιμος for interesting rhetorical purposes at 1 Cor 4:10 and 2 Cor 11:19. The figure implicit in Plutarch's ἀδούλωτος has general parallels throughout ECL (see, e.g., Bauer, s.v. δουλεία [2], δουλεύω [2.b-c], δοῦλος [1.e, 3, 4], δουλόω [2]; K. H. Rengstorf, *TDNT*, s.v. δοῦλος, C.2-3; *PECL* 1:17).

ὥσπερ ἐπὶ ζυγοῦ ῥοπὴν τῷ ἤθει προστιθέντα καὶ βάρος. This Plutarchan simile-metaphor has no ECL parallel. On ἦθος, see on 750E.

(754C)

It is the smile at Pisias, "the most austere of Bacchon's lovers" (749C), which accompanies Plutarch's remark about Ismenodora's being no older than her rivals (ἀντερασταί) and not having their gray hair, that points up the difference in emotional content between Plutarch's and Paul's reaction to homosexuality (see Rom 1:26-27; cf. on 749C [καλός]).

τὰ νέα . . . μόλις ἐν χρόνῳ πολλῷ τὸ φρύαγμα καὶ τὴν ὕβριν ἀφίησιν. Plutarch here uses φρύαγμα metaphorically (it literally designates the snorting or neighing of a horse) to describe the self-willed behavior of young newlyweds toward one another; at Acts 4:25 (= Ps 2:1) the cognate verb is figuratively used to describe the insolent treatment of Jesus by gentiles and Jews alike. On ὕβρις, see on 750B.

τὰ νέα . . . κυμαίνει καὶ ζυγομαχεῖ. Plutarch continues with his metaphorical description of the conduct of young newlyweds toward each other. With the wave metaphor, cf. Eph 4:14 (κλυδωνιζόμενοι καὶ περιφερόμενοι παντὶ ἀνέμῳ τῆς διδασκαλίας), Jas 1:6 (ὁ γὰρ διακρινόμενος ἔοικεν κλύδωνι θαλάσσης ἀνεμιζομένῳ καὶ ῥιπιζομένῳ), Jude 13 (κύματα ἄγρια θαλάσσης ἐπαφρίζοντα τὰς ἑαυτῶν αἰσχύνας), and on 751E. With the yoke metaphor, cf. the figurative uses of ζυγός in ECL (see Bauer, s.v., 1) and on 752C-D.

(754C-D)

ἂν Ἔρως ἐγγένηται καθάπερ πνεῦμα κυβερνήτου μὴ παρόντος ἐτάραξε καὶ συνέχεε τὸν γάμον. Plutarch now offers a nautical metaphor in his description of the behavior of young newlyweds. Cf. Mart Pol 19:2 (Χριστόν, τὸν . . . κυβερνήτην τῶν σωμάτων ἡμῶν), the figurative use of κυβερνήσεις at 1 Cor 12:28, the preceding comment, and on 751E.

(754D)

Plutarch's manner of presenting his thesis that throughout life every man is always subject to some higher temporal authority is strikingly Greek, especially his examples of the gymnasiarch ruling the ἔφηβος (cf. on 749E) and the ἐραστής the youth (cf., e.g., on 749C [καλός], 749D-E, 754C). Yet the thesis per se has loose ECL parallels at, e.g., Rom 13:1-6, Eph 5:21-6:9, Col 3:18-22, Tit 2:5, 2:9, 3:1, 1 Pet 2:13-14, 2:18, 3:1-6, 5:5, Barn 19:7, 1 Clem 1:3, 57:1, 60:4-61:1, Ign Eph 2:2, Ign Magn 2, 13:2, Ign Pol 6:1, Ign Trall 2:1-2, 13:2. ECL writers, however, generally regard temporal subordination as ordained of God, while Plutarch here treats it as merely part of the normal social order. And Plutarch's pederastic example would certainly be offensive to Paul (Rom 1:26-27, 1 Cor 6:9), Polycarp (5:3), and the author of 1 Tim (1:10), of Did (2:2), and of Barn (10:6, 19:4).

γυνὴ . . . κυβερνήσει νέου βίον ἀνδρός. On the nautical figure, see on 754C-D; cf. on 751E, 754C.

Ch. 10

(754E-F)

Βάκχων . . . ἀπιὼν ἐκ παλαίστρας. On the palaestra, see on 749C, 751A.

(754F)

κοσμίως. An adverb descriptive of Bacchon's gait. See on 753B. On Bacchon as καλός, see on 749C.

After seizing Bacchon and carrying him into Ismenodora's house, τὰς θύρας εὐθὺς ἀπέκλεισαν. Almqvist (47 [sec. 42]) notes close verbal parallels, but in contexts that are far different, at Matt 25:10, Luke 13:25, Acts 21:30.

(755A)

ἡ δ' αὐλητρὶς αὐλοῦσα. In ECL, there is no mention of flute playing in connection with a wedding.

(755A-B)

The references to the supervision of the ephebes by the gymnasiarchs and to the desertion of the theatre, where contests were being held, give this passage an especially Greek flavor (cf. on 749E, 749C, 754D). With the uproar at Thespiae, cf. that at Ephesus described at Acts 19:23-40.

Ch. 11

(755B)

ὥσπερ ἐν πολέμῳ προσελάσας τὸν ἵππον. On the military simile, see on 749C, 750A.

τί πέρας ἔσται τῆς ἀνατρεπούσης τὴν πόλιν ἡμῶν ἐλευθερίας; In his cry of indignation at Ismenodora's behavior, Pisias uses ἐλευθερία pejoratively as "license." Though Plato sometimes uses this term or a cognate with such force (e.g., at *Grg.* 492C, *R.* 561A, *R.* 575A), among classical authors ἐλευθερία is a political catchword that normally carries highly favorable connotations (see, e.g., Herodotus 5.62.1, 7.103-104; Thucydides 1.124.3; Plutarch *gen. Soc.* 595D [Ch. 27]; V. Ehrenberg, *The Greek State* [New York and Toronto, 1960] passim [s.v. "freedom" and ἐλευθερία in Index] and 252, on Section 5, for bibliography [hereafter cited as Ehrenberg]; H. Schlier, *TDNT*, s.v. ἐλεύθερος, A; *PECL* 1:284 [595D]). In ECL also, ἐλευθερία and its cognates are normally used in a highly favorable sense, though they often refer to spiritual, rather than political or social, freedom (see Bauer, s.v. ἐλευθερία, ἐλεύθερος, ἐλευθερόω and H. Schlier, *TDNT*, s.v. ἐλεύθερος, C). At Gal 5:13 and 1 Pet 2:16, however, a distinction is made between true spiritual ἐλευθερία and another ἐλευθερία that amounts to license.

εἰς ἀνομίαν τὰ πράγματα διὰ τῆς αὐτονομίας βαδίζει. Pisias' *pejorative* use of αὐτονομία, another Greek political catchword (see, e.g., Plutarch *Rom.* 27.1 and Ehrenberg, passim [s.v. "autonomous" in Index] and 252, on Section 5, for bibliography), is also quite uncharacteristic. αὐτονομία does not appear in ECL.

(755B-C)

περὶ νόμων καὶ δικαίων. νόμος and δικαιοσύνη are associated in various ways at Acts 13:38, Rom 3:21-31, 6:19, 10:3-5, 2 Cor 6:14, Gal 2:21, 3:21, Phil 3:6-9, 1 Tim 1:8-9, Heb 1:9 (= Ps 44:8 [45:7]), 1 Clem 45:4, 56:11, Diogn 9:5, Herm Man 4:1:

3, Mart Pol 3:1. On νόμος and δικαιοσύνη in Greek authors and in ECL, see, in addition to the appropriate entries in Bauer and *TDNT*, e.g., E. D. Burton, *A Critical and Exegetical Commentary on the Epistle to the Galatians* (Edinburgh, 1921) 443-74 (hereafter cited as Burton, *Gal.*); W. Jaeger, *Paideia,* passim (s.v. "Dikaiosyné," "Diké," "Law," "Nomos" in Index); Jaeger, *The Theology of the Early Greek Philosophers* (Oxford, 1947) passim (s.v. "Law," νόμος in Indexes); P. Friedländer, *Plato* (New York and Evanston, 1958) passim (s.v. "law," "*Nomos*" in Index) [hereafter cited as Friedländer]; Ehrenberg, passim (s.v. "Nomos," δικαιοσύνη, δίκη, and νόμος in Index); North, *Sophrosyne,* passim (s.v. "*Dikaiosynê*" in Subject Index); *PECL* 1:19-20, 42 (352C), 151 (416C), 166 (423D), 188 (548E-F), 189 (549A), 193 (550A), 200 (551C), 251f. (578D).

(755C)

ἡ ... φύσις παρανομεῖται γυναικοκρατουμένη. On the argument from nature, here put forward in a rather unusual form by Pisias, see on 750C-D, 751C-D.

Pisias sarcastically proposes that the gymnasium and bouleuterion be handed over to women. These were structures characteristic of Greek cities of all periods. See, e.g., D.S. Robertson, *A Handbook of Greek and Roman Architecture* (Cambridge, 1943) passim (s.v. "Bouleuterion," "Gymnasium," "Palaestra" in General Index); W. B. Dinsmoor, *The Architecture of Ancient Greece* (London, 1950) passim (s.v. "Bouleuterion," "Gymnasium," "Palaestra" in Index C); and Marrou, passim (s.v. "gymnasium," "palestra" in Analytical Index II). Cf. on 749C, 750A, 751A, 751F-752A.

σφόδρ' ἐρώσης γυναικός. On Ismenodora's erotic passion, see on 749D-E, 752C, 753B-C, 753C-D.

In reference to the previous announcement (755B) that Ismenodora has kidnapped (ἥρπακεν) Bacchon, Soclarus addresses a question to Anthemion: οἴει ... ἁρπαγήν ... γεγονέναι καὶ βιασμόν; Cf. Jesus' statement at Matt 11:12: ἡ βασιλεία τῶν οὐρανῶν βιάζεται καὶ βιασταὶ ἁρπάζουσιν αὐτήν (Luke 16:16 reports what appears to be the same statement quite differently). Almqvist (38 [sec. 18]) offers exegesis of the Matthean passage and lists several passages where Plutarch similarly associates ἁρπάζω and βιάζομαι (*reg. et. imp.* 203C, *num. vind.* 562D, *amat. narr.* 772E, *Herod. mal.* 857A).

(755D)

εἰ μὴ φύσει τὸν τρόπον ἁπλοῦς ἦν καὶ ἀφελής, ἐμέ γ' οὐκ ἂν ἀπεκρύψατο. Anthemion is the speaker and Bacchon the subject. ECL can use φύσει (Rom 2:14, Gal 2:15, 4:8, Eph 2:3), ἐκ φύσεως (Rom 2:27), and κατὰ φύσιν (Rom 11:21-24, Ign Trall 1:1) in reference to a natural characteristic or condition (cf. *PECL* 1:86 [384F]); Ign Trall 1:1 probably offers the nearest thing to a conceptual parallel to Anthemion's use of φύσει ("by nature"). Anthemion seems to be personalizing the argument from nature, for which see on 750C-D, 751C-D, 755C. On the accusative of respect (here τρόπον), see on 749D; on contrary-to-fact conditions, on 752E.

τί κοσμιώτερον Ἰσμηνοδώρας . . .; On κόσμιος, see on 753B.

πότε δ' εἰσῆλθεν ἢ λόγος αἰσχρὸς ἢ . . . Cf. ἤ πότε σοι αἰσχρὸν ῥῆμα ἐλάλησα; (Herm Vis 1:1:7). The ECL parallel is rather close. Surely context requires, and Koine syntactical usage justifies (see BDF, sec. 151.1), taking Hermas' σοι/ῥῆμα as a syntactical equivalent of the double-accusative construction of classical Greek (on which, see Goodwin-Gulick, sec. 1071 and Smyth-Messing, sec. 1622).

(755E)

ἔοικε θεία τις ὄντως εἰληφέναι τὴν ἄνθρωπον (Ismenodora) ἐπίπνοια καὶ κρείττων ἀνθρωπίνου λογισμοῦ. ἐπίπνοια does not appear in ECL, though it is moderately well attested in the literature covered by Lampe. Probably the nearest thing in ECL to the "religious" phenomenon referred to by Anthemion, viz. Ismenodora's non-rational behavior, is glossolalia and prophesying inspired by the Holy Spirit, for which see Acts 10:44-46, 19:5-6, 1 Cor 12:10, 12:28-30, 13:1, 13:8, 14:1-33, 14:39-40. Paul's behavior at his conversion (Acts 9:1-22) and the glossolalia of Pentecost (Acts 2:1-13) are distinctive in that both are instigated by concrete and carefully described supernatural occurrences. Cf. *PECL* 1:104, 107 (396C), 124 (406D, F), 133, 148 (414 E), 269 (588E).

Ch. 12

ψυχῆς τὸ μανικώτατον πάθος καὶ μέγιστον ἱερὸν καὶ θεῖον ἔνιοι προσαγορεύουσιν. On erotic love as a divinely aroused passion, see the preceding comment and on 750F. Pemptides' remark is too brief to reveal whether by ψυχή he presently has in mind anything more than the seat of one's emotional and inner life. On ψυχή in this sense in ECL, see Bauer, s.v., 1.b and E. Schweizer, *TDNT*, s.v., D.I.3; cf. *PECL* 1:41 (352B).

(755E-F)

In Pemptides' simile, Ἔρως corresponds to the snake (ὄφις) he saw in Egypt and the champions of pederastic and of hetero-sexual/conjugal love to the two neighbors vying for possession of the snake as an ἀγαθὸς δαίμων. Pemptides' simile approaches being a parable, and ὄφις is common in ECL imagery (see Bauer, s.v.); but there is no ECL parallel to this use of δαίμων.

(755F)

οὐκ ἐθαύμαζον (Pemptides) εἰ τηλικαύτην δύναμιν ἔσχε καὶ τιμὴν τὸ πάθος. On δύναμις and τιμή, see on 752B; on ἔρως as a πάθος, on 750F.

(756A)

ἂν . . . ἀκούσαιμι. On the potential optative, see on 750A.

Ch. 13

τῶν γυμνασιάρχων ἦν διαφορά. The two gymnasiarchs are at odds as to how to react to Ismenodora's untoward behavior. On this distinctively Greek official, see Marrou, passim (s.v. "gymnasiarch" in Analytical Index II); cf. on 754D, 755C.

(756A-B)

At this point, in response to a query just lodged (756A [Ch. 12]) by Pemptides, Plutarch begins his defense of Eros' divinity. On this defense, see Intro. II.4, III. For concentrated parallels to ECL, the present passage (756A-B: μεγάλου . . . ὕποπτος) is probably the richest in *amat.*

δοκεῖς (Pemptides) . . . ὅλως τὰ ἀκίνητα κινεῖν τῆς περὶ θεῶν δόξης ἣν ἔχομεν, περὶ ἑκάστου λόγον ἀπαιτῶν . . .· ἀρκεῖ γὰρ ἡ πάτριος καὶ παλαιὰ πίστις . . . , ἀλλ' ἕδρα τις αὕτη . . . κοινὴ πρὸς εὐσέβειαν. The only exclusively classical element in this quotation as here presented is δόξης, which ECL never uses in the sense of "opinion," "belief" (see G. Kittel, *TDNT*, s.v. δόξα [under δοκέω], A-B; cf. *PECL* 1:21). Plutarch's use of εὐσέβεια, ("piety," "religion") is distinctively within the semantic and conceptual framework of ECL (see Bauer, s.v. εὐσέβεια, εὐσεβέω, εὐσεβής, εὐσεβῶς and *PECL* 1:9, 35), and his use of πίστις as "doctrine," "body of belief" has parallels at Jude 3 (ἐπαγωνίζεσθαι τῇ ἅπαξ παραδοθείσῃ τοῖς ἁγίοις πίστει), 1 Cor 15:11 (οὕτως κηρύσσομεν καὶ οὕτως ἐπιστεύσατε), John 20:31 (. . . ἵνα πιστεύητε ὅτι Ἰησοῦς ἐστιν ὁ χριστὸς ὁ υἱὸς τοῦ θεοῦ), and elsewhere in ECL (see Bauer, s.v. πιστεύω [1], πίστις [3] and R. Bultmann, *TDNT*, s.v. πιστεύω, D.II.2.b and d-e, D.III.1.a, D.IV.1; but, for a different point of view, see Burton, *Gal.*, 483 [at asterisk]); for πίστις in another sense in Plutarch, with many ECL parallels, see *PECL* 1:118 (402B), 190 (549B). Verbal parallels to this passage are present at Ign Smyrn 1:1 (ἐν ἀκινήτῳ πίστει; cf. Ign Phld 1:2 and *PECL* 1:121 [404E]), 1 Cor 15:58 (ἑδραῖοι γίνεσθε, ἀμετακίνητοι), Col 1:23 (τῇ πίστει . . . ἑδραῖοι καὶ μὴ μετακινούμενοι ἀπὸ τῆς ἐλπίδος τοῦ εὐαγγελίου), Ign Pol 1:1 (τὴν ἐν θεῷ γνωμὴν ἡδρασμένην ὡς ἐπὶ πέτραν ἀκίνητον), Ign Eph 10:2 (ἑδραῖοι τῇ πίστει), Ign Smyrn 13:2 (ἑδρᾶσθαι πίστει; cf. Ign Pol 3:1, Smyrn 1:1), 1 Pet 3:15 (ἕτοιμοι . . . πρὸς ἀπολογίαν παντὶ τῷ αἰτοῦντι ὑμᾶς λόγον περὶ τῆς . . . ἐλπίδος; cf. Bauer [s.v. λόγος, 2.a], A. Debrunner [*TDNT*, s.v. λέγω, A.2.b.ii-iv], H. Kleinknecht [*TDNT*, s.v. λέγω, B.1.b], G. Kittel [*TDNT*, s.v. λέγω, D.2.a], and the various ECL occurrences of the λόγον ἀποδίδωμι περί/ὑπέρ idiom [Matt 12:36, Acts 19:40, Herm Vis 3:9:10]), 2 Cor 12:9 (ἀρκεῖ σοι ἡ χάρις μου; cf. Herm Vis 3:10:8), Gal 1:14 (ζηλωτὴς . . . τῶν πατρικῶν μου παραδόσεων), Acts 22:3 (τοῦ πατρῴου νόμου; cf. *PECL* 1:192 [549E]), 24:14 (τῷ πατρῴῳ θεῷ), 28:17 (τοῖς ἔθεσι τοῖς πατρῴοις), 1 John 2:7 (γράφω ὑμῖν . . . ἐντολὴν παλαιὰν ἣν εἴχετε ἀπ' ἀρχῆς . . . ἡ ἐντολὴ ἡ παλαιά; cf. 2 Cor 3:14, Herm Sim 9:2:2, 9:12:1), Tit 1:4 (κατὰ κοινὴν πίστιν; cf. Jude 3, 1 Clem 51:1, Ign Eph 21:2, Phld 5:2, 11:2).

(756B)

Plutarch exalts traditional belief (πίστις) above intellectual speculation, represented by τὸ σοφόν ("clever notion," "ingenious thought") in the verse (203) quoted from Euripides' *Ba.*, as a reliable source of knowledge about the gods. Cf. Ign Eph 18:1, where ὁ σοφός is by implication ὁ ἀπιστῶν, and the absolute rejection of σοφία as a means of comprehending God at Rom 1:22-23, 1 Cor 1:17-27, 2:11-14, 3:18-20, Matt 11:25//Luke

10:21, 1 Clem 13:1 (cf. 38:2); also U. Wilckens, *TDNT*, s.v. σοφία, E.3.c and *PECL* 1:89 (385C).

ἕδρα τις αὕτη καὶ βάσις (=ἡ πάτριος καὶ παλαιὰ πίστις) . . . , ἐὰν ἐφ' ἑνὸς ταράττηται καὶ σαλεύηται τὸ βέβαιον αὐτῆς . . . , ἐπισφαλὴς γίνεται πᾶσα . . . . The deluge of verbal parallels continues: see 1 Clem 1:2 (τὴν . . . βεβαίαν . . . πίστιν), 6:2 (τὸν τῆς πίστεως βέβαιον δρόμον), Pol Phil 1:2 (ἡ βεβαία τῆς πίστεως . . . ῥίζα), Col 2:7 (βεβαιούμενοι τῇ πίστει), Ign Smyrn 8:2 (ἵνα ἀσφαλὲς ᾖ καὶ βέβαιον πᾶν ὃ πράσσετε). Cf. Rom 4:16, 2 Cor 1:7; H. Schlier, *TDNT*, s.v. βέβαιος, B; *PECL* 1:222 (on τεταραγμένην at 564A), 278 (592A). ECL is fond of architectural figures and parables: see, e.g., Col 1:23 (τῇ πίστει τεθεμελιωμένοι καὶ ἑδραῖοι), 1 Clem 33:3 (γῆν . . . ἥδρασεν ἐπὶ τὸν ἀσφαλῆ τοῦ ἰδίου βουλεύματος θεμέλιον), 1 Tim 3:15 (στῦλος καὶ ἑδραίωμα τῆς ἀληθείας), Luke 6:48-49 (architectural parable containing the phrase σαλεῦσαι αὐτήν [= οἰκίαν]).

(756C)

On δόξα as "opinion," see on 756A-B.

οὐδ' ἔπηλυς (Eros) ἔκ τινος βαρβαρικῆς δεισιδαιμονίας. On the Plutarchan treatise about δεισιδαιμονία, see M. Smith (*PECL* 1:1-7), who questions its authenticity. In the Plutarchan corpus, δεισιδαιμονία is regularly (as in ECL only at Diogn 1, 4:1; cf. *PECL* 1:30 [169B-C]) a pejorative quality (cf. the misleading observation by W. Foerster, *TDNT*, s.v. δεισιδαίμων [under δαίμων]) and is often paired with ἀθεότης as the other of two religiously wrong extremes: see *superst.* and *PECL* 1:41 (352B), 44 (353E), 47 (355D), 75 (378A), 77 (379E), 78 (380A), 206 (555A), 209 (556B), 254 (579F), 255 (580A), 257 (580C).

Ἔρως . . . οὐδ' . . . τιμὰς οὐ προσηκούσας καρπούμενος. Cf. on 750E (καρπὸν ἤθους), 752B (first comment).

ὥστε παρεισγραφῆς δίκην φεύγειν καὶ νοθείας τῆς ἐν θεοῖς. Cf. on 751F. Though ECL lacks a direct parallel to Plutarch's legal metaphor, cf., e.g., Rom 8:16-17, Gal 3:15, 4:1-5 and see, e.g., Bultmann, *Der Stil*, 30 (no. 5). Both Plutarch and Paul are aware of the need to speak κατὰ ἄνθρωπον (Gal 3:15) about deity.

(756D)

Plutarch here identifies Ἔρως with Empedocles' φιλότης. See my "Plutarch's Citation of Empedocles at *Amatorius* 756 D," *GRBS* 10 (1969) 57-63.

οὐ γάρ ἐστιν ὁρατὸς ἀλλὰ δοξαστὸς ἡμῖν ὁ θεὸς οὗτος (Eros) ἐν τοῖς πάνυ παλαιοῖς. Cf. on δόξα at 756A-B. It is unclear whether Plutarch is stating an aesthetic fact ("this god is not to be seen by us among the most ancient deities [viz., in art and drama] but is to be conceived of as there") or a theological principle ("we are to recognize this god among the most ancient deities not through sight but through belief"). Esp. if the latter, cf. W. Michaelis, *TDNT*, s.v. ὁράω, C.2.f, D and ὁρατός (under ὁράω); the Johannine statements that no one has seen (ἑώρακε) God (John 1:18, 6:46, 1 John 4:20); the ECL application of ἀόρατος to God (Col 1:15; 1 Tim 1:17; Heb 11:27; 2 Clem 20:5; Diogn 7:2; Ign Magn 3:2; Pol 3:2; Ker Pet 2, p. 13, 24) and his δύναμις (Herm Vis 1:3:4 [?], 3:3:5; cf. on 752B); the related uses of ἀόρατος at Col 1:16, Ign Smyrn 6:1, Ign Rom 5:3, Ign Pol 2:2, Barn 11:4 (= Isa 45:2-3); and Rom 1:20 (τὰ ... ἀόρατα αὐτοῦ ... τοῖς ποιήμασιν νοούμενα καθορᾶται ...) and Ign Trall 5:2 (δύναμαι νοεῖν τὰ ἐπουράνια ..., ὁρατά τε καὶ ἀόρατα), where νοούμενα and νοεῖν bear comparison with Plutarch's δοξαστός. The dative of agent (here ἡμῖν), common in classical Greek (see Goodwin-Gulick, sec. 1174 and Smyth-Messing, secs. 1488-94), is extremely rare in ECL (see BDF, sec. 191).

Continuing his defense of traditional belief (πίστις), Plutarch characterizes Pemptides as παντὸς ἁπτόμενος ἱεροῦ καὶ παντὶ βωμῷ σοφιστικὴν ἐπάγων πεῖραν. Cf. 1 John 5:18 (ὁ πονηρὸς οὐχ ἅπτεται αὐτοῦ [the man who has been sanctified]) and on 756B; also, the NT passages which employ cognates of Plutarch's πεῖρα to describe man's testing of God, Jesus, or the Holy Spirit: Matt 4:7//Luke 4:12 (= Deut 6:16), Luke 10:25, Acts 5:9, 15:10, 1 Cor 10:9, Heb 3:8-9 (= Ps 94 [95]:9). On the OT and NT concept of the testing of God by man, see H. Seesemann, *TDNT*, s.v. πεῖρα, B.2, C.II.2.

(756E)

τὸ μέγα τοῦτο καὶ θαυμαστὸν Ἀφροδίτης μὲν ἔργον Ἔρωτος δὲ πάρεργόν ἐστιν. As I interpret this phrase, the meaning of ἔργον is (work in the sense of created) "product," that of πάρεργον "by-product"; and the referent of both is the "desire" (ἔρος) that is mentioned in the Euripides quotation at the end of 756D; cf. below (756E), where ἔργον more clearly has this sense in Plutarch's statement to the effect that Parmenides regarded Ἔρως as the eldest of the ἔργα of Aphrodite. ἔργον as a product created of God is rare in ECL and perhaps only as an OT reminiscence: see Heb 1:10, Barn 5:10, 15:3 and note Ps 101:26 (102:25); cf. G. Bertram, *TDNT*, s.v. ἔργον, B.1. A striking verbal parallel to Plutarch's statement, however, is offered by Rev 15:3 (μεγάλα καὶ θαυμαστὰ τὰ ἔργα σου, Κύριε ... ; cf. Pss 111:2, 139:14); cf. John 7:21, Acts 13:41.

ἀνέραστος γὰρ ὁμιλία καθάπερ πεῖνα καὶ δίψα πλησμονὴν ἔχουσα πέρας (= τέλος, for which see on 750E) εἰς οὐδὲν ἐξικνεῖται καλόν. With this hunger and thirst simile, cf. *cohib. ira* 460B and *PECL* 1:197 (550F). διψάω, both alone (John 4:14, 7:37, Rev 21:6, 22:17) and in combination with πεινάω (Matt 5:6, John 6:35), is an important ECL metaphorical term (see Bauer, s.v. διψάω, 2 and πεινάω, 2 and J. Behm and G. Bertram, *TDNT*, s.v. διψάω); and the two verbs are coordinated in their literal significance at 1 Cor 4:11, Rev 7:16, Ign Smyrn 6:2. In ECL, ὁμιλία is never used to designate sexual intercourse.

φιλότητα ποιεῖ (Aphrodite). φιλότης does not appear in ECL, and φιλία is rare. See on 750D and cf. on 750B-751B, 751B-752B.

(756F)

Ἡσίοδος δὲ φυσικώτερον ἐμοὶ δοκεῖ ποιεῖν Ἔρωτα πάντων προγενέστατον, ἵνα πάντα δι' ἐκεῖνον μετάσχῃ γενέσεως. Note the verbal and conceptual parallels in the references to Christ at Herm Sim 9:12:2 (ὁ ... υἱὸς τοῦ θεοῦ πάσης τῆς κτίσεως αὐτοῦ προγενέστερός ἐστιν, ὥστε σύμβουλον αὐτὸν γενέσθαι τῷ πατρὶ τῆς κτίσεως αὐτοῦ), the prologue to John (esp. ἐν ἀρχῇ ἦν ὁ λόγος ... πάντα δι' αὐτοῦ ἐγένετο [1-3] .... ὁ κόσμος δι' αὐτοῦ ἐγένετο [10]), and Col 1:13-20 (esp. πρωτότοκος πάσης κτίσεως, ὅτι ἐν αὐτῷ ἐκτίσθη τὰ πάντα [15-16] .... τὰ πάντα δι' αὐτοῦ ... ἔκτισται .... αὐτός ἐστιν πρὸ πάντων [16-17]). Cf. Rom 8:29, Heb 1:6, Rev 1:5, and W. Michaelis, *TDNT*, s.v. πρωτότοκος (under πρῶτος). On the argument from nature, see on 750C-D, 755D.

(757A)

Ἔρωτι λοιδοροῦνται ... τῶν ἄλλων θεῶν σχεδὸν ἀλοιδόρητος οὐδεὶς ἐκπέφευγε τὴν εὐλοιδόρητον ἀμαθίαν. Plutarch is here formulating a concept of blasphemy. And we are again at a point at which his verbal and conceptual framework overlaps, if only to a limited degree, that of ECL, in which λοιδορέω (though in the active-passive rather than the middle voice as here) is used twice with reference to reviling Christ (1 Pet 2:23, Mart Pol 9:3) and once the High-priest (Acts 23:4-5) and those who distort the meaning of scripture are designated ἀμαθεῖς (2 Pet 3:16); also, Plutarch and Paul (as reported by Acts) resort to the same basic idiom as a synonym for λοιδορέομαι/λοιδορέω, though Plutarch chooses its passive (κακῶς ἀκούω at 757A) and Paul its active (κακῶς ἐρέω at Acts 23:5 [= Exod 22:28]) variety. Cf. H. Hanse, *TDNT*, s.v. λοιδορέω and *PECL* 1:58 (363C), 68 (371C), 186 (λοιδορίᾳ).

(757B)

Χρύσιππος ἐξηγούμενος τοὔνομα τοῦ θεοῦ (Ares). On this verb in the sense of "explain," "interpret," see Bauer, s.v. ἐξηγέομαι and ἐξήγησις, 2.

(757B-C)

Plutarch here decries the brand of atheism (ἀθεότης) that rationalizes the traditional deities into personified designations for our emotions (πάθη), faculties (δυνάμεις), and virtues (ἀρεταί), instead of recognizing them for what they are, real and vital beings that patronize and superintend these human attributes (Ch. 14:757C-D); note Plutarch's opposition to similar forms of rationalistic atheism at *Is. et. Os.* 359D-360B, 377D-E. Though early Christianity was confronted with a sort of practical atheism (see, e.g., Rom 1:28-32; 3:9-20; 1 Cor 15:32; Eph 2:11-13, where such "atheists" are described as ἄθεοι ἐν τῷ κόσμῳ), its definable opposition was not atheism per se but belief in false gods (see, e.g, Acts 14:8-18, 17:23-31, 19:23-40, Rom 1:18-23, 1 Cor 8, 12:2, 1 Thes 1:9-10, 1 John 5:21, 2 Clem 17:1, Did 3:4, Herm Man 11:4, Sim 9:21:3, Mart Pol 3, 9-12) and in what was eventually classified as heretical doctrine (see, e.g., Ign Trall 10 [where the docetists are called ἄθεοι; cf. 3:20] and Smyrn). This state of affairs is perhaps summed up in the fact that ἀθεότης does not appear in ECL and ἄθεος is quite rare, being applied to Christians by pagans in two (Mart Pol 3, 9:2a) of its six or seven occurrences, only one of which is in NT (Eph 2:12). On all this, see Bauer, s.v. ἄθεος; E. Stauffer, *TDNT*, s.v. ἄθεος (under θεός); *PECL* 1:52, 74-75 (cf. *PECL* 1:2-35 [passim]).

Ch. 14

(757C-D)

The sense is not seriously marred by the textual corruption near the beginning of 757D (see the texts and apparatus of Hubert, Flacelière, and Helmbold): Eros is the patron deity (θεός) of a particular human attribute, τὸ δὲ φιλητικὸν καὶ κοινωνικὸν καὶ συνελευστικόν; and in this capacity he helps φιλότης issue into ὁμοφροσύνη and κοινωνία. Of these terms and their cognates, only the κοινωνία complex looms large within the conceptual framework of ECL (of the others, the φιλία complex is the most significant, on which see on 750D, 756E and cf. on 750B-751B, 751B-752B). There are, however, fundamental differences between what Plutarch here means by κοινωνία and what is meant by the term in ECL, esp. Paul and 1 John, in both of which we encounter a fully developed concept of κοινωνία. Plutarch is thinking of a fellowship derived from an innate attribute and, as the overall context of *amat.* demonstrates, between only two individuals; in ECL, fellowship is a communal bond among all believers and is derived from their shared participation in fellowship with Christ. For Plutarch, κοινωνία is merely an aspect of φιλία; in ECL, it is itself the common denominator that defines a relationship. On κοινωνία in ECL, see F. Hauck, *TDNT*, s.v. κοινός, D and κοινωνός (under κοινός), D and *PECL* 1:166 (423D), 290 (926F); cf. *PECL* 1:213 (559A).

(757D)

οὐδεὶς θεῶν μάρτυς οὐδ' ἐπίσκοπος οὐδ' ἡγεμὼν ἢ συνεργὸς ἡμῖν γέγονεν; The reference is to Eros and his patronizing of τὸ φιλητικόν, though it is unclear as to how he functions as μάρτυς. In ECL, we encounter God or Christ never as ἡγεμών, once or twice as συνεργός (Mark 16:20, Rom 8:28 [see v.l. and Bauer, s.v. συνεργέω]), and more often as ἐπίσκοπος (esp. 1 Pet 2:25, 1 Clem 59:3, Ign Magn 3:1, Ign Rom 9:1, Ign Pol *inscr.*, 8:3) or μάρτυς (esp. Rom 1:9, 2 Cor 1:23, Phil 1:8, 1 Thes 2:5, Ign Phld 7:2, Acts 13:22, 14:3, 15:8, Barn 15:4). On μάρτυς and its cognates in general, see H. Strathmann, *TDNT*, s.v. and *PECL* 1:59 (364E), 91 (385F).

(757E)

ἀνδρὶ δὲ τὸ κάλλιστον ἐπιχειροῦντι θήραμα φιλίαν ἑλεῖν οὔτε θεὸς οὔτε δαίμων ἀπευθύνει καὶ συνεφάπτεται τῆς ὁρμῆς; The correct answer to Plutarch's question is, of course, "Yes, Eros!" On φιλία, see on 749F, 750B-751B, 750D, 751B-752B, 756E. With Plutarch's hunting metaphor, cf. the metaphor at Rom 11:9 (cf. Ps 69:22-23) and the figure at Luke 11:53; it may also be that the Plutarchan passage involves a nautical figure (cf. at Jas 3:4 ἡ ὁρμὴ τοῦ εὐθύνοντος, "the impulse of the steersman"). Plutarch is here not interested in a firm distinction between θεός and δαίμων (cf. θεῶν ἢ δαιμόνων at 757F; Intro. IV; *PECL* 1:2-3, 272 [589D]) and is using δαίμων in a non-pejorative sense. In ECL, δαίμων in its single occurrence (Matt 8:31) and δαιμόνιον in its numerous occurrences invariably designate "evil spirits," except at Acts 17:18, where in the mouths of some among Paul's pagan audience at Athens δαιμόνια has the neutral sense of "divinities." On demonology in Plutarch and ECL, see on 755E-F, 756C; Bauer, s.v. δαιμόνιον, δαίμων; W. Foerster, *TDNT*, s.v. δαίμων, C; *PECL* 1: passim (s.v. "Demonology" in Indices); F. E. Brenk, "From Mysticism to Mysticism: the Religious Development of Plutarch of Chaironeia," *Society of Biblical Literature: 1975 Seminar Papers*, G. MacRae ed. (Missoula, 1975) 1:194-95.

With Plutarch's metaphorical comparison of a human being to a plant (φυτόν), cf. the metaphorical usage of φυτεία/φυτεύω at Matt 15:13, 1 Cor 3:6-9, 9:7, Ign Trall 11:1, Phld 3:1; Bultmann, *Der Stil*, 89 (no. 4); on 750C, 750E, 752B.

Ch. 15

(757F)

With Plutarch's figure wherein he speaks of boys ἐν ὥρᾳ καὶ ἄνθει, cf. the ἄνθος simile borrowed from Isa 40:6-7 at Jas 1:10-11 and 1 Pet 1:24.

(758A)

Eros is here incidentally depicted as the deity that superintends the arrival of fair youths at ἀρετή. On this peculiarly Greek notion, see, e.g., Intro. II.4, III and on 749C (καλός), 750B-751B, 750D.

τοῦ θείου τοῦ φιλανθρώπου πανταχόσε νενεμημένου καὶ μηδαμοῦ προλείποντος (sc. human beings) ἐν χρείαις. It is not clear whether the nominative of the opening expression is to be construed as τὸ θεῖον τὸ φιλάνθρωπον, the semantic and syntactic equivalent of τὸ φιλάνθρωπον θεῖον ("the benevolent godhead"), or as τοῦ θείου τὸ φιλάνθρωπον ("the benevolence of the godhead"). Perhaps it all amounts to the same thing. At any rate, Plutarch goes on (758A-B) to illustrate this divine benevolence by citing the deities that assist human beings at birth, during illness, and on their journey from this world to the next. The present passage (758A-B) is the nearest Plutarch ever comes in *amat.* to formulating a notion either of a godhead that subsumes the various θεοὶ ἢ δαίμονες or of deity as endowed with love for humanity. Plutarch is here at least looking in the direction of ἀγάπη, as a substitute for which later Christian writers often chose φιλανθρωπία (e.g., Theophilus Antiochenus *Autol.* 2:27:89 = *PG* 6:1096; Origenes *Cels.* 4:15:54, 4:17:58 = *PG* 11:1045, 1049; Athanasius Alexandrinus *inc.* 1:31, 8:75 and 78, 12:1 = *PG* 25:97, 109, 117; Gregorius Nyssenus *hom. in Cant.* 10 [*PG* 44:988 A], *or. catech.* 15 [*PG* 45:48 A]): see Nygren, viii (n. 1), 374, 428, 430, 434, 601. The seeds of this later development are apparent (1) in Hellenistic ethics (see, in addition to the present passage, my article "The Concept of *Philanthropia* in Plutarch's *Lives*," *AJPh* 82 [1961] 164-175, together with the bibliography there cited, and U. Luck, *TDNT*, s.v. φιλανθρωπία, A-B; cf. Intro. V.4 and n. 16 and *PECL* 1:202 [551F], 280 [593A]) and (2) at several points in ECL (cf. on 749D): Tit 3:4 (ἡ φιλανθρωπία . . . τοῦ σωτῆρος ἡμῶν θεοῦ), Diogn 9:2 (ὢ τῆς ὑπερβαλλούσης φιλανθρωπίας καὶ ἀγάπης τοῦ θεοῦ!), 8:7 (θεός . . . φιλάνθρωπος ἐγένετο), Agr 7 (ἡ φιλόθεος καὶ φιλάνθρωπος ἀγάπη). Plutarch often uses τὸ θεῖον for deity (see, e.g., *PECL* 1:4 [n. 4], 22, 51 [358E], 100 [393B], 221 [563D], 292 [941F]); but τὸ θεῖον appears only once in ECL, at Acts 17:29 where Paul so designates God while addressing his pagan audience in Athens in their own terms (cf. *PECL* 1:22).

On θεῖος ἐπίσκοπος, an expression Plutarch here applies to the goddess of childbirth, see on 757D.

(758B)

οὐκ ἔστιν εἰπεῖν ἔργον ἱερώτερον (sc. than Eros'). ἔργον appears to mean "activity" or "function" here, a meaning it lacks in ECL in references to divine behavior (see Bauer, s.v., 1.C; cf. on 756E).

(758B-C)

On Eros as the god that superintends the courting of the καλοί by their lovers and directs such courting πρὸς ἀρετὴν καὶ φιλίαν, see, e.g., the material cited at 758A.

(758C)

δεσπότην ... Ἔρωτα. In ECL, δεσπότης is used often of God and occasionally of Christ. See Bauer, s.v.; K. H. Rengstorf, *TDNT*, s.v., B.2-3; *PECL* 1:168 (426C).

Ch. 16

(758C-D)

To my knowledge, there is nothing in ECL corresponding to the fourfold classification of φιλία that Plutarch here reports.

(758D)

ἐπιστάτην θεόν. In Luke, Jesus is six times addressed by ἐπιστάτης in the vocative (5:5, 8:24, 8:45, 9:33, 9:49, 17:13). See Bauer, s.v.; A. Oepke, *TDNT*, s.v.; *PECL* 1:177 (436F).

ἐπιμελείας καὶ κυβερνήσεως δεόμενον. It is friendship of the erotic class that is here described as "needing care and guidance." ἐπιμέλεια is rare in ECL and is not used of God or Christ (note Plutarch's similar use of the word, e.g., at 758B and cf. *PECL* 1:169 [426E]); but κυβέρνησις in its single ECL occurrence (in the pl. at 1 Cor 12:28) also has a figurative meaning, close to its present one (cf. on 754C-D). On δέομαι, see on 749A.

ἔχει καὶ ταῦτα ... οὐ μικρὰν ἀλογίαν. This is Zeuxippus' reply to Plutarch. Cf. the procurator Festus' ἄλογον γάρ μοι δοκεῖ at Acts 25:27. On litotes and on alpha-privative, see respectively on οὐκ ὀλίγον χρόνον (749D) and on 751B.

(758D-759D)

τά γε τοῦ Πλάτωνος ἐπιλάβοιτ' ἂν τοῦ λόγου (on the potential optative and on λόγος as "discussion," see respectively on 750A and on 748E). With this statement Plutarch begins summarizing the Platonic matter that will occupy his primary attention up to nearly the end of 759D; this matter is drawn chiefly from *Phdr.* 244A-245C, 265A-C, and *Ti.* 86E-87A (on which passages, see, e.g., R. Hackforth, *Plato's Phaedrus* [Cambridge, 1952] 56-62, 131f.; F. M. Cornford, *Plato's Cosmology* [New York,

1957] 343-49; and, more generally, Dodds, 64-101). According to Plutarch's summary, there are two basic types of madness (μανία). One, a kind of disease and purely internal in origin, derives from the effect of disorders of the body (σῶμα) on the soul (ψυχή). The other is of exterior, divine origin and is aptly called ἐνθουσιασμός, which may be subdivided according to the god that inspires it and its effect on human behavior: prophetic frenzy is imparted by Apollo, bacchic by Dionysus, poetic by the Muses, martial by Ares, and erotic by Eros. Plutarch is here, as always in *amat.* (cf. κάλλος ἅμα σώματος καὶ ψυχῆς at 757E and esp. Ch. 19: 764E-Ch. 20:766B), arguing within the framework of a Platonic, dualistic anthropology that identifies a human being essentially with the immortal ψυχή that is temporarily lodged in his perishable σῶμα. With the possible exception of Diogn 6, such a dualistic anthropology is foreign to ECL: see, e.g., Bultmann, *TNT*, secs. 17-20, 22, 42-44; *Primitive Christianity*, 190-208; E. Schweizer, *TDNT*, s.v. σῶμα, D-E; *TDNT*, s.v. ψυχή, D; the second part of J. Hershbell's Intro. to *virt. mor.* in this vol., and cf. Nygren, 169-72, 222-25, 280-87, 330-31, 336-40, 404-408 and *PECL* 1:295f. (943A). Again, with regard to vocabulary, this section of *amat.* stands in general contrast to ECL. While there are loose ECL parallels to Plutarchan ἐνθουσιασμός (on which parallels, see *PECL* 1:103-30, esp. 103f.) in the matter of prophecy, revelation, and glossolalia (see, e.g., Acts 2:1-21, 10:44-48, 19:6, 1 Cor 14, Gal 1:11-17, 1 Thes 5:20, 1 Tim 4:14, 2 Pet 1:20-21, Rev 1, 22:6-21, Did 11:7-12, Herm Vis) and of the overall working of the Holy Spirit (see, e.g., John 14:26, 15:26, 16:12-15, Acts 7:55, Rom 8:26-27, 15:17-19, 1 Cor 2:4-5, 12, 1 Thes 1:5, 4:8), neither ἐνθουσιασμός nor any of its cognates appears in ECL; and much of the rest of Plutarch's key descriptive vocabulary is absent or rare in ECL (e.g., μανία, ἐπίπνοια, μαντικός, βακχεῖος, μουσικός, ἐρωτικός). Indeed, in its single ECL occurrence μανία is a charge levelled at Paul by a pagan, the exasperated procurator Festus (Acts 26:24-25); and of the five occurrences of μαίνομαι, two are from the same context (Festus' μαίνῃ, Παῦλε and Paul's οὐ μαίνομαι) and one (μαίνεσθε at 1 Cor 14:23) is the prospective response of pagans to a Christian congregation should all its members be engaged in glossolalia. At the same time, Plutarch's tendency to slur the distinction between θεός and δαίμων (see on 757E) brings him at least near the conceptual atmosphere of John 10:20, where μανία is virtually equated with demon-possession (δαιμόνιον ἔχει καὶ μαίνεται); and Plutarch's explanation that ἐνθουσιασμός is so named κοινωνίᾳ θειοτέρας δυνάμεως is fully within the verbal and conceptual framework of ECL (see the occurrences of θεῖος in ECL, esp. θείας δυνάμεως at 2 Pet 1:3, and on 757C-D).

(758E)

παρατροπὴ τοῦ λογιζομένου καὶ φρονοῦντος. This is part of Plutarch's definition of the second basic type of μανία (cf. *PECL* 1:223 [discussion of τὸ φρονοῦν]). παρατροπή does not occur in ECL; and to my knowledge ECL never designates the rational faculty in man by τὸ λογιζόμενον, τὸ φρονοῦν, or any such expression. The substantivized participle in the neuter singular, however, has an occasional existence in ECL as well as Plutarch and other classical authors (see Weissenberger, 27-28; Goodwin-Gulick, sec. 932; Smyth-Messing, sec. 1025; BDF, sec. 413.3); and we find ἐφρόνουν and ἐλογιζόμην, along with ἐλάλουν, keeping close company at 1 Cor 13:11.

(759A)

Plutarch asks Pemptides which of the gods arouses τὸν φιλητικὸν τοῦτον περὶ παῖδας ἀγαθοὺς καὶ σώφρονας γυναῖκας ἐνθουσιασμόν, the expected answer being of course Eros. On the verbal and conceptual matter of this question, see on 757E and 753C-D, where all the passages are listed to which my basic comments on, respectively, φιλία and σωφροσύνη are keyed. Implicit in Plutarch's question is a presumption of a single Eros, who patronizes both pederastic and heterosexual love.

(759B)

ἡ Πυθία τοῦ τρίποδος ἐκβᾶσα καὶ τοῦ πνεύματος ἐν γαλήνῃ καὶ ἡσυχίᾳ διατελεῖ. On all this, see *Pyth. or.*, *def. or.*; *PECL* 1 passim (s.v. πνεῦμα and "Pythia" in Indices); Dodds, 68-75; and, for the γαλήνη figure, on 751E.

ἐρωτικὴν μανίαν . . . διακαύσασαν (sc. a man). On the fire metaphor, see on 752D, 753A.

Plutarch's observation that lovers νήφοντες καλοῦσι τοὺς καλοὺς καὶ πίνοντες ᾄδουσι indicates that he has relapsed into the conceptual framework of Greek pederasty, from which only a moment before (759A) he seemed to begin extricating himself. See on 749C (καλός).

(759C)

Both the metaphor and the simile employed by Plutarch in this section are difficult of interpretation, but neither seems to have a parallel in ECL.

There are a number of general ECL parallels to Plutarch's use of διάνοια as "mind" here and at 392B. See Bauer, s.v., 1; J. Behm, *TDNT*, s.v. διάνοια (under νοέω); *PECL* 1:97-98.

εἴδωλα (sc. of the beloveds) ... παραμένοντα (sc. in the memory of lovers) τὸν ἄλλον χρόνον. εἴδωλον lacks this non-material sense in ECL (cf. *PECL* 1:101). On the accusative to express duration of time, see on οὐκ ὀλίγον χρόνον at 749D.

ἔλεγε (Cato) τὴν ψυχὴν τοῦ ἐρῶντος ἐνδιαιτᾶσθαι τῇ τοῦ ἐρωμένου (cf. *Cat. Ma.* 9.8: τοῦ δ' ἐρῶντος ἔλεγε [Cato] τὴν ψυχὴν ἐν ἀλλοτρίῳ σώματι ζῆν). Cato's remark is probably an expression of the same dualistic anthropology described in my comment to 758D-759D.

On the lacuna at the end of this section, see Helmbold, 367, n. e and the *apparatus criticus* to the editions of Hubert and of Flacelière.

(759D)

τὸ εἶδος καὶ τὸ ἦθος καὶ ὁ βίος καὶ αἱ πράξεις (sc. of the beloved), ὑφ' ὧν ἀγόμενος ταχὺ συναιρεῖ (the lover) πολλὴν ὁδόν. See, on εἶδος as "outward appearance" in ECL, Bauer, s.v., 1 and G. Kittel, *TDNT*, s.v., 1; on ἦθος (here "character"), on 750E; on βίος as "manner of life" in ECL, Bauer, s.v., 2; on πρᾶξις as "deed" in ECL, Bauer, s.v., 4 and C. Maurer, *TDNT*, s.v. (under πράσσω), 4-5. With Plutarch's ὁδός metaphor, cf. the frequent occurrence of ὁδός in ECL figures and metaphors (see Bauer, s.v., 2; W. Michaelis, *TDNT*, s.v., C.2-3, D; *PECL* 1:188 [548E]).

Plutarch enhances the appositeness of his quotation from the Cynics by adding ἐπὶ τὴν φιλίαν to the ἐπ' ἀρετήν of the quotation. On φιλία καὶ ἀρετή in *amat.*, see on 750D and on all the passages listed in my comment to φιλία at 757E.

Despite the lacuna here (on which, see Helmbold, 369, n. b and Hubert's *apparatus criticus*), it is reasonably certain that in the simile following it Plutarch compares to a κῦμα the πάθος aroused by Eros. On the simile, cf. on 754C; on πάθος, see on 750F, 755E.

ὁ τῶν ἐρώτων ἐνθουσιασμός . . . οὔτ' ἄλλον ἔχει θεὸν ἐπιστάτην καὶ ἡνίοχον ἢ τοῦτον, ᾧ νῦν ἑορτάζομεν καὶ θύομεν. On Eros as ἐπιστάτης, see on 758D; though ἡνίοχος does not appear in ECL, cf. with Plutarch's charioteer metaphor the appropriate ECL passages listed in my comments to 752C-D. On ἑορτάζω and θύω, see on 749B.

(759D-E)

Despite textual corruption at two points in this section (near the end of D and in the midst of E), the overall sense is clear. Plutarch now turns to a eulogy of Eros for his δύναμις and ὠφέλεια, the former attribute to occupy Plutarch's attention through 762A and the latter from 762B to the middle of 762E (for the manner in which this eulogy fits into the course of Plutarch's argumentation, see Intro. II.4). ὠφέλεια will receive comment in conjunction with 762B. Plutarch begins by contending that Eros is inferior to no god in δύναμις (as a synonym for which ἰσχύς is used at 759E and 762B), as is shown by the fact that his "power" surpasses that both of Aphrodite and of Ares, in each of whom one of the two types of divine δύναμις is concentrated, ἡ οἰκειωτικὴ πρὸς τὸ καλόν in Aphrodite and ἡ ἀντιτακτικὴ πρὸς τὸ αἰσχρόν in Ares. And each type is innate in men's souls (ἀρχῆθεν ἐγγέγονε ταῖς ψυχαῖς), presumably conferred by its respective deity. In arguing, on a theological level, that Eros is more powerful than either Aphrodite or Ares, Plutarch is also arguing, on an anthropological level, that erotic passion is stronger than either sexual passion or martial passion (on the distinction between Eros and Aphrodite and between erotic and sexual passion, see Intro. III). The notions of a two-fold and of an innate δύναμις are derived from Plato (see Plutarch's reference to Plato at 759E; Hubert's *testimonium* to this reference; and Helmbold, 369, n. d) and are foreign to ECL, as is the dualistic anthropology implicit in Plutarch's reference to ψυχαί (see on 758D-759D). That of δύναμις conferred on men by a deity, however, has some slight affinity to the ECL conception of δύναμις as something that God and the Holy Spirit impart to or exercise through believers (see, e.g., Acts 1:8,

4:33, 6:8, Rom 15:13, 15:19, Eph 1:19, 3:20, Col 1:11, 2 Tim 1:7, Herm Man 11 [passim]). But it is the very fact of δύναμις-ἰσχύς as a divine attribute that calls forth the greatest number of ECL parallels, where δύναμις constantly and ἰσχύς not uncommonly appear as divine attributes (see Bauer, s.v. δύναμις [1], ἰσχυρός [1.a], ἰσχύς; W. Grundmann, *TDNT*, s.v. δύναμαι, D; *TDNT*, s.v. ἰσχύω, 2-3). Finally, as here in *amat.*, δύναμις and ἰσχύς are rather often closely associated in ECL: e.g., at Eph 1:19, 6:10, Phil 4:13, 2 Pet 2:11, Rev 5:12, 7:12, 1 Clem 39:2, Herm Sim 9:1:2 (cf., e.g., Matt 12:29//Mark 3:27, 1 Cor 1:25-28, 10:21-22, Heb 11:34, 1 Clem 27:4-5, Diogn 9:6, Herm Vis 1:3:4).

(759D)

τῶν ἀνθρωπίνων ἀγαθῶν δύο ταῦτα, βασιλείαν καὶ ἀρετήν, θειότατα καὶ νομίζομεν καὶ ὀνομάζομεν. The attitude summed up in this observation clashes with the whole tenor of ECL, excepting perhaps a few references to ἀρετή by Hermas (see on 750D).

(759E)

τρόπον τινά. On the accusative of respect, see on 749D, 755D.

τὸ καλὸν . . . τὸ αἰσχρὸν. The neuter singular of adjectives is commonly substantivized in this fashion in both classical Greek and ECL (see Goodwin-Gulick, sec. 931; Smyth-Messing, sec. 1023; BDF, sec. 263.1-2; cf. on 758E). In fact, Paul so uses τὸ καλόν at Rom 7:18-19, 7:21, 2 Cor 13:7, 1 Thes 5:21, as does the author of Barnabas at 21:2 (cf. Jas 4:17). Yet, in all these ECL passages καλός is exclusively moral in reference (cf. W. Grundmann, *TDNT*, s.v., D-E), for it is in each instance, either explicitly or by obvious implication, synonymous with ἀγαθός and/or antonymous to κακός or πονηρός; while, as is revealed both by the general usage of καλός throughout *amat.* (see, e.g., on 749C, 750B, 752A) and by the immediate context in which τὸ καλόν is here used (see on 759D-E), Plutarch's τὸ καλόν, in keeping with its Platonic origins (see Hubert's *testimonium* to 759E and Helmbold, 369, n. d; note, e.g., Plato's *Smp.* 210A-212A and *Phdr.* 250C-256E; cf., e.g., R. G. Bury, *The Symposium of Plato* [Cambridge, 1932] xxxvi-li; R. Hackforth, *Plato's Phaedrus*, 92-109; Friedländer, 32-58; and W. Grundmann, *TDNT*, s.v. καλός, C), has physical beauty as its primary referent and only secondarily assumes a moral referent. αἰσχρός is never substantivized in ECL.

σκοπῶμεν. On the hortatory subjunctive, see on 749A (εὐχώμεθα).

Ἀφροδίτης τοὔργον ... ὤνιόν ἐστι δραχμῆς. Since the ἔργον can be purchased, it is probably a "product" (cf. on 756E). The genitive of price or value (here δραχμῆς) is perhaps more common in classical literature than in ECL (see Goodwin-Gulick, secs. 1133-35; Smyth-Messing secs. 1372-74; BDF, sec. 179).

ὅπως ... μὴ ... ὀνομάζωμεν. This purpose clause depends, at least syntactically, on παροδεύεται. Its basic grammatical features (ὅπως as the introductory conjunction, μή as the negative particle, and the subjunctive mood after a primary tense) are typical of both classical and Koine Greek. See Goodwin-Gulick, secs. 1371-74, 1377; Smyth-Messing, secs. 2193, 2196; BDF, sec. 369; Bauer, s.v. μή, A.I.2 and ὅπως, 2.a; and on 749F-750A.

(759F)

τοῦτο ... ταλάντων καὶ ... ἀρχῆς ἀντάξιον ἐποίησεν. See on 759E for discussion of the genitive of price or value. In ECL, this construction abounds after ἄξιος, ἀξιόω, ἀξίως, and καταξιόω (see these entries in Bauer), though ἀντάξιος and its cognates are not represented in ECL. Plutarch's ἐποίησεν is quite obviously a gnomic aorist (note, in addition to the context, the translations of Flacelière and of Helmbold and the present tense of παροδεύεται), a usage common enough in classical Greek but infrequent in ECL (see Goodwin-Gulick, secs. 1293-94; Smyth-Messing, secs. 1931-32; BDF, sec. 333.1).

ἡ τῆς Ἀφροδίτης χάρις. Cf. χάρις θεοῦ at Luke 2:40 and the many similar phrases throughout ECL (see Bauer, s.v. χάρις, 2-4).

ἂν συνίδοις. On the potential optative, see on 750A.

(759F-760D)

No ECL writer ever speaks so dispassionately or uncensoriously as does Plutarch here and in Chs. 17-18 about what, by the ethical standards of ECL, is quite simply fornication, adultery, and homosexuality.

(760A-B)

ἐπίδοξος ἦν διὰ τῆς γυναικὸς ὁ Φάυλλος ἐκπρεποῦς οὔσης, εἰ συγγένοιτο τῷ Φιλίππῳ, διαπράξασθαι (so Hubert and Flacelière, following the MSS; Helmbold reads [note his and Hubert's *apparatus*] the future διαπράξεσθαι, which tense of the infinitive is rare in ECL [see BDF, secs. 65.1.c, 338.3, 350, 356])... δυναστείαν αὐτῷ. Cf. Herm Vis 3:10:5, where ἐκπρεπής is also used of a beautiful woman. Hein, 127-28, would apparently analyze this sentence as a condition with an optative in the protasis (συγγένοιτο) and an imperfect indicative in the apodosis (ἦν); one might also view εἰ συγγένοιτο ... διαπράξασθαι ... as a conditional sentence reduced to indirect discourse after ἐπίδοξος ἦν (see Goodwin-Gulick, secs. 1512-14; Smyth-Messing, secs 2617-21). Whichever analysis one follows, the sentence bears comparison with the similar constructions at Acts 20:16 (ἔσπευδεν ...; εἰ δυνατὸν εἴη ..., ... γενέσθαι εἰς Ἰεροσόλυμα [note the aorist infinitive dependent on a main verb in the imperfect indicative]), 24:19, and 27:39 (ἐβουλεύοντο, εἰ δύναιντο, ἐξῶσαι ... [again, an aorist infinitive dependent on a main verb in the imperfect indicative]); cf. BDF, secs. 371, 385.2. The optative, however, is exceedingly rare in ECL, esp. in comparison with its frequency in Plutarch and all classical literature (see BDF, secs. 65.2, 357, 359.2, 367, 371.2 and 5, 384-86; cf. on 749F-750A, 750A, 751F, 752D.

(760B)

γυναῖκα ... παρεισέπεμψε (Phayllus) λαθοῦσαν. λαθών (here in the form λαθοῦσαν, "secretly") is not used as an adverbial participle in ECL (on which usage in classical Greek, see Goodwin-Gulick, sec. 1567; Smyth-Messing, sec. 2062.a), though λανθάνω once takes a supplementary participle, at Heb 13:2, where it, therefore, conveys an adverbial idea (cf. BDF, secs 414.3, 435). Early Christian as well as classical writers, including Plutarch, occasionally choose the adverb λάθρᾳ to express such an idea: see D. Wyttenbach, *Lexicon Plutarcheum* 2, s.v. λάθρα; LSJ, s.v. λάθρῃ; Goodwin-Gulick, sec. 412; Smyth-Messing, secs. 1443, 1700; BDF, secs. 26, 435.

ἐπὶ ταῖς τοῦ Διὸς τιμαῖς. Cf. on 752B.

τυράννοις ... ἀντερῶντες ... καὶ φιλοτιμούμενοι περὶ τῶν καλῶν καὶ ὡραίων. Cf. on 748F, 749C, 752A. The common classical political terms τυραννίς and τύραννος are limited to two or three occurrences in ECL (Acts 5:39 [v.l.], Diogn 7:3, Mart Pol 2:4). On these terms and the political institution they represent, see, e.g. A. Andrewes, *The Greek Tyrants* (New York and Evanston, 1956) and V. Ehrenberg, *OCD*, s.v. "Tyranny".

(760C)

ὥσπερ ἱεροῖς (their beloveds) . . . ἀθίκτοις ἀμύνοντες (the ἐρασταί referred to at 760B-C). With Plutarch's simile, cf. the metaphorical use of τὰ ἄθικτα ἀρχεῖα at Ign Phld 8:2. It is unclear whether Plutarch's ἱερά (nominative of ἱεροῖς) is to be taken as the plural of the noun ἱερόν ("temple") or as a substantivized neuter plural ("holy things") of the adjective ἱερός. In ECL, τὸ ἱερόν is, with the exception of Acts 19:27, the temple at Jerusalem; and ἱερός is only an occasional adjective. On classical and ECL usage of both terms, see G. Schrenk, *TDNT*, s.v. ἱερός, A-B, E-F and τὸ ἱερόν, A-C, E.

τυγχάνεις ἐρῶν. The supplementary participle with τυγχάνω, common in classical authors (see, e.g., Goodwin-Gulick, sec. 1588 and Smyth-Messing, secs. 1873, 2095-96), never appears in ECL, except possibly in the form of an understood but unexpressed ὤν at Diogn 5:8 and 10:7 (see BDF, sec. 414.1, where a supplementary participle is wrongly assigned to Luke 10:30 as v.l.; Blass-Debrunner-Rehkopf correctly omit this reference to Luke).

(760D)

ἀπόλοιο. The optative of wish, a typical classical and Plutarchan usage (see Hein, 53-58; Goodwin-Gulick, sec. 1355; Smyth-Messing, secs. 1814-15, 1820), is chiefly, but not exclusively, in evidence in ECL in the Pauline formula μὴ γένοιτο (see BDF, sec. 384). Yet on one point of this construction the usage of ECL and of Plutarch nearly coincide: ECL completely eschews the introductory particles εἴθε and εἰ γάρ (see BDF, sec. 384), Plutarch uses only the former, and that very rarely (see Hein, 55). Cf. on 760A-B.

Ch. 17

(760E)

οἱ περὶ Πεμπτίδην. Cf. οἱ περὶ Παῦλον (Acts 13:13) and the similar uses of περί listed by Bauer, s.v., 2.a.δ.

ἡδέως ἂν πυθοίμεθα. Note the similar idiomatic use of ἡδέως in ECL (see Bauer, s.v.). On the potential optative, see on 750A.

ἄξιον (understand ἐστί). Cf. the impersonal ἄξιον at 1 Cor 16:4, 2 Thes 1:3.

ἄνδρα λαμπρὸν ὄντα τὴν ψυχήν. On λαμπρός and on the accusative of respect (here ψυχήν), see on 748F, 749D. At 749D, Plutarch's figurative λαμπρός was qualified by a dative of respect, the more common of the two respect constructions in ECL.

(760F)

φιλοφρόνως. In ECL, only at Acts 28:7. Cf. 1 Pet 3:8 (t.r.) and *PECL* 1:261 (582D).

τοὺς ἀρίστους τῶν Θεσσαλῶν. On ἄριστος, replete with social, political, and moral connotations throughout classical literature but absent from ECL, see, e.g., LSJ, s.v.; W. Jaeger, *Paideia*, 1:5-8; A. R. Burn, *The Pelican History of Greece* (Baltimore, 1966) 64-65.

ἐξήλασε (Cleomachus) λαμπρῶς. On the figurative use of this adverb, see on 748F.

(761A)

τάφον (sc. of Cleomachus) ... δεικνύουσιν (the Chalcidians) ἐν ἀγορᾷ ..., ἐφ' οὗ μέχρι νῦν ὁ μέγας ἐφέστηκε κίων. Cf. μέχρι νῦν at Ign Magn 8:1 and the fifteen or so additional instances of the temporal use of μέχρι listed by Bauer, s.v., 1.b. With this and other statements by Plutarch indicating autopsy (on which statements, see C. Theander, "Plutarch und die Geschichte," *Bulletin de la Société royale des lettres de Lund* [1950-51] 2-32), cf. the "we" portions of Acts (16:10-17, 20:5-21:18, 27:1-28:16). ECL can use δείκνυμι in a generally similar sense (see Bauer, s.v., 1.a [first half] and H. Schlier, *TDNT*, s.v., A.1-2).

τὸ παιδεραστεῖν ... ἠγάπησαν. On Greek pederasty as presented in *amat.*, see, e.g., Intro. III and on 749C, 750B-751 B. The force of ἀγαπάω in classical authors is generally "weak and variable", esp. in comparison with that of ἐράω, and of ἀγαπάω in Christian writers (see E. Stauffer, *TDNT*, s.v. ἀγαπάω, B and *PECL* 1:73 [376A]); but ECL too can use ἀγαπάω with an abstract object (e.g., ἀλήθειαν; see Bauer, s.v. ἀγαπάω, 2).

τὸν δ' ὑπὸ τοῦ ἐρωμένου φιληθέντα. Plutarch a moment before (760F) described the incident here referred to with the genitive absolute τοῦ νεανίσκου ... φιλοφρόνως αὐτὸν ἀσπασαμένου. φιληθέντα is probably better rendered into English as "kissed" (so M. Hadas [tr.], *On Love, the Family, and the Good Life: Selected Essays of Plutarch* [New York, 1957] 33) than as "embraced" (so Helmbold); cf. Flacelière's perhaps appropriately ambiguous "embrassé." On φιλέω as "kiss" in classical authors, LXX, and ECL, see LSJ, s.v., 4; Bauer, s.v., 2; G. Stählin, *TDNT*, s.v., A.4, B.II, C.II, D. ἀσπάζομαι too, at least in classical Greek, can occasionally bear the rendering "kiss" (see LSJ, s.v., 2 and Plutarch *Rom.* 1.3 [ἀσπάζεσθαι τοῖς στόμασι]); and in NT the epistolary imperative ἀσπάσασθε may be accompanied by the explicit phrases ἐν φιλήματι ἁγίῳ (Rom 16:16, 1 Cor 16:20, 2 Cor 13:12, 1 Thes 5:26) or ἐν φιλήματι ἀγάπης (1 Pet 5:14). We must suppose that an ἀσπασμός ("greeting" or "embrace") in both pagan and Christian practice commonly included a kiss. Cf. H. Windisch, *TDNT*, s.v. ἀσπάζομαι, passim and Stählin's proposal (*TDNT*, s.v. φιλέω, C.II.1) that in NT "in many cases where one might expect greeting or parting kisses to be mentioned, they are perhaps implied in other words like ἀσπάζομαι."

(761D)

Plutarch speaks of Achilles, Epaminondas, and several other heroes of legend and history (the distinction between the two is mine, not Plutarch's) as belonging to οἱ παλαιοί ("the ancients"). ECL does not use this term in reference to OT figures.

Ἰόλαον . . . μέχρι νῦν σέβονται καὶ τιμῶσιν. The cult of Iolaüs, Heracles' beloved (ἐρώμενος), was still functioning in Plutarch's day (see Flacelière, 129, n. 38 and Helmbold, 381, n.d; cf. on 761A). ECL uses both σέβομαι and τιμάω, though not in combination as here, of the worship of God (cf. on 752B and Bauer, s.v. σέβω and τιμάω, 2; W. Foerster, *TDNT*, s.v. σέβομαι, C; J. Schneider, *TDNT*, s.v. τιμή, II.1; *PECL* 1:50 [358A], 151-52 [416C]).

(761E)

ὅρκους τε καὶ πίστεις . . . παρὰ τῶν ἐρωμένων λαμβάνοντες. "Receiving oaths and pledges from their beloveds" (not "exchanging . . . with," as Helmbold, or "qui échangent avec," as Flacelière); see LSJ, s.v. λαμβάνω, A.II.1.f and πίστις, II.1 and Bauer, s.v. λαμβάνω, 1.d. In ECL, ὅρκος is moderately common (see Bauer, s.v. and J. Schneider, *TDNT*, s.v., B). But πίστις is never associated with ὅρκος in ECL, and is used in NT in the sense of "oath" or "pledge" only at 1 Tim 5:12 and, possibly, Acts 17:31 (see Bauer, s.v., 1.b-c); both this sense and the association with ὅρκος are common in classical literature (see LSJ, s.v. πίστις, II.1).

λέγεται ... Ἄλκηστιν ἰατρικὸς ὢν (Heracles) ἀπεγνωσμένην σῶσαι τῷ Ἀδμήτῳ χαριζόμενος. It is a moot point whether Plutarch's ἰατρικός is meant literally or metaphorically, but his vocabulary has many obvious ECL parallels (bear in mind that Heracles was cultically worshipped as a hero, and occasionally as a god; see, e.g., H. J. Rose and C. M. Robertson, *OCD*, s.v. "Heracles" and "Hero-Cult"): Christ is variously depicted, literally as well as metaphorically, as an ἰατρός (see, e.g., Ign Eph 7:2, Diogn 9:6, Matt 9:11-13//Mark 2:16-17//Luke 5:30-32, Mark 5:25-34, Luke 4:23; A. Oepke, *TDNT*, s.v. ἰάομαι, C.2-3, D; *PECL* 1:87 [384F], 193 [549F], 225 [564F]), who "saves" men from sickness and death "out of favor" to them (see, e.g., the passages just listed; Eph 2:4-9, esp. the twice uttered χάριτί ἐστε σεσῳσμένοι; Pol Phil 1:3 [same phrase]; Tit 2:11 [χάρις τοῦ θεοῦ σωτήριος]; Luke 7:21; Acts 15:11 [διὰ τῆς χάριτος ... Ἰησοῦ πιστεύομεν σωθῆναι]; Bauer, s.v. σῴζω [2.a.α], σωτήρ [1-2], σωτηρία [2], σωτήριος, χαρίζομαι [1], χάρις [2.a and 3.b]; W. Foerster, *TDNT*, s.v. σῴζω, D-E and σωτήρ [under σῴζω], D-E; H. Conzelmann, *TDNT*, s.v. χάρις [under χαίρω], D-E; *PECL* 1:29 [169B-C]), even if they have despaired of life (see the use of ἀπογινώσκω at Herm Sim 9:26:4-6 [note σωθῆναι in 6], Man 12:6:2 [note ἴασιν], and Vis 1:1:9 [note ἰάσεται]).

ἡ δ' ἐξ Ἔρωτος κατοχὴ προάγεταί τι τολμᾶν παρὰ φύσιν καὶ ἀποθνήσκειν. ECL never uses κατοχή. But cf. παρὰ φύσιν at Rom 1:26, the ECL usage of φύσις described on 750C-D and 755D, and at Rom 5:7 τολμᾷ ἀποθανεῖν.

εἰ ... μύθων πρὸς πίστιν ὄφελός ἐστιν. It is highly unlikely that an ECL writer would ever have appealed to μῦθοι to support his case; see on 749A (near end). In ECL, πίστις never means "proof," except possibly once, at Acts 17:31 (see Bauer, s.v., 1.c); on this meaning in classical literature, see LSJ, s.v., II.2.

(761F-762A)

The semi-technical members of Plutarch's religious vocabulary at this point (τελετή, ὀργιαστής, μύστης) are absent from ECL, though μυστήριον is common (see Bauer, s.v. and G. Bornkamm, *TDNT*, s.v., C-D) and μυέω occurs once, at Phil 4:12 (on which occurrence, see Bornkamm, s.v. [under μυστήριον, 4:828]).

(762A)

οὔτι τοῖς μύθοις πειθόμενος οὐ μὴν οὐδ' ἀπιστῶν παντάπασιν. With Plutarch's strictly qualified acceptance of μῦθοι and his allegorical (or existential?) explanation of those under consideration, cf. Bultmann's demythologizing (see, e.g., his essay "New Testament and Mythology" in H. W. Bartsch and R. H. Fuller [eds.], *Kerygma and Myth* [New York, 1961] 1-44).

εὖ ... λέγουσι ... τοῖς ἐρωτικοῖς ἄνοδον εἰς φῶς ὑπάρχειν, ὅπῃ δὲ καὶ ὅπως ἀγνοοῦσιν, ὥσπερ ἀτραποῦ διαμαρτόντες ἣν πρῶτος ... διὰ φιλοσοφίας Πλάτων κατεῖδε. This "upward journey of lovers to the light" is a metaphor, as is clear from Plutarch's approving reference to Plato's philosophic explanation (or rather vision, if we maintain the figure in κατεῖδε) of the journey, an explanation that will be fully set forth at 764A-766B. The Plutarchan metaphor, doubtlessly inspired by countless passages in Plato, calls to mind the metaphorical use in ECL of ὁδός (see on 759D; ἄνοδος itself is absent from ECL) and φῶς (see Bauer, s.v., 3; H. Conzelmann, *TDNT*, s.v., E-F; *PECL* 1:65 [369E], 69 [372A], 81 [Ch. 77:382C], 93 [387A], 110 [397C], 230 [566D], 271 [589B]; and cf. on darkness imagery at 751F). With Plutarch's figurative κατεῖδε, cf. a similar use of καθορᾶται at Rom 1:20.

ἀπορροαὶ ... τῆς ἀληθείας ἔνεισι ταῖς Αἰγυπτίων ... μυθολογίαις, ἀλλ' ἰχνηλάτου δεινοῦ δέονται ... Cf. the roughly similar use of ἀλήθεια ("truth") throughout ECL (see Bauer, s.v., 2.b; R. Bultmann, *TDNT*, s.v., D; *PECL* 1:93 [387A]) and the metaphorical occurrences of ἴχνος at Rom 4:12, 2 Cor 12:18, 1 Pet 2:21, Ign Eph 12:2, Mart Pol 22:1.

(762B)

At 759D-E, Plutarch began a eulogy of Eros for his power and ὠφέλεια. Having completed his treatment of the former attribute, he turns to the latter, now defined as ἡ πρὸς ἀνθρώπους εὐμένεια καὶ χάρις, which Plutarch undertakes to demonstrate by enumerating the multitude of ἀγαθά ("blessings"; cf. 759D-E, where ἀγαθά has the same sense) Eros bestows on lovers, after observing parenthetically that all men recognize the many blessings beloved youths receive from this god. (The ἀγαθά Plutarch has in mind are chiefly moral qualities, as is apparent from 762B-E and as was alluded to at 759D-E, where he remarked a connection between divine ὠφέλεια and human ἀρετή.) An appropriate translation of ὠφέλεια is, therefore, "benevolence" or "beneficence," depending on whether one stresses, respectively, the εὐμένεια or the χάρις element in Plutarch's definition. A unique feature of Plutarch's vocabulary in this matter is the very occurrence of ὠφέλεια, which is absolutely without theological significance in both classical literature (see LSJ, s.v.) and ECL, where it occurs only twice (Rom 3:1, Jude 16) and in the sense "use" or "advantage" (neither the term nor its cognates merits an entry in *TDNT*). Plutarch's theological use of χάρις, however, is of course fraught with ECL parallelism (on this term, see on 759F, 761E), and his ἀγαθά as "blessings" bears comparison with a similar use of this neuter plural in ECL (see Bauer, s.v. ἀγαθός, 2.b). εὐμένεια, which along with its cognates is absent from ECL, is here characteristically used to designate the "favor" or "goodwill" of the divine (see LSJ, s.v.).

Plutarch begins his description of the ἀγαθά Eros bestows on the lover by contending that the god makes him συνετός even if he is ῥάθυμος, and, as men harden soft wood (ξύλα) in fire, ἀνδρεῖος if he is ἄτολμος. In ECL, σύνεσις is a significant spiritual quality (see Bauer, s.v. σύνεσις, συνετός, συνίημι and H. Conzelmann, *TDNT*, s.v. συνίημι, D-E); and τόλμα, chiefly through its cognate τολμάω, enjoys a modest prominence (see G. Fitzer, *TDNT*, s.v. τολμάω, D and *PECL* 1:188 [548E], 248 [575C]; ἄτολμος does not occur). But the cardinal Platonic virtue ἀνδρεία (see, e.g., *R*. 429A-430C, 441D) is represented in ECL merely by the infrequent appearance of several of its cognates (cf. *PECL* 1:55 and the observation by A. Oepke that "ἀνδρεία occurs in the LXX only in books strongly influenced by Hellenism" [*TDNT* 1:363]), and ῥαθυμία is virtually non-existent (a cognate occurs once, at Herm Vis 1:3:2). There is to my knowledge nothing in ECL in the way of a counterpart to Plutarch's simile, though ξύλον in the sense of "tree" is used in a simile by Clement (1 Clem 23:4, 2 Clem 11:3) and metaphorically at Diogn 12.

(762B-C)

Plutarch next describes the moral improvement Eros induces in the lover vis-à-vis his beloved: instead of γλίσχρος, he becomes δωρητικός, ἁπλοῦς, and μεγαλόφρων; and his μικρολογία and φιλαργυρία melt away δίκην σιδήρου διὰ πυρός. The ethical terminology here is actually or virtually absent from ECL, except for ἁπλοῦς and φιλαργυρία. In ECL, ἁπλότης and ἁπλοῦς are moderately important ethical terms, esp. for Hermas, with at least strong connotations of generosity or liberality, as Plutarch's ἁπλοῦς, at Rom 12:8, 2 Cor 8:2, and 9:11-13 (twice). Though φιλαργυρία is not treated in *TDNT*, one of the ten ECL occurrences of the term and its cognates is at 1 Tim 6:10 (ῥίζα ... πάντων τῶν κακῶν ἐστιν ἡ φιλαργυρία; cf. Pol Phil 4:1). With Plutarch's reference to molten iron, cf. πεπυρωμένος σίδηρος at Apoc Pet 13:28 and the figurative expression ἐν ῥάβδῳ σιδηρᾷ at Rev 2:27, 12:5, 19:15 (cf. Ps 2:9).

(762C)

Anytus, the lover of Alcibiades, was entertaining his guests φιλοτίμως καὶ λαμπρῶς. On the adverbial expression, see on 748F. But Plutarch would certainly not have us take this anecdote too seriously; by way of comparison, one notes the absence of humour from ECL.

Anytus insists that Alcibiades treated him φιλανθρώπως rather than ὑβριστικῶς and ὑπερηφάνως, as his guests insisted. On φιλανθρωπία and ὕβρις, see Intro. V.4 and n. 16 and on 749D, 750B, 758A, ὑπερηφανία is an occasional vice in ECL (see G. Bertram, *TDNT*, s.v. ὑπερήφανος, D-E), and is associated with ὕβρις at Rom 1:30 and 1 Clem 59:3.

Ch. 18

(762D)

At the conclusion of Plutarch's Anytus-Alcibiades anecdote, Zeuxippus characterizes Anytus as πρᾶος ... περὶ ἔρωτα καὶ γενναῖος. Clement and the author of Mart Pol like the terms γενναῖος and γενναιότης, but they are the only ECL writers to use them (see Bauer, s.v.). πραότης (predominantly πραΰτης in NT) is a significant Hellenistic and ECL virtue (see, in addition to Bauer, my article "The Concept of Prāotēs in Plutarch's *Lives*," *GRBS* 3 [1960] 65-73; F. Hauck and S. Schulz, *TDNT*, s.v. πραΰς; *PECL* 1:105, 197-98 [550F], 202, 261).

Plutarch now begins his description of the changes in character and behavior that Eros produces in a lover vis-à-vis the world at large. First, if he is δύσκολος καὶ σκυθρωπός ("grouchy and sullen") the god makes him φιλανθρωπότερος καὶ ἡδίων ("more agreeable and more pleasant"). φιλανθρωπία and its cognates appear infrequently in ECL (but note on 758A); and only in two occurrences in Acts (27:3, 28:2), where, respectively, the adverb and the noun describe deeds of hospitality and kindness, do we encounter a sense that approaches the present one (cf. on λόγους φιλανθρώπους at 749D). The other ethical terms Plutarch employs at this point display varying degrees of insignificance in ECL: σκυθρωπός stresses appearance rather than character in one (Matt 6:16) of its two ECL occurrences (cf. W. Bieder, *TDNT*, s.v. and *PECL* 1:61, 154 [417C]), and ECL does not use δύσκολος/δυσκόλως in an ethical sense (see Bauer, s.v.), as is also true of the single occurrence of ἡδύς (Herm Sim 8:9:1, in the non-classical comparative form ἡδύτερος, on which see BDF, sec. 61.1).

A man becomes φαιδρότερος ("brighter" with cheerfulness), Plutarch contends, ὑπὸ τῆς ἐρωτικῆς θερμότητος. φαιδρός is absent from ECL, which offers no exact parallel to Plutarch's metaphor. But cf. 1 Cor 7:9, where Paul likens sexual passion to πῦρ, the word employed to designate fire in the "Homeric" (see Helmbold, 386, n.b) quotation which introduces and generates Plutarch's metaphor; also, on 752 D, 753A.

If men see a light in a house at night, θεῖον ἡγοῦνται καὶ θαυμάζουσι. Cf. τὸ θαυμαστὸν αὐτοῦ (God's) φῶς at 1 Pet 2:9, the use of θαυμάζω and its cognates in ECL descriptions of human reaction to Jesus and God (see G. Bertram, *TDNT*, s.v. θαῦμα, C-D), and the ECL application of the adjective θαυμαστός to God (1 Clem 60:1) and things related to him (see Bauer, s.v.). On θεῖος, cf. on 758A, 758D-759D (near end).

(762E)

ψυχὴν δὲ μικρὰν καὶ ταπεινὴν καὶ ἀγεννῆ ὁρῶντες (people in general) ἐξαίφνης ὑποπιμπλαμένην φρονήματος, ἐλευθερίας, φιλοτιμίας, χάριτος, ἀφειδίας, οὐκ ἀναγκάζονται λέγειν ... "... τις θεὸς ἔνδον" (*Od.* 19.40). Plutarch here appears to be using ψυχή in a non-philosophical sense to designate the whole man from the perspective of his emotional and inner life, a sense with general parallels throughout ECL (see Bauer, s.v., 1.b-d and E. Schweizer, *TDNT*, s.v., D; cf. on 755E, 758D-759D). Plutarch's figurative use of μικρός is striking; for this term lacks an ethical sense in

ECL (cf. on μικρολογία at 762B-C), and in only one of the illustrative passages cited by LSJ (Sophocles *Aj.* 1120) does it have noticeably moral connotations, its figurative use in both ECL and classical literature being generally confined to the depiction of basically amoral qualities (see LSJ, s.v., I.3; Bauer, s.v., 1.C; O. Michel, *TDNT*, s.v., 4-5). The pejorative force of ταπεινός here, characteristic of classical usage (see LSJ, s.v. ταπεινός, 2-4 and ταπεινότης and W. Grundmann, *TDNT*, s.v. ταπεινός, A, B.5; but note *PECL* 1:191 on the use of the adjective in a favorable sense by one of the speakers in Plutarch's *num. vind.* [549C-D]), clashes sharply with the usage of ECL, where, with *possibly* a few exceptions (see, e.g., Bauer's treatment of ταπεινός at 2 Cor 10:1 [s.v., 2.a] and of the two occurrences of ταπεινοφροσύνη at Col 2:18-23 [s.v.]), ταπεινός, ταπεινοφροσύνη, and their cognates have a morally positive force (see Bauer, s.v. and Grundmann, *TDNT*, s.v. ταπεινός, B.5, D-E): in fact, ταπεινοφροσύνη and πραΰτης, antithetically presented through their respective adjectives in the present *amat.* passage (762D-E; note above on πρᾶος at 762D), are on several occasions in ECL treated as complementary virtues (Matt 11:29, Eph 4:2, Col 3:12, 1 Clem 30:8, Ign Eph 10:2, Herm Man 11:8); and the ψυχὴ ταπεινή, here held up for reproach by Plutarch, is twice extolled in ECL (Herm Man 4:2:2, Barn 3:1). ἀγενής occurs once in ECL (1 Cor 1:28); cf. on γενναῖος at 762D. ECL employs φρόνημα only at Rom 8:6-7 and 27, where it always has a sense quite different from its present one (see Bauer, s.v., and G. Bertram, *TDNT*, s.v. [under φρήν], D.3.b). Plutarch's use of ἐλευθερία in a moral and spiritual, rather than a political or social, sense has a number of general parallels in ECL (see on 755B). φιλοτιμία as used by Plutarch can convey the senses of "ambition," "zeal," or "generosity" (see my article "The Character of Plutarch's Themistocles," *TAPhA* 92 [1961] 327 and n. 4), the first two of which have loose ECL parallels in the use of its cognate verb at Rom 15:20, 2 Cor 5:9, and 1 Thes 4:11; for more on φιλοτιμία, see on 748F. χάρις as a quality inspired in the lover by Eros is perhaps a reflection of ἡ πρὸς ἀνθρώπους εὐμένεια καὶ χάρις that is a primary attribute of Eros (on which phrase, see on 762B); cf. Acts 6:8 (Stephen was full of χάρις), Mart Pol 12:1 (Polycarp's countenance was filled with χάρις), and the other passages cited by Bauer along with these (s.v. χάρις, 4). In its single ECL appearance (Col 2:23), ἀφειδία has a sense almost antithetical to its present one.

Plutarch asks ἐκεῖνο ... οὐ δαιμόνιον; and goes on to describe the marvelous behavior of ὁ ἐρωτικός. As here used, δαιμόνιον contrasts notably with ECL usage (see on ἀγαθὸς δαίμων at 755E-F and esp. on 757E). And the description of the lover's behavior, inspired by Plato *Phdr.* 252A, is without conceptual parallel in ECL.

(762E-F)

Plutarch figuratively describes the effect on the lover of the appearance of his καλός (on which term, see on 749C): τὸ θράσος ἐκκέκλασται καὶ κατακέκοπταί οἱ τὸ τῆς ψυχῆς γαῦρον. Cf., for a superficial verbal parallel, the injunction of Barn 19:3 and Did 3:9: οὐ δώσεις τῇ ψυχῇ σου θράσος. Paul uses ἐκκλάω metaphorically, though the context is far different from Plutarch's, at Rom 11:16-21.

(762F)

ἄξιον (understand ἐστί) ... μνημονεῦσαι. See on the impersonal use of ἄξιον at 760E. At 1 Cor 16:4, however, Paul puts his infinitive in the articular construction (cf. BDF, sec. 400.3).

μεμιγμένα πυρὶ φθέγγεται καὶ διὰ τῶν μελῶν (i.e., her poetry) ἀναφέρει τὴν ἀπὸ τῆς καρδίας θερμότητα. The subject of each verb is Sappho. On Plutarch's "fire" and "heat" metaphor, see on 752D, 753A, 762D. Both classical authors and ECL commonly employ καρδία as here, to designate the seat of the emotions: see LSJ, s.v., I.1-2; Bauer, s.v., 1.b.ε; J. Behm, *TDNT*, s.v., B.2.a, D.2.a.

(762F-763A)

It is noteworthy, from the point of view of contrast with ECL, that Sappho's erotic passion, which Plutarch cites to illustrate the overwhelming power of Eros, is homosexual (cf. on 749C [καλός]). On Lesbianism in Greece and on the poem by Sappho (2 [= fr. 31]) here summarized by Plutarch, see, e.g., D. Page, *Sappho and Alcaeus* (Oxford, 1955) 19-33, 140-46 and Flacelière, *Love*, 92-100.

(763A)

Plutarch describes the passion Eros inspires as a δαιμόνιος σάλος τῆς ψυχῆς. Again, as at 762E and in contrast to ECL usage, δαιμόνιος in a neutral, if not favorable, sense; see on 755E-F, 757E, 762E.

(763A-B)

On the prophetic frenzy of the Pythia and the bacchic frenzy of the devotees of Cybele, see on 758D-759D, 759B.

(763B-C)

Plutarch's distinction between the sensible and the intelligible world and his discussion of the means (the μῦθος of the poets, the νόμος of the lawgivers, and the λόγος ["rational thought"] of the philosophers; cf. *PECL* 1:181-82, 272 [589F], 280 [592F], 319 [Frag. 157]) whereby we develop "belief" (πίστις) and an "opinion" (δόξα) about the gods (concerning whose number, nature, and relationship poets, lawgivers, and philosophers debate) strike me as basically the product of Greek thought and as alien to the modes of thought we encounter in ECL (cf. on μῦθος at 749A and 761E, φιλοσοφία at 749C and 752A, and δόξα at 756A-B; also, note that λόγος does not carry the sense "rational thought," "reason" in ECL [cf. H. Kleinknecht, *TDNT*, s.v. λέγω, B.5 and *PECL* 1:319 (Frag. 157)]). But it cannot be denied that Plutarch's present conceptual framework has accommodated πίστις in a sense that is fully suggestive of *ECL* usage (see Bauer, s.v., 2 and R. Bultmann, *TDNT*, s.v. πιστεύω, esp. D.II.1.a, D.II.2.a and d, D.IV.7; cf. *PECL* 1:118, 190 and on 756A-B, 756B), though not without ample precedent in earlier classical literature (see LSJ, s.v., 1; the classical parallels cited by Bauer, s.v., 2; Bultmann, *TDNT*, s.v. πιστεύω, A.I.3.a, D.I.1-3; and, e.g., Sophocles *OT* 1445 [. . . ἂν τῷ θεῷ πίστιν φέροις.]).

(763C)

Plutarch's use of οὐσία in the philosophical sense in reference to the nature or essence of the gods (on which sense, see LSJ, s.v., II) is without parallel in ECL, where the term means "property" or "wealth" in its two occurrences (Luke 15:12-13).

μάχονται (the philosophers) . . . τοῖς νομοθέταις. Plutarch is referring to the theological disputes between the philosophers and the lawgivers. ECL also uses μάχομαι in this figurative manner (see Bauer, s.v., 2 and O. Bauernfeind, *TDNT*, s.v.; cf. on 749C, 750A), but never with the dative of hostile association, though once with πρός plus the accusative to syntactically express hostile association (John 6:52; cf. 2 Tim 2:24). Both the dative and the πρός-accusative construction are characteristic of classical usage (see LSJ, s.v. μάχομαι; cf. Goodwin-Gulick, sec. 1189; Smyth-Messing, sec. 1523.b, and on Ἔρωτι πολεμήσων at 750A).

(763D)

Poets and lawgivers, Plutarch continues, either refuse to listen or are unable to comprehend when philosophers treat as gods certain ἰδέαι, ἀριθμοί, μονάδες, and πνεύματα. The last term of course permeates ECL (see Bauer, s.v. and E. Schweizer, *TDNT*, s.v., E-F; cf. *PECL* 1:118 [402C], 134, 171 [432DE], 180 [438B, 438C]) and is by comparison more or less insignificant in Greek thought (see H. Kleinknecht, *TDNT*, s.v., A.IV); but μονάς is absent from ECL, which also never uses ἰδέα or ἀριθμός with philosophical signification (see Bauer, s.v. and O. Rühle, *TDNT*, s.v. ἀριθμέω), though the former is a favorite term with Hermas.

ἀνωμαλίαν ἔχουσιν αἱ δόξαι καὶ διαφοράν. Again, δόξα in a sense typical of classical Greek but foreign to ECL (see on 756A-B).

(763D-E)

Plutarch twice uses στάσις in the sense "faction" (political at 763D, theological at 763E; cf. LSJ, s.v., II-III), a sense it never quite reaches in ECL (see Bauer, s.v. and G. Delling, *TDNT*, s.v., C-D).

(763D)

πάντες ἐν ταὐτῷ γενόμενοι. Cf. the adverbial uses of τὸ αὐτό in ECL (see Bauer, s.v. αὐτός, 4.b and BDF, sec. 233.1).

(763E-F)

βασιλεὺς καὶ ἄρχων καὶ ἁρμοστὴς ὁ Ἔρως . . . ἐστεφανωμένος. In ECL, βασιλεύς is used once of a chthonic spirit (Rev 9:11) and frequently of Christ or God (see Bauer, s.v., 2 and K. L. Schmidt, *TDNT*, s.v., E; cf. *PECL* 1:43 [353B], 48 [355E], 67 [370D], 82 [383A]); ἄρχων, once of Christ (Rev 1:5), once of an angelic being (Diogn 7:2), and often of evil spirits (see Bauer, s.v., 1, 3 and G. Delling, *TDNT*, s.v. [under ἄρχω], 2-3; cf. *PECL* 1:167, 193 [550A]); ἁρμοστής does not occur; and there are two references to Christ "crowned" (ἐστεφανωμένος; Heb 2:9 [cf.

2:7 and Ps 8:4-6], Barn 7:9), one to his golden στέφανος (Rev 14:14), and four to his στέφανος of thorns (Matt 27:29//Mark 15:17, John 19:2-5). On the significance of the crown in NT and the early Church, see W. Grundmann, *TDNT*, s.v. στέφανος, D-E.

(763F)

Eros is κεκοσμημένος . . . πολλαῖς συνωρίσι φιλίας καὶ κοινωνίας. In ECL, God and Christ are neither direct objects of κοσμέω (but note Tit 2:10) nor modified by any of its passive participles. On φιλία and κοινωνία in Plutarch and ECL, see on 757C-D; it is clear, both from συνωρίσι and from the overall substance of *amat.*, that Plutarch is thinking in terms of a "friendship and fellowship" limited to two individuals.

The φιλία and κοινωνία inspired by Eros figuratively soars aloft ἐπὶ τὰ κάλλιστα τῶν ὄντων καὶ θειότατα. Plutarch is now moving in a verbal and conceptual framework alien to ECL: as we know from the immediately succeeding references to Plato (763F-764A) and from 764E-765D, Plutarch has in mind Plato's distinction between the real and the phenomenal world and that Platonic vision of eternal beauty, the "form" τὸ καλόν, which Eros makes available to human souls. See Flacelière's and Helmbold's notes to these portions of *amat.* and, on the Platonic doctrines being utilized by Plutarch, e.g., Friedländer, 3-84 and J. E. Raven, *Plato's Thought in the Making* (Cambridge, 1965) passim (s.v. εἶδος, "Eros," "Idea," "Ideas" in General Index) [henceforth cited as Raven].

Ch. 19

(764A)

τὰ . . . εἰρημένα Πλάτωνι . . . μηδ' . . . εἴπῃς. The dative of agent, common enough in classical Greek (see Goodwin-Gulick, sec. 1174 and Smyth-Messing, secs. 1488-94), is virtually non-existent in ECL (see BDF, sec. 191); the prohibitive subjunctive (in the aorist), however, is characteristic of both bodies of literature (see Goodwin-Gulick, sec. 1345; Smyth-Messing, secs. 1800, 1840-44; BDF, secs 335, 337.3, 364.3).

ὑπηνίξω τὸν Αἰγυπτίων μῦθον εἰς ταὐτὰ τοῖς Πλατωνικοῖς συμφέρεσθαι περὶ Ἔρωτος. Soclarus addresses this statement to Plutarch, having in mind Plutarch's reference at 762A to Plato and the μυθολογίαι of the Egyptians. See, on μῦθος, my comments to 749A, 761E, 762A. Cf. on ἐν ταὐτῷ at 763D.

(764B)

ἀγαπήσομεν ("we shall be delighted," "pleased"). The force of ἀγαπάω is here even weaker than that at 761A. See on this passage for more on ἀγαπάω.

Plutarch observes that the Greeks recognize two Erotes, a Vulgar one (πάνδημος) and a Heavenly one (οὐράνιος). Throughout *Agape and Eros*, e.g., on p. 51, Nygren wrongly attributes this very distinction between two Erotes to Plato. It is not Plato's at all, but Pausanias' (*Smp.* 180C-182A), and is incompatible with Plato's own concept of a single Eros, which is set forth through the agency of Socrates and Diotima at *Smp.* 199C-212B (cf. Bury, *The Symposium of Plato*, lii-lx, esp. lviii). Plutarch's observation is undoubtedly derived, partially if not entirely, from Pausanias' speech in *Smp.*

(764B-C)

Throughout Plutarch's set of four similes, Eros and the sun (ἥλιος) function as analogues; and in the first and fourth, Ἔρως: ψυχή:: ἥλιος:σῶμα. Cf. the simile at Rev 1:16, in which the countenance of Christ is likened to ἥλιος, and the NT metaphors presenting Christ as φῶς (in Plutarch's first simile at 764B, as the sun furnishes φῶς to the body, so does Eros to souls; cf. *PECL* 1:173 [433D]): John 1:4-9, 8:12, 9:5, 12:46, Luke 2:32 (Isa 42:6). Cf. Matt 4:16 (Isa 9:1-2), Eph 5:13-14, 1 John 2:8; Bauer, s.v. φῶς; H. Conzelmann, *TDNT*, s.v. φῶς, E-F. On the dualistic anthropology implicit in Plutarch's first and fourth similes, see on 758D-759D.

(764C)

σώματος ἀγύμναστος ἕξις. Note the verbal parallel at Heb 5:14: διὰ τὴν ἕξιν τὰ αἰσθητήρια γεγυμνασμένα.

(764C-D)

But, Plutarch continues, there is a difference between Eros and the sun: δείκνυσιν ἥλιος μὲν . . . τὰ καλὰ καὶ τὰ αἰσχρὰ τοῖς ὁρῶσιν· Ἔρως δὲ μόνων τῶν καλῶν φέγγος ἐστὶ καὶ πρὸς ταῦτα μόνα τοὺς ἐρῶντας ἀναπείθει βλέπειν καὶ στρέφεσθαι. This statement points up the dangers of pressing too far any analogy between Plutarchan Ἔρως (and, by implication, φιλία, which for Plutarch is inspired by Eros; see, e.g., Intro. III) and early Christian ἀγάπη, which is not contingent upon the beauty, either physical or moral, of its object, whether it is being expressed by God toward humans or by a man toward his neighbor (see, e.g., Nygren, passim [s.v. ἀγάπη in Index of Greek Words, "Love" in Index of Subjects]; Bultmann, *TNT*, secs 32.3, 39.3, 50.4, 60.2 and *Primitive Christianity*, 75, 78, 205; E. Stauffer, *TDNT*, s.v. ἀγαπάω, D-F; and, for a different [contradictory?] philological slant, Burton, *Gal.*, 520f.). On καλός and αἰσχρός, see on 759D-E and esp. 759E. Cf. the φέγγος radiated by two heavenly beings at Gos Pet 9:36.

(764D-E)

Plutarch now calls attention to *the* essential difference between Eros and the sun: οὐ γὰρ ψυχῇ σῶμα ταὐτὸν ἀλλ' ἕτερον, ὥσπερ ἥλιον μὲν ὁρατὸν Ἔρωτα δὲ νοητόν. Again, Plutarch's dualistic anthropology shows through, together with a firm indication that here his distinction of ψυχή from σῶμα is fully metaphysical and not, as in ECL and perhaps previously at 755E and 762E, primarily analytical (on all this, see on 755E, 758D-759D, 762E, 764B-C); for ἥλιος (explicitly) and σῶμα (implicitly) are assigned to the sensible and Ἔρως (explicitly) and ψυχή (implicitly) to the intelligible world. In fact, Plutarch adds as a corollary, the sun turns the "mind" (διάνοια, on which term see on 759C) ἀπὸ τῶν νοητῶν ἐπὶ τὰ αἰσθητά, persuading it that reality (ἀλήθεια) is located in the sensible rather than the intelligible world and inducing λήθην ὧν ὁ Ἔρως ἀνάμνησίς ἐστιν. This whole passage, with its dualistic anthropology, distinction between the real and the phenomenal world, and notion of anamnesis is thoroughly Platonic and in some respects alien to the conceptual framework of ECL (see, in addition to my comments just cited, on 763F and the following comment on anamnesis); it is significant that λήθη occurs only once in ECL and νοητός and αἰσθητός not at all (but see on ὁρατός and δοξαστός at 756D), and that in the three NT occurrences of cognates of αἰσθητός the reference is to non-sensible perception (Luke 9:45, Phil 1:9, Heb 5:14; cf. Bauer, s.v. αἰσθάνομαι, αἴσθησις, αἰσθητήριον and G. Delling, *TDNT*, s.v. αἰσθάνομαι, B). At the same time, Plutarch's assigning of Eros to the intelligible world at least calls to mind the NT notion that God is invisible (John 1:18, 1 Tim 1:17) and a πνεῦμα (John 4:24) and must be worshipped accordingly (John 4:23-24); cf. *PECL* 1:116 (400D).

Also, Plutarch's use here and in the closely related context of the remainder of Ch. 19 of ἀλήθεια to designate (764E, 764F-765A) and ἀληθῶς to describe (764F, 765D) the true and ultimate reality of the intelligible world as against the appearances of the sensible world, though classical in character (see LSJ, s.v. ἀλήθεια [I.2], ἀληθής, ἀληθινός [I.2, II] and R. Bultmann, *TDNT* s.v. ἀλήθεια, C) and Platonic in immediate origin (see Plato *Phdr.* 248B; Flacelière, 133, n. 134; Helmbold, 402f., nn. b and d), has affinities with the common occurrence in ECL of ἀλήθεια and its cognates to designate and describe "reality," often as opposed to appearance (see Bauer, s.v. ἀλήθεια [3], ἀληθής [3], ἀληθινός [3], ἀληθῶς and R. Bultmann, *TDNT*, s.v. ἀλήθεια [D.3, 6], ἀληθής [3, 6; under ἀλήθεια], and ἀληθινός [under ἀλήθεια]). For present purposes, the most significant of such ECL occurrences involve the use of the adjectives ἀληθής and ἀληθινός to depict a world of spiritual reality that is somehow set off against the phenomenal world; esp. John 1:9 (Christ was τὸ φῶς τὸ ἀληθινόν coming into the κόσμος; note H. Sasse, *TDNT*, s.v. κόσμος [under κοσμέω]: "Like all that is created, the κόσμος has only limited duration. . . . Transitoriness is of the very essence of the κόσμος as the sum of everything created" [C.2.b] and "the term κόσμος, which derives from pagan philosophy, is reserved for the world which lies under sin and death" [C.4.c]), 1 John 2:8 (darkness is passing away and τὸ φῶς τὸ ἀληθινόν is now shining; cf. *PECL* 1:93 [387A]), John 6:30-35 (Christ represents himself as ὁ ἄρτος ὁ ἀληθινός, who/which gives ζωή to the κόσμος and satisfies hunger eternally), John 6:46-58 (Christ represents his flesh as ἀληθὴς βρῶσις and his blood as ἀληθὴς πόσις), John 15:1-6 (Christ represents himself as ἡ ἄμπελος ἡ ἀληθινή), Ign Eph 7:2 (Christ is ζωὴ ἀληθινή), Smyrn 4:1 (Christ is τὸ ἀληθινὸν ἡμῶν ζῆν; cf. the use of substantivized adjectives and participles by Plato, Plutarch, and classical authors in general to express abstract thought [see on 758E, 759E, 764E-765D]), Trall 9:2 (without Christ, we do not have τὸ ἀληθινὸν ζῆν), Eph 11:1 (let us be found in Christ εἰς τὸ ἀληθινὸν ζῆν), Diogn 12:4 (apparently a distinction between ζωή and ζωὴ ἀληθής), 1 John 5:20 (Christ has given us διάνοια to know ὁ ἀληθινὸς θεός, who is not to be confounded with idols; note the intimate connection between διάνοια and ἀλήθεια in the *amat.* passage under scrutiny), 1 Thes 1:9 (the Thessalonians turned to God from idols δουλεύειν θεῷ ζῶντι καὶ ἀληθινῷ), John 17:3 (Christ associates eternal ζωή with the knowledge of ὁ μόνος ἀληθινὸς θεός), 1 Clem 43:6 (a reference to ὁ ἀληθινὸς καὶ μόνος θεός), Heb 8:1-6 (the risen Christ is a minister of ἡ σκηνὴ ἡ ἀληθινή, which was established by the Lord, not by man, and which is the model of which the earthly tabernacle is but a copy and a shadow; cf. *PECL* 1:93 [387C]), and Heb 9:24 (Christ has entered, not into χειροποίητα . . . ἅγια, ἀντίτυπα τῶν ἀληθινῶν, but into heaven itself).

(764E-765D)

Plutarch now expounds and summarizes the Platonic doctrine of ἀνάμνησις, as it relates to Eros and τὸ καλόν (or κάλλος) and as it appears in Plato's *Phdr.* (244A-257B) and *Smp.* (199C-212B). Plutarch's thought, itself an incomplete outline of Plato's concepts, runs, in barest outline, as follows. The immortal ψυχή, before it entered the phenomenal world to abide temporarily in a mortal σῶμα, existed in the real world and there had concourse with, among other eternal forms, τὸ καλόν, that pure, abstract "beauty" that is the ultimate source of all the beauty, ethical as well as physical, that we discern in the world of phenomena, where beauty never appears in a pure, unmixed form. But upon entering the phenomenal world, the ψυχή is so dazzled by sensible "reality" that it *forgets* the eternal forms and confuses beauty with beautiful objects, unless it accepts as its guide Eros, who will lead it out of its confusion to a "perception" and comprehension of τὸ καλόν, which it has forgotten. It is through ἀνάμνησις that Eros carries out this metaphysical function, for Eros *reminds* the ψυχή of the forgotten beauty by directing its attention, first, to beautiful σώματα (which reflect τὸ καλόν on an immediate, sensible level) and, then, after its μνήμη has been stirred, to the beautiful ἦθος within a beautiful σῶμα, thus reintroducing the ψυχή to beauty of a purely abstract sort. For more on all this, and on its derivation from Plato and relation to ECL, see on 750E (for ἦθος), 758D-759D, 759E (for τὸ καλόν), 764C-D, 764D-E and cf. *PECL* 1:295-96 (943A), 300 (945A, 945B). In the passage under immediate scrutiny, Plutarch is moving in a conceptual atmosphere quite distinct from that of ECL; and though ἀνάμνησις, μνήμη, and related terms are of some importance in ECL (see J. Behm, *TDNT*, s.v. ἀνάμνησις and O. Michel, *TDNT*, s.v. μιμνήσκομαι etc.), their occurrences, so it seems to me, fail to yield any significant parallels.

(764E-F)

Charmed by the sun (ἔοικε ... φαρμάττειν τὴν διάνοιαν ὁ ἥλιος) and filled with ἡδονή and wonder, we focus our attention on the world about us and forget the world of true reality. On ἡδονή, which here, as customarily in ECL, has pejorative connotations, see on 750C-D, 751B. φαρμάττω itself is absent from ECL, but its cognates invariably exhibit pejorative force, excepting φάρμακον at Ign Eph 20:2.

(764F)

One cannot comprehend the nature of beauty, ἂν μὴ τύχῃ ... σώφρονος ("chaste," I think; so also Flacelière and Helmbold) Ἔρωτος ἰατροῦ καὶ σωτῆρος. On the terms with which Plutarch here describes Eros, see on 752A, 761E (the reference to Heracles).

(765A)

Eros guides his devotee ἐπὶ τὴν ἀλήθειαν ... εἰς τὸ ἀληθείας πεδίον (Plato *Phdr*. 248B), οὗ τὸ ... καθαρὸν καὶ ἀψευδὲς ἵδρυται κάλλος. On these occurrences of ἀλήθεια, see on 764D-E. καθαρός as here used to describe the form beauty (on which form, see on 763F, 764D-E, 764E-765D), probably taken over from Plato (see, e.g., *Smp*. 211D-E, *Phdr*. 250C), is without true parallel in ECL, where the term usually refers to physical, ritual, or moral cleanness or purity (see Bauer, s.v. and F. Hauck, *TDNT*, s.v., D; cf. *PECL* 1:81 [382E], 95 [388F], 176 [435D], 322-23); but note Ignatius' metaphorical use of καθαρός with the connotation "unmixed" at Rom 4:1. The antithesis that Plutarch sets up through his use of ἀλήθεια and ἀψευδής, however, has loose parallels throughout ECL (see, e.g., Bauer, s.v. ἀψευδής, ψεῦδος; H. Conzelmann, *TDNT*, s.v. ψεῦδος, D-E; *PECL* 1:97 [392A]).

διὰ χρόνου, "after an interval." On this classical construction, see LSJ, s.v. διά, II.2; Smyth-Messing, sec. 1685.c; Goodwin-Gulick, sec. 1213.a.3. διά is similarly used in ECL (see Bauer, s.v., A.II.2 and BDF, sec. 223.1).

Plutarch describes Eros as εὐμενής (on which term, cf. on 762B) and likens him to a μυσταγωγός at an initiation (τελετή) into a mystery religion. The three terms given in Greek are not represented in ECL, though μυέω occurs once (Phil 4:12), significantly enough in a figurative sense, and μυστήριον is common. Plutarch's simile is undoubtedly inspired, at least partially, by Plato's initiation metaphor, involving the verb μυέω, at *Smp.* 209E-210A. Toward the end of 765A, there is a figurative use of μυέω (τὰ νοητὰ μυηθῆναι . . . εἴδη) that bears comparison with the one at Phil 4:12.

Teachers of geometry, Plutarch observes, offer ἁπτὰ καὶ ὁρατὰ μιμήματα of abstract geometric forms to pupils not yet able to comprehend τὰ νοητὰ . . . τῆς ἀσωμάτου καὶ ἀπαθοῦς οὐσίας εἴδη. Cf. the use of ὁρατός and ἀόρατος in ECL (see on 756D), Christ's assertion at John 5:37 (οὔτε εἶδος αὐτοῦ [God] ἑωράκατε; cf. Kittel's exegesis of διὰ εἴδους at 2 Cor 5:7, *TDNT*, s.v. εἶδος, 2), and Pol Phil 1:1 (τὰ μιμήματα τῆς ἀληθοῦς ἀγάπης; note W. Michaelis, *TDNT*, s.v. μιμέομαι, 6 [at end] and cf. *PECL* 1:55-56 [361E], 196 [550E] and on ἀλήθεια at 764D-E). Yet Plutarch's reference to geometry and distinction between the sensible and intelligible worlds are thoroughly Platonic in spirit (see, e.g., Plato *Men.* 81E-85D; Raven, 56-70; and on 764D-E, 764E-765D), as is his use of εἶδος (see, e.g., Friedländer, Ch. 1 and Raven, passim [s.v. εἶδος, "Ideas" in General Index]; cf. *PECL* 1:164 [422B]); and in ECL οὐσία is both rare and without philosophical, much less metaphysical, import (see Bauer, s.v. and on 763C). Ignatius, however, can speak of a δαιμόνιον ἀσώματον (Smyrn 3:2; cf. Smyrn 2) and, with striking metaphysical connotations, characterizes the pre- and post-existent Christ as ἀπαθής, as against the Christ of history, who was παθητός (Eph 7:2, Pol 3:2).

(765B)

ὁ οὐράνιος Ἔρως (cf. on 764B). Cf. the Matthean formula ὁ πατὴρ ὑμῶν (or μου) ὁ οὐράνιος (5:48, 6:14, 6:26, 6:32, 15:13, 18:35, 23:9; note the discussion of this formula by H. Traub, *TDNT*, s.v. οὐράνιος [under οὐρανός], 5:538) and the application by ECL writers of the adjective ἐπουράνιος to God (1 Clem 61:2), Christ (1 Cor 15:47-49, Mart Pol 14:3), and heavenly beings in general (Phil 2:10, Ign Trall 9:1). ECL regularly conceives of οὐρανός as the abode of the divine (see Bauer, s.v., 2-3 and H. Traub, *TDNT*, s.v. οὐρανός [D-E], οὐράνιος, ἐπουράνιος, οὐρανόθεν).

Ἔρως ἔσοπτρα καλῶν καλά, θνητὰ μέντοι θείων (so Hubert, Flacelière, and Helmbold, after Wyttenbach and Herwerden; θεῶν EB) ⟨καὶ ἀπαθῶν⟩ (add. Hubert, Flacelière, and Helmbold, after Wyttenbach and Bernardakis) παθητὰ καὶ νοητῶν αἰσθητὰ μηχανώμενος ἔν τε σχήμασι ... καὶ εἴδεσι νέων ὥρᾳ στίλβοντα δείκνυσι καὶ κινεῖ τὴν μνήμην ... διὰ τούτων ἀναφλεγομένην. Several ECL parallels come to mind: at 1 Cor 13:12, βλέπομεν ... ἄρτι δι' ἐσόπτρου ἐν αἰνίγματι, τότε δὲ πρόσωπον πρὸς πρόσωπον (on which, see G. Kittel, *TDNT*, s.v. αἴνιγμα; cf. Jas 1:23, commented on by Kittel, *TDNT*, s.v. ἔσοπτρον); Rom 1:20 (τὰ ... ἀόρατα [sc. of God] ... τοῖς ποιήμασιν νοούμενα [but cf. on 764D-E] καθορᾶται, ἥ τε ... θειότης); the antitheses involving θνητός and ἀθάνατος or ἀθανασία (1 Cor 15:53-54, Did 4:8, Diogn 6:8 [cf. on 758D-759D], 9:2; cf. *PECL* 1:136 [409F] and the life-death contrasts at Rom 8:11, 2 Cor 4:10-12, 5:4, 1 Tim 5:6, Herm Sim 8:7:1, 9:21:2-4); Ignatius' antithetical use of ἀπαθής and παθητός at Eph 7:2 and Pol 3:2 (on which use, see W. Michaelis, *TDNT*, s.v. παθητός [under πάσχω], 3 and on 765A; cf. *PECL* 1:268 [588D]); and the use of σχῆμα (Phil 2:7, Herm Vis 5:1; cf. the exegeses of these two passages by J. Schneider, *TNDT*, s.v. σχῆμα, B and μετασχηματίζω, C) and of εἶδος (Luke 9:29; cf. Luke 3:22 and on 759D) with reference to a person's external appearance. On εἶδος as intelligible, rather than sensible, "form," see on 765A. On μνήμη, see on 764E-765D. With Plutarch's metaphorical use of ἀναφλέγω, though the word itself is absent from ECL, cf. 1 Cor 7:9; note my comments on 752D, 753A, 762D, 762F. Almqvist (101-3 [sec. 205]) brings 1 Cor 13:12 into connection with the present and two other *Mor.* passages where Plutarch employs ἔσοπτρον metaphorically (*Is. et Os.* 382A, *princ. ind.* 781F).

σβεννύναι ... τὸ πάθος. Plutarch is criticizing those who wrongfully try "to extinguish erotic passion" in friends or relatives. Cf. τὸ πνεῦμα μὴ σβέννυτε (1 Thes 5:19) and on πάθος at 750F.

πρὸς ἡδονὰς σκοτίους ... ῥυέντες ... ἐμαράνθησαν. Plutarch is referring to those who wrongly turn "to dark pleasures" (on which, see on 750C-D, 751B, 751F) as a means of extinguishing their erotic passion. With Plutarch's figure, cf. perhaps the simile at Jas 1:11: as the grass is withered by the scorching heat of the sun, so also ὁ πλούσιος ... μαρανθήσεται.

(765B-C)

σώφρονι λογισμῷ μετ' αἰδοῦς οἷον ... πυρὸς ἀφεῖλον τὸ μανικόν, αὐγὴν δὲ καὶ φῶς ἀπέλιπον τῇ ψυχῇ μετὰ θερμότητος. Plutarch is talking about those who handle their erotic passion in the proper way. On the vocabulary, metaphors, and conceptual framework of this passage, see on 752A (σωφρονεῖν), 752D (πῦρ), 753B (σωφρονεῖ), 758D-759D, 762A (φῶς), 762D (ὑπὸ τῆς ἐρωτικῆς θερμότητος). Cf. the association between αὐγάζω and φωτισμός at 2 Cor 4:4 and that between αἰδώς and σωφροσύνη at 1 Tim 2:9.

(765C)

τό τε σῶμα τὸ τῶν ἐρωμένων παρελθόντες (the lovers) ἔσω φέρονται καὶ ἅπτονται τοῦ ἤθους. On the concepts and vocabulary involved in this statement, see on ἦθος and on σῶμα at 750E, 758D-759D, 764B-C, 764D-E, 764E-765D.

(765C-D)

Plutarch is describing proper behavior on the part of lovers: they abide with their beloved youths, ἂν (ἄν for ἐάν is quite rare in Koine; see Bauer, s.v. ἄν [at end] and BDF, sec. 107) ... τοῦ καλοῦ ... εἴδωλον ἐν ταῖς διανοίαις ἔχωσιν (the beloveds); but if not, the lovers forsake them as bees (αἱ μέλιτται) do flowers without honey (μέλι). See, on τὸ καλόν, on 759E, 763F, 764E-765D; on διάνοια, on 759C; and on Plutarch's bee simile, on 750C. In ECL, εἴδωλον always means "idol" and is never used even of a sensible "reflection," much less a purely intelligible one (see Bauer, s.v.; F. Büchsel, *TDNT*, s.v., 2-3; *PECL* 1:101; and on 759C). The Platonic ἔρως Plutarch has in mind contrasts emphatically, it seems to me, with early Christian ἀγάπη (cf. on 764C-D).

(765D)

Wherever lovers find within the character and thoughts of young men ἴχνος τι τοῦ θείου (on which phrase, see on ἴχνος at 762A and τὸ θεῖον at 758A) ... καὶ ὁμοιότητα σαίνουσαν (on the single occurrence of σαίνω in ECL, see Bauer, s.v. and F. Lang, *TDNT*, s.v.), ὑφ' ἡδονῆς καὶ θαύματος ἐνθουσιῶντες (on which phrase, see on ἡδονή at 750C-D and 751B, θαυμάζουσι at 762D, and ἐνθουσιασμός at 758D-759D) ..., εὐπαθοῦσι τῇ μνήμῃ (for the Platonic-Plutarchan epistemology that accounts for this phrase, see on 764E-765D).

Plutarch continues with his description of the lovers' reaction to the moral and intellectual beauty of young men: ἀναλάμπουσι πρὸς ἐκεῖνο τὸ ἐράσμιον ἀληθῶς καὶ μακάριον καὶ φίλιον ἅπασι (I take ἅπασι as neuter, "in all respects," and not, with Flacelière and Helmbold, as masculine and referring to persons) καὶ ἀγαπητόν. That in the presence of which lovers "light up" and which is so magnificently qualified with this profusion of adjectives is τὸ καλόν, reflected in the thoughts of the youths. See, on Plutarch's light imagery, on φῶς at 762A and, on ἀληθῶς, on 764D-E. Cf. πρὸς τὸν θεόν (John 1:1-2), πρὸς τὸν πατέρα (1 John 1:2), and the other passages cited by Bauer, s.v. πρός, III. 7; BDF, sec. 239.1; B. Reicke, *TDNT*, s.v. πρός, C.1.c. Cf. also the ECL application of ἀγαπητός to Christ (see Bauer, s.v., 1 and E. Stauffer, *TDNT*, s.v. ἀγαπάω, D.2.b, F) and of μακάριος to God and to what is closely related to God (see 1 Tim 1:11, 6:15; Bauer, s.v., 2, 3.b; F. Hauck, *TDNT*, s.v., D.3); but I can not avoid the feeling that the application of these two adjectives to τὸ καλόν is completely alien to ECL modes of thought. ἐράσμιος and φίλιος are absent from ECL.

Ch. 20

It seems, Plutarch observes, that when poets write or sing about the god (ὁ θεός = Eros) they are usually either poking fun at him or in their cups, ὀλίγα δὲ εἴρηται μετὰ σπουδῆς αὐτοῖς, εἴτε κατὰ νοῦν καὶ λογισμὸν εἴτε σὺν θεῷ τῆς ἀληθείας ἁψαμένοις. See, on Eros' being designated a θεός, Intro. IV and on 757E; on the dative of agent (here αὐτοῖς), on 764A; on divine inspiration, on 758D-759D; and on ἀλήθεια as "truth," on 762A. Plutarch's νοῦς and λογισμός appear loosely consistent with ECL usage (see Bauer, s.v.; H. W. Heidland, *TDNT*, s.v. λογίζομαι, B.1; J. Behm, *TDNT*, s.v. νοῦς [under νοέω], C-D). Despite μετὰ σπουδῆς at Mark 6:25, Luke 1:39, Mart Pol 8:3, and Diogn 12:1 (on which occurrences, see Bauer, s.v. σπουδή and G. Harder, *TDNT*, s.v. σπουδάζω, C.3, D.3), there is in ECL no true semantic parallel to Plutarch's use of the phrase here in the sense of "seriously." νοῦς is not a significant term in *amat.*, though it is elsewhere in Plutarch (see, e.g., *PECL* 1, passim [s.v., Index of Greek Words]).

(765F)

Plutarch speaks of the effect of erotic passion "on souls that [truly] love beauty" (περὶ . . . φιλοκάλους ψυχάς). On Plutarch's conceptual and semantic framework, see on 749C (καλός), 758D-759D, 759E (τὸ καλόν), 763F (τὸ καλόν), 764C-D, 764D-E, 764E-765D.

ἀνάκλασιν ποιεῖ (Eros) τῆς μνήμης ἀπὸ τῶν ἐνταῦθα φαινομένων καὶ προσαγορευομένων καλῶν εἰς τὸ θεῖον καὶ ἐράσμιον καὶ μακάριον ὡς ἀληθῶς ἐκεῖνο καὶ θαυμάσιον καλόν. On all this, see, in addition to the preceding comment, on 758D-759D (at end), 762D (θαυμάζουσι), 765D (Ch. 19).

(765F-766A)

Misguided lovers, Plutarch continues, by pursuing merely the εἴδωλον of τὸ καλόν, an εἴδωλον that appears ἐν παισὶ καὶ γυναιξὶν ὥσπερ ἐν κατόπτροις, are able to obtain nothing more substantial than ἡδονή mixed with pain. See, in addition to the material cited in the two previous comments, on εἴδωλον at 765C-D, on ἔσοπτρα καλῶν καλά at 765B, and on ἡδονή at 750C-D and 751B. For exegesis of Paul's problematic τὴν δόξαν Κυρίου κατοπτριζόμενοι τὴν αὐτὴν εἰκόνα μεταμορφούμεθα ἀπὸ δόξης εἰς δόξαν (2 Cor 3:18), see Bauer, s.v. κατοπτρίζω and G. Kittel, *TDNT*, s.v. εἰκών, B.3.

(766A)

εὐφυοῦς δ' ἐραστοῦ καὶ σώφρονος ἄλλος τρόπος. Plutarch is contrasting the τρόπος ("character," "conduct," "manner," a sense this term exhibits in ECL only at Heb 13:5, Did 11:8, and Herm Vis 1:1:2; see Bauer, s.v., 2) "of the noble and chaste lover" with that of the misguided one. εὐφυής and cognates are not represented in ECL. On σώφρων, see on 752A.

ἀνακλᾶται πρὸς τὸ θεῖον καὶ νοητὸν καλόν. The syntactical subject of the verb is the ἐραστής mentioned in the preceding clause; yet the context makes clear that Plutarch has in mind as actual subject the lover's soul, conceived of as the essential man, or else the implied "vision" of his soul. On this statement, cf. on 765F (ἀνάκλασιν κτλ.), 765F-766A and see on 758D-759D (at end), 764D-E, 765B (Ἔρως ἔσοπτρα κτλ.).

ὁρατοῦ δὲ σώματος ἐντυχὼν κάλλει καὶ χρώμενος οἷον ὀργάνῳ τινὶ τῆς μνήμης ἀσπάζεται καὶ ἀγαπᾷ, καὶ συνὼν . . . μᾶλλον ἐκφλέγεται τὴν διάνοιαν. The noble and chaste lover is the subject of each verb. Cf. the figurative uses of ὄργανον at 2 Clem 18:2 and Ign Rom 4:2 and of φλέγω at Gos Pet 12:50; for discussion of concepts and vocabulary, see on 749C (καλός), 756D, 758D-759D, 759C (διάνοια), 759E (τὸ καλόν), 761A (ἀσπάζομαι), 763F (τὸ καλόν), 764B-C, 764C-D, 764D-E, 764E-765D, 765A (ὁρατὰ μιμήματα). Plutarch's use in this passage of ἀγαπάω in a strong sense is striking, especially in view of the weak sense it carries at 761A and 764B (see my comments on these occurrences; but cf. *PECL* 1:196 [550D]). There is, nevertheless, no parallel to ECL usage, since for Plutarch the object of ἀγάπη is not a person but a person's physical beauty, which is itself only a mnemonic device that helps the lover's soul remember τὸ καλόν (cf. on 764C-D).

(766B)

μετὰ τὴν τελευτήν. In its single ECL occurrence at Matt 2:15, τελευτή is also used as a euphemism for death (cf. *PECL* 1:81 [Ch. 77:382C]).

δυσόνειρα φαντασμάτια φιληδόνων καὶ φιλοσωμάτων ἀνδρῶν καὶ γυναικῶν οὐ δικαίως ἐρωτικῶν προσαγορευομένων. Plutarch is referring to the "ghosts," described as "nightmarish" (on δυσ- as a compounding prefix characteristic of Greek of all periods, see Weissenberger, 12; Goodwin-Gulick, secs. 568, 861.b; Smyth-Messing, secs. 103.a, 105, 452, 885.3, 898.C; Bauer, s.v. beginning with δυσ-; BDF, sec. 117.1), of men and women who spent their earthly lives in the pursuit of sexual pleasure. Cf. my comments on 765F-766A and 766A; φιλήδονοι μᾶλλον ἢ φιλόθεοι at 2 Tim 3:4; and Matt 14:26//Mark 6:49, where the disciples mistake Christ walking on water for a φάντασμα (cf. Luke 24:37D and R. Bultmann and D. Lührmann, *TDNT*, s.v. φάντασμα [under φαίνω]).

ὁ . . . ὡς ἀληθῶς ἐρωτικὸς ἐκεῖ (the metaphysical world) γενόμενος καὶ τοῖς καλοῖς ὁμιλήσας ᾗ θέμις. Cf. the impersonal use of θεμιτόν at 1 Clem 63:1 and Diogn 6:10, and see my comments at 764D-E and 765A on ἀλήθεια and ἀληθῶς. Again (cf. on 766A, ἀνακλᾶται κτλ.), although the ἐρωτικός is the grammatical subject of the sentence, its essential subject is his soul, or the ἐρωτικός conceived of as soul. Both the immediately following description of his soul's "activity" in the metaphysical world and the reference to reincarnation (ἑτέρας ἄρχηται γενέσεως) with which 766B ends are derived from Plato (see esp. *Phdr.* 246A-253C, *R.* 614B-621D [the myth of Er]; cf. Helmbold, 411, n. a). ECL is without any notion of metempsychosis (cf., e.g., Bultmann, *Primitive Christianity*, 190-91, 201-202).

(766C)

Eros is εὐμενέστατος to those who receive him, but βαρύς to those who reject him. εὐμενής and cognates are absent from ECL (cf. on 762B). ECL uses βαρύς figuratively (see Bauer, s.v. and G. Schrenk, *TDNT*, s.v. [under βάρος]), but offers no true parallel to its figurative occurrence here.

Eros is τῶν . . . ὑπερηφάνων κολαστής. ὑπερήφανος is here pejorative (cf. on 762C), as usually in classical Greek and always in ECL (see LSJ, s.v.; Bauer, s.v.; G. Bertram, *TDNT*, s.v.). In ECL, God often opposes directly the ὑπερήφανοι (see esp. Luke 1:51 [2 Sam 22:28], Jas 4:6 [Prov 3:34], 1 Pet 5:5 [Prov 3:34], 1 Clem 30:2 [Prov 3:34], 59:3, Ign Eph 5:3 [Prov 3:34]; cf., e.g., Rom 1:30, 1 Clem 35:5-6, 57:2). Though κολαστής is absent from ECL, its cognates κολάζω and κόλασις are not uncommon there with reference to divine retribution (see Bauer, s.v.; J. Schneider, *TDNT*, s.v.; *PECL* 1:26, 191, 231, 279).

(766D)

νέος ἐπιεικὴς καὶ γένει λαμπρός. See on γυνὴ . . . γένει λαμπρά at 749D. The occurrences in ECL of ἐπιείκεια and ἐπιεικής, though moderately common (see Bauer, s.v. and H. Preisker, *TDNT*, s.v.), do not offer any parallels to the present passage.

ἐκ . . . λαμπρῶν εἰς ταπεινὰ πράγματα. Cf. τὰ λαμπρά as "splendor" at Rev 18:14 and, if it is a neuter rather than a masculine plural (cf. Bauer, s.v. συναπάγω and W. Grundmann, *TDNT*, s.v. ταπεινός, D.3.c), τοῖς ταπεινοῖς at Rom 12:16. Cf. on ψυχὴν . . . ταπεινήν at 762E.

αὐτὸν οὐδενὸς ἀπηξίου (so Helmbold, after Bernardakis; Hubert and Flacelière read ἀπηξιοῦτο with the MSS). Cf. in ECL the syntactically and semantically similar usage of ἀξιόω with an accusative plus a genitive (see Bauer, s.v., 1.a).

Ch. 21

(766D-E)

On the great lacuna at the end of 766D and the dramatic situation and tenor of Plutarch's argument when the MSS resume, see Intro. I (first paragraph), II.6-7.

ἃς λέγουσιν αἰτίας καὶ γενέσεις ἔρωτος, ἴδιαι μὲν οὐδετέρου γένους εἰσὶ κοιναὶ δ' ἀμφοτέρων. Hubert, Flacelière, and Helmbold capitalize Ἔρωτος, to my view incorrectly (cf. at 767A ποιεῖται τοὺς ἔρωτας, "expresses his desires"). I would translate: "what they [perhaps the Epicureans; see Helmbold, 413, n. b] call the causes and origins of desire are peculiar to neither sex and common to both." Plutarch will momentarily claim explicitly (766E-767A) that women, as well as youths, are capable of reflecting ideal beauty and, therefore, of arousing the recollection and desire of it. ECL also uses αἰτία in the sense of "cause," "reason" (see Bauer, s.v., 1); but γένεσις does not mean "origin," "source" in ECL, except possibly at Matt 1:1 (see Bauer, s.v., 3). Also, despite such an expression as μήτε κατ' ἰδίαν . . . μήτε κοινῇ (Ign Smyrn 7:2), it should be borne in mind that ECL never uses ἴδιος and γένος in their present sense and, to my knowledge, never allows ἴδιος and κοινός to govern a genitive of the present sort (I take the genitive in τὸ κοινὸν τῆς ἐλπίδος at 1 Clem 51:1 as appositive).

(766E-F)

Though this section of the *amat.* text is mutilated at several points, the gist of Plutarch's argument is clear. Women as well as youths, he claims, can quicken recollections (ἀναμνήσεις) of τὸ θεῖον καὶ ἀληθινὸν καὶ ὀλύμπιον ἐκεῖνο κάλλος . . . , ὅταν ἦθος ἁγνὸν καὶ κόσμιον ἐν ὥρᾳ καὶ χάριτι μορφῆς διαφανὲς γένηται. Much of the conceptual and terminological matter of this statement has already received comment (see on 750E [ἦθος], 753B [κοσμίως], 758D-759D [at end], 763F [κάλλιστα and θειότατα], 764D-E, 764E-765D). Some additional commentary, however, is in order. As to differences between Plutarchan and ECL usage, ὀλύμπιος is absent from ECL; ὥρα, which often in classical Greek has its present sense of "beauty" (see LSJ, s.v., B. II), always has a temporal designation in ECL (see Bauer, s.v. and G. Delling, *TDNT*, s.v., C-D; but note that ὡραῖος can mean "beautiful," "fair" in ECL); and in ECL, except possibly at

Mart Pol 12:1 (τὸ πρόσωπον αὐτοῦ χάριτος ἐπληροῦτο), χάρις never denotes "physical beauty" or "gracefulness," as it does here and not uncommonly in classical authors (see LSJ, s.v., I.1). There are also two points of similarity, since μορφή can denote "external appearance" in ECL (see Bauer, s.v.), as it does here and regularly in classical literature (see LSJ, s.v., 1-2 and J. Behm, *TDNT*, s.v., A.1-3), and since ἁγνός is descriptive of women at 2 Cor 11:2 and Tit 2:5, of conduct or behavior at 1 Pet 3:2 and 1 Clem 48:1, and of συνείδησις at 1 Clem 1:3 and Pol Phil 5:3.

(766F)

Amidst a corrupt text (see the readings and *apparatus* of Hubert, Flacelière, and Helmbold), Plutarch makes a reference to what οἱ δεινοὶ τῶν τοιούτων αἰσθάνεσθαι perceive ἐν εἴδεσι καλοῖς καὶ καθαροῖς σώμασιν (doubtless, of women). δεινός never carries this common classical sense of "skillful," "clever" (see LSJ, s.v., III) in ECL, where it always means basically "fearful," "terrible" (see Bauer, s.v.). On the terms and conceptual framework of Plutarch's prepositional phrase, see on 759D (where εἶδος also denotes "outward appearance"), 764E-765D, 765A (where καθαρός describes the form beauty rather than, as here, something in the sensible world).

(766F-767A)

With Plutarch's reference to the φιλήδονος whose clever reply to a question suited his preoccupation with ἐπιθυμία, cf. Intro. III and on 750D (second comment), 766B (φαντασμάτια φιληδόνων).

(767A)

In a sentence of unusually complex structure, Plutarch asserts that the φιλόκαλος καὶ γενναῖος directs his erotic desires only toward τὸ καλόν and εὐφυΐα, and ignores differences in sex. He adds that, as the φίλιππος admires mares as well as stallions and as the huntsman raises female as well as male dogs, so the φιλόκαλος καὶ φιλάνθρωπος is attracted to both sexes (ἀμφοτέροις τοῖς γένεσιν). All this reflects social and ethical traditions and principles quite out of harmony with those that prompted Paul's castigation of pagan homosexuality at Rom 1:24-27 and the condemnation of the παιδοφθόρος at Did 2:2, Barn 10:6, and Barn 19:4. Also, Plutarch's coordinating of the love of beauty and of mankind (in the phrase φιλόκαλος καὶ φιλάνθρωπος) clashes somewhat with the force of φιλανθρωπία in its few, but pregnant, ECL occurrences, in which the quality is *never* associated with an attraction to the beauty of its object (see on 758A, 764C-D; cf. Intro. V.4 and n. 16 and on τὸ καλόν at 759E, 763F, 764E-765D). For comments on Plutarch's γενναῖος and γένος vis-à-vis their usage in ECL, see on 762D (at beginning), 766D-E. Neither φιλόκαλος nor εὐφυΐα appears in ECL, though φιλο- is a most common Koine prefix (see BDF, sec. 118.2 and the words in Bauer beginning with this prefix).

(767B)

Plutarch now argues that women have a natural capacity for ἀρετή (on which term, see Intro. III and on 750B-751B, 750D): τήν γ' ὥραν "ἄνθος ἀρετῆς" εἶναι λέγουσι, μὴ φάναι δ' ἀνθεῖν τὸ θῆλυ μηδὲ ποιεῖν ἔμφασιν εὐφυΐας πρὸς ἀρετὴν ἄτοπόν ἐστι. Cf. ἄτοπόν ἐστιν plus the infinitive at Ign Magn 10:3 and see, for comments about ὥρα and ἄνθος, on 757F, 766E-F. Although εὐφυΐα is not an ECL term, cf. on φύσις at 750C-D, 755D.

πότερον . . . ἰταμοῦ μὲν ἤθους καὶ ἀκολάστου καὶ διεφθορότος σημεῖα τοῖς εἴδεσι τῶν γυναικῶν ἐπιτρέχει, κοσμίου δὲ καὶ σώφρονος οὐδὲν ἔπεστι τῇ μορφῇ φέγγος; Much of this vocabulary has already received sufficient comment: see on ἦθος at 750E, 764E-765D; on εἶδος at 759D; on κοσμιότης at 753B; on σωφροσύνη (also in ECL regarded as especially appropriate to women) at 752A, 752C, 753B, 753C-D; on μορφή at 766E-F. Though ἀκόλαστος and cognates are absent from ECL and ἰταμός appears only at Herm Man 11:12, cf., in the way of loose ECL parallels, διαπαρατριβαὶ διεφθαρμένων ἀνθρώπων τὸν νοῦν (1 Tim 6:5), the use of σημεῖον to denote a "sign" by which something is known (see Bauer, s.v., 1; cf. K. H. Rengstorf, *TDNT*, s.v., D. II.1), and the figurative use of τρέχω, especially by Paul (see Bauer, s.v., 2; O. Bauernfeind, *TDNT*, s.v., C-D; Bultmann, *Der Stil*, 90 [no. 7]).

οὐδέτερον γὰρ εὔλογον οὐδ' ἀληθές. At Ign Magn 7:1 and Smyrn 9:1, εὔλογος also means "reasonable," "right" (see Bauer, s.v.). On ἀληθής as "true," "right" in ECL, see Bauer, s.v., 2 and R. Bultmann, *TDNT*, s.v. (under ἀλήθεια), 4; cf. on ἀλήθεια at 762A.

(767C)

Plutarch in summarizing asserts that the characteristics he has been talking about belong "to both sexes alike" (κοινῶς ... τοῖς γένεσι). See on γένος at 766D-E, 767A.

Zeuxippus is described by Plutarch as ἐπιθυμίᾳ τὸν Ἔρωτα ταὐτὸ ποιῶν ἀκαταστάτῳ καὶ πρὸς τὸ ἀκόλαστον ἐκφερούσῃ τὴν ψυχήν. ἀκόλαστος and cognates are absent from ECL. But ἐπιθυμία is also used pejoratively of sexual desire at 1 Thes 4:5, Did 3:3, Herm Man 6:2:5, Ign Pol 5:2 (cf. my comment on this term at 750D); and ἀκατάστατος (here "disorderly," "unstable") and its cognates have generally parallel meanings in their several occurrences in ECL (see Bauer, s.v.). Zeuxippus, Plutarch avers, heard this nonsense from ἀνδρῶν δυσκόλων καὶ ἀνεράστων (cf. on δύσκολος at 762D).

Plutarch refers to grasping, ill-tempered husbands who thrust their wives εἰς οἰκονομίαν καὶ λογισμοὺς ("accounts") ... ἀνελευθέρους. λογισμός is not used as a business term in ECL. Though ἀνελεύθερος does not appear in ECL, cf. on ἐλευθερία at 755B 762E.

(767D)

Plutarch speaks of the εὔνοια (on which term, see on 749C) between husband and wife that is fostered by time and συνήθεια ("intimacy," "fellowship," a meaning this term has in ECL only at Ign Eph 5:1; cf. on συνήθης at 749B).

(767E)

On the heels of a corrupt text, Plutarch refers to couples (apparently, married couples) who τοῖς σώμασιν ὁριζόμενοι τὰς ψυχὰς βίᾳ συνάγουσι καὶ συντήκουσι. One thinks of Jesus' remarks concerning marriage at Matt 19:3-6//Mark 10:2-9 (cf. Gen 2:24). Yet Jesus' ὥστε οὐκέτι εἰσὶν δύο ἀλλὰ μία σάρξ points to a different conceptualization of a human being, for the dichotomous anthropology inherent in Plutarch's contrast between σῶμα and ψυχή is strikingly missing from Jesus' σάρξ. Paul actually uses σῶμα as a synonym for σάρξ at 1 Cor 6:16-17 (cf. Eph 5:29-31), when he quotes the same Gen passage on which Jesus' remarks are based. Cf. E. Schweizer, *TDNT*, s.v. σάρξ, E.I.2 and on 758D-759D, 764D-E, 764E-765D.

With Plutarch's mention of mutual σωφροσύνη as a thing which marriage especially requires, cf. on 752A, 752C, 753B, 753C-D.

Eros is described by Plutarch as richly endowed with ἐγκράτεια (see on 753B, 754B), κόσμος (see on 753B), and πίστις ("faithfulness," on which meaning in ECL, see Bauer, s.v., 1.a and R. Bultmann, *TDNT*, s.v. πιστεύω, D.I.2) and as, even if he touch an ἀκόλαστος ψυχή (see on 750B), ἐκκόψας ... τὸ θράσος καὶ κατακλάσας τὸ σοβαρὸν καὶ ἀνάγωγον (though the last two terms are missing from ECL, see on 762E-F).

(767E-F)

Eros is further described by Plutarch as ἐμβαλὼν αἰδῶ καὶ σιωπὴν καὶ ἡσυχίαν καὶ σχῆμα περιθεὶς κόσμιον. Cf. the admonition to wives at 1 Tim 2:9 ἐν καταστολῇ κοσμίῳ μετὰ αἰδοῦς ... κοσμεῖν ἑαυτάς; nevertheless, αἰδώς, though prominent in classical ethics, is the rarest of early Christian virtues (see, e.g., R. Bultmann, *TDNT*, s.v. and North, *Sophrosyne*, passim [s.v. "*Aidôs*" in Subject Index]; cf. *PECL* 1:142). Also, Hermas is told (Man 11:8) that he who has the Holy Spirit is ἡσύχιος, and ἡσυχία and σιωπή are very loosely associated at Ign Eph 15:1-2. In ECL, however, ἡσυχία is commonly a quality to which Christians are exhorted, rather than a gift of the Spirit: see 1 Thes 4:10-11, 2 Thes 3:12, 1 Tim 2:2, 2:11-12, 1 Pet 3:3-4, Barn 19:4, Did 3:8, Herm Man 8:10.

(767F)

Ἴστε ... ἀκοῇ Λαΐδα τὴν ἀοίδιμον ἐκείνην. In ECL too, ἀκοή can mean "report," "fame" (see Bauer, s.v., 2.a and G. Kittel, *TDNT*, s.v. [under ἀκούω]).

(767F-768A)

After Eros touched Laïs, ᾤχετο κοσμίως. Cf. on 753B.

(768A)

The women of Thessaly stoned Laïs to death ὑπὸ φθόνου καὶ ζήλου. In ECL, these are rather common vices, though ζῆλος has a good sense as well (see Bauer, s.v. ζῆλος, ζηλόω, φθονέω, φθόνος; A. Stumpff *TDNT*, s.v. ζῆλος [C], ζηλόω [D]; *PECL* 1:55, 208 [555E], 227, 229). They are emphatically coordinated by 1 Clement at 3:2 and 4:7.

Plutarch speaks of those who receive Eros as their δεσπότης, and soon adds: οἷς ἂν Ἔρως κύριος ἐγγένηται, τῶν ἄλλων δεσποτῶν καὶ ἀρχόντων ἐλεύθεροι καὶ ἄφετοι καθάπερ ἱερόδουλοι διατελοῦσιν. There are countless parallels in ECL, where δεσπότης is used often of God and occasionally of Christ (see on 758C), where κύριος regularly functions as a designation or title of God and of Christ (see Bauer, s.v., 2; W. Foerster, *TDNT*, s.v., E.2-3; *PECL* 1:43 [353B], 47 [355E], 60 [365A], 79 [381E], 167 [426A], 193 [550A], 294-95 [942D]), where those who have a right relation to God or Christ are frequently designated his δοῦλοι (see Bauer, s.v., 4 and K. H. Rengstorf, *TDNT*, s.v., C.2), and where ἐλεύθερος-ἐλευθερία and δοῦλος-δουλεία are rather commonly brought into contrasting association (as at Rom 8:21, 1 Cor 7:21-22, 9:19, 12:13, Gal 2:4, 3:28, 4:21-31, 5:1, Eph 6:8, Col 3:11, 1 Pet 2:16, 2 Pet 2:19, Rev 6:15, 13:16, 19:18, Ign Pol 4:3, Ign Rom 4:3, Herm Sim 5:2:7). Especially noteworthy in this last respect are those passages describing the ἐλεύθερος as simultaneously the δοῦλος of God or Christ (1 Cor 7:22, 1 Pet 2:16, Ign Pol 4:3). Regarding δεσπότης and κύριος, note esp. Jude 4, where these two terms are coordinated as titles of Christ. Though ἄφετος does not appear in ECL, at Luke 4:17-21 Jesus, quoting Isa 61:1, identifies himself as the one appointed to proclaim αἰχμαλώτοις ἄφεσιν (cf. Barn 14:9).

(768B)

ἡ δὲ γενναία γυνὴ πρὸς ἄνδρα νόμιμον συγκραθεῖσα δι' Ἔρωτος. Cf. on 762D (γενναῖος).

Ch. 22

οὐκ ἄξιόν ἐστι . . . παρελθεῖν. Cf. on 760E and 762F, where we find similar uses of ἄξιον.

Plutarch tells a story involving Sinatus, a tetrarch in Galatia, who is murdered by Sinorix (also a Galatian tetrarch, as we learn from *mul. virt.* 257E). In ECL, only Herod Antipas bears the title tetrarch (Matt 14:1, Luke 3:19, 9:7, Acts 13:1, Ign Smyrn 1:2).

Ch. 23

(768E-F)

Plutarch is here condemning ὁμιλία ("sexual intercourse," a meaning this term does not have in ECL, as was pointed out at

756E) between males, not the institution of pederasty as such. Plutarch's position is predicated on a firm distinction between erotic love and sexual desire (cf. Intro. III). Plutarch characterizes young men who take pleasure in "being sodomized" (τὸ πάσχειν; on this verb's present meaning, which it lacks in ECL, see Flacelière, 134, n. 158) as guilty of the worst sort of κακία ("depravity," "wickedness," on which meaning in ECL, see Bauer, s.v., 1.a and W. Grundmann, *TDNT*, s.v. [under κακός], 3:484) and as devoid of πίστις ("faithfulness," on which meaning in ECL see on 767E), αἰδώς (see on 767E-F), and φιλία (see esp. Intro. III and on 750B-751B, 750D). Plutarch would probably have endorsed the commandment οὐ παιδοφθορήσεις (Did 2:2, Barn 19:4; cf. Barn 10:6), though it is doubtful that its authors would have accepted Plutarch's position.

(769A)

Plutarch regards sexual union between man and wife as ἀρχαὶ . . . φιλίας, ὥσπερ ἱερῶν μεγάλων κοινωνήματα. Plutarch's language is virtually sacramental; cf. on 767E, where I mention Jesus' remarks about marriage at Matt 19:3-6//Mark 10:2-9.

Plutarch mentions the mutual ἀγάπησις of man and wife. This particular noun is not used in ECL.

(769A-B)

There is again an almost sacramental tone to Plutarch's assertion that man and wife should sexually unite on a regular basis, not for the sake of pleasure but that they may renew their marriage ἐν τοιαύτῃ φιλοφροσύνῃ. This last term is represented in ECL only by a cognate adverb at Acts 28:7 and a cognate adjective at 1 Pet 3:8 (t.r.).

(769B)

Plutarch speaks of the φαῦλα (neuter plural with the meaning "bad," "base") involved in the wrong kind of passion for either women or boys. This same neuter plural is twice used with a similar moral force in ECL (John 3:20, 5:29). Cf. Bauer, s.v. φαῦλος, 1 and on 753F.

To demonstrate that women are capable of ἀρετή (see Intro. III and on 750B-751B, 750D), Plutarch cites their σωφροσύνη (see on 752A, 752C, 753B, 753C-D), σύνεσις (see on 762B), πίστις (see on 767E, 768E-F), δικαιοσύνη (see on 755B-C), τὸ ἀνδρεῖον (see on 762B), τὸ θαρραλέον (a quality represented in ECL only by some occurrences of θαρρ[σ]έω and, rarely, of θάρσος; cf. Bauer, s.v. and W. Grundmann, *TDNT*, s.v. θαρρέω), and τὸ μεγαλόψυχον (a quality prominent in Aristotle's ethical thinking [see *EN* 2:1107.b.22-27, 4:1123.a.34-1125.a.35] but not recognized in ECL; cf. on μεγαλόφρων at 762B-C).

(769C)

To demonstrate that women have the capacity for φιλία (see esp. Intro. III and on 750B-751B, 750D), Plutarch asserts that they are φιλότεκνοι καὶ φίλανδροι καὶ τὸ στερκτικὸν ὅλως ἐν αὐταῖς, ὥσπερ εὐφυὴς χώρα καὶ δεκτικὴ φιλίας, οὔτε πειθοῦς οὔτε χαρίτων ἄμοιρον ὑπόκειται. Cf. Tit 2:4, where young wives are urged to be φίλανδροι and φιλότεκνοι; 1 Clem 1:3 and Pol Phil 4:2, where wives are instructed to be affectionate (στέργειν) toward their husbands; and the parabolic use of χώρα at Luke 12:16 and John 4:35. In ECL, however, πειθώ is actually or virtually non-existent (see Bauer, s.v. πειθός, πειθώ) and χάρις never denotes physical grace (cf. the following comment and on 766E-F).

(769C-D)

Just as poetry, through its aesthetic allurements, both enhances the educative power (τὸ παιδεῦον) of language and, at the same time, makes its power to harm (τὸ βλάπτον) more difficult to resist, οὕτως ἡ φύσις (cf. on 750C-D, 751C-D, 755D) γυναικὶ περιθεῖσα χάριν ὄψεως (on χάρις as physical "beauty," see on 766E-F, 769C) καὶ φωνῆς πιθανότητα (πιθανότης does not occur in ECL; cf. the preceding comment) καὶ μορφῆς ἐπαγωγὸν εἶδος (cf. on εἶδος at 759D, 765B and μορφή at 766E-F), τῇ μὲν ἀκολάστῳ (absent from ECL; cf. on 750B) πρὸς ἡδονὴν καὶ ἀπάτην (Bauer recognizes "pleasure" as a possible meaning for ἀπάτη in ECL [s.v., 2]) τῇ δὲ σώφρονι (see on 752A, 752C, 753B, 753C-D) πρὸς εὔνοιαν (see on 749C) ἀνδρὸς καὶ φιλίαν (see esp. Intro. III and on 750D, 769C) μεγάλα συνήργησεν. For some ECL appearances of παιδεύω in a sense generally parallel to that which it has here, see Bauer, s.v., 1, 2.a (cf. G. Bertram, *TDNT*, s.v., D); only at Mart Pol 10:2 does ECL use βλάπτω of spiritual or moral harm. On Paul's problematic συνεργεῖ εἰς at Rom 8:28, see Bauer, s.v. συνεργέω and G. Bertram, *TDNT*, s.v. συνεργός, C.1 (7:875).

(769D)

Plutarch refers to one Xenocrates, who, though γενναῖος, was αὐστηρότατος in character (τῷ ἤθει). Comments on this descriptive vocabulary have been made at 749E-F (αὐστηρός), 750E (ἦθος), and 762D (γενναῖος).

χρηστῇ δ' ἄν τις γυναικὶ καὶ σώφρονι παραινέσειε τῷ Ἔρωτι θύειν, ὅπως εὐμενὴς (on which term, see on 762B) συνοικουρῇ τῷ γάμῳ. This statement is reminiscent of Plutarch's assertion at 753C-D (cf. my comment) that a wife's σωφροσύνη needs tempering with erotic passion for her husband. Only at 1 Cor 15:33 does χρηστός have its present meaning of "morally good" in ECL (see Bauer, s.v. and K. Weiss, *TDNT*, s.v., C). παραινέω is used with the dative of the person at Ign Smyrn 4:1 and with the accusative of the person plus an infinitive at Acts 27:22; the dative is regular in classical authors (see LSJ, s.v., 1; cf. BDF, sec. 152.3). For related comments, see on 749B (θύω), 749F-750A (ὅπως), 750A (potential optative), 762B (εὐμενής).

(769D-E)

τὸ γὰρ ἐρᾶν ἐν γάμῳ τοῦ ἐρᾶσθαι μεῖζον ἀγαθόν ἐστι· πολλῶν γὰρ ἁμαρτημάτων ἀπαλλάττει. I find no ECL parallel to Plutarch's dictum. ἁμάρτημα in ECL, I think, carries stronger moral connotations than it does here (cf. Bauer, s.v., and G. Stählin, *TDNT*, s.v. ἁμαρτάνω, D.2). On ἀγαθόν as "blessing," cf. on 762B.

Ch. 24

(769E)

Plutarch speaks in encouraging terms of the breaking of the bride's hymen: τὸ ... δάκνον.... μὴ φοβηθῇς ὡς ἕλκος ἢ ὀδαξησμόν ... μεθ' ἕλκους ἴσως οὐδὲν δεινὸν ὥσπερ τὰ δένδρα συμφυῆ γενέσθαι πρὸς γυναῖκα χρηστήν. Cf. the metaphorical use of δάκνω at Gal 5:15, the grafting metaphor of Rom 11:17-24, and the OT-NT notion of man and wife's becoming μία σάρξ (Gen 2:24, Matt 19:3-6//Mark 10:2-9; cf. on this notion at 767E). On the prohibitive subjunctive and on χρηστός, see, respectively, on 764A and 769D.

(769E-F)

Plutarch uses ταράττω and τάραξις to describe the internal agitation produced in boys and young men by their lessons or philosophical studies and in the newly married by Eros. Cf. the figurative use in ECL of these words and their cognates.

(769F)

Plutarch, borrowing the vocabulary of science (see *conjug. praec.* 142F-143A, and Helmbold, 431, n. c), speaks, in obvious reference to the union that Eros works between man and wife, of ἡ δι' ὅλων λεγομένη κρᾶσις. He adds a reference to the ἑνότητα . . . οἵαν Ἔρως ποιεῖ γαμικῆς κοινωνίας ἐπιλαβόμενος. On the related ECL concept of married union as μία σάρξ, see on 767E, 769A, 769E. To my knowledge, however, ECL never designates marriage as a κοινωνία, as Plutarch and other classical authors sometimes do (see LSJ, s.v.; Bauer, s.v., 1 [at beginning]; and on 769A).

(770A)

Plutarch speaks approvingly of the ἡδοναὶ . . . ἀπ' ἄλλων and the χρεῖαι . . . πρὸς ἄλλους which are inherent in the erotic fellowship of man and wife. Cf. on ἡδονή at 750C-D, 751B. Despite its frequency in ECL, χρεία there denotes "service," a common meaning in classical authors (see LSJ, s.v., III), only at Acts 6:3.

τοὺς θεοὺς Ἔρωτος ἡ φύσις ἀποδείκνυσι δεομένους. Cf. on φύσις at 750C-D, 751C-D, 755D.

(770A-B)

γῆν . . . μητέρα καὶ . . . γένεσιν οὐκ ἀναγκαῖον ἀπολέσθαι . . . , ὅταν ὁ δεινὸς Ἔρως . . . τὴν ὕλην ἀπολίπῃ καὶ παύσηται ποθοῦσα . . . τὴν ἐκεῖθεν ἀρχὴν καὶ κίνησιν; ECL lacks the notion of mother earth and does not, except possibly at Matt 1:1 (cf. on 766D-E), use γένεσις as "source," "origin;" nor is δεινός in any of its occasional ECL appearances (cf. on 766F) applied to God, Christ, ἀγάπη or φιλία. For a few, tenuous ECL parallels, see the references to Christ as creation's ἀρχή (Col 1:15-18, Rev 3:14; note the discussion of these two passages by G. Delling, *TDNT*, s.v. ἀρχή, C.3 and cf. *PECL* 1:60 [365B], 72 [374A], 81 [Ch. 77]), the use of ὕλη as "matter" (see Diogn 2:3 [φθαρτῆς ὕλης]; Bauer, s.v., 2; *PECL* 1:72 [Ch. 56], 81 [382C], 147 [414D]), and Acts 17:28 (ἐν αὐτῷ . . . ζῶμεν καὶ κινούμεθα καὶ ἐσμέν). Plutarch also juxtaposes ἀρχή and κίνησις at *Pyth. or.* 397C and 398C. On the former as a philosophical term in classical literature, see, e.g.,

G. S. Kirk and J. E. Raven, *The Presocratic Philosophers* (Cambridge, 1960) 88, 92, 97, 105, 107-8, 111 and G. Delling, *TDNT*, s.v., A.1.

(770C)

πάσης πίστεως κοινωνίαν. Plutarch so characterizes any erotic relationship between genuine lovers (cf. γνησίων ἐραστῶν near the beginning of 770C), even a pederastic one; yet it is evident that he has in mind chiefly marriage grounded in erotic devotion (cf. on 769F). πίστεως, as I take it, is a genitive of quality and embraces the notions of both "trust" and "fidelity" (cf. my last comment on 767E; Bauer, s.v., 1-2; R. Bultmann, *TDNT*, s.v. πιστεύω, A.I, A.II.3, D.I.2-7). Cf. at Phlm 6 the enigmatic ἡ κοινωνία τῆς πίστεώς σου, taken by Bauer as "your participation in the faith" (s.v. κοινωνία, 4), where the words are the same as Plutarch's but their meaning, whether or not Bauer is correct, is obviously quite different.

Ch. 25

(770C-D)

Plutarch here uses Γαλατία to designate Gaul, not Galatia. In ECL, only at 2 Tim 4:10 (with Γαλλία as v.l.) is there the possibility that this term is so used (see Bauer, s.v. Γαλατία, Γαλλία); elsewhere (1 Cor 16:1, Gal 1:2, 3:1, 1 Pet 1:1) Γαλατία and cognates refer to Galatia of Asia Minor. Bauer briefly summarizes scholarly opinion as to whether this Galatia is to be understood as an ethnic district or the Roman province.

(771A)

τὰ ... ἄλλα παρὰ τῆς γυναικὸς ... συνετραγῳδεῖτο. Plutarch is describing the convincing manner in which Empona pretends to be grieving for her husband Sabinus, who is not dead but in hiding. Plutarch's verb and dramatic metaphor are absent from ECL (cf. my comments on the earlier dramatic metaphors at 749A, 753B-C).

διὰ χρόνου δ' εἰς πόλιν ἐφοίτα. It is Empona who "from time to time would make trips into town." Both the phrase διὰ χρόνου and its present sense would probably be at home in either classical literature or ECL: see LSJ, s.v. διά, A.II.1 and Bauer, s.v. διά, A.II.1 (cf. on 765A, where the same phrase occurs in the sense "after an interval"). The iterative imperfect, as at Acts 2:45, is also a feature of the Koine: see BDF, secs. 318.3, 325.

(771B)

ἔλαθε κύουσα (Empona). The supplementary participle with λανθάνω is common enough in classical literature (see Goodwin-Gulick, sec. 1588 and Smyth-Messing, secs. 1873, 2095-96), but occurs in ECL only at Heb 13:2 (see BDF, sec. 414.3). Cf. on 760C, where I comment on the supplementary participle with τυγχάνω.

ECL offers no close parallel to the simile in which Plutarch compares Empona to a lioness. The lion, however, appears in several ECL similes (1 Pet 5:8, Rev 9:17, 10:3, 13:2, 1 Clem 35:11) and metaphors (2 Tim 4:17, Rev 5:5). Cf. W. Michaelis, *TDNT*, s.v. λέων and *PECL* 1:94 (387E).

(771C)

Plutarch deprecates the fact that Vespasian put Empona to death: οὐδὲν ... ἤνεγκεν ἡ ... ἡγεμονία σκυθρωπότερον. His act offended both gods and spirits (καὶ θεοὺς καὶ δαίμονας). ἡγεμονία is used to designate the principate of Tiberius at Luke 3:1 (cf. 1 Clem 61:1). σκυθρωπός has received comment at 762D; θεός and δαίμων in Intro. IV and on 755E-F, 757E, 762E.

τὸ θαρραλέον and τὸ μεγαλήγορον on the part of Empona aroused the ire of Vespasian and the pity of onlookers. The former term received comment at 769B, the latter is absent from ECL.

Ch. 26

(771D)

The genitive absolute, used three times in this section (Σωκλάρου ... εἰπόντος, γάμων ὄντων, and θυσίας περιμενούσης), is frequent in both classical authors and ECL: see Goodwin-Gulick, secs. 1156, 1570, 1595.b; Smyth-Messing, secs. 2032.f, 2058, 2070-75; BDF, secs. 417, 423. A comparison of Smyth-Messing, sec. 2073 with BDF, sec. 423 suggests that the non-classical tendencies of this construction in Koine are perhaps not so prominent as the latter supposes.

οὐκ εὐφημήσετε ... καὶ προάξετε; Acts 13:10 offers a syntactical parallel to this interrogative future with imperative force (οὐ παύσῃ διαστρέφων ... ;); see BDF, sec. 387.3 and Smyth-Messing, sec. 1918. I know of no reference to auspicious silence in ECL, where εὐφημέω does not appear.

(771E)

ἴωμεν, ὅπως ἐπεγγελάσωμεν τἀνδρὶ (Pisias) καὶ τὸν θεὸν προσκυνήσωμεν. On the hortatory subjunctive, characteristic of both classical and Koine Greek, see Goodwin-Gulick, sec. 1343; Smyth-Messing, secs. 1797-99; BDF, sec. 364, and on εὐχώμεθα at 749A. ὅπως is a regular final conjunction in ECL (see BDF, sec. 369 and on 749F-750A), in which capacity it is, as here, commonly followed by an aorist subjunctive (see Bauer, s.v. ὅπως, 2.a). Plutarch here, as at *gen. Soc.* 590B, follows earlier, classical practice in using an accusative after προσκυνέω (see LSJ, s.v., I and BDF, sec. 151.2); while Koine may use the accusative, it prefers the dative (see Bauer, s.v. and BDF, secs. 151.2, 187.2). On this verb, which is exceedingly common in Matt, John, and esp. Rev and moderately to sparsely so throughout the remainder of ECL, see Bauer, s.v.; H. Greeven, *TDNT*, s.v.; *PECL* 1:15-16 (166 B), 23 (167 D-E), 273 (590 B). The object of adoration in ECL may be God, Christ, idols, angels, Satan and Satanic beings, or humans regarded as belonging to a supernatural realm.

Eros is described as χαίρων καὶ παρών. Cf. John 15:11 (Jesus refers to ἡ χαρὰ ἡ ἐμή), 1 Clem 33:7 ("and the Lord himself . . . rejoiced" [ἐχάρη]), and Ign Magn 9:2 (Christ described as παρών).

INDEXES

The index to passages from the Septuagint and early Christian literature is complete in that it includes all passages cited in this volume. The index to Greek words and the index to subject matters are selective, giving only those words and subjects that are discussed.

1. PASSAGES FROM ANCIENT LITERATURE

a) *Old Testament including Pseudepigrapha*

b) *New Testament*

c) *Other early Christian literature*

2. GREEK WORDS

3. SUBJECT MATTERS

CORRIGENDUM

p. 156, line 21 read: Heb. 5:14